Rhetorical Agendas

Political, Ethical, Spiritual

Rhetorical Agendas

Political, Ethical, Spiritual

Edited by

Patricia Bizzell

College of the Holy Cross

Routledge
Taylor & Francis Group
New York   London

First published by Lawrence Erlbaum Associates, Inc., Publishers
10 Industrial Avenue
Mahwah, New Jersey 07430

Transferred to digital printing 2010 by Routledge

Routledge

270 Madison Avenue
New York, NY 10016

2 Park Square, Milton Park
Abingdon, Oxon OX14 4RN, UK

Cover design by Tomai Maridou

Library of Congress Cataloging-in-Publication Data

Rhetoric Society of America. Conference (11th : 2004 : Austin, Tex.)
    Rhetorical agendas : political, ethical, spiritual / edited by Patricia
Bizzell.
        p. cm.
Proceedings of the 11th biennial Conference of the Rhetoric Society of
    America, held May 28-31, 2004, Austin, Texas.
    Includes bibliographical references and index.
ISBN 0-8058-5310-3 (cloth : alk. paper)
ISBN 0-8058-5311-1 (pbk. : alk. paper)
    1. Rhetoric—Congresses.   I. Bizzell, Patricia.   II. Title.

PN171.6.R54 2004
808—dc22   2004065023
                                                        CIP

Table of Contents

III   Theory

VI   Gender

Preface

Conference themes seldom withstand precise parsing, and that's as it should be. At their best they are evocative and draw forth a multiplicity of scholarly responses, rather than hailing only a selected few. I had hoped that the "political" and "ethical" strands in my conference title would recognize the extent to which work on publics, counterpublics, and public spheres, particularly as these might be gendered, had dominated the biennial conferences of the Rhetoric Society of America (RSA) recently, and would invite that trend to continue. At the same time, a more personal interest prompted me to add "spiritual" to the mix—and as well, I suspected that there might be a pent-up need among rhetoricians to address religious discourses of all sorts. I counted on the RSA's tradition of providing a hospitable home for historical work to continue. I also hoped to encourage more pedagogical work by specifically mentioning it in the Call for Proposals.

The patterns that emerged in both the proposals for conference presentations and the submissions for inclusion in the present proceedings volume confirmed that my terms were indeed generative. These patterns are indicated in the broad-cut categories into which I have grouped most of the essays here: "History," "Theory," "Pedagogy," "Publics," and "Gender." The "Rhetorical Agendas" section collects the talks of the conference's featured speakers, whose titles indicate the variety of their interests and where in these categories they might be placed. It will be seen that the category boundaries are highly permeable. An essay in the pedagogy section may be highly theorized; an essay in the gender section may provide important historical insights. And there is no separate section on the "spiritual" because so many essays, to be found in every section, treat religious discourses in one way or another. Nevertheless, I hope the attempt at sorting will indicate the areas that seem most productive now of exciting scholarship.

Foregrounding the notion of "rhetorical agendas" in the conference theme also recognizes something that I regard as distinctive of work that has found a scholarly home at the Rhetoric Society of America. I mean work that deals comfortably with notions of rhetorical agency. Only human agents—and perhaps their textual creations—can have agendas. Of course, the postmodern critique of the idea of an autonomous human agent is well known, as is rhetoric theory that convicts most work in the field of propagating this ideology of autonomy. Yet were rhetoricians to accept this critique in toto, it would appear to leave little for us to do: one could not instruct students to make better rhetorical choices if they really were unable to make choices, and one could not analyze how accomplished rhetors had done so. Moreover, were we to accept this critique, we would have to accept as illusory not only the agency of powerful political orators, but also that of marginalized people who have only in recent years begun to find their public voices. What has happened instead is that rhetoricians have come increasingly to investigate the conditions that produce rhetorical agency, in terms of individual abilities, training, and social, cultural, and historical contexts. As Karlyn Kohrs Campbell articulated in her brilliant plenary address to the inaugural conference of the Alliance of Rhetoric Societies (ARS), we are coming to understand that "agency is communal, social, cooperative, and participatory" (5). In Cheryl Geisler's account of discussions about agency at the ARS conference, she provides an extremely helpful overview of this work, and many of its theoretical premises can be detected in essays in this volume.

I am very grateful to the people who reviewed submissions for this proceedings volume: Fred Antczak, Michelle Ballif, Davida Charney, Rosa Eberly, Richard Leo Enos, Diana George, Michael Halloran, Bruce Herzberg, Gesa Kirsch, Lu Ming Mao, Carolyn Miller, Peter Mortensen, Carol Rutz, Jack Selzer, and Art Walzer. These generous people also reviewed proposals for presentations at the 2004 conference, as did Dale Bauer, Beth Daniell, Jane Donawerth, Lisa Ede, Robert Gaines, Jerry Hauser, Susan Jarratt, Nan Johnson, Michelle Kendricks, Janice Lauer, Shirley Logan, Glen McClish, Alisse Portnoy, Krista Ratcliffe, Barbara Warnick, Sue Wells, Molly Wertheimer, and David Zarefsky. I very much appreciate all their help, without which the conference, and this volume, could not succeed. Such professional service is never adequately compensated except by the gratitude of all of us for the work that allows our scholarly community to continue.

I also thank Susan Pfeiffer, my administrative assistant for Rhetoric Society work, whose tireless attention to detail has made all my projects for the Society possible; and thanks as well to Stephen Ainlay, Vice President for Academic Affairs and Dean of the College of the Holy Cross, who arranged for me to have her help. Finally, I must thank Bruce Herzberg, who was my husband while this volume was in preparation, not only for his professional assistance as a reviewer, noted above, but also for his personal support.

WORKS CITED

Campbell, Karlyn Kohrs. "Agency: Promiscuous and Protean." 15 August 2004 date of access. http://www.rhetoricsociety.org/ARS/pdf/campbellonagency.pdf
Geisler, Cheryl. "How Ought We to Understand the Concept of Rhetorical Agency? A Report from ARS." *Rhetoric Society Quarterly, 34* (Summer 2004): 9–17.

Contributors

Lois Agnew is an Assistant Professor of Writing and Rhetoric at Syracuse University. Her specializations include history of rhetoric, classical rhetoric, British rhetorical theory and composition theory and pedagogy. Her current research interests include exploring ways in which assumptions about rhetoric's civic function change in response to particular social concerns. She is working on a manuscript that examines the influence of Stoic ethics on British rhetorical theory across several centuries. Her most recent publications include "The Stoic Temper in Belletristic Rhetoric." *Rhetorical Society Quarterly* 33.2 (April, 2003) and "The 'Perplexity' of George Campbell's Rhetoric: The Epistemic Function of Common Sense." *Rhetorica* 18.1 (Winter 2000).

Patricia Bizzell is a Professor and Chair of the Department of English at the College of the Holy Cross in Worcester, Massachusetts. Among her publications are *Academic Discourse and Critical Consciousness* (University of Pittsburgh, 1992) and, co-authored with Bruce Herzberg, *The Rhetorical Tradition: Readings from Classical Times to the Present* (Bedford Books, second edition, 2001). Her current research interests include nineteenth-century American women's rhetoric and Jewish intellectual history. She is the President of the Rhetoric Society of America.

Jerry Blitefield is an Associate Professor in the Department of English at the University of Massachusetts (Dartmouth). His research focuses on the physics of rhetoric about which he is currently developing a book length manuscript. His recent publications have appeared in the 2000 and 2002 RSA proceedings, and he has a book chapter forthcoming in Lawrence Prelli's *Rhetorics of Display* (University of South Carolina Press).

Julie A. Bokser is an Assistant Professor in the Department of English at DePaul University. Her teaching interests include history of rhetoric, composition, composition theory and advanced non-fiction writing. Among her publications are "Pedagogies of Belonging: Listening to Students and Peers," in *Writing Center Journal*, 25.1 (2005) and "Straining to Hear the Center" in *Lore: An E-journal for Teachers of Writing*" (Spring, 2003).

Danika M. Brown is an Assistant Professor of English at The University of Texas, Pan American where she teaches undergraduate and graduate courses in rhetoric, composition, critical pedagogy, and critical rhetorical theory. Her publications include the monograph, *Pulling it Together: A Method for Developing Service Learning and Community Partnerships Based in Critical Pedagogy*, "Hegemony and the Discourse of the Land Grant Movement: Historicizing as a Point of Departure" in *The Journal of Advanced Composition*, and "At Work in the Field" (with Thomas P. Miller) in *Culture Shock and the Practice of Profession*.

Beth Burmester is an Assistant Professor in the Department of English and Director of the Writing Studio at Georgia State University in Atlanta. Her research and teaching interests include writing center studies, composition theory and pedagogy, and histories of rhetoric and composition, with an emphasis in classical rhetoric and feminist historiography. Professor Burmester's publications include a book chapter co-authored with Jim Sosnoski, "Reconfiguring the Education of Rhetoricians" in *Culture Shock: Training the New Wave in Rhetoric and Composition*, edited by Susan Romano and Virginia Anderson (Hampton Press, Fall 2004), and articles in *Composition Studies, Southern Discourse, IWCA Update, On Campus with Women*, and the online journal *Lore*. Part of the research in her chapter in this volume was sponsored by an American Dissertation Fellowship from The American Association of University Women (AAUW).

Jami Carlacio is a Lecturer in the Department of English at Cornell University. Her areas of study include rhetorical history and theory, nineteenth-century African American women's rhetorics, and American literary studies. Her publications include "What's So Democratic About CMC?: The Rhetoric of Techno-Literacy in the New Millennium," in *Electronic Collaboration in the Humanities: Issues and Options*. Eds. James Inman, Cheryl Reed and Peter Sands. (Lawrence Erlbaum Associates 2003), "Alternative Articulations of Citizenship: The Written Discourse of an African American Woman." *Rhetorical Democracy: Discursive Practices of Civic Engagement* (Lawrence Erlbaum Associates, 2002), "African American Women's Autobiography," in *Encyclopedia of Women's Autobiography*. Ed. Jo Malin and Victoria Boynton (Greenwood P. Forthcoming, 2005); and "Speaking With and To Me: Discursive Positioning and the Unstable Categories of Race, Class and Gender," in *Calling Cards: Theory and Practice in the Study of Race, Gender and Culture*. Ed. Jacqueline Jones Royster and Ann Marie Simpkins (State U of New York P. Forthcoming 2005).

Sue Carter is Associate Professor in the English Department at Bowling Green State University. She holds a Ph.D in English with Rhetoric Specialization from University of Texas. Her research interests include rhetorical history, history of rhetoric and writing instruction in US colleges and universities, women's rhetoric and rhetorical theory. Her most recent publications are *Perspectives on Academic Writing* (Allyn & Bacon, 1997) and *The Teaching of Writing* which is under contract with Allyn & Bacon.

Gregory D. Clark is a Professor in the English Department at Brigham Young University where he directs the English composition program and teaches courses in rhetoric and in American literature. His most recent book is *Rhetorical Landscapes in America: Variations on a Theme from Kenneth Burke* (University of South Carolina Press, 2004). Professor Clark is currently editor of *Rhetoric Society Quarterly*, the journal of the Rhetoric Society of America.

Dana L. Cloud is a Professor in Communication Studies at the University of Texas at Austin. Professor Cloud's areas of research include the American labor movement, race and popular culture, feminist and Marxist theory and criticism and arguments against the post-structuralists turn in discourse theory. Professor Cloud has published one book, *Control and Consolation in American Culture and Politics: Rhetorics of Theory* (Sage 1998) and a number of articles and essays in *Critical Studies in Mass Communication, the Western Journal of Communication* and several edited books.

Barbara A. Couture was appointed Senior Vice Chancellor for Academic Affairs at the University of Nebraska in August, 2004. Her scholarly interests include rhetoric and philosophy, technical communication, composition and writing theory. Her publications on these topics include: *The Private, the Public and the Published: Reconciling Private Lives and Public Rhetoric* (USUP 2004, edited with Thomas Kent); *Toward a Phenomenological Rhetoric: Writing, Professional, and Altruism* (SIUP 1998); *Functional Approaches to Writing Research Perspectives* (Ablex 1986); and *Cases for Technical and Professional Writing* (Little Brown 1985, with Jone Rymer Goldstein).

Christy Desmet is an Associate Professor in the Department of English at the University of Georgia and Director of the First-Year Composition Program. Her book, *Reading Shakespeare's Characters, Rhetorical Ethics and Identity*, was published in 1992 by the University of Massachusetts Press. She is also co-editor of three books: *Shakespeare and Appropriation* (1999), *Harold Bloom's Shakespeare* (2001), and *Argument: A Prentice-Hall Pocket Anthology*. With Deborah Miller and Alexis Hart, she is currently working on *Literature: A Portfolio Anthology*.

Christa Downer is a Ph.D candidate in rhetoric at Texas Woman's University. She is currently working on her dissertation "The Making of a Civic America: Reconceptualizing the Rhetoric of Multiculturalism in the 21st Century." During her Ph.D studies, she completed a graduate certificate in Women's Studies. Her research interests include the theories and criticism(s) of rhetoric, composition and multicultural feminism.

Lester Faigley holds the Robert Adger Law and Thos. H. Law Centennial Professorship in Humanities at the University of Texas at Austin. He was the founding director of both the Division of Rhetoric and Composition and Concentration in Technology, Literacy, and Culture at Texas, and he served as the 1996 Chair of the Conference on College Composition and Communication. He currently directs the Undergraduate Writing Center at Texas. Professor Faigley has published ten books, including *Fragments of Rationality* (Pittsburgh, 1992) which received the MLA Mina P. Shaughnessy Prize and the CCCC Outstanding Book Award.

Kristie Fleckenstein is an Associate Professor of English at Ball State University. She is the author of *Embodied Literacies: Imageword and Poetics of Teaching* (Southern Illinois University Press 2003).

Richard R. Glejzer is Associate Professor of English in the Department of English and Director of First Year Writing at North Central College in Naperville, Illinois. He is the co-author of *Between Witness and Testimony: The Holocaust and the Limits of Representation* (SUNY 2001), the co-editor of *Witnessing the Disasters: Essays on Representation and the Holocaust* (Wisconsin 2003), and *Rhetoric in an Antifoundational World: Language, Culture, Pedagogy,* (Yale 1998). Professor Glejzer's current research considers the intersections between critical theory, rhetorics and ethics.

Catalina González is a graduate student of comparative Literature in the Graduate School of Arts and Sciences at Emory University.

G. Thomas Goodnight is a Professor and Director of Doctoral Studies at the Annenberg School of Communication at the University of Southern California. He has been accorded career awards in Rhetoric and Communication Theory by the NCA and has been named among the five top scholars in argumentation of the last 50 years by the AFA. He is a regular contributor to the *Quarterly Journal of Speech* and a former editor of *Argumentation and Advocacy*.

David C. Gore is a Ph.D candidate in Rhetoric and Public Affairs at Texas A & M University. His more recent publications have dealt with the interplay of rhetoric, ethical and economic issues in the work of Adam Smith, and separately, in contemporary inflation rhetoric. He is currently writing a dissertation entitled "Rhetoric and Economics" that focuses on the moral dimensions of the invention of economics as an academic discipline.

Gerard A. Hauser is a Professor of Communications at the University of Colorado at Boulder. He is a specialist in rhetoric and has published numerous articles and books on the subject of rhetorical theory and criticism, including *Introduction to Rhetorical Theory*, 2nd ed (2002) and *Vernacular Voices: The Rhetoric of Publics and Public Spheres*(1999). Professor Hauser is a Fellow of the Rhetoric Society of America and its immediate past President. He is recipient of the National Communication Association's Hochmuth-Nichols Award for public address scholarship, RSA's Kneupper Article Award and George E. Yoos Award for Services. His research focuses on classical rhetorical theory, dissident rhetoric and rhetorical features of public spheres. He is currently investigating the rhetoric of prisoners of conscience as a source of self-identity and as a call for civic society.

David Henry is chair and member of the academic faculty in Communication Studies at the University of Nevada in Las Vegas. He is Executive Director of the Rhetoric Society of America and Editor of the *Quarterly Journal of Speech* for 2005-07. His scholarship focuses on public advocacy in a variety of contexts, including presidential rhetoric and nuclear politics. He is co-author of a book on Ronald Reagan's political oratory and has published articles and reviews in the *Quarterly Journal of Speech, Communication Monographs, Communication Studies* and the *Rhetoric Society Quarterly*.

David Hingstman is a Professor in Communication Studies at the University of Iowa. He is Director of the A. Craig Baird Debate Forum and of the A. Craig Baird Center for Public Advocacy and Debate. His scholarly interests include argumentation, rhetorical criticism and freedom of expression as applied to the study of legal and political discourse.

Kristen E. Hoerl is a graduate student in the Department of Communication Studies at the University of Texas at Austin. Her scholarly interests include public memory, popular culture, and the rhetorics of dissent.

Mara Holt is Associate Professor of English at Ohio University in Athens. A graduate of the University of Texas at Austin with a Ph.D in English with a Rhetoric concentration, she is the author of many publications, most recently including "Collaboration and Conflict in a Faculty Mentoring Relationship" (with Albert Rouzie), Dialogue 8.2 (Spring 2003) and "Making Emotion Work Visible in Writing Program Administration" (with Leon Anderson and Albert Rouzie) in *A Way to Move: Rhetorics of Emotion and Composition Studies*. Eds. Dale Jacobs and Laura Micciche. Portsmouth, NH: Boynton/Cook, 2003. Professor Holt is currently at work on a book titled *Collaborative Learning in Composition Studies*, part of a series of reference guides edited by Charles Bazerman and published by a joint collaboration between Parlor Press and WAC Clearinghouse.

Julie Jung is an Assistant Professor in the Department of English at Illinois State University where she teaches courses in rhetorical theory, composition theory and writing, with an emphasis on theories and practices of revision. A graduate of the University of Arizona with a Ph.D in English, her professional affiliations include the College Composition and Communication, National Council of Teachers of English and the Rhetoric Society of America. Her articles have appeared in *JAC* and *Composition Studies*. A book titled *Revisionary Rhetoric, Feminist Pedagogy, and Multigenre Texts* is forthcoming in summer 2005 from SIUP.

Connie Kendall is currently writing her dissertation for a Ph.D in English at Miami University (Ohio). Her research interests include New Literacy Studies, linguistic pragmatics, American pragmatism and the history and politics of literacy/language assessment in US contexts. Connie teaches first-year college composition courses and cross-disciplinary courses in the study of language and literacy, has co-directed the Portfolio Placement Program, and held a two-year appointment as a writing consultant to Miami University's College of Business Administration faculty, both in Oxford, Ohio and in London, England. Her two most recent publications are "The Pedagogical Legacy Left to Us," a book review for *Peitho* (Summer 2002) and "Legislating Literacy: The Politics of Proficiency," a chapter in *The Literacy Standard* (Hampton Press 2002).

Thomas J. Kinney is a Ph.D candidate in the Rhetoric, Composition and Teaching program at the University of Arizona. He specializes in the history of classical, modern and contemporary rhetoric; political theories of rhetoric and composition; and comparative rhetorics. His publications include "Remapping the Archive: Recovered Literature and the Deterritorialization of the Canon" in *Recovering the U.S. Hispanic Literary Heritage*, Vol. 4 and "Civic Humanism, A Postmortem?" (co-written with Thomas P. Miller) forthcoming in *The Viability of the Rhetorical Transition*. He is currently working on his dissertation, "The Political Unconscious of Rhetoric: Remapping the Rhetorical Tradition," which is an analysis of the material conditions of rhetorical theory and practice.

Kevin D. Kuswa is Director of Debate in the Department of Rhetoric and Communication Studies at the University of Richmond. He earned his Ph.D at the University of Texas in 2001 and his research areas include cultural studies, rhetoric, globalization, argumentation and debate. Dr. Kuswa's recent work appears in *Law in Society*, *Controversia* and *Rhizomes*, and he teaches a class on the rhetoric of terrorism that has been profiled on CNN.com.

Lisa Langstraat is an Associate Professor in the Department of English at Colorado State University. Among the courses she teaches are Composition Theory and Pedagogy, Literacy

Studies, Service-Learning, Cultural Studies, History of Rhetoric and Feminist Theories. She also teaches victim empathy classes to juvenile offenders at a local non-profit agency that serves at-risk youth. Co-author of a textbook, *Four Worlds of Writing: Inquiry and Action in Context* 4th ed., Dr. Langstraat has published articles in such journals as *JAC: A Quarterly Journal for the Interdisciplinary Study of Rhetoric, Writing, Multiple Literacies and Politics, Composition Forum, Works and Days* and in several collections.

Peter Mack is a professor of English at Warwick University who specializes in the field of medieval and renaissance European intellectual, cultural and literary history. Most of his publications are connected with Renaissance rhetoric and dialectic, including *Renaissance Argument: Valla and Agricola in the Traditions of Rhetoric and Dialectic* (1993). He has also published articles on rhetoric and literature, Chaucer and fifteenth and sixteenth century practices of reading. His *Elizabethan Composition* (2002) studies the impact of grammar school and university training on early modern practices of reading and writing in ethics, history, politics and religion. He has been editor of *Rhetorica* (University of California Press) from 1998-2002. He is currently writing a book comparing Shakespeare's and Montaigne's use of the resources of humanist rhetorical and ethical education.

Beth Innocenti Manolescu is an Assistant Professor in Communication Studies at the University of Kansas. Her teaching and research interests are in the history of rhetoric and argumentation theory. Her publications include "Formal Proprietary as Rhetorical Norm" in *Argumentation* (2004), "Kames's Legal Career and Writings as Precedents for Elements of Criticism" in *Rhetorica* (in press), and "Traditions of Rhetoric, Criticism and Argument in Lord Kames's Elements of Criticism," *Rhetoric Review* (2003). She has served on the Steering Committee of the American Society for the History of Rhetoric.

Danielle Mitchell is Assistant Professor in Liberal Arts at Pennsylvania State University (Fayette)-The Eberly Campus, where she teaches courses in composition and literature. Her primary research interests are in rhetoric and composition, cultural studies and queer theory. In addition to the article in this volume, publications addressing the representations of sexuality in popular culture are forthcoming in *The Journal of Popular Culture* and *Queer TV* (McFarland Press).

Terese Guinsatao Monberg is an assistant professor in the Department of English at the University of Kansas, where she teaches courses in writing, composition studies, and cultural rhetorics. Her research interests include Filipino and Asian American rhetoric(s), emergent writing publics, and public memory. She is currently working on a book-length manuscript based on her study of the Filipino American National Historical Society (FANHS). Her article, "Re-Centering Authority, Social Reflexivity and Re-Positioning in Composition Research" (written with Ellen Cushman) appeared in *Under Construction: Working at the Intersections of Composition Theory, Research, and Practice*.

Joddy Murray is an Assistant Professor in Writing and Rhetoric at Washington State University. He currently directs the Writing Center as well as the Digital Technology and Culture degree on the Tri-Cities campus. His specializations include image rhetoric, language theory, and the connections between the affective domain and multimodal, non-discursive texts. His most recent publication is "Michel de Certeau's Language Theory," *Journal of College Writing*: 6.1 (2003).

Ellen Quandahl is Associate Professor of Rhetoric and Writing Studies and director of the Lower Division Writing Program at San Diego State University. Her teaching and research interests include rhetorical history and theory, the intersection of theory and pedagogy, the teaching of writing and reading and Kenneth Burke. Her essays have appeared in *College English, Rhetoric Review, Rhetoric Society Quarterly* and *JAC*.

Thomas Rickert is Assistant Professor of English at Purdue University. His areas of interest include histories and theories of rhetoric, composition theory, modern/postmodern theory, cultural studies and network culture. His most recent publication is "'Hands Up, You are Free': Composition in a Post-Oedipal World" in *JAC*:21.2 (Spring, 2001). He is an editor for the online journal *Enculturation*.

Beth Ann Rothermel is an Associate Professor teaching writing and American literature at Westfield State College. While a graduate student at UT, Professor Rothermel found an interest in the field of rhetoric and composition. While studying in Europe, she was curious about the ways in which writing and literature are taught in other countries. Her dissertation, compared language-arts instruction in Sweden and the USA. Based on this research, she published an article in a Dutch language-arts journal. More recently, she has been doing research on the history of women's education in reading, speaking and writing at Massachusetts Normal Schools. Her essay on the experiences of 19th century women at the Westfield Normal School appeared in *Rhetoric Society Quarterly* (Winter, 2003).

Albert Rouzie is an Associate Professor of Rhetoric and Composition in the Department of English at Ohio University. He has published articles in *CCC, Computers and Composition, JAC,* and *Dialogue.* His book, *At Play in the Fields of Writing: A Serio-Ludic Rhetoric,* is forthcoming in 2005 from Hampton Press.

Jacqueline Jones Royster is Professor of English at The Ohio State University. She is the author of *Traces of a Stream: Literacy and Social Change Among African American Women* (University of Pittsburgh Press, 2000); editor of *Southern Horrors and Other Writings: the Anti-Lynching Campaign of Ida B. Wells* (Bedford, 1997); and co-editor of *Double Stitch: Black Writers About Mothers and Daughters* (Beacon Press, 1991) and *Calling Cards: Theory and Practice in the Study of Race, Gender, and Culture* (2005). Her textbooks include: *Critical Inquiries: Readings on Culture and Community* (Addison Wesley Longman, 2003); *Writer's Choice* (Glencoe/McGraw-Hill, 1994-2005), and *Reader's Choice* (Glencoe/McGraw-Hill, 2002). She is also the author of several articles and reviews in composition studies, rhetorical studies, and women's studies.

Christine Mason Sutherland teaches courses in rhetoric and the history of rhetoric and also the senior seminar in Communications in the Faculty of Communication and Culture at the University of Calgary. She has published essays on the rhetoric of St. Augustine of Hippo, but her work has mostly been on women in the history of rhetoric. Her publications include: In press: *The Eloquence of Mary Astell* to be published by the University of Calgary Press in

Spring, 2005; "Augustine, Ethos and Integrative Nature of Christian Rhetoric," in *Rhetor*, (Fall, 2004) [E. Journal, www.cssr.scer.ca/rhetor], "Margaret Cavendish, Duchess of New Castle" in *Dictionary of Literary Biography: British Rhetoricians and Logicians 1500-1660.* Vol. 281, 2nd Series: Ed. Edward A. Malone, Detroit: Gale, 2003. "Feminist Historiography: Research Methods in Rhetoric" in RSQ 32:1 (Winter 2002). Principal editor of *The Changing Tradition: Women in the History of Rhetoric.* Ed. Christine Mason Sutherland and Rebecca Sutcliffe. Calgary: University of Calgary Press, 1999. "Women in the History of Rhetoric: The Past and the Future." (Plenary Address from ISHR conference, 1997) in *The Changing Tradition*.

Lisa Storm Villadsen is an Assistant Professor of Rhetoric at the Department of Media, Cognition and Communication at the University of Copenhagen. A graduate of Northwestern University with a Ph.D in Communication Studies, she currently pursues her interest in contemporary American rhetorical scholarship in her native Denmark. Her teaching and research interests focus on rhetorical criticism and modern rhetorical theory. Among her publications are articles on the concept of genre in rhetorical criticism and on the relationship between theory, methods, and models in rhetorical criticism. Her current research project concerns the basis and nature of normativity in rhetorical criticism. Professor Villadsen is Danish Editor of the Scandinavian Journal *Rhetorica Scandinavica*.

Lynda Walsh is an Assistant Professor of English at the New Mexico Institute of Mining and Technology, where she coordinates the Freshman Writing program and the Writing Center. Her current research interests include pragmatic methodologies for studying scientific writing, gender equity in science education, and non-western philosophies of science and rhetoric. Her most recent publication is "A Rhetorical Perspective on the Sokal Hoax: Genre, Style, and Context" with Marie Secor in *Written Communication* (January 2004). A book manuscript based on her dissertation, "Sins Against Science: Scientific Media Hoaxes in Nineteenth-Century America," is currently under review at SUNY Press.

I

Rhetorical Agendas

1

Rhetorics Fast and Slow

Lester L. Faigley
University of Texas at Austin

Remember the 2000 Presidential election? It seems now like ancient history. Looking back, the election gave out-of-favor nations the chance to poke the ribs of the know-it-all super-power that loves to preach about the ideals of democracy. Robert Mugabe's administration in Zimbabwe offered to send observers to help Floridians run a fair election, Havana's daily, *Granma*, ran a headline calling the United States a "banana republic," and other recipients of American advice over the years—China, Russia, even Saddam Hussein's Iraq—all got in their digs (Freedland). But nearly every American newspaper missed the humor. They failed to report the international teasing, choosing instead to draw morals that every vote counts and that the framers of the Constitution were wise to allow so much time to sort out muddled elections.

This pontificating, however, underscored the opposite of what was being claimed. The 2000 Presidential election demonstrated that every vote *doesn't* count, and I'm not speaking of discarded ballots. It revealed that unless an election is effectively tied, only those votes tabulated immediately end up counting. The absentee votes of one million Californians became relevant only because the outcome of the popular vote remained in doubt. Most remarkable was the case of Oregon, where ballots were cast entirely by mail. Even though the election was called an incredible success by leading politicians in the state, the recipient of Oregon's seven electoral votes was not decided until nine days after the election because of the slowness in counting—not recounting—the ballots (Egan).

Oregon's choice of mail ballots indicates the depth of nostalgia for eighteenth-century voting practices and a rebellion against exit polls and media-driven politics. Nonetheless, Oregonians cannot pretend to live in a world without instantaneous communication any more than Amish buggy drivers can pretend they do not share highways with cars and trucks traveling more than a mile a minute. If the national election had been ordinary, the voters of Oregon would have been consigned to the equivalent of garbage time in basketball games, where substitutes determine the final score long after the outcome has been determined.

The lesson of the 2000 election was not that every vote counts, or even that the electoral college, which worked effectively only during George Washington's lifetime, is obsolete.[1] If there is a lesson to be drawn, it was perhaps most visibly displayed on CNBC, where for days

3

one window showed a frozen electoral vote awaiting Florida's results beside another that gave nearly instantaneous values of the volatile Dow, NASDAQ, and S&P 500. Our institutions operate today on radically different speeds, which has been the case for many decades, but digital technologies have greatly magnified the differences and they have intensified a global culture that affects us daily in large and small ways.

This essay is about fast versus slow, and I'm keenly aware of how anachronistic was its original presentation, read to a seated audience. I'm the Amish buggy driver in the slow lane. I used one of the oldest of literate technologies—reading an extended written text aloud— the epitome of what I'm calling slow rhetoric. And the auditors, at least those who didn't nod off, performed an increasingly rare act of cognition—making connections among ideas in an extended monologue while simultaneously engaging in a mental dialogue with the speaker. And yet, if you're anything like me, you find this act more difficult than ever. It's hard even for us, educated in the culture of the book, to stay focused on an extended presentation delivered at slow speed and low bandwidth.

Fast rhetorics dominate our world—e-mail, cell phones, instant messaging, digital photographs, Web sites, running headlines across the bottom of news programs. We all have messages waiting for which quick replies are expected. In fast rhetoric, rapid fire, visual intensity, wit, and originality win out over lengthy exposition, explicit logical relations, sobriety, and order. But fast rhetorics alone have not created a disciplinary crisis in rhetoric or in any other discipline for that matter. Fast electronic rhetorics have been around since the telegraph, and the predecessors like semaphore communication go back even further. Even the graffiti on the walls of Pompeii could be considered fast rhetoric.

Likewise, the comparison of fast and slow is hardly novel. I first met the idea that media shape the message in Marshall McLuhan's *Understanding Media* as a college freshman in 1965. And the idea wasn't new with McLuhan either. (McLuhan drew heavily on the work of his teacher, Harold Innis.) Debates about fast versus slow communication technologies closely follow the appearance of new media; recall Thoreau's remark about the telegraph in *Walden*: what if "Maine and Texas ... have nothing important to communicate" (52).

Much of contemporary communications studies is devoted to fast rhetorics and many of the key findings, like the shortening of segments in news broadcasting, have become general knowledge. And many writing teachers, including me, encourage students to produce multimedia texts. So what is different now? I would argue that the difference lies in how fast rhetorics are embodied in larger cultural trends. The proliferation of digital technologies since 1990 has accelerated the pace of global capitalism, uncertainty, complexity, and individualism.

The much talked about digital divide is usually represented as a divide between rich and poor. Certainly digital technologies have aided the enormous expansion of wealth among the richest people in the world over the past decade, but digital technologies arrive too late to be counted as a major cause of glaring poverty. Rather, the digital divide is one of speed. Put simply, institutions, organizations, and people who travel fast and light now dominate those that move slowly and are tied to particular locations. For those who travel fast, for example, transnational corporations and global investors, slow institutions like national governments are viewed as little more than potential impediments.

Increasingly, national governments have become what the German social scientist, Ulrich Beck, in a 1999 interview, called "zombie institutions"—institutions which are "dead and still alive" (quoted in Bauman 6). We live in a world where many institutions appear on the outside to have changed little. They carry the same names and still occupy the same buildings, but what goes on inside has changed to the extent that original missions have been relegated to the margins or forgotten altogether. At this point we have to ask to what extent is the university, as traditionally conceived, a "zombie institution"? By traditional, I mean an institution with most of its members physically proximate and with the liberal arts at the core of its undergraduate curriculum. By "zombie," I mean an institution that is dead but still alive—dead in the sense that its primary mission has been vacated but still alive in the sense that it performs important secondary functions that justify its existence.

The mission of higher education as traditionally articulated in the United States aims at preparing students for citizenship through the liberal arts component of the undergraduate curriculum. The place of rhetoric, real or imagined, in the undergraduate curriculum has been closely tied to this mission. Arguments for the centrality of rhetoric have maintained that rhetoric provides the means for reuniting the fragmented disciplines of the liberal arts and restores the liberal arts as a manual for living. While these arguments have been criticized as nostalgic, some version of the polis without the exclusions of gender, class, race, ethnicity, disability, and sexual orientation remains implicit even in the best arguments for rhetoric as the means to participatory democracy.

This vision of people talking with each other and more importantly listening to each other has been invoked with every new electronic communications technology. The following statement is typical:

> It is impossible that old prejudices and hostilities should longer exist, while such an instrument has been created for an exchange of thought between all the nations of the earth. Such is the vista which this new triumph of the might of human intelligence opens to us. Every one must feel stronger and freer at the accession of such an increase of power to the human family. (Briggs and Maverick 22)

These words were written to celebrate the completion of the transatlantic cable in 1858, yet they remind us of the hype written about the Internet and particularly the World Wide Web just a decade ago. Celebrants of the Internet issued sweeping claims that it would resolve ethnic and national conflicts, create a new sense of community, revitalize participatory democracy, and bring about global cohesion.

Looking at these claims for new technologies in retrospect, we can see that observers were correct in noting that change was occurring, but they seldom predicted accurately the direction change would take. Indeed, the primary effects were not those that could have been anticipated. The major examples are now familiar. The electric telegraph, invented primarily for railroad control, led to the modern concept of late-breaking news and made possible a national commodities market. The telephone, envisioned as a broadcasting medium, turned out to be used for two-way communication. The wireless, invented as a form of the telegraph, evolved into radio, the broadcasting medium imagined for the telephone. And more recently, the World Wide Web, imagined as a global library, became in a few months a global home shopping network.

The reason those who predicted the impacts of new technologies turned out to be so uniformly wrong was that they believed in technological determinism. Instead, new technologies quickly became implicated in larger social, economic, and political forces. While echoes of technological determinism remain in advertisements, the belief that world peace and world understanding will result from connecting people is gone. I think we know how the next chapter of the Internet will turn out: the new technologies will be faster, smaller, and more ubiquitous—integrating text, voice, and images. (Computers are now in eyeglasses frames and jewelry; reduction of battery size is the nagging issue.) We're entering a time when many forms of digital content—movies, music, games, the Web—will be delivered in multiple forms to anybody with disposable income.

But it's hard to imagine the world as a more harmonious place just because people have the increased potential to talk with each other. Just the opposite is happening as vividly demonstrated by the cell phones used to detonate the bombs on Madrid railroads on March 11, 2004. Fundamentalism is on the rise. The thesis that fundamentalism is a reaction to modernity offered by Benjamin Barber in *Jihad vs. McWorld* does not explain why people do not seem to be getting along very well within developed nations either. The tone of public discourse—be it in political campaigns, opinion in print and in pixels, talk radio, and discussion boards—has taken a turn toward the ugly. More information seems to have led to less understanding. Brenda Laurel, one of the more insightful commentators on the effects of digital media, observes:

> I see a world where dominator politics prevail, where human rights abuses multiply in direct relation to increasing poverty and overpopulation. I see world religions in a state of rigor mortis, with a death grip on science, art, and the exchange of ideas. I see the ecology of the Alaskan Arctic devoured by petro-gluttony and the forest of Indonesia in flames. Worst of all, I see a world where people can't talk to each other in any meaningful way. Global networking will be a tool of business communication, consumerism, propaganda, banal conversations, and mindless entertainment. We will have forgotten how to tell stories or how to hear them. The majority of the world's population will be very young people without extended families or intact cultures, with fanatical allegiances to dead religions or live dictatorships. We have what Jonas Salk called a "wisdom deficit." (102–03)

Perhaps McLuhan was right to proclaim a global village, but the village has become claustrophobic and oppressive. Paul Virilio says the world has become an echo chamber; interactivity is nothing more than our words bounced back immediately.

So what has happened? In one sense, to call the present the Information Age seems silly. Any society where animals interact—bees, ants, wolves, chimpanzees, and, of course, humans—is an information society. Without the ability to communicate information about the location of food sources, bees could not survive. The ability to communicate more complex subjects effectively gave our human ancestors an evolutionary edge over competing primate species, eventually leading to urban centers and empires.

What is different about the present era from earlier centuries is the amount of information available. The potent combination of digital and satellite technologies has brought a deluge of information to affluent people in affluent nations that could not have been imagined a few years earlier. We can safely predict the volume will increase over the next few years as the delivery becomes faster, cheaper, and more portable.

The glut of information that is readily accessible has not led to broader global understanding but instead to increased fragmentation, confusion, and exhaustion. And it has changed our daily lives. Think for a moment about the following statements. Do they apply to you?

1. I carry a cell phone.
2. Too much of my day is occupied by e-mail.
3. I check my e-mail frequently, even at times when I know I will receive nothing of importance.

4. I purchase more books that I'm able to read.
5. I have too little time to do sustained reading for pleasure.
6. I have too little time to pursue interests outside work.
7. I have so many competing demands on me that I often find it difficult to decide what to do first.
8. I find myself more impatient when I feel I am losing seconds, such as when an elevator door is slow to close or a computer is slow to boot up.

For me, all the above is true except for a cell phone. And, except for time to read for pleasure and to pursue interests outside work, none was true for me twenty years ago.

Information beyond what a person could acquire from a particular location or remember from past experience was a scarce resource until recent times. Now the scarce resource is filters for those deluged with information. Fast has overwhelmed slow. No wonder the simplistic filters of fundamentalism are spreading. And no wonder we feel threatened.

Speed brings risks. We live in a world of risks beyond our control to the extent that it difficult to think of anything that is risk free down to the most basic human acts—sex in an era of AIDS, eating in an era of genetically altered food, walking outside in an ozone-depleted atmosphere, drinking water and breathing air laden with chemicals whose effects we do not understand. Should we eat more fish in our daily diet? Nutritionists tell us that eating fish reduces the risk of heart disease. But other scientists tell us that fish are contaminated with a new generation of synthetic chemicals.

Our era, of course, is not unique as a time of uncertainty. Disease, famine, and natural disasters were the daily reality for most humans in times before modernity and for many living in it now. But today, most risks are produced by humans. Beginning with Rachel Carson's *Silent Spring* in 1962, we stopped worrying so much about what nature was doing to us and more about what we were doing to nature. Science and technology, which had been viewed as the solution to problems, suddenly became their cause.

Going faster and faster leads to more and more accidents. We are consuming resources at a pace far beyond what can be sustained, and we already see the effects in our deteriorating ecosystems and the widening gap between rich and poor. Many of us sense that we're compromising future generations.

A sustainable future demands that our society finds it unacceptable to act in disregard of our descendants. Such changes of social outlook have happened in the not too distant past. Less than two centuries ago most Americans accepted slavery, which very few people would now defend. Attitudes toward slavery changed because of debates in slow rhetoric.

The musician Brian Eno says:

> Humans are capable of a unique trick: creating realities by first imagining them, by experiencing them in their minds. When Martin Luther King said, "I have a dream," he was inviting others to dream it with him. Once a dream becomes shared in that way, current reality gets measured against it and then modified towards it. As soon as we sense the possibility of a more desirable world, we begin behaving differently—as though that world is starting to come into existence, as though, in our minds at least, we're already there. The dream becomes an invisible force which pulls us forward.

Slow rhetoric is the means for dreams to be articulated. Our courses are a major site where slow rhetoric can be practiced. We know how to teach slow rhetoric and what slow rhetoric can accomplish. Many examples were given at the 2004 Rhetoric Society of America (RSA) conference, including Jerry Hauser's examination of the rhetorics of conscience produced by Dietrich Bonhoeffer, Vaclav Havel, and Nelson Mandela (ch. 2, this vol.) and Jackie Royster's exploration of Bernice Johnson Reagon's statement, "Silence in a democracy is a dangerous thing," in the writing of African American women (ch. 4, this vol.). Indeed, an academic conference is a celebration of the power of slow rhetoric.

At the same time, however, we are challenged by trends I've described that affect our daily lives and those of our students. It's difficult to be an effective teacher of slow rhetoric if you cannot slow down yourself. I experienced how pace affects seeing and thinking when just before the 2004 RSA conference, I paddled one hundred miles down the Green River in Utah and hiked in several of the side canyons. Hiking or paddling the deep canyons of the Four Corners region is a profound experience in time travel. Down and down through layer after layer of sedimentary rock—mud frozen into stone. Back and back in time to 300 million years ago. On the sides of the canyons are 800-year-old Anasazi ruins that look as if they were abandoned only a few decades ago, a mistake John Wesley Powell made on his first descent of the Green and Colorado Rivers in 1869. In other places are the remains of uranium mines, with one dead bulldozer that has barely rusted in fifty years. On a time scale, we humans represent the dust atop 1500-foot cliffs.

Many people each day see canyons similar to the ones I paddled from viewpoints at the top. They drive up, take a snapshot, and if they pause long enough to read the brochure they were handed when they paid to enter the park, they can identify 300 million years of geological history. What is missing from that quick look is the narrative provided by going slowly downward. Each stratum is different because you experience it directly: you walk on it, you camp on it, you eat your lunch on it. Moreover, you become more aware of yourself as a porous bag of water, where a strenuous side hike can require six quarts to replenish. The Green River is so muddy that it is extraordinarily difficult to filter, and the few puddles in the side canyons are undependable. How long you can stay in the desert depends on how much water you can carry.

Finally, neither the Anasazi nor the white settlers who tried to farm and ranch on the upper Green River were able to remain in the canyons. Their fate speaks to us now. They could not survive extended droughts. Today we are threatened not so much by drought, famine, and disease, but by the ways we have chosen to live. We now face a crisis of sustainability that poses a real threat to the survival of humans and other forms of life. Within a hundred years, loss of habitat along with climate change will doom as many as half the species on earth to extinction or ghost status, surviving in zoos or as DNA samples. The evidence for accelerating climate change is now overwhelming and unavoidable. While there will be some regions that benefit from global warming, the effects on coastal regions and aquatic ecosystems are already becoming evident. For example, hundreds of thousands of seabirds in the islands along the coast of Scotland failed to breed in 2004 because of starvation. The cause was the disappearance of the sandeel, a small fish that sustained larger fish, marine mammals, and seabirds. The plankton, on which the sandeel feed, moved north because the water around Scotland became too warm.

The situation for humans is not all that much better. Along with degradation of the environment and the depletion of natural resources, poverty, unemployment, and the disintegration of communities have accelerated. A sustainable future depends not only on a healthy environment; sustainable communities and institutions must be based on social justice. People in rich countries can no longer deny opportunities for safe, productive lives to people in poor countries, not to mention opportunities to the poor in their own countries.

That most of our problems are human-created is both a cause for optimism and depression. Many problems could be addressed if people choose to do so. Yet a sense of inevitability—that nothing can be done—pervades our culture. Fast rhetorics are manifestation of a culture that suffers from attention deficit disorder, a culture where things are quickly used and discarded, a culture where the abuse of the environment and gaping inequalities are ignored. As Jackie Royster puts it, we need better ways of being and better ways of doing (see ch. 4, this vol.). We need pedagogies that encourage students to develop a sense of place, a sense of stewardship, a sense of equity, and a sense of connectedness to the world around them. We need to make better arguments about the value of slow rhetoric and be more imaginative about creating spaces where slow rhetoric can be practiced. The fate of future generations will depend on how well the students we teach can use slow rhetoric.

NOTES

1. In the nation's third election in 1796, thirteen candidates received votes, with John Adams winning the most, becoming President, and Thomas Jefferson second, becoming Vice President. But when two political parties appeared on the scene in 1800, the candidates from one party—the Democratic-Republicans—tied for electoral votes, forcing the House of Representatives to decide that Jefferson would become President and Aaron Burr Vice President. The Twelfth Amendment to the Constitution patched the immediate problem, but the fundamental flaw was exposed.

WORKS CITED

Barber, Benjamin. *Jihad vs. McWorld*. New York: Times, 1995.

Bauman, Zygmunt. *Liquid Modernity*. Cambridge: Polity, 2000.

Briggs, Charles F., and Augustus Maverick. *The Story of the Telegraph and a History of the Great Atlantic Cable*. New York: Rudd, 1858.

Carson, Rachel. *Silent Spring*. Boston: Houghton, 1962.

Egan, Timothy. "Days After Its Historic Vote, Oregon Still Trying to Pick a Winner." *New York Times* 11 Nov. 2000, late ed.: A15.

Eno, Brian. "The Big Here and Long Now." *Digitalsouls.com*. 2001. 27 May 2004 <http://www.digitalsouls.com/2001/Brian_Eno_Big_Here.html>.

Freedland, Jonathan. "Mechanical Politics." *Guardian* 11 Nov. 2000: 26.

Innis, Harold. *Empire and Communications*. Oxford: Clarendon, 1950.

Laurel, Brenda. *Utopian Entrepreneur*. Cambridge: MIT UP, 2001.

McLuhan, Marshall. *Understanding Media: The Extensions of Man*. New York: New American Library, 1964.

Thoreau, Henry David. *Walden*. Ed. J. Lyndon Shanley. Princeton: Princeton UP, 1971.

Virilio, Paul, and Sylvere Lotringer. *Crepuscular Dawn*. Trans. Mike Taormina. Los Angeles: Semiotext(e), 2002.

2

Moral Vernaculars and Rhetorics of Conscience

Gerard A. Hauser
University of Colorado–Boulder

The only lost cause is the one we give up on before we enter the struggle.

—Vaclav Havel (*Summer Meditations* 3)

Two years ago, the theme for the Rhetoric Society of America's biennial conference was "Rhetorical Democracy." The conferees discussed its prospects against the backdrop of September 11, 2001, and the rhetorical construction of national understanding of that event and its aftermath. We are still on the same question—shocked by the devastation of 9/11, fearful for our safety, concerned about the consequences it has had on U.S. domestic and foreign policy, divided about the language used to discuss it, wary of the extreme rhetoric it has launched and rhetorical repression it has ushered in, and disturbed by the extent to which basic civil rights of citizens and human rights of foreign nationals are now being legally abrogated.

> Today, all the talk is of globalization. But far too often, both its advocates and its critics have portrayed globalization as an exclusively economic and technological phenomenon. In fact, in the new millennium, there are at least three universal "languages": money, the Internet, and democracy and human rights. (U.S. Department of State, "Introduction")

With these words, the U.S. Department of State begins its 1999 annual report on international human rights practices. Framing human rights in conjunction with money and the Internet suggests too easily that there is growing international discourse on human rights because moral individualism is somehow joined to economic individualism and that it has become a global language because it serves the interests of the powerful. In fact, the opposite is the case. Money and human rights are more commonly antagonists, as the pressure brought against large conglomerates for abusive labor practices in Third World nations demonstrates. The globalization of human rights is rather a function of localization; its success as an international movement depends on its ability to embed itself in the language and culture of nations independent of the United States and the West. I wish to examine this localizing discourse, a discourse of the *moral vernacular*. I will explore it through the lens of resistance rhetoric in hopes that its moral vernaculars might provide insight into our present circumstances and what rhetoric scholars might contribute to advancing the political, ethical, and spiritual health of the body politic.

HUMAN RIGHTS AND THE PROBLEM OF MORAL UNIVERSALISM

Shortly after World War II had ended and the United Nations had formed, world leaders set to drafting what became the Universal Declaration of Human Rights. This document was intended to enunciate the rights of all human beings and the obligations of sovereign states to respect them. This was a remarkable endeavor, considering the condition of the world in 1947 and the differences between states over their relations to their citizens and their respective assumptions of sovereignty. Were it not for the unsurpassed leadership of Eleanor Roosevelt, the endeavor likely would have failed. Her skill at keeping self-interested arguments of national representatives in check and the drafting committee's focus clear were critical.

More challenging than competing interests for the final document's ultimate shape and present-day consequences for human rights rhetoric were deep philosophical differences already present when Mrs. Roosevelt first convened a drafting committee in her Washington Square apartment in February 1947. At that meeting two philosophers, Peng-Chun Chang, a Chinese Confucian who had studied under John Dewey at Columbia, and Charles Malik, a Lebanese Greek Orthodox Thomist, got into a row over the bases of human rights. At stake was how far to go in the direction of pragmatic compromise without putting truth, and thereby moral universality, up for grabs (Glendon 47). At one point the argument became so heated that Mrs. Roosevelt concluded the only way to make progress were if West and East agreed to disagree (Ignatieff, "Human Rights" 58). Her choice was wise since it also allowed all parties to avoid the uncomfortable discussion that would have ensued had the skeletons been brought from the closet. The Soviet Union had no more interest in explaining the Red Terror than the United States had in its Jim Crow laws or the British in its colonial practices. Everyone had something to be ashamed of, but the point was not to embarrass each other with indictments of what *is* but to keep themselves focused on the high principles of *ought*.

High principles also skirted the question of enforcement. The Universal Declaration provides no mandate for intervention to stop human rights abuses, leaving Mrs. Roosevelt's uncertainty that "a mere statement of rights, without legal obligations, would inspire governments to see that these rights were preserved" (qtd. in Urquhart 32) as the real question ever since. The Universal Declaration left untouched the U.N. Charter's guarantee of state sovereignty. "Instead," as Michael Ignatieff observes, "the delegates put their hopes in the idea that by declaring rights as moral universals, they could foster global rights consciousness among those they called 'the common people'" ("Human Rights" 58).

The rhetorical character of moral universalism without the undergirding of a specific philosophy or theology makes the Universal Declaration an affirmation of a secular creed left ambiguous in its justification so as to better move among different political systems and cultural frames (Taylor 126). With Nazi atrocities fresh on everyone's mind, the framers asserted the priority of each person's basic humanity as entailing fundamental rights that nations must agree to accept and respect. It may not have set forth specific consequences for failure to respect these rights, but the world has acted *as if* abusing human rights could go neither unnoticed nor unpunished, at least as this view is reflected in the rhetoric of human rights on the international stage.

The ideals of moral perfectionism, however, are hard to live by, especially when trouble hits. Their abstract righteousness offers a language of anti-politics, which inspires rhetorical neutrality toward national interests in order to privilege the inherent worth of every human regardless of national origin, belief, or creed. This rhetorical position is problematic when your nation is under attack. It is difficult to criticize your government when you can be attacked for being unpatriotic. Defending, say, the human rights of "enemy combatant" detainees at Guantánamo accused of being part of the Al Quaeda network or part of the Taliban, with the language of moral universals seems, to an audience of angry and fearful citizens, not only unpatriotic but also impudent and irrelevant (Ignatieff "Rights Stuff" 18).

MORAL VERNACULARS

Such conditions are not new, and the moral panic they inspire is not unique to the United States. They are as ancient as Antigone's placing of her familial obligation to Polynices's slain remains above that to the edict of a spiteful king. To make sense of her act as resistance required that she explain not only to Creon but also to herself why she had to pay final service to her brother's corpse. She prefaces her explanation by reflection on the question: What law lies behind these words? (Sophocles 39) It is a question that pertains to all manifestations of resistance.

Since adoption of the Universal Declaration, resistance discourse has appropriated the language of human rights to serve its rhetoric of opposition. The laws behind its words are moral universals, whose decontextualized language requires refitting to meet local demands. The rhetorical problem of moral universalism, whose premises lack transcultural supporting assumptions, is to convert them into the moral vernacular of the society and culture to which their claims on conduct are addressed.

This conversion is not entirely straightforward, at least if we are to judge by the rhetoric of political prisoners. The rhetorical animus of their call to conscience seldom begins with the inherent responsiveness of an audience of virtuous citizens who act on the basis of what moral conviction demands; nor is the rhetorical animus the actor's virtue. Their rhetoric is situated within the frame of the rhetoric to which it responds. To counter the state's monopoly on power and violence, the moral vernacular of resistance flows, instead, from the orientation of the vice to which it responds, and more specifically, which vice the rhetor puts first. I wish to explore this thesis through appeals by three prisoners of conscience. Their rhetoric translates moral universals into the moral vernacular of three different societies and times through the prism of what Judith Shklar calls ordinary vices: Dietrich Bonhoeffer, Vaclav Havel, and Nelson Mandela.

Dietrich Bonhoeffer

For Germany in the 1930s, the line of conflict was not clearly drawn. The evil of Nazism was not evident to the majority of Germans as it was to citizens in occupied territories of France, Holland, and Norway, where issues of sovereignty and human rights sparked resistance movements. There was terror in Germany, but matters were confused by the semblance of legitimacy to the Nazi government (Burke) that appeared legal, respectable, and even clean. The Nazi promise of national rebirth, overcoming economic crisis and unemployment, breaking from the chains of Versailles, and its vision of *Volksgemeinschaft* over-coming the haggling of party interests and class proved a great temptation (Stern). Resisters in Germany were without widespread social support; they were called "'strang-ers' among our own people" (von Klemperer 144).

Dietrich Bonhoeffer was a protestant theologian whose writings during the late 1920s and through the 1930s earned him international acclaim. He held a faculty appointment at the University of Berlin, served as a pastor, was a founder of the Confessing Church, an ecu-menical protestant sect, and was a pacifist. He also was active in the German counter-intelligence group within *Abwehr,* the Nazi intelligence agency, and had participated in the ongoing plot to assassinate Hitler, for which he was hanged, at age 39, on April 9, 1945, mere weeks before Germany surrendered.

Bonhoeffer maintained that the true Christian is not a member of a religion but a be-liever who sees Christian life in this world and who acts, as we must, for peace and social justice while accepting that what is required of us will not be delivered by a shaft of divine light. Christians could not, as Karl Barth and the Confessing Church had advised, "en-trench ourselves persistently behind the 'faith of the Church,' and evade the honest ques-tion as to what we ourselves really believe" (von Klemperer 203). Asking "What does it mean to do good?" raised the wrong question. Since evil exists in the world, it must be con-fronted by manifesting Christian moral agency through worldly practice. The real ques-tion, Bonhoeffer insisted, is "What is the will of God, what is required of us at this time, what are we called to do?"

During the decade of the 1930s, Bonhoeffer had urged the Lutheran Church to take stands opposing both Nazi oppression of Jews and the war. In terms of ordinary vices, the Nazis were guilty of cruelty, and Hitler was its public exemplar. Cruelty inspires fear, which seemed to grip the Church and the ecumenical movement. They had chosen a path of accom-modation by remaining silent rather than accepting the political repercussions of speaking out. Silence in the face of cruelty left morality in abstract terms. Moreover, silence was self-deception, a form of hypocrisy that made cruelty easier by quieting the one voice able to dissent with moral authority. The Church had succumbed to what Bonhoeffer called "cheap grace," grace without the cross (*Discipleship* 41–102). Christians could only defeat evil with "costly grace," attained through the discipleship dictated by the Sermon on the Mount. The price of following a homily whose political trajectory leads to activism and passive resistance was high. It cost them their lives.

On one hand, Bonhoeffer's commitments of conscience as a pacifist, as a Christian, and as a pastor were not easily reconciled with acts of duplicity, violence, and the risk of death for the sake of Christianity and Germany's honor. Confronted by evil, civilized and cultured Germans, who were morally righteous Christian believers, had collapsed under the weight of their own ineffectual rationalizations. At the same time, acts that violated Christian morality for a righteous cause were still violations of fundamental commitments of one's own con-science. Bonhoeffer had these considerations in mind when he wrote his Christmas letter at the end of 1942, "After Ten Years," to assess the consequences of Hitler's decade in power and the work he shared with Claus Oster and Hans von Dohnanyi, his collaborators in the re-sistance and to whom, along with his friend Eberhard Bethge and his parents, the letter was sent. The letter is a remarkable synthesis, drawing together thoughts and actions of resistance during the preceding decade; it is an aria to agency.

The letter is written from the perspective of the outcasts and those who suffer, seeing the great events of world history from below. In this frame Bonhoeffer and his friends have acted in ways that violated their conscious commitments. He writes of the toll this has taken and the fundamental question it raises:

> We have been silent witnesses to evil deeds; we have been drenched by many storms; we have learnt the arts of equivocation and pretense; experience has made us suspicious of others and kept us from being truthful and open; intolerable conflicts have worn us down and made us cynical. Are we still of any use? (17)

Against cruelty, the question, "Are we still of any use?" haunts his reflections. He returns to it repeatedly in his search for a stance of effective opposition capable of reconciliation with God.

The problem of resistance went deeper than acting from political conviction. Evil was disguised to appear as "light, charity, historical necessity, or social justice" (2). For Germans, whose traditional virtues placed community above the individual and encouraged acting out of duty, the disguise was bewildering. Being of use meant finding a moral anchor that would hold against Nazi depravity. How could a people to whom every available alternative seemed equally intolerable, repugnant, and futile, have become paralyzed by philosophic misanthropy? Responsible Germans, horrified by Nazism and in a constant state of outrage, were without firm ground beneath their feet. Foreshadowing the emphasis his prison letters would later place on this as *a world come of age*, Bonhoeffer captured this Kantian theme[1] in his assessment of their dilemma. Resistors hoping to displace the authority of the state's totalizing claim to agency could no longer rely on the counterauthority of traditional Christian righteousness. Resistance must come from their sense of Christian responsibility.

Bonhoeffer's argument is theologically based. He wrote, "The great masquerade of evil has played havoc with all our ethical concepts" (2). Reason, enthusiasm, conscience, duty, freedom, private virtue—moral traits that had sustained earlier generations—had become quixotic weapons and, therefore, the wrong weapons for this battle. Each arose from a sense of its own efficacy for overcoming the monsters that had taken control of German life, only to find itself lost in the fog of self-deception and resigning in defeat. The values of the human world—the German tradition of custom, history, and culture—had crumbled before an evil beyond its horizon of experience and to which it had become an unwitting accomplice.

Reason, enthusiasm, conscience, duty, freedom, and private virtue respectively offered only an illusion of agency while absent civil courage. Bonhoeffer's opening catechism inverts these traditional German virtues, recasting them as ineffectual and guilty of the primary Christian vice, pride. In their place, he invokes the values of faith.

Who stands fast? For Bonhoeffer, it is the large-hearted Christian.

> We are not Christ, but if we want to be Christians, we must have some share in Christ's large-heartedness by acting with responsibility and in freedom when the hour of danger comes, and by showing a real sympathy that springs, not from fear, but from the liberating and redeeming love of Christ for all who suffer. Mere waiting and looking is not Christian behavior. (14)

The spiritual basis for his argument justifying the conspirators' moral transgressions and answering the question "Are we still of any use?" is the theology of faith without religion. It is the moral vernacular of a Christian faith that foregoes the precedent of the preceding nineteen hundred years when Christianity had rested on a religious *a priori* (*Letters and Papers* 139). It is adapted to the last hundred years, when "man has learnt to deal with himself and all questions of importance without recourse to the working hypothesis called 'God'" (168). If a solely religious understanding of Christianity made Jesus disappear from sight, as Bonhoeffer believed, and with him the rationale for action found in the gospels, his large-hearted Christian would find the path back to responsible action through communion with God. He would not require recourse to abstract principles of ethics, which ran counter to what a person was called to do in the face of evil, but would act, Bonhoeffer concluded, in "a bold venture of faith while believing that there is forgiveness and consolation to the person who becomes a sinner in that venture" (5).

Vaclav Havel

A different vice provides tension for the moral vernacular invoked by Vaclav Havel. In his New Year's Day 1990 address, Havel reflected on the astonishing political developments of the previous year in Central and Eastern Europe. For him, the spontaneity of widespread harmonious revolutionary action posed important questions about political consciousness:

> Everywhere in the world people wonder where those meek, humiliated, skeptical, and seemingly cynical citizens of Czechoslovakia found the marvelous strength to shake the totalitarian yoke from their shoulders in several weeks, and in a decent and peaceful way. And let us ask: where did the young people who never knew another system find their desire for truth, their love of free thought, their political ideas, their civic courage and civic prudence? How did their parents—the very generation that had been considered as lost—come to join them? How is it possible that so many people immediately knew what to do, without advice or instruction? (Havel, *Art* 5)

Havel may not have shared everyone's surprise, since his writings predicted the way these developments transpired.

From a distance, his essays appear to be attacking hypocrisy as the ordinary vice corrupting his nation. Certainly he has hypocrisy in mind when he depicts life in communist Czechoslovakia as living within a lie and describes a national yearning for living within truth. More fundamentally, however, Havel was concerned with how post-Prague Spring life had sapped the reserves of human spontaneity from his fellow Czechs. The problem was less the regime's hypocrisy than its treachery. Close up, his essays and letters during the 1970s and 1980s, a period he dubs "post-totalitarian," are morose reflections on the treachery of a system that strips away all pretense of hope.

The post-totalitarian state no longer required physical violence to gain compliance. Since its subjects believed there was no alternative, they were coerced into obeying appeals detached from their personal convictions in order to avoid trouble. The state's treachery lay in requiring citizens to be unfaithful to themselves and, through their infidelity, live a life of hypocrisy.

How treachery evokes conscience is exemplified by Havel's distinguished essay "The Power of the Powerless." Havel wrote the essay in 1978 to explain the significance of Charter 77, of which he was a founder. It was banned from official publication in Czechoslovakia but had circulated as *samizdat* and was printed in the West (Keane 281). It explores the state's violation of the moral universal to respect each person's inherent dignity through its memorable parable of the greengrocer.

The parable portrays a world of stultified thought and compliant behavior enacted through a poster proclaiming, "Workers of the world unite!" The party has given the poster to shopkeepers, and the greengrocer automatically displays it in his shop window. Its display signifies he is living in a lie. Havel observes that the greengrocer need not believe the mystifications of the state that "enslave the working class in the name of the working class," falsify national history, misrepresent the material conditions of life, and present the very circumstances that degrade the individual as the source of the individual's liberation. However, the greengrocer must behave *as if* he believed them. He acts in this way to get along in life, to avoid being reproached for failing to have the right decoration in his window or being accused of disloyalty. He displays the poster with indifference to its semantic meaning and the ideal it expresses for one reason: so he will be left alone (42).

Significantly, the greengrocer was not directed to put the sign in his window. Had a party official instructed him to display a sign proclaiming "I am afraid and therefore unquestioningly obedient," he would not be nearly as indifferent to its semantic content. It would be a source of embarrassment and shame because it would be an unequivocal statement of his degradation and violate his sense of human dignity, even though it spoke the truth. To overcome this complication, the greengrocer's expression of loyalty must take the form of a disinterested sign. It hides him from the low foundations of his own obedience while simultaneously concealing the low foundations of power behind the façade of something high: *ideology.*

Havel positions the power of the post-totalitarian world to control life in ideology's excusatory function. What is wrong with supporting the workers of the world? How could one question whether they should unite? The sign's ideological content provides those below and above with an *illusion* of identity, dignity, and morality while making it easier for everyone in a post-totalitarian world to *part* from them. The illusion "that the system is in harmony with the human order and the order of the universe"(43) gives ideology a transcendent power. It goes beyond physical power to dominate it by providing power with its inner cohesion and by becoming a pillar supporting the system's external stability. Havel depicted the treachery of exerting control out of a conscience lacking objective content but infinitely certain of itself and also the cause of the state's undoing. Its ideology is an unstable pillar because, he says, "it is built on lies. It works only as long as people are willing to live within the lie" (50).

The power of the powerless, on the other hand, lay in their ability to act differently, to decide not to live within the lie. Prefiguring 1989's "Velvet Revolution," Havel continues his parable of the fruit and vegetable store manager:

> Let us imagine that one day something in our greengrocer snaps and he stops putting up slogans merely to ingratiate himself. He stops voting in elections he knows are a farce. He begins to say what he really thinks at political meetings. And he even finds strength in himself to express solidarity with those whom his conscience commands him to support. In this revolt the greengrocer steps out of living within the lie. He rejects the ritual and breaks the rules of the game. He discovers once more his suppressed identity and dignity. He gives his freedom a concrete significance. His revolt is an attempt to *live within the truth.* (55)

There will be consequences for breaking the façade and exposing the nakedness of post-totalitarian power. Of course, he will pay a price for his assertion of autonomy. He will lose his position as manager of the shop, be transferred to a warehouse, have his pay reduced, lose his vacation time for a holiday in Bulgaria, and even see his children's success in higher education threatened. Nonetheless, his act will have confronted living within the lie with its alternative, and these two alternatives cannot coexist. People may not queue up publicly to support him, but everyone will know the mendacity of the regime has been exposed.

> In the post-totalitarian system, therefore, living within the truth has more than a mere existential dimension (returning humanity to its inherent nature), or a noetic dimension (revealing reality as

it is), or a moral dimension (setting an example for others). It also has an unambiguous *political* dimension. (57)

Havel's parable of the greengrocer is representative of the problematic addressed by oppositional writers in post-totalitarian states. Unlike dictatorships, which impose their will through violence, the post-totalitarian regime exerts its power through its web of influence in every aspect of life, dividing the person from himself or herself with a force, Havel says, that eludes description.

His argument, then, relies on an ethical commitment to the primacy of human dignity. In this respect, it fits with a fundamental argument for human rights in which human dignity is invoked as a universal, albeit ambiguous, first principle from which other moral universals follow. Importantly, the parable of the greengrocer translates its moral first principle into a Central/Eastern European vernacular. It is questionable whether Western audiences would feel the compelling force to display the sign in the first place or grasp the political understanding of the parable as an exemplar of the moral universal it represents. Havel's efforts here, as elsewhere, explained to Western readers that they typically misunderstood the realities of Czech political stances because they suffered from what I refer to as *the Todorov problem*, whereby they habitually misrepresented the local meaning of Central/Eastern European discourse critical of the state through their own filter of cold war ideology.[2] Havel's concern was to quicken his *native* readers' sense that everyone shared the private thoughts they harbored with each act of self-betrayal. In this supersaturated condition of moral alienation, someone braking ranks and exposing the nakedness of the regime would be the seed that catalyzed a revolution of independent conduct typical of a functioning and vibrant civil society.

Mandela

The line of conflict for Nelson Mandela was more publicly apparent than for Bonhoeffer or Havel. Oppressor and oppressed were delineated by color and Mandela was a public figure among those leading a campaign to oust the regime. Mandela's position as well as his rhetorical circumstances meant that the ostensible audience for his discourse often was an official branch of the government he was opposing. Perhaps this accounts for his distinctive voice. Mandela, the outlaw, the prisoner, the African lacking political and legal status, addresses power as its peer. Although we might expect an emphasis on his legal status in public statements made in courts of law and the quasi-official prison contexts where he is the prisoners' spokesperson, even his letters to South Africa's Prime Ministers—Verwoerd, Botha, and de Klerk—were written in the voice of a person who operates outside his official identity as an African prisoner lacking political identity and rights. He addressed power with the voice of a free man who is an official entitled to equal rights and privileges.

Apartheid's legalized racism had institutionalized the ordinary vice of snobbery. This is not to say that racism is not a form of cruelty or hypocrisy, because it is. However, these vices flowed from apartheid's fundamental premise of racial superiority on which it justified unequal human treatment. Apartheid's racism promised "the comprehensive separation of all volkere [ethnic nations] of South Africa into their own national units" (Sparks 149). A smokescreen of tribalism ritualized snobbery into orthodoxy through laws that restricted movement, association, location, education, opportunity, distribution of wealth, and power.[3]

Mandela engaged apartheid power through the rhetoric of law. He assumed that as a human he was a rights-bearing individual entitled to equal treatment under the law. Whatever failed to meet this criterion failed to meet the standard of a just law and, therefore, had no legitimate claim on his allegiance or obedience. In contrast to apartheid law, he invoked the moral vernacular of democratic law. He understood democratic law to grant rights, preserve equality, and protect against arbitrary treatment. It manifested the moral universals contained in the Universal Declaration of Human Rights and provided the moral framework that exposed apartheid's lack of moral and political ethos. It was manifested locally in the Freedom Charter, a document composed in the 1950s as the African National Congress's (ANC's) political platform. The Freedom Charter expressed the ANC's political vision in terms of basic human rights, many of which are found in the Universal Declaration. The Freedom Charter translated the moral universalism of the Universal Declaration into localized moral principles on which to found a just South African democracy in which all South Africans have equal rights regardless of color.

The opposition of apartheid law and democratic law is illustrated in Mandela's remarks and cross-examination of state witnesses during his 1962 trial on charges of inciting persons to strike illegally and of leaving the country without a valid passport. The charges against Mandela arose from his leadership of a stay-at-home strike in protest against the Verwoerd government's implementation of a national referendum on whether South Africa should remain part of the British Commonwealth or become an independent republic. The referendum, in which the African majority had no vote, passed in favor of independence and was to go into effect on May 31, 1961. In response, a conference of 1,500 delegates from across the country representing 145 organizations formed the All-in African National Action Council.[4] Since the government represented a small minority of the South African population, the Council contended that political reform of the nation's status was not its decision to make without first consulting the African people.

Pursuant to that belief, Mandela, as secretary of the body, wrote to Prime Minister Verwoerd on April 20 pointing out that the government's savage treatment of South Africans had led to a serious deterioration of relations and that the only way to prevent this dangerous situation from deteriorating further was to call a national convention representative of all South Africans to discuss the nations problems and to work out their solutions. His letter went on to indicate that if the government did not call the convention before the May 31 implementation date, countrywide demonstrations of protest would be held on the eve of the republic. Verwoerd did not acknowledge or reply to Mandela's letter. On May 29, a general strike was called and workers refused to report to their jobs for three days. The government reacted by rushing a special law through Parliament authorizing detention without trial of those who had organized the strike. More than 10,000 Africans were arrested under the pass laws, and meetings were banned throughout the country. On June 26, 1961, Mandela again wrote to Verwoerd calling for a national convention and vowing that unless such a convention were called, the African people would persist in non-co-operation with the republic. Again, Verwoerd neither acknowledged nor replied to the letter (Mandela, *Long Walk* 187–88).

Two features of Mandela's defense are especially relevant to this discussion: his use of "law" as a topos for isolating South Africa's apartheid regime from the community of civilized nations and his insinuation of snobbery into his defense. Mandela set the tone for arguing his case in terms of a political philosophy—democracy—and its correlative understanding of justice. He reminded the court of South Africa's human rights commitment to the Universal Declaration, which provides in Article 7 that "All are equal before the law and are entitled without discrimination to equal protection of the law." "In May 1951," he continued, "Dr. D. F. Malan, then Prime Minister, told the Union parliament that this provision of the Declaration applies in this country" ("Black Man" 3). Drawing on the premise that law is based on the principle of equal treatment, he argued that, with respect to its citizens of color, South Africa did not establish laws conforming to a principle of justice, but to a political policy. That policy placed the government at odds with the understanding of justice of all other civilized nations.

Mandela used the frame of law as an inventional wedge to develop a moral indictment of the National Party and the apartheid state. He made repeated reference to the specific practices of the government that abridged the rights of some of South Africa's citizens or ignored their reasonable requests or treated their reasonable acts of disagreement as illegal for no reason but color. The implication of apartheid's lack of civility pierced the surface during his cross-examination of Mr. Bernard (see also *Long Walk* 326–67), Prime Minister Verwoerd's private secretary, on the reason "why I was not favoured with the courtesy of an acknowledgment of the letter, irrespective of what the Prime Minister is going to do about it?" Bernard tried to evade answering, and Mandela asked: "I see. This is not the type of thing the Prime Minister would ever consider responding to?" Bernard replied it was the letter's tone. In light of Bernard's earlier concession that the letter raised important issues, Mandela's incredulity over the excuse of "tone" is palpable: "The tone of the letter demanding a National Convention? Of all South Africans? That is the tone of the letter? That is not the type of thing your Prime Minister could ever respond to?" (9–11). Mandela's incredulity suggests that Verwoerd didn't reply because he regarded its author and the group he represented beneath acknowledgment. Later, Mandela concluded: "[That] I was not favoured with the courtesy of an acknowledgment of the letter [shows] once again, government standards in dealing with my people fell below what the civilized world would expect" (21).

More generally, in his statements to the court, Mandela refused to speak from within the system of a subject of a racist state, assuming instead the stance of the moral universals expressed in the first 13 articles of the Universal Declaration of Human Rights. These expressions of equality and rights are translated into the moral vernacular of law through a series of contrasts that pit the practices of the National Party regime against reason and the civilized world. For example:

- The African majority cannot be tried by their African peers. Why? "To ensure that the justice dispensed by the courts should conform to the policy of the country, however much that policy might be in conflict with the norms of justice accepted in judiciaries throughout the civilized world" (3).
- Africans are not legally or morally obliged to obey laws they have not made nor have confidence in the courts that enforce them. Why? "The will of the people [as] the basis of the authority of government is a principle universally acknowledged as sacred throughout the civilized world, and constitutes the basic foundations of freedom and justice" (5).
- Faced with Antigone's dilemma of obeying laws that were "unjust, immoral, and intolerable" or obeying their conscience, the Africans and the regime are contrasts in civility. Why? Because Africans chose peaceful dissent, seeking that the stay-at-home demonstrations "should go through peacefully and peaceably, without clash

and conflict, as such demonstrations do in every civilized country" (22). In response, "The government behaved in a way no civilized government should dare behave when faced with a peaceful, disciplined sensible, and democratic expression of views of its own population. It ordered the mobilization of its armed forces to attempt to cow and terrorize our peaceful protest" (23).

Mandela's use of law as the moral vernacular for making arguments presupposes universal principles of justice. Although addressed to the court, they are less concerned with the specifics of his case or South African law than with establishing in the public record of the trial transcript a critique of the verdict to follow as unjust, as outside the frame of expected conduct by a civilized government, and as condemned by "the overwhelming majority of mankind both in this country and abroad" who despise its "racial arrogance" (26–27).

The moral vernacular of democratic law both challenged apartheid's aura of legality by reducing it to another form of snobbery and exposed its misanthropy—not the misanthropy of Machiavelli, whose prince personalized his hatred, but in the form expressed by a political system. In the impersonal state, personal qualities no longer make a difference. In fact, they might interfere with the primary obligation of justice. Mandela's framing of himself as a black man in a white man's court uses the particular case to express the principle of equal justice for all on which a state's legitimacy must rest. An impersonal legal system respected basic human rights and allowed for the distribution of power among intermediary groups that protected each citizen by limiting the opportunities for violence (Shklar 211). It offered the impersonal instrument to combat the misanthropy of the apartheid state.

LESSONS LEARNED

I began with a claim that the globalization of human rights is a function of localization of the moral vernacular. The three cases I have presented found their moral voice in God, living in truth, and law—the spiritual, ethical, and political. Their specificity to their culture and circumstances cautions against general conclusions. However, they do share a positive image of human possibilities. Their favoring of the powerless is a way of escaping misanthropy and of finding an ethos that, unlike revealed religion, leads neither to zeal nor cruelty (Shklar 17). They share a sense of their opponent as embodying an ordinary vice that seeps through every fiber of society and that explains, in the case of Bonhoeffer and Mandela, the need for extreme measures. In focusing on vice from which the call to conscience emanates, they reduce a monolithic force to one that, while no less formidable, is considerably less than grand.

They also avoid valorizing victims. A rhetoric encouraging us to think of victims as valorous risks misusing them to serve our own interests as onlookers. It forces them to serve as a means to nourish our own self-esteem and control our own fears. Nor do they position us to respond as a mass of self-mortified Dimmsdales, mean-spirited weaklings salving our conscience through pity of the victims, which performs a version of mass social work for the onlookers. Pity is the ideology of the weak, as Nietzsche taught us. The moral vernacular uses moral cruelty as its priestly weapon, forcing us to recognize the discontinuity, at times, between public and private life, how the state becomes remote from the actualities of its public acts, and how responding to extreme circumstances sometimes exacts the personal cruelty of being divided against ourselves. Sometimes it is impossible to be both a good person and a good citizen. Sometimes you have to be one or the other.

Finally, these considerations bear on our current situation in the United States, as citizens confront both the acts and threat of terror targeting its civilian population, the responses of its government, and the disturbing practices—both sanctioned and unsanctioned—in treating enemy detainees. The issues are complicated, and the official and vernacular rhetorics addressing them are often confusing.

It is hard to imagine, for example, anything more extreme than the genocide witnessed during the twentieth century.[5] The Universal Declaration of Human Rights, as a codified refusal to let the slaughter go unnoticed and affirmation of the value of every life, is genocide's dialectical partner. Yet its mobilization of political power opposing the inhumane exercise of obliterating entire peoples often undergoes a curious inversion.

The normative force of the Universal Declaration's moral universals is challenged by the practices of *real politik*. Paramilitary forces, the new armies of the twenty-first century, do not observe the rules of war that prohibit committing atrocities, while sovereign nations confronted by evidence of such practices typically look the other way, often saying they look more like the results of civil war than a crime against humanity, or with standoffishness, as Secretary of State James Baker infamously represented when he explained the U.S. rationale for backing away from involvement in Bosnia as, "We have no dog in this fight" (in Blocker). Such rhetoric works when we lack a sense of the problem's underlying causes. It works because the problem has not been translated into our moral vernacular.

A case in point is the widespread revulsion of Americans to photographic evidence of U.S. treatment of enemy detainees in Abu Ghraib prison in Iraq. National outrage is appropriate and also indicates the more basic problem of mobilizing moral universals. The disturbing practices came to us through visual images of humiliated bodies. Islamic militants retaliated with horrifying images of Nicholas Berg's decapitation. Although our own bodily experiences help us to empathize with a body in pain because we can imagine its anguish, as Michael Ignatieff has argued, the image of a suffering body does not *assert* a moral claim; it can only *instantiate* a moral claim *if* the observers feel under a potential obligation to those who are suffering. As long as we remain fixated by the images and in emotional states of horror and empathy without knowing the root causes for the suffering and humiliation, our compassion unleashed by these emotions risks succumbing to a form of amnesia, a mechanism for forgetting the role of the West in the causes of famine and war, or to social work for onlookers, as just noted (Ignatieff et al. 16). Without a moral vernacular to connect political and economic practices to moral universals, it is difficult to imagine how we will escape being tossed by the waves of emotion that rationalize responses but do not resolve political, moral, and spiritual problems of public life.

If the rationalizations of powerful nations or horrified citizens for standing on the sidelines make the efficacy of moral universalism suspect, there are redeeming lessons contained in the way the powerless appropriate them to challenge oppressive power. Without guns and an army, the powerless gain momentum by activating moral universals capable of resistance within their oppressive cultural milieu. Perhaps our most valuable lessons on how to respond to oppression come not from states (or from political theory) but from the writings of dissident activists. Their rhetorical achievements suggest agendas for confronting the moral panic that accompanies, uninvited, the masquerade of vice.

NOTES

1. In "An Answer to the Question: What is Enlightenment?" Kant had posited, "Enlightenment is the human being's emergence from his self-incurred minority [*Unüdigkeit*, immaturity]. *Minority* [immaturity] is inability to use one's own understanding without direction from another." (p. 17)

2. *The Todorov problem* refers to a mode of argumentation employed by Tzvetan Todorov in *Voices from the Gulag*. Todorov uses the narratives of camp survivors, who are providing testimony to witness what took place, to make an anticommunist argument suited to Western cold war ideology. It is doubtful his anticommunist intent was that of the storytellers. The term *gulag* is not used by Bulgarians; they refer to the camps. The survivors' stories are excerpted and edited into a different narrative intended to make a political indictment of the regime. The problem refers to the rhetorical strategy of appropriating testimony offered for one purpose to serve a different ideological end. I am indebted to Nadia Keneva, whose seminar discussion of Todorov's book and whose native insights into Bulgarian camp survivors helped in formulating the problem. For Havel's critique of Western misunderstanding of the Czech moral vernacular, in addition to "Power of the Powerless," see "Politics and Conscience," and "An Anatomy of Reticence," in *Living in Truth*.

3. In 1948 the National Party gained a small majority in Parliament and introduced apartheid. The legal control of its citizens of color was enacted through a series of acts that required the racial classification of the population (Population Registration Act of 1950), prohibited marriage and sexual relations across racial boundaries (Mixed Marriage Act of 1948, Immorality Act of 1950), allowed geographic zones to be defined according to race and for people to be confined within these zones (Group Areas Act of 1950, Prevention of Illegal Squatting Act of 1951), provided for separate but unequal public amenities (Reservation of Separate Amenities Act of 1951, which led to the "petty apartheid" practices of white-only swimming pools, buses, parks, beaches, post office counters and liquor outlets), separate and highly discriminatory education system for Africans (Bantu Education Act of 1953), and prohibition of political parties not based on racial lines, restriction of democratic political action, and reservation of power for the government, or National Party rule (Suppression of Communism Act of 1950, Public Safety Act of 1953, and Criminal Laws Amendment Act of 1953).

4. The numbers offered in Mandela's letter to Verwoerd, as read into evidence at the trial, and those he reported in his autobiography have minor differences. I have used the numbers he reported in his letter to Verwoerd.

5. Estimates of genocide during the twentieth century include 800,000 Armenians by the Turks at the beginning of the century, 5 million Jews at Hitler's hand, 2 million Cambodians during Pol Pot's four-year reign, 100,000 Kurds gassed and executed by Hussein, 800,000 Tutsi Rwandans executed by Hutu Rwandans in 100 days, 200,000 Bosniacs, and at least 100,000 Albanian men unaccounted for and presumed killed under Milosovic's orders, in addition to the loss of approximately 20 million Chinese slaughtered by the Japanese Empire and tens of millions more in the Soviet gulag. These figures are cited in Power, xix-xx, 9; and Newman, 167-68.

WORKS CITED

Blocker, Joel. "Bosnia: Holbrooke Describes the Difficult Path to Peace." 3 May 2004 <http://www.b-info.com/places/Bulgaria/news/98-07/jul14c.rfe>.

Bonhoeffer, Dietrich. *Letters and Papers from Prison.* Ed. and trans. Eberhard Bethge. Rev. ed. New York: Macmillan, 1967.

—. *The Cost of Discipleship.* Trans. R. H. Fuller. New York: Touchtone, 1995.

Burke, Kenneth. "The Rhetoric of Hitler's Battle." *Philosophy of Literary Form.* 3rd ed. Berkeley: U of California P, 1973. 191–220.

Glendon, Mary Ann. *A World Made New: Eleanore Roosevelt and the Universal Declaration of Human Rights.* New York: Random, 2001.

Havel, Vaclav. *The Art of the Impossible: Politics as Morality in Practice.* Trans. Paul Wilson et al. New York: Fromm, 1998.

—. "The Power of the Powerless." Trans. Paul Wilson. *Living in Truth.* Ed. Jan Vladislav. Boston: Faber, 1996.

—*Summer Meditations.* Trans. Paul Wilson. New York: Alfred A. Knopf, 1992.

Ignatieff, Michael. "Human Rights: The Midlife Crisis." *New York Review of Books* 46.19 (1999): 58–62.

—. "The Rights Stuff." *New York Review of Books* 49.10 (2002): 18.

Ignatieff, Michael et al. *Human Rights as Politics and Idolatry.* Ed. Amy Gutmann. Princeton: Princeton UP, 2001.

Kant, Immanuel. *Practical Philosophy.* Trans. Mary J. Gregor. Cambridge: Cambridge UP, 17–22.

Keane, John. *Vaclav Havel: A Political Tragedy in Six Acts.* New York: Basic, 2000.

Mandela, Nelson. "Black Man in a White Court." 13 May 2004 <http://www.anc.org.za/ancdocs/history/mandela/1960s/nm6210.html>.

—. *Long Walk to Freedom.* Boston: Little, 1994.

Newman, Robert P. *Truman and the Hiroshima Cult.* East Lansing: Michigan State UP, 1995.

Power, Samantha. *"A Problem from Hell": America and the Age of Genocide.* New York: Basic, 2002.

Shklar, Judith N. *Ordinary Vices.* Cambridge: Belknap, 1984.

Sophocles. *Antigone.* Trans. Richard Emil Braun. New York: Oxford, 1973.

Sparks, Allister. *The Mind of South Africa.* New York: Ballantine, 1990.

Stern, Fritz. "National Socialism as Temptation." *Dreams and Delusions.* New York: Knopf, 1987. 147–91.

Taylor, Charles. "Conditions of an Unforced Consensus on Human Rights." *The East Asian Challenge for Human Rights.* Ed. Joanne R. Bauer and Daniel A. Bell. Cambridge: Cambridge UP, 1999.

Todorov, Tzvetan. *Voices from the Gulag: Life and Death in Communist Bulgaria.* Trans. Robert Zaretsky. University Park: Pennsylvania State UP, 1999.

United States Department of State. "Introduction." *1999 Country Report on Human Rights Practices.* 12 Feb. 2004 <http://www.state.gov/www/global/human_rights/1999_hrp_report/99hrp_toc.html>.

"Universal Declaration of Human Rights." 14 May 2004 <http://www.udhr.org/UDHR/default.htm>.

Urquhart, Brian. "Mrs. Roosevelt's Revolution." *New York Review of Books* 48.7 (2001): 32–34.

von Klemperer, Klemens. "'What Is the Law That Lies behind These Words?' Antigone's Question and the German Resistance against Hitler." *Resistance Against the Third Reich.* Ed. Michael Geyer and John W. Boyer. Chicago: U of Chicago P, 1994.

3

Rudolph Agricola's Contribution to Rhetorical Theory

Peter Mack
University of Warwick

My aim in this paper is to persuade you that Rudolph Agricola (1444–85) was one of the major theorists of rhetoric, someone whose ideas we still need to take account of as well as someone who made a significant contribution to the development of rhetorical theory.[1] In the past Agricola has been underrated. Historians of rhetoric have tended to exclude him from consideration because his most famous work, *De inventione dialectica* (completed 1479; first printed 1515) appears to be a work on dialectic (which in the Middle Ages and the Renaissance was almost a synonym for logic), whereas historians of logic thought that he betrayed logic by making it rhetorical (Agricola).[2] We must set this disciplinary rivalry to one side. In the Renaissance, logic and rhetoric were taught together. In literature and composition departments today, we aim to teach people to read critically, to argue, and to write. Agricola is a great example to us in putting these concerns together.

My main procedure will be to give a reasonably detailed account (with enough quotation to give you some of the flavor of the work) of eight of the principal doctrines of Agricola's most successful work, *De inventione dialectica*, of which there were seventy-six printings (forty-four of the whole text and thirty-two of epitomes) in the sixteenth century (Huisman). So it was a very successful and much used work. My claim will be both that Agricola's contributions were innovative in relation to the rhetoric of his time and that some of them are of enduring interest to teachers and theorists of composition even today. I will not have time to give a thorough account of the historical contexts of these doctrines, but my implication is always that these doctrines were either original to Agricola or adapted by him in innovative ways. In one place, my point will be that he reestablishes, generalizes, and makes more widely available a doctrine of Aristotle that had fallen into disuse in fifteenth-century rhetoric. The eight topics of the paper are:

1. Exposition and Argumentation
2. Handling of Emotions
3. Amplification and *Copia*
4. Exploring the Question
5. Disposition
6. The Topics
7. Dialectical Reading
8. Dialectical Invention: A Synthesis of Rhetoric and Dialectic

My ideal outcome would be that some of you will want to read *On Dialectical Invention* for yourselves. If I can persuade you that Agricola really is one of the major theorists of rhetoric, then we really ought to have an English translation of the whole work to complement and replace the very useful selections which the late James McNally published in 1967 (McNally).[3]

Like most Renaissance teachers of the use of language, Agricola believed that logic and rhetoric had to be taught together. Later, I will describe his views on the connections between rhetoric and dialectic and on some subjects which he considered to be part of dialectic. But I would like to begin with four subjects with clear connections to rhetoric.

Near the beginning of *De inventione dialectica*, Agrciola proposes that there are two ways of using language to teach an audience. If the audience is willing to believe what we say, we can use exposition, that is, stating our view as clearly as possible. But if the audience is likely to resist our ideas, we will need to use argumentation in order to make them believe what we say.[4]

The distinction between exposition and argumentation has two aspects. At the level of the speaker's intention, it reflects the speaker's view about what the audience will believe willingly and what it will resist. And this is a distinction we need to make whenever we speak. No audience will tolerate us proving everything we say; we need to work out what they will agree to easily and what we shall have to labor to persuade them of. This distinction is also reflected at the level of style. In exposition, we concentrate on clarity and order; in argumentation, we add reasons and emotions. We must consider this to be a rhetorical distinction because it has to do with the speaker's estimate of the audience's reaction and because it affects the choices the speaker will make about the verbal expression of particular sections of the speech. Later in the work, Agricola gives some advice about argumentation, but I am not concerned with that here. Typically Agricola makes his point about the difference between exposition and argumentation by analyzing two passages from Vergil's *Aeneid*.

> Exposition, as we say, recounts only that a certain thing is such, as if to a hearer disposed to believe. Argumentation tries to prove that a certain thing is such, using reason. So that this is exposition:
>
> (I give Agricola's quotation from Vergil in Fitzgerald's translation and at more length than Agricola does.)
>
> Tyrian settlers in that ancient time
> Held Carthage, on the far shore of the sea,
> Set against Italy and Tiber's mouth,
> A rich new town, warlike and trained for war.
> And Juno, we are told, cared more for Carthage
> Than for any walled city of the earth.

More than for Samos, even. There her armour
And chariot were kept, and, fate permitting,
Carthage would be the ruler of the world.
So she intended, and so nursed that power,
But she had heard long since
That generations born of Trojan blood
Would one day overthrow her Tyrian walls [...]
In fear of this and holding in memory
The old war she carried on at Troy
For Argos' sake [...]
Saturnian Juno, burning for it all,
Buffeted on the waste of sea those Trojans (i.e., Aeneas and his men)

The poet reviews the reasons why Juno hated Aeneas. If he had considered them in such a way that he made it doubtful whether Juno hated Aeneas and wanted to prove it by rehearsing these reasons, it would have been argumentation. Now, because the hatred of Juno is taken as certain and beyond doubt, the causes are subjoined to it, not to show that Juno hated Aeneas (for that is regarded as certain as we have said) but to show the reasons why the hatred itself arose, so it is exposition.

But now if we should change the sentence and say: 'there is no doubt that Juno hated Aeneas because she loved Carthage, whose ruin would be brought about by descendants of Aeneas and because she stood against the Trojans on the side of her Argives in the war' and the other things the poet has put in, it would become argumentation.

Incidentally, we should point out that on occasion the same thing can be exposition and argumentation, provided that the linguistic form is altered, just as the same thing can be both the cause of a thing and its reason. The reason is that by which a thing is known, the cause is that by which it is.

(Here Agricola illustrates his point that the reason and the cause can be the same with a discussion about the apparent shape of the moon.)

What the poet introduces a little later *is*, however, argumentation:

(Again I give Juno's soliloquy at more length than Agricola's brief citation)

"Give up what I began?
Am I defeated? Am I impotent
To keep the king of the Teucrians from Italy?
The Fates forbid me, am I to suppose?
Could Pallas then consume the Argive fleet
With fire and drown the men ...
But I who walk as queen of all the gods,
Sister and wife of Jove, I must contend
For years against one people! Who adores
The power of Juno after this?

Juno is not saying to herself, as if to someone disposed to believe, that she does not want to give up her plans; rather with the addition of reason she explains to herself why it would be unworthy for her to give up; and she encourages herself to persist in the same frame of mind."[5]

For Agricola, the argumentative and emotional force of Juno's soliloquy makes it argumentation rather than exposition. Agricola uses quotation of Vergil (and an imagined rewriting of Vergil's text) to illustrate the distinction between argumentation and exposition. He shows that the same material could be expressed in either form depending on the kinds of connections made, the elaboration of the material, and the writer or character's intention. Argumentation here is a matter of density of texture, of the way material is presented. We would also think of this passage from Juno, argumentative though it is, as emotional. As Agricola says, Juno uses arguments to stoke up her anger.

A little later, Agricola discusses Sinon's speech to the Trojans from book 2 of the *Aeneid*, in which he explains the value of the wooden horse, and in effect persuades them to take it within their walls, to illustrate the ways in which exposition can contribute to persuasion. His analysis of this speech shows that Sinon sets out a series of propositions (some true, some so connected to the true ones as to be plausible, some not unlikely) which the Trojans then gather together into arguments to persuade themselves that taking the horse inside the walls will give them an advantage (262–63).[6] The psychological insight that people are more likely to believe what their own reasoning has persuaded them of is linked to an argument about the way in which an exposition can be organized in order to create belief. Agricola suggests that when we wish to write a convincing exposition, the logical connections between the propositions must be there in our minds but should not be stated explicitly. Argumentation, by contrast, is a matter of setting out logical connections and of repeating important points.

Now Agricola's distinction between exposition and argumentation is, as he admits, related to the classical distinction in the plan of the oration between narration and confirmation (258). But Agricola insists that his way of putting it is more useful, first because it is of more general application outside the oration, second because it recognizes the fact that you may need exposition within your confirmation or arguments in your narration, and third because it makes the link between features of linguistic form and decisions which the speaker makes about his or her audience. Now these features of linguistic form can be syllogisms or enthymemes, but they can also be figures of emphasis and repetition. Agricola shows too that there is a close connection between composing persuasive expositions and making arguments. That relation is based on using the topics (of which more later) in order to find the connections.

I now move to the second rhetorical doctrine: the handling of emotions. Agricola begins by confronting the argument that emotional manipulation has nothing to do with argument. If this means that plainly presented syllogisms will be unhelpful in arousing emotions, Agricola agrees.

> But if we call argumentation everything by which we consider what is doubtful and uncertain, I would have thought not only that it is necessary for arousing emotions but that it ought to be very dense and even thickly packed. For strength is necessary for the intellect to be seized and for the mind itself to be carried away from itself and as it were placed outside itself. This technique of argument is so much imitated by creative writers that if they are short of arguments they pile on the same point, changing the words, as if they were making several points. What else does Vergil express when Dido says in his work:

Per ego has lachrymas, dextramque tuam te …
Per connubia nostra, per inceptos Hymenaeos
(I beg you by your tears, by your own right hand, by our sleeping together, by the marriage rites
we began)

The *dextra* and the *connubium* and the *Hymenaei* were the same thing: he means by these three
things nothing other than the faith of married people: however by repeating it in other words he
has driven it home as if it were more than one thing (199).[7]

Agricola uses his example to show that an emotional effect can be created by an intense
and repetitive linguistic formulation of an argument, in this case, the reason why she ought
to be able to trust him. Dido feels betrayed. She expresses her anger by repeating the signs
of Aeneas's faith which have proved so false. Agricola urges rhetoricians to study the por-
trayal of emotion in tragedy and history. He provides a long commentary on the peroration
of *Pro Milone* to demonstrate that each of Cicero's moves is intended to show that Milo
does not deserve the harsh fate which awaits him if found guilty. To this end, he emphasizes
Milo's bravery, the debt which Rome owes him, and the disaster which will befall his
friends if he is exiled (199–201).

In book 3, Agricola sets out a general theory of emotion. He defines emotion as an impetus of mind by which we are impelled to desire or reject something more vehemently
than we would in a relaxed state of mind (378).[8] We desire the good or the apparent good,
and we reject what we believe to be harmful. Therefore, in arousing emotion, the orator
needs to consider two elements: the thing which happens and the person to whom it happens. If the person deserves the thing which happens (whether it is good or bad), the audience is pleased. If the person does not deserve what happens, the audience is moved, to
anger if the thing undeserved is good, to pity if it is bad. Therefore, in arousing the emotion
of pity, the orator will need to establish both the harshness of the fate and the degree to
which it is undeserved. The particular circumstances of the case (or the previous opinions
of the audience) may lead the orator to emphasize one or other of these arguments in the
speech. Agricola refers to the second book of Aristotle's *Rhetoric* for a comprehensive
treatment of the different emotions (380).

Agricola's main point is that arousing emotions involves a logical calculation based on
the way in which an audience can be made to regard a person and a past or future event. In this
logical approach to arousing emotion, he is generalizing and simplifying Aristotle's view.
But Aristotle's account of emotion had not really featured in the most widely used rhetoric
textbooks of the fifteenth century, Cicero's *De inventione* and the pseudo-Ciceronian
Rhetorica ad Herennium. So Agricola was directing attention back to Aristotle, presenting
Aristotle's views in a form that could be used by students and analyzing Latin texts to show
the effectiveness of his theory. Within this framework, Agricola describes three ways to convey emotions in compositions. First, emotion may be a matter of style, in particular of the
choice of vocabulary and of the tone of a passage. Agricola illustrates this by comparing the
tone of the three famous Latin satirists and the very different emotional impacts of Horace
and Juvenal. Second, the writer may describe someone in the grip of an emotion. Agricola
gives examples from tragedy and epic. Finally, an author may wish to arouse a particular

emotion in the audience. In this case, it will be necessary to focus on the person involved and the thing which happens (382–84).

Agricola linked the theory of emotional manipulation to the technique of amplification, which is the third rhetorical doctrine I shall mention. If emotions are aroused too quickly, they also pass quickly. Orators use amplification to build up emotion gradually. By making the subject they talk about seem great, they prepare their audience to expend great emotion on it. You can make something seem important to an audience by linking it to things which are important to everyone or to the deepest interests of a particular audience. More generally, things can be made to seem great by comparisons, by dividing a topic into sections and considering each section, and by descriptions (386–91). In this section, Agricola relies on Quintilian's account of amplification.

But he adds to this a little later in his discussion of *copia* and brevity. Agricola links *copia* to the aim of pleasing an audience. Pleasing can be brought about either by the intrinsic interest and delight of the subject-matter or from the skillfulness of the language in which something is expressed. The doctrine of *copia* teaches writers to add detail to descriptions and fullness of incident to narratives. It encourages writers to multiply questions, to add further arguments and propositions (400–03). Although *copia* is presented as an ideal of style, many of the techniques which Agricola recommends for achieving *copia* are derived from dialectic. Taken together, Agricola's accounts of amplification and *copia* constitute a major source for Erasmus's *De copia* (1511), perhaps the most influential rhetoric textbook of the sixteenth century.

The practicality of Agricola's approach to the teaching of writing is illustrated by his teaching on the question, which is the fourth doctrine I shall discuss. For Agricola the subject-matter of dialectic is the question (206). Dialectic offers to make arguments about anything which can be expressed as a question. Therefore, it is very important for the orator to understand the nature of the question posed. To start with Agricola divides questions into different types because the type to which a question belongs will have an impact on the most appropriate way of answering it. Then he begins considering the way in which an orator (or indeed any writer) will approach a question which has been set. The key is to get beyond the overt question to the real issue on which the argument must turn. To help with this, he summarizes traditional rhetorical teaching on status theory (241–42), the theory which helped an ancient orator determine the key point at issue. Agricola acknowledges that the key question in any assignment is likely to depend on the genre of speech or composition and the expectations of that genre. Once a likely key question has been identified, the orator must analyze the implications of the question, breaking it down into the subsidiary questions implied by the words in which it is formulated. Using the example of the historical question, "Did Cato rightly hand Marcia over to Hortensius?" Agricola argues that some subsidiary questions are implied in the words of the main question (Did Cato hand her over? Was it right for him to do so?), while some depend on general ethical considerations (Could it ever be right to act like this? How much consideration should be given to the feelings of other people in comparison with the expectations of society?) and others still on the nature of the particular people involved (Should a Roman senator behave in this way? Should a Stoic philosopher? [247–50]). Any of these subsidiary questions may lead to powerful arguments which may alter one's perception of the key point at which all persuasive efforts must be directed. Any of these newly formulated questions may subsequently be subjected to topical invention in order to generate new arguments. By directing attention to the formulation of questions, Agricola offers ways of approaching the task of composition which later experience shows to be important but which the textbook tradition of rhetoric had neglected.

In the fifth place, I must say something about disposition. In the rhetoric textbook, disposition could become a rather empty category since the treatise on invention was usually organized according to the contents of the oration, beginning with the exordium, continuing with narration and confirmation, and ending with the peroration. This left disposition to discuss occasions when one of the four parts might be omitted or when their order might be altered. Disposition could not really be discussed because the textbook assumed that there was only one practical system of organization for a speech.

Agricola, by contrast, starts his account with a general theory: Disposition is defined as "the ordering and distribution of things which shows what belongs and what should be positioned in which places (413)."[9] He distinguishes three kinds of order: natural order (broadly temporal), arbitrary order (when there is no natural order or we choose not to follow it), and artificial order (when we deliberately place later things first, as when the account of Aeneas's voyage precedes the account of the fall of Troy). These three orders are then connected with four kinds of natural order (or four senses of the word *prius* [413–15). Then Agricola describes the organization of a number of texts: Vergil's *Aeneid;* Terence's *Andria;* the histories of Tacitus, Livy, and Valerius Maximus; and Ovid's *Metamorphoses* (416–23). He aims to show that the best authors have provided models of a large number of different forms of organization. This enables him to reject the traditional rhetorical assumption that the four-part oration is the only acceptable form for a work. From such questions of overall organization (and still working with examples), Agricola descends to consider the order in which one might discuss a series of questions, the order in which a series of arguments might be placed, the ordering of propositions within an argument, and the tactical ordering of arguments in a disputation. He shows that in all these cases, the ordering of points will depend on the position one wishes to uphold and the audience for whom one is writing. He concludes this section of the work with a broad summary.

> Let us now bring all that pertains to disposition into some sort of summary. The first requirement for anyone who wishes to do well at disposition is that he should lay out in front of him the whole raw material of his invention, that is everything he is thinking of saying. Then he should decide carefully what he wishes to bring about in the mind of the hearer. Then he should compare the things themselves, the parts of the things, the force and nature of them singly and together, first among themselves and then all together with the precepts. Then he will see without difficulty when the order of time should be followed, when things should be separated into their species and single things should be distinguished as if by certain boundaries: when one should be derived from another, depending on whichever is nearest or most suitable. The he should determine how to please the audience, how to make his point and win it, and what order of questions, argumentations and propositions to observe. Disposition is to be treated thoroughly and with great care, since skill in this part is rightly praised. (449–50) [10]

For Agricola, each composition needs to be planned on the basis of full information about subject-matter, speaker's intention, and audience. The writer needs to have an understanding of the principles of ordering and a knowledge of a range of structural forms which have been created by previous writers. Only at the point when all the material for the work has been gathered together should the writer attempt to determine the organization of the particular work. We need to see this perhaps rather utopian position as a strong and practical response to the rather empty role assigned to disposition by the rhetoric textbook. At the same time, we should see it as consonant with one of the abiding principles of rhetoric, which is that rhetoric concerns itself with a very wide range of different skills in the use of language. Where the traditional rhetoric textbook makes this range of skills comprehensible to the student by separating issues and simplifying them, Agricola insists that the most effective way to intervene in practice is to gather all the relevant information together and to apply general principles to each particular case.

After exploring some of Agricola's rhetorical ideas, it is time to turn to dialectic and first to the topics which are the heart of *De inventione dialectica*. The topics of invention are a series of headings (e.g., definition, genus, species, adjacents, actions, cause, effect, similar, opposite). By applying these headings to any subject, one can generate associations which may lead to arguments. For example, if one wants to make an argument about rhetoric, it may help to recall that rhetoric is *defined* as the art of speaking well, that it belongs to the *genus* of language arts, that its *species* are judicial, deliberative, epideictic, and educational, and so on.

Agricola improves on the traditional treatment of the topics in four main ways (Mack, "Agricola's Topoics"). Unlike Cicero and Boethius, he gives very clear instructions on the practical use of the topics and exercises and worked examples to help his readers understand them.

Second, he provides an explanation for the effectiveness of the topics in generating material. The topics work because they list the common connections between things in the world. Although the things in the world are almost infinitely various, they are connected to each other in certain specifiable ways. Thinking about the ways in which a particular item is connected to other things helps us understand the nature of that item. The topics serve as prompts which enable us to turn an object over in our minds and consider it (Agricola 2–3, 9).

Third, Agricola provides an organization and a rationale for the list of topics. Agricola's first commentator, Phrissemius, provides a diagram illustrating the division of topics into groups (25). Topics are divided into internal and external. Internal topics are either within or around the thing. External topics are either necessarily joined or joined without necessity. In broad terms, Agricola's topics are organized into groups corresponding to their distance from the thing itself, starting with elements which are part of the identity of the thing and ending with opposites. Organizing the topics in this way is an attempt to instill some order and logic into the list of headings. While this has some explanatory power, it is not entirely successful. The list of topics is not logically exhaustive. The topics remain an arbitrary list of headings, but Agricola has done more than earlier writers to introduce order into the list.

Fourth, Agricola takes a different approach to describing the individual topics. Where Cicero or Boethius simply defines the topic, provides an example of an argument derived from it and, in the case of Boethius, adds a justifying maxim, Agricola thinks that the reader needs to become familiar with the nature and parts of each topic in order to find arguments and to understand the relative strength of these arguments. The topics present a set of viewpoints with which to analyze things in the world. The better you understand the topics, the more perceptive you will be in making arguments about the world. Equally, exploring the connections you find through a particular topic will refine your understanding of the nature of that topic and enable you to use it better in the future. As you apply this set of tools to the world, you continually improve your understanding both of the world and of the tools you are using to explore it.

For example, to help us understand definition, Agricola first defines it and then defines its parts. Then he shows how definitions can be built up by naming the genus to which something belongs and excluding the other members of the genus. He provides worked examples of definitions of law and city. Then he provides some laws which apply to good definitions.

TABLE 3.1
Organization of the Topics

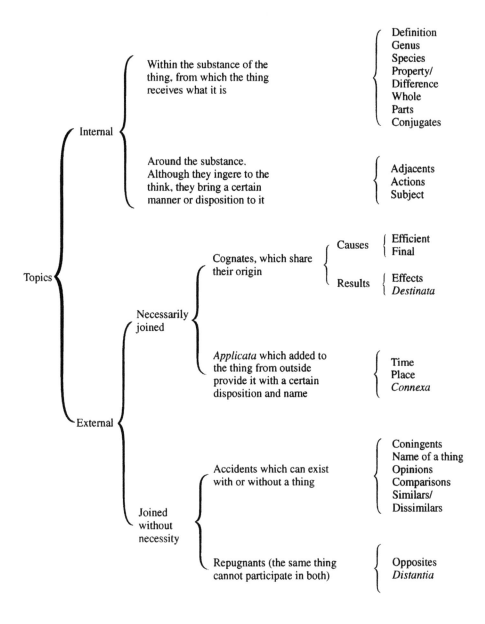

Finally, he discusses the language in which definitions should be set out and the way they can be used to begin arguments and confer authority on the speaker. Throughout, Agricola insists that a definition is a verbal construct intended to circumscribe the nature of a thing but also to provide the person who composes it with footholds for further arguments (26–29).

In looking at causes, Agricola tries to understand the different ways in which causes come together in particular instances. He emphasizes the complexity and interrelatedness (sometimes even the provisionalness) of the idea of causation (78–92, Baxandall). He is particularly illuminating on the generally neglected topic of similitudes.

> Of all the topics from which arguments are drawn almost none has less strength against a resistant reader than similitude. On the other hand there is none more suitable for the hearer who follows willingly and shows himself apt to be taught. For if it is correctly applied, it opens up a thing and places a sort of picture of it before the mind so that although it does not bring with it the necessity of agreeing, it does cause an implicit reluctance to disagree. Therefore it is not so frequently used for proving things but it is often used by orators for exploring and illuminating things, and is even more often used by poets. In spite of this similitude often has an appearance of proving by the very fact that it shows how something is. Thus when you read that similitude of Quintilian: "just as a vase with a narrow mouth rejects an excess of liquid but is filled by flowing or pouring gradually" it does not therefore follow that, on account of this, the delicate minds of boys must be taught according to their own strengths, but nonetheless, once someone has conceived the matter in his mind according to this image, he persuades himself that it cannot be otherwise.[11]

Agricola's comment here is extremely subtle and perceptive, registering the power of arguments from similitude as well as their limitations. Similitude is not proof, but it can be very powerful in conditioning a mind to think in a particular way. Agricola's accounts of the topics often provide this type of insight into the functioning of our thinking about texts, categories, and the world more generally.

Anyone who reads and digests these short articles will enhance their thinking about their tools of analysis and improve their skills as a reader.

As part of the training intended to familiarize his readers with the topics, Agricola proposes the exercise of dialectical reading, which is my seventh doctrine. This technique trains the reader to uncover the argumentative structures which underlie texts. The reader must first establish the nature of the subject-matter and the audience and recover the main question which the writer has posed in answer to the particular assignment. Individual arguments can then be compared with this overarching question in order to establish the main lines of reasoning. Later, particular syllogisms will be reconstructed and the reader will trace individual arguments back to the topics which generated them (353–62). Agricola provides an extended example of dialectical reading in his commentary on Cicero's *Pro lege Manilia*, which became the model for the later humanist genre of the dialectical commentary.[12] By considering segments of argumentation in relation to the overall aims of the speech Agricola is able to reconstruct the assumptions implicit in the argument.

> [Cicero] gives one reason for the greatness of the war with an argument derived from efficient causes. "The war which two great kings wage and which many warlike peoples undertake must be great and dangerous ..." A twofold argument is needed so that what the speech proceeds to say is understood from these words of Cicero. He treats the first argument as established. It can be formed in this way: "for a necessary and dangerous war the best general must be chosen; this war is both necessary and dangerous; for this reason the best general must be chosen for this

war." The other argument is; "Precisely the man who is the best general must be put in charge of this war." But Pompey is the best general of our age; therefore Pompey alone must be put in charge of this war." (466)[13]

Agricola is able to reconstruct the argument of the entire speech and to place each element in relation to Cicero's overall argumentative aim. Demonstrating the logical structure which governs the speech is an important step in showing the use of logic in practical life and the close interrelation between rhetoric and dialectic.

The eighth and final subject of this chapter is dialectical invention, which Agricola describes as the subject of his book. Dialectical invention includes many elements from the traditional syllabuses of rhetoric and dialectic. Agricola treats dialectical invention as the stage of writing at which everything is planned. The author works out what approach will be taken, what the chief arguments are, how the work will be organized, where and how particular emotions will be aroused, which passages will be amplified, and how this will be done. So dialectical invention involves most of rhetoric apart from the figures and tropes and most of dialectic apart from the doctrines of the proposition and the syllogism. But the logic is always envisaged as having a practical aim, providing the means of persuasion in a real situation to be expressed not in formal logic or the artificial language of the syllogism but using the full resources of neoclassical Latin writing. So I would want to argue that the highly original choice of subject-matter and structural organization of Agricola's book contributes to the increasing realization in the Renaissance (and now) that rhetoric and dialectic have to be studied together, in combination rather than in competition.

Below I have tried to summarize in Table 3.2 how Agricola's text is organized and in Table 3.3 how it draws its material from the very differently organized logic and rhetoric textbooks of the classical tradition. In Table 3.2 I divide each book into three or four main sections, on the basis of Agricola's comments.

Even on the basis of this short summary, it is clear that the organization of *De inventione dialectica* is very different from the traditional textbook of rhetoric. In Table 3.3 I try to reinforce this by listing the main contents of the manuals of rhetoric and dialectic in the usual order in which they occur (in textbooks like *Rhetorica ad Herennium* or Peter of Spain's *Tractatus*). The cross-references aim to show which elements from the traditional syllabi of both subjects are found in both subjects and where Agricola puts them. So, for example, in Table 3.3, the letters 2C and 3C against *exordium* indicate that the issue of the *exordium* is discussed both in part C of book 2 (specifically in chapter 24 on the parts of the oration) and in part C of book 3 (in Agricola's account of disposition).

By combining Tables 3.2 and 3.3, it should be evident that most of Agricola's teachings draw on the traditional contents of the manuals of rhetoric and dialectic but that he chooses selectively among the materials in both subjects and combines them together in an original framework.

My argument has been that Agricola produced an original synthesis of the doctrines of rhetoric and dialectic. He placed the emphasis firmly on the process of planning, in which estimates of the audience, ideas about possible arguments, and awareness of the range of means of persuasion and forms of expression must be brought together. Putting the topics of invention at the center of the process of writing, he proposed a close connection between logical argument and emotional persuasion. He understood that the speakers' estimates about the nature of an audience will be reflected in the techniques employed and in the stylistic texture of a work. Although he was not primarily concerned with style, he explored the distinc-

TABLE 3.2

Plan of *De inventione dialectica*

Section		Chapter Nos.
	Book 1	
A	Introduction	1
B	The Topics	
	Introduction to the Topics	2–4
	The Topics	5–19, 21–27
	Discussion of other treatments of them	20, 28, 29
	Book 2	
A	Introductory	
	The deficiency of contemporary dialectic	1
	What is dialectic?	2–3
	Teaching, Moving and Pleasing	4–5
B	Matter	
	The nature of the question	6–8
	Divisions of the question	8–11
	The chief question and its dependents	12–14
C	Instrument	
	Kinds of language use	15–17
	Argumentation	18–21
	Exposition	22–23
	The parts of the oration	24
	The topics belong to dialectic	25
D	Treatment	
	Knowing the topics and using them	26–30
	Book 3	
A	Moving	
	The handling of emotions	1–3
B	Pleasing	
	Pleasing and Digression	4
	Copia and brevity	5–7
C	Disposition	
	Overall disposition	8–11
	Arranging questions and arguments	12–15
	Exercises, reading and conclusion	16

These tables are taken, with slight corrections, from my *Renaissance Argument*, pp. 121–23.

TABLE 3.3

Courses in Rhetoric and Dialectic Compared With *De inventione dialectica*

Rhetoric	DID	Dialectic	DID
Invention:		**Predicables**	1B
Exordium	2C 3C	**Categories:**	
Narration	2C	Substance	1B
Status theory	2B	Quantity	
Special topics		Relatives	
General topics	1B	Quality	1B
Forms of Argumentation	2C	Post-predicaments	3C
Refutation	2C	**Proposition:**	
Amplification	3AB	Quantity	2B
Emotional appeals	3A	Quality	2B
Humour		Contraries	1B
Disposition:		Modals	2B
Varying 4 part form	3C	**Syllogism:**	
Argument order	3C	Figures	2C
Deliberative Speech		Moods	2C
Epideictic Speech	2B	Advice	2C
Style:		**Topics:**	
3 kinds		Forms of argumentation	2C
Qualities		Maxims and Differences	
Tropes		List of Topics	1B
Figures		Definition	1B
Memory		Division	1B
Delivery		**Sophisms:**	
		Kinds	
		Strategy	

tion between plain and more elaborate styles, argumentative, amplified, and copious. He investigated the effects of these differences of texture on an audience.

He restored emotional persuasion and disposition to their central role in rhetorical theory and opened up new ways of thinking about both. He understood the force of the argumentative structure of a text and taught his pupils how to uncover and reconstruct these structures in the speeches and poems they read. He insisted that logic needed to become involved with practical persuasion in natural language and that logical techniques could be applied to all aspects of composition. For him, rhetoric and dialectic, understood in the broadest possible way, always belonged together.

Because Agricola's guides to the use of argument in practical reasoning are always the great Latin poets and orators, he joined literature to rhetoric and dialectic. He showed that the tools of analysis of rhetoric and dialectic needed to be applied to the masterpieces of classical literature in order to provide lessons in how to write and how to think. In fact, his book is a record of his highly perceptive and technically aware reading as much as it is a textbook of composition. I hope that the examples I have quoted have shown the value of the book as an example of close reading and literary criticism. But it is as a textbook of composition and a textbook in analyzing the world and thinking about it that I would recommend *De inventione dialectica* to anyone interested in the history and practice of reading and writing.

NOTES

1. Agricola was born in Baflo near Groningen. He was educated at Erfurt and Louvain before going on to study law at Pavia (1469–74). There he abandoned law for the study of Latin literature. His desire to learn Greek took him to Ferrara (1475–79) where for a time he was employed as a musician by Duke Ercole I. He completed his major work *De inventione dialectica* during his return journey to the north where he worked for a time as town secretary to Groningen before moving to Heidelberg (1484) to assist his friend Johann von Dalberg, who had been made Bishop of Worms. Following a journey to Italy in 1485, he was taken ill in Trento and died shortly after his return to Heidelberg. A slightly fuller life with sources in P. Mack, *Renaissance Argument: Valla and Agricola in the Traditions of Rhetoric and Dialectic* (Leiden, 1993), pp. 117–20, 125–29. A very good account of the sources and secondary literature in F. Akkerman and A. J. Vanderjagt eds, *Rodolphus Agricola Phrisius* (Leiden, 1988), pp. 313–44.
2. R. Agricola, *De inventione dialectica* (Cologne, 1539, reprinted Nieuwkoop, 1967).
3. Readers are warned that McNally was using a slightly different edition with different chapter numberings to the Cologne 1539). Several key passages are translated in my *Renaissance Argument*, pp. 117–256 which provides a full justification for many of the arguments advanced in this paper. Agricola's whole text is translated into German in R. Agricola, *De inventione dialectica* (Tubingen, 1992) and there are good French translations of some chapters in Agricola, *Ecrits sur la dialectique et l'humanisme*, ed. Marc van der Poel.
4. Marc van der Poel and I are exploring the possibility of a new complete English translation.
5. DID, pp. 258–59: Expositio ergo (quemadmodum dicimus) est, quae rem recenset solum talem aliquam esse velut credenti auditori. Argumentatio, quae talem esse rem ratione pervincere nititur. Ut sit expositio: Urbs antiqua fuit, Tyrii tenuere coloni, Carthago, quaeque sequuntur. Causas enim propter quas oderat Aeneam Iuno recenset poeta. Easque si sic accepisset, ut dubium faceret an odisset Aeneam Iuno, harumque commemoratione causarum vellet id docere, argumentatio esset. Nunc quia odium Iunonis velut certum indubitatumque sumitur, cui causae subduntur, non ut ostendatur odisse Aeneam Iuno, quippe pro certo est, quemadmodum diximus, sed propter quas odium ipsum provenerit, expositio est. Quod si iam

convertamus orationem dicamusque, non dubium est quin oderit Aeneam Iuno, quoniam Carthaginem amabat, cui exitium ab Aeneae posteritate venturum erat, et quia contra Troianos steterat pro Argivis suis in bello, et reliquae poeta subdidit, argumentatio fiet. Ut obiter admoneamus, idem quandoque expositionem et argumentationem, mutata tantum orationis forma fieri posse, cum possit idipsum et causa rei esse et ratio. Rationem in praesentia dico, perquam res cogniscitur; causam, per quam est ...

Argumentatio autem est, quod paulo post subiecit poeta: Mene incepto desistere victam/Nec posse Italia Teucrorum avertere regem? Et reliqua, noti enim sunt loci. Non dicit Iuno sibi ipsi tanquam credenti nolle se desistere proposito, sed addita ratione docet ipsa se, quare indignum sit ut desistat; hortaturque, ut in sententia permaneat. *Aeneid*, I, 12ff, 37ff.

6. Analyzed in Mack, "Rudolph Agricola's Reading of Literature", *Journal of the Warburg and Courtauld Institutes* 48 (1985), pp. 23–41.

7. Quod si omne id vocemus argumentationem, quo dubia incertaque colligimus, non modo opus ea esse ad affectus evocandos crediderim, sed crebriorem etiam densioremque esse oportere. Viribus enim opus est et rapeienda mens auferendusque ipse sibi animus et velut extra se ponendus. Imitantur hoc in eloquendo autores, ut si minus [MSS and early editions read quominus] sint ipsis plura quae dicant, idem tamen mutatis subinde verbis velut plura ingerant. Quid aliud Virgilius expressit cum dicit apud eum Dido: Per ego has lachrymas, dextramque tuam te,/ Per connubia nostra, per inceptos Hymenaeos. Idem erant dextra et connubium et Hymenaei. Non enim aliud quam fidem coniugii his tribus significat, repetendo tamen aliis verbis tanquam plura inculcavit. *Aeneid*, IV, 314–16.

8. Affectus autem mihi non aliud videtur esse quam impetus quidam animi, quo ad appetendum aversandumve aliquid vehementius quam pro quietu statu mentis impellimur.

9. Ordo et distributio rerum, quae demonstrat, quid quibus locis conveniat et collocandum sit.

10. Ut ergo quae ad dispositionem pertinent, in summam quandam redigamus: opus est in primis, quisquis bene disponere volet, ut totam inventionis suae sylvam, hoc est, omnia quaecunque dicturus est, velut conspectui suo subiiciat. Tum quid in animo auditoris efficere velit, diligenter expendat. Deinde res ipsas, rerumque partes, et vim naturamque singularum, omniumque, et inter se conferat, et cum praeceptis omnia. Tum non difficulter videbit ubi temporum sequenda ratio, ubi per species res digerenda, et quibusdam velut limitibus singula discernenda, ubi aliud ex alio, et quicque proximum aptissimumve fuerit, ducendum. Tum quid tribuendum voluptati, quomodo victoriae certaminique serviendum, quis quaestionum ordo, quis argumentationum, quis propositionum servandus. Est autem diligenti multaque cura tractanda dispositio, quando veram haec pars ingenii laudem meretur.

11. Omnium locorum e quibus ducuntur argumenta, nulli fere minus est virium contra renitentem auditorem, quam similitudini. Ad eum vero qui sponte sequitur, docendumque se praebet, accommodatior nullus est. Aperit enim rem (si recte adhibeatur) et quandam eius imaginem subiicit animo, ut cum assentiendi necessitatem non afferat, afferat tacitum dissentiendi pudorem. Quapropter ad probandum non ita crebro, ad explanandum illustrandumque saepe ab oratoribus, a poetis saepius adhibetur. Habet tamen persaepe probantis speciem similitudo, eo ipso, quod rem qualis sit indicat. Itaque cum legis Quintiliani illud: Vascula oris angusti superfusam humoris copiam respuunt, sensim autem influentibus vel instillantibus etiam replentur, non conficitur utique, debere propter hoc tenera puerorum ingenia pro modo virium suarum doceri. Sed tamen concipiendo quisque rem apud animum suum sub hac imagine, persuadet sibi, aliter fieri non posse. Quintilian, *Institutio oratoria*, 1.2.28.

12. Van der Poel, Meerhoff, 25–62, 171–90, Mack, "Meharchtran's Commentaries," "Ramos Reading."

13. Magnitudinem belli una ratione ostendit ducta argumentatione a causis efficientibus. Quod enim bellum duo magni reges gerunt, quod multae ac bellicosae gentes suscipiunt, id magnum ac periculosum sit oportet ... Duplici argumentatione est opus ut ex his Ciceronis verbis intelligatur id quo haec tendit oratio, quarum priorem velut notam iam accipit Cicero, potestque ea formari hoc modo: ad bellum necessarium ac periculosum deligendus est imperator optimus; hoc autem

bellum, et necessarium et periculosum est; proinde ad hoc bellum optimus imperator deligendus est. Altera est: is demum huic bello praeficiendus est, qui imperator sit optimus; proinde solus Pompeius huic bello praeficiendus est.

WORKS CITED

Agricola, Rodolphus. *De inventione dialectica*. Cologne, 1539, reprinted Niewkoop: De Graaf, 1967.

Agricola, Rodolphe. *Ecrits sur la dialectique et l'humanisme*. Ed. and Trans. Marc van der Poel. Paris: Champion, Geneva: Slatkine, 1997.

Agricola, Rudolf. *De inventione dialectica*. Ed. and Trans. Lothar Mundt. Tubingen: Max Niemeyer, 1992.

Akkerman, Fokke and A. J. Vanderjagt, eds. *Rodolphus Agricola Phrisius*. Leiden: E. J. Brill, 1988.

Baxandall, Michael. *Words for Pictures*. New Haven: Yale UP, 2003, 69–82.

Huisman, Gerda C. *Rudolph Agricola: A Bibliography*. Nieuwkoop: De Graaf, 1985.

Mack, Peter. "Melanchthon's Commentaries on Latin Literature." In *Melanchthon und Europa II, Westeuropa*. Ed. G. Frank and K. Meerhoff. Stuttgart: Jan Thorboeke, 2002: 29–52.

Mack, Peter. "Ramus Reading: The Commentaries on Cicero's *Consular Orations* and Vergil's *Ecologues* and *Georgics*." *Journal of the Warburg and Courtauld Institutes* 61 (1998): 111–41.

Mack, Peter. *Renaissance Argument: Valla and Agricola in the Traditions of Rhetoric and Dialetic*. Leiden: E. J. Brill, 1993.

Mack, Peter. "Rudolph Agricola's Reading of Literature." *Journal of the Warburg and Courtauld Institutes* 48 (1985): 23–41.

Mack, Peter. "Rudolph Agricola's Topics." In Akkerman ed. *Rodolphus Agricola:* 257–69.

McNally, James R. "Rudolph Agricola's *De inventione Libri Tres:* A Translation of Selected Chapters." *Speech Monographs* 34 (1967): 393–422.

Meerhoff, Kees. *Entre logique et littérature*. Orleans: Paradigme, 2001.

Van der Poel, Marc. "The Scholia in Orationem Pro Lege Manilia" of Rudolph Agricola." *Lias* 24 (1997): 1–35.

Virgil. *The Aeneid*. Trans. Robert Fitzgerald. Harmondsworth: Penguin, 1985.

4

Responsible Citizenship: Ethos, Action, and the Voices of African American Women

Jacqueline Jones Royster
The Ohio State University

Silence in a democracy is a dangerous thing.

—Bernice Johnson Reagon
Protest Music and Responsible Citizenship

On March 19, 2003, during the annual convention of the Conference on College Composition and Communication (CCCC) in New York City, at the hands of President George W. Bush, the United States of America found itself at war with Iraq, a conflict that was positioned in public discourse by the White House as a "quick and just" war. As might be expected, since then, there has been much evidence to indicate that this discourse was propagandistic, deliberately designed to achieve political and economic goals, and perhaps even the personal goals of the Bush administration. An astute observer might easily make the case that this administration operated in selfish terms and with alarming disregard for both the citizens of the nation and the world. Whether one makes such an assertion or not, clearly, we now find that our nation has functioned as an invader of another nation, as the crafter—without invitation by the invaded nation—of a military occupation, and in the very difficult, if not impossible situation, of trying to figure out options for simultaneously extricating ourselves from the scene, needing to create a better image for ourselves on the world's stage, and needing to expend considerable national resources on rebuilding the nation that we will be leaving in our wake.

Against this backdrop, as experts in rhetoric and composition, how do we see ourselves as complicit? What are our social and cultural obligations as teachers, researchers, and scholars? What do we have to offer as one set of people among many others in the nation who exist in the worlds beyond the Bush administration, groups who seek to operate as responsible citizens dedicated to bringing knowledge, experience, and expertise to bear in finding workable, more positive solutions to contentious problems and challenges, rather than choosing

41

war and other imperialist actions? How do we respond reactively and proactively to foundational questions: What would a "safe," "secure," "peaceful," "prosperous" world look like? How can we do our parts to make it so? Where are the cautionary tales? Where is the hope for peace? How does the work and activism of academic humanists matter?

RESPONSIBLE CITIZENSHIP AND ACADEMIC HUMANISTS

One response to the last question is a project that we have launched at The Ohio State University. In describing this project, my intention is to connect it to the historical imperatives of African American women's public discourse in a way that illuminates a critical point about responsible citizenship: the need to bring critical attention to dynamic relationships between a continuity of commitment to social activism and the continuity of need in the United States for responsible and respectful global citizenship. My intent is to suggest that the enactment of democracy, as an illusive political concept, is yoked to a continuous commitment to sociopolitical critique as exercised through sustained ethical behavior, just actions, and socially and politically conscious public discourse.

In the fall of 2002, a year after the September 11th tragedy and with the rise of national homeland security policies, the College of Humanities at Ohio State was invited by our University Homeland and International Security Office to prepare a position paper in response to the two national documents that constitute the basic policy of the United States with regard to homeland security and international relationships: *The National Security Strategy* and *National Strategy for Homeland Security*.

We recognized that the College of Humanities, with three hundred tenure line faculty in the humanities disciplines alone (not including the arts), is arguably the largest collection of humanists in the United States and that we have a social obligation to bring our knowledge and expertise to bear in helping the nation to operate more responsibly. A team of thirty-five people from across the humanities, from other areas at the university, and a small group of external consultants developed a response that we completed and made available in print and on the web in October 2003 (www.humanities.osu.edu). The rationale from that statement says:

> *The National Security Strategy of the United States of America* and the *National Strategy for Homeland Security* present an integrated framework for United States policy that attempts to link the government's economic and political policies and ground them in United States history, culture, and values. *The National Security Strategy* (NSS) examines a wide range of international security issues and (foreign) terrorism concerns, and the *National Strategy for Homeland Security* (HS) outlines a reorganization of disparate governmental agencies in order to prioritize domestic security. Neither document is adequately informed by the cultural and historical knowledge and expertise that humanists can provide. The humanities promote disciplined reflection and research on histories, languages, and cultures, and on how individuals and communities in different times and places have understood themselves and their environment. One hallmark of this approach is critical analysis, self-reflection, and the deliberate creation of interpretive, explanatory contextual frames. Neither of the two national security documents shows adequate evidence of this perspective in its conceptual or analytical framework. As a result, neither benefits from the insights and accumulated knowledge of the humanities. The purpose of this analysis is to make clearer the benefits of consistently incorporating humanities knowledge and expertise in public policy making in order to rectify what we see in the two national documents as conceptual—if not ethical—problems.

Over the course of the 2003–2004 academic year, we moved forward with several follow-up activities. First was the college-sponsored annual spring forum on a pressing issue. The 2004 forum, which occurred on April 22nd, was titled Language, Culture, Media, and (Inter)National Security, and we were pleased to have the external consultants who worked with us on the production of the position paper to serve as the panelists for the forum. They are:

- Kathleen Woodward, Director of the Simpson Center for the Humanities at the University of Washington in Seattle
- James C. Early, Director of Cultural Heritage Policy at the Smithsonian Institution, Washington, DC
- Richard Brecht, Director of the Center for the Advanced Study of Languages at the University of Maryland, College Park
- Nathan J. Citino, Assistant Professor in Diplomatic History at Colorado State University, Fort Collins
- Laura J. Gurak, Professor and Department Head, Department of Rhetoric, Program in Scientific and Technical Communication, University of Minnesota

Moreover, the forum also constituted the thematic focus of our annual college magazine, *Humanities Exchange* (2004). This issue highlights the forum and includes several essays written on issues of language, culture, media, and (inter)national security written by faculty in the College of Humanities who are experts in related areas.

Second, faculty with interests in these thematic areas (i.e., language, culture, media, and [inter]national security) have formed working groups, mainly through the Center for Public Humanities and Collaborative Research, the Center for Folklore Studies, and the Office of International Affairs, to engage in issues of mutual interests and pursue collaborative, cross-disciplinary research projects. The individuals in these groups are actively engaged in their own research but, through the working groups, have the opportunity to cluster their concerns in cross-disciplinary ways with the concerns of others in an effort to create synergies. The interactions have given rise to brown-bag dialogues, conferences, presentations, and other programming that have energized not only the individuals directly involved but also the audiences that have developed around them.

Third, in January 2005, the College of Humanities opened its newest building, Hagerty Hall, which houses the World Media and Culture Center and brings together our language departments (through which we offer over thirty languages annually) and the Department of Comparative Studies. Hagerty is our most technologically sophisticated building in the humanities. It permits us to use cutting-edge technologies to connect with sites around the globe and to engage more vibrantly with languages and cultures both internationally and intranationally.

Fourth, with this evolving program we are in the process of pulling various related projects together under a general umbrella for which we have a working title: Humanities in Action: Language, Culture, Media, (Inter)National Security, and Global Responsibility. It is a multidisciplinary initiative designed to bring together as core participants several units at the university, including departments and centers across the arts and sciences and our radio and television stations, to participate in projects focused on expanding the notion of global responsibility to include varying roles for the knowledge and expertise that we have accumulated across the disciplines and interdisciplines associated with the arts and sciences. At Ohio State, these areas comprise five colleges: Arts, Biological Sciences, Humanities, Mathematical and Physical Sciences, and Social and Behavioral Sciences. From a collective view, the projects question sovereignty, self-determination, political boundaries, national security, international security, language, culture, global interconnectedness, media, peace, and so forth, while serving to help anchor the question, "What does it mean to be a responsible citizen in today's world?"

The foci are manifold. Among the topics most directly related to the humanities are:

- Citizenship and Security, which examines issues of national and international security and their relationship to culture, humanities research, and the media.
- Citizenship in Contention, which focuses on conflict zones and the particular role of cultural exchange and the media in these disputed contexts, examining in particular the circulation and functioning of culture, media, and art in places where the interactions among polarized communities are restricted.
- Citizenship in a Democracy, which explores the notion of protest, what it means to have participatory democracy, and how literature, art, and other cultural expressions help to construct the sociopolitical conscience of a nation and foment social change. The largest and most visible project under this third theme is a project on protest music. Under the leadership of my colleague, Amy Horowitz, a musicologist who works with the Melton Center for Jewish Studies and the Mershon Center for the Interdisciplinary Study of International Security and Public Policy, we are working on a documentary film: *Protest Music and Responsible Citizenship: A Conversation with Harry Belafonte, Holly Near, Bernice Johnson Reagon, and Pete Seeger.*

In the fall of 2003, Amy Horowitz and Amy Shuman, the Director of our Center for Folklore Studies, in collaboration with several campus units, convened in a historic event on the anniversary of the September 11th attacks. This project brought the four performers just mentioned to Columbus, Ohio, to engage in two days worth of conversation with each other about their music and their social, political, and cultural activism. The event ended with a joint performance by all four artists. We videotaped the two days of their time with us and are in the process of putting together a documentary on the relationships between music, public discourse, and the development of a national sociopolitical consciousness.

ETHOS, ACTION, AND THE VOICES
OF AFRICAN AMERICAN WOMEN[1]

In the video clip from *Protest Music and Responsible Citizenship*, as indicated in the quotation that opens this essay, Bernice Johnson Reagon says, "Silence in a democracy is a dangerous thing." Her statement forms a springboard from which to highlight two points. First, it is Reagon's direct response to our request that she think about and articulate the ways in which she sees her work as writer, scholar, musician, activist, and so forth to be connected to the notion of responsible citizenship. Second, and more salient for my own research, her statement emerges from a long-standing expressive tradition and exemplifies an ethical viewpoint and commitment to social action that is traceable over two centuries in the writing of African American women. This springboard directs us toward the connection that I posited in the beginning of this essay between the historical imperatives of African American women's public discourse and responsible citizenship. Reagon's statement highlights the critical tension between a continuity of commitment to social activism and the continuity of need in the United States for responsible and respectful global citizenship.

Over the generations African American women writers have habitually demonstrated, as Reagon's statement suggests, an urgent desire to participate in public discourse with the intention of raising the consciousness of a nation and creating a world that is better than the one in which these women have quite persistently, if not inevitably, found themselves. In doing so, these writers have performed yet an additional service beyond their contributions to aesthetic traditions. They have offered patterns of language and action that form a vibrant and vital legacy for what it means to live consciously in a democratic society and to enact responsible global citizenship in a world where injustices, inequities, inequalities, and complex oppressions persistently prevail.

As a versatile performer with both words and music, Reagon exhibits patterns of language and action that clearly place her within this group of writer-activists. With this short statement, "Silence in a democracy is a dangerous thing," she underscores in provocative terms what I posit as a deeply seated system of belief that intricately links ethos, action, and transformative rhetorics. In an essay titled "Coalition Politics: Turning the Century," Reagon states:

> You must believe that believing in human beings in balance with the environment and the universe is a good thing. You must believe [...] that having a society that doesn't solve everything with guns is a good thing.[...] The thing that must survive you is not just the record of your practice, but the principles that are the basis of your practice [...] what counts is not what you do this weekend [at the West Coast Women's Music Festival 1981, Yosemite National Forest, California] but take what this weekend has meant—try to digest it. And first thing, Monday, Tuesday morning at work, before twenty-four hours go around, apply it. And then do it everyday you get up and find yourself alive. (366, 368)

In this essay, Reagon connects ethical principles to conscious and deliberate action. This inclination to connect ethos and action forms a resonating thread among African American women writers, as demonstrated also by the writing of Maria W. Stewart, the earliest known African American woman to write political essays. In 1831, Stewart published an essay titled "Religion and the Pure Principles of Morality, the Sure Foundation on Which We Must Build" in *The Liberator,* the abolitionist newspaper published by William Lloyd Garrison and Isaac Knapp. A point to emphasize is that the frames for these two essays indicate several evolutionary shifts with regard to the context for action, the imperatives for language use, the ideological perspectives of the writers, and so forth, illustrating in fact that we actually have in this case a continuum of transformative rhetorics. We can chart trajectories from the Black Jeremiad tradition of the abolitionist rhetorics, in which Stewart's essay participated, to the civil and women's rights rhetorics of the 20th century, in which Reagon's essay participated, to the rhetorics that are emerging in the 21st century in contemporary arenas of popular culture, as evidenced, for example, by the participation of African American women in hip-hop culture. The research of several scholars is relevant in this regard, including Marilyn Richardson, 1987; David Howard-Pitney, 1990; Robbie Jean Walker, 1992; the Black Public Sphere Collective, 1995; Philip S. Foner and Robert James Branham, 1998; Shirley Wilson Logan, 1999; Houston A. Baker, Jr., 2001; and Gwendolyn D. Pough, 2004. However, despite the evolutionary dimensions of these rhetorical practices that are discernable through recent scholarship, over the various reform movements, there remains evidence of some remarkable resonances as well.

In 1831, Stewart said:

> Truly, my heart's desire and prayer is, that Ethiopia [used as a signifier during Stewart's day of people of African descent rather than people from the modern nation of Ethiopia] might stretch forth her hands unto God. But we have a great work to do. Never, no, never will the chains of slavery and ignorance burst, till we become united as one, and cultivate among ourselves pure principles of piety, morality and virtue ... my heart's desire and prayer to God is that there might come a thorough reformation among us. Our minds have too long groveled in ignorance and sin. Come, let us incline our ears to wisdom, and apply our hearts to understanding [...] [L]et us make a mighty effort, and arise; and if no one will promote or respect us, let us promote and respect ourselves. (qtd. in Richardson 30, 36–37).

Stewart and Reagon are writers separated in time by 150 years but bound by the continuity of their struggles for freedom and social justice. Like the work of other African American women writers, their essays are part of an expressive tradition that makes evident the urgency of connecting ethos and action. African American women writers have trod and retrod this ground, gaining expertise through their enactments of what it means to use language variously to resist oppression and injustice and to engage in social reform. They have done this so persistently that collectively their lives and words constitute a substantial body of knowledge and wisdom. Such wisdom, in being so well rooted in experience, serves reflexively, and perhaps even instinctively, as a springboard for ongoing action. These writers have demonstrated over two centuries that they are indeed wise women, forwarding an intellectual tradition that remains instructive for a world that today remains equally persistent in its need for social justice and social reform.

This view of African American women writers' wisdom was articulately explained in an article first published in 1991 by Mae Gwendolyn Henderson and often quoted since then. Henderson states:

> Also interesting is the link between the gift of tongues, the gift of prophecy, and the gift of interpretation. [...] If to speak in tongues is to utter mysteries in and through the Spirit, to prophesy is to speak to others in a (diversity of) language(s) which the congregation can understand. The Scriptures would suggest that the disciples were able to perform both. I propose, at this juncture, an enabling critical fiction—that it is black women writers who are the modern day apostles, empowered by experience to speak as poets and prophets in many tongues. (150–51)

In effect, Henderson claims the power of vision, interpretation, and eloquence for African American women writers, a claim that as late as the 1990s was still considered to have a modest and somewhat questionable scope of believability in that African American women writers who had received acclaim to that point were seen as rather "exotic" or unusual, and habitually marked as "exceptional" rather than "normal" in elite literate circles. In other words, these writers as a group were still marked quite fundamentally as "unnatural" and outside of the normative range of those expected to have the capacity to set and sustain the terms of performance in lettered domains. By contrast, as indicated by the quotation above, Henderson proclaims for this group interpretive vision and the gift of prophecy. She goes on to suggest that what typically happens with African American women writers is that the conditions around them require them to create multivocal texts and to participate in a multiplicity of discourses even in one text in order to succeed expressively and, I would add, rhetorically as well.

As Henderson explains, African American women writers are heteroglossic, in that they "speak from a multiple and complex social, historical, and cultural positionality which, in effect, constitutes black female subjectivity" (147). Further, she says that this social positionality functions also to constitute a consciousness:

a kind of "inner speech" reflecting "the outer word" in a process that links the psyche, language, and social interaction [...] a social positionality that enables them to speak in dialogically racial and gendered voices to the other(s) both within and without. If the psyche functions as an internalization of heterogeneous social voices, black women's speech/writing becomes at once a dialogue between self and society and between self and psyche. (146)

Henderson posits that this complex embodiment of difference enriches the ability of African American women to speak in the multiple languages of public discourse, to bring a multivocal analysis to complex problems, and to interpret the world in dialogic ways, all of which she characterizes as their ability to "speak in tongues."

In *Feminist Theory: From Margin to Center*, bell hooks offers a different rendering of this phenomenon. She says:

To be in the margin is to be part of the whole but outside the main body. [...] Living as we did—on the edge—we developed a particular way of seeing reality. We looked both from the outside in and from the inside out. We focused our attention on the center as well as on the margin. We understood both. This mode of seeing reminded us of the existence of a center. Our survival depended on an ongoing public awareness of the separation between margin and center and an ongoing private acknowledgment that we were a necessary, vital part of that whole.

This sense of wholeness, impressed upon our consciousness by the structure of our daily lives, provided us an oppositional world view—a mode of seeing unknown to most of our oppressors, that sustained us, aided us in our struggle to transcend poverty and despair, strengthened our sense of self and our solidarity. (Preface)

Similar to Henderson, hooks recognizes that the positionality of African American people includes both an outsider perspective and an insider perspective, a view also articulated at the turn of the twentieth century by W. E. B. DuBois, in *The Souls of Black Folk*. Hooks asserts that, instead of the warring souls that DuBois suggests, the duality constitutes a wholeness of vision that enables African American people (women in this instance) to have a transcendant viewpoint that aids the understanding of both public and private mandates and that helps those with such vision to resist being overcome spiritually, ideologically, and politically by the realities of poverty, despair, and other contending social and political forces.

In contrast to Henderson, hooks directs attention to how this positioning functions to enable action rather than to the action itself. My interests are directed toward both, taking into account not just duality or multiplicity but the notion that positionality is constituent in an instrumental process. From my perspective, in the ephemeral space between vision and action, ethos forms. Individuals in a particular place and time come to voice, exhibiting a desire to have agency in the world. They take a stance (sometimes a shifting one) in response to social and political conditions and mandates and as an enactment of their own desires and imperatives, and they act, in this case, as speakers and writers. Ethos formation can be framed thereby as a constituent part of a process which links dynamically viewpoint, whether characterized as vision or positionality, and action as it is rendered broadly to include rhetorical action. I articulated this relationship in *Traces of a Stream* as a kaleidoscopic model that merges context, ethos, and action.

Shifting attention to the interconnections between context, ethos, and action recasts the analytical anchor so that multi*focality*, as a way of seeing and being, rather than just multi*vocality*, as an effect of positionality, gains saliency as a term that encapsulates these practices in two specific ways. On one hand, it acknowledges overtly the existence of a foveal view (see Chafe, 1994) with regard to what is centered on the retina at the point of acute vision versus what is also visible simultaneously in the peripheral areas surrounding that sightline. Using this concept helps us to see that the shifts described by Henderson, as illustrated for example by African American women's essay writing, can be rendered as rhetorical moves. Moreover, given the historical positionality of African American women, many such moves can actually be rendered as ritualized, that is, as part of a patterned response to persistent social and political conditions. In essay writing, these rhetorical practices function to increase the capacity of the writers to complicate the foveal view, to bring texture and vibrancy to it, and thereby, hopefully, to help audiences to gain a viewpoint that is more useable with regard to the writers' interests and ultimately with regard to their desire to connect communicatively with others and to persuade them to see their views of the world as reasonable, viable, worthy, and compelling.

A second feature is that multifocality sets in motion a stronger imperative to use multivariant appeals in the development of sense-making strategies. The writers quite necessarily shift perspectives, shift voicing, and shift often the audiences directly and indirectly addressed in light of the complexity of the external and internal mandates that they face. These shifts activate a companion move to deploy persuasive appeals just as variously toward logos, ethos, or pathos. In other words, these writers use sense-making strategies flexibly as they determine them to be useful in talking to whatever part of the sensory system that offers a connection, whether it is the head, the backbone, the heart, or the stomach. In making these choices, they operate with tacit and sometimes overt understanding of *kairos,* or opportune moments, appropriateness, social obligation, and sometimes dramatic effect as they attune their texts with their persuasive goals.

In focusing on essay writing as an instructive example of these types of discursive practices, I have added to Henderson's assertions the notion that when we look at African American women's essays, we see that they have gone one step farther than multivocality, multifocality, and multiple discourses. I add that they also habitually express themselves across multiple genres as well. In looking organically and developmentally at their patterns of literate practices, I have noted the following:

- Some of the writers choose essays as a primary genre of choice, as in the case of Ida B. Wells-Barnett, who was a journalist, and bell hooks, who is a public academic—even though in the case of these two writers both have published occasionally using other forms. For example, Wells-Barnett wrote "Two Christmas Days: A Holiday Story," and bell hooks has published several children's books: *Happy to Be Nappy,* 1999; *Be Boy Buzz,* 2002; *Homemade Love,* 2002).
- Others in this group use essays more as a companion form, publishing essays occasionally amid other writing that they continue to do more often, as in the case of

Frances E. W. Harper, who was more celebrated as a poet and novelist, or any of the more contemporary writers who publish mainly as poets, novelists, and playwrights, but who also write essays—for example, Audre Lorde, Alice Walker, June Jordan, Toni Morrison, Nikki Giovanni, Pearl Cleage, Maya Angelou, and so on.

- Last but not least, sometimes, especially in the case of the contemporary writers, they strategically use a combination of generic strategies within their essay writing, as demonstrated by Alice Walker and June Jordan, who use poetic and narrative devices in their essays along with other more typical expository and persuasive ones.

Even a preliminary surveying of nineteenth- and twentieth-century African American women essayists shows that they tend to write using more than one literate form. Often, as illustrated by nineteenth- and twentieth-century writers, they combine two or more forms—nonfiction, fiction, poetry, or drama. The point to be emphasized is that from an analytical perspective, this habit facilitates an analysis of their discursive practices in that, because of the generic features of this particular form, their essay writing easily emerges as an important lens for illuminating a fifth, perhaps even more salient, feature. African American women essay writers consistently use written language, not only to fulfill expressive mandates, but also to fulfill sociopolitical ones as well, and they do so across genres.

A point to be highlighted is that the type of essay writing that dominates among this group is the personal essay, a form that is particularly useful from an analytical perspective in identifying features that suggest an author's vision and ethical stance (i.e., the ways by which the author comes to voice and establishes a place from which to speak or write). As I summarize in *Traces of a Stream,* African American women's essay writing consistently shows the following features:

- The writer is self-authorized.
- The "I" perspective is foregrounded.
- Knowledge and understanding are grounded in experience.
- There is a sense of a mind at work.
- The thinking is exploratory, unfinished, open-ended.
- The writer recognizes a listening audience and expects response.
- The writer invites skepticism and thereby often situates the text as going quite appropriately against the grain of current thought or practice, a feature that I underscore as evidence of radicalism.
- The text is situated in time and place and is thereby responsive to its context—the material realities of time, place, and person/writer.
- The writer's knowledge, experience, and insight can intersect in variable ways. For example, either focal point might be foregrounded in the organization and development of the text while retaining the other in a complementary or suggestive way.
- As a non-fiction form, a distinctive generic feature of the essay itself is that it is protean and flexibly lends itself to an incorporation of a full range of expressive and organizational devices. (*Traces* 22–23)

In using the essay writing of African American women as an example of heteroglossia, a critical point to underscore is that this form actually goes well beyond being simply an instructive example of an applicable analytical concept. It functions also as a lens through which to gain a clearer understanding of other elements of their discursive practices more generally. I find that through their uses of essay writing, African American women writers demonstrate a desire to cast attention quite directly and forthrightly as they flesh out foveal concerns in more complex ways, rather than addressing these concerns more symbolically or inferentially. They make overtures at will to more than one audience within a single essay and thereby amplify messages that they might well have treated through other literate forms in a more narrowly deployed way (e.g., in their poetry, plays, novels, etc.). They engage audiences, multiple or singular, by means of more than one persuasive appeal (i.e., in terms of logos, pathos, and ethos); speak to those audiences using multiple registers; and most saliently, engage them through direct address on issues of social and political consequence and thereby exercise their desires, often in provocative terms, to change the world. Further, with regard to developmental strategies, the writers sometimes use narrative, poetic, or dramatic devices in support of expository or persuasive purposes within a single essay. When this essaying practice is connected with their practices across expressive forms, we gain a clearer understanding of their multigeneric approach to expressiveness, whether across multiple generic forms or through the use of multiple generic strategies within one form.

So, what does this analysis suggest? Well, it suggests many things, but fundamental to this list is a pattern that may not be so evident in more surface analyses. Consider the following line of thought: African American women have experienced in this country a continuity of oppressions (with regard to race, gender, culture, class, etc.). This continuity of oppressions has engendered continuity also in their responses to both the oppressions and the persistent continuity of them. These responses have been heartily defined by what is now demonstrable as habits of resistance that get enacted rhetorically as well as in other ways. Rhetorically, these habits of resistance are evident in their habit of using writing: to participate in the circles of public discourse that relate variously to their lives, to engage in social and political reform in their own interests and in the interests of others, and to exercise their socially defined commitments to nation building and responsible citizenship, which in their renderings are more typically articulated as a commitment to make the world a better place. This schema for positioning the ethos formation and rhetorical actions of African American women offers a different framework for interpreting their discursive practices and connecting them to the larger world of rhetorical performance.

RECASTING THE *WARRIOR WOMAN* IMAGE

A second concept that comes into play in connecting ethos formation and rhetorical action for African American women writers is intellectual history, as this term embodies the wisdom accumulated in the substantial body of work that they have produced over the generations. The point to be underscored, as I have done in past publications ("Perspectives"), is that *intellectual* is not typically a term that has been used to frame our understanding of African American women's writing. Instead, their writing is keyed more often by a framing that I have found to be increasingly problematic, that is, that their writing results from the fact that they are warrior women. My view is that warrior women serves mainly as a window onto an area that has permitted us to articulate various dimensions of socially conscious writing so that we can now recognize such writing and its purposes. Ultimately, however, such analyses are too shallow and too narrow. These essentially descriptive accomplishments do not actually constitute an adequate assessment, interrogation, or interpretive umbrella in accounting for the fairly broad array of rhetorical actions encoded by the metaphor. We just have not gone far enough with the warrior image as a springboard to explain the nature or persistence of certain patterns and habits of rhetorical performance or to connect these practices in a substantive and instructive way to the history of rhetoric as a long-standing but, by academic tradition, ethnocentrically defined arena.

In recent years, the metaphor of African American women writers as warriors for social justice has been consistently deployed by many scholars. It was invoked, for example, by Pamela Klass Mittlefehldt in "'A Weaponry of Choice': Black American Women Writers and the Essay" (1993). She says:

> In these essays, Black women have refused silence, and have shattered the calm with their words. An array of selves speaks through these works; grounded, disrupting, their words demand response. They put us all "On Call." Throughout these essays, I as a reader am called beyond contemplation to action. These are not platonic abstractions pondering metaphors of truth; these are passionate injunctions declaring the immediacy of battle. The essay has become a form that melds the eloquence and urgency of poetry with the precision and potency of fine rhetoric. A weaponry of choice, which demands transformation. (206)

This view is also alluded to in an edited volume by Beverly Guy-Sheftall, *Words of Fire: An Anthology of African-American Feminist Thought* (1995); an edited volume by Shirley Wilson Logan, *With Pen and Voice: A Critical Anthology of Nineteenth-Century African-American Women* (1995); and even in my own work, as illustrated by my discussion of Ida B. Wells in "To Call a Thing by its True Name: The Rhetoric of Ida B. Wells" (1995).

Moreover, the writers themselves also use this image frequently, as evidenced, for example, by the autobiographies of Ida B. Wells, titled *Crusade for Justice* (1970) and June Jordan, titled, *Soldier: A Poet's Childhood* (2000). As illustrated by Jordan, they also do so in their essays. In *Civil Wars: Observations from the Front Lines of America* (1981), for example, Jordan speaks eloquently about herself as a writer using this image:

> Early on, the scriptural concept that "in the beginning was the Word and the Word was with God and the Word was God"—the idea that the word could represent and then deliver into reality what the word symbolized—this possibility of language, of writing, seemed to me magical and basic and irresistible. [...] I loved words and I hated to fight. But if, as a Black girl-child in America, I could not evade the necessity to fight, then, maybe, I could choose my weaponry at least. ("Foreword")

This passage was the source of Mittlefehldt's title.

In similar manner, Audre Lorde established her identity as a warrior woman in an essay titled "The Transformation of Silence into Language and Action" (*Sister Outsider*, 1984). She says:

> What are the words you do not yet have? What do you need to say? What are the tyrannies you swallow day by day and attempt to make your own, until you will sicken and die of them, still in silence? Perhaps for some of you here today, I am the face of one of your fears. Because I am woman, because I am Black, because I am lesbian, because I am myself—a Black woman warrior poet doing my work—come to ask you, are you doing yours? (41–2)

As evidenced by Jordan, Lorde, and so many other African American women writers, the warrior woman image captures a well-grounded and easily documented view of them as passionate thinkers and activists who use the pen as a mighty sword. The image suggests that their words bite and sting as they lay out truths and engage in advocacy and activism for various causes. The truth of these assertions, as indicated by the preceding account of various writers, is indeed trackable.

After years of using this image as central to my own work, however, I have become increasingly aware of the limitations of this truth, and I am suggesting that it is time to move beyond this viewpoint. In working to meet this challenge, I have looked again and again at the textual evidence, and I have become aware of another thread, as illustrated by the quotation from Bernice Johnson Reagon, "Silence in a democracy is a dangerous thing" or by Audre Lorde's essay, "The Transformation of Silence into Language and Action." I suggest that the image of silence, or more specifically not being silent, is equally compelling and perhaps key to a deeper understanding of the rhetorical practices of African American women.

What does it really mean for African American women writers to conjure warrior images so persistently? What does it mean to remember that these images emerge from a history of experience and a history of intellectualism? What does it mean to see that within such a compelling image are other images that are equally compelling, like the image of not being silent, of speaking, of acting, of dedicating oneself every day all day to responsible citizenship, to making the world a better place?

In the larger project from which this essay is taken, my goal is to respond to these questions and pick up on a line of argument that I started in *Traces of a Stream*. In *Traces of a Stream*, I presented a model of literacy and sociopolitical action designed to explain essaying practices in a way that enables us to see how African American women writers have used literacy (with essay writing being an instructive example) as an act of resistance to disempowering conditions and in support of agenda for positive action. The main thesis of that study was that these women used writing to facilitate their abilities to operate with vision, insight, passion, and compassion in making sense of their lives and seeking to improve their conditions. As I stated in that publication, "Symbolically their lives became literacy in action, that is, an empowered use of literacy in the interests of action, social consciousness, and social responsibility" (*Traces* 61).

My effort was to document the continuity of African American women's experiences within an essentially hostile context of racism, sexism, economic oppression, and the like, and to assert that this context has given rise over time to a set of rhetorical practices, as evidenced by their use of the essay, geared toward advocacy, activism, and social reform. The primary assertion was that African American women writers have developed a habit of re-setting the terms of engagement with the intent of creating more accommodating spaces for sense-making and for action.

As demonstrated by all of the writers that I have referenced here, African American women writers hold fast to a notion of social responsibility that pushes them not to be silent but to speak up and out about the circumstances and conditions that surround them, to think critically about what they see, and to suggest pathways to action that they believe build the capacity of our society to create a better world. They enact variously the notion of responsible global citizenship, sharing the wisdom of their experiences as people who look back, look around, and also look forward.

As a researcher of these practices, I find wisdom in a quotation from Hans-Georg Gadamer in *Philosophical Hermeneutics*:

> The understanding of a text has not begun as long as the text remains mute. But a text can begin to speak [...]. When it does begin to speak, however, it does not simply speak its word, always the same, in lifeless rigidity, but gives ever new answers to the person who questions it and poses ever new questions to him who answers it. To understand a text is to come to understand oneself in a

kind of dialogue. This contention is confirmed by the fact that the concrete dealing with a text yields understanding only when what is said in the text begins to find expression in the inter-preter's own language. Interpretation belongs to the essential unity of understanding. One must take up into himself what is said to him in such a fashion that it speaks and finds an answer in the words of his own language. (57)

The general goal with my book length project, for which I use the working title, *Nubia Lives*, is to listen to the writing of African American women—again and again and again—and to find my own words to interpret the transformative rhetorics that I have come to under-stand that African American women deploy. As Reagon has recommended, I have tried to savor these women's words, to digest them, and to be instructed by them every day that I have gotten up and found myself alive. My intention is to have their words speak, to help their experiences to find expression in the world of research and scholarship so that they inform our theoretical frameworks, to use the knowledge that I've gained from their practices to gen-erate new frameworks that have greater interpretive power and that offer a means to a clearer understanding of the capacity of human beings to be eloquent, and to have their words partic-ipate in more vibrant and vital ways in the "discourses of MAN" so that they can claim the intellectual authority that I believe they so richly deserve.

With regard to the connection between the imperatives of African American women writers and responsible citizenship in the contemporary context, my view is that the need in the world still exists for the types of vision and voices that African American women writers have persistently exhibited as citizens of the nation and world who are passion-ately committed to being socially conscious and socially responsible. Clearly, they do not wish to be among the "missing" voices in these vital discourses, and in my view the very least that we can do as researchers and scholars is to pay more critical attention, to listen well, and to bring a more insightful critical view of what in the end may indeed be bold and outrageous but wholly noble efforts in the interest of a world that really does have an urgent need for better ways of being and better ways of doing in our highly con-tentious global arenas.

NOTE

1. The remainder of this essay is excerpted from a book length project, *Nubia Lives: Utopian Desire and Radical Action in the Discursive Practices of African American Women* (in progress).

WORKS CITED

Angelou, Maya. "And Still I Rise." *And Still I Rise*. New York: Random, 1978. 41–42.

Baker, Houston A., Jr. *Critical Memory: Public Sphere, African American Writing, and Black Fa-thers and Sons of America*. Athens: U of Georgia P, 2001.

Black Public Sphere Collective. *The Black Public Sphere: A Public Culture Book*. Chicago: U of Chicago P, 1995.

Chafe, Wallace. *Discourse, Consciousness, and Time: The Flow and Displacement of Conscious Experience in Speaking and Writing*. Chicago: U of Chicago P, 1994.

Cleage, Pearl. *Mad at Miles: A Black Woman's Guide to Truth*. Southfield: The Cleage Group, Inc., 1989.

—. *Deals With the Devil: And Other Reasons to Riot*. New York: Ballantine, 1993.

DuBois, W. E. B. *The Souls of Black Folk*. 1903. New York: Gramercy, 1994.

Foner, Philip S., and Robert James Branham, eds. *Lift Every Voice: African American Oratory, 1787–1900*. Tuscaloosa: U of Alabama P, 1998.

Gadamer, Hans-Georg. *Philosophical Hermeneutics*. Trans. and ed. David E. Linge. Berkeley: U of California P, 1976.

Giddings, Paula. *When and Where I Enter: The Impact of Black Women on Race and Sex in America*. New York: Bantam, 1984.

Giovanni, Nikki. "Ego-Tripping." *Ego-Tripping and Other Poems for Young People*. New York: Hill, 1973.

Guy-Sheftall, Beverly, ed. *Words of Fire: An Anthology of African-American Feminist Thought*. New York: New, 1995.

Henderson, Mae Gwendolyn. "Speaking in Tongues: Diaologics, Dialectics, and the Black Women Writer's Literary Tradition." *Feminists Theorize the Political*. Ed. Judith Butler and Joan W. Scott. New York: Routledge, 1992. 144–66.

hooks, bell. *Feminist Theory: From Margin to Center*. Boston: South End, 1984.

——. *Happy to Be Nappy*. New York: Hyperion, 1999.

——. *Be Boy Buzz*. New York: Jump at the Sun, 2002.

——. *Homemade Love*. New York: Jump at the Sun, 2002.

Howard-Pitney, David. *The Afro-American Jeremiad: Appeals for Justice in America*. Philadelphia: Temple UP, 1990.

Jones, Beverly. *Quest for Equality: The Life and Writing of Mary Eliza Church Terrell, 1863–1954*. Vol. 13. *Black Women in United States History*. Ed. Darlene Clark Hine. Brooklyn: Carlson, 1990.

——. "Mary Eliza Church Terrell." *Black Women in America: An Historical Encyclopedia*. Vol. 2. Ed. Darlene Clark Hine. Brooklyn: Carlson, 1993. 1157–59.

Joeres, Ruth-Ellen Boetcher, and Elizabeth Mittman, eds. *The Politics of the Essay: Feminist Perspectives*. Bloomington: Indiana UP, 1993.

Jordan, June. *Soldier: A Poet's Childhood*. New York: Basic, 2000.

——. "Foreword." *Civil Wars: Observations from the Front Lines of America*. New York: Touchstone, 1981.

Kelley, Robin D. G. *Freedom Dreams: The Black Radical Imagination*. Boston: Beacon, 2002.

Logan, Shirley Wilson, ed. *With Pen and Voice: A Critical Anthology of Nineteenth-Century African-American Women*. Carbondale: Southern Illinois UP, 1995.

——. *We Are Coming: The Persuasive Discourse of Nineteenth-Century Black Women*. Carbondale: Southern Illinois University Press, 1999.

Lorde, Audre. "Litany for Survival." *Black Unicorn*. New York: Norton, 1978. 31–32.

——. *Sister Outsider: Essays and Speeches by Audre Lorde*. Freedom: Crossing, 1984.

Mittlefehldt, Pamela Klass. "'A Weaponry of Choice': Black American Women Writers and the Essay." *The Politics of the Essay: Feminist Perspectives*. Ed. Ruth-Ellen Boetcher Joeres and Elizabeth Mittarian. Bloomington: Indiana UP, 1993.

Morrison, Toni. *Playing in the Dark: Whiteness and the Literary Imagination*. Cambridge: Harvard UP, 1992.

Peterson, Carla L. *"Doers of the Word": African American Women Speakers and Writers in the North (1830-1880)*. New Brunswick: Rutgers UP, 1998.

Pough, Gwendolyn D. *Check It While I Wreck It: Black Womanhood, Hip-Hop Culture, and the Public Sphere*. Boston: Northeastern UP, 2004.

Ratcliffe, Krista. "Rhetorical Listening: A Trope for Interpretive Invention and a 'Code of Cross-Cultural Conduct'." *CCC* 51.2 (Dec. 1999): 195–224.

Reagon, Bernice Johnson. "Coalition Politics: Turning the Century." *Home Girls: A Black Feminist Anthology*. Ed. Barbara Smith. New York: Kitchen Table, 1983. 356–68.

Richardson, Marilyn, ed. *Maria W. Stewart, America's First Black Women Political Writer*. Bloomington: Indiana UP, 1987.

Royster, Jacqueline Jones. "Perspectives on the Intellectual Tradition of Black Women Writers." *The Right to Literacy*. Ed. Andrea A. Lunsford, Helene Moglen, and James Slevin. New York: MLA, 1990. 103–12.

——. "To Call a Thing by Its True Name: The Rhetoric of Ida B. Wells." In *Reclaiming Rhetorica*. Ed. Andrea A. Lunsford. Pittsburgh: University of Pittsburgh Press, 1995.

—. *Traces of a Stream: Literacy and Social Change among African American Women.* Pittsburgh: U of Pittsburgh P, 2000.

—, facilitator. *College of Humanities Response to National Security Documents.* <www.humanities.osu.edu>.

Salem, Dorothy. *To Better Our World.* Vol. 14. *Black Women in United States History.* Ed. Darlene Clark Hine. Brooklyn: Carlson, 1990.

Stewart, Maria W. "Religion and the Pure Principles of Morality, The Sure Foundation on Which We Must Build." *Maria W. Stewart, America's First Black Woman Political Writer: Essays and Speeches.* Ed. Marilyn Richardson. Bloomington: Indiana UP, 1987. 28–42.

Terrell, Mary Church. *A Colored Woman in a White World.* 1940. New Hampshire: Ayer, 1986.

Walker, Alice. *In Search of Our Mothers' Gardens: Womanist Prose.* New York, Harcourt, 1983.

Walker, Robbie Jean, ed. *The Rhetoric of Struggle: Public Address by African American Women.* New York: Garland, 1992.

Wells, Ida B. *Crusade for Justice: The Autobiography of Ida B. Wells.* Chicago: U of Chicago P, 1970.

—. "Two Christmas Days: A Holiday Story." *Ida B. Wells-Barnett: An Exploratory Study of an American Black Woman, 1893–1930.* Ed. Mildred I. Thompson. Brooklyn: Carlson, 1990.

Wesley, Charles Harris. *The History of the National Association of Colored Women's Clubs: A Legacy of Service.* Washington, DC: National Association of Colored Women's Clubs, 1984.

White, Deborah Gray. *Too Heavy a Load: Black Women in Defense of Themselves, 1894-1994.* New York: Norton, 1999.

II

History

5

The Centrality of *Ethos* in Eighteenth-Century Methodist Preaching

Lois Agnew

Syracuse University

The unique feature of eighteenth-century Methodist sermons is generally described as an emotional intensity that deviated from the more restrained Anglican norm. James Downey describes British Methodism as influential in an eighteenth-century shift in homiletics consisting of "a movement away from a style of oratory that is ethical and rational in its content, disciplined and precise in its language, and unimpassioned in its presentation, towards a preaching the content of which is evangelical, the language emotive, and presentation histrionic" (228). Like Downey, Bernd Lenz emphasizes the role of British Methodism in this evolution, noting that "a theological position which stressed inner holiness and spiritualization must inevitably affect the style of sermons and preaching, too, since it favours, perhaps even requires, more intrinsic and extrinsic emotionalism" (115). Although Lenz acknowledges that the level of emotion differs among Methodist preachers and varies from one sermon and audience to the next, he generally characterizes Methodist preaching as a development in homiletics that "parallels the rise of sentimentalism in literature" (124).

There is no doubt that John Wesley's sermons in many instances employ rhetorical devices that would be classified as emotive and that the fervor in Methodist sermons differs substantially from the style typically found in Anglican preaching of the same era. In part, a passionate delivery reflects the strong convictions that led one critical observer to describe Wesley as "a rigid zealot" who spoke with such "zeal and unbounded satire as quite spoiled what otherwise might have been turned to great advantage" (Kennicott 86). However, the strong and consistent emotional response of Wesley's audiences cannot be explained entirely in terms of his strategic use of emotional language. In fact, the form of Wesley's sermons is highly structured, and the content generally follows a logical progression of thought that is intended to appeal to the audience's reason.[1] Moreover, Wesley deliberately used plain language rather than the elevated literary style typically associated with eloquence in his day; he was highly critical of a popular style of preaching that featured what he described as an "unconnected rhapsody of unmeaning words" (qtd. in Heitzenrater, *Wesley and the People* 185). The primary distinguishing characteristic of Wesley's preaching lies not in a direct and intense appeal to the emotion, but in Wesley's ability to employ a type of *ethos* that simultaneously reveals himself to the members of his audience and establishes a personal connection with them that accounts for their emotional response to his message.

This application of ethical proof draws the speaker and audience together in an intricate relationship that departs substantially from Aristotle's division between *pathos*, which lies "in disposing the listener in some way," and *ethos*, which resides "in the character [*ethos*] of the speaker" (1356a). In offering his definition of the three forms of proof, each of which corresponds to one of the parties in a rhetorical interaction, Aristotle appears to assume the possibility of defining the function of proofs based on characteristics each one possesses in relative isolation from the other two. However, the rhetorical context for Wesley's sermons demanded that those classical boundaries be challenged, which supports James Baumlin's contention that "*ethos*, like versions of the self, must change over time and among cultures" (xxii). Understanding the factors that help to form the complex relationship between Wesley and his audience can help to illuminate ways in which *ethos* functions in eighteenth- and nineteenth-century sermons in response to particular cultural circumstances.

This change in *ethos*, which is an important component of Wesley's rhetorical technique, reflects the insight of contemporary theorists who argue that a speaker's success in interacting with an audience requires a connection between the audience's perception of the speaker's character and its emotional response to his or her message. Building on Kenneth Burke's notion of identification, Marshall W. Alcorn Jr. suggests that a modern notion of *ethos* involves the creation of texts that "contain devices that connect the self-structure of authors with the self-structure of readers" (22). In Alcorn's view, *ethos* must therefore be defined as "an argument in which rhetorical force derives not from the logic of what is said but from the perceived personality of the agent behind what is said" (23). Alcorn therefore follows the lead of Max Weber in linking *ethos* to "the power of charisma" (23) and adds, "Charismatic authority is a different mode whose legitimacy comes neither from special knowledge nor from the leader's special place in a social hierarchy of power" (22). For Alcorn, the rhetor evokes *ethos* not simply through revealing his or her character to an audience conceived as passive spectators, who form judgments about his or her authority based on external standards. Instead, he or she builds *ethos* through sharing his or her personality in a manner that connects with the audience, a strategy that actively engages audience members in appreciating the value of a message delivered by a speaker dedicated to addressing their concerns on multiple levels.

The model of *ethos* as the formation of a relationship between speaker and audience accommodates the unique challenges John Wesley faced as he began his ministry. After completing his baccalaureate degree at Oxford in 1724, Wesley, the son of a Church of England clergyman, initially embarked on what appeared to be an ordinary career. He received a fellowship from Lincoln College, accepted his father's offer of the curacy at Epworth and Wroot, and eventually returned to Oxford to assume the tutorial duties required as part of his fellowship. However, Wesley's return to Oxford in 1729–30 marked his participation in a small group of enthusiastic Christians who formed the beginning of a Methodist movement, featuring both a systematic approach to life that Wesley viewed as the foundation for holy living and regular charitable visits to disenfranchised citizens that included prisoners and the poor (Heitzenrater, *Wesley and the People* 34-41).

The group's determination to visit those who were unlikely to receive the notice of the Church of England establishment also provided a foundation for Wesley's expansion of his preaching ministry. Wesley was himself initially shocked at the phenomenon of open-air preaching that he encountered when he went to Bristol in 1739 for the purpose of taking over George Whitefield's ministry there. Like many of his colleagues in the Church, Wesley acknowledged that his adherence to convention inclined him to believe "the saving of souls almost a sin if it had not been done in a church" (qtd. in Heitzenrater, *Wesley and the People* 99). However, his observation of the vast numbers of people that Whitefield was able to reach outside the church walls helped to resolve his doubts about the propriety of field preaching, and Wesley went on to become a founder of an itinerant revival movement that reached thousands who responded eagerly to the message he, and the lay preachers under his direction, brought to them.

Wesley continued to maintain his ties to the Church of England and to resist separation from it; he insisted that his goal was simply "to follow the rubrics and canons of the Church with a more 'scrupulous exactness' than most of his clergy compatriots" (Heitzenrater, *Wesley and the People* 131). However, his determination to lead an "extraordinary ministry" that could be spread far beyond the church walls constituted an implicit challenge to the established church. Mounting this challenge presented Wesley with a unique dilemma as he attempted to establish his *ethos* as a preacher. While most eighteenth-century ministers achieved their authority through representing the Church to their parishioners, Wesley sought to establish his authority as a spokesperson for Christianity while simultaneously challenging the formal structures through which the Church maintained and disseminated that authority. At the same time, the audience's standards for judging the speaker's credibility were unpredictable since Wesley's task included the creation of an audience that had not previously existed.

In seeking to live out what he perceived to be the essential message of the gospel, Wesley embarked on a campaign directed toward sharing the Christian gospel with "the bulk of mankind" ("Preface," *Works* I. 103), a goal sparked by his love of preaching and determination to take his message to others wherever he could find the opportunity to do so. In his journal entry of 07/28/1757, Wesley writes: "About noon I preached at Woodseats, in the evening at Sheffield. I do indeed *live* by preaching!" (118). However, Wesley's explicit intention of maintaining his ties to the Church of England was increasingly difficult as he continued his leadership of a movement that raised serious questions about the established Church's ability to meet the social needs that were so important to Wesley and his followers. Wesley's practice of field preaching was therefore a direct challenge to authority even as he attempted to maintain his allegiance to the Church. Thus, the goal of presenting their extraordinary message about the Gospel required Wesley and other Methodist leaders to respond effectively to this unique rhetorical context, which included devising an *ethos* based, in Alcorn's terms, on the development of "a charismatic authority" distinct from the speaker's representation of "a social hierarchy of power" (22).

Wesley's strength in creating this type of *ethos* lies in the fact that his detachment from the "social hierarchy of power" actually provided the means for forming the type of relationship with his audience that was central to the creation of that *ethos*. Wesley's deviation from the bounds of church propriety, specifically with regard to the expectations for the venue in which preaching should take place, limited his authority in conventional terms; in fact, Wesley was regularly barred from returning to those churches where he had preached on a single occasion due to the challenge he posed to the Church's established views. However, his determination to preach wherever he found those whom he perceived to be in need of his message provided him with the charismatic authority that emerged from his audience's emotional response to his very presence in their midst. Wesley's famous statement, "I look upon all the world as my parish" (qtd. in Heitzenrater, *Wesley and the People* 93; Outler 22) reveals his recognition of the significance of a ministry that moved beyond the conventional assignments made to Church of England clergymen. Using terms that resonate with Burke's rhetorical theory and Alcorn's discussion of modern *ethos*, Wesley scholar Albert Outler attributes Wesley's popularity to his relationship with the audience: "The harvest of a unique career had come, more than he or the others realized, from a radical role-reversal from his original identity as academic don and regular cleric to a virtual identification with the English underclass" (18). Outler notes that, in reaching those who had previously been excluded from the Church's notice, Wesley's "unconventional ministry had given them not only a new hope of grace and salvation *in this life* but also a new sense of human dignity, also *in this life*" (18).

Wesley's insistence upon the human dignity of his audience unquestionably held emotional power for those who had previously received little respect from the established church, and it is through the complex relationship with his audience that Wesley's rhetoric challenges rigid boundaries between logical, ethical, and emotional proof. Although the sometimes hysterical responses of Wesley's audiences have led to the assumption that his preaching relies heavily on direct emotional appeal, Wesley's effort to communicate with those who had not previously had access to the message of hope that he sought to share in fact relied most heavily upon his attempt to engage the audience's reason. Each of his sermons is carefully structured, and in most of them Wesley dissects the topic at hand into parts that can be carefully studied. Definition of terms is one of the hallmarks of Wesley's rhetorical strategies. After introducing the technical distinction between justification and being born again in "The Great Privilege of those that are Born of God," Wesley prefaces his further discussion with the statement, "In order to apprehend this clearly it may be necessary, first, to consider what is the proper meaning of that expression, 'whosoever is born of God'; and, secondly, to inquire in what sense he 'doth not commit sin'" (*Works* I. 432). Similarly, his explanation of the "plain and simple" truth of Christianity is presented in "The Scripture Way of Salvation" in the form of three sections that explore discrete questions related to the nature of faith: "I. What is salvation? II. What is that faith whereby we are saved? And III. How we are saved by it" (*Works* II. 156). In "The Duty of Constant Communion," Wesley involves his audience in a complex hypothetical exchange in which he raises possible questions and then responds to them in a dialectical fashion:

> The case is this. God offers you one of the greatest mercies on this side heaven, and commands you to accept it. Why do not you accept this mercy in obedience to his command? You say, 'I am unworthy to receive it.' And what then? You are unworthy to receive any mercy from God. But is that a reason for refusing all mercy? God offers you a pardon for all your sins. You are unworthy of it, 'tis sure, and he knows it: but since he is pleased to offer it nevertheless, will not you accept of it? (*Works* III: 433).

In addition to presenting the audience with a reasoned argument about theological issues, the content of Wesley's sermons often focuses on encouraging his listeners and readers to develop the use of reason alongside their faith. His sermon warning of the hazards of enthusiasm advocates that people instead rely upon "the plain, scriptural, rational way to know what is the will of God in a particular case" ("The Nature," *Works* II. 55), and he concludes with the advice: "Never dream of forcing men into the ways of God. Think yourself, and let think. Use no constraint in matters of religion. Even those who are farthest out of the way never 'compel to come in' by any other means than reason, truth, and love" (*Works* II. 59). His "Caution against Bigotry" suggests that people seek "sufficient, reasonable proof" before reaching a judgment about others (*Works* II. 73). Even "The Case of Reason Impartially Considered," a sermon that explores the limitations of reason in attaining salvation, which Wesley holds to be based purely on faith, acknowledges reason to be a significant "gift of God" (*Works* II. 599) and contains a highly logical exploration of ideas that requires the reader to reason carefully about the matter at hand.

In addition to the fact that the structure and content of Wesley's sermons more consistently appeal to reason than emotion, Wesley's style also lacks the florid quality that is frequently associated with discourse that evokes an emotional response. At the same time, his plain style does reflect his ethical orientation, as it reflects a conscious attempt to support an unconventional ministry geared toward reaching "the bulk of mankind." Wesley viewed style as a moral issue and, although an erudite speaker, made a deliberate effort to simplify his textual references to facilitate the comprehension of the "plain people" whom he perceived to be his primary audience (Outler 31–35). In responding to a critic who suggested that his plain style reflected a decline in his faculties, Wesley replied: "I *could* even now write as floridly and rhetorically as even the admired Dr. B[lair]. But I dare not, because I seek the honour that cometh of God only! […] Let who will admire the French frippery. I am still for plain, sound English […]. This is the style, the most excellent style, for every gospel preacher" ("Preface to Sermons on Several Occasions," *Works* II. 356–57). Wesley's cultivation of a simple style was also reflected in his advice to others. His 1747 rules for preaching include injunctions to "choose the plainest texts you can," "always suit your subject to your audience," and "take care of anything awkward or affected, either in your gesture or pronunciation" (qtd. in Heitzenrater, *Wesley and the People* 164). Wesley's insistence upon plain, sincere, and direct communication with the audience illustrates an important feature of his attempt to establish a meaningful relationship with his listeners rather than simply mesmerizing them with powerful language.

Wesley's belief in the importance of a lasting relationship with the audience is evident not only in his preaching itself, but also in his systematic work in establishing Methodist societies that sought to provide people with ongoing support as they continued to develop their commitment to Christianity. Through the societies, which provided social outreach programs as well as spiritual support, Wesley showed himself to be an individual whose desire to share his message was one part of his genuine concern for the community. It was first through this direct demonstration of his character, rather than through the immediate impact of his words, that Wesley generated the emotional fervor in his audiences for which he was well known. In describing Wesley's preaching before an audience of over 4,000 people in 1769, Swedish professor Johan Henrik Liden wrote: "He has not great oratorical gifts, no outward appearance, but he speaks clear and pleasant […]. His talk is very agreeable, and his mild face and pious manner secure him the love of all rightminded men. He is the personification of piety, and he seems to be as a living representation of the Apostle John" (88).

One of Wesley's lay preachers, John Hampson, also supports Liden's assessment of the impact of Wesley's person upon his hearers: "Few have seen him without being struck with his appearance; and many who had been greatly prejudiced against him have been known

to change their opinion the moment they have been introduced into his presence"
(Heitzenrater, *The Elusive* 84).

Wesley's conviction that preaching involved an interpersonal encounter with others
(Outler 24), coupled with what appeared to be his visible representation of compassion and
piety, enabled him to move readily from sharing his own inner conviction to establishing
connections with those who listened to him. These connections established Wesley's enduring influence in spite of the fact that his quiet manner of speaking was not considered as technically exciting as that of his Methodist colleague and friend, George Whitefield
(Heitzenrater, *Wesley and the People* 94). In his collection of eyewitness accounts of Wesley's preaching, nineteenth-century evangelical historian Thomas Haweis writes:

> His mode of address in public was chaste and solemn, though not illumined with those corusca-
> tions of eloquence which marked, if I may use that expression, the discourses of his rival, George
> Whitefield. But there was a divine simplicity, a zeal, a venerableness in his manner which com-
> manded attention and never forsook him in his latest years [...]. Never man possessed greater
> personal influence over the people connected with him [...] (qtd. in Outler 18)

Wesley's skill as a preacher consistently comes through language that invites readers and
listeners to active engagement with the speaker's thought. Wesley repeatedly draws the
reader into his thought process as he develops his sermons. In "Salvation by Faith," he first
sets out to prove that everyone merits God's grace and then adds: "Now, that we fall not short
of the grace of God, it concerns us carefully to inquire: I. What faith it is through which we
are saved. II. What is the salvation which is through faith. III. How we may answer some objections" (*Works* I. 118). Thus, Wesley creates a tightly structured logical argument that simultaneously establishes his *ethos* through establishing a dialogue with the audience—a
strategy that in turn generates a sympathetic emotional response on the part of listeners who
find that they are included in Wesley's consideration of important theological matters. While
Wesley's discussion at the end of the sermon of "the adversary" who rages against the message of "salvation by faith" is unquestionably emotional, his encouraging message to the audience maintains the personal connection that was Wesley's hallmark: "Go forth then, thou
little child that believest in him, and his right hand shall teach thee terrible things! Though
thou art helpless and weak as an infant of days, the strong man shall not be able to stand before thee" (*Works* I. 130).

Wesley's willingness to encourage his audience and to reveal ways in which his own personal struggles connected with theirs exemplifies what Dale Sullivan describes as the
epideictic requirement that "the audience must think of the rhetor as one of their own, preeminent among them, no doubt, but still one who belongs to them" (126). In transgressing established social boundaries to create a "timeless, consubstantial space that enfolds participants
in epideictic exchange" (Sullivan 127), Wesley creates an *ethos* that enables his listeners to
see themselves as a community authorized to act upon the message they hear. This sense of
community in turn evokes a strong emotional response that cannot be located in the audience
alone, but instead must be examined in connection with the ethical appeal of Wesley himself.

The significance of this community is something that Wesley directly represents both
through the style of his language and through his commitment to the audience, most strik-
ingly illustrated by his action of delivering his message "in the fields" beyond the church's
formal structures. Moreover, Wesley's sermons explicitly articulate the theological import
of the relationships that were formed among those who participated in the Methodist
movement. A sermon titled "Catholic Spirit" argues for the need to enact the loving rela-

tionship with others that Wesley saw as a central feature of Christianity, a practice that would in turn eliminate the divisions that frequently interfere with the prospect of community within the larger church:

> But although a difference in opinions or modes of worship may prevent an external union, yet need it prevent our union in affection? Though we can't think alike, may we not love alike? May we not be of one heart, though we are not of one opinion? Without all doubt we may. Herein all the children of God may unite, notwithstanding these smaller differences. (*Works* II. 82)

Wesley points out that Christians who form a right relationship with each other are in turn able to encourage each other to live a holy life. On the other hand, the schisms that threaten to divide the church represent "evil itself" ("On Schism," *Works* III. 64). Wesley therefore strongly advocates Christian unity that derives from "a love of our neighbour that can only spring from the love of God" ("On Charity," *Works* III. 295). While he acknowledges that reproof may in some instances be necessary, he urges his followers to find ways of expressing their concern "in the spirit of *love;* in the spirit of tender goodwill to our neighbour [...]. Then, by the grace of God, love will beget love" ("The Duty of Reproving," *Works* II. 516). In keeping with this vision of Christian communication, Wesley insists that members of the Church must "preserve inviolate the same spirit of lowliness and meekness, of long-suffering, mutual forbearance and love; and all these cemented and knit together by that sacred tie, the peace of God filling the heart," adding, "the church is called 'holy' because it is holy; because each member thereof is holy, though in different degrees, as he that called them is holy" (*Works* III. 55–56).

This personal holiness requires an ongoing commitment to each person in the community. Wesley builds on this theme in "Catholic Spirit" with the repeated question, "'Is thine heart right, as my heart is with thy heart?' [...] Do you show your love by your works? [...] If thou art thus minded, may every Christian say [...] then 'thy heart is right, as my heart is with thy heart'" (*Works* II. 87–89). As the sermon develops, Wesley provides his audience with the following approach to attaining Christian charity: "I mean, first, love me. And that not only as thou lovest all mankind [...] I am not satisfied with this. No; 'If thine heart be right, as mine with thy heart', then love me with a very tender affection, as a friend that is closer than a brother; as a brother in Christ [...] " (*Works* II. 90). Wesley's view of Christian love, then, requires the formation of a true relationship that involves direct knowledge of another person rather than an abstract notion of love offered to an impersonal ideal of humanity. Wesley's *ethos* lies in his own effort to embody this type of direct personal commitment to his audience and to offer them the experience of Christian community that such a relationship entailed. For those who had previously had only a nominal presence in public life, Wesley's personal attention and offer of full membership in a supportive community undoubtedly held substantial emotional power.

Wesley's ability to touch his audience's emotions therefore can best be accounted for not based on his direct use of *pathos,* but instead as a result of Wesley's *ethos* in presenting an authoritative statement about the Gospel that was directly enacted through his ministry to an audience that had previously been excluded from hearing that message. Exploring the ethical foundation of Wesley's appeal contributes to a more complete assessment of the unique role of Methodist sermons in eighteenth-century homiletics in the midst of social change.

Understanding the complex relationship between Wesley's *ethos* and the emotional appeal of his sermons also promotes a better understanding of the strategic function of *ethos* in the formation of shared values. Wesley lived in a period of dramatic transition, as England endured the changes associated with the rise of industrial society and the formation of a class system that offered expanded social and economic opportunities to a small portion of the population, relegating others to poverty and obscurity. The complicated public sphere that evolved over the course of the eighteenth century lacked the assumptions about shared values that had sustained the notion of *ethos* during the classical period. Wesley's strategy can be seen as an early modern response to the challenge of revitalizing *ethos*, as he facilitated the formation of shared values through encouraging the audience's emotional investment in a community that came into being through his rhetorical agency.

NOTE

1. Of course, Wesley's written sermons would necessarily differ from those he delivered orally. However, eyewitness accounts of Wesley's preaching indicate that there were key points of similarity. Moreover, Wesley's own statements about his decision to publish his sermons also support the argument that Wesley's written as well as oral sermons emphasize his desire to establish a relationship with the audience. Albert Outler takes note of Wesley's belief that preaching must involve "an interpersonal encounter between the preacher and his hearers" (24), adding that written sermons for Wesley should be seen "as either preparatory for more effective oral utterance or else distillates of it: the written word as substitute for personal presence" (24). In Outler's view, the primary difference between Wesley's oral and written sermons is in aim: the oral served the purpose of "proclamation and invitation," while written sermons guided the reader in "nurture and reflection" (24). However, even this difference maintains Wesley's emphasis on *ethos*—the connection the writer or speaker develops with the audience. In addition, Wesley's education at Oxford in the eighteenth century involved training in formal extemporaneous speaking, as well as extensive oral examination and deliberation, which would suggest that his oral sermons would have evinced the reasoned disputation that he had practiced and later transferred to written form for broader dissemination. Thus, it can be assumed that a similar logical and ethical structure would have been present both in Wesley's oral and written sermons.

WORKS CITED

Alcorn, Marshall W., Jr. "Self-Structure as a Rhetorical Device: Modern *Ethos* and the Divisiveness of the Self." *Ethos: New Essays in Rhetorical and Critical Theory*. Ed. James J. Baumlin & Tita French Baumlin. Dallas: Southern Methodist UP, 1994. 3–35.

Aristotle. *On Rhetoric*. Trans. George A. Kennedy. New York: Oxford UP, 1991.

Baumlin, James S. "Introduction: Positioning *Ethos* in Historical and Contemporary Theory." *Ethos: New Essays in Rhetorical and Critical Theory*. Ed. James S. Baumlin and Tita French Baumlin. Dallas: Southern Methodist UP, 1994. xi–xxxi.

Downey, James. *The Eighteenth Century Pulpit. A Study of Butler, Berkeley, Secker, Sterne, Whitefield and Wesley*. Oxford: Oxford UP, 1969.

Heitzenrater, Richard P., ed. *The Elusive Mr. Wesley*. Vol. II. Nashville: Abingdon, 1984.

——. *Wesley and the People Called Methodists*. Nashville: Abingdon, 1995.

Kennicott, Benjamin. "A Rigid Zealot." *The Elusive Mr. Wesley*. Vol. II. Ed. Richard P. Heitzenrater. Nashville: Abingdon, 1984. 85-87.

Lenz, Bernd. "Preachers and Preaching: Emotionalism in Eighteenth-Century Homiletics and Homilies." *Telling Stories: Studies in Honour of Ulrich Broich on the Occasion of his 60th Birthday*. Ed. Elmar Lehmann and Bernd Lenz. Amsterdam: Gruner, 1992. 109–25.

Liden, Johan Henrik. "The Personification of Piety." Trans. K. A. Jansson. *The Elusive Mr. Wesley*. Vol. 2. Ed. Richard P. Heitzenrater. Nashville: Abingdon, 1984. 87–89.

Outler, Albert. *John Wesley's Sermons: An Introduction*. Nashville: Abingdon, 1991.

Sullivan, Dale. "The Ethos of Epideictic Encounter." *Philosophy and Rhetoric* 26.2 (1993): 113-33.

Wesley, John. "A Caution against Bigotry." Vol. II: Sermons. *The Works of John Wesley*. 26 vols. Ed. Albert C. Outler. Nashville: Abingdon, 1987. 61-78.

——. "The Case of Reason Impartially Considered." Vol. II: Sermons. *The Works of John Wesley*. 26 vols. Ed. Albert C. Outler. Nashville: Abingdon, 1987. 587-600.

——. "The Catholic Spirit." Vol. II: Sermons. *The Works of John Wesley*. 26 vols. Ed. Albert C. Outler. Nashville: Abingdon, 1987. 81–95.

——. "The Duty of Constant Communion." Vol. III: Sermons. *The Works of John Wesley*. 26 vols. Ed. Albert C. Outler. Nashville: Abingdon, 1987. 427–39.

——. "The Duty of Reproving our Neighbour." Vol. II: Sermons. *The Works of John Wesley*. 26 vols. Ed. Albert C. Outler. Nashville: Abingdon, 1987. 511–20.

——. "The Great Privilege of those that are Born of God." Vol. I: Sermons. *The Works of John Wesley*. 26 vols. Ed. Albert C. Outler. Nashville: Abingdon, 1987. 431–43.

——. Journal #10. Vol. XXI: Journals and Diaries. *The Works of John Wesley*. 26 vols. Ed. W. Reginald Ward. Nashville: Abingdon, 1992. 117–18.

——. "The Nature of Enthusiasm." Vol. II: Sermons. *The Works of John Wesley*. 26 vols. Ed. Albert C. Outler. Nashville: Abingdon, 1987. 46–60.

——. "Of the Church." Vol. III: Sermons. *The Works of John Wesley*. 26 vols. Ed. Albert C. Outler. Nashville: Abingdon, 1987. 46–57.

——. "On Charity." Vol. III: Sermons. *The Works of John Wesley*. 26 vols. Ed. Albert C. Outler. Nashville: Abingdon, 1987. 292–307.

——. "On Schism." Vol. III: Sermons. *The Works of John Wesley*. 26 vols. Ed. Albert C. Outler. Nashville: Abingdon, 1987. 59–69.

——. "The Preface." Vol. I: Sermons. *The Works of John Wesley*. 26 vols. Ed. Albert C. Outler. Nashville: Abingdon, 1987. 103–07.

——. "Preface to Sermons on Several Occasions." Vol. II: Sermons. *The Works of John Wesley*. 26 vols. Ed. Albert C. Outler. Nashville: Abingdon, 1987. 355–57.

——. "Salvation by Faith." Vol. I: Sermons. *The Works of John Wesley*. 26 vols. Ed. Albert C. Outler. Nashville: Abingdon, 1987. 117–30.

——. "The Scripture Way of Salvation." Vol. II: Sermons. *The Works of John Wesley*. 26 vols. Ed. Albert C. Outler. Nashville: Abingdon, 1987. 155–69.

6

Between Iconophilia and Iconophobia: Milton's *Aeropagitica* and Seventeenth-Century Visual Culture

Kristie S. Fleckenstein
Ball State University

"I deny not," John Milton writes in *Areopagitica,* "that it is of greatest concernment in the church and commonwealth to have a vigilant eye how books demean themselves as well as men" (720). But, he goes on, too much vigilance, too much "good" "can kill a man as kill a good book," and whoever "kills a man kills a reasonable creature, God's image; but he who destroys a good book, kills reason itself, kills the image of God, as it were, in the eye" (720).

This metaphor, an amalgam of image and word, begins and encapsulates Milton's argument against the Licensing Order of June 16, 1643. It reflects two contentious ways of seeing dominant during seventeenth-century England—iconophilia, or love of the image, and iconophobia, or fear of the image—a dynamic that shapes the manuscript speech. In this essay, I argue that we can fully understand neither Milton's argument nor the complexity of that argument without considering the scopic regimes—the dominant ways of seeing—that organized visual culture in the seventeenth century. Specifically, *Areopagitica* draws its power from and manifests a conflicted visual culture, one that simultaneously loved and hated the image.

Except as an element of style, imagery is rarely considered central to understanding rhetorical performances. Even more peripheral to discussions of rhetoric are ways of seeing, the shared conventions by which a culture perceives its reality and organizes its image-word relationships. However, rhetoric can be, and should be, plotted according to and against a history of ways of seeing. W. J. T. Mitchell in *Iconology* argues that "The dialectic of word and image seems to be a constant in the fabric of signs that a culture weaves around itself," and the history of a culture is in part a narrative of the tug of image and word (43). By extension, a history of rhetoric and the story of rhetorical performances in any one era are also subject to the tug of image and word. To understand political discourse, we have to "picture" that discourse through the lens of its visual culture.

According to Martin Jay, a culture organizes itself by means of a dominant way of seeing, or a scopic regime, a term that he reclaims from Christian Metz. A scopic regime consists of visual conventions that determine what we see and how we see. For example, Jay argues that the dominant way of seeing in the West is Cartesian perspectivalism. Trained from childhood in the West, we detach ourselves from the object we wish to perceive and treat it as something that can be analyzed. Like a discursive formation, scopic regimes exercise a formative power over what is knowable, sayable, and doable (*Downcast*). In addition, again like discursive formations, scopic regimes are multiple (Jay, "Scopic"). A culture is rarely organized by means of a single hegemonic regime. Instead, competing ways of seeing clash and contend for organizational power within any culture. To illustrate, the detached, analytical vision of Cartesian perspectivalism contests with the highly participatory vision Ernest G. Schachtel calls "allocentric perception," which is characterized by "profound interest in the object, and complete openness and receptivity toward it, a full turning toward the object which makes possible a direct encounter with it" (220).

Three points concerning vision and imagery are important to my argument. First, a culture is shaped as much by its scopic regimes as by its discursive formations. Second, like discursive formations, scopic regimes are never singular. A dominant regime jostles with competing, even if repressed, ways of seeing. Third, scopic regimes implicate discursive formations. Visual conventions affect discourse conventions. The dominant means of persuasion within a period cannot be excised from the shared ways of seeing—from the visual culture—of that period. This brings me back to my argument. To understand the political rhetoric of the seventeenth century requires taking into consideration the era's competing scopic regimes: iconophilia, or love of the visual image, as played out in the era's fascination with all things visual, and iconophobia, or fear of the visual image, as played out in the denigration of all things visual. These two dominant orientations to imagery provide the context within which Milton shaped *Areopagitica*.

SEVENTEENTH-CENTURY ICONOPHILIA AND ICONOPHOBIA

Iconophilia is easily traced. Let me point out two examples. First, the explosion of print options, especially the pamphlet, or, what Michael Mendle calls ephemera, provided multimedia opportunities to meld graphic image and word.[1] Mendle claims that England experienced a culture shock in the 1640s: an explosion of cheap books and broadsides, or pamphlets, "commenting on and manipulating public events" (201). Mendle refers to the England of this period as the "pamphlet culture," (201), and this pamphlet culture gloried in graphic images that innovations in print technology linked ever more successfully with word in print. Thus, the seventeenth century in Britain, unremarkable for any artistic excellence in visual art (Parry), is remarkable for the explosion of print boasting verbal and graphic images.[2]

Second, the science of the image, of optics, prospered. During the seventeenth century, the telescope was invented or at least patented in Belgium. In addition, this century saw the invention of both the simple and compound microscopes. Philosophy kept pace with science. In 1637 Descartes published *Dioptics*, an appendix to his *Discourse on the Method,* in which he presented his observations on refraction and the operations of vision. Fascinated by the cellular, Robert Hooke published *Micrographia,* and Johann Kepler, entranced by the celestial, published *Astronomia Nova*. Finally, Newton, as early as 1670, was lecturing on optics, exploring light, prisms, and color, an exploration that ultimately resulted in the reflecting telescope as well as *Optiks,* published in 1704.

The combination of these factors reveals the fascination that visual imagery exercised on the seventeenth-century imagination. However, at the same time that iconophilia flourished, iconophobia flourished. Even as images attracted, images repelled. This, after all, was the tail end of Reformation, where the attack on idolatry, on devotional images, called for a literal pulling down and breaking up of those images. In addition to physical images, however, the image-making power of the mind was suspect, for that power was tainted by a carnality that misdirected the attention of the devout from God to God's creations. Imagery's carnal taint contributed to its denigration in the culture at large. As Alastair Fowler points out, "Iconographic symbols, in particular, seem to have informed the substrate of dreams, fantasies, and imaginative thought" (8). This imagistic substrate may not seem particularly invidious to the modern or postmodern temperament. However, when we factor in the seventeenth-century attitude toward imagination, which conceived of imagination—the image-making facility—as the link between body and mind, we can better understand the era's fear of the image. For instance, popular during this time and well into the eighteenth century was the belief that gestating women should be protected from grotesque and gruesome visual images for fear that the embryo they nourish would be imprinted and a monstrous birth result. Visuality and corporeality were intertwined; imagery was inextricable from desire and deviance. Because images were associated with the irrational, chaotic, and illusory, they called forth distrust and a drive to control their power.

This iconophobia is manifested in a variety of ways. First, the mistrust of imagery, both verbal and visual, was a central part of the growing discipline of science. While scholars investigated the nature of light and vision, relying on vision to validate empirically their evolving scientific knowledge, at the same time they distrusted vision. Interest in optics stemmed in part from a simultaneous interest in optical illusions, such as the resurfacing in the Renaissance of trompe l'oeil, or paintings that fooled the eye, and magical prestidigitations popular during this era, in which sleight of hand, again, fooled the eye. This divided attitude toward vision and its suspect reliability is illustrated by the rigorous standards necessary for scientific witnessing, where the vision of only certain individuals—generally upper-class, English men—could be trusted (Haraway). Women could not testify because their vision was despoiled, subject to carnal confusion. A similar effort was afoot to strip metaphor—all schemes and tropes—from the scientific language of the fledging Royal Society, as Thomas Sprat's efforts reflect. Here language was shorn of images and of metaphors because they distracted the reader from the truth of the scientific insight. The conventions of science and the language of science each manifests a denigration of what Lana Cable calls "carnal rhetoric," language rich with imagery, metaphor, and emotion (*Carnal*).

Second, the popularity of multimedia ephemera was off set by efforts to license those very publications. Prior to, during, and even after the end of the Protectorate, politicos on both sides of the political divide sought to control verbal and visual images. Like the Catholic Church's hegemonic efforts to curtail the circulation of certain books and information in the sixteenth century, English religious-political leaders sought to gatekeep, choosing which images and metaphors were safe to be loosed on the public. By controlling the seductive allure of verbal and visual images, the ruling party could control what was thought within the population at large, particularly among the more radical elements. In 1660, Samuel Parker, an official licenser and later bishop of Oxford argued: "Had we but an Act of Parliament to abridge Preachers the use of fulsome and luscious Metaphors, it might perhaps be an effectual Cure of all our present Distempers," for it is the "gawdy Metaphor" and "lascivious Allegories" that authorize the workings of private, and dissenting, conscience (qtd. in Cable, "Licensing" 244).

Drawing on Ernest B. Gilman's *Iconoclasm and Poetry in the English Reformation,* Cable argues that the tension between the "iconic plenitude of the Renaissance imagination and the Reformist conception of a language purified of affective intent" released the creative impulse (*Carnal* 3). I argue that the same tension between a love and a fear of the image fueled the creation of counterhegemonic systems of belief and behavior. Milton's *Areopagitica* is iconoclastic in that it breaks with the edicts and intellectual hegemony of his fellow reformists holding power in Parliament. The conflict between iconophilia and iconophobia is central to both Milton's argument in his polemical *Areopagitica* and his ability to make that argument.

MILTON'S *AREOPAGITICA*
AND SEVENTEENTH-CENTURY SCOPIC REGIMES

Fashioned deliberately to mimic Isocrates's manuscript speech, *Logos Areopagiticos,* addressed to the Areopagus, in which Isocrates argues that morality cannot be legislated by an ever-increasing number of laws, Milton's *Areopagitica,* also a manuscript speech, was addressed to Parliament and disseminated as an unlicensed pamphlet. Like Isocrates, Milton maintains the fiction of a speech by addressing his audience—the House of Commons and the House of Lords—directly and consistently. He claims that their love of truth and their uprightness of judgment will lead them to rescind the censorship laws. As their "prudent spirit acknowledges and obeys the voice of reason" they will be rendered "willing to repeal any act" that is obviously outside the bounds of reason (79). Milton organizes the speech into four parts: he argues that the current administration will not want to be associated with those who invented licensing; he demonstrates how the nature of reading suffers from the cruelty of licensing; he proves that censorship doesn't work; and, finally, he details the harm to learning caused by censorship.

I first consider the ways in which iconophobia and iconophilia are manifested in general through the speech. Then, I focus on the way in which the very logic of Milton's argument derives from the tension between these two scopic regimes.

Iconophobia is evident is a variety of ways, both obvious and subtle. First, *Areopagitica*'s title page has no images. Reflecting the plain style, it contains only the title of the speech, the author's name, its aim and audience, a quote from Euripides (in the original Greek and Milton's translation), the city, and the year printed. No printer's emblem, no illustration, no image evoking the ethical appeal of classical Greece. Instead, the text seemingly stands alone. Second, again mimicking Isocrates, Milton writes, but does not perform, his speech, eschewing the visual spectacle of an oration.

More subtle is the iconophobic emphasis on the power of reason. For example, Milton addresses the members of Parliament as men of reason who are persuaded by reason. His entire argument is predicated on the assertion that books are reason, for "he who destroys a good book, kills reason itself" (720). He who licenses "strikes at the ethereal and fifth essence, the breath of reason itself, and slays an immortality rather than a life" (720). Reason is also central to his argument, for it is through God's "gift of reason" that men possess the ability and the right to choose for themselves what to read. "When God gave him [humanity] reason," Milton argues, "he gave him freedom to choose, for reason is but choosing" (733). Ergo, reducing the scope of a man's choice reduces the scope of his reason (733). Conversely, increasing that scope increases reason. Milton says that the "the benefit of books promiscuously read" is greater virtue, greater reason (729).

Contending with iconophobia, however, even in the same sentence, is iconophilia, for he who destroys a good book destroys not only reason but also the image of God in the eye. He who licenses *slays* an immortality. Lush, sensual, openly corporeal images permeate Milton's speech. Let me provide just a brief sampling, beginning with the first part of his argument, the section in which he argues that Parliament does not want to associate themselves with those who originated censorship. For example, Milton describes the radical censorship of the Catholic Church during the early Middle Ages—specifically, the policy of sifting through indexes and expurging all suspect titles—as raking "through the entrails of many an old good author" (724). Before the "antichristian council," "books were ever as freely admitted into the world as any other birth," and if a monster issued forth, of course, it must be destroyed, but it has to be born—published—first. Later, in the second part of his argument, Milton refers to books as "meats and viands" (727), the universal diet of man's body. Building on the connection between bodies and books, in the third part of his argument, Milton describes the injurious effects of licensing as "infections" (729), and a response to those infections are the "useful drugs and materials" represented by books. In one of his most dramatic corporeal images, Milton argues that Truth's lovely form has been mangled, "hewed" into a "thousand pieces" (741). Knowledge is a process of searching for and reassembling those scattered limbs. Therefore, he pleads, "Suffer not these licensing prohibitions [...], that [we may] continue to do our obsequies to the torn body of our martyred saint [truth]" (742).

Beyond the metaphors *in* the argument, the argument itself is poised *between* love for and rejection of image. First, a harmful outcome of licensing is that it blinds; it kills vision. Milton contends that Catholic Church following the Council of Trent sought through licensing to extend "their dominion over men's eyes" (723). Now, the reformatory spirit is enacting an analogous blinding. Milton warns: "We boast of our light," that is, the light of the Reformation, "but if we look not wisely on the sun itself, it smites us into darkness," just as "we are stark blind" if we think there is nothing left to look into and reform (742). However, without the blinkers of licensing, the nation becomes an eagle "kindling her undazzled eyes at the full midday beam; purging and unscaling her long-abused sight at the fountain itself of heavenly radiance" (745).

Second, licensing is doomed to failure because the supposed threat books pose are replicated in other elements of the culture, and those elements are impossible to regulate. For instance, Milton argues that for censorship to achieve its desired end, licensers will have to censor all recreations and pastimes, an impossibility: "And who shall silence all the airs and madrigals that whisper softness in chambers," he asks (732). Along with regulating the words in art, music, and conversation, the licensers must also regulate the image, for, he mockingly points out, "there are shrewd (mischievous) books, with dangerous frontispieces, set to sale" (732). Again, this regulation of dangerous images is impossible.

Third, and most important, no true knowledge can exist without temptation. Adam's doom, Milton points out, is not just knowing good and evil; it is knowing good through evil. "That which purifies us is trial, and trial is by what is contrary" (728). It is only through exposure to trial that we hone our virtue, which means that part of our testing consists of exposure to imagery; imagery contending with words sharpens the efficacy of reason, the scope of our virtue. Without imagery, virtue could not exist. Milton asks, "Wherefore did he [God] create passion within us, pleasures round about us, but that these rightly tempered are the very ingredients of virtue?" (733). We need the threat of seductive knowledge, of seductive images, so that we can be intellectually vigilant (739). Without that "exercise," knowledge, virtue, and reason are fettered; we are shut up "all again into the breast of a licenser" (739). To promote just this atmosphere of trial, we must set open the temple of Janus with his two controversial faces, Milton urges. "Let [Truth] and Falsehood grapple" (746), let image and word grapple, I would add, for from this clash a "'new light' that will shine in upon us" (746).

This analysis of Milton's *Areopagitica,* coupled with an analysis of its cultural matrix, offers two values. First, it suggests that radicalism—positions contesting hegemonic edicts— might depend on the productive tension between scopic regimes for its existence. A conflicted visual culture might open up aporia within which a participant can turn around on hegemony, recognize its tyranny, and evolve a response to it. Second, my analysis highlights that an orientation to vision, a subtle but pervasive way of seeing that holds within it a tacit theory of imagination and being in the world, implicates a political orientation to and use of language. Gilman asks, "How does any age [...] conceive of the relationship between the word and the image, writing and drawing, linguistic and visual perception" (3). To this list, I would add, "How does any age conceive of the relationship between image and rhetoric?" Understanding the rhetoric of a period involves understanding the scopic regimes within that period. If world history can be plotted according to the fortunes of the image, so, too, can rhetorical history. Thus, we are charged with exploring the politics of vision as we explore the politics of discourse and the discourse of politics. These two benefits highlight the need to continue charting the connections between ways of seeing and rhetoric.

NOTES

1. Focusing on literature, particularly poetry, Ernest B. Gilman argues that seventeenth-century England offers a particularly rich area of investigation because it is a transitional century, a liminal era during which the image-word relationships were shifting from those current in the Renaissance to those that presaged modernism.
2. The wedding of all things visual and verbal via technology is reflected as well in the popularity of emblem books, a phenomenon that evolved in the Renaissance and proliferated in seventeenth-century England (Fowler 6). The emblem, Alastair Fowler argues, is a literary genre that combines picture/emblem with epigram and/or motto; it functions many times as terms in "quasi-logical propositions, or to formulate more complex ideas" (8). The emblem book and the pamphlet culture highlight the era's fascination with visual images.

WORKS CITED

Cable, Lana. *Carnal Rhetoric: Milton's Iconoclasm and the Poetics of Desire.* Durham: Duke UP, 1995.

—-. "Licensing Metaphor: Parker, Marvell, and the Debate over Conscience." *Books and Readers in Early Modern England: Material Studies.* Ed. Jennifer Andersen and Elizabeth Sauer. Philadelphia: U of Pennsylvania P, 2002. 243–60.

Fowler, Alastair. "The Emblem as a Literary Genre." *Deviceful Settings: The English Renaissance Emblem and its Contexts.* Ed. Michael Bath and Daniel Russell. New York: AMS, 1999. 1–32.

Gilman, Ernest B. *Iconoclasm and Poetry in the English Reformation: Down Went Dagon.* Chicago: U of Chicago P, 1986.

Haraway, Donna J. *Modest_Witness@Second_Millenium.FemaleMan©_Meets_OncoMouse™: Feminism and Technoscience*. New York: Routledge, 1997.

Jay, Martin. *Downcast Eyes: The Denigration of Vision in Twentieth-Century French Thought.* Berkeley, CA: U of California P, 1993.

—. "Scopic Regimes of Modernity." *Vision and Visuality.* Ed. Hal Foster. Seattle: Bay Press, 1988. 3–23.

Mendle, Michael. "Preserving the Ephemeral: Reading, Collecting, and the Pamphlet Culture of Seventeenth-Century England." *Books and Readers in Early Modern England: Material Studies.* Ed. Jennifer Andersen and Elizabeth Sauer. Philadelphia: U of Pennsylvania P, 2002. 201–16.

Mitchell, W. J. T. *Iconology: Image, Text, Ideology.* Chicago: U of Chicago P, 1986.

Milton, John. *Areopagitica: For the Liberty of Unlicenced Printing. John Milton: Complete Poems and Major Prose.* Ed. Merritt Y. Hughes. New York: Odyssey, 1957. 716–49.

Parry, Graham. *The Seventeenth Century: The Intellectual and Cultural Context of English Literature, 1603–1700.* London: Longman, 1989.

Schachtel, Ernest G. *Metamorphosis: On the Development of Affect, Perception, Attention, and Memory.* New York: Basic, 1959.

7

Vico's *Institutiones Oratoriae*: Acumen, Memory, and the Imaginative Universals

Catalina González
Emory University

The position that the *Institutiones Oratoriae* holds in the context of Vico's work has been very disputed in Vico's recent scholarship. It is the general opinion that the *Institutiones* is merely Vico's textbook for his lectures on rhetoric and that his most original ideas are either unconnected to it or, if contained in it, only in an incipient manner. Indeed, the *Institutiones* is a much less original work than the *New Science*. Even though Vico's selection of the principal teachings of the rhetorical tradition shows an unusual understanding of rhetoric for his time, the textbook is still, mostly, a compilation of Aristotle's and Quintilian's main teachings. It seems that Vico's *Institutiones Oratoriae* is no more than a peculiar manual of rhetoric among others in Latin Renaissance Humanism. For this among other reasons,[1] it does make sense to give little importance to Vico's rhetorical work, as traditional scholarship does.[2] However, recently, commentators have argued that the *Institutiones* contains some of the "seeds" of the *New Science* intertwined with practical teachings on eloquence. They also agree in seeing Vico's interest in rhetoric as an important element of his philosophical rehabilitation of Humanism.[3] Perhaps the most paradigmatic of those interpretations is Mooney's: "Properly reflected upon, the principles of discourse contain in themselves *the seeds* of historical consciousness, if not a full and proper historicism, such that *one may doubt whether Vico, apart from the tradition of rhetoric, could ever have written a science of humanity*" (83, emphasis added).

In attempting to stress even more the relationship between the Vico of the *Institutiones* and the Vico of the *New Science*, I would like to claim that the *Institutiones* shows not only a very original interpretation of the rhetorical tradition but also an especially clear epistemological posture that may accurately be interpreted as the *grounds*, and not just as the *seeds*, of Vico's major work, the *New Science*. Were Vico alive, I am certain that he would not understand why we find such a great disparity between rhetoric and philosophy. After all, for him, eloquence was defined as "wisdom speaking." The fact that rhetoric was not only an art of persuasion but also a reflection on truth and an epistemological stance needed no explanation for Vico. It was indeed plain for him that the *New Science* arose from his reflection on rhetoric; hence, it could not be accurately appreciated without a fundamental recognition of the value of the rhetorical tradition. It is, thus, my opinion that the *Institutiones* is not just to be interpreted in the light of the *New Science*, but to the contrary, that the *New Science* can only be properly understood in the light of the *Institutiones*.

To support this thesis, I will refer to some of the key concepts of both the *New Science* and the *Institutiones*. I will begin by discussing the notion of "imaginative universals" in the *New Science*, and will then show how can it be understood in terms of the *Institutiones'* account of the art of invention and its relation to ingenuity or wit.

POETIC WISDOM AND IMAGINATIVE UNIVERSALS

"The first gentile peoples," says Vico, "were poets who spoke in poetic characters" (New Science 21). These "poetic characters" are not words yet; they are a sort of "primordial thoughts" which the first people communicated through mute signs—gesturing or signaling at things. Vico also calls them "imaginative genera." Imaginative genera (or imaginative universals) resemble logical genera in that they encapsulate many particulars; however, they are not universals; they are just particulars to which the primitive minds, led by their imagination, attributed a set of other particulars.

Vico compares them with the "fables of human times, such as those of late comedy [which] are the intelligible genera reasoned out by moral philosophy, from which the comic poets form imaginative genera, which are the persons of the comedies" (New Science 22). To use an example, in Molière's *The Miser*, avarice is embodied in Harpagon, a closefisted bourgeois. Molière transferred the meaning of the concept to this character so that, throughout the comedy's plot, the public could appreciate all the aspects inherent to avarice. The difference between the imaginative universals of the first human beings and their characterization in comedies is that the latter consist in this *transferring* of a universal concept into a particular, whereas in the former there are no conceptual universals to transfer; thus, the activity performed by the imagination should be rather seen as that of *identifying* one particular with other particulars (Verene 76).[4] In other words, what takes place here is rather the identification of Harpagon's aspects of miser behavior with all the other physical entities (not only humans) that show the same behavior, and the formation of a corresponding thought, that is, the thought of "Harpagon."

It could be said, *á la* Nietzsche, that this primitive operation reveals a sort of metaphorical origin of thought and language. This way of understanding the imaginative universals finds further support in the fact that Vico also calls them "poetic characters." However, Vico affirms that this first operation of the human mind was not metaphorical, in the ordinary sense of it, that is, analogical. As he says: "[...] the true poetic allegories [...] gave the fables *univocal, not analogical, meanings* for various particulars comprised under their poetic genera" (New Science 75). Analogical meanings can only exist in the human times of reflection, when men already have an array of logical universals whose meanings they can pass on to particular terms. As in primitive times there was no transference of meaning from a universal term to a particular one, "poetic universals" had indeed "univocal" or "literal" meanings—which also amounts to saying that they were "true."

Vico, however, gave these thoughts the title and dignity of "Poetic Wisdom." Why? In my view, Vico is here making an *epistemological and methodological* claim: he is saying that we can only glimpse these first truths through metaphorical transferences—that we, readers of his time, can only obliquely understand this peculiar phenomenon by appealing to an operation of the imagination that somehow attempts to reproduce the primordial one, although it fails by nature.

Now I would like to turn my attention to the *Institutiones* and see how this primordial operation of the mind may be understood in rhetorical terms. Regarding this text, Vico's commentators are divided in their allegiances. Some of them, especially Andrea Sorrentino, want to stress Vico's theory of tropes, which appears in his discussion of "style" or "elocution," whereas others, in particular Mooney and Giuliani, see as more valuable the connection between Vico's rhetoric and the theory of argumentation (which corresponds to "invention"). I would like to side with the latter tendency. It is my opinion that, as important as the theory of the tropes is to Vico's rhetoric, it cannot be properly interpreted without a previous understanding of his *topica*. I will come back to this idea at the end of the paper. For the moment, it is important to approach some of the reasons why Vico's *Institutiones* can be seen as a handbook on argumentation.

THE PECULIARITY OF VICO'S *INSTITUTIONES ORATORIAE*

Vico's *Institutiones Oratoriae* is certainly a very peculiar manual of rhetoric for its time. One of its most original features, for example, is the fact that it does not develop the last two of the five constitutive parts of rhetoric—namely, memory and delivery. Surprisingly enough, Vico considers memory as not deserving further explanation and not requiring any specific art for its development (Art of Rhetoric 206).[5] This is a curious view given Vico's treatment of memory in *On the Method of Studies of Our Time*, where he asserts that memory is *almost* the same as imagination (Method of Studies 14).[6] The best way to train memory, according to *On the Method of Studies of Our Times,* is by learning languages. Correspondingly, the best way to train the imagination is by learning rhetoric, poetry, and jurisprudence. But curiously enough, in the *Institutiones* Vico shows himself suspicious of the importance of training memory and especially of the art of *mnemonics*. Perhaps Vico mentions this art here just out of regard for its antiquity and only in order to avoid further controversy in this respect. In fact, if Vico considers memory and imagination as almost identical, one can presume that, apart from the learning of languages, the same technique that trains the imagination also develops memory, and this technique, in the realm of rhetoric, is not the art of mnemonics, but the art of "invention."

As in *On the Method of Studies of our Time*, in the *Institutiones* too Vico's understanding of rhetoric strongly emphasizes the first part of it: the topics. For Vico, this art is the core of rhetorical training; indeed, without *topica*, Vico believes, there would be no rhetoric at all. Although the idea appears to be self-evident, this certainly was not the case in Vico's time. From the Renaissance and up to the eighteenth century, the rhetorical tradition suffered a substantial transformation: it was torn apart by two contrary tendencies which I would like to call the Christianization and the logicization of rhetoric.[7] Both brought about a momentous consequence for the tradition of rhetoric in early modernity, namely, the gradual oblivion of the art of topics and the final identification of rhetoric with pure matters of style. Vico is reacting against both trends. The evident prominence that he gives to the topics in *On the Method of Studies of Our Time* is clearly not only a response to Cartesianism, which, after all, is just a consequence of a long-lasting process of enervation of the rhetorical tradition. Vico is well aware that, without invention, rhetoric would lose all its epistemological value. It would be reduced (as it has been, at last) to a matter of composition and style. Vico's rhetoric, therefore, retrieves the ancient value of the topics in an attempt to rescue the epistemological import of rhetoric from such an impending fate (Mooney, 26).[8]

Vico's high regard for the *topica* supports the view that the *Institutiones* is more a manual of argumentation than a manual of style. This is further confirmed by the fact that, when Vico refers to the three offices of the orator and its corresponding styles, he gives more weight to the plain than to the ornate and the sublime styles. In the very opening of the *Institutiones*, Vico presents his position on this matter. Vico stresses the value of a plain argument over that of an ornate or sublime speech (Art of Rhetoric 7). [9] At first sight, this tendency seems compatible with the Christianization and logicization of rhetoric. However, not only the capacities that Vico assigns to the offices are rather peculiar—teaching requires sharpness (*acumen*); pleasing, gentleness (*lenitas*); and moving, forcefulness (*vis*)—but, among them, sharpness or acumen is not in any way the quality of a logical or dogmatic mind. Indeed, it is the trait of a quick mind, one that does not need to make recourse to long derivations or to truths of faith. This sharpness Vico also calls *ingenium* or ingenuity. It is to be expected, then, that Vico's *topica* illustrate how this sharp mind can be cultivated. In what follows, I will summarize the central issue of Vico's topics, namely, his discussion of enthymeme, and the connection between enthymeme and this quality of the mind called sharpness or ingenuity.

The Enthymeme as the Practical or Conjectural Inference

Vico's definition of an argument is taken from the rhetorical notion of enthymeme. An enthymeme is usually defined as a syllogism in which one of the premises is omitted. The effect of this omission is that the listener is given a task to perform during the speech, that is, that of filling in the blanks of the argument as he listens to it. As a result, the enthymeme is highly persuasive; the delight that the listener feels in completing the reasoning easily provokes his approval. Indeed, a good orator is she who entices the minds of the public so as to make them reach, by their own means, the conclusions that she has preconceived. Here, Vico faithfully adheres to Aristotle's definition (Art of Rhetoric 89).[10]

Furthermore, the use of the enthymeme is not only rhetorical but also dialectical. In other words, the enthymeme is not only highly persuasive, but is also a valid form of reasoning. It brings about approval as it expresses a sound inference. Nonetheless, the enthymeme is only formally comparable to the syllogism, for it involves a qualitatively different operation of inference. The procedure of going from the premises to the conclusion in the enthymeme is not logical or demonstrative—it has a rather atypical nature. It could be said that both syllogism and enthymeme are deductive forms of reasoning, but the former is demonstrative and the latter conjectural and practical. In the section concerning the "Arguments for Teaching," Vico distinguishes between *loci* of certainty and *loci* of reasoning. The former, says Vico, contain apodictic and demonstrative arguments, namely, syllogisms. Their conclusions are, thus, either true or false. The latter, on the other hand, contain enthymemic arguments, which lead to "probable or verisimilar conclusions." Logicians deal with the *loci* of certainty, while dialecticians and orators deal with the *loci* of reasoning (Art of Rhetoric 27).[11]

There is, in turn, a difference between probable and verisimilar conclusions: "The conclusion is probable when the question concerns knowing, or, when it is, as the schools normally call it, 'speculative.' The conclusion is verisimilar, when a question is proposed for a course of action which is called by the schools 'practical.'" (AR 27). In brief, the loci of reasoning, or the enthymemic loci, are of two kinds: conjectural or *speculative*, which have probable conclusions; and practical, which have verisimilar conclusions. The arguments proper *only* to the orator are the practical arguments. The conclusion of a practical enthymeme is what Aristotle called a maxim. A maxim asserts what kind of behavior is beneficial in view of the known circumstances; hence, it is tightly related to a value judgment (Aristotle 1394a 20–30). The orator, says Vico, "speaks in maxims." But he must produce these maxims offhandedly; as practical matters always require immediate solutions, he does not have the time of the dialectician. He must be able to quickly think in enthymemic terms. In sum, the orator must have the capacity to make certain kind of deductions, which are based on particular premises, and which bring about conclusions that are both feasible and good.

Now, let us examine whether this capacity of making up enthymemes is what Vico calls ingenuity or sharpness of mind. In the discussion of style, Vico further elaborates the notion of maxim.[12] Here, Vico uses one of his (controversial) philological proofs to introduce the notion of conceit.

A maxim (in Latin, *sententia*) has, according to Vico, its equivalent in the Italian word *concetto*, which could be translated as "acute saying."[13] A maxim, then, is best stylistically expressed in the manner of an acute saying (Art of Rhetoric 125).[14] The stylistic trait of a conceit is its brilliance. This brilliance Vico also calls "entymemic power," and it shows that peculiar quality of the mind of the orator or dialectician identified as ingenuity (Art of Rhetoric 127).[15]

This manner of creation, again, consists in joining two extremes of the inference, with a middle term, which is hidden or implicit. In other words, it consists in being able to abridge the inference as it is created. The good orator is not one who makes the complete argument beforehand and hides one of the premises during the delivery, but one who can see the relationship between the two extremes, without having to make the middle term explicit, even for himself. It oftentimes happens that, when someone states a witticism and the listeners ask her how she came up with that idea, she answers, "I don't know, I just made it up." This is precisely the kind of phenomenon that Vico is addressing. The middle term is not one that the orator can easily supply after having made the enthymeme. In order to do so, she would have to further reflect upon it. Perhaps this is the most important difference between the dialectician and the orator. Through a judicious reflection, the former acquires an actual grasp of the middle terms of her arguments, whereas the latter has this nonreflective brilliance, which allows her to make sound, although offhanded, arguments.

The Newness of the Idea and the Beauty of the Argument

The persuasiveness of the conceit, Vico has shown, is tightly related to this procedure of thought—the abridged operation of the orator finds its complement in the listener. The listener, as it were, fills in the blanks of the enthymeme and, in doing so, feels delight. Vico claims to be following Aristotle in this argument, as he quotes the latter: "By them [the acute sayings], men learn many things quickly and easy" (Art of Rhetoric 127). Here, however, in my view, Vico is making a rather neo-platonic move.[16] For Aristotle, it is the "newness" of the ideas brought up by the saying that gives delight to the public (Aristotle 141065–10).[17] But Vico wants to add to the authority of Aristotle that of Sforza Pallavacino who claimed that the delight of an acute saying comes rather from the beauty of the relationship between the extreme premises and the middle term. Thus, Vico affirms:

> Truth […] is the object of intellect, beauty, the object of ingenuity. […] The orator in proposing an acute saying brings about the beautiful, which he leaves to the listener himself to discover. Surely,

in offering an acute saying, that is, by suggesting the reason of the bond, the listener explores it, comes up with the medium, joins the extremes, and contemplates the harmonious joining, and he himself discovers the beautiful, which the orator produces. Hence, he sees himself to be ingenious and delights in the acute saying, not so much as having been presented by the orator but as he himself has understood it. (AR, 128)

Undoubtedly, the idea that the contemplation of a harmonious whole brings delight to the listener is derived from Vico's appreciation of the platonic Academy. For, in order for the listener to see this whole, he must somehow be *already familiar* with the missing piece of the argument, the middle term. It could be said then, that the persuasiveness of the enthymeme relies on an operation of *recollection* that makes possible the contemplation of a harmonious whole. Vico is implying, perhaps against Aristotle, that if the persuasiveness of the argument were derived solely from the newness of the idea, there would be no delight at all, but just intellectual wonder and the subsequent satisfaction of it. Delight, however, is what keeps the attention of the public—wonder is too unsteady a passion for the orator to rely on.

This interpretation is further supported by an etymological consideration, which, although Vico does not explicitly explore, he must undoubtedly have had in mind. This is the etymology of the word *enthymeme,* which Walter Ong has explained in his argument on the middle ground that rhetoric occupies between the conscious and the unconscious. He writes: "*Enthymêma* primarily signifies something within one's soul, mind, heart, feelings, hence something not uttered or 'outered' and to this extent not a fully conscious argument, legitimate though it might be" (12). There is, thus, a connection between the hidden premise of the enthymeme and a nonconscious but somehow known or familiar judgment. Once this argument comes up to consciousness in an act of recollective imagination, the listener can appreciate the harmonious whole of the argument and feel delight in it. If the hidden element was completely unknown, completely new, it would not fit the argument harmoniously. It would have, as it were, too much weight and, in consequence, the whole would be unbalanced.

Thus, the knowledge of the hidden premise must be one in which both the orator and the listener partake, although not consciously or reflectively. By filling in the blanks of the argument, the listener brings to consciousness an element of his own beliefs, and puts it in relation to the rest of the orator's speech. As a result, the listener recognizes a similarity between the orator's motives and his own and feels prone to identifying or sympathizing with him. There is in this phenomenon a tacit agreement between the orator and the listener on the basis of a common belief, upon which the listener has never reflected before, but which lies in the realm of his pre-reflective knowledge. The beauty of the whole argument is, then, sustained by a positive feeling of self-approbation and participation in a common way of feeling and believing, that is, in the *sensus communis* of the whole human race.

POETIC WISDOM AND ENTHYMEMIC RECOLLECTION

Let us now pick up the thread of the initial argument of this paper. My primary challenge was to show that the key notion of the *New Science,* the imaginative universals, could be most properly understood in terms of the rhetorical theory developed in the *Institutiones Oratoriae.* I have argued that Vico's textbook stresses the importance of the topics as the core of the rhetorical enterprise, and so that, if we were to look for a place to find a rhetorical explanation of the imaginative universals, this place should be Vico's discussion of the enthymeme and the conceit. Now, I have arrived at the point where this connection between the art of topics and the imaginative universals can be more clearly observed.

Vico could have given a different name to the first thoughts of the giants, but instead he chose to call them "imaginative universals" or "poetic characters." With this denomination, Vico is not saying that those first thoughts were metaphorical or poetic in nature (at least not in the sense we give to "poetic" nowadays), but that in order for us to approach them, we have to appeal to a sort of poetic, metaphorical or imaginative operation of the mind. This operation is, in my view, the same we have been examining here, namely, the enthymemic inference.

In the enthymeme, says Vico, we state the two extremes of an inference while leaving implied the middle term. This middle term corresponds to the universal that holds together two particular statements. Vico's example of an enthymeme is: "Shall we, who have the gift of speech neglect to speak with eloquence?". Here, the hidden universal corresponds to the practical maxim, "All human beings shall cultivate their endowments." This maxim is indeed part of our common human beliefs, part of our common sense.

The whole purpose of the enthymemic argument is, thus, to bring to consciousness this oblique contemplation or awareness of those common but forgotten first thoughts that compose the so-called human *sensus communis*. As Schaeffer explains, this *sensus communis* has an aesthetic as well as an epistemological side. The enthymeme or conceit is a sort of argument in which "the ingenuity (wit conceived as a faculty) by-passed usual ratiocinative processes and seized upon a truth in a way that fused logical certitude with aesthetic beauty" (64). The imaginative universals of the first people reside in this *sensus communis* that Vico called "judgment without reflection" (New Science, 63). Reaching back to them is an operation of the mind that can only be carried out rhetorically and that corresponds to the invention of arguments. Only through it can the imagination excel in the form of ingenuity and the memory go beyond its limits in the form of recollection. It becomes clear now why Vico left untouched the art of mnemonics in the *Institutiones*. The true art of memory is the art of recollective imagination. Mnemonics is just a secondary technique, one that trains, as it were, our short-term memory, but not our natural bond with the primordial, collective memory of humanity.

Vico's *Insititutiones*, then, gives us more than clues to interpret the *New Science*. It teaches us that the epistemological reflection and the method of the humanities are to be found in the rhetorical tradition. It remains to explain, however, why Vico himself was less adamant than expected in explicitly stressing the connection of rhetoric with the *New Science*. Perhaps Vico was not completely conscious of the enormous task he had in hand at this point. Perhaps he believed that the cause of rhetoric was already a lost one and that Cartesianism would, after all, prevail. Perhaps Vico thought that the barbarism of reason was unavoidable, unless there eventually came a third *corso* in which rhetoric would resuscitate and his *New Science* could then be read and seen with less barbaric eyes. Perhaps the time has not come yet, but we are approaching it.

NOTES

1. Also, the fact that Vico himself tells us very little about the *Institutiones* in his autobiography, whereas he devotes many pages of it to account for the process of composition of the *New Science*, as well as his permanent complaint that his philosophical ideas were not sufficiently recog-

nized, and his frustration for never having been able to replace his position in the University of Naples as the chair of Rhetoric for a more distinguished one in Jurisprudence.

2. As accounted by M. Mooney: "Croce [...] had already read them [the *Institutiones*] and confessed to find in them nothing but a dry rhetoric manual, prepared for school use in which one looks in vain for a shadow of Vico's ideas. M. Mooney, *Vico in the Tradition of Rhetoric*, p. 26. Croce's citation appears in: *Aesthetic and Science of Expression and General Linguistic* 230.

3. Among them, Grassi, Sorrentino, Donati, Battistini, Mooney, Verene and Schaeffer. For further reference, see the Introduction to the English edition of the *Institutiones*, xvii–xxviii.

4. This operation of identification is at the same time one of distinction since, by identifying qualities, the primitive men also began to distinguish among physical entities. As D.P. Verene has shown, before this operation first happened, there was, for the human mind, only a 'flux of sensations' that it could not fully grasp. Imaginative universals are, thus, the first organizing principles for experience and, indeed, the first thoughts of humanity.

5. He writes: "There is nothing we can say on memory. It is indeed an innate virtue which is maintained and kept by usage, and if there is an art to this, *which I do not think there is*, the proper one is that which is called *mnemonics*." (emphasis added)

6. "The teacher should give the greatest care to the pupils memory which, though not exactly the same as imagination, is *almost identical* with it." (emphasis added)

7. In the former trend, rhetoric was appropriated by the Catholic Church, which saw in it a very effective instrument to spread out the Christian message. The best representative of this tendency is Augustine, whose main argument in *On Christian Doctrine* is that, since the power of rhetoric has proved to be very efficacious to argue in favor of both true and false civil matters, the Church should now put it in service of the religious truth, so that it can defend itself from blasphemy and incredulity. In the latter trend, dialecticians of the early Enlightenment, such as Peter Ramus, prepared the French scene for Cartesian philosophy by reducing invention to a method of arguing from oppositions and circumscribing rhetoric to matters of style.

8. In Michael Mooney's words: "Seen within its age, Vico's Principles of Oratory is indeed reactionary [...]. Deprived by Ramus of its 'logical' operations, rhetoric had become increasingly a formal enterprise, a theory of ornate form or an art of communication. In the force of this trend, Vico recalls the full program of classical rhetoric, insisting with Aristotle that its relation to dialectic is its distinguishing, and unifying feature."

9. "The parts or duties of the orator ... are to 'please' (*delectare*), to 'teach' (*docere*), and to 'move' (*connovere*) ... the first requires gentleness (*lenitas*), the second sharpness (*acumen*) and the third, forcefulness (*vis*) ... in this manner, the orator seizes the listeners with pleasure, he holds them with truth, and turns them about by feelings. In the first part, there is the danger of the insidious, while in the third part there is the danger of treachery. But indeed it is in the argument where we find the abundance of the power of eloquence."

10. "Philosophers often use imperfect syllogisms which they call the 'enthymeme' or the incomplete syllogism in which they omit one of the premises, the one assumed [...]. Orators, for purposes of variety, may omit general statements (*effata ex genere*) most of the time, so that the one who is listening would never be aware of the technique or be bored by repetition, and so that the listener may supply the argumentation with something of his own in which he would take delight."

11. "The lawyer (orator) does not derive arguments from this type of *loci* [the *loci* of certainty] because whenever those arguments occur there is no case, and therefore the lawyer takes no part in defending; they are cases only for the judge in sentencing. [...] Of the *loci* of these kinds of arguments [the *loci* of reasoning], either probable or verisimilar, some are common to the dialecticians as well as the orators, and others proper to the orator."

12. This chapter has the appearance of a digression, especially as it is situated right after an extended discussion on the roots of the Latin Language and before the beginning of the properly stylistic matters, i.e. tropes and figures. It seems to be an *addendum*, in terms of style, to the explanation of the arguments.

13. Whether Vico's association between the two ideas is sound or not is open to question.
14. "… from among the maxims, those are so named by the Latins which, because of certain brilliance, show the most of ingenuity, and the same by the Italians, because of that brilliance are called *concetti*."
15. "All of the worthiness of an ingenious saying, must be referred not to the topic or the subject matter but to the manner of the form of creation, so that the name fitting to the thing itself is justly said to be *ingeniosum dictum*."
16. It is reminiscent of Plotinus' treatise on beauty in his *Enneads*. I.6, 46–56.
17. "We all naturally feel it agreeable to get hold of new ideas easily: words express ideas, and therefore those words are the most agreeable that enable us to get hold of new ideas."

WORKS CITED

Aristotle. "Rhetoric." *The Complete Works of Aristotle*. Ed. Jonathan Barnes. Princeton: Princeton UP, 1984.

Augustine. *On Christian Doctrine*. New York: Macmillan, 1987.

Croce, Benedetto. *Aesthetic as Science of Expression and General Linguistic*. London: Macmillan, 1922.

Mooney, Michael. *Vico in the Tradition of Rhetoric*. Princeton: Princeton UP, 1985.

Ong, Walter. *Rhetoric, Romance and Technology*. Ithaca: Cornell UP, 1971.

Plotinus. *The Enneads*. London: Penguin Classics, 1991.

Verene, D. P. *Vico's Science of Imagination*. Ithaca: Cornell UP, 1981.

Vico, Giambattista. *The Art of Rhetoric*. Amsterdam: Value-Inquiry Book Series, 1996.

—. *The New Science*. Ithaca: Cornell UP, 1984.

—. *On the Method of Studies of Our Time*. Ithaca-London: Cornell UP, 1990.

Schaeffer, J. D. *Sensus Communis: Vico, Rhetoric and the Limits of Relativism*. Durham: Duke UP, 1990.

Sorrentino, Andrea. *La retorica e poetica di Vico, ossia la prima concezione estetica del linguaggio*. Turin: Fratelli Boca, 1927.

8

The Spiritual and Secular Rhetoric of Happiness in Joseph Smith and John Stuart Mill

David Gore
Texas A&M University

Søren Kierkegaard wrote of the revolutionary upsurge in Europe in 1848 that it looked now as if politics were everything; "but it will be seen that the catastrophe (the Revolution) corresponds to us and is the obverse of the Reformation: then everything pointed to a religious movement and proved to be political; now everything points to a political movement, but will become religious" (qtd. in Bloom 13). The strange intermixture of politics in religion during the Reformation is, in one sense, the obverse of all things religious now appearing in political guise since 1848. The Mormon prophet Joseph Smith, mayor of the largest town in Illinois during his day and once a candidate for President of the United States, had as much, if not more to say about the U.S. Constitution than he did about sacred happiness. John Stuart Mill, "his satanic free-trade majesty," in the words of Henry Adams, has inspired nearly as many religious-like followers and heretics as Smith, even as his rhetoric was primarily secular (72). Reading Smith and Mill together reiterates Kierkegaard's observation and highlights central differences between American communitarians and British libertarians in the nineteenth century. For Smith, happiness comes from obedience to God's laws within a community devoted to keeping them; for Mill, happiness is derived from an appreciation of self-interest in political and social life, an appreciation that includes reason as the critical factor. For Smith, like much of nineteenth-century America, happiness carried religious and democratic, almost revolutionary, overtones; whereas, for Mill and much of nineteenth-century Britain, happiness was defined by reason and an increasingly democratic policy meant to secure the foundation of reason.

Though it is true that Mill's focus was more secular, it cannot be said that Smith's focus was solely on the hereafter. It cannot be said either that Mill's conception of happiness employed a pure rhetoric of secularism given his propensity to emphasize religious language and imagery, especially in his account of Utilitarianism in his *Autobiography*. Their contrasting claims about happiness indicate how religion is often used to organize people for

87

happiness and how secular liberalism encourages privatism. Indeed, the social organization achieved by Smith can be contrasted with the one advocated by Mill, and in that contrast the roots of communitarian and libertarian visions of happiness are exposed for our view and consideration.[1]

Of course their differences extend even to the level of rhetoric, and setting their claims about happiness in juxtaposition is useful for the insight it gives to nineteenth-century rhetorical practice. Namely, Smith's words draw heavily on what Kenneth Cmiel has called the "democratic idiom," the propensity to value "truth over politeness," a "middling poetics" of "calculated bluntness" (63). Like Americans of all ages, Smith expressed contempt for politicians with their "peculiar tact," decrying the "insolence" of President Van Buren, the "soft to flatter, rather than solid to feed" words of Henry Clay (Evans 254). In fact, Smith's use of words renders it impossible to forget his prophetic claim. Like the prophetic logos of the Old Testament and American politics, Smith's words are those of a messenger, calculated to convert, radical, unreasonable, at times inflexible, and finally characterized by martyrdom (Darsey 16–22). Smith's discourse evokes a strong emotional response and induces beliefs in auditors and is thus best characterized by Edwin Black's term, "exhortative discourse."

Mill, by contrast, uses words in a much more deliberate and systematic manner, and, like Black's genre of "argumentative discourse," it always occurs in a situation of controversy. By young adulthood, Mill had studied closely Aristotle's *Rhetoric*, translated Plato's dialogues, read Quintilian's *Institutes* and Cicero's orations and writings on oratory, and studied Richard Whately's *Elements of Logic* and *Elements of Rhetoric*. He was in every possible way the consummate professional rhetorician, publishing widely throughout his lifetime as well as working for most of his life as a professional correspondent for the East India Company. Karen Whedbee argues that Mill carefully divided scientific argument from practical argument, the former concerned with what is, the latter with what ought to be, and thus argues persuasively that Mill used his understanding of classical rhetoric to construct a distinct rhetorical theory. Moreover, John F. Tinkler has observed that debating societies were the paradigm for Mill's intellectual work and that his "whole political system—perhaps his whole society—is a kind of constantly contested rhetorical controversy" (186). The dominant form of Mill's rhetoric, then, is the deliberative, and his solution to controversy, Tinkler claims, is *moderatio*—the sense of balance; proud of the English tendency to steer between extremes, Mill's rhetoric promotes and responds to a constant controversy and produces a constant balance between contrasting arguments (185). It is characterized best as professional rhetoric designed to promote debate and solutions that balance contrasting arguments.

As it relates to happiness, reading Smith and Mill together offers insight into the simultaneous but very different changes occurring in American and British society during the nineteenth century. Smith is founding an American religion and argues for happiness within a community of like-minded believers. Mill's rhetoric occurs in the context of Christendom's decline within the British Empire and argues for a private happiness within a plural community. Smith indeed struggles with the problem of how to maintain community happiness, knowing that that community will always exist inside of a larger society. Mill is concerned with a happiness that is private in very different ways but that still contributes to an overall happiness quotient. Questions remain over the best ways to define and seek happiness while still maintaining a commitment to larger societal issues, and investigating how Smith and Mill approached these questions is fruitful for providing new answers. Matters of religious happiness, particularly how to talk about religious visions of happiness inside of a plural society, cannot always be conveniently reduced to utility, and thus the contrast presented below can lead to further insight on the question of religious talk in public discourse.

HAPPINESS AS COMMUNITY IN OBEDIENCE TO GOD

Joseph Smith's purported vision of God and Jesus Christ and the subsequent founding of The Church of Jesus Christ of Latter-day Saints is well documented.[2] The Church he founded was, he claimed, a restoration of the gospel as opposed to a reformation of what he agreed was an already corrupted version of Christianity. The Book of Mormon was presented as a tool of the restoration, meant to convince both Jew and Gentile that Jesus is the Christ, and is read by Latter-day Saints as a companion book of scripture to the Bible. During his lifetime, Smith led the church amidst some very perplexing times, including heated and controversial schisms or coups for church control, national financial market crashes, life-threatening mob attacks, and religious persecution that was not relieved by the U.S. government. Smith successfully convinced church members of his authority to lead despite personal imperfections.

What many critics have noted is Smith's personal charisma. Harold Bloom argues that Smith was a "religious genius," though given Bloom's propensity to use the latter term liberally we can reasonably ask, even of Bloom, what makes it so (80)? Bloom writes:

> Like St. Paul (whose theology is almost totally cast out by the Mormons), Smith implicitly understood not only his own aims but the pragmatics of religion making, or what would *work* in matters of the spirit. For that remains the center of his achievement: the Mormons have continued for over a hundred and sixty years; they change, but they do not die. There are now about as many Mormons in our nation and the world as there are Jews, and as I remarked earlier, the Mormons, like the Jews before them, are a religion that became a people. That, I have come to understand, always was Joseph Smith's pragmatic goal, for he had the genius to see that only by becoming a people could the Mormons survive. (83)

What qualifies Smith as a genius was his recognition that in order for the spirit of Mormonism to survive, it must become a people, by which we are to understand it must become a distinct nation of sorts, as the Jews are known. Smith's success in establishing a people, a community of like-minded believers must always inform our measurement of his rhetoric.

Smith's most recent biographer, Robert V. Remini, prefers to see Smith in the light of the Second Great Awakening and the Jacksonian era. The Book of Mormon is, Remini argues, as much a product of nineteenth-century America as anything, especially its stories about crossing oceans, settling wilderness, "revivalist passion," and "democratic impulses" (72). Smith's "tremendous creative energy and verbal fluency" added to his ability to capture the attention of listeners and to persuade them to follow (85). Consequently, Remini sees Smith's "King Follet Discourse," a eulogy preached at the funeral of one King Follet, as the representative anecdote of Smith's religious energy. By contrast, however, Bloom reads the Wentworth Letter, a letter written to John Wentworth, a Chicago newspaper editor, as the representative anecdote of Smith's religious discourse, choosing to emphasize the Gnostic elements in Smith's writings, as all religion is, for Bloom, a kind of "spilled poetry, good and bad" (80). The "King Follet Discourse," by contradistinction, is much more democratic in its ambitions and tends to emphasize an American approach to religion with its disdain for educated authorities. Both works are good introductions to Smith's rhetorical oeuvre and support the notion that his central concerns were spirituality and democracy, usually in that order.

Smith's rhetoric is ingeniously creative, vibrant, captivating, and resonant with its age, if not altogether un-intellectual and oft times poorly written. It was Mark Twain who said the Book of Mormon was "chloroform in print," choosing of course to pun instead of speak clearly seeing as one of the books making up the Book of Mormon is titled "Ether." Most criticism of Smith's writing is, too often, lightly made. His writings in the Doctrine and Covenants, a collection of revelations received by him between 1823 and 1843, especially sections 121 and 122, deserve to rank at least with the highest of all "spilled poetry," even if Bloom is right that Smith was an "indifferent writer" whose "visions far transcended his talents in the composition of divine texts" (80-82). Smith's "Essay on Happiness" surely falls into the category of indifferent writings, but what it lacks in directness it makes up in clarity and consistency. That is, Smith's claims about happiness are clear and direct if his writings on those claims are not always.

What Smith says about happiness is that it can be obtained by any who want it, and that it comes through obedience to God. For Smith there is not a limited amount of happiness in the world. Instead there is infinite happiness, though it is always dependent on our keeping the commandments of God. Smith's "Essay on Happiness" opens:

> Happiness is the object and design of our existence and will be the end thereof, if we pursue the path that leads to it; and this path is virtue, uprightness, faithfulness, holiness, and keeping all the commandments of God. But we cannot keep all the commandments without first knowing them, and we cannot expect to know all, or more than we now know unless we comply with or keep those we have already received. That which is wrong under one circumstance, may be, and often is, right under another (5: 134).

The premise Smith begins with is that God has designed things to work for our happiness and that we are also participants by choosing whether we want the happiness God freely offers. The "plan of happiness," as the Book of Mormon calls it, is to seek virtue, uprightness, faithfulness, holiness, and most importantly obedience. If sought and attained, Smith claimed, these virtues provide happiness now and in the next life. Note that the rhetoric of this passage echoes the language found in the King James Version of the Bible. Smith's sentences are also long, and the passage seems to ramble over many diverse topics. The rambling is probably the result of the fact that Smith's rhetoric is more often heard than read. Smith's rhetoric does not often translate well as effective writing.

At the end of the first paragraph, the essay becomes most consistent with Mormon theology and rhetoric. Smith asserts that the path to virtue, uprightness, faithfulness, holiness, and obedience is dependent on circumstance. It is always changing; that is, God's commands sometimes change but our duty is always to obey them. Revelation is the "principle on which the government of heaven is conducted" (5: 135). Revelation is "adapted to the circumstances in which the children of the kingdom are placed," the essay continues (5: 135). Revelation is the key to knowing what God requires. Doing whatever it is God requires is the key to happiness. Knowledge and action form the mainspring of happiness insofar as they inform us of God's will. To know what God requires, however, is not so simple as doing whatever the prophet says. Instead, like the Jews before them, the Mormons recognize that one important function of the prophet, as Bloom has noted, is to make a people, to build a community.

In addition to founding and leading the church, Smith was instrumental in settling several cities in Ohio, Missouri, and Illinois, and his city planning directed Brigham Young in settling Great Basin cities in present-day Arizona, California, Idaho, Nevada, Northern Mexico, Utah, and Wyoming. It can be said, then, without exaggeration that Smith had a tremendous impact on the settlement of communities throughout the United States. His plans suggest that the optimal size for a city is fifteen to twenty thousand inhabitants, with city lots for all members of the community. The small size, Smith thought, was necessary to ensure democratic participation. However, proximity to the city was also necessary so that all could enjoy the "benefits of society," and thus size had to be limited so that farmers could easily commute to their farms. Smith writes:

> [T]he tiller of the soil as well as the merchant and mechanic will live in the city. The farmer and his family, therefore, will enjoy all the advantages of schools, public lectures and other meetings. His home will no longer be isolated, and his family denied the benefits of society, which has been, and always will be, the great educator of the human race; but they will enjoy the same privileges of society, and can surround their homes with the same intellectual life, the same social refinement as will be found in the home of the merchant or banker or professional man (Roberts 1: 311).

Smith recognized that all members of the community must participate in government, but as importantly, in society. Access to "intellectual life" and "social refinement" was a critical aspect of his city planning. Without carefully planned cities, opportunities for livelihood, and a rich home life, happiness was unattainable.

Smith's "Essay on Happiness" is rounded out by the example of a child stealing fruit. Smith argues that had the child simply asked his parents for the fruit, he would have eaten with a better appetite instead of receiving "stripes." The example is illustrative of Smith's claim about happiness: happiness comes when we obey God and live with attention to the obligations of society, in this case the obligation of a child to ask for food from a parent. For Smith, the example illustrates man's relationship with God:

> [I]n obedience there is joy and peace unspotted, unalloyed; and as God has designed our happiness—and the happiness of all His creatures, he never has—He never will institute an ordinance or give a commandment to His people that is not calculated in its nature to promote that happiness which He has designed, and which will not end in the greatest amount of good and glory to those who become the recipients of his law and ordinances (5: 135).

Smith argues that God has designed for the happiness of his people and that if they will receive God's laws and ordinances, they will receive happiness. Cooperating with a community of believers is a step on the path to happiness. The model for Latter-day Saint (LDS) happiness is the family, one reason why many church members today still refer to Joseph Smith as "Brother Joseph." It is indicative of the LDS community that family relationships constitute happiness in time and eternity. Happiness, thus, in Smith's view, requires that certain moral principles be followed, and Smith argues that by following God's moral principles, happiness is "designed" a priori. It is still, however, dependent on man to discover God's design and conform his life to it. Smith was ever confident that such discovery and conformity was possible, and his "Essay on Happiness" is consistent with that claim.

One criticism that can be leveled at Smith's claims is that he was a "true believer" in Eric Hoffer's sense of the term. In other words, what place might non-Mormons have in a community envisioned on Smith's pattern of happiness, or, to put it in Mill's terms, what are the consequences of a Smithian community? In a civic sense, Smith was concerned with consequences, especially the separation of church and state. Furthermore, Smith argued that God inspired the U.S. Constitution "for the rights and protection of all flesh."[3] His civic vision included a definite pluralism and was never intended to trample on rights of association or conscience. It could be said that Smith may have personally put too much faith in the U.S. Constitution to protect religious liberty, but it cannot be said that he supported a philosophical or civic system that would undermine the U.S. Constitution's general principles, like freedom of religion, speech, press, and association.

HAPPINESS AS INDIVIDUAL AND RATIONAL CALCULATION

Mill's early life varies absolutely from Smith's. Mill was, under the tutelage of his father, raised for a life of scholarship. By age three he was reading Greek, by six he was writing independently, and at eight reading Latin. Around age seventeen his intellectual life broadened considerably as he left home to travel and work for the East India Company. His collected works fill over thirty volumes and contain essays published during his teenage years through the entirety of his adult life and beyond. Under the direction of James Mill and Jeremy Bentham, Mill's younger years were spent preparing him for a life in the publishing world, as well as a life advocating the philosophy of his tutors: Utilitarianism.

Though the most widely read of Mill's works are *On Liberty* and the *Autobiography*, *Utilitarianism* is in fact the cornerstone of Mill's philosophical system. Often scholars in the humanities, excepting philosophy, mistakenly think that the principles of liberty are at odds with utility, and that, if pressed, Mill would side with liberty. Alan Ryan, however, has been one of the most forcible advocates against this view. Instead, Ryan argues that the happiness principle of Utilitarianism is Mill's guiding light and that liberty is only a component of happiness. Ryan stresses that the conversion experience recorded by Mill in the *Autobiography*, and often used by many to evidence Mill's escape from Utilitarianism, is in fact part of Mill's "theoretical work" (9). This approach to the *Autobiography* reframes utility as Mill's central interest.

As the story goes, Mill experiences in his teenage years the euphoria of a religious conversion to Bentham's philosophy and then, with the passage of time, suffers a severe depression from the intense internal admission that Utilitarianism, as presented by his father and Bentham, is a narrow and shortsighted philosophy. Mill's depression, says the popular reading of the *Autobiography*, is softened by a new conviction that the beauty of art and especially poetry can offer something more than utility offers. Mill recounts his happiness crisis:

> From the winter of 1821, when I first read Bentham, and especially from the commencement of the *Westminster Review*, I had what might truly be called an object in life; to be a reformer of the world. My conception of my own happiness was entirely identified with this object. The personal sympathies I wished for were those of fellow labourers in this enterprise. [...] I was accustomed to felicitate myself on the certainty of a happy life which I enjoyed, through placing my happiness in something durable and distant, in which some progress might be always making, while it could never be exhausted by complete attainment. This did very well for several years, during which the general improvement going on in the world and the idea of myself as engaged with others in struggling to promote it, seemed enough to fill up an interesting and animated existence. But the time came when I awakened from this as from a dream. (*Autobiography* 111–112)

What Mill awakens to is a sense that Utilitarianism, as advocated by James Mill and Jeremy Bentham, is without "charm" and has "nothing in it to attract sympathy" (*Autobiography* 113). The rest of the chapter is devoted to Mill's rebirth in feeling. Note additionally the contrast between those passages from Smith earlier in the chapter. Particularly, Mill's rhetoric is more direct, and although in this selection on a very personal note, his rhetoric is still much more efficient than Smith's. Mill writes clearly, uses shorter clauses, and does not carry any burden of oral discourse.

Slowly but surely, Mill writes, he became aware that feeling itself, in contradistinction to rational calculation, could produce happiness. "Of the truth of this I was convinced," Mill writes, "but to know that a feeling would make me happy if I had it, did not give me the feeling. My education, I thought, had failed to create these feelings in sufficient strength to resist the dissolving influence of analysis" (*Autobiography* 115). What finally brings feeling, after months without it, is reading Marmontel's *Memoirs* wherein the author relates his father's death. This "small ray of light" was enough for Mill to realize that he "was no longer hopeless," "not a stock or a stone" (*Autobiography* 117). Mill then reads Wordsworth for the first time and relates how it opened him up to a "pleasurable susceptibilit[y]," to the "power of rural beauty" (*Autobiography* 121). Wordsworth's poetry was "medicine" for his state of mind and delivered him from the grips of depression "and I felt myself at once better and happier" and was made to "feel that there was real, permanent happiness in tranquil contemplation"(*Autobiography* 121).

This narrative gives the impression that Mill was converted as it were from the depressingly stark Utilitarianism of his father and Bentham to an enlightened and poetic view of truth and happiness. I argue that this is not the case. Instead, as I alluded earlier, Ryan argues that this narrative functions to support Utilitarianism. I go further by saying explicitly that Mill never fully inverts the hierarchy of analysis over feeling. Additionally, he never places the two on equal ground. Analysis and rational calculation are always the sure means to happiness though, it is admitted, feeling can play a part. Ryan writes:

> Since the concept of utility or happiness is a disputed one, a moralist's value must depend very heavily on how well he understands the diversity of human happiness. [...] Mill wanted to expand, not renounce his inheritance. Utilitarianism had to be enlarged to cover those aspects of human life which Bentham did not see; majority rule had to be rendered compatible with due deference to elite opinion, and the underlying social theory had to expand to take in cultural and historical factors of a new kind. (54–56)

Mill's autobiographical narrative does not undermine Utilitarianism. Rather it seeks to reinforce Mill's version of Utilitarianism. One of the problems resolved by reading Mill in this manner is that utility and liberty are no longer seen at odds. Furthermore we can more fully appreciate the fact that Mill never relinquished his preference for induction, econometrics, and objectivity.

Another passage written around the same time as *On Liberty* and *Utilitarianism* corroborates the view that Mill's outlook on life is of a slightly antipoetic kind. The passage comes from Mill's *Three Essays on Religion* that was, like the *Autobiography*, published posthumously though written much earlier. In one essay, "On the Utility of Religion," Mill writes, "Religion and poetry address themselves, at least in one of their aspects, to the same part of the human constitution: they both supply the same want, that of ideal conceptions grander and more beautiful than we see realized in the prose of human life" (*Three Essays* 103). Thus, another way of stating Ryan's insight is to say that human life, for Mill, is prose, not poetry.

The observation that life is prosaic and that religion and poetry simply run interference for the heart is critical for appreciating Mill's works, especially his conception of human happiness. It is that privation of feeling attached to Mill's writings in *Utilitarianism* that flavors all his works. Mill writes:

> The creed which accepts as the foundation of morals "utility" or the "greatest happiness principle" holds that actions are right in proportion as they tend to promote happiness; wrong as they tend to produce the reverse of happiness. By happiness is intended pleasure and the absence of pain; by unhappiness, pain and the privation of pleasure. (*Utilitarianism* 7)

I need not go on at greater length. Mill's writing carries a burden of objectivity and prose, especially, as ever, the burden of nonfiction prose—that burden is one that would see "happiness" as the "greatest happiness principle," and finally, then, as "utility."

Coupled with his interest in utility is Mill's assertion that individuals will make rational decisions and will seek to improve the utility of themselves and their neighbors. Some critics of Mill claim that utility choices will inevitably lead to selfish, calculating behaviors that will restrict the overall happiness quotient. Mill argues in response that they have represented human nature in a degrading light. Mill's libertarianism is designed to shield the individual from societal encroachment and the "tyranny of the majority." Still, in order to work, it requires that the individual choose higher order virtues. Mill argues that human happiness or "human well being" derives principally from "the internal culture of the individual" (*Autobiography* 118). That Utilitarianism is more often presented as a political and public system for creating and regulating happiness, I do not deny. However, I argue that Mill's notion of happiness is one absolutely and clearly dependent on individual calculation, and regardless of utility calculations of a public nature, Mill thinks happiness is private and personal.

The consequences of Mill's arguments are tremendously broad and powerful. Mill has impacted generations of thinkers, especially economists, and promoted thinking about how to calculate happiness in public affairs. One obvious impact of Mill's overall argument was to elevate induction in policymaking by establishing it as the central method of investigation. Furthermore, Mill can be credited with making the method of economics a tool for social change. James Buchanan and Gordon Tullock's *The Calculus of Consent* and their work on Public Choice Theory and even to some extent the application of economics to law and literature, primarily by Richard Posner, are all prominent examples of how Mill's thinking has been updated to include a stronger and clearer delineation of rights while preserving Millian method. Mill's classical liberal theory and method, thus, continue to spawn new ideas about how to calculate happiness for polities and how to see happiness as primarily personal and private, while his rhetorical preference for prose is found nowhere so clearly as in the writing of contemporary economists.

CONCLUDING REMARKS

Joseph Smith, influenced heavily by Jacksonian democracy and the Bible, sees happiness as a function of God's will and community solidarity. B. H. Roberts said of Smith that he "made no attempt to create a 'system' of philosophy. His philosophical utterances were flung off without reference to any arrangement or orderly sequence. In the main they were taught in independent aphorisms ... " (2: 411–12). Smith presented an American vision of democratic happiness in the middle years of the nineteenth century, a communitarian vision where knowledge of God and righteous action cohere in happiness. Mill, on the other hand, wishes to protect individuals from community consensus and defines happiness as a function of individual, rational calculation. Mill's systematic British libertarianism promotes the happiness of the individual over the happiness of the group and views group happiness as merely the sum of individual feelings.

A further note, an insight gleaned from Harold Bloom, emphasizes my central point. Bloom's oeuvre, from his *Anxiety of Influence* through *The Book of J* and beyond, revolves around a central contention: the contention that life is poetic. Mill, were he around to do so, would turn all of that on its head by arguing that human life is prose. Bloom judges Smith a religious genius because he is the representative American exemplar of the art of "spilled poetry." The dissidence between Smith and Mill represents the dissonance between metaphor and realism, the distance between communitarian and libertarian philosophies. Bloom might say that distance explains why Smith died a martyr at an early age and why Mill continued to publish prose posthumously, why one chose death as a commitment to his philosophy and the other retirement. Smith's democratic happiness was always part of a city of friendly followers. Mill's is always democracy without a buddy; Mill's is always individual, personal happiness—most emphatically not the American democratic, communitarian vision of the nineteenth century. That poetic and prosaic rhetoric are still active in our discursive consciousness is enduring testimony that the dissimilarity Smith and Mill embody abides.

ACKNOWLEDGMENT

The author wishes to thank Jim Aune and Patricia Bizzell for their helpful comments on earlier drafts of this essay.

NOTES

1   Michael Sandel argues that republicans and liberals differ in their conception of how to organize for liberty, which is another way of saying, I think, how they would organize for happiness. Sandel sees liberty as a "sharing in self-government" while liberals see it as "the capacity of persons to choose their values and ends." I read Smith, by this categorization, as a republican, Mill as a liberal. This distinction informs my understanding of their rhetoric. See Michael J. Sandel, *Democracy's Discontents* (Cambridge: Harvard University Press, 1996) and *Debating Democracy's Discontents*, Ed. Anita L. Allen and Milton C. Regan, Jr. (Oxford: Oxford University Press, 1998) for more on Sandel's conception of liberty, its strengths and weaknesses.
2. See discussion by Arrington and Bitton and "Joseph Smith's First Visions, 1820–1830" by Bushman and Bushman.
3   See Smith's *Doctrine and Covenants* 101: 77–80 and Hancock's edited volume for an overview of Smith's thoughts on the U.S. Constitution.

WORKS CITED

Adams, Henry. *The Education of Henry Adams*. New York: Modern Library, 1999.
Arrington, Leonard J., and Davis Bitton. *The Mormon Experience: A History of the Latter-day Saints*. 2nd ed. Urbana: U of Illinois P, 1992.

Black, Edwin. *Rhetorical Criticism: A Study in Method.* Madison: U of Wisconsin P, 1978).

Bloom, Harold. *The American Religion: The Emergence of a Post-Christian Nation.* New York: Simon, 1992.

Bushman, Claudia Lauper, and Richard Lyman Bushman. *Building the Kingdom: A History of Mormons in America.* Oxford: Oxford UP, 2001.

Cmiel, Kenneth. *Democratic Eloquence: The Fight over Popular Speech in Nineteenth-Century America.* New York: Morrow, 1990.

Darsey, James. *The Prophetic Tradition and Radical Rhetoric in America.* New York: New York UP, 1997.

Evans, John Henry. *Joseph Smith: An American Prophet.* New York: Macmillan, 1933.

Hancock, Ralph C., Ed. *Just and Holy Principles: Latter-day Saint Readings on America and the Constitution.* Needham Heights: Simon, 1998.

Hoffer, Eric. *The True Believer.* New York: Harper, 1951.

Mill, John Stuart. *Autobiography.* New York: Penguin, 1989.

——. *Three Essays on Religion.* Amherst: Prometheus, 1998.

——. *Utilitarianism.* Indianapolis: Hackett, 1979.

Remini, Robert V. *Joseph Smith.* New York: Penguin, 2002.

Roberts, B. H. *A Comprehensive History of the Church of Jesus Christ of Latter-day Saints.* 6 vols. Salt Lake City: Deseret News, 1930.

Ryan, Alan. *J. S. Mill.* London: Routledge, 1974.

Smith, Joseph. *The History of the Church.* 7 vols. Salt Lake City: Deseret, 1980.

Tinkler, John F. "J. S. Mill as a Nineteenth-Century Humanist." *Rhetorica* 10 (Spring 1992): 165–91.

Whedbee, Karen. "John Stuart Mill's Theory of Practical Argument and Political Advocacy." University of Wisconsin, 1993.

9

Nooses and Neck Verses: The Life and Death Consequences of Literacy Testing

Connie Kendall

Miami University (Ohio)

The said Paul reads, to be branded;

The said William does not read, to be hanged.

—Sussex Gaol records (1613)

"Linguistic competence [...] is a political judgement about legitimacy."

—Bruce Horner and John Trimbur ("English Only")

HANGING IN THE BALANCE, OR HOW LITERACY CAN SAVE YOUR NECK

One of the oldest institutionalized uses of a standardized literacy test on record is that of the reading test[1] which originally accompanied a criminous[2] cleric's testimony during trial in medieval and early modern British lay courts. The test's legal function was to ensure the prudent use of the "benefit of clergy" exemption—a privilege extended to felonious clerics that facilitated their dismissal from trial in the King's court, which frequently imposed the death penalty, in favor of a trial held in the Bishop's court, which rarely, if ever, imposed the death penalty. Popularly dubbed the "neck verse" for its ability to quite literally "save the necks" of all literate religious (and later, all secular) clerks accused of capital crimes, this early literacy test claims an extraordinary, though virtually ignored, history that spans more than four hundred years of British common law (c. 1278 [6 Edward I] – 1707 [5 Anne]) and extends across the reigns of not less than nineteen British monarchs.

While in use, the legal authority granted to this singular test of a prisoner's literacy was both daunting and unequivocal: successful reading of the neck verse meant life, and failure meant death. Although arguably implicated in the summary judgment of death by hanging

97

for thousands[3] of (presumably "illiterate") clerks, both religious and secular alike, the history of this literacy test is noticeably absent from the field's authorized accounts[4] of the development and spread of literacy in the Western world. I seek to address this curious gap in the field's recounting of the history of literacy, in an effort to provide a new way of thinking about the meaning(s), use(s) and consequence(s) of standardized literacy tests, especially for those individuals who are (as yet) being put to the trial of their literacy.

I take for my point of entry into this discussion of the complexities surrounding literacy testing practices Horner and Trimbur's remark, my epigraph, which arguably looms large in the current debates surrounding the resurgence of high-stakes testing policies and their sweeping and, to my mind, dangerous effects on the nature and goals of U.S. public education. That is to suggest that, as researchers interested in interrogating the educational institution's increasing reliance on large-scale, legislatively mandated literacy testing practices, we would do well to position ourselves within the standpoint Horner and Trimbur's words provide; namely, to regard all institutionally authorized assessments of an individual's literacy practices as necessarily linked to political judgments about his or her claims of legitimacy. In so doing, we may be able to disrupt the prevailing notion that the testing situations into which we routinely place various populations of people—situations that have historically held seriously "high stakes" for individual test-takers—are far from neutral occasions. On the contrary, standardized tests of literacy are always ideologically freighted, and the idea that tests centering on language use can reveal hidden meanings relative to an individual's class, gender, race, nationality, or other social and/or political affiliations claims a particularly long and, I would add, a noticeably bloody history. The history of the neck verse presents us with an especially striking example of this well-forged link between acts of literacy and judgments of legitimacy. Thus, I suggest that a fuller examination of this early reading test will afford new insights with which we can (re)theorize the meaning of standardized tests of literacy in our own time.

My discussion of the neck verse centers on two related claims: (1) that the literacy test which stood between a criminous cleric and his[5] impending doom had little to do with certifying literacy, but was instead aimed at certifying the prisoner's legitimacy as a member of the clergy who was thereby entitled to clerical immunity from secular trial; and (2) that, within the context of the trial, a prisoner's singular act of literacy (i.e., successful reading of the neck verse) constitutes a rhetorical action aimed at persuading court authorities to both belief and (favorable) action. Since four hundred years of British legal, religious and secular history comprise a vast expanse of time and entail a complexity that obviously can not be fully accounted for here, I will direct my remarks specifically toward the question of exigency,[6] and the ways in which shifting perceptions of exigency (or exigencies) condition the meaning(fulness) of the reading test differently and in accordance with its context(s) for use.

Toward that end, I examine two distinct transformations regarding the perceived exigential conditions for the test. The first transformation I will describe, whereby the sociopolitical exigency (i.e., increasing abuses of clerical immunities) is reinterpreted by the secular courts as an institutional exigency that became known as the problem of "doubtful clergy," allows me to situate the neck verse within its historical context and point to the ways in which the "original"—a modifier I use advisedly—exigency is obscured by the authority granted to the reading test. The second transformation I will propose, whereby the court's problem of "doubtful clergy" is reinterpreted by the prisoner as a rhetorical exigency that requires the persuasive use of his literacy, will help me to reconfigure testing situations as rhetorical occasions and, by extension, test-takers as rhetorical agents.

PRIVILEGIUM CLERICALE AND THE PROBLEM
OF "DOUBTFUL CLERGY"

When William the Conqueror ordered the separation of the "temporal" courts from the "spiritual" courts in 1072, he disrupted the balance of power between Church and Realm that had existed throughout Anglo-Saxon times, where Bishops and ealdormen sat side-by-side in shire courts and jointly adjudicated both secular and canonical law. While not inconsistent with the ideological tenor that defined the political circumstances of the period—a moment when the early Norman kings were establishing the laws of the British Empire to accord with Christian ideals—the Conqueror's Ordinance, which required that all spiritual persons, regardless of the nature of the offense, be tried before the Bishop, set the legal precedent for what came to be known as the benefit of clergy exemption[7] and provoked a political struggle that would trouble the relationship between England's two great authorities for the next seven centuries. A struggle that, at its outset, had nothing to do with the idea of literacy per se, but would eventually take the form of a literacy test by which the secular courts could determine the legitimacy of a criminous cleric's right to "personal immunity from lesser secular authorities."

The problem of the criminous cleric was an especially thorny one for medieval court authorities. Recognized as *personae mixtae*—a "mixed person" who, like the anointed and crowned *Rex unctus*, belonged equally to both God and country—clerics enjoyed a privileged social and political status that was substantially respected by the Norman kings; a status that was seriously jeopardized, however, when the cleric in question committed a crime against the Realm. The problem was really one of overlapping jurisdictional claims regarding the (mixed) legal status of criminous clerics: secular authority argued that clerics, who had first and foremost broken the King's peace, should be tried in the King's court, and ecclesiastical authority countered that clerics were already protected from all forms of secular law by virtue of the Conqueror's Ordinance and so could only be tried in the Bishop's court. Given the ideological constraints in place—where the expectation was that a *real* Christian king would yield to the deity's judgment as delivered by the Bishop—it was the benefit of clergy exemption, a privilege (originally) made available only to *legitimate* members of the clergy (i.e., the ordained or "higher" orders, including bishops, priests, deacons, and monks), that would function as the compromise between the two courts.

However, the benefit of clergy compromise held disastrous implications for secular authority throughout the twelfth century, a period of time that was witness to a dramatic increase in abuses to clerical privileges. This now-legal exemption was being regularly invoked for every imaginable felony, from murder and rape to petty larceny and counterfeiting, by "legitimate" clerics throughout England. Almost needless to say, the authority granted to the benefit of clergy quickly became a thorn in the sides of the royals and their secular court judges, who generally believed that clerics were deliberately exploiting the privilege for their own gain, and who thus actively sought ways to stem the abuses to the legal system.[8] From their viewpoint, these repeated legal misapplications of clerical privilege, which signified the vast power of the Church, had grown dangerously out of control and demanded reform. But of course, (re)shifting the balance of power is always a delicate matter; and, if Henry II's debacle at the end of the twelfth century taught the secular courts nothing else, it demonstrated clearly that direct (secular) challenges to the competence of canonical law brought about political ruin. To avoid the fate that befell Henry, the lay courts would instead engage in a subtle shifting of the question of the Church's competence to the question of an individual cleric's (linguistic) competence. After all, it is much safer to accuse a power-less prisoner of treachery and incompetence than to accuse the Bishop of witting malefaction and the deliberate miscarriage of justice.

I suggest that it was within this context that the "original" sociopolitical exigency (i.e., uncontrolled abuses of clerical immunity) was transformed into an institutional exigency specific to the lay courts and reinterpreted as the problem of "doubtful clergy." That is, the exigency facing thirteenth- and fourteenth-century judges was simply this: How can the secular courts ascertain the legitimacy of a criminous cleric's claim to the benefit of clergy exemption? For, the wide berth legally granted to the benefit of clergy exemption not only drew the attention of "legitimate" clergy intent on breaking the law, but was also attractive to a number of "illegitimate" felons, laymen who posed as clergy in order to receive the benefit. The increasing frequency of faked first tonsures, forged Holy Orders, and the wearing of stolen clerical vestments[9] placed an additional burden on the court's determination of clerkship and called for the institution of a new mode of proof, one that was less available to fakery or forgery, one that was not dependent on the externals of clerkship but could instead provide a more internal measure of criminous cleric's legitimacy—his literacy. Enter the reading test, circa 1278.

That the secular courts regarded the reading test as "proof competent" of a cleric's legitimacy[10] implies its ideological character. The phrasing itself is a key indicator: the descriptor *competent* refers to the intrinsic nature of the proof, not the intrinsic nature of the cleric's literacy. In fact, surviving transcripts indicate that a prisoner could be a very poor "reader" of the neck verse—sometimes barely able to *sillabicare*—yet still be pronounced *"legit"* and claimed by the Ordinary for the Bishop. Take for example, the case of William Pernill [18 Edward III], who faced the justices at Colchester Prison on the felony charge of robbery and clearly had only a rudimentary knowledge of "letters" learned in a very short amount of time.

> The Ordinary, upon being asked if he wished to claim the prisoner, was explicit enough in his re-fusal; for, in the words of the entry, [...] *eo quod legere ignorat.* And William, being pronounced guilty by the jury, was doomed to hang. Before the sentence was carried out, however, the Ordi-nary appeared once more before the justices, this time asserting that William could read, and claimed him as a clerk. The Ordinary may have erred on the first occasion, though it is difficult to see how. *It is much more probable that the doomed prisoner had improved his last days or hours by a diligent study of the neck-verse, perhaps with the assistance of a well-disposed gaoler.* (Gabel 72, emphasis added)

Pernill's case presents a most interesting question: How can we account for the apparent contradiction between his "literacy," which was minimal at best, and the court's final judgment of legitimacy? The answer, I contend, rests in the (already meaningful) ideological linkage between the ideas of "literacy" and "legitimacy," in the ways in which the test obscures the contradiction between a material practice (i.e., reading the neck verse) and its authorized institutional meaning (i.e., legitimacy). That is, the courts were operating within a kind of axiomatic logic (i.e., literate = legitimate; illiterate = illegitimate) that derives from what literacy theorist M. T. Clanchy describes as a commonplace medieval construction, also axiomatic in nature; namely, that *cleric* meant "literate" and *layman* meant "illiterate" (cf. Clanchy 177–81). And while space constrains my ability to more carefully tease out the implications of the secular court's reliance on this axiomatic model of jurisprudence, suffice to say that, as the meaning of *litteratus* was "reduced" from "having a reputation for erudition" to meaning "a person with a minimal ability to read, albeit in Latin" (Clanchy 185), and as the meaning of *clericus* was concomitantly widened to include all those who had acquired first tonsures (i.e., the "minor orders," including subdeacons, acolytes, exorcists, lectors, porters, all monastic persons, and choristers), the reading test became more of a problem than a solution.[11] Perhaps ironically, it was the way in which the reading test upheld the older axiomatic pairings *and* functioned ideologically to smooth over any contradictions between the newly defined concept of literacy and its attendant sociopolitical meaning of legitimacy that eventually compromised the test's intended purpose. In other words, these dramatic semantic shifts were effectively stabilized under the interpretive authority granted to the reading test. So stabilized, it is hardly implausible to speculate that the prospect of becoming literate (read: minimally competent in Latin) in order to access a form of legitimacy that could "save your neck" provided incentive for the lower classes to acquire literacy and further encouraged the criminal classes to abuse existing clerical privileges. It is also possible to recognize the secular courts' complicity with the so-called exploitation of literacy—or what might be more accurately described as the exploitation of legitimacy through literacy—as it had been institutionally authorized for certain types of people via the reading test. "A little Latin," Clanchy quips, "like a little literacy in recent times, could get a man a long way [...] deplorable as that was in the eyes of scholars" (191). And of course, in the context of a secular court trial, one of the things that a "little Latin" could quite literally "get a man" was his neck out of the hangman's noose.

LITERATE ACTS OF PERSUASION: MOVING THE COURT FROM DOUBT TO BELIEF

Since the reading test aims not at the certification of a criminous cleric's literacy, but at the certification of his (presumed) legitimacy, I suggest that this testing situation is best regarded as a rhetorical occasion—a site that occasions the cleric's purposeful *use* of literacy in the negotiation of (the meaning of) his life. In other words, I want to propose the idea that a second and, at least in my opinion, an as-yet undertheorized reinterpretation of exigency is visible in the context of this (or for that matter, any) "trial" regarding an individual's literate condition. For inasmuch as the problem of "doubtful clergy" represents an institutional exigency for the secular courts, I contend that, from the perspective of the cleric on trial, the problem of "doubtful clergy" (re)presents a rhetorical exigency.

My position is informed by contemporary literacy and language theorists, who argue that an individual's literate practices are culturally shaped social practices and not merely a set of discrete and transferable skills that can either be acquired or employed in isolation.[12] Regarded as a social practice, then, literacy has been productively recast as an individual's "*ways of using* written language" (Ivanic 58). Stressing its contextualized nature, literacy theorist Roz Ivanic further argues that "literacy (in the sense of 'using written language') serves some specific social purpose: it is used in order to respond to some particular life demand, not practised for its own sake" (61). The importance of Ivanic's reformulation should not be overlooked, for it not only acknowledges that literacy is an always situated practice (i.e., purposeful, aimed, and responsive to perceived exigential conditions) but also presumes that the individual language user, as a social being likewise situated within a given culture, is an always "knowing subject" (i.e., an agent) putting his/her literacy into action toward specific ends. This revised perspective on literacy is, to my mind, a decidedly rhetorical perspective, one which prompts me to ask: What would it mean to recast the criminous cleric as a knowing subject who exists in a situated discursive exchange and uses literacy to achieve a particular effect? How might that change our understanding of literacy testing situations and those we (continue to) put to the test?

To our modern sensibilities, of course, it might seem that merely reading a standardized Latin verse constitutes a less than reliable method of establishing proof of (even) minimal literacy—let alone a rhetorical action—especially if such "reading" was shown to be more an act of rote memorization and delivery than the actual decoding of written script. Clanchy's research, however, importantly reminds us that many of our strongest twentieth-century assumptions about literacy (i.e., that reading and writing are complementary skills, that the "spread" of literacy indicates that a majority of people possess a minimal ability to read/write in the language they speak, that the development of literacy is a consequence of advancing culture and mass education rather than a consequence of "practical" demands in everyday life) are "products of recent history and not invariable norms" (263). Clanchy remarks that, throughout medieval times, "[r]eading was linked to hearing rather than seeing" (218) and was viewed as "part of the mastery of speech," which was acquired formally like training in the *ars dictaminis* and thus was able to furnish proof of a "literate mentality" (226). And of course, these are the assumptions which appear to inform secular courtroom practices, where the spoken word (i.e., reading aloud the neck verse) was understood as providing the "proof competent" necessary for the determination of legitimate clerkship. Furthermore, and with regard to the presumed reliability of courtroom evidence, Clanchy reports that two principles were as-yet accepted as legal commonplaces during the thirteenth and fourteenth centuries: (1) that oral witness was to be privileged over written evidence and (2) that whenever possible, a litigant must speak on his own behalf "because only words from his own mouth were authentic" (221). Thus, it is within these conditions that I suggest we can re-theorize the criminous cleric's use of literacy as rhetorical action.

The theoretical turn I am proposing is simply this: if it is the court's doubt that precipitates the institution of the reading test, then it becomes the cleric's rhetorical task to find a way to resolve the court's doubt via the use of his literacy. And the since the resolution of doubt is not found in truth but instead resides in belief—or maybe better put, in the belief of the possibility of a truth—the criminous cleric's use of literacy is more accurately understood as an act of persuasion. That is, rather than "mere" reading, the prisoner's act of literacy constitutes a rhetorical action, aimed at persuading an audience (i.e., secular court authorities) to belief in the (probable) truth of his literacy in a deliberate effort to move them to favorable action (i.e., to find him "*legit*") and thereby save his life.

IN OUR OWN TIME: CONTEMPORARY IMPLICATIONS
FOR MODERN-DAY NECK VERSES

Reconceptualizing the cleric's use of literacy as an act of persuasion, as opposed to a display of literate skill, changes the way we might view all tests of literacy. Rather than regarding literacy tests as decontextualized mechanisms unilaterally deployed in response to institutional exigencies alone, we can reconfigure tests as discursive sites that present rhetorical exigencies for test-takers—sites that occasion the use of persuasive rhetorical action in the negotiation of the meaning(s) of an individual's literacy. Such a reconfiguration would importantly shift our analytical focus away from the literate "product" itself and toward the rhetorical relationship that (always) exists between test-takers and test-makers, wherein the meaning of a person's literacy is made. Admittedly, the rhetorical relationship between test-takers and test-makers is highly constrained by the institution within which the literacy testing situation occurs. There can be no doubt that institutionally mandated tests of literacy authorize asymmetrical arrangements of power and maintain the ideological and political investments of the dominant groups in society—two critical, not to mention problematic, aspects of literacy testing that call for further and consistent interrogation. And while the authority granted to institutional interests and exigencies works to mask the rhetorical exigencies operating in testing situations, such authority does not preclude the test-taker as an agent of his or her literacy from recognizing the rhetorical nature of literacy tests and/or the possibility of actively negotiating the meaning of his or her literacy within these particular constraints. For, acts of literacy (re)conceived as acts of rhetoric must always account for situational constraints; it is, of course, the very nature of all (successful) rhetorical action to do so.

NOTES

1. The procedure for examining an individual's literacy was fairly clear-cut. After a guilty verdict was rendered for the capital offense, the presiding judge would ask the prisoner if he knew any reason why the court should not move directly to sentencing. At this point, the (now) *clericus convictus* could choose to invoke his right to the "benefit of clergy" and call for the reading test, a formal examination of his literacy to be administered by the court's Ordinary (i.e., the cleric assigned to the secular trial by the Bishop of the diocese). The Ordinary would present the felon with the *clergy*, the term used for the courtroom copy of the Psalter, ceremoniously opened to the Fifty-first Psalm, a psalm of contrition aptly named *"Miserere mei, Deus,"* and require the prisoner to read the first verse: *Have mercy upon me, O God, after thy great goodness; according to the multitude of mercies do away mine offences.* Once the convicted cleric "read" the verse, the judge would ask the Ordinary one question only: *"Legit vel non?"* If the Ordinary answered *"Legit,"* thereby claiming the prisoner as a legitimate member of the clergy, the felon was immediately dismissed from secular court and remanded to his Bishop's prison in the care of the Ordinary to await ecclesiastical trial. If, however, the Ordinary replied, *"Non legit,"* the prisoner's claim to the benefit of clergy was rendered invalid and sentencing in the lay court, which usually resulted in the death penalty, proceeded without further interference from the Church.
2. For medievals, the term *criminous* meant "felonious" and referred to someone accused of a capital crime. The phrasing "criminous cleric" was common usage and so I use this phrasing here.
3. Historian L. C. Gabel's research suggests that nearly fifty percent of the criminous clerics on trial during the thirteenth, fourteenth, and fifteenth centuries were convicted (945/2001 cases examined across three county court registers; see Table A, pp. 128–9). And while Gabel rightly holds the opinion that one can merely speculate on the role that the neck verse played in a prisoner's failed attempt to save his life, the reading test's growing prominence in existing court records makes plausible the claim that it was a significant factor in the secular court's decision-making process. Interested readers are encouraged to consult Gabel's research directly.
4. One notable exception is M. T. Clanchy's (1979) *From Memory to Written Record.* Other texts where the neck verse and its implications are considered in greater detail include George Dalzell's *Benefit of Clergy in America* and L. C. Gabel's *Benefit of Clergy in England in the Later Middle Ages.* It may also be of interest to note that, while scholarly references to the neck verse are either noticeably absent or are otherwise held in footnotes or in the space of a few short paragraphs, "vulgarized" references to the reading test can be found in surviving popular texts of the period. The *British Apollo* newspaper (circulated in the early 1700s) published several poems that parodied the meaning of the neck verse for those unfortunate enough to be put to the (reading) test in a court of law, and Shakespeare's play, *Henry VI, Part 2,* includes a scene where Jack

Cade's rebels turn the tables on the Clerk of Chatham and "convict" him *on account of* his literacy (see Act IV, sc. ii). Thus, it seems entirely plausible to me that, despite the fact that the neck verse warrants only marginal comment from recent literacy historians (see especially Cressy's dismissal of the test's relevance for the lives of "most people" [16–17]), the reading test's meaning was quite well-known to the general public, and its dire consequences were equally well-feared.

5. I employ pronouns in the masculine form advisedly, for the reading test—as the legal mechanism intended to ensure the prudent use of the benefit of clergy exemption—was offered only to "legitimate" members of the clergy, a profession that was at the time unavailable to women. In fact, it was not until very late in the history of the benefit of clergy exemption that the privilege was extended to women at all, with the possible exception of nuns; and, on that point, the existing records are not very clear. The formal inclusion of women within the purview of the benefit was legislated in 1692, during the reign of William and Mary. It was only after this time that the reading test was offered to all women prisoners, regardless of their criminal offense.

6. I recognize that the question of exigency, specifically in its relationship to the meaning of and/or participation in any "rhetorical situation," remains a strong point of contention in the field. Bitzer's famous essay, "The Rhetorical Situation," and the various responses it has drawn from the field (most notably Vatz; Consigny; Hunsaker and Smith; Brinton; Biesecker; Garrett and Xiao; and Smith and Lybarger) provide a number of perspectives on the ways we might define the term and/or theorize its function in discursive situations that are viewed as "rhetorical." To my way of thinking, however, the examination of the idea/meaning of exigency relative to large-scale, legislatively mandated literacy testing situations remains seriously undertheorized, perhaps even owing to the resilience of Bitzer's model which, despite these compelling critiques, still informs much of our thinking about testing situations as being somehow divorced from any (real) rhetorical concerns. Much of my research is, therefore, directed at re-theorizing the testing situation as constituting a (real) rhetorical situation, especially for those individuals whom we continue to require to take literacy tests—(real) people who face (very real) consequences and who are, in my opinion, fully aware of the social, political, and economic exigencies that prompt the institution of the test(s) and thus remain operative in the testing situation itself. That is to say that, my work aims to extend the scholarship that is already responding to this need to better theorize the meaning(s), use(s), and consequence(s) of all forms of literacy assessment for actual test-takers and, in this way, seeks to more fully address the impact of legislating "high-stakes" testing policies.

7. The *privilegium clericale* in its full significance in canon law is a much more inclusive term than the "benefit of clergy" legal exemption which is my focus here. Clerical rights have historically included: Personal immunity from lesser court authority; Freedom from taxation; Freedom from military and civil service, impressments, or obligation; Privilege of free travel (no tolls or curfews); Privilege of room and board; Privilege of sanctification; Privilege of sanctuary; and the General Rights of Respect (see Revised Catholic Encyclopedia). The specific point of the *privilegium clericale* upon which the courts Christian relied was the privilege of "personal immunity from lesser secular authorities," which stipulates that priests are inviolate and, as direct spokesmen of the deity, may not be touched or restrained in a hostile manner. It is also worth mentioning that the benefit of clergy exemption, which underwent a number of legal permutations from its inception until it was abolished from British common law in 1827 [7 George IV], was also adopted and recognized in American colonial, and later, U.S. state legislation until the middle nineteenth century (abolished in Virginia in 1848; Kentucky in 1852; and North and South Carolina in 1854). George Dalzell's *Benefit of Clergy in America* provides an excellent history of the uses and implications of the exemption in its American context(s).

8. The struggle between Henry II and Archbishop Thomas Becket is perhaps the most famous clash between secular and ecclesiastical authority. Excellent sources concerning the significance of Henry II and Becket's dispute include H. W. C. Davis (1905) *England Under the Normans and Angevins, 1066–1272;* and J. C. Robertson (1875–1885) *Materials for the History of Thomas Becket, Archbishop of Canterbury,* 7 vols.

9.   Since the original beneficiaries of the privilege were the *clericus* (read: ordained clergy including monks), any one of three modes of "proof" was generally accepted by the secular judge: (1) evidence of first tonsure (i.e., the first step preparatory to entering the priesthood, conferred by the Bishop, who shaves the crown of the candidate's head); (2) examination of Holy Orders; and (3) appearance in court *in habitus clericus* (i.e., wearing full clerical habit). However, and as Gabel remarks, in reality "there was nothing to prevent any person's securing for himself the externals of clerkship if he were not too sensitive to the spiritual censures thus to be incurred. A gaoler himself might confer a tonsure!" (64). A "faked" first tonsure was apparently an especially common occurrence. In her book, Gabel relates a remarkable story of Robert de Neuby, a prisoner at Newgate Prison, who earned the secular court judge's suspicion by appearing in court with a fresh tonsure (*quod corona sua de novo rasa est*). And although the results of the court's inquiry into the case are not reported, Gabel concludes that "one gathers from the close scrutiny with which the judge observed the prisoner that the ruse was not unfamiliar to him" (64). Likewise, it is not difficult to imagine that minor order clerics, who may have well been studied in "letters" and certainly had access to priestly vestments, could (and did) forge Holy Orders and/or could (and did) procure clerical habits in less than honest ways.

10. The reading test which appeared in secular courtrooms with increasing regularity was not the result of a singular legislative event per se, but instead took shape slowly, over the course of the late thirteenth and early fourteenth centuries, throughout which time the test frequently occurs side-by-side with the three "older" modes of proof and merely constitutes "accessory proof." For example, in 1300 [28 Edward I] William Asshendene, a cleric charged with murder, was able to prove his literacy but was ultimately sentenced to death because he failed to appear in *habitum et tonsuram clericalem* (Gabel 65). By the middle 1300s, however, the reading test was more regularly regarded as "proof competent." Gabel provides a wonderful example of the vast power granted to the neck verse by relating the case of John, son of Thomas Dennyson Trotter senior, in 1366 [39 Edward III]. She writes,

> On being summoned before the justices to answer a charge of murder as well as to several indictments, the accused said he was a clerk and could not answer without his Ordinary. Thereupon the Vicar of St. Lawrence's, Appleby, as the Ordinary of the Bishop of Carlisle, handed him a Psalter. The results were extremely dubious, for John, as the record says, could neither read nor "syllabicare," yet seemed to know certain passages by rote. At this point the secular judge gave him the book upside down, but the prisoner "read" as before, in nowise disturbed by the altered circumstance. [...] The jury took an inquest, the findings of which are curious. The prisoner was discovered to have been a layman and illiterate at the time of his arrest, but had been taught what he knew by two boys from Appleby, who had been admitted to the gaol through the good offices of the gaoler. [John] was pronounced guilty of the charges and remitted to prison, as a layman refusing to stand to the common law of the realm. *The offence as regards the pretended literacy was really the gaoler's, for if the prisoner had actually succeeded in learning to read while in gaol, his claim to clergy would have held, though the gaoler might have been punished.* (73, emphasis added)

11. That the reading test caused more problems for the courts than had been anticipated is implied by the number of legislative changes made to the benefit of clergy exemption itself. Put plainly, the reading test came to be viewed as not restrictive enough for the determination of a felon's "legitimacy." It is telling that, over time, the reformations made to the benefit of clergy exemption were directed in one of two ways: (1) restricting the kinds of offenses for which no one would be able to claim the privilege and (2) redrawing the boundaries between "legitimate" religious clerics and "legitimate" secular clerks. On the subject of non-clergyable offenses, historian Frank McLynn suggests the following dramatic progression: in 1225, only two felonies would have been outside the pale of the benefit (i.e., high treason and sacrilege); in 1688, 50 felonies were listed as non-clergyable for secular clerks (including murder, petit treason, rape, arson, burglary, counter-

feiting, and poisoning); in 1765, the list grew to include 160 non-clergyable offenses; and by 1815, at the height of the infamous "Bloody Code" of England, a full 225 offenses were outside the benefit of clergy exemption (xi). These later restrictions were applied to secular clerks only, due in large measure to Henry VII's reactionary legislative maneuvers. Henry VII's famous statute "An Act to Take Awaye the Benefytt of Clergye from Certayne Persons" (1489), which forcefully reestablished the line between religious and secular clerks, was by far the most drastic of all the restrictions applied to the exemption. The statute asserts that

> bicause they have ben contineully admitted to the benefifice of the Clergie as ofte as they did offend in any of the premisses: In avoiding of such presumptuous boldnes, be it enacted ordeyned and stablisshed by thauctorite of this present parliament that every persone not being with orders, whiche onys hath ben admytted to the benefice of his Clergie, eftsonys arayned of eny suche offence, be not admytted to have the benefice or privilege of his Clergie; And that every suche persone so convicted for murder, to be marked with a M upon the brawne of the lefte thumbe, and if he be for eny other felony, the same persone to be marked with a T in the same place of the thumbe, and theis markes to be made by the Gaillor openly in the Courte before the Jugge, er that such persone be delivered to the Ordinary. (qtd. in Gabel 123–24)

The legal rationale for branding the thumbs of all secular literate felons was, of course, to provide evidence should this same criminal be brought before the courts at any time in the future.

12.   Notable contributions to the recent refiguring of literacy as an inherently social practice, conditioned by the ideological and political interests and values of a given society, include: Barton (1994) *Literacy: An Introduction to the Ecology of Written Communication;* Graff (1987) *The Legacies of Literacy;* Heath (1983) *Ways with Words;* Ivanic (1998) *Writing and Identity;* and Street (1984) *Literacy in Theory and Practice.*

WORKS CITED

Barton, David. *Literacy: An Introduction to the Ecology of Written Communication.* Oxford: Blackwell, 1994.
Biesecker, Barbara A. "Rethinking the Rhetorical Situation from within the Thematic of Différance." *Philosophy and Rhetoric* 22 (1989): 110–30.
Bitzer, Lloyd. "The Rhetorical Situation." *Philosophy and Rhetoric* 1 (1968): 1–14.
Brinton, Alan. "Situation in the Theory of Rhetoric." *Philosophy and Rhetoric* 14 (1981): 234–48.
Clanchy, M. T. *From Memory to Written Record, England 1066–1307.* London: Edward Arnold, 1979.
Consigny, Scott. "Rhetoric and Its Situations." *Philosophy and Rhetoric* 7 (1974): 175–86.
Cressy, David. *Literacy and the Social Order: Reading and Writing in Tudor and Stuart England.* Cambridge: Cambridge UP, 1980.
Dalzell, George. *Benefit of Clergy in America & Related Matters.* Winston-Salem: Blair, 1955.
Davis, H. W. C. *England Under the Normans and Angevins, 1066–1272.* London: Methuen, 1912.
Gabel, L. C. *Benefit of Clergy in England in the Later Middle Ages* (1928–29). Rpt. New York: Octagon, 1969.
Garrett, Mary, and Xiaosui Xiao. "The Rhetorical Situation Revisited." *Rhetoric Society Quarterly* 23.2 (1993): 30–40.
Graff, Harvey. *The Legacies of Literacy: Continuities and Contradictions in Western Culture and Society.* Bloomington: Indiana UP, 1987.
Heath, Shirley Brice. *Ways with Words: Language, Life, and Work in Communities and Classrooms.* Cambridge: Cambridge UP, 1983.
Horner, Bruce, and John Trimbur. "English Only and U.S. College Composition." *CCC* 53.4 (2002): 594–630.
Hunsaker, David M., and Craig R. Smith. "A Constructive Approach to Situational Rhetoric." *Western Speech Communication* 40.3 (1976): 144–55.

Ivanic, Roz. *Writing and Identity: The Discoursal Construction of Identity in Academic Writing.* Amsterdam: John Benjamins, 1998.

McLynn, Frank. *Crime and Punishment in Eighteenth-Century England.* New York: Routledge, 1989.

Revised Catholic Encyclopedia, Vol. II. Robert Appleton Company, 1907. Online edition. K. Knight *Imprimatur* and John M. Farley, Archbishop of New York, 2003. <http://www.newadvent.org/cathen/02476a.htm>.

Robertson, J. C., ed. *Materials for the History of Thomas Becket, Archbishop of Canterbury,* 7 vols. London: Longman, 1875–1885.

Smith, Craig R., and Scott Lybarger. "Bitzer's Model Reconstructed." *Communication Quarterly* 44.2 (1996): 197–213.

Street, Brian V. *Literacy in Theory and Practice.* Cambridge: Cambridge UP, 1984.

Vatz, Richard. "The Myth of the Rhetorical Situation." *Philosophy and Rhetoric* 6 (1973): 154–61.

10

Campbell's View of Argument as Comparison Advances His Religious Agenda

Beth Innocenti Manolescu
University of Kansas

Not all scholars maintain that Campbell's *Philosophy of Rhetoric* covers invention (Walzer, *Campbell* 4, 27, 103), but those who do have connected it to style. One has described the inventional problem as how to enliven ideas (Bitzer, "Hume's" 158, 160; Bitzer, "Introduction" xxxii) and another as how to balance thought and language to achieve the ends of discourse (Ulman 107). Despite attention to invention and style, however, neither these scholars nor others have explicated Campbell's view of the relationship between style and argument. Doing so is worthwhile for three reasons. First, style is the most discussed canon in *Philosophy of Rhetoric*, so a better understanding of the relationship between style and argument will lead to a better understanding of the book. Second, argument is as essential as emotion in Campbell's analysis of persuasion—"the speaker must always assume the character of the close candid reasoner: for though he may be an acute logician who is no orator, he will never be a consummate orator who is no logician" (61; see also 78)—but only his treatment of emotion has received scholarly attention (Walzer, "Campbell," *Campbell*). Third, scholars continue to find the relationship between style and argument worth theoretical and critical attention for understanding, analyzing, and evaluating rhetoric and argumentation (see, e.g., example Conley; Fahnestock; Leff, "Relation" 56–57, "Rhetoric" 246–47; Manolescu, "Formal"; Tindale), so a study of Campbell can contribute to this research program.

I argue that *Philosophy of Rhetoric* offers a theory of inventing arguments that makes them equivalent to style only if they involve comparison. I outline implications of Campbell's view of the relationship between style and argument; and conclude by arguing that Campbell's view of their relationship is shaped in part by his spiritual agenda. Thus, the essay also contributes to the project of identifying religious principles that shape Campbell's rhetorical theory (Bitzer, "Introduction" xlvii–li; Bitzer, "Religious"; Walzer, *Campbell*) and offers a case study of how a religious agenda can shape rhetorical theory.

Campbell holds that discovering the grounding in human nature of rhetorical precepts will enhance inventional faculties. In the introduction to *Philosophy of Rhetoric*, he notes that the orator's own faculties contribute to proficiency in the art and that "a more thorough investigation of the latent energies [...] whereby the instruments employed by eloquence produce their effect upon hearers, will serve considerably [...] to enrich the fancy" which, in turn, will suggest "the proper mediums [...] whereby the necessary aids of topics, arguments, illustrations, and motives, may be procured" (lxxiv). So understanding how rhetorical precepts are founded in human nature enriches rhetors' imaginations which enables invention.

Campbell describes argument in *Philosophy of Rhetoric* in terms of style. First, he describes argument as the "predominant quality" of addresses to the understanding designed to prove a position disbelieved or doubted (2). The "quality" of argument in addresses aimed at conviction corresponds to the quality of perspicuity that characterizes addresses aimed at instruction. Second, he asserts that "all argument is a kind of comparison" (14). The simplest case is argument by analogy. As Campbell puts it, "What are rhetorical comparisons, when brought to illustrate any point inculcated on the hearers [...] but arguments from analogy" (74). He then cites a passage from Quintilian that claims the significance of the need for education for the mind by considering the importance of culture to the ground. But Campbell means to class other kinds of comparison as arguments. Following his observation about rhetorical comparisons being arguments from analogy, he asserts:

> Now if comparison, which is the chief, hath so great an influence upon conviction, it is no wonder that all those other oratorical tropes and figures addressed to the imagination, which are more or less nearly related to comparison, should derive hence both life and efficacy. Even antithesis implies comparison. Simile is comparison in epitome. Metaphor is an allegory in miniature. Allegory and prosopopoeia are comparisons conveyed under a particular form. (75)

So the range of forms that may count as arguments include antithesis, simile, metaphor, allegory, and prosopopoeia. They may serve as arguments because they involve comparison and are tied to conviction.

Campbell limits the overlap between style and argument to comparison because in his view, argument is comprised of thought and language, and thought and language overlap only in comparison. It is noteworthy, first, that for Campbell there is a hard and fast distinction between language and thought; and, second, that the laws of thought are universal while language is relative. Campbell speculates that "[i]n every region of the globe we may soon discover, that people feel and argue in much the same manner, but the speech of one nation is quite unintelligible to another. The art of the logician is accordingly, in some sense, universal; the art of the grammarian is always particular and local" (34). These ideas not only shape his view of the relationship between style and argument but also serve to advance his spiritual agenda.

For Campbell, reasoning is comparing. Like his contemporaries, Campbell describes the function of the faculty of understanding as comparison. He describes reasoning as a comparison of past and present facts to identify similarities and differences. For example, comparing a falling tile, apple, and other objects over time provides an initial idea of gravitation. Dogs and other animals, according to Campbell, have "an original incapacity of classing, and [...] of generalizing their perceptions," but humans are superior to animals, and some humans are superior to other humans (48). Campbell asserts that we call this activity of mind "reasoning" to the extent that we deliberately exert it and are therefore conscious of it (49). So style involving comparison makes use of the same mental acts as reasoning.

Campbell conceives of invention as comparison and describes it in terms of both argument and style. When taking up the question of the difference between addressing the understanding and addressing the imagination, Campbell suggests that there is a continuum of appeals. One end marks addresses primarily to understanding, the other end marks addresses primarily to imagination, and the midpoint marks addresses equally to both. An address primarily to the understanding would involve comparisons of individuals of the same species, such as "man to man, eagle to eagle, sea to sea" (74); or comparison between one species to another species of the same genus such as lion to tiger or alder to oak. Imagination notes these kinds of comparison, according to Campbell, but "to the faculty of imagination, this resemblance appears rather under the notion of identity; although it be the foundation of the strongest reasoning from experience" (74). Significantly, he notes that comparisons between species of the same genus can serve as "a considerable fund of argumentation" (74). A third case involves the midpoint of the understanding-imagination continuum, to which both faculties "have an equal claim" (74): analogy. Here he mentions the passage from Quintilian that compares education with cultivation and continues with cases that may address imagination more than understanding, namely, different kinds of comparison such as simile, metaphor, and allegory. Presumably these figures can also serve as a "fund of argumentation." Although Campbell holds that figures originate in principles of the human mind rather than "inventions of art" (316), he would certainly hold that, as reason itself, the comparisons involved are voluntary to at least some degree. His use of the "allegoric style" to compare probability and plausibility, as well as his request for indulgence for the style, are signs that figures involving comparison may be invented (85–86).

In sum, for Campbell, style and argument overlap with the act of comparison, and comparison is an act of invention. This is a potentially rich conception of the relationship between style and argument. If we take comparison in a broad sense, as a way of seeing different kinds of relationships, then we could generate an inventional system consisting of different kinds of relationships like Perelman and Olbrechts-Tyteca's liaisons in *The New Rhetoric*. But Campbell does not take us nearly this far. Style and argument overlap incidentally rather than fundamentally, a point illustrated by how Campbell positions figures on a thought-expression continuum. At the thought end are figures that are on the understanding-imagination continuum, namely, antithesis, simile, allegory, and so on. He positions metaphor at the midpoint—as holding equally of thought and expression. But, according to Campbell, other figures such as syncecdoche and metonymy hold more of expression than thought. For Campbell, this means that the figure is founded on language use rather than the nature of things (295-96); prosopopoeia may be translated into other languages, but metonymy may not make sense when translated into another language. Thus translation becomes a test or sign of the extent to which style represents thought or is merely conventional.

This conception of the relationship between style and argument advances Campbell's spiritual agenda. During his lifetime, Campbell staked his reputation not on *Philosophy of Rhetoric* but on his translation of the gospels, first published in 1789. Linking the two is justified, first, by the fact that he was working on them around the same time. The preface of each work states that he began working on it around 1750 (*Philosophy*, lxv; *Gospels*, i); *Philosophy of Rhetoric* was first published in 1776 while in *The Four Gospels* Campbell mentions that part of it "was written towards the end of the American war" (56). Second, he brings up

Biblical translations at a number of points in *Philosophy of Rhetoric* (see, e.g., 177, 181, 183n8, 189, 210, 230, 234, 235, 238-39, 296–97n2, 307n7, 313, 314, 347-48, 352, 360-61, 361n2), a sign that translation was on his mind while composing it. Third, in both he describes argument in terms of style. We have seen this in *Philosophy of Rhetoric*. In *The Four Gospels*, describing Jesus' style as often didactic and argumentative, Campbell notes that he is using "arguing" according to "popular language" rather than "strict propriety" (32). In "strict propriety," argument takes a deductive form; but "popular language" would call a parable an argument. Both the "strict" and "popular" senses of "argument" involve reasoning, but the reasoning is presented in different styles. As Campbell puts it:

> when a similitude or an example is made to supply the place of argument, in support of a particular sentiment, he [Jesus] does not formally deduce the conclusion, but either leaves it to the reflections of his hearers, or draws it from their own mouths by a single question. This, without the parade of reasoning, is, in practical subjects, the strongest of all reasoning. After candidly stating an apposite case, it is appealing for the decision, not to prejudice or the passions, but to the natural sense of good and evil, even of his adversaries. (32)

A similar desire to avoid a "parade of reasoning" is evident in one of his objections to the syllogism in *Philosophy of Rhetoric*: the syllogism "bears the manifest indications of an artificial and ostentatious parade of learning, calculated for giving the appearance of great profundity to what in fact is very shallow" (62). So his broader conception of argument derives from his attention to audience.

Campbell's role as translator of the Gospels and interest in defending the authority of revealed religion help to account for his position that logic is universal while language is relative and therefore why argument and style overlap only in comparison. First, he conceives of his role as a translator as putting the author's thoughts into the words of his own language. As he puts it in *The Four Gospels*: "The thoughts are the author's; the translator's business is to convey them unadulterated, in the words of another language. To blend them with his own sentiments, or with any sentiments which are not the author's, is to discharge the humble office of translator unfaithfully" (vi). The aim of maintaining the thought while changing only the language presumes a clear distinction between the two. But it is important for him to maintain the distinction so he can claim to present the substance of divine revelation in spite of the translation.

Second, he enters a debate regarding the eloquence of the Gospels, taking issue both with those who praise their style as a way of defending their authority and with those who argue that their lack of eloquence is a sign that they are not divinely inspired since everything that comes from God must be perfect in its kind (5–6; Manolescu, "Clerics"). Campbell holds that, besides features of style relevant to the ear such as harmony, "every excellency of style is relative, arising solely from its fitness for producing, in the mind of the reader, the end intended by the writer" (8). Excellence in style for Campbell, then, consists in how well it achieves desired effects, and this is relative to the audience. Thus, he has another religious motive for viewing style as relative.

Third, he offers an explanation for the diversity in style of divinely inspired writers:

> that the Holy Spirit should always employ the same style in conveying celestial truths to men, is no more necessary than that he should always use the same language. People do not sufficiently advert, when they speak on this subject, to the difference between the expression and the sentiment, but strangely confound these, as though they were the same; yet no two things can be more widely

different. The truths implied in the sentiments, are essential, immutable, and have an intrinsic value: the words which compose the expression, are in their nature circumstantial, changeable, and have no other value than what they derive from the arbitrary conventions of men. (10)

Thus, a clear distinction between thought and language as well as an elevation of thought to universal status with language as merely relative allow Campbell to defend the authority of revelation despite the Gospels' stylistic flaws and diversity.

In sum, Campbell advances provocative starting points for thinking about the relationship between argument and style. Conceiving of argument as a kind of comparison offers the potential for bridging the apparent thought-language dichotomy, since comparisons partake of both thought and language. It offers the potential for conceiving of reasoning more broadly—beyond deductions or inferential leaps to "seeing" the point for which a parable, metaphor, wit, or irony serves as an argument. But Campbell's spiritual agenda is partly to blame for these potentials remaining unexplored in *Philosophy of Rhetoric*. As a translator of the Gospels and defender of the authority of revealed religion, Campbell accepts a hard and fast distinction between thought and language and holds that style is merely relative while thought is universal. In any case, I think Campbell's description of argument in terms of style is worth exploring as a starting point for a productive and substantive conception of invention, argument, and style.

WORKS CITED

Bitzer, Lloyd F. "Hume's Philosophy in George Campbell's Philosophy of Rhetoric." *Philosophy and Rhetoric* 2 (1969): 139–66.

——. "Introduction." *Philosophy of Rhetoric*. Ed. Lloyd F. Bitzer. Carbondale: Southern Illinois UP, 1988. vii–li.

——. "Religious and Scientific Foundations of 18th-Century Theories of Rhetoric." Van Zelst Lecture in Communication. Northwestern University, Evanston, IL. 11 May, 1995.

Campbell, George. *The Four Gospels, Translated from the Greek, with Preliminary Dissertations, and Notes Critical and Explanatory*. Philadelphia, 1799.

——. *The Philosophy of Rhetoric*. Ed. Lloyd F. Bitzer. Carbondale: Southern Illinois UP, 1988.

Conley, Thomas. "What Jokes Can Tell Us about Arguments." *A Companion to Rhetoric and Rhetorical Criticism*. Ed. Walter Jost and Wendy Olmsted. Malden: Blackwell, 2004. 266–77.

Fahnestock, Jeanne. *Rhetorical Figures in Science*. New York: Oxford UP, 1999.

Leff, Michael. "The Relation between Dialectic and Rhetoric in a Classical and Modern Perspective." *Dialectic and Rhetoric: The Warp and Woof of Argumentation* Analysis. Ed. Frans H. van Eemeren and Peter Houtlosser. Dorcrecht: Kluwer, 2002. 53–63.

——. "Rhetoric and Dialectic in the Twenty-First Century." *Argumentation* 14 (2000): 241–54.

Manolescu, Beth Innocenti. "Clerics Competing for and against 'Eloquence' in Mid-Eighteenth-Century Britain." *Rhetoric Society Quarterly* 30 (2000): 47–67.

——. "Formal Propriety as Rhetorical Norm." *Argumentation* 18 (2004): 113–25.

Tindale, Christopher W. *Acts of Arguing: A Rhetorical Model of Argument*. Albany: State U of New York P, 1999.

Ulman, H. Lewis. *Things, Thoughts, Words, and Actions: The Problem of Language in Late Eighteenth-Century British Rhetorical Theory*. Carbondale: Southern Illinois UP, 1994.

Walzer, Arthur E. "Campbell on the Passions: A Rereading of the *Philosophy of Rhetoric*." *Quarterly Journal of Speech* 85 (1999): 72–85.

——. *George Campbell: Rhetoric in the Age of Enlightenment*. Albany: State U of New York P, 2003.

III

Theory

11

Aristotle, Kenneth Burke, and the Transubstantiation of Place

Jerry Blitefield
University of Massachusetts–Dartmouth

In his *Grammar of Motives,* Kenneth Burke titles the first section "Ways of Placement," and the first chapter within that section, "Container and Thing Contained." Perhaps it is coincidental that *container* and *thing contained* are the identical terms that Aristotle uses when theorizing ways of placement in Book IV of his *Physics.* More likely, Burke uses Aristotle's figuration of place as a metaphor for constructing the all-encompassing "scene." If Burke borrows from Aristotle to get at place, he gives no indication; but as he is talking about ways of placement, and as Aristotle's Book IV develops a theory of place which may have been originary to the dramatistic notion of "scene," it is useful to compare Burke's and Aristotle's approach to place.

The coordinating conjunction in Burke's "Container and Thing Contained" identifies his subject as not just a definition of two objects but rather as an analysis of the relationship between the two, in this instance, "scene" and "act," also known as "the scene-act ratio." Prior to exploring that relationship, Burke says, "Using 'scene' in the sense of setting or background, and 'act' in the sense of action, one could say that 'the scene contains the act'" (3). If Burke's goal, however, is to explain ways of placement, as the title to Part I suggests, ultimately, he misconstrues place, at least from an Aristotelian perspective. In "Container and Thing Contained," Burke conflates scene with place, burying it within so much Ibsenian, O'Neilian, and Shakespearean signification that the container itself, place, cannot be genuinely discerned. Referring to it variously as "setting, or background" and "stage-sets" (3), Burke goes on to read a bit of Ibsen's *An Enemy of the People* as "a good instance of the scene-act ratio, since the correlations between scene and act are readily observable" (3).

For Burke, those "correlations" are symbolic and largely dialogic: scene and act prove each other, both guiding and affirming for the audience what they, the audience, experience as the play unfolds. Scene murmurs act; act restates scene. As an interpretive tool for drama this is fine, but for rhetoric, it is insufficient. For while the scene-act ratio may offer a way to probe the meaning of the play, it does so at the expense of glossing over the real issue of "Container and Thing Contained." If we are to understand this play *fully* from a rhetorical perspective then, we have to see more than just the act contained within the scene: we must see the play contained within the playhouse. That is, we must understand that the success or failure of Ibsen's play is as much contingent upon the building, the place of the play, as upon the script, the acting, the direction, or anything else which goes into its production. And by "building," I mean simply that thing in which the play comes to be, that thing whose existence allows the play to unfold, from curtain rise to curtain fall. At this most basic level, unless the play gains access to the place which is the playhouse, Ibsen's scene will matter little to its acts, because no one will see either.

From Aristotle, we get "container" and "thing contained" as means of arriving at a universal understanding of what place is and what it does. From Aristotle, place arrives as a slippery notion. He describes it in terms of an urn, a vessel which can hold water or wine or air, but which remains unchanged regardless of contents. The slippery part is that only the two-dimensional, innermost surface coming into contact with the contents constitutes their place; the material outside that two-dimensional surface, for example, the actual urn, constitutes matter and form. And though I anticipate that defining place as that innermost surface could undermine what I have to say later in this chapter, it must be understood that form too exists within a place, met at its outermost surface. In a sense, form allows place to do its thing, both on its innermost and outermost surfaces. Sticking with Aristotle's innermost criterion for now, he goes on to say the effectiveness of that innermost containing surface determines the quality of it as a place; that is, the extent to which it is able to contain the things it contains is the degree to which it functions as a place for its contents: even though form may enhance that innermost surface's ability to contain, only that innermost surface is the containing place, according to Aristotle.

Admittedly, this is an oversimplification of Aristotle's theory (even when it is fully elaborated, it's got problems). Yet, even incomplete, Aristotle's sense of place offers us a useful hermeneutic to set alongside Burke's. Though both use "container" and "thing contained," we get from each radically different concerns. Burke directs our focus toward the play: "In any case, examining first the relation between scene and act, all we need note here is the principle whereby the scene is a fit 'container' for the act, expressing in fixed properties the same quality that the action expresses in terms of development" (3).

Aristotle steers us toward the playhouse: "Another thing is plain: since the vessel is no part of what is in it (what contains in the strict sense is different from what is contained), place could not be either the matter or the form of the thing contained, but must be different—for the latter, both the matter and the shape, are parts of what is contained" (210b27). While scene and act, as container and thing contained, are for Burke symbiotic, container and thing contained for Aristotle are necessarily separable, as place is always prior and indifferent to that which it contains. Burke may give scene-as-place a certain hardness or texture—setting, background (and later context, condition, even "situation")—another lexicon (or perhaps culture?) with which to understand act, but its power is symbolically interpretive of human action. For Aristotle, however, because the place and things in place can never be the same, and as place is always prior to the things it contains, place has not only physical power but also ontological power. Edward Casey sums up the ontological significance for Aristotle's place this way: "Without place things would not only fail to be located; they would not even be *things:* they would *have no place to be the things they are*" (71). This makes place materially prior to something's "isness," for, from a physical standpoint, something cannot be nowhere; it must be somewhere and, as such, must inhabit something else in order to be and to become. Before something can come to be, there must be a place prior to it which can contain it.

From a rhetorical standpoint (and other standpoints as well, such as politics), the implications of Aristotle's simple dictum are remarkable, for the "thing" of physical/material discourse, then, is also either nowhere or in something else. Burke is right that scene contains act, but he elides the true significance of place in the process of his analysis. Case in point: this past winter Adbusters, the Canadian culturejammers, bid to purchase airtime during the Superbowl in which they would have delivered one of their anticonsumerist messages. FOX refused to run it. According to *Adbusters* magazine, Tim Souris, of the network's broadcast standards department, offered Adbusters this defense: "You must understand, for a broadcast TV network things like boycotting television and anti-consumerism might not go over very well with our other advertisers" (*Adbusters* npn).

From a scenic perspective, we can look at the consumerist culture which the ad sought to admonish, or even the celebration of capitalist competition which the Superbowl has come to be, and from these understand FOX's rejection of the Adbuster bid. But from an Aristotelian perspective, simply put, as the Adbusters message never found a place within the game's broadcast, at least on that day, for that audience, it remained not only nowhere, but as a result, physically nothing. As the ad never took place, literally, it never was, rhetorically, either. Another example would be Judy Chicago's sizeable and controversial installation *The Dinner Party*. Though recently purchased for permanent exhibition by the Brooklyn Museum of Art, *The Dinner Party* has led a nomadic life since its creation in 1979. A dramatistic analysis might argue that *The Dinner Party* (act) is rarely exhibited for its feminist message (agency) which critiques the larger patriarchal society (scene, container); from a placial perspective, one might examine whether the installation—a triangular table whose three sides each measure forty-eight feet—is so large and needs so much room in which to be exhibited that few galleries and museums can actually host it. Regardless, the results have been the same: without a place, for most of its days *The Dinner Party* remained boxed in storage, mute and rhetorically nowhere.

There is a second element crucial to place, implied in Aristotle but unstated: place contains (surrounds), but it also protects, seals out, serves as a boundary. Referring to a statement on place by the fourth-century mathematician and philosopher, Archytas of Tarentum, Edward Casey writes this about Aristotle: "Aristotle surpasses Archytas, however, in his eagerness to show just how 'it is obvious that one has to grant priority to place', and just why 'it is the first of all things'. He does so by demonstrating that place, beyond providing mere position, gives bountiful aegis---active protective support---to what it locates" (71).

Though Burke doesn't point to it directly, his sense of place conveyed through scene likewise sets boundaries, for while setting and such may contribute to the play, they also proscribe the ways in which the audience should see the play, literally and figuratively. That is, while apt scene properly contextualizes act, it does so by making the relationship between scene, act, and audience consistent and intuitive. Scene identifies with act: it allies itself with act to ensure discursive discipline. It works to actively hone audience imagination as it directs that imagination back to act; similarly, it restricts the imagination from interpreting act any old way.

For Aristotle, however, because place is indifferent to its contents, because it will hold water as impartially as it will hold wine, it can never be allied with its contents as can scene be with act. Place is always a matter of resistance. How well it resists the escape of that which it contains, coupled with how well it resists the challenges by that which it excludes, determines its completeness. To serve well, place must exert sufficient force to keep its contents under control and to keep other contents from penetrating.

The function of place then is of two kinds: to keep in that which is within and to keep out that which is without. As it performs these Janus-like functions, it can be assumed that place has power. The degree to which place has power is the degree to which it can function as container and boundary. For Burke, this function is symbolic. Using his dramatic analogy, the power with which a scene is set will present a calculus for invoking audience imagination vis-à-vis act: The stronger the scene, the less imagination the audience needs bring to the performance; the weaker the scene, the more imagination the audience needs to bring to the performance. In some ways, this is a basic distinction between stage and screen.

As a matter of physics, though, place takes on a much more elemental, though perhaps less perceptible role than scene. For example, a small drama company in my town recently purchased a restaurant-turned-theater in which to make its home. The building is old but sturdy. Its roof does a good job of keeping out the rain and snow and most anything else which could fall from the sky, but that same roof also does a good job of trapping heat, so that in the summer the theater's temperatures can be stifling. Lacking the resources, that is, power, at present to install air conditioning, in order to release the heat in that place, the building's (container's) windows must be opened to allow an exchange of hot air for cool. But opening the windows also admits the roar of the many open-tailpipe Harleys which cruise the streets summer nights, whose loud throttling drowns out spoken lines, gobbling up bits and pieces of dialogue, which, unheard, are lost to the audience.

In this instance, we can see how the power of place is a primary rhetorical concern; but it is also a primary political concern, for the power to exercise a place, to control a place, clearly determines the discourse which can transpire within: robust power imperceptibly ensures air conditioning, soundproof windows (if windows at all), and thick walls; an undisturbed performance. Marginal power has to contend with Harley Davidsons and the corruption, even interruption, of delivery. If place, with its ability to physically include/exclude, is by its very being already an instantiation of power (for how else could it include or exclude?), then the power in place can remain intact only so long as its power is greater than that of whatever power(s) may challenge it. The power of place as a double-edged container is therefore the predominant determinant of rhetorical discourse, the ability to control place as a site of inclusion, coupled with the power to control place as a site of exclusion, will determine the potential rhetorical parameters of that place. The relationship of the rhetor to that power in place is therefore also contingent upon the relative power in and over place: the stronger the relationship, the greater the opportunity and control of discourse; the weaker the relationship, the more tenuous the opportunity and control of discourse. Place, then, is always an expression and definition of power.

Let's return to Burke and an elaboration on the scene-act ratio. Speaking of how scene contains act, he says,

> Thus, when the curtain rises to disclose a certain stage-set, this stage-set contains, simultaneously, implicitly, all that the narrative is to draw out as a sequence, explicitly. Or, if you will, the stage-set contains the action *ambiguously* (as regards the norms of action)—and in the course of the play's development this ambiguity is converted into a corresponding *articulacy*. The proportion would be: scene is to act as implicit is to explicit. (7)

This corresponds with what I mentioned earlier regarding the dialogic and disciplinary nature of scene and act, but by extrapolation this excerpt has interesting results for place as the locus of power (and again, it is important not to conflate symbolic power with physical power, even though symbolic power is materialized in place *ipso facto*). Suppose, then, we substitute *place* for *scene* and *power* for *act,* so that we get "The proportion would be: place is to power as implicit is to explicit"? If the place is an expression of power, an implicit representation of the power explicit either within it or somewhere else, then place automatically becomes not just a site for discourse but a medium *of* discourse, an outward expresser of will and resources: place as agent. More than just a projection of power into the world, it also stakes a claim for that power on the future. Consequently, once power assumes materialization in place and as such projects that power into the world and becomes an agent of power, that place immediately becomes the very medium, perhaps the most potent medium, by which the power inherent in that place can be challenged. Consequently, it becomes a viable site of (contentious) discourse. Where before there was no medium for directly challenging power, place, once established, presents a lingering threshold for accessing that power. So here is the irony: As an extension of power, place also serves as the locus for undermining the very power it extends. Place becomes a double-agent. Here again Aristotle rings true. Dissent out of place is nowhere, and hence nothing: only place can bring discord into material being. Physical place becomes symbolic agent.

Does this mean that as materializations of power all places are by nature sites of struggle? Earlier I stated that places are by nature contested, both from within and from without. Generally, though, as the interface between power and public, most places achieve a benign equilibrium. But as power is both mutable and relative, places of power are by nature unstable and therefore vulnerable. Most cars, for instance, do not become sites of struggle. Yet, if gas prices continue to rise, and if emissions tolls on the environment increase, we may see more action against automobiles, especially the gas-guzzling SUVs, such as we had earlier this year when several Hummers got torched at a California dealership. As expressions of power, the greater the disequilibrium of power expressed between those who hold it and those who look upon it, the more salient that place becomes as a rhetorical medium, as a double-agent. That is, in its very corporeal nature, place presents a facade upon which to inscribe rhetorical discourse, even if only temporary in duration. It becomes an open page upon which to address not only the powerholders but also those others outside who look upon the discourse from a distance. That is, using the boundaries of place as rhetorical media addresses several audiences. Ostensibly, the first audience is the placeholders themselves. But inscribing a place also creates public discourse and can, when conducted properly, compose a public text. Political graffiti does this. So too can we see this polyvalent discourse in demonstrations outside houses of government. Universal to all pickets is the tacit statement, "If we had your power, if we were in your place, these are the changes we'd make," coupled with the implied warning/threat, "Pay attention to us or you may find yourself out of power, out of place." But the very fact of the demonstration proves that the demonstrators lack power. With the respect demonstrators accord place, they validate the power in place.

We can see more aggressive discourse, however, with activist groups such as Greenpeace, Earth First!, PETA, Act-Up!, and others, who hack into the power of place and once inside, create havoc outside. Perhaps Greenpeace has best understood the rhetorical double-agent potential of place, as their history is chronicled with invasive gestures which expose the explicit limits of power implied in place and act to publicly repudiate them; how often have we seen Greenpeace scale corporate buildings to hang banners embarrassing the very companies from whose buildings those banners hang, or disrupt whole military armadas with a few buzzing zodiacs? Still, despite its prankish activism to expose and mock oafish power, Greenpeace leaves those places intact and, as a consequence, tacitly and ultimately acknowledges the power expressed therein.

Surely the World Trade Center and the Pentagon were attacked as symbols, but targeting them was as much an assault on the physics of America as a secure place as on America as purveyor of Western lifestyle. It is unlikely that the hijackers thought they would actually bring down Western civilization with four airplanes; in fact, they may have even doubted that their launch into the Twin Towers would have produced such devastating results. But it is evident that they wanted to prove to the United States and to the world that America as a physical place was not as secure and untouchable as most of us assumed it to be, wanted it to be.

A dramatistic scene-act reading of 9/11 could produce endless possibilities: the hostility of radical Islam to Western culture produced an unprovoked attack; the profaning of Muslim culture by Western capitalism produced an act of resistance or retribution. As the stream of editorials have shown since, there are myriad competing scenes with which to contain those fiery acts. But, from a placial perspective, I offer a more efficient accounting. The destruction of those places was set in motion from the moment the first spade broke ground for those buildings. From the moment they began to materialize the colossal power of their maturity, they presaged their own destruction. If not in 2001, then sometime earlier or later; if not from planes, then from bombs; and if not from Al Qaeda, then from some other group. More than symbols of "America" or of American values, the Twin Towers and the Pentagon were targeted because they were the embodiment, the identifiable agents, of a massive disequilibrium of power and because as places they were, therefore, targetable. Now that security around the Pentagon has no doubt been elevated to apparently impervious levels, one of two possibilities exists (or maybe both): either terrorists will plot new ways to confound Pentagon security, or they will simply move on to a next-level place of power. And it is incontrovertible, as Daniel Benjamin wrote recently in *The New York Times*, that the proposed "Freedom Tower" planned for construction on so-called ground zero will immediately become a "1,776-foot-tall target." Not only will the "Freedom Tower" be targeted for what it will represent symbolically, it will also be targeted for what it will make present materially: power coalesced, and therefore captive, in place. In a piece prepared for *Le Monde*, Jean Baudrillard said,

> An allergy to all definitive order, to all definitive power is happily universal, and the two towers of the World Trade Center embodied perfectly, in their very double-ness (literally twin-ness), this definitive order. As if every domination apparatus were creating its own antibody, the chemistry of its own disappearance; against this almost automatic reversal of its own puissance, the system is powerless.

The attacks were intended to show the ultimate failure of America as a place. Whether or not that failure is correctable is a question never to be fully and finally answered, and as such, already has been.

WORKS CITED

Adbusters: Journal of the Mental Environment. No. 51: Jan/Feb, 2004.

Aristotle. *Physics.* Trans. R. P. Hardie and R. K. Gaye. *The Works of Aristotle Translated into English. Vol. 2.* Ed. W. D. Ross. Oxford: Oxford UP, 1930.

Baudrillard, Jean. "The Spirit of Terrorism." *Le Monde.* Trans. Rachel Bloul. November 2, 2001. <http://www.egs.edu/faculty/baudrillard/baudrillard-the-spirit-of-terrorism.html>.

Benjamin, Daniel. "The 1,176-Foot-Tall Target." *The New York Times,* 23 Mar. 2004, late ed.: A23.

Burke, Kenneth. *A Grammar of Motives.* Berkeley: U of California, 1945.

Casey, Edward S. *The Fate of Place: A Philosophical History.* Berkeley: U of California, 1997.

12

Private Commitments and Public Rhetoric: Implications for Ethical Practice

Barbara Couture
University of Nebraska–Lincoln

The ethical practice of public rhetoric reflects a private commitment. In stating this, I do not intend to enter the debate about whether private and public language can be descriptively distinguished, but rather to suggest a set of prescriptive criteria for the ethical practice of public rhetoric—criteria that, in my view, demand that speakers examine private commitments as they shape public rhetoric.

Public rhetoric, for my purposes here, is speech that represents a private or personally held commitment to an idea, a proposed action, or a point of view that is expressed publicly with the intention that it be accepted, adopted, or supported by a public audience. Such public rhetoric, if effective in realizing the speaker's intentions, is characterized by the mutual benefit of the speaker who accrues public support for a personal or privately held idea and of the public audience who gain a new perspective of potential value to them. I shall argue, in this chapter, that the ethical practice of public rhetoric so defined brings the speaker into a more fully responsible relationship with his or her audience and instantiates the personal responsibility of one for another that underlies all ethical social relationships.

The ethical practice of public rhetoric responds to three criteria:

- the speech overtly translates a private commitment to a public responsibility;
- the speech acknowledges acceptance of the mutual obligation of speaker to audience and audience to speaker; and
- the speech equates public responsibility with the public good.

I have derived these criteria from my interpretation of contemporary rhetorical scholarship on public and private speech and on the relationship between private intention and public rhetoric. I shall elaborate them by drawing on these sources and citing examples that show implications of their application.

123

CRITERIA FOR THE ETHICAL PRACTICE OF PUBLIC RHETORIC

Overtly Translate Private Commitment to Public Responsibility

To overtly translate a private commitment to a public responsibility, my first criterion for ethical public rhetoric, a speaker must first, intend his or her speech to be public and second, intend to move a private commitment to an arena where it is subjected to public judgment and its consequences. Let me illustrate.

One popular way that public rhetoric is defined is by the audience to whom it is directed. This definition limits the role of the speaker who decides to make a private commitment public and to take responsibility for that commitment by dealing with the reaction of his or her audience. As Christian Weisser notes in a recently published essay entitled "Public Writing and Rhetoric: A New Place for Composition," writing instructors in general have advanced a rather anemic notion of public rhetoric, assuming that it is simply writing for the general public about public issues, a typical example of such discourse being the newspaper editorial or letter to an editor.

Weisser challenges writing teachers to think beyond genres that are so defined and even beyond what theorists, such as Jürgen Habermas, have defined as the "public sphere," that is, the sites where "private persons deliberate about 'public issues,'" or "matters of common concern to all or nearly all members of a society" (244). In contrast, Weisser defines public rhetoric as that where speakers not only address matters commonly identified to be of public concern, but also make "through their sustained discursive contestation" issues formerly considered private "a matter of common concern" (245). Referring to the work of Nancy Fraser, Weisser notes that common definitions of public and private matters can function ideologically to keep matters private that should be of public concern, such as the issue of domestic violence (245). Weisser effectively distinguishes, in my view, public rhetoric from its ethical practice. The latter requires a far more deliberative view toward the speaker's intention to be public, one that does not assume rhetoric to be public by mere description of its audience, but rather by virtue of the author's intention to take an issue to the public.

Beyond having an intention to complete his or her translation of a private commitment to a public responsibility, the speaker must expose that commitment to public judgment. Although arguably, a letter to an editor of a newspaper does just this—the writer certainly subjects himself or herself to the possibility that the newspaper editor or another reader may respond in debate—in reality, such consequences are often remote or the repercussions fairly limited; there may be a couple of written exchanges over a period of days or weeks, but generally the matter is dropped. But there are many other contemporary arenas where the potential for judgment and its consequences are more keenly felt; a few examples might be a speaker defending a commercial use for personal property to an audience of city council members and citizens, a university professor defending a curricular approach to members of the faculty senate, or a church leader defending a position on abortion to a social agency. These are situations with the potential for the speaker to risk loss of personal stature or belief.

Jacques Derrida provides a philosophical insight into the nature of this risk in *Politics of Friendship*, a work that explores the bonds between human beings as articulated by kinship, friendship, and citizenship and their implications for truth-seeking. Derrida's discussion of these matters reveals that when a speaker subjects a private commitment to public scrutiny, such subjection could obliterate the security of the speaker's identity and shake foundations upon which the speaker's notions of truth are based. Yet if men and women in their public discourse cannot overcome their fear of these possible outcomes, a larger threat looms—the very dissolution of modern democracy.

In an extended exposition of the classical notion of friendship among aristocratic peers as it differs from modern democratic citizenship, Derrida explains that classical friendship was defined as one friend selflessly and reliably loving another; friendship, in this model, "demands an equality of virtue between friends, in what assign them reciprocally to one another" (23). The bonds of friendship, though mutually shared among friends, are by definition exclusive. The virtuous friend is advised not to have too many friends because one cannot love them all well, a fact which raises the specter of friendship's antithesis: the existence of enemies. To believe in friendship is to hold the possibility of there being enemies. But more than this, Derrida tells us, to believe in friendship is to close a circle against a presumed enemy, a circle that hides from knowledge that would deny the friendship, a circle that hides friends from truth. The closed classical conception of friendship involves, as Derrida tells us "making each other laugh about evil. Among friends" (56).

Within the security of sharing beliefs among friends, one does not have to face truth that lies beyond that friendship, such as the evil persecution of enemies in the name of that shared belief. We do not need to look far for modern-day examples of this kind of closed friendship, the delusions shared by Hitler's Nazi sympathizers, the justification of suicide and murder by Osama bin Laden's Al Qaeda.

What a democracy requires is the potential to dissolve the friend/enemy dichotomy by defining friendship as a bond of love that not only overlooks the faults of friends, but also admits the possibility of an untold truth that can be revealed by someone who is not one's friend now but may be in the future. To participate in a democracy, one must be willing to subject the beliefs which now bind one to a group of friends to the judgment of those who would be future friends. In short, one must be willing to make one's private commitment a public responsibility to others who, standing in judgment, have the potential to be our friends. This commitment entails more than enduring the risk to one's identity that comes from exposing one's commitment to others and more than defending one's beliefs when subjected to the judgment of others; it requires one's acceptance of the reciprocal obligations of a speaker to an audience and an audience to a speaker, my second criterion for the ethical practice of public rhetoric.

Accept the Reciprocal Obligation of Speaker to Audience and Audience to Speaker

The reciprocal obligation of speaker to audience and audience to speaker both implicates the speaker's development of an ethical self and creates the potential for new knowledge.

Contemporary rhetorical theory is replete with examples of the obligation of the speaker to the needs of his or her audience and of the importance of anticipating audience response to a message. But few theorists speak to the implications of this relationship for self-development; likewise, although some theorists acknowledge that interaction with others enables knowledge production, few identify the ethical stance of the speaker as a critical component of that interaction.

Rhetoricians' and linguists' descriptions of the speaker's relationship to an audience range from pragmatic analyses of how language responds to social contexts, such as those presented by Michael Halliday, Gunther Kress, or Lester Faigley; to analyses of speakers' arguments as they address known principles of logic or constraints of the rhetorical situation, as reflected in the work of Stephen Toulmin or Kenneth Burke, for example; to extended rubrics to assist the speaker in analyzing audiences and situations, such as the tagmemic matrix presented by Young, Becker, and Pike in their classic text *Rhetoric, Discovery, and Change* or the strategies for analyzing internal and external audiences presented by Mathes and Stevenson in *Designing Technical Reports*. Although these methods aim at preparing a speaker to relate more effectively to an audience so that he or she might better persuade them, they do not hint at the ontology of the speaker's obligation to an other nor speak to its consequences.

A few contemporary theorists do acknowledge the mutual benefits for speaker and audience when the speaker achieves public understanding of the value of his or her private commitments and when the audience in turn learns about a new perspective. I am thinking here of Carl Rogers's claim that successful persuasion depends on the speaker's ability to empathize with the audience's point of view or Donald Davidson's theory that successful communication is dependent on the participants' charitable belief that a person who is speaking wishes to be understood. Although these language theorists acknowledge that the success of communication is at stake should a speaker not understand the reciprocal obligations of speaker to audience, they do not press beyond this to suggest much more.

I wish to suggest that what is at stake in the speaker's acknowledgment of reciprocal obligations to an audience is both the speaker's very development of an ethical self and his or her potential to develop new knowledge. To illustrate this point, I shall turn briefly to theories of the social nature of ethical and intellectual development presented by James R. Mensch and Luce Irigaray.

In *Ethics and Selfhood: Alterity and the Phenomenology of Obligation*, James R. Mensch argues that responsibility to others is not only requisite for ethical behavior but is also essential to selfhood. Mensch forwards "a model of the self that recognizes its essential situatedness within the human framework" (8). He argues that it is our very situatedness which allows us to create the conditions for autonomy that lead to moral judgment. Mensch bases this view on the claim that selfhood is developed through "the opposition of the individual and the collective aspects of our selfhood" (9). Individuals cannot fully choose the self they wish to become without seeing the other possibilities for selfhood expressed by those they encounter. An epistemological or moral theory which is based on principles that reduce to abstractions the ways that individuals interpret the world or make choices, Mensch believes, fails to address what he calls the "exceeding quality" (14) of life, that is, the stuff of life that can not be accounted for by reductive theories of knowledge or moral behavior, such as the Cartesian scientific method or the Kantian categorical imperative, which requires a separation of "the willing subject from all motivations springing from its particular circumstances" (6) in order to determine whether choices are justifiable universally.

Mensch interprets an individual's freedom to act as a direct consequence of life's exceeding quality and one that is enabled through interactions with others: "Others, in their informing me of life's possibilities, inform me of the choices that make freedom real" (15). And he demonstrates that encounters with others help individuals make difficult choices, despite social pressure, such as the choice some citizens made to assist their Jewish neighbors facing Nazi persecution: "Facing death, through the other [that is, the Jew facing annihilation], I experience the contingency of my own life" (14–15).

To extend Mensch's argument to the rhetorical situation of public rhetoric, we might say this: A speaker who makes a choice to reveal a private commitment has the ethical obligation to do so while acknowledging the possibility that the other with whom he or she speaks may have commitments that account for life in ways that the speaker's own experience cannot encompass. In short, the speaker must be open to the possibility of being changed by the audience in order to develop a truer assessment of his or her own situation.

As I noted, Mensch's theory of ethical self-development suggests that an individual's interaction with others has significant consequences for individual freedom and autonomy to exercise the agency which is key to effective written expression. But beyond even this consequence for individual selves, empathetic response to another is critical for the development of new knowledge.

Luce Irigaray offers an interesting perspective on the phenomenon of human relationship as it implicates not only individual development, but also knowledge creation. In *The Way of Love*, Irigaray presents what she calls an alternate perspective on man's relationship to the world, that is, "a philosophy in the feminine, where the values of intersubjectivity, of dialogue in difference, of attention to present life, in its concrete and sensible aspects, will be recognized and raised to the level of a wisdom" (vii). Irigaray claims that knowledge develops when the relationship of difference that becomes apparent when speakers regard themselves to be in constant dialogue with others generates information that cannot be obtained when one regards the world and others in it as mere objects to be observed. The latter behavior subjects others to one perspective, a mistake that only can be corrected by allowing each participant in communication to bring something of his or her own into the conversation. She says, "In order for the relation in difference not to fall back into submission, subjection to one sole subject, to values univocally established, each must bring a meaning of one's own into the dialogue" (8). It is this continuous state of openness to others that creates the space where new knowledge is developed. Irigaray explains this space and condition for it as "never a completeness of the One, but constitution of two worlds open and in relation with one other, and which give both to a third world, as work in common and space-time to be shared" (10).

Irigaray's unsettling conclusion is that knowledge so formed in dialogue is indeterminate. She says, "In an exchange between two, meaning quivers and always remains unstable, incomplete, unsettled, irreducible to the word" (28). To regard knowledge-making in this way is to turn the tables on previous, long-standing views of the purpose of knowledge-seeking as the love of wisdom which results in mastery. Irigaray translates the very word *philosophy* as both the love of wisdom and the wisdom of love (Intro. 1–4). If we cannot regard knowledge as dependent on loving relationships, she claims, we cannot address the most pressing problems that now confront us as a world society. She challenges the belief that language is precoded, and she denies that the things it names and defines are located and stabilized in a people or in an accepted epistemology. Rather, she suggests language and knowledge are developed through a relationship of reciprocal exchange between speaker and audience. The implications for public rhetoric are clear; public rhetoric must create the possibility of a new language that communicates more successfully how participants' views are transformed by their relationship, rather than subjected to observation. Irigaray asks, "How [else] will we respond, or correspond, to the challenges of globalization, if not through the invention of another language? Through making our way toward finding a language that is more communicative and less subjected to information?" (42).

Equate Public Responsibility with Public Good

Irigaray's question elicits what I call the third criterion for the ethical practice of public rhetoric: public rhetoric must equate public responsibility with the public good.

This criterion, like the others I have named, places a primary value on productive social interaction, one that supersedes the desires of individuals. Some philosophers have argued that for individuals to thrive, their primary goal should be to do only what allows them to excel, burn brightly, be brilliant, regardless of how others react to this exhibition of individual will, or in my terms, this public exposure of a distinctly private commitment. It is the very tendency to tout one's individual perspective that makes the work of artists exceptional, for instance. One could argue, by extension, that a similar goal of individual achievement ought to guide a speaker's decision to bring ideas to the public—at some level, such public rhetoric ought to be regarded for its own merit, irrespective of public response. After all, what meaning can individual lives and contributions have, if they do not strive to set themselves apart from others? To burn brilliantly? If we don't strive to set ourselves apart, is not life meaningless?

In an interesting book about the human fear of meaninglessness, M. A. Casey examines modern-day solutions to this problem posed by Nietzsche, Freud, and Rorty. Casey believes these philosophers attempt to overcome meaninglessness by trying to deny the very need for meaning. For this reason, Nietzsche advocates the "superman" who employs power to overcome the fruitless search for truth, Freud advances therapy to overcome repression of desire, and Rorty proposes ironic distance to overcome one's sense that life is senseless. Casey argues that what these philosophers overlook is the fact that man can transcend himself, through his "ability, through love, to make a gift of [himself] to other people" (125). It is this possibility of transcendence that gives life meaning. By extension, it is this possibility of transcendence that demands the speaker of public rhetoric to address the public good; by so making of himself or herself a gift to others, the speaker makes his or her own life meaningful.

But other than the benefit of engaging the speaker in meaningful work, why ultimately should public rhetoric address the public good? Public rhetoric should address the public good because in doing so, it creates the conditions for democracy. As I noted earlier, democracies are sustained by the possibility of individuals being able to create an ever-widening circle of potential friends, people who in some way share the same desires of peaceful and productive coexistence. The engine, if you will, that drives this process is public rhetoric directed for the public good.

Several modern-day scholars of citizenship support this view. Cornel West, for example, argues that a modern democracy demands citizens who invest in the well-being of all in society through actively questioning whether the society is treating everyone well, regardless of their status. He says, "Democracy always raises the fundamental question: What is the role of the most disadvantaged in relation to the public interest? It is similar in some ways to the biblical question: What are you to do with the least of these? If we do not want to live in a democracy, we are not obliged to raise that question" (9). West continues:

> Any civilization that is unable to sustain its networks of caring and nurturing will generate enough anger and aggression to make communication near impossible. The result is a society in which we do not even respect each other enough to listen to each other. Dialogue is the lifeblood of democracy and is predicated on certain bonds of trust and respect. (10)

But beyond sustaining a "dialogue of care" that is essential for democracy, public rhetoric also should define the aims of a good society, challenging the relationship between individual prosperity and the public good. Some argue that a society is good when it maximizes individuals' wealth and power, such productivity and efficiency being at least one measure of a public good. Michael Lerner, editor of *Tikkun*, a journal of scholarship on social and political values, argues in contrast that a society is "productive or efficient to the extent that it tends to create human beings who are capable of having and sustaining loving and caring relationships and being ethically, spiritually, and ecologically sensitive and alive" (73). What benefit is there in maintaining this definition of the good society? The benefit of advocating this model of a good society is that such a society restores meaning to human lives.

Lerner is quite didactic in his assertion of the inherent value of action for the public good, and he advocates for a new politics of meaning. In short, he proposes a new public rhetoric that acknowledges the fundamental value that all human beings place on connecting with others:

> There is in everybody, including those who will be the quickest to ridicule [this] politics of meaning, this hunger for a different way of life, for a different way of being in society. [...] When enough of us start to interfere with that discourse of selfishness, materialism, and cynicism, to challenge the media, and to articulate the values that we really want, we will have this kind of movement happening. (77)

And we will have along with it, I would maintain, a system where the ethical practice of public rhetoric is the norm.

Among the examples of public rhetoric that meets the ethical criteria I have established, rhetoric that translates private commitment to public responsibility, accepts the reciprocal obligations of speaker to audience, and equates public responsibility with the public good are those cited by Gerard Hauser (ch. 2, this vol.). He demonstrates the relationship between private commitments and public responsibility which girded the powerful and ethical rhetoric of Bonhoeffer, Havel, and Mandela. In any case, the fundamental project for teachers of rhetoric as I see it is to, on a smaller but more personal scale, help students see how this relationship must guide their own practice of public rhetoric and the consequences if it should not.

WORKS CITED

Casey, M. A. *Meaninglessness: The Solutions of Nietzsche, Freud, and Rorty.* Lanham: Lexington, 2002.

Derrida, Jacques. *Politics of Friendship.* Trans. George Collins. London: Verso, 1997.

Irigaray, Luce. *The Way of Love.* Trans. Heidi Bostic and Stephen Pluhácek. London: Continuum, 2002.

Lerner, Michael. "The Crisis of Values in America: Its Manipulation by the Right and Its Invisibility to the Left." *The Good Citizen.* Ed. David Batstone and Eduardo Mendieta. New York: Routledge, 1999. 65–80.

Mensch, James R. *Ethics and Selfhood: Alterity and the Phenomenology of Obligation.* Albany: State U of New York P, 2003.

Weisser, Christian R. "Public Writing and Rhetoric: A New Place for Composition." Ed. Barbara Couture and Thomas Kent. *The Private, the Public, and the Published: Reconciling Private Lives and Public Rhetoric.* Logan: Utah State UP, 2004. 230–48.

West, Cornel. "The Moral Obligations of Living in a Democratic Society." *The Good Citizen.* Ed. David Batstone and Eduardo Mendieta. New York: Routledge, 1999. 5–12.

13

Reading Talmud: Levinas and the Possibility of Rhetoric

Richard R. Glejzer
North Central College

The face of a neighbor signifies for me an unexceptionable responsibility, preceding every free consent, every pact, every contract. It escapes representation; it is the very collapse of phenomenality.

—Emmanuel Levinas (*Otherwise Than Being* 88)

[S]peach, in its original essence, is a commitment to a third party on behalf of our neighbor: the act *par excellence*, the institution of society. The original function of speech consists not in designating an object in order to communicate with the other in a game with no consequences but in assuming toward someone a responsibility on behalf of someone else. To speak is to engage the interests of men. Responsibility would be the essence of language.

—Emmanuel Levinas (*Nine Talmudic Readings* 21)

The respect for the stranger and the sanctification of the name of the eternal are strangely equivalent.

—Emmanuel Levinas (*Nine Talmudic Readings* 27)

There is a problem in any attempt to link rhetoric and ethics: How one proceeds from speaking to acting, from acting to speaking involves some articulation of causality; there must be some agency at work, some being, some substance, some body that might guarantee the grounding of action as well as the grounding of speaking. Emmanuel Levinas might suggest that such placeholders for cause only thematize or occlude an other on the side of the infinite with a more mundane, finite other. For Levinas, the ethical begins and ends with such an infinite other, not the mundane other of common everyday morality. In fact, Levinas is most concerned with how we might speak about this infinite other, this other of pure causality, pure agency, that calls the subject into being as a subject of responsibility. This turn away from being and its finite wisdom (a turning away from knowledge) is an important challenge to rhetoric since it demands us to consider how the very language we speak as neighbors must first act in relation to this cause, this other that is otherwise-than-being, otherwise than a face across a divide since the very divide is the face of the infinite.

In considering how one approaches this infinite divide, Levinas presents a complicated ambivalence to language. On the one hand, Levinas consistently argues that to place the obligation of the other in language is to elide the ethical with a specific thematization. On the other hand, Levinas suggests that it is only through language that the absence of the other in thematization is represented. As he says in *Otherwise than Being*: "The mode in which a face indicates its own absence in my responsibility requires a description that can be formed only in ethical language" (94). Put another way, Levinas here suggests that causality—which, I argue here, binds ethics to rhetoric—is manifest in language, albeit as absence. Levinas offers us a specific instance of this binding of rhetoric and ethics in his consideration of forgiveness in *Nine Talmudic Readings*. Here, Levinas follows this ethical mode by presenting a paradoxical notion of forgiveness, one that stems not from a moral transgression but rather from an elision between such a transgression and the other itself, where the demand for the chance to forgive is an effacement of one's own responsibility to the other. Here I will examine this ethical "mode" of language in Levinas, as a way toward establishing a rhetoric that maintains a place for causality in the now of language, allowing for a causal arc in which the movement between rhetoric and ethics may be traced.

To speak about an ethical possibility for rhetoric in Levinas is perhaps, at best, just wishful thinking. Throughout all of his major works, Levinas is pretty clear about the function of rhetoric as a means away from a recognition of one's obligation to the other, and thus as a means toward violence. In fact, Levinas goes so far as to suggest that rhetoric (both as trope and as persuasion) rests on a demand for the same, where the other is required to enter the realm of identification with the I. In *Totality and Infinity*, Levinas makes his dismissal of rhetoric from the field of ethical inquiry plain:

> Our pedagogical or psychagogical discourse is rhetoric, taking the position of him who approaches his neighbor with ruse. And this is why the art of the sophist is a theme with reference to which the true conversation concerning truth, or philosophical discourse, is defined. Rhetoric, absent from no discourse, and which philosophical discourse seeks to overcome, resists discourse (or leads to it: pedagogy, demagogy, psychagogy). It approaches the other not to face him, but obliquely—not, to be sure, as a thing, since rhetoric remains conversation, and across all its artifices goes unto the Other, solicits his yes. But the specific nature of rhetoric (of propaganda, flattery, diplomacy, etc.) consists in corrupting this freedom. It is for this that it is preeminently violence, that is injustice—not violence exercised on an inertia (which would not be a violence), but on a freedom, which, precisely as freedom, should be incorruptible. (70)

Jill Robbins offers an interesting connection here to an early essay by Levinas where he similarly connects violence with an oblique glance: "Violence consists in ignoring this opposition, ignoring the face of being, avoiding the gaze, and *catching sight of an angle* whereby the *no* inscribed on a face by the very fact that it is a face becomes a hostile or submissive force. Violence is a way of acting on every being and every freedom by approaching it from an *indirect angle*" (qtd. in Robbins 17–18). This "indirect angle," this "oblique" vision, rests not on the face of the Other in its radical infinity, but rather glances aside the very radical otherness of the other in favor of an equal other, an other with whom one can speak as equals, an other whom we might persuade. And such an equality between the I and the other is antithetical to Levinas's project that argues for an ethics that sees the first and only obligation point back to the other as a precursor to any I whatsoever. Thus for Levinas, rhetoric is not possible in the field of the other since one is not face to face with the other as other. Rather, it is only through the face of the other that the I may then be. There is no "give and take" with the other and thus there is no rhetorical means by which one may encounter the other, be obliged to the other, or even probe an ethics of the other. Levinas is both clear and consistent through all of his philosophical work about this danger of rhetoric where language is but a ruse.

But how does one approach a neighbor without such a ruse? And if one can approach a neighbor without a ruse, how is this not rhetorical? These worldly questions do not enter into Levinas's philosophical writings explicitly, but they do found the core of his reading of Talmud. The Greek or Western philosophical tradition is only one part of Levinas's consideration of ethics, and his dismissal of rhetoric stems from his reading of Plato, from within the Western philosophical tradition. However, Levinas's project rests on a translation enterprise between what he describes as Biblical and Greek traditions, where Jewish thought offers something that the Greek tradition does not. And it is within this Jewish tradition that Levinas will eventually find a place for rhetoric, although he does not call it by that name. Levinas situates what is particularly unique about Jewish tradition within an implicitly rhetorical frame: "Herein, no doubt, lies the originality of Judaism: the existence of a tradition, uninterrupted through the very transmission and commentary of the Talmudic texts, commentaries overlapping commentaries" (*Nine Talmudic Readings* 6–7). Whereas Levinas clearly admonishes rhetoric as a tool or mode in Western tradition, what he sees as a unique contribution to ethics within Biblical tradition is clearly a rhetorical one.

In all of his readings of Talmud, Levinas consistently praises the very nature of Talmudic learning, the tradition that layers commentary upon commentary, that shows a deep concern for the method of truth. At no point does Levinas ever try to resolve the readings into one correct or even more fruitful interpretation. Rather, his approach is to keep all the commentaries active and to plot out the terrain that they cover in their aggregate. One of the points that he finds most important in Talmudic thinking is the axiom do first, understand later, where one is supposed to act in accordance with the demand of the other prior to any overt ethical consideration or system. For Levinas, such pure action precedes speaking, precedes knowing. It is in such a context that Levinas reads the various commentaries, as acts. For, he argues, only in such action can one thus encounter the other's face, not as an object of the gaze (one interpretation), but rather as a positioning toward the other, a certain kind of relation that does not represent the other as an object. It is in this relation that Levinas places the divine.

In his first of four readings of Talmud, Levinas interestingly chooses a passage addressing forgiveness, specifically focusing on Yom Kippur. Here he considers the distinction between God's forgiveness, which is guaranteed, versus human forgiveness, which is never guaranteed. From the Mishna:

> The transgressions of man toward God are forgiven him by the Day of Atonement; the transgressions against other people are not forgiven him by the Day of Atonement if he has not first appeased the other person. (*Nine Talmudic Readings* 12)

It is interesting that Levinas chooses to begin with this particular Tractate (Yoma 85a-85b), where the first obligation is to appease the other. From the Gemara, Levinas then presents two stories that explore what it might mean to "appease" the other person, that consider explicitly the rhetorical kernel of such forgiveness: One of Rab who, on the eve of Yom Kippur, goes to a butcher who has wronged him with the hopes that the butcher will ask for forgiveness. While hammering away on an ox head, the butcher refuses, saying, "Go away Abba. I have nothing in common with you" (13). As the butcher hammers, the skull shatters, a bone breaks loose and lodges in the butcher's throat, killing him. The second narrative has Rab commenting on a text before Rabbi. Each time Rab begins his commentary, he is interrupted by a latecomer and must then begin his commentary again. When the master of the school, Rab Hanina bar Hama, comes in, Rab says, "How many times am I to repeat myself?" and refuses to start again. Rab Hanina takes offense. "For thirteen years, on Yom Kippur eve, Rab went to seek forgiveness, and Rab Hanina refused to be appeased" (13).

Together, both narratives speak toward a rhetorical problem at the heart of forgiveness, where the other's refusal to either ask for forgiveness or to forgive when asked puts God's forgiveness in jeopardy, both in essence leading to violence. As the Mishna clearly states, "The transgressions against other people are not forgiven him by the Day of Atonement if he has not first appeased the other person" (12). Levinas's examination of the commentary rests on this notion of "appeasing" at the heart of both narratives. In the latter example, Levinas offers two strands of the Talmud commentary, the first considering the lengths that Rab goes to apologize to his teacher:

> The injury done to the master differs from all other injuries. But isn't the other man always to some degree your master? You can behave like Rab. For has anyone, in any case, ever finished asking for forgiveness? Our wrongs appear to us as we humble ourselves. The seeking for forgiveness never comes to an end. Nothing is ever completed. (*Nine Talmudic Readings* 24)

Secondly, Levinas also offers the reading that the reason Rab Hanina does not forgive Rab is that Rab has yet to recognize the nature of his transgression: Rab does not see that his refusal to begin again comes from his desire to take the place of his teacher, a desire that Rab Hanina recognizes. Thus, Rab does not yet understand the nature of his offense, which is why Rab Hanina refuses to forgive him. Both readings in the end demonstrate that one must approach the other humbly, without a preconceived knowledge of what one thinks one has done.

Likewise, the demand of Rab that the butcher apologize so that Rab can then forgive him also demonstrates the violence of preconceived knowledge. Commenting on the butcher's response, "I have nothing in common with you," Levinas remarks:

> The expression is marvelously precise and underlines one of the essential aspects of the situation. Mankind is spread out on different levels. It is made up of multiple worlds that are closed to one another because of their unequal heights. Men do not yet form one humanity. [...] It is certainly not of a miracle that the story wants to tell us but of this death within the systems in which humanity closes itself off. It also wants to speak to us of the purity which can kill, in a mankind as yet unequally evolved, and of the enormity of the responsibility which Rab took upon himself in his premature confidence of the humanity of the Other. (*Nine Talmudic Readings* 23)

On the one hand, Rab does show a remarkable responsibility for the other, such that he feels responsible for the unforgiven state of the butcher. However, his approaches to the other in "premature confidence" is one based on sameness and thus ultimately leads to violence. Who is Rab to place himself in the position of the infinite other to the other person? It is this equation of one for the other, where the other is not one's master, that leads to falling away from an ethical stance, a rhetorical position that demands a straight-on look at the face of the other.

Both examples from the Gemara rest upon this speaking to the face of the other as the ethical approach to one's neighbor. For Levinas, both examples illustrate the necessity of depending on the good will of the neighbor.

> My faults toward God are forgiven without my depending on his good will! God is, in a sense, the *other, par excellence,* the other as other, the absolutely other—and nonetheless my standing with this God depends only on myself. The instrument of forgiveness is in my hands. On the other hand, my neighbor, my brother, man, infinitely less other than the absolutely other, is in a certain

way more other than God: to obtain his forgiveness on the Day of Atonement I must first succeed in appeasing him. What if he refuses? As soon as two are involved, everything is in danger. The other can refuse forgiveness and leave me forever unpardoned. This must hide some interesting teachings on the essence of the Divine! (16)

In this sense, Levinas offers a point of contact between these two others, that is, the human other and the divine other. In both cases, there is an instrument for forgiveness: in the first case, the instrument isn't shared (God has no need of instruments!), and in the second case, the instrument is shared. The beginning of ethics, then, rests in this two-ness in relation to a one that is not part of two, is other than two, but that grounds the very possibility of two. Rather than banishing rhetoric as solely about the relation among ontological equals, Levinas shows in his reading of Talmud that there is a place for rhetoric at the very inception of the ethical, at the moment before the I when the responsibility for the other calls the I forth, an I that then rests in the face of its neighbor, a face that is not the same but demands a response. This is precisely the beginning of rhetoric, one end of rhetoric that may then lead to the very violence of persuasion and trope that Levinas fears. But this does not have to be the case. Rhetoric does not have to do the dirty work of ontology doing violence to freedom by demanding an other in being. Rhetoric is also about the saying and not just the said, as Derrida reminds us. In his careful reading of these two stories of forgiveness, Levinas shows this one end of rhetoric: that ethics—a relation with the infinite—demands a response that is otherwise than being, a response that begins, "What does one say to this neighbor who is not me?"

Although Levinas's explicit consideration of the question of the subject in relation to the imperative of a responsibility to the Other is the central focus of much of his theoretical work, most especially in his two major texts *Totality and Infinity* and *Otherwise Than Being*, it is perhaps in his most practical texts that the question of the other and one's responsibility to the other gets shaped. Specifically, in his readings of the Talmud, Levinas shows us a rhetorical means of investigation that takes one's responsibility for the other seriously. At some level, it's easy within a Greek or Western tradition to theorize the other abstractly. However, Judaism, defined by Levinas as a religion of adults, offers a consideration of the way the face of the other is the object of responsibility, preceding any responsibility for oneself. Throughout his Talmudic readings, Levinas demonstrates that it is the rhetorical end of the subject that defines an ethics of the other. Hence, his understanding of God not as a substance or even an agency, but rather as a position relative to the human: God is an ethical stance—a rhetorical claim, if you will—that points toward the thematizations necessary for any universal (see Aronowicz xxiii). God as a rhetorical claim, a relation to the infinite other: This does not mean that this is some originary movement or moment prior to subjectivity, a movement that is forever foreclosed by the establishment of the I or the self. Rather, Levinas argues that this rhetorical claim—a claim that ends (in) rhetoric—is a constant relation, an ever-present responsibility that serves to question and undermine the I as the common wisdom response to such a claim. In this sense, the I and its other are not the constituents of speaking and thus do not serve as the only field through which we study rhetoric. The I and its other only exits within the spoken, the statement, the claim of alterity that is only a ruse. For Levinas, a neighborly rhetoric would neither rest on a claim of universality nor fall into the trap of only privileging the radically particular. The claim of the other simply never goes away. "We" are forever in doubt of the ethics of our actions, of the rhetoric of our words. And thus, "we" do not make claims on the other. Levinas concludes his reading on forgiveness with a comment about revenge and justice: "The Talmud teaches that one cannot force men who demand retaliatory justice to grant forgiveness. It teaches us that Israel does not deny this imprescriptible right to others. But it teaches us above all that if Israel recognizes this right, it does not ask it for itself and that to be Israel is not to claim it" (*Nine Talmudic Readings* 28–29).

WORKS CITED

Aronowicz, Annette. " Introduction." *Nine Talmudic Readings*. By Emmanuel Levinas. Trans. Annette Aronowicz. Bloomington: Indiana UP, 1990. ix–xxxix.

Levinas, Emmanuel. *Nine Talmudic Readings*. Trans. Annette Aronowicz. Bloomington: Indiana UP, 1990.

——. *Otherwise Than Being or Beyond Essence*. Trans. Alphonso Lingis. Pittsburgh: Duquesne UP, 1998.

——. *Totality and Infinity: An Essay on Exteriority*. Trans. Alphonso Lingis. Pittsburgh: Duquesne UP, 1969.

Robbins, Jill. *Altered Readings: Levinas and Literature*. Chicago: U of Chicago P, 1999.

14

Rhetoric and Political Economy at the Aesthetic Nexus: A Study of Archbishop Whately

G. Thomas Goodnight
University of Southern California

David B. Hingstman
University of Iowa

[W]hat Aristotle says of Dialectics and rhetoric, that all men partake of them in a certain degree, since all occasionally aim (whether skillfully or unskillfully) to accomplish the objects of those arts—this will in a great degree, in such a country as this, apply to Political-Economy.

—Richard Whately (*Political Economy* 84).

This paper examines Whately's thesis that rhetoric and political economy are overlapping areas of study, mediated, according to the Archbishop, by directed action in the pursuit of a goal. We believe that in constructing this case, Whately borrows from Aristotelian aesthetics while modifying significantly this teleological view to meet a progressive sense of history and to address the paradoxes apprehended by modern sensibilities between individual purpose and collective outcome. In recovering the rhetorical tradition, Whately borrows Aristotle's perspective as a social scientist who sees the uses of language as a neutral tool for overcoming excess and deficiencies in informed motivation. On the other hand, Whately transforms classical aesthetics from a principle of adjustment of subject to audience through proportionate representation to a progressive aesthetic of discovery and arrangement that transforms deficiency into surplus in the interest of accumulation of moral and material progress. Thus, modern rhetoric preserves a portion of the classical tradition, setting on its way conditions for its own effacement and the social scientific study of individual and collective persuasion.

The relationship of modern rhetoric to political economy is complex. In one sense, the two follow completely distinct traditions. The recognition that many early modern, Enlightenment, and nineteenth-century figures wrote both political economies and rhetorics is often forgotten. Further, when recollected, the relationship between the two disciplines is read through "moral" concerns, as value becomes a common denominator for both disciplines. This essay proposes an alternative reading, namely an investigation into the relationship through the logic of appearances, an aesthetics that borrowed and transformed the problematics of perception, judgment, appreciation, and change in the ancient public sphere to a modern set of concerns and sensibilities.

As is well known, Whately makes the case that rhetoric uniquely is the art of argumentative composition. As such, it has two main tasks to perform: invention and arrangement. Invention is a process of discovery where experience is transformed to knowledge through a principle that appears to provide a solution to a problem where doing more of the same produces only the same results. People in general, he believes, are not deficient in the amount of knowledge they have, just in their ability to see how the particulars and general cohere as a useful means to an end. Generally, "though possessed of less knowledge than they ought to have, [they] yet possess more than they know what to do with." The rhetor is like one who enlarges "the prospect of a short-sighted man by bringing him to the top of a hill" (*Rhetoric* 14). In an analogy deployed both in the *Rhetoric* and the *Political Economy,* Whately deploys an architectonic metaphor. Confronted with the task of repairing a roof, one brother simply wishes to lay on more straw, which may delay soaking but not solve it; the other sees the problem as one requiring a pitched architecture, creating the new condition of runoff. (*Rhetoric* 15).

The task the Archbishop set for himself was daunting. The arts of language were held in high regard by neither the elites nor the masses. As to the opinion of logic and rhetoric, he quipped, neither is held in high esteem, "the one being generally regarded by the vulgar as the Art of bewildering the learned by frivolous subtleties; the other, that of deluding the multitude by specious falsehood" (*Rhetoric* xxxiv). Whately creates a modern rhetoric through transforming classical aesthetics in the way words and reasons, and speakers and audiences, could appear to each other in making choices, assessing authorities, forming passions, and envisioning relationships between speaker, audience, and world. In so doing, Whately preserves Aristotle's insights into rhetoric and judgment but transforms the logic of appearance to suit a modern society where presumptions, authorities, and passions are inherently conflicted. The price demanded by modern rhetoric was nothing less than the disappearance of the art into the discipline of political economy.

A MODERN RHETORIC

The testing procedure of invention depends upon retaining an equilibrium model of judgment. Aristotle's view of the passions was, in his received view of rhetoric, that such human capabilities are neither bad nor good, but could be addressed for purposes of motivating action proper to a situation. The position of rhetor is one who measures the audience relative to the occasion to see if a problem is created or a solution hindered by either excess or defects of the passion. Invention is a matter of discovery of the appropriate measure relative to audience and situation. This, the Archbishop shows to be the case in addressing a number of antinomies that place stress on the perceived reasonability of the speaker and the attained rational competence of the audience.

The first test is that of *choice* in the face of uncertain knowledge, figured by the well-known rhetorical figure of the traveler at the crossroads. In a world where sophisms abound, both internal rationalizations and external tricks, choice is hard. "[I]n numberless transactions of ordinary life," we are forced to "make up our minds at once to take one course of action, even where there are no sufficient grounds for a full conviction of the understanding" (*Rhetoric* 81). Some will make premature decisions without thinking through the situation, whereas a "smaller number of persons, among whom however are to be found a larger portion of the intelligent, are prone to the opposite extreme" will delay. "The one decide without inquiring, the other inquire without deciding (81)" Choice is given a modern twist because theory and experience do not necessarily point in a congruent direction. Experience may be reliable until it encounters novelty; change may be untested and unneeded, ballyhooed for reasons of self-interest.

The second test is that of *deference* to authority. In a world where authorities gain credibility by associating with successful figures and avoiding responsibility, figuring out whom to follow is difficult. Deference to the ancients, without good reason, may block innovative thinking; on the other hand, rhetoricians pander to our "wishes" making current authorities questionable. Further, the problem is compounded by legislation that reflects compromises that leave a "fence" and a "gap," directing a course of action with one hand and taking it away with the other. The most one can do is to set presumptions and deploy authority as supporting proof where there is a probability of error in acceding too much, to the wrong authority, or becoming "arrogant" in self-deference. The antinomy is given a modern twist by recognizing that there are multiple, changeable presumptions in a given situation rather than reasons pointing toward a single resolution of a case.

The third test is the deployment of *emotions* in the service of an end. Rhetoric itself is a suspicious art due to the tendency of rhetoricians to cloud the judgment by overly stimulating negative emotions such as fear or anger, on the one hand, or appealing to positive emotions that substitute wishful thinking for realistic appraisal on the other. Like Aristotle, Whately argues that emotions can be excessive for the uneducated or deficient for the elite. Though risky, emotions are necessary motivators for action. Reason can no more operate as a motive "than the eyes, which show a man his road, can enable him to move from place to place; or than a ship provided with a compass, can sail without a wind" (*Rhetoric* 180). The antinomy receives a modern twist by the recognition that the rhetor has to contend with a split between attributed norm and secret desire on the part of the audience. "We are often really under the influence of different, and even opposite emotions at once; e.g. we are in some respects gratified, and in others, pained, by the same occurrence." (*Rhetoric* 182). Reasons acquired from the norms of society about what one ought to feel are different than what one does feels in visceral experience. The rhetor has to address this paradox effectively so that a message cannot be offloaded as applying to others properly, but not to one's self. Thus, Whately opens the door to the development of a modern sense of self: "a good and wise man has to act the part of an orator towards himself" (*Rhetoric* 186).

The final test for rhetoric is that of the *imagination* that envisions a relationship between speaker, audience, and world. In the antinomies of choice, authority, and emotion, Aristotle's advice can be followed for the most part by the establishment of an equilibrium between excess and deficiency regulated by effective pursuit of ends. The case the rhetor makes and the understanding of the audience can be transparent to each other because there is no inherent difference between the two. The equilibrium, however, becomes progressively unstable as novelty risks judgment of experience, presumptions conflict, and mixed motives characterize the feelings. The result of these accumulating exceptions is a difficulty that becomes a defining characteristic of modern rhetoric, the radically conflicted imagination between speaker and audience.

The place of the imagination unfolds for the rhetor in the basic dilemma that is faced by achieving rhetorical success, through credible argument, in achieving a reputation for eloquence. The speaker is guided by Aristotle's injunction that rhetoric is a neutral art. Just as one cannot "any more pronounce on the Eloquence of any Composition, than upon the wholesomeness of a medicine, without knowing for whom it is intended" (*Rhetoric* 204). Thus, the speaker need adapt his arguments to the "opinions and the habits of the audience" (*Rhetoric* 207). The risk that is faced is that if the speaker asks for too much change, then the credibility of argument is diminished. On the other hand, if the speaker but flatters the audience, little may be accomplished. "Popularity, alone, therefore, is not test at all of the eloquence of the speaker. [...] There is but little Eloquence in convincing men that they are in the right, or inducing them to approve a character which coincides with their own" (*Rhetoric* 208–09). The optimal solution would be to vary from the audience as much as one dares while increasing, rather than diminishing, credibility. Note that if the speaker does not ask for change, his reputation is not secure, because the audience may conclude that the speech was a waste of time. Anyone can inflame a mob, Whately notes: that's no trick. The real art is to provide for an audience an argument with sufficient strength to break the misdirections of the passions and to cultivate the resolve to do what is right. The cost of resolving this dilemma for the rhetor is nothing less than the disappearance of his art altogether.

Whately notes that "whatever is attributed to the Eloquence of the speaker, is so much deducted from the strength of the cause." Further, he cites Thucydides' recapitulation of Pericles, who is described as "artfully claiming, in his vindications of himself, the power of explaining the measures he proposes, not, Eloquence in persuading their adoption" (*Rhetoric* 210). The unlearned are suspicious of the learned. The learned know how to bypass a telling argument by ignoring it; they also refrain from overemphasizing a weak argument by belaboring it. Whately tries to reduce the issue to his dependable equilibrium model: "[T]here is a danger of over-rating as well as of under-rating the eloquence of what is said; and what to attribute to the skill of the advocate what really belongs to the strength of the cause, is just as likely to lead to error as the opposite mistake" (*Rhetoric* 214). This balance is next to impossible to achieve overtly because the rhetor can only overcome vanity by falsely investing the audience with attributed knowledge, and moral lax with attributed desire for rectitude. Eloquence "is, in some degree, dreaded by all; and the reputation for it, consequently, will always be, in some degree a disadvantage." "The Orator attains his End the better the less he is regarded as an Orator" (*Rhetoric* 211). "If there ever could be an absolutely perfect Orator, no one would (at the time at least) discover that he was so" (*Rhetoric* 212). To make the transition to modernity, with its autonomous subject, not to mention its democratic and egalitarian virtues, rhetoric—unlike choice, authority, emotion, and imagination which are rendered visible in triangulations of audience and occasion—must disappear altogether!

THE DISCIPLINE OF POLITICAL ECONOMY

The domain of political economy, according to Whately, follows the old tradition of adjusting means to ends. In this light, the human being is "an animal that makes exchanges" (PE 53). The principle of exchange recognizes that "the same thing is different to different persons." Like rhetoric, which traffics in the art of adjustment, political economy faces the epistemological antinomy: to the extent its findings are new, it will face "angry declamation" (PE 17); however, because many of its observations are of ordinary interaction among humans, most of its conclusions will be dismissed as common sense. Just as rhetoric does not add new knowledge, but discovers in the existing knowledge of the audience scattered habits and beliefs that can be arranged for productive ends, so the brand new science of political economy "does not enable us to dispense with common-sense, but only to employ it more profitably." (PE 64). Similarly, as those trained in rhetoric benefit from the habit of inductively analyzing a situation through the testing and arrangement of a wide array of facts, so too theorists of political economy address wider situations through principles of discovery unique to the topics of politics and economy, including "taxation, tithes, the national debt, the poor-laws," wages, and charity, subjects of common and private interest that "are debated perpetually, not merely at public meetings, but in the course of conversation" (PE 77). Just as all people travel and encounter traffic in the broad avenues of dialectic and rhetoric, so in the modern streets of commerce "there is, in fact, no way to keep clear of Political-Economy" (PE 79). "[T]he world always in fact has been, and must be, governed by political-economists, whether they have called themselves so or not, and whether skilful or unskilful" (PE 83). Thus, the subject is "of deep interest to most men; and what is more, they are subjects on which most men will form opinions, whether well or ill-founded; and will act on those opinions, whether in their own immediate management of public affairs or in their choices of persons to be entrusted with the charge" (PE 79).

Despite the claims to universality across time and social space, there are two differences that distinguish political economy as a peculiarly modern or at least postclassical science. First, the term *political economy* is presented as a paradoxical one, conjoining decision making for the household and the public realm, two different spheres of the classical world. Second, the results of such collective activity are differentiated from the outcomes of individual choices. Enthralled with Mandeville's fable of the bees and the hive, Whately works out the implications of how different individual activities can create an order that would be impossible to fathom or design from the intent of a single individual or even expanded committee. The upshot of these differences, as Whately strives to persuade his audience, is that society can change in expanding its wealth through progressive achievements of civilization. Yet, the risks are that absent such attainment, the collective choices leading to war or ill-designed legislation can put society back on the slope toward barbarism. Key in this contest were the distinguishing polarities of party faction and public spirit. Party-faction substituted enmity for rhetorical address, envy and hatred for compromise; factions thirst for the power and rule that political victory brings. "Public spirit, either in the form of Patriotism which looks to the good of a community, or that of Philanthropy which seeks the good of the whole human race, implies, not merely benevolent feelings stronger than, in fact, we commonly meet with, but also powers of abstraction beyond what the mass of mankind can possess" (PE 93).

Just as Aristotle's acquisition of prudent political activity could be cultivated by a responsible rhetoric, so, too, the proper deployment of the principles of political economy could make clear the connections between cause and effect in promoting a progressive economy and preventing retrograde policies. Three examples substantiate the investiture of Whately's modern rhetoric in his notion of political economy.

The epistemic bedrock of political economy is lodged in the risks of *experience and expertise*. This dilemma materializes the rhetorical problem of reflective choice discussed earlier. Whately does not have a high estimate of common sense. He sees such rules of thumb as "an exercise of the judgment unaided by any art of system or rules; such as we must necessarily employ in numberless cases of daily occurrence; in which, having no established principle to guide us—no line of procedure, as it were, distinctly chalked out—we must needs act on the best extemporaneous conjectures we can form" (PE 62). Common sense is an unreliable guide because it results in a condition where one trusts one's own expertise but looks to common sense in any other situation: "[E]ach gives the preference to unassisted common-sense only in those cases where he himself has nothing else to trust to, and invariably resorts to the rules of art, wherever he possesses the knowledge of them" (PE 63). The problem with acquiring an expert, on the other hand, is that an expert is likely to see a problem only through the prejudgments of specialized training.

This epistemic situation leaves rhetoric (transformed into the heart of political economy) in a rather nifty position. Experience is an unreliable guide because it provides no avenue of abstraction, cannot respond to situations for which it is not applicable, and is slow to recognize and adapt to change, whether it be based on common sense or expertise. A science of discovery and arrangement is needed to figure the principles of exchange more generally upon which the needs and capacities of a group are adapted to its ends. Thus, a space for doctrines of utility is formed. Sanford and Merton, the two brothers who working on the roof issue in the *Rhetoric* reappear as rational decision makers in the *Political Economy* (PE 236).

Whately analyzes the relationship between *apparent* and *real* purposes to social activity. He poses the question, How did England come to acquire a modern civilization where wealth is accumulating and other nations remain in a state of savagery? The answer is to be found in "natural theology" where "providence" provides initial moments that "spark" the self-feeding development of a booming economy. The four principles that evolve civilization are the simple arts, the division of labor, the security of property, and a medium of exchange. Without the arts, people are left to subsistence; without specialization, labor is inefficient; without protection of property, people have an incentive only to consume, not accumulate, wealth; and without a neutral medium of exchange, work and wealth are not universally convertible. The results are not always apparent, but always generative of greater wealth. The printing press made publishing existing books more efficient, but it also generated new publishing and facilitated spreading literacy in Western Europe, Whately avers. Technology has positive spinoffs that overcome nature's limits, one might say. Those innovations that are deployed for an apparent purpose to solve one problem are, in reality, innovations that can be ingeniously deployed for others.

The dialectic of the apparent and the real makes itself felt also in assessment of human conduct. In one context, consumers who desire goods and "emulate" their neighbors (buying to keep up with the Jones's) may be seen as committing "Avarice or Covetousness," both "base and odious" motives (PE 146). However, when acquisition of goods is seen as really a motive for supporting one's family, this is noble. Further, while emulation can degenerate "into Envy" which is detestable, "when duly controlled and directed to the best of objects […] it is a useful and honourable ally of virtue" (PE 147). Further, even actions that are seen as hoarding resources can be in an economy quite useful as an accumulation of wealth necessary for investment for needed activities. Conversely, displays of consumption by the wealthy result in jobs for the community. Thus, apparent vices becomes virtues, luxuries necessities, socially suspect behavior prized, all in the name of a political economy with its plurality of needs and pursuits. In sum, Whately wishes his modern audience to understand that contentment is not happiness, and unhappiness is not discontent. "[O]ne who is exerting himself all his life in the pursuit of rich and fresh advancement, whether in Wealth, Learning, Fame, Virtue, or any other object, is not necessarily discontented or unhappy" (PE 148). On the contrary, a pursuit seems to be a main ingredient of happiness. What is the pursuit? "The race [to advance] never comes to an end, while the competitors are striving, not to reach a certain fixed goal, but, each either permanently to keep a-head of the rest, or at least, not be among the hindmost" (PE 148). Rhetoric as rivalry in the pursuit of fame is thus transmuted into the modern notion of acquisition as competition in the pursuit of reward. The reality is the process, the appearances are the goods that offer ways of keeping score.

Whately is a nominalist; words serve as means to ends. He is not comfortable, however, with the outcome of the relativistic positions adumbrated in his epistemology or axiological dynamics of political economy. Rather, he tries to sustain the connection between science and commerce pushing innovation and the law and the church retarding innovation. He develops a "virtue" theory that inscribes political-economy risks within a dialectic of *civilization* and *savagery,* a relationship that serves as a barely disguised allegory of relationship among classes. The lower classes are similar to savages. "Savages it should be remembered, and all men in proportion as they approach the condition of savages, are men in respect of their passions, while, in intellect, they are children" (PE 76). Civilization broadens perspective, stimulates thinking, and fuses motivation and calculation into acts of production. This amalgam Whately describes in terms of a virtue logic.

> For that Integrity, Temperance, and other Virtues, which often require us to forego present gratification, do, in the long run, conduce to our temporal prosperity and enjoyment, is a truth which is perceived more and more as our views become enlarged; and cannot be comprehended at all by those who are so dull and unthinking as hardly to look beyond the passing moment. (PE 170)

On the other hand, those with virtues are "always the better Christians in proportion as they advance in refinement and intellectual cultivation" (PE 170).

Whately believes that moral progress is requisite to material progress, but due to the accidental outcomes of a political economy, material progress as a whole does not always generate moral individuals. He blames the savagery of the lower classes upon a lack of skill, the absence of a drive for the acquisition of property, and a tendency toward sluggishness that inhibits planning beyond immediate rewards. The "dregs of civilized community" are "idle, thoughtless, improvident" and "thievish" (PE 149). The result of this outrageous description of the working class is not without its felicitous outcomes, however, for justifying reform on the only grounds that might have been acceptable to those who governed. The hallmark of civilization is specialization, the equation of a person's worth with the single operation he or she is able to perform. Reducing a man to "one part machine" is harmful because it "narrows the mind," leaving "intellectual faculties underdeveloped" (PE 195). Such a worker "loses, therefore, the habit of such exertion [invention] and generally becomes as stupid and ignorant as it is possible for a human creature to become" (PE 196). Reducing a modern member of society to an impoverished state through exploitation impairs the judgments, stifles intercourse, reduces dexterity, and comes at the expense of "intellectual, social, and martial virtues" (PE 196). True, if you educate the masses, some may become "puffed up with conceit," while others demand unwise "innovation" derived "from an idea that all ancient institutions must be either obsolete remnants of a state of general barbarism and darkness, or contrivances of fraudulent oppressors for imposing on the simple" (PE 211). Yet, it is equally fanciful and unjustified to view the past as a place of pastoral virtue or the present as the apex of progress. Importantly, through his *Political Economy,* Whately's views invite into the realm of evaluation a notion of responsibility for education related to the generation of new material wealth, not to mention the necessity for what, in his audience's estimation, would be prudent action forestalling revolution. This progressive view is a lynchpin of modernity in its shift from stable, rural, agricultural society to a progressive, pluralistic, urban world. Accepting the classical distinction between civilization and savagery, Whately twists the trope to argue that civilization is at risk unless the modern world recognizes the self-persuading nature of the social conditions availed to oppressed classes. Ironically, this argument is a powerful motivator for political change, even as it bulwarks nineteenth-century colonialist expansion.

CONCLUSION

In this work, we found that Whately retained the variability of choice known to the ancients but expanded judgment into the epistemic domain concerning permanence and change. He retained authority as a standard of rhetoric but relativized it across communities. Additionally, he recapitulated Aristotle's logic of excess and deficit in relation to the passions but differentiated private and public emotions in figuring recesses of resistance. Finally, he enlisted the imagination in aid of understanding, conferring the office upon rhetoric to render relationships vivid, an aesthetic act known to Aristotle, but he removed the distance between speaker and audience and placed them into a self-questioning line of sight. The modern rhetor is thus equipped with an expansive range of choice, relativized authority, conflicted emotions, and skeptical relation to the compositions of knowledge. Only this rhetor can come to terms with the complexity of changing relationships among experience and expertise, perspectives on appearance and reality in the conflicted spaces between individual purpose and collective results, and the eternal struggle between the conditions of civilization and savagery. Reading Whately's rhetoric across his political economy imparts a fuller picture of the predicaments of modernity as a master rhetorician deploys rhetoric to erase his art.

WORKS CITED

Whately, Richard. *Elements of Rhetoric*. 1846. Ed. Douglas Ehninger. Carbondale: Southern Illinois UP, 1963.
Whately, Richard. *Introductory Lectures on Political Economy*. 1832. New York: Kelley, 1966.

15

White Space as Rhetorical Space: Usability and Image in Electronic Texts

Joddy Murray
Washington State University, Tri-Cities

What exactly is the appeal of white space in regard to the usability of text, especially in terms of the layout and design of electronic texts such as web pages? Recent work done in the research on silence in discourse may begin to explain the use and effect of white space as image—as non-discursive text important to the rhetoricity of web pages and electronic communication. White space within electronic texts is especially important because it can provide relief to a user who is otherwise overrun with content and options. Just as silence can be used to emphasize or amplify a verbal statement for maximum effect on an audience, white space allows for ease, even pleasure, in the usability of complex documents: it highlights by making room, and it is associated with materiality and luxury.

White (or blank) space in discursive text operates in much the same way as it does in verbal discourse; it is an interpretive moment filled with many possible meanings. In exploring a few examples of the rhetorical use of white space as silence in web pages, I will also begin to provide a framework of three categories for the analysis of white space based on Bernard P. Dauenhauer's book *Silence: The Phenomenon and Its Ontological Significance*: intervening white space, fore-and-after white space, and deep white space. These categories help to illustrate what happens in the spaces where discursive text stops and non-discursive meaning emerges. In an age in which technology generally and information culture specifically is much maligned as continuously bombastic and full of noise, it is especially important to analyze how white space is used as silence and, more important, to discover what that silence can mean.

SILENCE AND WHITE SPACE

Silence is variously theorized in discourse studies, but one thing remains consistent—silence is not just a still moment in communication. Silence is an interpretive moment filled with many possible meanings: as turn-taking (Schegloff and Sacks 1973); as metaphoric extension (Bruneau 1973); diffusing hostility (Malinowski 1974); as censorship (Foucault

1978); as relevant activity (Goodwin 1980); as a public strategy (Brummet 1980); maintaining a speech frame (Tannen and Wallat 1987); as the absence of usable forms of symbolic expression (Ehrenhaus 1988); as an essential mechanism of social interaction (Tatsis and Zito 1992); as a mode of expression in the arts (Jaworski 1993); as an active state in discourse (Scott 1993); as a genuine mode of knowing (Kalamaras 1994); and as a counter-image that society projects into the environment (Luhmann 1994).

But in glancing at the literature, the theorist which seems to say the most about silence and its rhetorical use is Bernard P. Dauenhauer. In his book *Silence*, Dauenhauer stresses how silence is "active": discourse is only possible to the extent that silence (or negative space) is present to give that discourse form. The same is true in electronic space, especially in terms of rhetorically constructed web space. Certain web pages convey completely different messages not only through the visual way the page uses white (or blank) space, but also in the way those pages convey their content through the image of negative space. Just as silence allows time for the readers or listeners of text to "fill in" their own interpretation, or reflection, of what they are experiencing, white space can do the same: the user has time to pause, to take in the "feeling" of the site, to construct meaning outside of the presented text.

A common definition of "negative space" is one that emphasizes the shapes that are between or behind other shapes (Ocepek 118). Specifically, "a carefully considered correlation between positive and negative shapes enhances the design concept while energizing the layout" (118). But how do these "negative spaces" or shapes operate rhetorically? What do they do?

In *An Introduction to Discourse Analysis*, James Paul Gee asserts the following:

> We continually and actively build and rebuild our worlds not just through language, but through language used in tandem with actions, interactions, non-linguistic symbol systems, objects, tools, technologies, and distinctive ways of thinking, valuing, feeling, and believing. Sometimes what we build is quite similar to what we have built before; sometimes it is not. But language-in-action is always and everywhere an active building process. (11)

In building and rebuilding discourse, we may not attend to silence or white space because to participants in the process, silence is never silent: whether the focus of interpretation is on the speaker, the audience, or the web site, meaning is continually being built even when utterance or text is no longer present. Building discourse must depend, therefore, on silence as both a structural component *and* an integral and meaningful part of the receiver's (listener, viewer, reader, etc.) experience.

THREE SILENCE CATEGORIES

Dauenhauer's first category is intervening silence. Specifically "involved in the pacing of utterances, intervening silences punctuate those components—word phrases, musical notes, gestures, painted or sculpted shapes, etc.—which belong to an utterance taken as a whole" (6). An occurrence of intervening silence "terminates one sound phrase and, in some fashion, clears the way for the next sound phrase" (6–7). This kind of silence is rhythmically significant. In printed or oral text, this type of silence often comes in the form of punctuation (pauses and full stops), meter, and even the lack of physical expression or gesticulation (in the case of oration).

In electronic texts, intervening silence operates in much the same way. Even in the case of a web page consisting mostly of photos and illustrations, intervening silence is useful in the way text is organized into frames (the ability to display more than one web page within a single browser window), or the way images are organized next to each other (i.e., a calm image after a few frenetic ones, or the reverse). You can find this kind of silence often in gallery or museum web pages that deal with many images (or textual artifacts) organized into a collection: the Metropolitan Museum of Art (www.metmuseum.org), the Museum of Modern Art (www.moma.org), and the Guggenheim (www.guggenheim.org) provide just a few examples. The essential characteristic of this type of silence is in its pacing, rhythm, and/or the way this silence affects the viewer/reader *within* the utterance. In the case of galleries, the utterance is staying organized and labeled while the user is free to view images successively or in order of preference.

Dauenhauer's second category of silence is fore-and-after silence, defined as the silence that, in a sense, packages the text both before and after it is uttered, what Dauenhauer calls a "fringe of silence." There are two parts: the "fore-silence" and an "after-silence." Each component is constituted "by the occurrence of silence which immediately precedes the first sound phrase of an utterance and the occurrence of silence which immediately follows its last sound phrase" (9). In the case of electronic texts, this may be most readily translated to mean the amount and use of white space before and after a given web object, and it is most directly related to a document or web page's usability. Unlike intervening silence, these two occurrences of fore-silence and after-silence are not rhythmically significant, and they surround, rather than are located within, the utterance.

Fore-and-after silence is the white or blank space that exists between headings, Flash or ActiveX scenes, and even the space surrounding the web site in the first place (or the background). This type of silence literally constructs the content of the web space: it provides delineation, definition, and structure and is often what technical writers and web page designers mean when they declare a web site as "usable" or not. Web pages that are the most reliant of this kind of silence include news source web pages such as CNN, NPR, and MSNBC; web catalogs such as Wal-Mart, Best Buy, and Amazon.com; and reference web sites such as Reference.com and the Virtual Learning Resource Center (www.virtuallrc.com). As web sites become more cinematic and less based on layouts found on paper and advertisements, fore-and-after silence will still operate as boundaries around topics, subjects, and products.

Dauenhauer's last category of silence is called deep silence. He states, "Occurrences [...] do not appear to be subordinate to utterance. In fact, [...] they appear to enjoy a primacy over utterance" (16). Deep silence is the most rhetorical of these categories: it is rife with meaning that participants supply, reassess, and resupply. Dauenhauer specifies three modes of deep silence: "silence of intimates, liturgical silence, and the silence of the to-be-said" (17), but for my purpose here I will focus only on the latter. Dauenhauer defines the "to-be-said" as "the silence beyond all saying, the silence of the what-ought-to-be-said in which what-is-said is embedded" (19). In other words, this mode of silence "tests all that is said," which is an appeal "beyond the utterance for the authentication of the utterance" (19). Dauenhauer stresses that "whatever is uttered is either validated or invalidated by the silent to-be-said which the encountered world presents" (20). In addition, the silent to-be-said can be likened to "tact," or the act of contextualizing silence in such a way as to lead the listener to believe that what-ought-to-be-said is not being said on the grounds of being responsive either to the audience or to the audience's perception of the speaker. In short, deep silence of this sort functions rhetorically by *seeming* arhetorical.

In web texts, this form of "to-be-said" or "what-ought-to-be-said" is, of course, largely a matter of interpretation: by definition it has to be. But this form of silence is also very close to "what-cannot-be-said" or the unsayable or ineffable. In fact, this form of silence is close to what I would call the non-discursive use of silent image: the ability to mean many things and nothing at the same time. Ben-Ami Scharfstein, in his book *Ineffability: The Failure of Words in Philosophy and Religion*, defines the term *ineffability* as a more-or-less common phenomenon:

> We are the animals that use words and that complain rather often that they fail us. [...] [I]t is my strong conviction [...] that the various forms of ineffability are relevant to one another. [...] The reason for this [...] is the mutual inclusiveness and entanglement of worlds: each of us alone and in company is an approximately unified world in itself; and all these approximately unified worlds constitute a single, encompassing, unimaginably various world of worlds; and in all these worlds, as in the encompassing maybe limitless world of all worlds, every distinguishable quality is related to every other in somewhat the same way as our bodily activity is related to our emotionality, to our social needs, to our logic, and to the rhythms and intonations, both individually and generically human, in which we speak and remain silent. (xvii–xviii)

That is to say, our very social nature makes the interaction of our individual "worlds" both necessary and difficult. Writing discursively, whether online or on paper, can often become ineffable because the connections or relationships between these worlds are too complex for discursive logic. Deep silence in the form of the "to-be-said" allows us to inhabit these different worlds of discourse: to simply interact: to *be*. In that space, we allow images to form and become somehow combined or contrasted with experience and personal identities. This form of silence, then, exists because it allows us the time we need to anticipate and reformulate: the silence of the to-be-said allows the non-discursive to interact with the discursive.

Deep silence on the web can often, but not always, be found on splash pages (introductory pages). Whenever the web page seems to offer us very little, or highlight only a simple design or small amount of text, we are left in deep silence: there is space for us to interact with the site, to "fill in" our world with the world being presented. Just like in the printed realm, such pages paradoxically convey luxury and a level of materiality that can afford the time and money to create a space with so much emptiness, so much silence. The splash page to the Guggenheim site mentioned earlier, provides an example. Other than four slender images and the words *Guggenheim.org,* the page is completely white. After running the mouse pointer over each of the slender images, we can see that, if selected, each links to a different Guggenheim museum (New York, Bilbao, Venice, Berlin, and Las Vegas). Other than this, the page confronts us only with ourselves: an interaction that seems to convey the relative cultural importance of the museum and the treasure that may be found there.

In another example, the web page for the well-known designer Philippe Starck (www.philippe-starck.com) contains a grayed-out image of the designer, a scrolling gallery of some of his designs in a far corner, and simply the word *STARCK* typed vertically on the left. The user must pass over the word *STARCK* in order to get the menu of items the web site offers, but until then, there is very little left on the page with which to interact. Other than the scrolling marquee, the page is largely silent. Only when the user engages the page do more options become available, and even then they are constrained to the far left of the overall design. With deep silence, *copia* is replaced with meditative ambiguity: the appeal is to whisper rather than shout.

Silence exists in electronic texts as a way to construct non-discursive meaning in between discursive meaning. There are many other important kinds of silence in new media to investigate, especially in terms of how negative space/white space affects an audience directly. Rhetoricians have long noted the importance of the pause in orality; graphic designers also know the value of negative space. As rhetoricians continue to investigate new media and multimodal texts, we must also take note of the spaces between, among, and around utterances. As George Kalamaras has noted in his valuable book *Reclaiming the Tacit Dimension*, "the awareness of silence is not a transcendental state but is itself an act of interpretation and, consequently, a symbolic form" (187). He also emphasizes the importance of non-discursive language:

> I have been attempting to locate meaningfulness within a realm outside of discursive language, but not necessarily outside the domain of the Word. Indeed, we can never escape discursive ways of making meaning altogether, without using the discursive as a way of short-circuiting itself. Therefore, language can become a vehicle that enables one to experience the nondiscursive or nonconceptual realm of understanding. (121)

This may be the place for rhetorical studies to begin looking at silence in electronic texts because, as such, electronic texts struggle with both discursive and non-discursive logics. Silence, then, may be the place where these two forces in language intersect. Each silence, as such, helps build a world, and each world operates as a way to consider our own connection to it.

WORKS CITED

Brummett, B. "Towards a Theory of Silence as a Political Strategy." *Quarterly Journal of Speech* 66 (1980): 289–303.

Bruneau, T. J. "Communicative Silences: Forms and Functions." *Journal of Communication* 23 (1973): 17–46.

Dauenhauer, Bernard P. *Silence: The Phenomenon and Its Ontological Significance.* Bloomington: Indiana UP, 1980.

Ehrenhaus, Peter. "Silence and Symbolic Expression." *Communication Monographs* 55.1 (1988): 41–57.

Foucault, Michel. "The Incitement to Discourse." (1978) *The Discourse Reader.* Ed. Adam Jaworski and Nikolas Coupland. New York: Routledge, 1999. 514–22.

Gee, James Paul. *An Introduction to Discourse Analysis: Theory and Method.* New York: Routledge, 1999.

Goodwin, Charles. "Practices of Color Classification in Professional Discourse." *The Discourse Reader.* Ed. Adam Jaworski and Nikolas Coupland. New York: Routledge, 1999. 474–92.

Jaworski, Adam. *The Power of Silence: Social and Pragmatic Perspectives.* Newbury Park: Sage, 1993.

Kalamaras, George. *Reclaiming the Tacit Dimension: Symbolic Form in the Rhetoric of Silence.* Albany: State U of New York P, 1994.

Luhmann, Niklas. "Speaking and Silence." *New German Critique* 61 (1994): 25–37.

Malinowski, Bronislaw. "On Phatic Communication." (1974) *The Discourse Reader.* Ed. Adam Jaworski and Nikolas Coupland. New York: Routledge, 1999. 302–05.

Ocepek, Louis D. *Graphic Design: Vision, Process, Product.* Upper Saddle River, NJ: Prentice Hall, 2003.

Scharfstein, Ben-Ami. *Ineffability: The Failure of Words in Philosophy and Religion.* Albany:
    SUNY Press, 1993.
Schegloff, Emanuel A., and Harvey Sacks. "Opening Up Closings." (1973) *The Discourse Reader.*
    Ed. Adam Jaworski and Nikolas Coupland. New York: Routledge, 1999. 263–74.
Scott, Robert L. "Dialectical Tensions of Speaking and Silence." *Quarterly Journal of Speech,*
    79.1 (1993): 1–18.
Tannen, Deborah, and Cynthia Wallat. "Interactive Frames and Knowledge Schemas in Interac-
    tion: Examples from a Medical Examination/Interview." (1987) *The Discourse Reader.* Ed.
    Adam Jaworski and Nikolas Coupland. New York: Routledge, 1999. 367–75.
Tatsis, Nicholas, and George Zito. "The Social Meanings of Silence." American Sociological
    Association (1992). Abstract. 13 Apr 2001 <http://newfirstsearch.oclc.org>.

16

On a Rhetorical *Technē*
of the Moral-Emotions

Ellen Quandahl
San Diego State University

I begin with a few lines by a Bedouin girl, Kamla, from her essay written for ethnographer Lila Abu-Lughod on how young Bedouin women's lives are changing:

> [*The Bedouin*] *did not know that a girl had something she valued more than food and such things—and that was feelings.* (Feelings were forbidden to the girl.) *But she had feelings and sensitivity and affections just like any other person on this earth.* (This is true. There is no person God has created without feelings and sensitivity). (*Worlds* 213)

In previous work, Abu-Lughod had described her observations that among the Bedouin of Egypt, two apparently conflicting discourses—one of honor and modesty, and one of intimacy, sentiment, and sexual love—circulate in radically different social situations. The former underpins a social hierarchy and limits individual freedoms, especially women's freedoms to make life choices. The strength of this ideology of honor and modesty, she writes, is that "by framing ideas as values, in moral terms, it guarantees that people will desire to do what perpetuates the system" (*Sentiments* 238). Nor does this ideology merely mask the private and authentic feelings or inner reality expressed in the other, poetic discourse of sentiment and sexual love, which is also culturally sanctioned, and frames yet another set of ideals about cohesion among equals, thus also solidifying the social ranks. Such ethnographic work, like much recent scholarship, overturns the still-forceful *doxa* that emotions are simply internal, irrational, and natural (Lutz and Abu-Lughod 2), giving us good cause to reexamine *pathos*.

Kamla's essay appears in a chapter called "Honor and Shame," from a later collection of women's stories from the same period of Abu-Lughod's research, detached from generalizing moves such as the ethnographic impulse to say that this or that culture thinks and feels in this or that way. It may be a useful text for considering *pathos*, because it makes visible the link between one girl's feeling sense and her moral compass, since her most heated claims about wanting to go to school and to marry an educated Egyptian rather than a Bedouin kins-

151

man are at the same time bound up in distinctions about Bedouin piety, generosity, and mutual helpfulness, as against what she calls Egyptian or European immorality. Neither the essay nor Abu-Lughod's framing of it is written in an especially moving way. There is no high pathetic appeal nor elegant representation of the course of Kamla's emotions. Yet the text reveals that Kamla's reasons for what of the past she thinks should be kept and what abandoned have the force of reasons because of a moral-emotional orientation. Here one might think of Lynn Worsham's now indispensable definition of emotion as the "tight braid of affect and judgment, socially and historically constructed and bodily lived, through which the symbolic takes hold of and binds the individual, in complex and contradictory ways, to the social order and its structures of meaning" (216). Worsham theorizes, as Aristotle had done in a differently inflected way, a link between the sphere of ethics and that of emotion, which is evident in Kamla's essay. I want to briefly develop this side of a theory of *pathos* in order to raise the following question: What might be the role of *pathos*, with its ethical dimension, in a rhetorical pedagogy and a pedagogy of rhetoric?

I use the chiasmus to distinguish, on the one hand, rhetorical pedagogy as a structure of address, as what happens between teachers and students in the particular moment and with all of the complexities of rhetorical situation. So conceived, this is a situation where neither teachers nor students fully own their discourses and where *pathos* is at work, perhaps making unruly or unknowable the ways in which designs for students' development and knowing will operate, a scene of very high complexity. On the other hand, the pedagogy of rhetoric surely includes *information*, the concepts that structure curricula in a field where one works with students on their practices of reading and writing, their ways of working with language, their coming to know how to argue and communicate, to evaluate arguments and engage in ongoing research and discussions, which I take to be the broad territory of teaching in rhetoric at any level.

Where *pathos* is concerned, these two senses of pedagogy begin to be very engagingly linked, and I suggest that one might think of them together as part of a rhetorical craft which, like ancient *technai*, cuts across science and art, and which recently has been treated primarily by thinkers in hermeneutics or reader-response theory and in psychoanalysis somewhat more than by those in rhetoric. Such a craft is perhaps different from the two senses of pedagogy delineated by Worsham: the familiar sense of "pedagogy as a philosophy (or ideology) of teaching, including classroom practices and instructional methods; and the broad sense of pedagogy as education in general," the social *paideia* that shapes members of a culture, including what she calls primary education, the schooling of emotion (221, 223). (It's been rather stunning to me the extent to which it's necessary to think with and through these many prevailing definitions as I struggle toward a teachable theory of *pathos*. And so with emotion-words as well.) I want to stay with *pathos* here, in order to have recourse to rhetorical scholarship on the Greek term, and with the ordinary word *emotion*, in order to have recourse to scholarship about language practices, rather than that scholarship which struggles mightily to escape these to theorize and exploit an unbounded and wordless phenomenon, *affect*. I hope to show why I haven't begun at the end, with the inevitable move from rhetorical theory to practice, but at a necessary beginning, thinking about what pedagogy *is*.

Most often, our literature and mission statements about teaching make its enterprise an ethical and a teleological one, aiming at assisting students to become most fully themselves and to participate fully and equally in society. In this regard, it shares in the areas that Aristotle called politics and its subfield, ethics (of which rhetoric, as we know, is a "certain kind of offshoot" [*Rhetoric* 1356a]), since politics and ethics for him have as their aim people's flourishing, or living well over time. And in this realm of ethics-politics, Aristotle frequently says something quite surprising about the virtues or excellences—that they concern action and emotion, *praxis* and *pathos* (*Ethics* 1104b). Indeed a virtue, for Aristotle, is a characteristic or habit (*hexis*) of action and feeling. Kenneth Burke, at his most Aristotelian, claims that "insofar as ethics is treated *in its own terms*, as a special context of inquiry, rather than being reduced to non-ethical terms, one is pledged in advance to discourse on the subject of action and passion. For that is what the study of ethics is" (*Grammar* 137). Like Aristotle, Burke claims what Kamla's story illustrates, that the emotions are bound up with the ethical or moral sense.

The Greek term *pathos* helps us get at this nexus, because it means both what one experiences and what one feels. Aristotle uses the same word for both (Lear, *Open Minded* 211). One could say, as feminist Alison Jaggar does, that what one experiences linguistically and in social scenes are the preconditions for emotional life, within which the emotions come into being (135). In one of those great moments of clarity, Aristotle writes that the dispositions to act and feel are quite different from the innate capacities like seeing and hearing, which we first have and then use (*Ethics* 1103a). Rather, it is as people act in situations that they develop their interanimating moral and emotional habits. That is, if social culture educates emotions, it does so at least in part by setting the scene in which they are enacted and become dispositions.

This view interests me very much because it suggests that the place where our ethical ideas and histories come together is in emotion. Jonathan Lear, the philosopher turned psychoanalyst, amplifies two dimensions of this complex phenomenon that are useful for an inquiry into rhetoric and pedagogy. Lear notices that Aristotle conceives of emotions as "providing a *framework* through which the world is viewed," giving "pride of place to the way in which emotions locate the individual in the world" (*Love* 47-48). This is in line with Aristotle's suggestion that the rhetorician needs to know "what is their *state of mind* when people are angry and against *whom* are they usually angry, and for what sort of *reasons*" (*Rhetoric* 1378a). It is, Lear reminds us, through manipulating the "frame through which his audience interprets the world" that "the battle of persuasion is virtually won" (*Love* 48). But beyond orienting the individual, Lear argues, the emotion seems to come "packaged with its own *justification*." One is angry *because* one's wishes are frustrated, and the emotion, while it may involve bodily responses, awareness of them, fantasies of various kinds, "has not reached full development until it is able to express an explanation and justification of its own occurrence" (*Love* 50).

Now, as an analyst, Lear stresses that the emotion is also a significant psychological achievement, reached as the nameless events that befall one are converted into experiences of emotion and the equipment for handling them. To do this, he re-reads Freud's famous description of a child's fort/da (gone/there) game, tossing away and pulling back a spool on a string. Freud, as you recall, reads the game as a staging of the goings-away and returnings of the child's mother. But I don't think we even need the details of the case to appreciate Lear's calling it "a profile in (the development of) courage." He writes, "Aristotle insists that we need to be habituated into the ethical virtues, and I think we can here see Freud examining the prehistory of that psychic development" (*Happiness* 92). Fascinatingly, Lear reads the same occasion as one in which the child begins to feel what can be referred to as loss and to develop what can be referred to as the courage to face loss. In this amplifying of the psychology that Aristotle began in the *Ethics*, Lear shows that it is as people act in the face of life's contingencies that they develop and install what can then be reflected on and drawn upon as experiences of courage, loss, happiness, fortitude, and so on. This set-up suggests that emotions, as they develop together with the various dispositions of character, are significant motivators of moral responses. As Martha Nussbaum has suggested, they are components of judgment and motivators of action (392).

I think, then, that one might do well to call the *hexeis* or dispositions of character *moral-emotions*, and take them to be orientations in a broad sense. As I have argued elsewhere (20), they are much like what Kenneth Burke called *piety*, the overall "sense of what properly goes with what" (*Permanence* 74). That is, the emotions not only have their life in a social world, which educates them by setting the scene in which they are enacted and become dispositions, but they also bind the individual to ethical commitments and to the sense of how things are and ought to be. People are ethicized and emotionalized at once, and so what are to them good reasons have the force of "goodness" because goodness involves what one has experienced and what one feels. In other words, that the object of an emotion is its cause, the so-called cognitive view of emotions developed by Aristotle and many recent philosophers, needs to be complicated by the fact that emotions also occur within a skein of thoughts (to use Marcia Cavell's phrase [145]) that assimilate various causes and that take shape within the story of all that one has experienced, which also includes a developed, dispositional element. Moreover, as Burke shows in his discussion of orientation as *piety*, one's sense of what goes with what, how things are done, what is appropriate and good, has about it a non-churchly morality that is deeply felt and to which one feels, perhaps even unthinkingly, a kind of devotion which I would count as part of emotional life. Small wonder that students may feel and respond as if assaulted by arguments from other frames of reference and that entering into them may have the vague feeling of doing something wrong.

Now, Kamla's essay gives a rich illustration of *pathos* as conjoining what one experiences and what one feels, which is both social and individual, and which contributes so much to the apparent rationality and force of reasons. It is a text replete with rhetorical information—not about how one appeals to audiences' emotions, but about the operation or function of feeling in relation to values, judgments, and the arguments grounded in them. Guided by Burke, Aristotle, and Lear, one could frame questions inviting students to follow this thread of the ethnography, to bring it into high relief, and to make it a part of rhetorical knowledge.

A newly popular textbook featuring Kamla's story asks students to begin an engaged re-reading of the text by making a chart of all the relationships among the people in her complex family and community (Miller and Spellmeyer 52). Given that beginning, one might move with students to selecting passages that also show the mores that determine proper relationships and passages that trace, as Abu-Lughod suggests readers can do, "the outlines of the new world [Kamla] hoped to gain by marrying" outside her immediate community (*Worlds* 206). In preparation for a paper, students could also notice both where Kamla shows her feelings and where they respond as readers to this young woman, who both chafes against and fiercely defends her traditional Bedouin life. These could include not only Kamla's heated refusal to marry the cousin chosen for her, but also her claims that a Bedouin girl "has feelings for Egypt that may be even stronger than the Egyptian girl's" (*Worlds* 224) despite her father's fear of the influence of Egyptians on the Bedouin community. Alongside this, they might note Kamla's own defense of Bedouins as, for example, more modest and as better at mothering then Egyptians since Bedouins are not afraid to hit their errant daughters (*Worlds* 227-28). These readings may produce some confusion and/or resistance, since Kamla's feelings and her aspirations line up neatly neither with each other nor with American senses of romantic love and opportunities for women, for which, at first glance, Kamla seems to long. Students' responses to these facts may indeed be the most significant element of the work, as they begin to explore the interrelated workings of feeling and argument. Out of such note-taking and discussion, a writing project could ask students to explore whether and how their readings bear out or perhaps complicate Abu-Lughod's claim that her ethnographic works shows that "sentiments can actually symbolize values and that expression of these sentiments by individuals contributes to representations of the self, representations that are tied to morality, which in turn is ultimately tied to politics in its broadest sense" (*Sentiments* 34).

Such a project would complicate textbook notions of pathos, which, as Moon has shown, is usually the bastard in the trio with logos and ethos, something outside of or added to reason, or consulted and appealed to when all else fails (38). It would explore what Cintron, in his ethnography of the emotions, has called their "public dimension," the idea that emotions "do not just well up from the interior of a person but are distinctly shaped along systemic lines" (131). But Lear, as a practitioner, argues that "the concepts of theory, if they are to earn their theoretical living, are infused with meaning by the daily efforts of analysts and analysands, trying to come to grips with, to understand and react to, their lives" (*Love* 16). Similarly, a rhetorical pedagogy ought to infuse its concept of *pathos* with meaning by the daily efforts of teachers and students in their work of coming to grips with texts, the new material that one hopes will differently backlight their and our emotional and moral life. Thus, the text of students' comments in both discussion and writing on "Honor and Shame" must be the teachers' guide to facilitating whatever happens next in the class.

Consider, too, that assessment (which now drives curricula), demands, as Elizabeth Ellsworth has argued, a "correct fit" between curriculum and student understanding, a match between what teachers offer and students "get" (45–46). And yet the terms of curricular address necessarily misfire, since, as we've been saying for years now, our language knows more than we can know, speaks more than we intend; it belongs to social and cultural norms and to the narrative of individuals' lives, in which, as Peter Goldie and Dennis Lynch show, one's emotions and emotional dispositions are embedded. These are fairly settled notions for rhetoricians since Kenneth Burke, and they mean that there can never be a perfect fit between curricula and, to use a phrase from James Donald, the "psychic effect of *feeling*" of students encountering them (qtd. in Ellsworth 42). The moral-emotions alive and developing in students and their scholar-teachers are struggling into expression, lending their life and their meanings to what gets encountered in curricula, how it gets taken up and developed and used. We cannot, then, fully recognize "the learner's logic" (Britzman 26). That assessment must acknowledge this complexity is the subject of another paper. That this complexity is not a problem to be solved, or a theory to be translated into method, might be the first principle of a rhetorical pedagogy whose ethicality resides in an artful listening as much as in a democratic *telos*. Among its most crucial questions will be: How will I take up and develop the themes articulated by students, hand them back, work with them differently? (James Seitz, using Ellsworth, addressed such questions in a recent talk on responding to student writing.)

One last note: Aristotle suggests that not only the virtues and emotions, but also the *arts* are developed by enactment (*Ethics* 1103a). If rhetorical pedagogy is one such *technē*, its theory of *pathos* needs to be teachable, made visible in texts like Kamla's, and also artful, used by teachers who develop a feel for the fact that teaching misses its mark, since what students have experienced and felt is—productively, I would suggest—always getting in the way.

WORKS CITED

Abu-Lughod, Lila. *Veiled Sentiments: Honor and Poetry in Bedouin Society*. Berkeley: U of California P, 1999.
---. *Writing Women's Worlds: Bedouin Stories*. Berkeley: U of California P, 1992.
Aristotle. *Nicomachean Ethics*. Trans. Martin Ostwald. Englewood Cliffs: Liberal Arts, 1962.
---. *On Rhetoric*. Trans. George A. Kennedy. New York: Oxford UP, 1991.
Britzman, Deborah P. *Lost Subjects, Contested Objects: Toward a Psychoanalytic Inquiry of Learning*. Albany: State U of NewYork, 1998.
Burke, Kenneth. *A Grammar of Motives*. Berkeley: U of California P, 1974.
---. *Permanence and Change: Toward an Anatomy of Purpose*. 3rd ed. Berkeley: U of California P, 1984.
Cavell, Marcia. *The Psychoanalytic Mind: From Freud to Philosophy*. Cambridge: Harvard UP, 1993.
Cintron, Ralph. *Angels' Town: Chero Ways, Gang Life, and Rhetoric of the Everyday*. Boston: Beacon, 1997.
Ellsworth, Elizabeth. *Teaching Positions: Difference, Pedagogy and the Power of Address*. New York: Teachers College P, 1997.
Goldie, Peter. *The Emotions: A Philosophical Exploration*. Oxford: Clarendon, 2000.
Jaggar, Alison. "Love and Knowledge: Emotion in Feminist Epistemology." *Women, Knowledge, and Reality: Explorations in Feminist Philosophy*. Ed. Ann Garry and Marilyn Pearsall. Boston: Unwin, 1989. 129–55.
Lear, Jonathan. *Happiness, Death, and the Remainder of Life*. Cambridge: Harvard UP, 2000.
---. *Love and its Place in Nature* New York: Farrar, 1990.
---. *Open Minded: Working out the Logic of the Soul*. Cambridge: Harvard UP, 1998.
Lutz, Catherine A., and Lila Abu-Lughod. *Language and the Politics of Emotion*. Cambridge: Cambridge UP, 1990.
Lynch, Dennis. "Streams of Affect: An Integrative Approach to the Study of *Pathos*." Rhetoric Society of America Conference. Austin. 24 May 2004.
Miller, Richard E., and Kurt Spellmeyer. *The New Humanities Reader*. Boston: Houghton, 2003.
Moon, Gretchen Flesher. "The Pathos of *Pathos*: The Treatment of Emotion in Contemporary Composition Textbooks." *A Way to Move*. Ed. Dale Jacobs and Laura R. Micciche. Portsmouth: Heinemann, 2003. 33–42.
Nussbaum, Martha C. *The Therapy of Desire: Theory and Practice in Hellenistic Ethics*. Princeton: Princeton UP, 1994.
Quandahl, Ellen. "A Feeling for Aristotle: Emotion in the Sphere of Ethics." *A Way to Move*. 11–22.
Seitz, James. "Student Writing as Subject and Object." Conference on College Composition and Communication Convention. San Antonio. 25 March 2004.
Worsham, Lynn. "Going Postal: Pedagogic Violence and the Schooling of Emotion." *JAC* 18.2 (1998): 213–45.

17

Language's Duality
and the Rhetorical Problem of Music

Thomas Rickert
Purdue University

My title speaks to a duality in language hinted at in the early work of Nietzsche, a duality that challenges the traditional relation between language and music. Of course, rhetoric and music have often been conjoined. By this, I mean more than that forms of music and language come together, as in poetry, chant, and song. I mean that music and rhetoric inform each other not simply in the generation of such hybrid arts, but in the recursive development of discourses about music and rhetoric, whereby music provides a framework for understanding and practicing rhetoric, and vice versa. This is not to say that they are the same, but it is to suggest that rhetoric has not attended to how intimate they in fact are—and this is crucial—on music's terms, as opposed to rhetoric's or philosophy's terms. It is an understatement to say that the relations between the two are not equal. Overwhelmingly, the intellectual tradition has considered music suspicious if not dangerous. There have been two interrelated reasons for this: first, music's indeterminacy forestalls the kinds of control we seemingly achieve over language; second, while both music and language induce feelings, sensations, and emotions, music has been considered the more effective in doing so. One sees the problem: music is not only more affectively powerful, but indeterminately so, which opens the door, it is argued, for all manner of impropriety, decadence, and ill-virtue. To the extent that the language of rationality is elevated as the highest universal good and the key to ethical life, music and affect have been held in suspicion and tightly controlled.

Intriguingly, much contemporary thought, especially in the sciences, argues that music is not to be considered so much suspicious as unimportant. For example, the well-known evolutionary psychologist Steven Pinker has written books about how the mind works and how important language is to human evolution, but when it comes to music, he is less impressed. It communicates "nothing but formless emotion," and as far as biology is concerned, "music is useless" (528–29). Labeling music "auditory cheesecake," Pinker asserts that "[c]ompared with language, vision, social reasoning, and physical know-how, music could vanish from our species and the rest of our lifestyle would be virtually unchanged" (528, 534). While acknowledging the power of its effects on human life and culture, Pinker and like-minded scientists see music as, at best, decorative or palliative and, hence, parasitic on the truly great evolutionary advancements like language.

While Pinker shares with the historical tradition the valuation of language as primary, he is at odds with it concerning music's scope and affective power.[1] In the ancient Greek world, music was often integral to a conception of divine order. Representative here are Pythagoras and his followers, who held that the mathematical underpinnings of music "partook of the unity of numbers which were the realities underlying all manifestation" (Epperson 30). Music also concerned Plato and Aristotle. Plato was undoubtedly influenced by the Pythagoreans, but he focused on music's affective power to shape character. Music may reflect divine harmony and the moral order of the universe, but it remains perilous. Thus, one must listen to the right sorts of music. In *Laches,* he tells us that the true musician "has in his own life a harmony of words and deeds arranged—not in the Ionian, or in the Phrygian mode, nor yet in the Lydian, but in the true Hellenic mode, which is the Dorian, and no other" (188D). Forms of limitation and control are necessary because music's sensuousness, supposedly expressed in certain modes, rhythms, and melodies, creates pernicious effects. In the *Republic*, we are warned that music enters "the innermost part of the soul and powerfully [seizes] it" (401d).[2] Song, in moderation, helps create pliant and useful souls, but in excess, if one becomes spellbound, song ensures that the very sinews of one's soul will be cut out, leaving one discontent, touchy, and feeble (411b). Given music's affective power to sway ethical life, Plato argues for the censorship and the abolishment of all but the most proper forms of music. Further, he necessitates that words always be given priority over melody (398d, 400a, 400d).

In the *Politics*, Aristotle devotes a whole section to the problem of music and education. Like Plato, he sees the necessity for keeping the emotions in check, and he too is wary of music's affective potency. Further, he sees music as a leisure activity, tied to pleasure—in this regard, Pinker's conclusions about music as auditory cheesecake are old hat (Aristotle 1338a13). Insofar as one's virtue is tied to "taking pleasure aright and liking and disliking," then learning to judge properly the various forms of music, even if they are not directly useful, is necessary for education; Aristotle even goes so far as to recommend learning to perform when young, although he recommends giving it up when older (1340a14, 1340b31). Like Plato, Aristotle is attuned to the way music affects us; thus, the modes are one way of tying music to our emotional states: the Mixed Lydian induces grief and apprehension, the Phrygian enthusiasm, and, also like Plato, he finds the Dorian superior for its settling effects (1340a38). Like Socrates in *The Republic*, Aristotle is leery of Bacchic excitement and the frenzy of pipes. In short, music endows the soul with character, and one must be educated properly to judge it; musical education thereby serves as the means to mollify music's affective potency.

Plato's and Aristotle's cautions about music have been intellectual mainstays. St. Augustine, for example, valued music for its religious utility, but also feared its sensuous elements; he remained anxious that the words always take precedence over the melody, a concern shared by Plato (Epperson 44). Thus, he sees himself as falling into sin when he is deeply moved by a well-sung hymn, and the rhythmic and melodic elements tempt him to move beyond the sense of words (Augustine, Book X, 33). Over the next millennia, Church doctrine reinforced these basic moves of Augustine, seeing, in the Platonic way, each new musical innovation as the road to moral ruination. Thus, we get seminal moments like Pope John XXII's 1324 decree *Docta Sanctorum Patrum* and the Council of Trent's sixteenth-century pronouncement concerning the necessity of maintaining the intelligibility of the vocals over the affective forces of the music (Dolar 22). Similarly, Kant was suspicious of music for its shortcomings in relation to other fine arts—it produced enjoyment more than culture, feeling more than sense—and judged it as having the least value (328). Thus, Kant preferred vocal music, and so did Hegel, who deprecated "wordless music as subjective and indefinite" (Epperson 47). More recently, neoconservative critiques such as those of Allan Bloom, Robert Bork, and John McWhorter make arguments that contemporary music is culturally degenerative, thereby upholding an argument at least as old as Plato.

Brian Vickers, in his comprehensive essay "Figures of rhetoric/Figures of music?", traces out a more favorable approach to the relations among words, music, and affect in Renaissance rhetoric. Vickers, it should be noted, is nevertheless wary of running music and rhetoric together to the extent that someone like Joachim Burmeister did, who, writing between 1599 and 1606, developed "the first extended list of specific musical-rhetorical figures"; later writers in the seventeenth and eighteenth centuries further refined and extended his list of twenty-six to well over a hundred (Vickers 19–20). Vickers argues that the source for such a development was Quintillian, who first proposed the affinity between music and rhetoric, arguing in the *Institutes* that the orator should learn from the musician (Vickers 5). During the Renaissance, Quintillian was frequently cited in support of the idea that "music affected the passions" (6). The upshot was the repeated lesson that the affective power of music moves the passions in the same way as rhetoric (9), but as Vickers points out, this was primarily a one-way street involving the "rhetorization of music" (15). For example, musical terms like *theme, phrase, period, accent, figure, style, composition,* and *metrics* were all actually derived from the language arts (17). Ultimately, Vickers concludes that rhetoric and music can only share so much, but that rhetoric has throughout the centuries rightly been dominant, thereby falling in line with the general attitude toward music set out by Plato and Aristotle of making music subservient to the word.

In sum, we see here a general trend toward the overvaluation of reason over feeling, of determinate sense over indeterminate affect, and of more controlled aesthetic forms over the more unpredictable. All this may already be well known, especially since modern and postmodern critiques of this trend are commonplace. Another serious problem concerns the assumed mimetic function of music, in which music is thought to somehow imitate the emotions in order to evoke them. While this is an old and persistent idea, it is mistaken. Contemporary musicologists have argued that there is nothing to suggest that music mimics or reflects moral order, nor that any supposed licentiousness in music will lead to moral decay (Epperson 66; Kivy 3–18). Such arguments, however, are relatively recent, and it is important to have this historical background firmly in one's grasp in order to understand fully the radical import of the stance Nietzsche took with regard to music in *The Birth of Tragedy* and his short fragment from 1871, "On Music and Words." Nietzsche is significant for his attempt to counter millennia-old pronouncements about the dangers of music.[3]

The subtitle of Nietzsche's essay is "Or why great music—Dionysian music—makes us forget to listen to the words," and it is already indicative of his attempt to revalue music. Nietzsche notes that music in its origins begins in association with lyrical poetry and must traverse stages before it becomes absolute music; he then goes on to add that if we consider lyrical poetry to be imitative of the artistry of nature, then "we must find the original model of this association of music and lyrical poetry in the *duality* that nature has built into *the essence of language*" (103-04). Nietzsche's meaning is not immediately obvious. Nevertheless, the suggestion seems to be that lyrical poetry can only emerge if language has a musical component. In other words, the dual nature of language is such that we can no longer maintain so rigorous a distinction between the communicative and the melodic.

Such an assertion is obviously at odds with the tradition inherited from Plato, Aristotle, and the Church; yet it is also different from the Renaissance rhetoricians detailed by Vickers. Certainly these rhetoricians applied techniques from music to rhetoric and back, but they nevertheless maintained differences regarding their essences. One could deploy musical figures to further one's rhetorical purpose of evoking the proper affective response, for example, but this still fell far short of asserting, as Nietzsche appears to, that there is something already musical in language that allows for the emergence of lyrical poetry in the first place. This duality in the nature of language sets up two inversions: first, an emphasis on music over words, and second, affect over reason. Nietzsche offers as evidence a variety of phenomena: that while the musician may cross the bridge into the land of images, the lyric poet may not cross back to the land of the musician; or that Schiller's poem "To Joy" in Beethoven's Ninth Symphony is essentially unheard. Note: it is not that we cannot hear the words; rather, it is that the music blinds us in some essential way to their imagery and sense. As Nietzsche puts it, before the sublime wonder of Beethoven's music, all of the noble verve of Schiller's poem seems disturbing or distressing, even crude and insulting (112). He later claims that music can never become a means for words, and even in its "crudest and simplest stages it still overcomes poetry and reduces it to its reflection" (117).

These somewhat sketchy arguments were central, in more developed form, to *The Birth of Tragedy*, which appeared the following year in 1872. There Nietzsche claims that melody is primary and universal, over and above even poetry, which emerges from folk song (53).[4] He also claims that language inevitably falters before the sublime fulsomeness of music, finding in this revelation an argument for music's aesthetic superiority, contra the judgments of the philosophical tradition. Lyric arts, therefore, depend on the spirit of music, while music merely endures images and concepts as accompaniment (55). Nietzsche further holds that the lyric arts can express nothing that "did not already lie hidden in that vast universality and absoluteness in the music that compelled [the lyric artist] to figurative speech" (55). Thus, *The Birth of Tragedy* also traces out a duality, but this time from music's perspective: it is from out of music's "cosmic symbolism"—one of many such locutions Nietzsche devises—that the language arts emerge, meaning that music already bears language within it; it is as if language already rests within music in a nascent or virtual form.

Today, despite the claims of Pinker and other scientists that music is of little or no value, a number of empirical studies have emerged that support Nietzsche's arguments. Studies conducted in 1950 by Riesman, in the 1960s by Denzin, and in the 1970s by Robinson and Hirsch, and many more besides, have concluded that the majority of listeners respond vastly more to the sound of music than to the words (Frith 95, 105nn.52–55). Even in the case of protest music, listeners are typically unaware of what the words are or what the song is about. Often, when they do take the time to figure out the lyrics, they disagree with them (Frith 95–96). Simon Frith argues that while words may matter in assessing the cultural significance of song, words have at best an oblique relation to audience moods, beliefs, and ideologies (96). This further suggests that music primarily connects with audiences affectively and to such an extent that even disagreeable words may not be an impediment to music's power. It further suggests that the use of borderline nonsensical lyrics, as exemplified by rock artists such as T. Rex, Yes, The Cocteau Twins, Sigur Rós, and many more besides, can only be considered nonsensical from a linguistic perspective; from the perspective of the music, they do offer a kind of sense, and not only because they share in music's fulsome indeterminacy.

In addition to sociological and empirical researchers, some neurocognitivist scientists are also making claims that substantiate some of Nietzsche's views. For example, Antonio

Damasio argues in *The Feeling of What Happens* that the emotional tagging of experience is necessary for survival, suggesting that music has a special role to play in such tagging. These ideas concerning music's central role in the organization of our affective lives are given further credence in a recent collection, *The Cognitive Neuroscience of Music* (Peretz and Zatorre). Some basic claims, made by several researchers, are that music does serve an evolutionary function, that it is not useless or solely pleasurable, and that it should be considered a complex biological adaptation (see, e.g., Trehub, Cross, and Huron in Peretz and Zatorre). Huron, for example, discusses eight possible evolutionary needs for music, including social cohesion, mate selection, group effort, and motor skill development (61).[5] Trehub argues that mothers speak and sing to infants in highly idiosyncratic ways (e.g., with elevated pitch, slurred syllables) that infants respond to more favorably than they do to normal song and speech. She states, "Maternal music as a means of optimizing infant mood or arousal parallels adolescents' and adults' use of music for self-regulation" (11). Infants, she concludes, do not begin life with a "musical blank slate," but have a predisposition for sophisticated musical processing that is biological, not cultural (13–14).

Other studies show that the brain processes music and language independently of each other and that different parts of the brain are responsible for each. Although language tends to be processed first, one typically drowns out the other (Besson and Schön 281). From the perspective I have been developing here, it is music that tends to drown out words. Thus, a key question has been whether to see this as something positive, as Nietzsche attempts to do, or to seek protections against it, as the Platonic tradition demands.

As far as rhetoric is concerned, aside from the adaptation of musical motifs in developing rhythms and figures as described by Vickers, there has by and large been considerably more resisting than embracing of the musical component of language and its ties to the affective regulation or modification of audiences. A notable exception to this general reluctance is the work of Steven Katz, who argues in *The Epistemic Music of Rhetoric* that we should move beyond a "reliance on formalistic, rationalistic methods of investigating and knowing," not because they are wrong, but because they are limited (11). Katz seeks to understand how the dual indeterminacies of music and physical affective responses can be forms of knowledge (12). Katz, I argue, is aligned with Nietzsche in pointing to a kind of duality inherent in language. As Katz puts it, the challenge is to respond to "language as a musical trace of emotion in sound, rather than only as visual ideation, the imaging of meaning" (181–82).

My remarks here are necessarily sketchy and open-ended. In part, this open-endedness reflects an essential problem: music and affect lean toward subjective experience and, even in those terms, remain indeterminate. Furthermore, the problem takes its particular shape because of our dominant epistemological mindset, which is still heavily indebted to the very tradition that has overprivileged rationality and language at the expense of music and affect. Claiming epistemological status for what is defined as subjective experience is notoriously difficult; superlative efforts like those of Roland Barthes in *Camera Lucida*, where he essays to develop a science of the unique or irreducible, are given short shrift (Barthes 8, 71). It is difficult, then, in the face of the dominant will for determinate knowledge to side with indeterminacy and, even more precariously, make claims for it as a form of knowledge worth pursuing, one that is not just useful for rhetoric but already inscribed within all the language arts, rhetoric included. It might be objected that in relying on the young Nietzsche in making my argument, I have fallen prey to the problems of the romantic tradition he was working out of and was indeed highly critical of when he assessed *The Birth of Tragedy* in a new preface sixteen years later. However, as Katz's work shows, and as some of the work in neurocognitivist science makes plain, one need not remain in the romanticist framework to begin rethinking the importance of indeterminate knowledge for rhetoric. Thus, contra to the long dominant fears of the Platonic tradition, and indeed to the contemporary mindset, we should seek new ways of understanding, theorizing, and working with rhetoric as both an affective and musical art. This will mean, among other things, expanding greatly on our ability to theorize, codify, teach, and perform the musical aspects of language to achieve our goals at the level of affect. Any such project, however, will also face all the barriers established by a tradition that holds such a call in the greatest suspicion. But perhaps we can take heart from recent work that challenges this tradition, showing that the moral grounds upon which it stakes its claims are increasingly flimsy if not simply false. The challenge now is to build on such work and thereby extend rather than delimit the scope of rhetorical knowledge and practice.

NOTES

1. The argument that music is useless is actually quite old. For example, Democritus (c. 420 BC) made this same point; similarly, Aristotle saw music as pleasurable but lacking utility (Freeman 105).
2. The Greek term *mousik*, referring to the art of the muses, includes literary and artistic accomplishments generally, and not only music, but it can refer to our sense of music as well. It should be noted that some translators substitute "poetry" for music, but given that music, poetry, and literature formed the basis of Greek education, we should also keep in mind that "music" connotes education in general.
3. While I do not have the space to explore this further here, I should mention Hildegaard of Bingen, a twelfth-century abbess, who like Nietzsche also argued for music's primacy. For example, one of her works, *Ordo virtutum*, personifies the virtues in singing roles; the only speaking role—and incidently the only masculine character—is the devil. Perhaps unsurprisingly, in 1147 she barely escaped being condemned as a heretic (Dolar 22–23).
4. I do not have the space to explicate the romantic underpinnings of such an assertion, which can be seen to harken back to arguments such as those of Rousseau, who held that music was primary and that the first languages were sung not spoken, thus pointing to the importance of the affective prior to valuations of rationality (see Rousseau and Herder).
5. Although I cannot pursue the idea here, it would be of great interest to investigate to what extent Nietzsche's claim that Dionysian music achieves the dissolution of the principle of individuation dovetails with Huron's claims concerning music's role in social cohesion, group effort, conflict reduction, and so on. At this point, however, any such linkage must remain speculative.

WORKS CITED

Aristotle. *Politics*. Trans. Peter L. Phillips Simpson. Chapel Hill: U of North Carolina P, 1997.

Augustine. *The Confessions*. Trans. Rex Warner. New York: Mentor, 1963.

Barthes, Roland. *Camera Lucida: Reflections on Photography*. Trans. Richard Howard. New York: Hill and Wang, 1981.

Besson, Mireille, and Daniele Schön. "Comparison between Language and Music." *The Cognitive Neuroscience of Music*. Ed. Isabelle Peretz and Robert Zatorre. Oxford: Oxford UP. 2003. 269–93.

Damasio, Antonio. *The Feeling of What Happens: Body and Emotion in the Making of Consciousness*. San Diego: Harcourt, 1999.

Dolar, Mladen. "The Object Voice." *Gaze and Voice as Love Objects*. Ed. Renata Salecl and Slavoj i ek. Durham: Duk e UP, 1996. 7-31.

Epperson, Gordon. *The Musical Symbol: A Study of the Philosophic Theory of Music*. Ames: Iowa State UP, 1967.

Freeman, Kathleen. *Ancilla to the Pre-Socratic Philosophers*. Cambridge: Harvard UP, 1983.

Frith, Simon. "Why Do Songs Have Words?" *Lost in Music: Culture, Style and the Musical Event.* Ed. Avron Levine White. New York: Routledge, 1987. 77–106.

Huron, David. "Is Music an Evolutionary Adaptation?" *The Cognitive Neuroscience of Music*. Ed. Isabelle Peretz and Robert Zatorre. Oxford: Oxford UP, 2003. 57–75.

Kant, Immanuel. *Critique of Judgment*. Trans. Werner S. Pluhar. Indianapolis: Hackett, 1987.

Katz, Steven B. *The Epistemic Music of Rhetoric*. Carbondale: Southern Illinois UP, 1996.

Kivy, Peter. *Sound and Semblance: Reflections on Musical Representation*. Princeton: Princeton UP, 1984.

Nietzsche, Friedrich. *The Birth of Tragedy*. Trans. Walter Kaufmann. New York: Vintage, 1967.

——. "On Music and Words." Trans. Walter Kaufmann. *Between Romanticism and Modernism: Four Studies in the Music of the Later Nineteenth Century*. Ed. Carl Dahlhaus. Berkeley: U of California P, 1980. 103–20.

Peretz, Isabelle, and Robert Zatorre, eds. *The Cognitive Neuroscience of Music*. Oxford: Oxford UP, 2003.

Pinker, Steven. *How the Mind Works*. New York: Norton, 1997.

Plato. *Laches*. Trans. Benjamin Jowett. New York: Modern Library (n.d.).

——. *The Republic*. Trans. Raymond Larson. Arlington Heights: AHM, 1979.

Rousseau, Jean-Jacques, and Johann Gottfried Herder. *On the Origin of Language: Two Essays*. Trans. John H. Moran and Alexander Gode. Chicago: U of Chicago P, 1966.

Trehub, Sandra E. "Musical Predispositions in Infancy: An Update." *The Cognitive Neuroscience of Music*. Ed. Isabelle Peretz and Robert Zatorre. Oxford: Oxford UP, 2003. 3–20.

Vickers, Brian. "Figures of rhetoric/Figures of music?" *Rhetorica* 2.1 (Spring 1984): 1–44.

18

The Scientific Media Hoax:
A Rhetoric for Reconciling Linguistics
and Literary Criticism

Lynda Walsh
New Mexico Institute of Mining and Technology

In August of 1835, a scientific story sold a record number of copies of the brand new penny daily the New York *Sun*. It described in minute detail the observations of British astronomer J. F. W. Herschel, who had recently built a new observatory at Capetown with a telescope capable of viewing the moon's surface. To the astonishment of the scientist himself and the readers of the *Sun,* there were moon-bison, man-bats, and fields of poppies on the surface of the moon. New York was in an uproar over the news. A Baptist society reportedly began taking up a collection to send missionaries to the poor naked man-bats (Martineau 23). And then it came out that the story was in fact an elaborate fabrication by the *Sun*'s science writer, Richard Adams Locke. Interestingly, one of the critics who outed Locke was none other than Edgar Allan Poe. Ruthless in his enumeration of the scientific inadequacies of Locke's story, Poe's real motivation in exposing Locke seems to have been jealousy, for Poe had published his own moon hoax a few months earlier in the *Southern Literary Messenger,* and no one had paid it any mind.

Locke and Poe were not the only writers to toy with America's fascination with science. From the mid-1830s to the 1880s, at least a dozen similar major hoaxes appeared in penny dailies or literary monthlies. Poe could claim four of them. Other contributors included Mark Twain, who wrote a hoax about a petrified man, and his colleague Dan De Quille, who authored numerous scientific hoaxes including the "Solar Armor" hoax in which an inventor turns up a frozen corpse in the middle of Death Valley because the wet-sponge suit that he designed to cool himself down worked a little too efficiently (Fedler 40).

I discovered this strange antebellum media craze by accident, through a stray line mentioning it in Robert V. Bruce's *The Launching of Modern American Science*. I was fascinated and immediately had two questions I wanted answered: Why did august literary figures such as Poe and Twain bother to write fake science stories for newspapers? And how had they managed to fool so many people? I reviewed the scholarly work on these hoaxes, but my

165

questions remained unanswered. Previous treatments of the hoaxes were strictly literary, in that they ignored the reception of the hoaxes and instead preoccupied themselves with the physical texts—either shoehorning them into the authors' existing repertoire as science fiction, satire, tall tale, and so on, or treating them as fantasies that indexed the authors' psychological hang-ups.

It was quickly apparent that literary approaches to the hoaxes could not answer my questions because my questions were not literary: they were essentially questions of pragmatics—the social work that words do in the world. I wanted to know how the words of each hoax had temporarily altered the world inhabited by its reader so that it suddenly included petrified men and moon-bison. In short, I realized after my review of previous work on the hoaxes that answering my questions was going to entail a preliminary search for an analytical method capable of fielding them.

THE SEARCH FOR A METHOD: GRICE'S MAXIMS

I knew where to start. I knew what I needed to effect my analysis was something akin to Grice's maxims, which I had encountered in my semantics and pragmatics courses in linguistics. H. Paul Grice was a semantician who studied implicatures in conversation. Implicatures govern communication but are not hard-and-fast grammatical rules, as they can be and often are broken to create indirect speech acts. They are based on a common assumption of cooperativity that people make when they communicate. To formalize his intuitions about implicatures, Grice broke down the cooperativity principle into four basic maxims:

- Maxim of Quality: Tell the truth.
- Maxim of Quantity: Be as informative as expected.
- Maxim of Relevance: Make your contribution relevant to what has come before.
- Maxim of Manner: Be brief, orderly, and clear.

The maxims are usually adhered to in most "normal" communication, written and spoken, but they can be departed from in significant ways. Violation is unilateral departure, where one party is lying or otherwise secretly undermining the Cooperativity Principle; "flouting," in Grice's scheme, however, is a mutually obvious departure from the norms, and it structures indirect speech acts like sarcasm and irony. Clearly, in the process of hoaxing, violation and/or flouting of maxims (depending on whether the reader is duped or catches on) helps build the hoax's rhetorical effect. However, Gricean maxims are very general rules governing conversation, whereas writing and reading the hoaxes must have involved knowledge of certain specific conventions of the genre of the popular science article in the 1800s. So, although Grice's maxims would not exactly fit the bill, I knew I needed a similar methodology that reconstructed the meaning of a communicative act not as a function of the text or message itself but as an interaction of the text/message with the preconceptions and desires of both its author and its reader. I wanted to treat the hoaxes as rich textualities, as events that had social consequences at the time of their writing and reading.

I began to search for a suitable methodology among the schools of criticism whose interests seemed to converge in the problem of the hoax: reader-response (reception studies), new-historicism, sociolinguistics, pragmatics, and rhetoric. As it turned out, I had to build my own method of analysis from these traditions by a technique of *bricolage*. But in the course of my search, I encountered two fascinating critical genealogies, one constructing a disciplinary classism that predicted ultimate failure for my attempts to show how the hoaxes had worked on their readers, and one providing me with the pedigree I needed to justify my project and the tools to complete it.

THE SEARCH FOR A METHOD:
TWO GENEALOGIES OF PHILOLOGY

Both genealogies begin with the study of philology in the eighteenth century. The word *philology* was first used by Plato, most likely in the *Laches,* to denote a love(r) of debate or discussion. The term was revived in 1777 by Friedrich Wolf, a German scholar who used it to define the field he wished to study, overall an "attention to the grammar, criticism, geography, political history, customs, mythology, literature, art, and ideas of people" (qtd. in Graff 69). This ambitious program engendered both American linguistics and American English departments. Their short common history and famous parting of the ways during the World Wars are amply documented and analyzed by R. H. Robins, Julie Tetel Andresen, Gerald Graff, and most fully by Jacqueline Henkel in her landmark study *The Language of Criticism: Linguistic Models and Literary Theory.* But to sum up, the end result of this lineage was two incompatible programs, one working on writing and one working on speech, the disciplinary boundaries between them scarified by the trauma of Derrida's criticisms of John Searle and J. L. Austin in *Of Grammatology.*

However, I also discovered by working backward from Searle and Austin an alternate or subversive genealogy of philology that tells a story, against the traditional story of schism, about how certain linguists, critics, and rhetoricians have maintained the basic tenets of the philological program over almost three hundred years. This genealogy can be traced from Wolf's original prospectus for philology—a study of how words make the world—into America via its incarnation in William Dwight Whitney, the unacknowledged founder of American linguistics (Andresen 135,140), who insisted that the study of language must keep in view how it constructs publics. Roman Jakobson and the Prague School continued this focus, as did J. R. Firth and M. A. K. Halliday in Britain. Searle and Austin investigated the minute mechanics of how words were used to transact social business, and Grice followed their lead, inspiring a generation of sociolinguists including William Labov. Labov's influence in turn is felt in the work of Mary Louise Pratt and Elizabeth Traugott, who study speech acts in literature. A Gricean inheritance is also evident in work that borders on cognitive psychology, like Dan Sperber and Deirdre Wilson's relevance theory, which states that a reader/listener's preconception of relevance is the strongest single factor in determining her interpretation of a message.

Toward the end of following this second genealogy of philology, I began to encounter methods like Sperber and Wilson's that treated literary acts of reading and writing as communicative acts that negotiated meaning as a function of preconceptions held by readers and writers. This was exactly what I was looking for to help me understand how the hoaxes had duped their readers and what the authors were trying to communicate through this process of fooling and revealing. However, as I followed trails of footnotes from one relevant source to another, I found myself traveling in an ever-shrinking spiral among sociolinguistic, pragmatic, new-historicist, and reader-response methodologies. The center I was seemingly being drawn toward was rhetoric.

I have already described the sociolinguistic and pragmatic arcs of my methodological search. The reader-response sections of the spiral also follow from previous discussion—the adaptation of speech act and generative linguistic methodologies to the reconstruction of reading acts by critics like Jonathan Culler, Stanley Fish, and Robert Scholes. Scholes, in fact, put in a few words the very phenomenon I was out to capture in my methodology: "The supposed skill of reading is actually based upon a knowledge of the codes that were operative in the composition of any given text and the historical situation in which it was composed" (qtd. in Graff 77). In order to explain how the hoaxes worked, I needed to get at both of those things: the codes of reading science news that an individual newsreader at that time had in his or her head, and the historical context of that act of reading. The problem was that while I found statements like these by reader-response critics helpful and suggestive, many of their actual methods relied on a key factor unavailable to me—the ideal reader. The readers of my hoaxes, ideal or otherwise, had all died nearly a hundred years before I started studying them. I turned to new-historicist methods in an effort to recuperate my vanished readers, and indeed they helped me identify many of the conditions the readers must have faced as they read the hoaxes in newspapers—down to the quality of the paper the hoaxes were printed on and the light levels they were reading under. But these methods for all their contextual richness could not model the decision of a single reader to either believe or disbelieve Locke's Moon Hoax in the New York *Sun,* which was all I had to work with as data—the individual reactions to this hoax and to others preserved in archival sources. In short, after traveling through reader-response and new-historicist territories on my search, then, I found myself in an essentially Heisenbergian dilemma. If I fixed the experience of an individual reader, I lost the context of that reading, and if I fixed the context of the reading, the individual interpretive act was lost. I needed a method that could connect individual communicative acts to their historical and political contexts.

Fortunately, it is exactly this sort of analysis that rhetoricians excel at. By turning to rhetorical studies of historical reading acts, I found methods that combined the best of reader-response and new-historicist techniques to produce local histories of specific acts of reading. My technique for reconstructing the codes that governed antebellum science news reading was borrowed from three main sources: Charles Bazerman's *The Languages of Edison's Light,* Rosa Eberly's *Citizen Critics,* and Steven Mailloux's *Rhetorical Power.* This method writes local histories of specific acts of reading using contemporary reader responses. I applied this method to my own project first by reading the seventeen extant reader responses to Locke's Moon Hoax and gleaning from them common "sticking points" or *topoi* that the writers returned to again and again as they argued for the validity of their decisions to either believe or disbelieve the hoax. These *topoi* included the logical consistency of the story, the novelty of the reported discoveries on the moon, and the reputation of J. F. W. Herschel, the famous British astronomer credited with making them. While each reader made up his or her own mind, all of them made it up with reference to these same *topoi.* However, that set of readerly expectations was not enough in and of itself to describe how each individual hoax reader had come to his or her conclusion about the hoax. I needed some way of showing how these expectations interacted and perhaps competed with each other to produce belief or doubt.

Two models based on Gricean maxims helped me think about how to solve this problem. These were Sperber and Wilson's relevance theory and Ellen Schauber and Ellen Spolsky's preference rules. Both modeled interpretation as a sort of constraint-satisfaction game in which different expectations come into play and conflict with each other; the resolution of these conflicts produces an interpretation. The problems with the models were that relevance theory was not a reading theory and so did not allow for effects on relevance arising from the reader's selection of certain textual elements to attend to over others; it also did not provide for the multiple expectations I had already discovered in my research. The problem with Schauber and Spolsky's preference rules was that, while they were ranked in terms of importance and separated into linguistic, pragmatic, and literary conventions, the categories could not interact with each other in the model, and I knew the hoax-readers' understanding of the real world interacted freely with their understanding of the conventions of science news in their decisions about the hoaxes. I needed a way to model the interaction of multiple expectations in an individual reader's decision about the truth or falsity of the hoaxes.

THE SOLUTION: OPTIMALITY THEORY

Enter optimality theory, a constraint-satisfaction framework that models complex decisions made in the face of multiple competing constraints of varying strengths. Optimality theory (OT) is not actually a theory. It is a model for constraint-satisfaction processes in general (like workflow and decision problems, some cognitive processes, and biological processes like adaptation). Alan Prince and Paul Smolensky brought OT from economics into linguistics in 1993, where it proved useful for handling complex phonological problems previously inexplicable or oversimplified by generative grammar. I first encountered it as a phonological tool. However, OT is now being applied to syntax with a more limited degree of success, and a few studies have even applied OT to pragmatics, using Gricean rules for interaction, though these innovations are recent and relatively speculative. Bruce Hall's "Grice, Discourse Representation, and Optimal Intonation" is an example of this new work. How I used OT to model reader decisions about hoaxes is depicted below in Figs. 18.1 and 18.2.

In Fig. 18.1 is reproduced a direct quote from a contemporary reader justifying why he has decided to believe Locke's Moon Story until he reads confirmation or denial from famed British astronomer J. F. W. Herschel. What we see is the reader's suspicions about the plausibility and internal coherence of the story struggling against his desire not to besmudge the reputation of the astronomer. In the end, his respect for Herschel overcomes his doubts, and he chooses (provisionally) to believe the story. Modeling a relatively simple decision such as this in OT is straightforward. The decision is presented as a matrix. The top row is for the preconceptions the reader brings to the interpretive process. The left column lists all likely interpretations. Since the decision we are considering is whether or not to believe a hoax, the interpretive options are simplified to "true" and "false." Figure 18.2 represents the output state of the model. To get to it, one must work backward from the "true" interpretation and from the way the hoax satisfies or violates each of the reader's

*"After all, however, our doubts and incredulity may be a wrong to the **learned astronomer**, and the circumstances of this wonderful discovery may be correct. Let us do him justice, and allow him to tell his story in his own way" (Locke Moon Hoax 62).*	} = **"true"**

FIG. 18.1. Graphical representation of reader expectations at stake in a reader's decision to believe the moon hoax based on J. F. W. Herschel's reputation.

	Authority	Plausibility	Internal Coherence
✓TRUE		********	*
FALSE	*!		

FIG. 18.2.   An optimality theory model of decision in Figure 18.1.

preconceptions. What we want to end up with is a picture of which preconceptions "won" the contest and shaped the reader's final interpretation. The contest is indicated by a bold vertical line descending through the table. The preconceptions on the left of the line defeat those on the right side of the line.

The hoax contained, according to several readers' counts, at least eight implausible details and one violation of internal coherence (a change in the claimed optical power of Herschel's telescope). These violations are indicated by asterisks (*). To still believe the hoax as "true" would involve an overlooking or outweighing of these nine gaffs. Indeed, that is what we see in Fig. 18.2. The reader's chosen interpretation of "true," indicated by the check mark, reveals that his respect for Herschel's reputation as a scientific authority defeats the evidence of implausibility and incoherence in the moon story, a result which concords with the intuitive assessment of Fig. 18.1. If the reader had chosen to *dis*believe the moon story, his decision would be read across the columns in the "false" row. In this case, his conscience would have been clear in terms of his need to believe only science news stories that were plausible and internally consistent (this one wasn't); however, he would have had to publicly impugn Herschel's reputation, which was an unacceptable violation of his preconception that scientists tell the truth. That unacceptable violation is indicated by the exclamation mark (!). It knocks the "false" interpretation out of the running in the contest and secures the position of the Authority constraint as stronger than the constraints of Plausibility and Internal Coherence, as visualized by the bold black line dividing them. The dotted line between Plausibility and Internal Coherence indicates that they do not compete with each other but rather work in concert in this reader's decision to believe the hoax.[1]

This was just one interpretive game, representing a single reader's decision about one hoax. I repeated this analysis for thirty-two reader responses to hoaxes from 1835 to 1880, an exercise which produced insights that would have been impossible without a methodology capable of reconstructing and ranking historical reader expectations about science news:

> 1. My first set of OT analyses of Poe's and Locke's hoaxes revealed a consistent ranking of science news reading expectations by responders. The composite ranking or "filter" that operated in antebellum reading of science news is as follows, where the double angle brackets (>) indicate the loci of competition and therefore levels of rank, just as the bold black lines did in Fig. 18.2.

{Medium, Authority} > {Novelty, Sensation, Plaus.} > {Popsci., Foreign, Internal Coherence}

> Overall, the portrait of antebellum science newsreading that developed through my analysis is one in which the reputation of the medium and the author or source were the most important factors; in absence of that information, the novelty, sensation, and plausibility of the science story determined the reader's trust in it, and lacking all else, local de-

tails like the format, name-dropping of foreign luminaries, and internal coherence of the story decided the issue.

2. I discovered that this filter was not stable over time. Important historical changes and geographic changes insured that Western newsreaders read Twain's and De Quille's hoaxes differently in the 1860s and 1870s than New York readers read Poe's and Locke's hoaxes.

- The reputation of the medium (Medium) became a weaker constraint in decisions about truth in Western journalism, which was very new and still involved with folk practices of tall-tale telling and practical joking.
- The reactions to De Quille's hoaxes in the 1870s, particularly those from the reprinting papers, revealed that novelty and sensation (Novelty and Sensation) were not considered as reliable indicators of scientific truth as they were a few decades earlier. Eastern readers, especially, tended to evince suspicion without further proofs of plausibility.
- To model the Western hoaxes, I had to introduce a new expectation, Witness. The presence of eyewitnesses in the sparsely populated territories was important for readers to feel they had been provided with a vicarious experience of a real scientific phenomenon.
- The popular science article (Popsci.) changed over time to conform more to the format of a regular news article, front-loading the "who, what, when, where, why" and foregoing the "mystery" opening. This development goes hand-in-hand with the suspicion of sensation appearing in the reader reactions to the postbellum hoaxes. The popular science article also began to place background information at the end of the story instead of at the beginning, thus favoring a journalistic rather than a strictly narrative structure. The Foreign expectation eventually disappeared, as later Western newsreaders favored a local epistemology based on lay eyewitness over the word of far-flung foreign scientists.

3. I found, importantly, that the results of my models indicated why the hoaxers had chosen hoaxing over another rhetorical form in addressing their readers on scientific issues. Hoaxing, through its mechanism of illusion and revelation, singles out the preconceptions that drive readers' interpretation of science news. These are the expectations at the far left of Fig. 18.2. For example, the readers who chose to believe Locke's Moon Hoax ranked Novelty the highest. It was just this "belief in everything odd" that Poe claimed to be out to lampoon with his own moon hoax. Twain claimed to be out to puncture what he perceived as a "mania" for all things petrified. The portrait of his readers' reactions accordingly places their love of Sensation above their consideration of the logical facts of a story. In short, the authors chose hoaxes expressly to single out for criticism—and possibly for reform—the assumptions that were causing their readers to accept science uncritically as the new social epistemology of America.

Optimality theory, combined with a historical-rhetorical method for reconstructing reading expectations, served me powerfully in my analysis of scientific hoaxing in the nineteenth century. In short, OT answered my questions about hoaxes. I learned how the hoaxes worked—by performing reader expectations about science news. And I learned why these authors chose hoaxes—to bring into public discussion unstated assumptions about science's claims to be the new oracle of truth in American public life.

However, in her analysis of the historical borrowing of linguistic methodologies for literary projects, Jacqueline Henkel points out some traditional pitfalls of these attempts.

Critics may simply make an initially productive analogy account for literary facts too diverse: loosely applied at the outset, one notion (language as system, for example, or langue opposed to parole) applies to so many problems that it finally no longer provides enough resistance—a strong enough sense either of the goals of the original theory or of a coherent framework in which its various applications are articulated—to be usefully heuristic. The metaphor exhausts itself in local functions without pointing strongly toward an overall theory that will direct further critical practice. Or a (more strictly applied) metaphor starts as more genuinely parallel to a source concept (a literary rule analogous to a syntactic rule) but in a literary context accounts for so much more than was relevant in the linguistic theory that the literary version begins to collapse, and the literary facts the metaphor does not explain become increasingly obvious. (*Language* 11)

I had to ask myself if my adaptation of OT was not subject to those criticisms and so to the same doom that has befallen generative text structure and the ideal reader. While I am still engaged in answering Henkel's challenges, I can offer the following signs of hope. First, OT can produce useful results outside of the analysis of hoaxes. It can model any reading activity that foregrounds readers' preconceptions about a genre—particularly parody and satire. I have also used it to analyze a story that foregrounds the activity of reading itself—Jorge Luis Borges's "The Garden of the Forking Paths." In that project, OT produced unique results in terms of explicating the reader's relationship to the narrator and making clear the ways in which that relationship performs the central metaphor of the story—a maze. Finally, OT is also potentially applicable as a teaching tool to show students how the criteria for what makes a good sci-fi movie or a good American president can interact and compete with each other in the construction of an evaluative argument.

Henkel's second challenge to borrowed methodologies is that they miss crucial and/or interesting literary questions because they are not methods founded on literary values and assumptions. In other words, just as literary methods could not answer my questions about hoaxes because they were basically rhetorical and pragmatic questions, so my OT-based method could fail to answer literary questions. I found my method productive in addressing traditionally literary concerns such as the effects of history and politics on the reading experience, the effect of specific words and phrases on the reader, and even the sticky issue of authorial intention. That is because any application of OT relies on a method based in the field of application to derive the constraints that will drive the model. Since I had a primarily historical and rhetorical project, I used an established rhetorical method for analyzing historical acts of reading. A related objection along the lines of Henkel's second challenge to borrowed methodologies could be that my OT-based method is not rigorous enough to be predictive, that is, to predict whether a hoax will be successful or not in advance of reader responses. OT, as I have applied it, is primarily historical and descriptive, not predictive. It starts with historical data about a particular reading act and a recorded decision and works backward to model the varying strength of a reader's expectations on that decision. The model is testable, of course, against the final decisions readers made. If the model fails to locate the deciding factors in their reading processes, to reflect all of the interpretive conflicts apparent in the archived responses, then it must be edited until an explanatory description is achieved. But the model itself does not predict if a particular hoax will or will not be successful. The reason for this is that the expectations that form the engine of the model are expectations about science news, not about hoaxes. A hoax is a parasitic genre that borrows its conventions from the genres it apes. Now, as an interesting indirect project, one could apply the model to a particular hoax to see if it satisfied readers' top expectations of a good science news story, but this would be a probabilistic prediction that would likely miss idiosyncratic factors in a hoax's success, such as its serendipitous timing with other stories in the news or with the political climate at the time of the hoax's publication. OT works with historical judgments to open up the process of hoaxing for close examination. The conclusions that can be drawn from it pertain to the top-ranked reader expectations of science and why hoaxers chose to ridicule readers for these priorities.

Henkel does list as promising specifically cooperative projects between language and linguistics that efface the privilege accorded to literary language and treat it as a coordinated communicative activity governed by conventions similar to Grice's. I believe that my application of OT falls in line with those criteria. As a literary method, it also provides a way out of the Heisenbergian problem of individual versus context in the reading act; it provides a portrait of common reading codes in practice at a historical moment while still remaining capable of modeling one reader's reaction to a text. To put the case in linguistic terms, my OT-based method is able to account for both *la langue*, the communal possession of language, and *la parole*, the individual's creative practice of that communal possession. Thus, my methodology fits Andresen's desiderata for the future of linguistics in America as a discipline that "integrate(s) the study of language into use, society, history, and general cognition" (247). Both Andresen and Sampson argue that the rationalist "armchair" mode of linguistics inherited from the neogrammarian tradition is out of date and that linguists' projects and desires are coming ever closer to those of literary critics (Andresen 248). Andresen points in particular to the "rich and linguistically well-informed" work of Pierre Bourdieu and Barbara Herrnstein Smith as models in this reconciliation (251). Gerald Graff also sees a similar shift toward reconciliation at the end of his history of the literary disciplines:

> If there is any point of agreement among deconstructionists, structuralists, reader-response critics, pragmatists, phenomenologists, speech-act theorists, and theoretically-minded humanists, it is on the principle that texts are not, after all autonomous and self-contained, that the meaning of any text in itself depends for its comprehension on other texts and textualized frames of reference. (256)

So in conclusion, I propose optimality theory as a functional rhetoric for reconciling linguistic and literary critical methods on appropriate projects. Further, based on the subversive genealogy outlined above, I would like to propose the field of rhetoric as a meeting place for scholars who wish to synthesize linguistic and literary methodologies.

CONCLUSION: THE NEW PHILOLOGY

Few will protest the utility of rhetorical approaches to literature, but some may legitimately question the compatibility of linguistics and rhetoric. Linguistics is, in many ways, the study of what we do not choose when we use language. We cannot change the plural endings of English words or the syntax of relative clauses if we want to be understood. By contrast, rhetoric is about the choices we have and make when we use language and the politics that those choices inevitably invoke. However, if we consider the subversive genealogy of philology rather than the traditional one, there remains no reason for linguistic and rhetorical interests to remain divergent. In fact, when the Germans did philology, when William Dwight Whitney did his political linguistics, they were in many ways doing what we would now call either sociolinguistics or rhetoric, depending which discipline has formed our vantage point. This new-old way of looking at language does not stop with grammar but instead takes under its aegis literary and cultural expressions of language—the social goals, histories, values, and prejudices that the words automatically conjure when they are used.

Lest I be accused of painting an overly utopian picture of the melding of these various programs, I have not forgotten the disastrous political consequences of the old German philological projects that told a story of Aryan supremacy justified by the "inherent" superiority of Germanic languages in the world. By tying the study of language to politics, this is not a site we mean to revisit. However, the monolithic political foundation of academic power in America has fragmented some over the last century, and so the new philologists—sociolinguists, rhetoricians, and critics concerned with language—can tell stories of dominance and resistance, of the construction of identity in postcolonial societies. Post-post-modernism, these new philologists suddenly resemble the old philologists in terms of their stated fields and preferred methods much more than they do their more immediate linguistic, literary, current-traditional, or belletristic forebears.

NOTE

1. There could be other decisions in which they could compete with each other, say for instance in the reading of a plausible-sounding scientific discovery that nevertheless contained inconsistencies of reporting.

WORKS CITED

Andresen, Julie Tetel. *Linguistics in America, 1769–1924: A Critical History.* New York: Routledge, 1990.

Austin, J. L. *How to Do Things with Words.* Cambridge: Harvard UP, 1975.

Barthes, Roland. *Elements of Semiology.* New York: Noonday, 1977.

Bazerman, Charles. *The Languages of Edison's Light.* online ed. Cambridge: MIT P, 1999.

Bruce, Robert V. *The Launching of Modern American Science, 1846–1876.* 1st ed. New York: Knopf, 1987.

Clemens, Samuel Langhorne. "The Petrified Man: From *Sketches New and Old.*" *The Family Mark Twain.* New York: Harper, 1935.

Derrida, Jacques. *Of Grammatology.* Trans. Gayatri Chakravorty Spivak. Baltimore: Johns Hopkins UP, 1974.

Eberly, Rosa A. *Citizen Critics: Literary Public Spheres.* Urbana: U of Illinois P, 2000.

Fedler, Fred. *Media Hoaxes.* Ames: Iowa State UP, 1989.

Firth, J. R. *The Tongues of Men.* London: Oxford UP, 1964.

Graff, Gerald. *Professing Literature: An Institutional History.* Chicago: U of Chicago P, 1987.

Grice, H. Paul. "Logic and Conversation." *Syntax and Semantics.* Ed. Peter Cole and J. Morgan. Vol. 3: Speech Acts. New York: Academic P, 1975. 41–58.

Hall, Bruce. "Grice, Discourse Representation, and Optimal Intonation." *Papers from the Regional Meetings, Chicago Linguistic Society* 2 (1998): 63–78.

Halliday, M. A. K., and R. Hassan. *Cohesion in English.* Singapore: Longman, 1976.

Henkel, Jacqueline. *The Language of Criticism: Linguistic Models and Literary Theory.* Ithaca, New York: Cornell UP, 1996.

Locke, Richard Adams. *The Celebrated "Moon Story,": Its Origin and Incidents; / with a Memoir of the Author, and an Appendix, Containing, I. An Authentic Description of the Moon; Ii. A New Theory of the Lunar Surface, in Relation to That of the Earth.* Ed. William N. Griggs. New York: Bunnell, 1852.

Mailloux, Steven. *Rhetorical Power.* Ithaca: Cornell UP, 1989.

Martineau, Harriet. *Retrospect of Western Travel.* London: Saunders & Otley, 1838.

Plato. *Laches and Charmides.* Trans. Rosamond Kent Sprague. Indianapolis, Bobbs-Merrill, 1973.

Poe, Edgar Allan. "Hans Phaall—a Tale." *Southern Literary Messenger* June 1835: 565–80.

Poe, Edgar Allan. *The Literati of New York City: Richard Adams Locke.* October 1846. E. A. Poe Society. 4 Jan 2001< http://www.eapoe.org/works/misc/litratb6.htm. January 4 2001>.

Pratt, Mary Louise. *Toward a Speech Act Theory of Literary Discourse.* Bloomington: Indiana UP, 1977.

Prince, Alan, and Paul Smolensky. "Optimality Theory: Constraint Interaction in Generative Grammar." Ms., Rutgers U, New Brunswick and U of Colorado, Boulder, 1993.

Robins, R.H. *A Short History of Linguistics.* Ed. R. H. Robins, Geoffrey Horrocks, and David Denison. 4th ed. London: Longman, 1997.

Sampson, Geoffrey. *Schools of Linguistics.* Stanford: Stanford UP, 1980.

Schauber, Ellen, and Ellen Spolsky. *The Bounds of Interpretation.* Stanford: Stanford UP, 1986.

Searle, John. *Speech Acts.* Cambridge: Cambridge UP, 1969.

Smith, Carlota S. *Modes of Discourse.* Cambridge: Cambridge UP, 2003.

Sperber, Dan, and Deirdre Wilson. *Relevance: Communication and Cognition.* Cambridge: Harvard UP, 1986.

Traugott, Elizabeth, and Mary Louise Pratt. *Linguistics for Students of Literature.* New York: Harcourt, 1980.

IV

Pedagogy

19

Serving Academic Capitalism: The Cultural Function of Community-Based Partnerships

Danika M. Brown

University of Texas, Pan American

There has been much written to argue that higher education has historically functioned as a hegemonic institution to both facilitate the dominant economic system—liberal capitalism—as well as to contain resistance to that system by redefining social needs through the rhetoric of individual access and opportunity (see Aronowitz; Brown; Ohmann). At this historical moment, in order to understand our current political economy and the cultural and material implications of the work we undertake within higher education, we must complicate the ways we view the market and state and include a critical perspective on the role of voluntarism, service, and hybrid institutions such as higher education itself. I suggest that because there has been an apparent decline in state support for the "research culture" that has dominated higher education, the move toward privatized support of research and university's participating directly in market-driven research has engendered a shift in how universities define themselves in our current social context. I argue that the research culture has not disappeared, but that governmental support has shifted in the area of "service" activities, especially in the humanities, and that those activities function in important ways to enable and sustain the profit-oriented research functions of universities. In what follows here, I develop that claim by identifying this expanded culture of service and community development in higher education and by reading out the some of the ideological implications of those activities. I argue that in developing community-based partnerships around such sites as literacy and community development, the university reinscribes itself as the source of cultural authority and undertakes activities within the discourse of dominant ideology. Because the university reflects the ideological imperatives of the dominant economic system, the community development projects supported by the university perpetuate problematic discursive structures and provide "solutions" to communities by redefining the problems themselves. I encourage active critique of these activities in order to address the contradictions of motivations for community health while serving economic and ideological structures that depend on exploitation to expand. Finally, I suggest some possible ways to read radical potentials in these trends.

RHETORICS OF CRITICISM AND HIGHER EDUCATION

The theme of this volume is "rhetorical agendas." The theme itself suggests that material practices, policies, and political structures are shaped by the discourses that engage current practices. Such discourses are embedded in values and beliefs, and such discourses perpetuate, challenge, and define values and beliefs. The discourses that surround issues in higher education do not appear in a vacuum, but are deeply connected to broader social conditions. In fact, higher education has always been situated as an institution designed to respond to social need: economic and cultural. Currently (and over the past couple of decades at least), there are several conflicting strands of discourse aimed at shaping the direction of higher education or critiquing trends in higher education. On the one hand, there is a sustained argument that higher education has become detached from real social need and functions only to benefit itself or dominant interests. This critique we might call the "ivory tower argument."

The increasingly familiar rhetoric of this argument basically asserts that the research culture/agenda that has defined higher education (specifically universities) has separated institutions from the communities they ostensibly serve. The research culture of universities, it is argued, is often carried out at the expense of local communities (or on local communities), and the results or benefits of that research does not directly contribute to local communities. The "ivory tower argument" criticizes universities for a lack of accountability, for exploitation, and for directing resources outside of local communities where they are most needed. This argument has become a pervasive strand of critique of the modern university, seen in essays such as Zelda Gamson's "The Stratification of the Academy," where she outlines the attacks on the research culture. The trope of the "ivory tower" removed from the real social conditions that surround universities resonates precisely because of those features of the research culture that Gamson outlines. The allegiance to national concerns rather than local needs and the valuing of "pure" rather than applied research makes the work conducted within universities seem irrelevant at best to local communities. The emphasis on research at the expense of teaching, while the tuition paid by students has steadily increased, has led the paying public to demand more accountability of higher education. As many people face real declines in stable employment, increased costs of living not reflected in real wages, and growing economic insecurity, institutions of higher education appear in the cultural imagination to be profligate, unaccountable entities. And as Gamson points out, "[t]his concern has found its way into public policy and the media. Higher education has increasingly been treated as just another entitlement burden on taxpayers; decreasing support for higher education can be used to offset state deficits and as a trade-off with claims from other constituencies" (108). Gamson suggests that the "tide is turning" (107) and that the "research culture is losing its currency" (109).

Gamson's claim that the there is a decline in the research culture is certainly supported by fact that the millennial edition of the Carnegie Foundation's classification criteria for ranking universities has attempted to alter its system of classifying institutions of higher education. This move is explained in terms of the effects of the research culture as dictating university activities too narrowly. One of the major criteria for classifying types of institutions is research activities, and—up to the millennial edition of the classification—research activity was identified predominately by federal funding for research. While the Carnegie Foundation itself never intended the classification to be a ranking system, it clearly has functioned as such, as evidenced by this statement by the President of the Carnegie Foundation for the Advancement of Teaching in the foreword to the millennial edition of the classification:

> One of the greatest strengths of the higher education system in the United States is its diversity of institutions. One pernicious effect of the Carnegie Classification from the perspective of the Foundation is the tendency for many institutions to emulate the model of a large research university. It is our hope that the multiple lenses of the 2005 classification system will encourage institutions to fulfill their distinct missions (par. 11)

That the government spending and support which enabled the culture in the first place has significantly declined suggests that the research culture is indeed changing, although not necessarily disappearing. The research culture may be losing its cultural "currency" in some ways, but indications are that the research culture is increasingly using different currency. The Carnegie Foundation's own criteria for classifying institutions reflects this change. The millennial edition of the classification no longer uses federal funding to differentiate among doctorate-granting institutions. The Foundation explains that federal funding is no longer a reliable indicator of research activities and does not reflect the complexity of research activities among various institutions and funders. While this change does not suggest that the research culture has disappeared, it does indicate a couple of important trends. First, along with the Foundation's remarks that one of the major reasons for the change in criteria includes mitigating the use of the classification as a competitive ranking system, the change suggests that the research culture may become less of the primary model for emulation for other institutions. Second, the change reflects that more support for such activities is coming to institutions from nongovernmental sources (such as the private sector, foundations, and professional associations) and is being funneled into specialized areas of the university (those closest to direct market activity). Finally, the change suggests that the support from governmental sources to higher education may be being directed in areas other than direct research activities.

Gamson closes her essay by posing the question of what will replace the research mission which has dominated the function of higher education in this century: "What will replace the research culture in the majority of college and universities is still unclear [...]" (109). What is clear is that higher education has sought to address some of the ramifications of the loss of the research culture's legitimacy through corporatized solutions. This second critique of higher education we might call the "corporate U argument." This argument points out that, in a variety of ways, higher education has replaced state support with corporate partnerships and has itself begun emulating the corporate model. This trend is especially prevalent in disciplines that are most directly relevant to the market, such as in the sciences, technological fields, medicine, and business schools. Sheila Slaughter and Larry L. Leslie identify these changes as a move to "academic capitalism." Looking at the science and technology areas of higher education, Slaughter and Leslie make the argument that

> National policy makers in advanced industrialized countries are moving discretionary research and training moneys into programs focused on the production aspects of higher education, programs that complement areas of innovation in multinational corporations, such as high technology manufacturing, development of intellectual property, and producer services [ ] (14)

They argue that research funds, now brought in primarily through market sources, still function as a "critical resource" for which universities and their faculties compete: "Resource dependence theory suggests that faculty will turn to academic capitalism to maintain research (and other) resources and to maximize prestige" (17). The "Corporate U argument" suggests that the current problem with higher education is that institutions have become "Knowledge Factories," and the discourse constructs higher education as becoming narrowly defined by profit-generating activities.

However, this analysis fails to account for the complex cultural function of higher education. Higher education's trend toward "corporatization" does not adequately solve the crisis of cultural hegemony for the system of higher education. In order for higher education to fulfill its function as a means of asserting hegemony—both in the sense of contributing to the conditions of capitalism as well as containing the contradictions of that system through the articulation of needs and the solutions to those needs for the members of that system—its institutions cannot function merely as corporate entities. Higher education's ideological imperative requires it to be responsive to a larger cultural context; higher education does not have the luxury of limiting itself solely to the activity of generating profit. In this complex picture, the role of the humanities and other disciplines that tend to be somewhat more removed from direct market service, then, becomes a significant cultural one.

RHETORICS OF RESPONSE

One major response over the past decade to these simultaneous strands of critique has been a dramatic increase in community-based activities in higher education. One of the most popular of these practices is service learning, but also a host of other types of partnerships. Service learning has become nearly a mandated part of most colleges and universities' activities as those institutions have revised their mission statements to include and emphasize community accountability (see, e.g., Johns Hopkins's most recent mission statement). These practices are not only undertaken by individual programs or campuses; organizations such as Campus Compact and Community-Campus Partnerships for Health have developed to support community-based partnerships on a national level through conferences, funding, technical assistance, and resource sharing. Even more telling is the federal support structures that now exist to support university activities in communities. The Department of Education, the Department of Housing and Urban Development (HUD), and Fannie Mae all fund higher education partnerships with local community projects. Additionally, the Corporation for National and Community Service is a department created by Clinton and well supported by the Bush administration that deals exclusively with voluntarism. (The name of this department itself might give us pause, even more so since in 2003, David Eisner was named CEO of the "Corporation.") Through the Learn and Serve program of the Corporation, service learning and other community-based activities in higher education are supported, and through the VISTA (Volunteers in Service to America)/AmeriCorps (a domestic version of the Peace Corps) programs of the Corporation, many of these programs are staffed.

Most of the support of these programs emphasizes community access to higher education by having students volunteer in K-12 schools tutoring and mentoring younger students and by developing college preparatory programs. However, many of the programs, such as those funded through HUD for example, have universities deeply embedded in "community development" projects. The Center for Community Partnerships at University of Pennsylvania's

West-Philadelphia Improvement Corps (WEPIC) is an example of a partnership program that focuses on many areas, from community development and renewal to the promotion of health careers. The WEPIC initiative has the university deeply entrenched in delivering services to the community, from providing furniture, computer access, newspaper publication, day care, and actual instruction in topics ranging from aerobics to biology. WEPIC articulates its long-term goal as seeking "to create comprehensive, higher education-assisted community schools that are the social, service delivery, and educational hubs for the entire community. Ultimately, WEPIC intends to help develop schools that are open 24 hours a day and function as the core building of the community" (Center, par. 2).

Funding for these programs tends to de-emphasize research and privilege practical activities such as tutoring, building homes, or organizing after-school activities. Many of the programs enlist not only students in volunteer service delivery, but also VISTA/AmeriCorps members who work full-time for around $11,000 a year. These members often are charged with running whole programs, dramatically reducing the cost of such programs that would generally require oversight by paid professionals. Almost all these programs emphasize and seek to develop in their participants an "ethic of service" and encourage continued volunteer development.

The noble volunteer army these programs generate is, of course, laudable for their intentions and hard (uncompensated) work. However, it is most important to note the ways in which these "solutions" to the social problems and critiques of university activities actually redefine the problem and justify the cultural dominance of higher education. Social problems such as poverty, the inability to provide adequate supervision for children of parents who have to work several jobs to keep afloat, environmental and urban degradation, and so forth, are caused by corporate exploitation of people and resources in order to generate profit. The response of higher education through these community-based activities is not to address the real cause of the problem, but rather to redefine the problem as the need for access to higher education ("no child left behind") and places the responsibility of addressing the effects of an unjust economic system on the backs of unpaid volunteers delivering services that support the economic system to communities most exploited by that economic system. At the same time that institutions of higher education then serve as clearinghouses of volunteer labor, these activities reinforce higher education as a dominant cultural force, extending its ideological reach to kindergarten classes and day-care centers. The public relations is great: as Ira Harkavy, Director of the Center for Community Partnerships at Penn, says, "Altruism pays." In other words, such activities enable the institution of higher education (specific colleges and the institution more broadly understood) to appear accountable to communities; while areas of universities that are more market-oriented are able to continue profit-generating activities funded by the private sector, the humanities and other less market-oriented disciplines are meagerly subsidized by federal and philanthropic funding to produce not necessarily knowledge, but "citizens" and volunteers.

Despite my apparent blanket critique of the discourses and ideology of service as it is practiced by dominant institutions for dominant interests, I would like to conclude by suggesting that this critique enables us to glimpse some perhaps radical possibilities. What I have described here is, of course, the construction of service through the hegemonic lens and institutional imperatives. In practice, we know, it is not "institutions" that do the work, but individuals. As the opportunities for collaborating with communities are enabled and encouraged for academics and students, some interesting things occur. Such activities, while attempting to ameliorate social conditions, do render inequitable social conditions much more visible. That visibility is an essential part of motivating all of us to envision more radical change. Additionally, the visibility and proliferation of inequitable social conditions and having students engage with those conditions on an interhuman and immediate level renders the contradictions in dominant ideological beliefs about causes and the tendency to blame the victim for the necessary effects of an economic system based on exploitation much more likely. Another interesting radical possibility that this expanding trend in creating huge webs of volunteer-based services might create is a space where it becomes conceivable to envision communities functioning without dependence on a market or profit. Because capitalism, at least in its current global stage, fundamentally requires its subjects to live and breathe with recourse to the market for every activity (a necessary condition for our willingness to sell ourselves as commodities through wage-labor), it seems to me that even being able to begin imagining a non-market-driven existence carries significant radical potential. But the potential of these activities to contribute at all to any transformative agenda requires that we rigorously engage the implications of the dominant ways they are constructed and practiced. Analyzing the dominant discourse and discursive practices and the complicated social systems in which those discourses are embedded is, I believe, one of our significant responsibilities as rhetoricians.

WORKS CITED

Aronowitz, Stanley. *The Knowledge Factory: Dismantling the Corporate University and Creating True Higher Learning.* Boston: Beacon, 2000.

Brown, Danika M. "Hegemony and the Discourse of the Land Grant Movement: Historicizing as a Point of Departure." *JAC.* 23.2 (2003): 319–50.

Center for Community Partnerships. "West Philadelphia Improvement Corps (WEPIC)." *CCP.* 2 Feb. 2002. <http://www.upenn.edu/ccp/wepic_hist.shtml>.

Gamson, Zelda. "The Stratification of the Academy." *Chalk Lines: The Politics of Work in the Managed University.* Ed. Randy Martin. Durham: Duke UP, 1998. 103–11.

Harkavy, Ira. "School-Community-University Partnerships: Effectively Integrating Community Building and Education Reform." *Connecting Community Building and Education Reform: Effective School, Community, University Partnerships. Joint Forum U.S. Department of Education and U.S. Dept. of Housing and Urban Development,* Washington, DC, January 1998. 17 Jan, 2002. <http://www.upenn.edu/ccp/bibliography/ed_HUD_paper.html>.

Ohmann, Richard. "English and the Cold War." *The Cold War and the University: Toward an Intellectual History of the Postwar Years.* New York: The New Press, 1997. 73–106.

Slaughter, Sheila, and Larry L. Leslie. *Academic Capitalism: Politics, Policies, and the Entrepreneurial University.* Baltimore: Johns Hopkins U P, 1997.

20

Progymnasmata, Then and Now

Christy Desmet
University of Georgia

The Greco-Roman progymnasmata were graduated exercises in speaking and writing designed for boys before they took up the formal study of rhetoric. In form and content, they remained largely unchanged until around 1700, when the exercises disappeared suddenly from the pedagogical scene in Europe and England (Clark, "Rise and Fall"). In the twenty-first century, however, the progymnasmata are enjoying a renaissance, in arenas ranging from first-year composition to the classical education (e.g., Bauer), classical Christian education (e.g., Wilson), and home-schooling movements. While the motives and philosophy of the alternative educational systems, in particular, may prove surprising to historians of rhetoric, it is possible to construct a rhetorical genealogy for emerging uses of the progymnasmata in literacy education. In hypothesizing such a genealogy, I group together various classical education philosophies and programs, and, in turn, separate them from appropriations of the classical progymnasmata for composition pedagogy. I then analyze the cultural work performed by the classical progymnasmata in classical, Renaissance, and contemporary paideia and speculate on their cultural function at the present time.

PROGYMNASMATA NOW

Alternative Education

Philosophies of alternative literacy education that feature the progymnasmata began appearing in manifestos and curricula in the 1990s. When I did a web search on the term *progymnasmata* for this project back in 2002, I found a charming mixture of scholarly translations and postings by earnest parents to home-school discussion groups. Repeating the search in May 2004, I found links to popular classical education books on Amazon.com, posted curricula for parochial schools, online for-profit courses aimed at the Christian and home-school population, and a number of helpful web sites put up by individuals.[1] Finally, George Kennedy's collected translations of progymnasmata moved from being a soft-bound, privately disseminated text to a published book that is readily available on

185

Amazon.com and recommended by various writers. By 2004, the progymnasmata have become pretty big business.

What makes the progymnasmata attractive to a contemporary audience seeking alternative methods of educating children? A 2001 pamphlet titled "Classical Education and the Homeschool" (Wilson, Callihan, and Jones) justifies generally a curriculum grounded in the Trivium and Quadrivium for complex reasons. First and most obvious is a perceived harmony between classical methods of reasoning and Biblical hermeneutics. More broadly, the movement embraces classical methods as a corrective to narrow fundamentalism in Christian education, what Douglas Wilson calls "pious ignorance" (Wilson, *Recovering* 115; Wilson, Callihan, and Jones 5). A paper on the classical education movement in Lutheran schools claims more explicitly a connection between this variety of Christian education and the concept of "freedom" that ostensibly lies at the heart of education in the "liberal arts" (School Reform News; Veith and Ankergerb). Proponents of classical education, whether Christian or not, also promote the Great Books approach to reading and recommend authors ranging from Cicero to Adam Smith, Cotton Mather, and Jane Austen. More broadly, the curriculum aims to cultivate a sense of Western tradition (Wilson, Callihan, and Jones 11). Furthermore, the program is seen as descending specifically from early American—Puritan, but also Ivy League—methods of education (11). Classical education claims as a forefather Cotton Mather, but also the founding fathers of Harvard and Yale.

Finally, the classical education movement seeks to transform traditional power and class relationships. For-profit groups, in particular, stress the high performance of home-schooled and classical education graduates on standardized tests and college entrance exams (e.g., Veith and Ankergerb). Some, like the Lutheran schools, accept as their mission the dissemination of these tools specifically to minority students, who, by rigorous study and exercises such as the progymnasmata, can take their place in a new American meritocracy (School Reform News; Veith and Ankergerb). There is some sense that Christians, in particular, need the rhetorical agility that the progymnasmata putatively can provide.[2] Other writers stress the flexibility in employment that a solid grounding in logic and rhetoric will provide (Veith). Finally, a site on classical composition from a Christian organization recasts Quintilian's ideal of the "good man, speaking well" in a religious idiom: "For classical methodology, the mark of an educated person was the ability to write and speak well. We identify ourselves as part of the classical Christian school movement and so our mark might be described as graduating individuals with the ability to write and speak well about God and His creation—goodness, truth, and harmony" (Classical Composition, par. 1).

Rhetoric and Composition

At the same time as the alternative education movement was taking shape, a few voices in rhetoric and composition were urging the utility of the progymnasmata for college writing instruction. Several scholars recommended the progymnasmata as structured and sequenced heuristics to complement expressivist methods for invention, such as freewriting, clustering, and brainstorming (Comprone and Ronald; Hagaman; Murphy). Two notable textbooks aimed at the college composition market feature the progymnasmata: Frank D'Angelo's *Composition in the Classical Tradition* (2000), which is used by or recommended for some classical education curricula; and Sharon Crowley and Debra Hawhee's *Ancient Rhetorics for Contemporary Students*, now in its third edition (2004). The justifications offered for these texts are, of course, secular. D'Angelo offers six reasons why the progymnasmata are useful for today's students. First, the exercises are arranged in an "effectively graded sequence," moving from simple to complex and concrete to abstract. Second, these exercises "connect the spoken word to the written word," since they were both performed and written down. Third, the genres featured in the progymnasmata—such as myths, fables, and commonplaces—are familiar to non-Western societies. Like the Greek culture in which they developed, the progymnasmata are multicultural. Fourth, "the progymnasmata connect rhetoric to literary study," and more broadly, to other subjects in the liberal arts curriculum, such as history and philosophy. Fifth, the exercises promote moral instruction, and last but most important, the progynasmata "can help speakers and writers develop the rhetorical skill needed for participation in a civil society" (1–2).

Crowley and Hawhee offer a similar rationale. Their text considers the relationship between spoken and written argument; it considers the importance of belonging to a speech community; and it promotes civic literacy. As the Preface states,

> While writing *Ancient Rhetorics for Contemporary Students*, we adopted three ancient premises about composing: first, that nobody thinks or writes without reference to the culture in which he or she lives; second, that human beings disagree with one another often and for good reasons; and third, that people compose because they want to affect the course of events. (xiii–xiv)

The important guiding concept for Crowley and Hawhee's book is *kairos*, the importance of time and place to argument.

Obviously, the two groups dedicated to ancient rhetorics—classical education and rhetoric and composition—differ vastly in their epistemological orientation. The rhetoric and composition theorists assume that argument is better than agreement, or at least is a necessary prelude to agreement; they also assume that knowledge is situated rather than absolute. While most varieties of classical education recognize the importance of questioning texts, the "truth"—whether Christian doctrine or a sense of Western civilization—necessarily exists independent of both individuals and community. Knowledge may be situated, but the goals of knowledge—truth, beauty, goodness—are absolutes.

Despite these obvious and perhaps inevitable differences, however, the two groups share at least three attitudes. First is the importance of "imitation" for human development, whether spiritual, intellectual, or stylistic. Crowley and Hawhee write that "students can learn an art by imitating the example of people who are good at it" (353). Wilson argues that "[a] biblical aesthetic requires that true creativity be *built upon an inheritance*." Imitation keeps alive and improves that tradition. For the individual, "imitation brings the student 'up to speed,' and once this happens, the mystery of God's giftedness to him comes into play" ("The Case" 158, 159).[3]

Second, both groups embrace the dialectic between familiarity and estrangement that comes from applying "ancient" methods to "contemporary" students. In his textbook, D'Angelo pairs an "ancient" with a more up-to-date example for every exercise; the section on narrative, for instance, begins with a brief account of "The Fall of Icarus," followed by a police report on an incident in which "Man Test-Firing Gun Hits Bedroom" (34–35). Crowley and Hawhee provide examples from Aphthonius's *Progymnasmata*, followed by literary examples (e.g., from Shakespeare) and sometimes more contemporary ones. They also include visual examples, such as cartoons, for different exercises. The "Classical Composition" program mixes Biblical narratives with fairy tales ("The Frog Prince"), typical examples from Aphthonius, and recent, but not politically controversial, examples. The exotic lure of "classical texts" works harmoniously with the ability to recast ancient examples in a contemporary idiom

Last, but more subtly, all parties share a more or less stated commitment to challenging traditional class (although not necessarily gender) lines. The progymnasmata, as freestanding exercises whose content is malleable, are perceived as combating elitism, either because they are manageable, in a technical sense, or because they do not depend on an advanced state of knowledge.

PROGYMNASMATA THEN

Ancient Rhetorics

To what extent, then, do the contemporary progymnasmata conform to what scholars know about the form and function of these exercises in the Greco-Roman educational system? Virtually all contemporary writers label and sequence their exercises according to the pattern established by Aphthonius in the fifth century CE. (The exercises, in order of increasing complexity, are fable, narrative, chreia, maxim, refutation, confirmation, commonplace, encomium, invective, syncrisis, ethopoeia, ecphrasis, and on the introduction of a law [Kennedy, "Progymnasmata" 89–128].) Documents from the classical education movement suggest as well a self-conscious effort to imitate ancient classroom pedagogy. Aelius Theon provides a concrete look at the progymnasmata within a classroom context. Theon recommends that teachers collect good examples for each exercise from "ancient prose works" (Kennedy "Progymnasmata" 9), prefiguring Douglas Wilson's argument that the most important ingredient in home schooling is the amount and quality of the *teacher's* reading. Theon also recommends having students read aloud (66) and makes comments on the art of listening (69-71); both of these topics are addressed in the classical education literature as part of the project of imitation. In fact, the direct link may well be Kennedy's book of progymnasmata, which has developed an audience among Christian and classical educators.

The rhetoric and composition theorists, dealing as they do with a more advanced constituency of writers, focus less on the nuts-and-bolts of pedagogy. Crowley and Hawhee, in particular, offer a wide-ranging discussion of classical pedagogy from different schools and spend time discussing such topics as kairos, stasis theory, the difference between extrinsic and intrinsic proofs, and so forth. But in their discussion of imitation, they do discuss the goal of copiousness in terms of reading aloud and copying, imitation, translation, and paraphrase. From their varying perspectives, then, both sets of teachers attempt to re-create not just the form, but the cultural ethos behind the progymnasmata.

Renaissance Rhetorics

One feature—but an important one—of contemporary education in the progymnasmata that does not derive from ancient sources is the emphasis on producing eloquent speakers whose hallmark is copiousness, or facility with language. That ideal for education comes from the Renaissance. Although Greek and Roman rhetorical education provided pre-professional training for the law courts, in fact the compositions—particularly *written* compositions—were not necessarily characterized by copiousness or eloquence. Examining student narratives on papyrus, Teresa Morgan has found that most condensed rather than elaborated on their models, were simple in substance and diction, and showed little attempt to imitate literary sources. Morgan concludes that most students were destined not to produce persuasive rhetoric in the public sphere, but to be good bureaucrats (225 and passim).

While Crowley and Hawhee properly cite Cicero and Isocrates on the virtues and pleasures of cultivating copiousness through rhetorical exercise, the concept of eloquence as copiousness in current applications of the progymnasmata can be traced more directly to Erasmus, whose textbook *De Copia* was a staple of English early modern pedagogy (Baldwin 2: 176–96) and worked generally in tandem with Aphthonius's *Progymnasmata* (Baldwin 2: 301) as rendered into Latin by Johannes Maria Catanaeus (1507) and Reinhard Lorich (1542). (Lorich also supplemented the Greek text with scholia and additional model themes [Baldwin 2: 288–354; Clark 231–32, 233–49, and passim].)

The role of copiousness and the ethos it cultivated in Renaissance boys is perhaps more complicated and less intrinsically noble than we have come to expect. Assuredly, the period embraced Quintilian's ideal of the "good man, speaking well" and linked the exercises to Quintilian's status as a master of eloquence (Baldwin 2: 288). T. W. Baldwin's comprehensive but now largely forgotten account of Shakespeare's education nevertheless demonstrates that both the progymnasmata and other tricks for cultivating copiousness could be subject to irony. Erasmus's exercises can encourage melodrama: one of the sentences offered for systematic expansion, for instance, is "he lost all through excess" (Erasmus 43). They can also encourage outright silliness: another exercise involves ringing innumerable changes on the statement "I was happy to receive your letter." While for Shakespeare, the progymnasmata provide the impetus and form for such performances as Hamlet's "To Be or Not To Be" soliloquy and his impassioned invective, "Frailty, thy name is woman," as Baldwin's examples show, the most methodically copious speakers are Shakespeare's fools and clowns.

Other ironies accompany the wedding of a Renaissance ideal of copiousness to the ancient exercises. First, although the general goals of a Renaissance rhetorical education are broadly humanist (in the earlier rather than current sense), its methods were strict. If Shakespeare's schooling was not quite the rigorous Renaissance puberty rite described by Father Walter Ong, the Free School at Stratford would have subjected its boys to long hours and thorough discipline (Schoenbaum 50-55). Furthermore, although the Renaissance versions of Aphthonius offer tame examples for such early exercises as the fable (Aesop) and the narrative (how the rose became red), the culminating exercise in arguing for and against a law—as represented in Richard Rainolde's Englished Aphthonius, the *Foundacion of Rhetorike*—takes as its subject a law "which suffered adulterie to bee punished with death" (f. 59v-64r). This topic, of course, is the motivating force behind Shakespeare's *Measure for Measure*, where unlucky couples suffer under such a law while feckless philanderers leave their bastard children to be raised without support. Even the inoffensive exemplary "narrative," the etiological myth of how the rose became red, spawned a racy genre of mythological poetry, the epyllion; Shakespeare's *Venus and Adonis*, in which an overbearing and oversexed goddess wrestles amorously with a reluctant young boy, is merely a mild example of this poetic genre.

Even more at odds with contemporary uses of the progymnasmata is the model of selfhood that scholars have derived from the Renaissance love of copiousness. Prolonged encounters with Foucault have modified scholars' understanding of Richard Lanham's *homo rhetoricus*—a self-generating, mutable entity built up successively from linguistic performance in an ongoing social drama. But although in recent reconstructions, *homo rhetoricus* is moved by a depth of passion that qualifies his sophistic facility with language (e.g., Cockcroft), scholarship still recognizes that the rhetorical exercises, as practiced by Shakespeare, Milton, and Christopher Marlowe, promoted moral ends by *morally neutral means* (Lanham, Altman). Renaissance rhetorical education can produce a Dr. Faustus, or a Tamburlaine, as easily as it nurtures a Hamlet.

CONCLUSION

No vision of ethical practice could be further from the citizen rhetor or the learned, imaginative Christian envisioned by contemporary advocates of the progymnasmata. But perhaps the range of social and ethical positions that are perceptible in the history of the progymnasmata's transmission from ancient Greece to contemporary America provides proof positive not only of their pedagogical durability, but also of their social usefulness. Clearly, the progymnasmata work well as a self-contained sequence of graded exercises for speakers and writers. They can be used effectively with a wide range of content, from Aesop to crime reports to nearly pornographic mythological poetry. Perhaps most important, as Crowley and Hawhee emphasize, the ethical impact of the progymnasmata depends on kairos, the accommodation of rhetoric to community, time, and place. They can be employed profitably by students and teachers from the right as well as the left. Given the religious and cultural divide that continues to alienate from one another citizens raised in different educational climates, it is useful to consider the progymnasmata as perhaps offering a lingua franca for contemporary students. The writerly ethos cultivated by the progymnasmata can promote spiritual growth, political responsibility, or nothing more weighty than a love of language. But while the writers may differ, the progymnasmata can offer them a common rhetorical heritage.

NOTES

1. Evidence that the progymnasmata have become something of a fad among supporters of alternative education can be found in this admonition from one honest soul: "You will not ruin your child if you don't use the progymnasmata! If you have the time and inclination, the progym. may enhance your writing instruction. If you don't, 'regular' writing instruction is perfectly adequate" (Writing par. 1).
2. Wilson, Callihan, and Jones conclude their pamphlet with the sentiment that *"Christians ought to be the most skeptical and imaginative people on the face of the earth"* (44, italics in original). Less grandly, Regina Coeli Academy pledges that "[a]fter completing the progymnasmata, a student should be able to write more logically, concisely, and with fewer errors" (par. 15).
3. A more specific theological justification of imitation is as follows:
   Sinful man seeks autonomy from God, from neighbor, from the past. Autonomous man believes he is superior to the primitive, ancient cultures, which come before his time. [...] The whole idea of imitation is abhorrent to autonomous man. [...] However, true reasoning and learning are not based on expressing one's own opinion and thoughts but on the ability to understand the opinions and thoughts of others and to discern whatever truth exists in those other thoughts and opinions. In a more profound way our ability to "discover" any truth is simply the ability to understand God's opinions and thoughts expressed through Scripture or his Creation ("Narrative Curriculum Sample," in Classical Composition par. 4).

WORKS CITED

Altman, Joel B. *The Tudor Play of Mind: Rhetorical Inquiry and the Development of Elizabethan Drama*. Berkeley: U of California P, 1978.

Baldwin, T. W. *William Shakspere's Small Latine & Lesse Greeke*. 2 vols. Urbana: U of Illinois P, 1944.

Bauer, Susan Wise. *The Well-Educated Mind: A Guide to the Classical Education You Never Had*. New York: Norton, 2003.

Clark, Donald Lemen. "The Rise and Fall of the Progymnasmata in Sixteenth and Seventeenth Century Grammar Schools." *Speech Monographs* 19 (1952): 259–63.

——. *John Milton at St. Paul's School: A Study of Ancient Rhetoric in English Renaissance Education*. New York: Columbia UP, 1948. 230–49.

Classical Composition. "Developing Excellent Writers for Our Future: Using the Progymnasmata." 24 May 2004 <http://www.classicalcomposition.com/>.

Cockcroft, Robert. *Rhetorical Affect in Early Modern Writing: Renaissance Passions Reconsidered*. Houndsmill, Basingstoke, Hampshire: Palgrave, 2003.

Comprone, Joseph J., and Katharine J. Ronald. "Expressive Writing: Exercises in a New Progymnasmata." *Journal of Teaching Writing* 4.1 (1985): 31–53.

Crowley, Sharon, and Debra Hawhee. *Ancient Rhetorics for Contemporary Students*. 3rd ed. New York: Pearson, 2004.

D'Angelo, Frank. *Composition in the Classical Tradition*. Needham Heights: Allyn, 2000.

Erasmus, Desiderius. *On Copia of Words and Ideas*. Trans. Donald B. King and H. David Rix. Milwaukee: Marquette UP, 1963.

Hagaman, John. "Modern Use of the Progymnasmata in Teaching Rhetorical Invention." *Rhetoric Review* 5 (1986): 22–29.

Kennedy, George A. *Progymnasmata: Greeks Textbooks of Prose Composition and Rhetoric*. Atlanta: Society for Biblical Literature, 2003.

Lanham, Richard A. *The Motives of Eloquence: Literary Rhetoric in the Renaissance*. New Haven: Yale UP, 1976.

Morgan, Teresa. *Literate Education in the Hellenistic and Roman Worlds*. Cambridge: Cambridge UP. 1998. 198–226.

Murphy, James J. "The Modern Value of Ancient Roman Methods of Teaching Writing, with Answers to Twelve Current Fallacies." *Writing on the Edge* 1 (1989): 28–37.

Ong, Walter, S. J. "Latin Language Study as a Renaissance Puberty Rite." *Rhetoric, Romance, and Technology: Studies in the Interaction of Expression and Culture*. Ithaca: Cornell UP, 1971. 113–41.

"The Progymnasmata: Resources for Classical Writing." <http://home.wi.rr.com/penzky/progymnasmata.htm>.

Rainolde, Richard. *Foundacion of Rhetorike*. 1563; rpt. Menston, England: Scolar Press, 1972.

Regina Coeli Academy. "Restoring the Liberal Arts to Catholic Education." 24 May 2004 <http://wwww.reginacoeli.org./composition/agnusdeiwp.html>.

Schoenbaum, Samuel. *William Shakespeare: A Documentary Life*. New York: Oxford UP, 1975.

School Reform News. "Classical Education Makes a Comeback." 9 July 2002 <http://www.heartland.org/education/feb98/classical.htm>.

Veith, Gene Edward. "Renaissance, Not Reform: The Classical Schools Movement." Aug. 1996. 9 July 2002 <http://www.capitalresearch.org/publications/cc/1996/9608.htm>.

Veith, Gene, and Erik Ankergerb. "The Classical Education Movement and Lutheran Schools." Excerpts from *Lutheran Education* (Nov./Dec. 1999). 9 July 2002 <http://www.immanuelpeoria.org/plh/classical/cemls.htm>.

Wilson, Douglas. *Recovering the Lost Tools of Learning: An Approach to Distinctively Christian Education*. Wheaton: Crossways, 1991.

——. *The Case for Classical Christian Education*. Wheaton: Crossways, 2003.

Wilson, Douglas, Wes Callihan, and Douglas Jones. *Classical Education and the Homeschool*. Rev. ed. Moscow, ID: Canon, 2001.

21

The Traditional Made New: Jasinski's *Sourcebook on Rhetoric*

David Henry

University of Nevada, Las Vegas

James Jasinski's *Sourcebook on Rhetoric*, Herbert W. Simons notes in the work's foreword, began as an eight-page mimeograph Jasinski prepared to distribute to his contemporary rhetorical theory classes. Years later, he used the inventory of key terms as the basis for the proposal he submitted to Sage Publications' series in Rhetoric & Society, each book to be approximately 200 pages in length. Later still, scholars and students in rhetoric have before them a resource consisting of a 30-page introduction, a 602- page glossary of concepts, and a nearly 40-page index. The book is an important addition to such works as Bryant's "Rhetoric: Its Function and Its Scope," Ehninger's "On Systems of Rhetoric," Bitzer and Black's *The Prospect of Rhetoric*, Fisher's *Rhetoric: A Tradition in Transition*, Horner and Leff's *Rhetoric and Pedagogy*, and Lucaites, Condit, and Caudill's *Contemporary Rhetorical: A Reader.*[1] Though divergent in their purposes and approaches, these works and others in a similar tradition are unified by a focus on discerning key concepts, themes, ideas, and theories that define the rhetorical tradition, primarily from the perspective of research in communication studies. Jasinski's contribution to this tradition, to adapt Simons's words, is "a very odd but extremely useful reference work."[2] So it is. But in my view, it is much more useful than odd.

First, though, the odd. Following an extraordinary introduction, the text consists in an alphabetical orientation to more than 130 terms essential to an appreciation for rhetoric's history, theory, and practice. Beginning with "Accent" and concluding with "Vernacular," the *Sourcebook* provides in each entry a working definition of the concept; discussion of—as appropriate—major uses, influences, contributors, functions, effects, and so on of each term; and a list of references and additional readings that, if not exhaustive, promises a strong foundation for the reader's own work. Granted the organizational tack poses challenges, particularly when the table of contents lists a "Glossary of Concepts" limited to the nineteen letters of the alphabet that begin the concepts included. And there are sometimes curious choices of terms. Simons points to the absence of an entry for Example, for instance, and there is no independent entry for Metaphor. But the systematic and generally clearly explained scheme of finding aids—combining bold print. the use of italics, and extensive name and subject indexes—allows for the efficient location of most any topic.

And despite the broad range of ideas covered, Jasinski unifies his treatment of detail by returning consistently to, in Simons's words, "what he knows best, which is public address. past and present." Simons describes this focus as "at once a limitation of the book, but also a strength; it gives depth [...] albeit at a sacrifice to range" (viii). The depth of each entry's treatment is indeed impressive, but it is difficult to discern what more Jasinski might have done to increase the book's range. Are there concepts, contributors, or controversies not treated? Almost certainly. Would their inclusion have made for a stronger product? Perhaps. But taken on its own terms, what the *Sourcebook* offers is an indispensable orientation to the disciplines that constitute contemporary rhetorical studies.

Simons suggests the utility of Jasinski's work "across the terrain that is rhetoric." And it is the usefulness of this remarkable work that merits our attention. Those "readers who were reared in the literary/compositional/English department tradition of rhetorical studies," Simons writes,

> might begin with words such as *narrative* that already are familiar to them. but then. having become convinced that their tradition says not enough about rhetoric as an adaptive art. might venture to the oral/oratorical/communication studies side of the street for an introduction to *rhetorical situation*. The venturesome rhetorician in a communication studies department might likewise move from the familiar [...] to the unfamiliar. finding in Bloom's (1973) poetics of influence precisely the metaphor needed to analyze the oratory of Malcolm X. A decided virtue of this book is its broad range of pivotal terms—reason enough for students in English or communication studies to purchase it or make liberal use of it at their reference libraries. (vii)

Professor Simons is correct. Composition, literature, and communication studies students alike will benefit from Jasinski's orientations to the terms covered. Those that merit careful examination across the fields are numerous; they include **Criticism, Argument, Style, Polysemy, Text, Power, Narrative**, and many, many others. To illustrate the utility of Jasinski's approach to the terms, consider the previously mentioned **narrative**.[3] "Given the tremendous volume of thinking on the subject," Jasinski writes, "this entry is limited to discussion of four basic tasks." In one of the book's lengthier entries (389–405). he addresses these tasks as the *definitional, functional, formal,* and *evaluative.*

His treatment of *definition*—wherein he addresses such topics as plot, structure of action. the role of the narrator, and so on—is informed by Booth, White, Aristotle, Freytag, Martin. Scholes and Kellogg, and others. Narrative's *functions* occupy nearly half of the discussion. Jasinski addresses aesthetic rhetoric, ideological rhetoric, the art's *instrumental* and *constitutive* effects, and narrative as argument. Narrative argument, in turn, is manifested as *example,* as *generalization,* and as *analogy.* Drawing from Fisher, Cox, Perelman and Olbrechts-Tyteca, and his own case studies, Jasinski illustrates the types of narrative by examining narrative as argument in film, presidential oratory, literature, and extended foreign policy deliberations in legislative bodies. On *form,* he continues, narratives may be self-contained, autonomous texts; may be "embedded within other discursive practices," or "can exist, and be encountered, as underlying structural presences that shape or inform a number of seemingly unconnected messages" (401). These narrative forms, finally, may be evaluated by generally accepted standards of critical assessment such as "effects" and "quality." But criteria uniquely suited to the narrative form may also be applied. Jasinski directs readers to

Booth on *ethical criticism*; Fisher's theory of *narrative rationality*, and the roles of *narrative fidelity* and *narrative probability* therein; and White's notion of narrative inevitability.

This is an excellent orientation to narrative. Those well versed in the topic may notice omissions, dispute choices, argue interpretations, or debate with the author's areas of emphasis. But they will be hard pressed to deny the utility of this relatively brief, yet notably thorough, synopsis of narrative's dominant features, developments, uses, and theorists. The entry on narrative also demonstrates why Jasinski's treatments of the concepts to which he attends merit close reading and deep appreciation.

Equally if not more valuable than the orientation to rhetorical terms, however, is the book's "Introduction: On Defining Rhetoric as an Object of Intellectual Inquiry." This essay is a remarkable achievement. In two pages, Jasinski synthesizes the place in rhetorical history of Plato, Isocrates, Aristotle, Cicero, Quintilian, the humanist movement in the European Renaissance, Ehninger, Bryant, and Burke, among others. Following Burke, he concludes that rhetorical study divides historically into two tracks, "Rhetoric as Practice" and "Rhetoric as Theory." "Contemporary theorists and critics," he writes, "continue to use 'rhetoric' to refer to certain discursive practices as well as to certain forms of theory or modes of theorizing. But what specific types of discursive practice are rhetorical? What constitutes a theory or art of rhetoric?" (xiv) The pursuit of answers to these two questions is the business of the remainder of the introduction. In roughly the first half of the essay, Jasinski discerns no fewer than six

> prominent ways in which scholars have defined rhetoric as a form of discursive or language practice. These definitions include (a) rhetoric as practical persuasive discourse; (b) rhetoric as the use of tropes and figures; (c) rhetoric as a type of *middle ground* practice concerned with justice and/or creating and maintaining a community (intersubjectivity); (d) rhetoric as attitude, perspective, and/or discursive force (universalized rhetoric); (e) rhetoric as the persuasive *dimension* of discursive and symbolic practice; and (f) rhetoric as public or civic discourse. (xxiii)

These categories, he concludes, "are not mutually exclusive, and there are some affinities" among them. "But important tensions—rhetoric as form versus rhetoric as function, product versus process—persist" (xxiii–xxiv).

It is clearly beyond the scope of a short essay to detail these tensions and their consequences in relation to all six definitions. To illustrate Jasinski's point, though, and to highlight the insight of his analysis, we can turn to his treatment of "rhetoric as a *middle ground*." After detailing rhetoric, first, as persuasion or argument and, second, as language or style, he explains efforts to accommodate both in a single conception of the art. One alternative to the either/or treatment, he posits, "is to exploit the apparent human fascination with three-part schemes" (xviii). In his literary and legal scholarship, for instance, James Boyd White adapted the classical trivium that distinguished among rhetoric, poetics, and philosophical discourse. In White's scheme, philosophical discourse equates to the "pursuit of truth," aesthetic discourse parallels the "pursuit of beauty," and rhetorical discourse aligns with the "pursuit of justice." And for White, justice is the "essential ingredient in human communication" (xvii).

Habermas, on Jasinski's reading, posits a similar three-part approach to rhetoric when he addresses communication's objective, subjective, and intersubjective dimensions. Here, philosophical and scientific discourse are termed objective, aesthetic discourse and art more generally are subjective, and "rhetorical discourse (for Habermas this form of practice is restricted to legal and moral discourse) has an intersubjective orientation to the world; the objective of this form of practice is neither knowledge and truth nor self-expression and beauty but rather interaction with a world consisting of fellow creatures" (xix). Jasinski suggests that a virtue of the tripartite scheme is that

> rhetorical practice usually is positioned in the middle. As such, it inevitably will contain elements from the discursive forms that reside on either side; rhetorical discourse will raise issues of truth (the proper concern of philosophical and, more and more today, scientific discourse) and contain elements of formal beauty and self-expression (the focus of aesthetic practice). [...] Conceived as a middle ground between the traditional philosophical quest for truth and the aesthetic pursuit of beauty and self-expression, rhetorical discourse constitutes and reconstitutes intersubjective communities; it promotes intersubjective *identification* by overcoming the divisions that plague humanity. (xix)

Jasinski acknowledges that the middle ground is not without danger. Its proponents are vulnerable, for example, to Plato's admonition that the art has "no real *substance*" but is "simply a collection of discursive tricks" (xxiv). Yet another difficulty is that what Jasinski calls "real-world discursive practices" do not always accord with assigned categories. As sociologists of science and rhetorical critics of scientific advocacy increasingly demonstrate, "scientific discourse does not simply transmit objective knowledge; it also establishes and maintains a community of scientists." Despite these limitations with the *middle ground*, he asks, is "it possible to identify distinct forms of human communication and, in so doing, identify a specific form that can be considered 'rhetoric'?" (xix) He then proceeds to outline the constructivist or constitutive position as yet another potential approach to understanding rhetoric as discursive practice.

The purpose in detailing the treatment of the *middle ground* is not to advocate for this view as a "preferred" or "best" or "superior" means for achieving an understanding of "Rhetoric as Practice." Rather, it is to highlight the usefulness of Jasinski's work for apprehending the art's complexities. In all six areas he identifies, he culls from essential primary and secondary works the advocates' central arguments, modes of analysis, strengths of position, and weaknesses of the perspective advanced. And he does so in an extraordinarily accessible fashion.

These traits define as well his introduction to "Rhetoric as Theory." What "does it mean," he begins, "to talk about rhetoric as a way of thinking about practice or as a form of theory?" (xxiv). Acknowledging the difficulties posed by the question, Jasinski adopts the four-part scheme advanced by Donald Bryant in 1953 for discerning rhetoric as theory. In "Rhetoric: Its Function and Its Scope," Bryant identified four aspects of rhetorical theory that, Jasinski contends, "remain extremely useful as a way of sorting out the domain, or the meaning, of rhetorical theory" (xxiv). These are the instrumental or productive, the critical or interpretive, the social, and the philosophical.

Parallel to the earlier attention to *middle ground* as a way into discursive practice, Jasinski's analysis of "the social" serves here to explore his *Sourcebook*'s utility. In a relatively brief space, he defines "the social" by orienting readers to the significance of (1) where rhetorical practice takes place (he introduces the *rhetorical situation* and the *audience* in the process); (2) the concept of *genre;* (3) the "relationship between rhetorical practice and various social and political institutions"; (4) commentary on the "relationship between rhetorical practice and the *public* and *public sphere*"; and (5) "inquiry into the *effects of rhetorical practice*" (xxvii–xxviii).

On effect, Jasinski contrasts the concept's meaning early in the revival of rhetorical studies in communication departments with its more complex, nuanced meanings in recent scholarship. Initially, a rhetor's skill in moving an immediate audience to a particular action typically served as the dominant measure of effect. Voters' endorsements of candidates, consumers' purchases of products, congressional decisions that allied with a legislator's proposed course of action, and so on were taken to demonstrate the causal link between discourse and effect; assertions of such causality, moreover, served as evidence for theorizing about the rhetoric's social dimension.

Recent work, however, eschews rudimentary assertions of causality as the only, or even primary, means for theorizing about effect. Instead, scholars influenced by the *constructivist* intellectual movement "have begun to investigate the way in which language—in all its practical manifestations—helps to construct or constitute social reality" (xxviii). *Jasinski contends that in "exploring this capacity,"*

> scholars have moved well beyond the ways in which words can influence how people vote. Scholars now ask questions such as the following. How does rhetorical practice construct our understanding of the past […] and of what might be possible in the present? How does rhetorical practice construct our understanding of racial or ethnic categories? How does rhetorical practice shape and reshape the values and fundamental concepts or *ideographs* […] that make community possible? (xxviii)

Jasinski poses such questions not to limit theorizing about rhetorical theory's social aspect, but to distinguish simplistic early treatments of effect from the more sophisticated (and more productive) ventures characteristic of recent scholarship.

That Jasinski adopts Bryant's four aspects of rhetoric for his own orientation to "Rhetoric as Theory" is fitting. For the *Sourcebook on Rhetoric* is an important twenty-first-century addition to the tradition established in "Rhetoric: Its Function and Its Scope," and embodied in communication studies scholarship during the last fifty years. In the process of developing his eight-page handout into a 600-page essential resource, Jasinski has become, as Simons notes, "a singular[ly] adept teacher of contemporary rhetorical theory" (viii). Uninitiated readers and established scholars alike cannot help but appreciate how much he covers in the introduction, how concise the synthesis, and how productive the treatments of the concepts examined. This is indeed a useful project—even if a bit odd.

NOTES

1. A sample of representative works, both traditional and innovative, includes Donald C. Bryant, "Rhetoric: Its Function and Its Scope," *Quarterly Journal of Speech* 39 (1953): 401–24, and "'Rhetoric: Its Function and Its Scope' *Rediviva*" in Bryant's *Rhetorical Dimensions in Criticism* (Baton Rouge: Louisiana State University Press, 1973), 3–23; Lloyd Bitzer, "The Rhetorical Situation," *Philosophy and Rhetoric* 1 (1968): 1–14; Wayne E. Brockriede, "Dimensions of the Concept of Rhetoric," *Quarterly Journal of Speech* 54 (1968): 1–12; Carroll C. Arnold, "Oral Rhetoric, Rhetoric, and Literature," *Philosophy and Rhetoric* 1 (1968): 191–210; Douglas Ehninger, "On Systems of Rhetoric," *Philosophy and Rhetoric* 1 (1968): 131–144; Lloyd F. Bitzer and Edwin Black, ed., *The Prospect of Rhetoric: Report of the National Development Project* (Englewood Cliffs, NJ: Prentice-Hall, 1971); Walter R. Fisher, ed., *Rhetoric: A Tradition in Transition* (East Lansing: Michigan State University Press, 1974); Winifred Bryan Horner and

Michael Leff, *Rhetoric and Pedagogy: Its History, Philosophy, and Practice: Essays in Honor of James J. Murphy* (Mahwah, NJ: Lawrence Erlbaum, 1995); Thomas B. Farrell, ed., *Landmark Essays on Contemporary Rhetoric* (Mahwah, NJ: Lawrence Erlbaum, 1998); and John Louis Lucaites, Celeste Michelle Condit, and Sally Caudill, ed. *Contemporary Rhetorical Theory: A Reader* (New York: Guilford, 1999).

2.   Herbert W. Simons, "Foreword" to James Jasinski, *Sourcebook on Rhetoric* (Thousand Oaks, CA: Sage Publications, 2001), vii. Subsequent references from Simons' "Foreword," Jasinski's "Introduction" (xiii–xxv), and the "Glossary of Concepts" (3-602) all appear in the text of this paper.

3.   **[N]arrative** is in bold here to reflect its citation in Jasinski's work. Similarly, where terms are *italicized* or cited in what may seem a curious fashion, the citation form is intended to reflect Jasinski's treatment of the term.

WORKS CITED

Arnold, Carroll C. "Oral Rhetoric, Rhetoric, and Literature." *Philosophy and Rhetoric* 1 (1968): 191–210.

Bitzer, Lloyd. "The Rhetorical Situation." *Philosophy and Rhetoric* 1 (1968): 1–14.

Bitzer, Lloyd F., and Edwin Black. ed. *The Prospect of Rhetoric: Report of the National Development Project*. Englewood Cliffs: Prentice-Hall, 1971.

Brockriede, Wayne E. "Dimensions of the Concept of Rhetoric." *Quarterly Journal of Speech* 54 (1968): 1–12.

Bryant, Donald C. "Rhetoric: Its Function and Its Scope." *Quarterly Journal of Speech* 39 (1953): 401–424.

—. "Rhetoric: Its Function and Its Scope *Rediviva*." *Rhetorical Dimensions in Criticism*. Ed. Donald C. Bryant. Baton Rouge: Louisiana State UP, 1973. 3–23.

Ehninger, Douglas. "On Systems of Rhetoric." *Philosophy and Rhetoric* 1 (1968): 131–144.

Farrell, Thomas B., ed. *Landmark Essays on Contemporary Rhetoric*. Mahwah: Lawrence Erlbaum, 1998.

Fisher, Walter R., ed. *Rhetoric: A Tradition in Transition*. East Lansing: Michigan State UP, 1974.

Horner, Winifred Bryan, and Michael Leff, ed. *Rhetoric and Pedagogy: Its History, Philosophy and Practice*. Mahwah: Lawrence Erlbaum, 1995.

Jasinski, James. *Sourcebook on Rhetoric*. Thousand Oaks: Sage, 2001.

Lucaites, John Louis, Celeste Michelle Condit, and Sally Caudill, ed. *Contemporary Rhetorical Theory: A Reader*. New York: Guilford, 1999.

Simons, Herbert W. "Foreword." *Sourcebook on Rhetoric*, by James Jasinski. Thousand Oaks: Sage, 2001. vii–viii.

22

Electronic Versions
of Collaborative Pedagogy:
A Brief Survey

Mara Holt
Albert Rouzie
Ohio University

We begin by refusing a convention rampant in discussions of collaborative practice, that is, positioning oneself against the straw man of traditional, authoritarian, lecture-based, banking pedagogy. In examining the work of Ken Bruffee and similar scholarship in computers and writing, we found that everyone (including ourselves) uses progress narratives to establish their social constructionist credentials against the blighted epistemology of traditional, authoritarian models, which, as far as we can see, no one is defending. "Somebody's out there," sings Bob Dylan, "beating on a dead horse."

- We hereby *retire* the straw man of the rational subject riding the dead horse of traditional teaching.
- And we refuse a progress narrative.
- Thus, we free ourselves from the binary of *bad old days* and *good new ones*.
- Instead, we analyze how specific collaborative practices represent student subjects differently, with different implications for pedagogy.

Scholars of collaborative practice unanimously agree that "knowledge is socially constructed." However, as technology brings student discourse to center stage, the student subject is increasingly represented as (1) fragmented and/or multiple and (2) resistant to cultural and academic hegemony. Meanwhile, the combined power of digital technology and collaborative experimentation yields texts that are increasingly fragmented and multiple. Finally, the focus on student discourse leads the conversation to philosophical questions of individual responsibility and one's relation to difference.

Here we focus on representations of the student subject in, first, the work initiated by Kenneth Bruffee and, second, the work that developed in networked classrooms. Bruffee be-

199

gan the discourse of the pedagogical implications of social construction in 1972, before his textbook *A Short Course in Writing* helped disseminate his practice (the horse was alive and kicking when he landed the first blow). Bruffee's work was foundational in the design of Daedulus Interchange classroom software, which influenced the social direction of computer-mediated instruction. His focus on the role of collaboration in fostering collective action posits a socially constructed student subject who engages in productive, agonistic negotiation with peers in the context of an instructor-designed course. The computer-mediated communication model assumes a fragmented, self-questioning, socially constructed student subject who engages in unpredictable interactions with peers in the context of a software-designed course, originally based on Bruffee's design, but which soon developed a cyborgian mind of its own.

In his 1972 article "The Way Out," Bruffee offers the notion of a polycentric classroom dynamic. Rather than the teacher *sharing* power, which implies power as a possession, Bruffee maintains that a teacher can structure classroom activities so that students can collectively *take* power without the teacher losing any. In his pedagogy, in which conversation is the central metaphor, the teacher carefully designs tasks that structure students to converse with each other both face-to-face and in print. His plan of increasingly complex intellectual negotiation, evident in his series of written peer critiques, provides a method for student subjects to enter the fragmented discourse of uncertain knowledge and learn how to negotiate it. The site of his original project was an aggressive climate of early open admissions in New York higher education. The civil rights movement was beginning to bear fruit and the protest against the Vietnam War was following in its stead. Bruffee provided a structure in which his argumentative students could learn how to use their differences productively, coming to a provisional agreement, then testing that agreement against the provisional consensus of the academic community.

Bruffee's student subject is posited as, let's say, a modernist academic in training who, if given the right conditions, could argue his point in the face of stringent opposition. She is someone who likes to argue, but doesn't yet know that "good writing" is not a universally fixed category, but rather a matter of opinion based on a community's values. Bruffee wants to help students to think critically, to question authority, to point a skeptical gaze toward totalitarian thought. That it doesn't always work that way is due to unquestioned assumptions in Bruffee's notion of social construction. He doesn't question (1) the ability of students to stand up for themselves, (2) the tenuousness of the provisional consensus of academic communities, or (3) the fact that differences among students might not always be obvious and freely spoken. Consciously situated in a Vietnam War protest environment, with a new racially and ethnically diverse student population, Bruffee assumed strong agency and argued for the fragmented, clashing uncertainty of knowledge.

Bruffee's theory and practice, with most of its assumptions intact, was downloaded into the design of Daedalus software, and so, significantly influenced the shape of computer-mediated pedagogy. In Daedalus, Bruffee's social constructionist assumptions about knowledge are intact and the end product is still an argument essay. The difference lies in Daedelus's use of technology to alter the dynamics of student conversations, in effect, offering a social process for invention. Synchronous conferencing is used in a whole class discussion to generate thinking on a specific issue while allowing multiple threads of conversation to develop, disabling the instructor's control of the discussion. Students then discuss specific excerpts from the InterChange session, again in synchronous mode. This leads to developing argument enthymemes and eventually to individually composed essays taken through a version of Bruffee's peer critique process. As has been widely recognized, Daedalus pedagogy increased attention on and appreciation for student-centered discourse, which allowed students to resist teacher structure more freely than in face-to-face discussions.

Cooper and Selfe, in their 1990 article on asynchronous conferencing, articulate what we see as an increasingly student-centered philosophy that they theorize through Bakhtin's concept of internally persuasive discourse. Here, resisting authority is expanded to include the authoritative discourses of the academy. The goal of collaborative conversation is a new student subject position born of resistance to authoritarian discourse. Whereas with Bruffee authority is expandable, and for Daedalus pedagogy it is decentered and shifting, for Cooper and Selfe, authority should be resisted in favor of internally persuasive discourse. As the technology makes more space for student expression, then, Cooper and Selfe theorize that expression as playing an active role in challenging the idea of a stable identity and in defining alternative, politicized subjectivities.

The impact of technology becomes clearer with Beth Kolko's work. Kolko uses Daedalus to make the contingent nature of knowledge manifestly palpable. The student subject is fragmented, enabling a self-questioning critique that makes room for different, shifting, and ultimately politicized subject positions. So while early Daedalus pedagogy posited authority as decentered and shifting, Kolko's cultural studies approach further emphasizes this aspect in order to bring into dialectical relation collaborative practice *and* critical consciousness of the production of knowledge. Kolko's cultural studies approach directly articulates the problem of subjectivity by posing questions "that take issue with the ways in which society constructs individuals" and that focus on "the tension between the determined subject and the determining individual—the agent" (33). Kolko accomplishes this awareness in her students through collaborative practices in which they learn to treat each other's utterances and writing as worthy of citation. Students collaborate (as with Bruffee and Daedalus) not in group writing of formal documents but in "the intellectual process of brainstorming, refining, and challenging arguments" (34). Kolko assumes the resistant subject of Cooper and Selfe; she uses technology and Bruffean collaborative activities to foreground the cultural studies problematic of subjective agency, an approach that deconstructs received identities by assuming a fluid subject constituted in discourse that can be reconstructed through discourse.

In her experiment with group writing, Carol Winkelmann tracks what happens when composing is defined as the singular product and process of the entire class. Winkelmann begins with some assumptions that bear directly upon the question of the subject:

- that in the postmodernist, postfeminist digital era, identity ought to be seen as cyborg identity, which is by definition multiple, contradictory, and in dialectical relation to technology; (431)
- that electronic literacy is rooted in collaborative work that is anarchic, non-hierarchical, and transformative; (437–38) and
- that the resulting text will break the conventions of linear, academic texts. (440)

To enact these assumptions, she sets up parameters for students that refuse many of the usual decision-making roles of the instructor, placing all composing responsibility on students. The course readings immerse students in the discourse of computer textuality (Bolter's *Writing Space*) and cyberpunk literature and film. Students then take on various roles in relation to the emerging group identity. Here, the "group" is the whole class. Individuals clash, cooperate, negotiate, and confront individual difference, which leads to a transformation of social relations and expanded individual subjectivity. Through this conflictual, fragmented process of writing as role-playing, Winkelman's students "found themselves-in-community" (444) and they performed literacy through "shifting identities, dependencies, and combinations" (440). One result was that students spurned outside critique of their text, suggesting a shift to a dispersed community-based authority, "earned by the development of expertise" (441).

Myka Vielstimmig, the collaborative nom de plume of Michael Spooner and Kathleen Yancey, links with Winkelmann's cyborgian process through the unconventional text, which is based on reconfiguring the writing subject as plural. In the realm of collaborative writing, Vielstimmig's "Petals on a Wet Black Bough" represents an unconventional print text that foregrounds a postmodern practice of co-authorship that, in the process of exposing the conflicts and negotiations involved, multiplies the subject positions of the two authors and ultimately illustrates the process of creating and representing a kind of cyborg identity. Through the creation of a collaborative persona, the relationship of the writing subject to a real world self is made radically ambiguous. We see Winkelmann's self-organizing process honed down to the relational identity of two. Spooner and Yancey become Vielstimmig as they perform the erasure of the boundaries between two fragmented identities and in that erasure multiply subjectivities. And all this they represent on the printed page!

Marilyn Cooper's article, "Postmodern Possibilities in Electronic Conversations," theorizes the authority of students' subject positions within computer-mediated collaborative discourse in a way that retheorizes Bruffee's student subject, that relies on convention as the provisional authority, and that replaces it with a subject who, in a sense, redefines social construction against its most conventional implications. Drawing on the relationship between self and other articulated by Bauman and Levinas, Cooper's networked student subject is fully postmodern, free to exercise a range of options. Following Levinas, the subject creates its selfhood by both refusing to be categorized and by being responsible to "the other." Cooper's subject is encouraged rather than coerced to occupy an ethical stance open to "unassimilated otherness." Cooper's computer classroom is not Bruffee's Habermasian community, since the relations among individuals, much as in Winkelmann's experiment, are allowed to emerge without recourse to imposed social structure or externally authorized rules. Whereas Bruffee's pedagogy assumes strong student agency and argues for a postmodern account of knowledge, Cooper's pedagogy assumes the fragmented clashing uncertainty of knowledge and argues for responsible student agency. The student in Cooper's theory may choose to engage with peers in collective action, to remain silent, or to employ agonistic discourse. Furthermore, Cooper's focus on the dynamics of computer conferencing suggests a decentering of the academic essay also apparent in Winkelmann's multivoiced group text. Lastly, if the general trend since Bruffee has been to increasingly privilege student discourse, Cooper's student subject represents the highest level of individual autonomy within a collaborative framework.

Looking at collaborative learning from a cyborg perspective, one can defamiliarize it. One can refuse a progress narrative, value the tensions of contradiction and conflict, and assume hybridity. This perspective is important to our conclusion.

Each approach we've discussed grew out of particular social-historical situations and was appropriate to those conditions. The conversation metaphor popularized by Bruffee continues in the literature, morphing into different versions, including Cooper's radically different concept of conversation. Bruffee's site is Brooklyn College; Cooper's is Michigan Tech, a geographically isolated school populated with smart, white, conservative, science/engineering students. Her approach fits her particular conditions. It's not hard to imagine why Cooper, in a relatively homogenous student classroom, might find refreshing the chaos and combativeness of Lester Faigley's problematic interchange session as he reports it in *Fragments of Rationality* (163–99). Cooper, puzzled by Faigley's worried response to the session, sees it instead as full of useful tensions. In her teaching situation, she probably can assume the willingness of her students to be responsible to each other.

Just as student subjects can't be reified, neither can collaborative practices or the situations they are embedded in. "Best practices" in collaborative learning makes no sense as a frozen concept, because the idea of collaborative learning can't be imposed upon a situation. Even if you try, the situation will change it. Bruffee's pedagogy was put into Daedalus software and was changed by the electronic situation of networked computers. As an alternative to progress narratives, we have two suggestions: (1) situate collaborative practices historically and (2) embrace hybridity, not just of student subjects, but of the landscape of practices as well.

WORKS CITED

Bauman, Zygmunt. *Postmodern Ethics*. Oxford: Blackwell, 1993.

Bolter, Jay David. *Writing Space: The Computer Hypertext, and the History of Writing*. Hillsdale: Lawrence Erlbaum, 1991.

Bruffee, Kenneth A. "The Way Out." *College English* 33.4 (Jan. 1972): 457–70.

—. *A Short Course in Writing: Composition, Collaborative Learning, and Constructive Reading*. 4th ed. New York: HarperCollins, 1993.

Cooper, Marilyn. "Postmodern Possibilities in Electronic Conversations." Ed. Gail E. Hawisher and Cynthia L. Selfe. *Passions, Pedagogies, and 21st Century Technologies*. Logan: Utah State UP, 1999. 140–60.

Cooper and Selfe. "Computer Conferences and Learning: Authority, Resistance, and Internally Persuasive Discourse." *College English* 52.8 (1990): 847–69.

Dylan, Bob. "Man in the Long Black Coat." *Oh Mercy*. Columbia Records, 1989.

Faigley, Lester. *Fragments of Rationality: Postmodernity and the Subject of Composition*. Pittsburgh: U of Pittsburgh P, 1992.

Kolko, Beth E. "Cultural Studies in/and the Networked Writing Classroom." *The Online Writing Classroom*. Ed. Susanmarie Harrington, Rebecca Rickley, and Michael Day. Cresskill: Hampton, 2000. 29–44.

Levinas, Emmanuel. *Ethics and Infinity: Conversations with Philippe Nemo*. Trans. Richard A. Cohen. Pittsburgh: Duquesne UP, 1992.

Vielstimmig, Myka. "Petals on a Wet Black Bough: Textuality, Collaboration, and the New Essay." Ed. Gail E. Hawisher and Cynthia L. Selfe. *Passions, Pedagogies, and 21st Century Technologies*. Logan: Utah State UP, 1999. 89–114.

Winkelmann, Carol L. "Electronic Literacy, Critical Pedagogy, and Collaboration: A Case for Cyborg Writing." *Computers & the Humanities* 29. (1995): 431–48.

TABLE 22.1
Selected Table of Collaborative Learning Theory and Practice

Source	Subject	Difference	Goal(s)	Text	Authority
Bruffee (1970s–1980s)	Rational liberal humanist	Resolved though interaction	Mastery of academic process	Academic essay including peer critique essays	Expandable and prolific
Daedalus (late 1980s)	Rational liberal humanist	Usually unresolved	Social cooperation and academic skills	Academic essay and InterChange transcripts	Decentered, shifting
Cooper and Selfe (1990)	Alternative subjectivities	Used to question hegemony	Resistance to authoritative discourse	Asynchronous conferences	Decentered, shifting
Kolko (2000)	Fragmented, self-questioning	Used to question hegemony	Critical consciousness	Academic essay and InterChange transcripts	To be resisted. Persuasion is internal
Winkelmann (1995)	Multipolar Cyborg identity	Provisionally resolved and/or juxtaposed without synthesis to enable group composing	Effective transition to electronic community	Polyglot, multi-layered, communal	Radical decentering of teacher authority—emerging student-centered authority
Cooper (2001)	Emerges through acts of responsibility to others	Respected as unassimilated otherness	Individual responsibility	Synchronous conferencing transcripts	Untenable, defaults to individual
Vielstimmig (1998–2001) (AKA Spooner and Yancy)	Collaborative personae	Provisionally resolved and/or juxtaposed without synthesis to enable group composing	Collapse rhetoric/poetic and process/product	E-mail, polyglot, print "new essay"	Negotiated, conflictual

23

Reclaiming Hybridity: How One Filipino American Counterpublic Hybridizes Academic Discourse

Terese Guinsatao Monberg
University of Kansas

In the summer of 2004, Filipino Americans from across the nation gathered in St. Louis, Missouri, to participate in the Tenth Biennial Conference of the Filipino American National Historical Society (FANHS). The decision to hold the 2004 conference in St. Louis was a conscious one, for it marks a specific place and time in Filipino American history. St. Louis was the site for the 1904 Louisiana Purchase Exposition, a World's Fair commissioned by President McKinley who, when justifying U.S. imperialism in the Philippines, declared that Filipinos were "unfit for self-government" and that "there was nothing left for us [the U.S.] to do but to take them all, and to educate the Filipinos and uplift and civilize and Christianize them" (qtd. in Rusling 17). This imperialist narrative informed the design of the Fair's simulated, million-dollar Philippine village. Colonial administrators and academic anthropologists recruited some 1,100 native Filipinos to populate the village and perform their supposed "savageness" by repeatedly performing ordinarily mundane tasks, native customs, and special rituals for the American public according to a highly regimented, monotonous, daily schedule. The 1904 World's Fair is but one example of how images of the Filipino "savage" became amply available to an American public through various forms of publicity during the early twentieth century, in magazine articles, newspaper columns, and political cartoons. But the Fair also demonstrates how the American academy, particularly the discipline of anthropology, played an important role in "documenting" the Filipino "savage," therefore justifying U.S. imperialism in the Philippines and a self-proclaimed mission to benevolently "assimilate" Filipinos into more "civilized" ways of life. One hundred years later, Filipino Americans are still trying to negotiate the ways they have been represented by these narratives. Thus, it seems fitting that FANHS members came together during the St. Louis centennial to take stock of how far research-based knowledge of Filipino Americans has come "A Century Since St. Louis."[1]

FANHS defines itself as a community-based organization; its larger mission is to identify, gather, preserve, and disseminate materials on the history of Filipino Americans in the United States. As an organization that situates itself somewhere between academic and Filipino American communities, we might imagine its members adopting hybrid forms of academic discourse as they attempt to engage these two, sometimes overlapping audiences. But to reduce the rhetoric produced by FANHS members to a mere mix of academic and "home" or Filipino American discourse ignores the larger public and academic discourses that FANHS is working to counter. It neglects a large part of the intellectual work performed by this discourse. My purpose here, then, is to refine our notions of hybrid academic discourse by drawing on Mikhail Bakhtin's notion of the intentional hybrid utterance, and to redirect our attention to counterpublics as additional sources for exemplary models of hybrid academic discourse.

DEFINING AND REFINING NOTIONS OF HYBRIDITY: THEORIES OF HYBRID ACADEMIC DISCOURSE

The term *hybrid academic discourse* was defined in a 1999 article by Patricia Bizzell in her larger effort to recognize and encourage forms of written discourse that "are clearly doing serious intellectual work [...] even as they violate many of the conventions of traditional academic discourse" (8). Bizzell explains that she was attracted to the term *hybrid* because "it upsets the dichotomy established in [her] earlier work between academic and students' home discourses" ("Intellectual" 3). And, in many ways, this recent strand of work makes important strides toward breaking down that dichotomy. For example, she does not define *hybrid academic discourse* as a mix of "home" and academic discourses. She instead refers to the mix as one of academic and "previously non-academic" forms of discourse—which both widens her analytic lens and recognizes that these nonacademic discourses are changing and becoming forms of academic discourse ("Hybrid" 11). Citations of and responses to this new strand of her work, however, often shorten the phrase "hybrid academic discourse" to "hybrid discourse" and further reduce its definition to a mix between academic and "home" discourse. Judith Hebb, for example, begins an article on "mixed forms of academic discourse" with the following (somewhat reductive) definition: "broadly defined, a *'hybrid discourse'* is a mix of *home* and school languages" (21, emphasis added). Sidney Dobrin makes a similar move when responding to Bizzell's work by warning us that "talking about particular discourses as *hybrid discourses* risks nullifying or neutralizing *home* discourses" (46, emphasis added).

These modifications reduce the analytic power of Bizzell's concept in (at least) three ways. First, by dropping the qualifier *academic* from the phrase, we are simply left with "hybrid discourse." This phrase should enlarge our view; yet, the conversation has not focused on hybrid forms of medical, legal, political, journalistic, or novelistic discourse. The discussion continues to focus on academic discourses. Secondly, by defining "home" discourse as the only discourse that can be mixed with academic discourse, we make the faulty assumption that students, faculty, or community-based researchers do not have other discourses to draw upon in formulating and articulating new knowledge. My third point is that, taken together, these redefinitions potentially relegate hybrid forms of academic discourse to the multicultural margins of the discipline. This happens when members of the discipline begin to show a willingness to include, even welcome, the home and hybrid discourses of Others without always exhibiting an equal "willingness to recognize and respond to it as intellectual work" (Micciche, qtd. in Logan 41).

Bizzell has recently questioned and almost abandoned her use of the term *hybrid* in favor of *mixed* or *alternative* discourses (2000; 2002). What seems to remain constant in her work, however, is the notion that alternative forms of academic discourse are achieved through a process of mixing. I'd like to reverse these assertions. I argue that it is not so much the term *hybrid* as it is the assumptions behind the term that are problematic. And for my purposes here, I'd like to focus less on hybrid academic discourse as a mix and more on hybrid academic discourse as a discourse that is negotiating and questioning the assumptions behind academic discourse. For as Jacqueline Jones Royster reminds us, it's "not really about alternative discourses at all, but about alternative *assumptions* about discourses" (26). While Bizzell questions the usefulness of the term *hybrid* to describe *mixed* or *alternative* forms of academic discourse, Hebb argues the term need not be perceived so negatively. Drawing from Bakhtin's notion of "hybrid constructions," Hebb asks us to view hybrid forms of discourse "along a continuum of consciousness and empowerment" as their authors struggle with sometimes competing points of view (23). I'd like to take Hebb's reading of Bakhtin a bit further to emphasize these potentially competing points of view.

Bakhtin defines the "hybrid construction," as Hebb notes, as "an utterance that belongs [...] to a single speaker, but that actually contains mixed within it two utterances, two speech manners, two styles, two 'languages', two semantic and axiological belief systems" (23). But Bakhtin makes further distinctions between unintentional and intentional hybridizations. Unintentional, unconscious, or "organic" hybrids are, for Bakhtin, "one of the most important modes in the historical life and evolution of all languages" (358). Intentional hybrids, by contrast, are conscious, artistic images of language. The intentional hybrid is an act of language that brings (at least) two differing points of view into contact with one another. It doesn't mix these views as much as it dialogizes them, sets them against one another; it views one language—and its assumptions—through the lens of another.[2] Bakhtin writes:

> [A]s distinct from the opaque mixing of languages [...] the novelistic hybrid is *an artistically organized system for bringing different languages in contact with one another*, a system having as its goal the illumination of one language by means of another, the carving-out of a living image of another language. (361, emphasis original)

Bakhtin's notion of the intentional hybrid utterance, then, draws our attention to the dialogizing nature of the conscious hybrid. The intentional act of hybridization becomes not just a conscious mixing, but "a sociological probing, an exploring of values and beliefs [...] not a mere play of forms" (Morson and Emerson 312).[3] This reading of Bakhtin's intentional hybrid has affinity with notions of hybridity in postcolonial theory. Homi Bhabha, for example, reminds us that "[h]ybridity is a problematic of colonial representation and individuation that reverses the effects of colonial disavowal, so that other 'denied' knowledges enter upon the dominant discourse and estrange the basis of its authority—its rules of recognition" (114).

Given this refined notion of a hybrid that consciously dialogizes and attempts to estrange more authoritative forms of discourse, we might look to other sources for hybrid academic discourse. Traditionally, we have looked for hybrid forms of academic discourse in our classrooms and in published scholarship—both contexts in which academics hold the power to determine which hybrid forms hold merit for the field. I suggest that subaltern counterpublics may be another place to look for hybrid academic discourse. Because these publics generally emerge and situate themselves in relationship to more dominant publics—or at least in relationship to counterpublics with a more dominant voice—they offer us a view of the assumptions behind academic discourse from another standpoint.

Subaltern counterpublics, as defined by Nancy Fraser, are "parallel discursive arenas where members of subordinated social groups invent and circulate counterdiscourses, so as to formulate oppositional interpretations of their identities, interests, and needs" (14). These subaltern counterpublics exist both parallel to and in opposition to more dominant public spheres. Thus, according to both Rita Felski and Nancy Fraser, counterpublics direct their rhetorical activities both inward and outward. Fraser, for example, notes that "in stratified societies, subaltern counterpublics have a dual character. On the one hand they function as spaces of withdrawal and regroupment; on the other hand, they also function as bases and training grounds for agitational activities directed toward wider publics" (15).

These agitational activities stem from conflict and as Michael Warner reminds us, "the conflict extends not just to ideas or policy questions, but to the speech genres and modes of address that constitute the public, or the hierarchy among media" (424). Thus, counterpublics can offer us another view of the intellectual work performed by hybrid discourses.[4]

Recognizing the dual character of counterpublic discourse is not the same thing, in my view, as reinforcing a dichotomy between publics and counterpublics or between home discourses and academic discourses. The power of counterpublic theory, in my mind, is that it allows us to use the dual nature of counterpublic discourse as a heuristic lens without necessarily buying into false dichotomies. Let me illustrate my point further by turning to a discussion of one Filipino American counterpublic: the Filipino American National Historical Society (FANHS).

FANHS AS A COUNTERPUBLIC: HYBRIDIZING ACADEMIC DISCOURSE FOR A PURPOSE

As a counterpublic, FANHS emerged in response to larger structural changes that worked to place the voices of a particular group of Filipino Americans on the margins of multiple public and counterpublic spheres. For example, the influx of post-1965 Filipino immigrants tended to place the voices of American-born Filipinos (particularly those born before 1945) on the margins of Filipino American communities. Thus, it would be problematic to view the rhetoric of FANHS as a hybrid between something called "Filipino American discourse" and academic discourse. Instead, we might view FANHS as part of a larger Filipino American public sphere, one made up of heterogeneous, overlapping "emergent collectives."[5]

Viewed in this way, counterpublics may not just exist in opposition to a dominant public sphere, but in relationship to other counterpublics with similar goals. Social movements, as Phaedra Pezzullo reminds us, are often made up of "multiple critiques and actions" (361). Not only may there be multiple counterpublics that define themselves against a dominant public, there may also be counterpublics that define themselves against other counterpublics even as they work toward similar long-term goals. For example, a counterpublic emerged in 1968 when a group of Asian and Asian American students, professors, lecturers, and community activists came together to demand curricula more relevant to students and communities of color (Revilla 97; Wei 18). This movement prompted the founding of the first two Asian American Studies programs. But as Asian American Studies struggled for institutional recognition and legitimacy, community activists—once central to its mission—were placed on the margins of the knowledge-making and teaching activities of this discipline. FANHS emerged, in part, as a counterpublic to Asian American Studies. The relationship between FANHS and Asian American Studies might be defined as both an alliance—two counterpublics defined against a more dominant public sphere—and as an opposition—one counterpublic defined against another.

The history of FANHS, as a counterpublic, shows us the problem with labeling non-academic portions of academic hybrid discourses as "home" discourses. The mix of discourses and discourse assumptions present in FANHS publications cannot always be traced to an original parent; the nonacademic portions are not always distinctly Filipino or Filipino American or Asian American or Midwestern or Californian. For example, one of their key phrases, "Growing Up Brown," demonstrates the strong alliances these particular Filipino Americans had developed with other Black and Brown Americans during the 1970s. What I am proposing is that we read hybrid academic discourses differently, not as a mix of academic and nonacademic discourses, but as a view of academic discourse—and the assumptions embedded within that discourse—through the lens of another.

To illustrate how we might do this, I now turn to an example of hybrid academic discourse taken from the biennial *FANHS Journal*. The journal is similar to a conference proceeding; most of the articles appearing in the journal were presented by members at past biennial conferences. Its publication is overseen by an editorial board that includes community-based and academic researchers, and the journal is regularly deposited with university and college libraries across the United States. It is a journal that is consciously situated in relationship to a large and diverse audience: academics, community-based researchers, teachers, students, and a larger public audience. As such, many of its articles might be seen as using what we call hybrid academic discourse. The example I want to share with you is taken from an article written by community-based researcher Eloisa Gomez Borah, a research librarian at UCLA. By closely reading journal entries of the Spanish explorer Pedro de Unamuno, Borah found evidence of Filipinos setting foot in Morro Bay, California, in October of 1587. In recounting these events, Borah writes in the present tense, making Filipinos active subjects in her narrative. She writes:

The Filipinos, way ahead of the pack, encounter the first local Indians. They rush back to notify the captain that they have seen five persons. The captain hurriedly dispatches two soldiers and two Filipinos to make peace with these inhabitants, but the Indians have dispersed by the time the group returns to the point of the earlier encounter. [...] It is the Filipinos' eyewitness report of the five Indians, including the two women with two children they carried on their backs that the captain records in his journal. (16)

In this excerpt, Borah recounts her findings not by citing Unamuno's journal but by recounting the events as they might have happened. She explains that Filipinos were "way ahead of the pack," reminding her audience that as colonial subjects of Spain, Filipinos were seen as dispensable and were used as scouts. As scouts, Filipinos would be the first ones to encounter any perceived danger and the last ones to receive any acknowledgement for their crucial role in Unamuno's "discoveries." Borah's "storytelling" format would be largely avoided in academic forums but it allows Borah to represent Filipinos as active subjects of history rather than as passive objects of study.

Like an academic researcher, Borah reads historical documents within a larger historical context. Later in her article, Borah notes, "There is reason to be grateful to Unamuno, a relatively minor explorer of his time. Unlike others who made little or no note of 'Indios

Luzones' among their crew, his diary recorded in nineteen instances what the Filipinos were doing on those three days in Morro Bay" (17).

In this excerpt, Borah provides her audience with a methodology for reading historical documents. She situates her findings in relationship to what her audience already knows: that the Spanish did not always distinguish between Indians and Filipinos; Filipinos were, essentially, Indians from Luzon, the main island of the Philippines. Borah suggests to her readers that the histories of Filipinos and Filipino Americans will continue to elude researchers who don't understand the many ways Filipinos have traditionally been miscategorized, misrepresented, or miscounted. She further suggests there may be myriad documents that need to be revisited. She writes:

> There is often much more behind any single passing mention of Filipinos in historical accounts of the 15th, 16th, and 17th centuries. We need to revisit research that may be considered "already done" so that we may discover every incident of Filipino presence in early America and document Filipino contributions during this early period of settling this continent. (18)

Using a form of hybrid academic discourse, Borah not only asks her readers to see Unamuno's Filipino scouts as active subjects, she also asks her readers to see *themselves* as active, knowing subjects—capable of "revisiting" academic historical narratives with different assumptions and common knowledge. Knowing the history of Spanish and American colonization in the Philippines, knowing that Filipinos and Filipino Americans are often misrepresented in traditional categories, knowing that academic research has often ignored the experiences of Filipino Americans, members of Borah's audience are invited to re-read historical research through a different cultural lens.

When FANHS researchers represent Filipino Americans as sources and active subjects of knowledge, they implicitly call attention to the rhetorical contexts which frame all knowledge-making activities. Borah, for example, calls attention to the ways colonizing categories and academic research agendas created a rhetorical frame that kept Unamuno's Filipino scouts hidden from view. In doing so, she reminds her primarily Filipino American audience that their knowledge of their community, culture, and history can be used to create new knowledge about Filipino Americans.

To understand the intellectual work performed by hybrid academic discourses, we need to view these discourses as more than a mix of home and academic discourses. We need to see the author behind the hybrid as questioning and negotiating the assumptions behind academic discourse. We also need to look beyond academic contexts for exemplary models of hybrid academic discourse. FANHS members, for instance, employ hybrid academic discourse for very specific purposes—and these purposes offer us a view of our own academic practices.[6]

As a public sphere situated counter to the academy, FANHS invests its hybrid academic discourse with very different assumptions—assumptions that help promote a model of community-based research where research questions emerge from community concerns, where knowledge is made with community members and by community members, where primary and secondary research materials are owned by community-based archives, and where research findings are shared with community members in creative and interactive ways. FANHS seeks to empower community members not only with knowledge, but by affirming their experiences, giving them strategies for conducting and disseminating research, for starting their own FANHS chapter, and for organizing and maintaining archival materials. Through this hybrid academic discourse, it not just knowledge that is made accessible to the community; it is the very position of researcher and teacher that is made accessible to the community. These hybrid academic discourses carry very different assumptions from those behind the academic discourses generated in association with the 1904 St. Louis World's Fair, the nationalist agendas that informed Areas Studies of the Cold War era, and the evolution of Asian American Studies during the 1970s. These assumptions question what it means to sufficiently "educate" a Filipino American, or any American who lives in a racialized society.

NOTES

1. The CFP (call for papers) for the 2004 FANHS National Conference listed the conference theme as "The Filipino American Experience: A Century Since St. Louis." On the final program, the theme was listed as: "The Filipino American Experience ... 'A Century Hence, From the St. Louis World's Fair.'"
2. This is a different reading from Hebb's reading of Bakhtin's intentional hybrid. While Hebb cites the latter part of this same passage, she interprets intentional hybridization as a "purposeful mixing of languages [that] results in an enriched language [...]" (24).
3. See Morson and Emerson's discussion of Bakhtin's notion of the hybrid utterance as it relates to the novel—a form that works by dialogizing languages (see especially 311–17).
4. This is not a radically new insight. Much of the work that focuses on rhetoric and race recognizes the intellectual work and dual character of counterpublic and/or hybrid forms of discourse. See, for example, Juanita Comfort's work on African American women's rhetorics of "cultural negotiation," Shirley Wilson Logan's work on black women's rhetorical strategies of "identification and resistance," and Malea Powell's work on nineteenth-century American Indian "rhetorics of survivance (survival + resistance)."
5. While public sphere theory has increasingly recognized the multiplicity and diversity of any given public sphere, the concept of a counterpublic remains largely undertheorized (Asen; Pezzullo; Squires). As Robert Asen notes, counterpublics emerge and develop "as explicitly articulated alternatives to wider publics that exclude the participation of potential participants" (425). How counterpublics emerge and develop in relationship to more dominant public spheres or in relationship to other counterpublics is what remains undertheorized. Catherine Squires, for example, argues that the term *counterpublic* does not always "help us to understand the heterogeneity of marginalized groups" (447). For a discussion of different types of "marginal" or "counter" publics, see Squires's "Rethinking the Black Public Sphere: An Alternative Vocabulary for Multiple Public Spheres."
6. As researchers, we may need to develop a hybrid academic lens before we are able to see the larger purposes behind any given hybrid academic discourse. Being Filipino American does not mean I was born with a "natural" Filipino American interpretive lens. This interpretive lens, like an academic interpretive lens, is always in the process of development. Just as our academic training helps us recognize the genre, purposes, and uses of academic discourse, researchers may need to immerse themselves in other discourse contexts to develop "an ear" for particular forms of hybrid academic discourse. In the Q&A session that followed Jacqueline Jones Royster's 2004 RSA Plenary, she referred to this process as one of "standing under" discourse practices (as opposed to understanding them).

WORKS CITED

Asen, Robert. "What puts the 'counter' in counterpublic?" *Communication Theory* 10 (2000): 424–46.

Bakhtin, M. M. *The Dialogic Imagination: Four Essays.* Trans. Caryl Emerson and Michael Holoquist. Ed. Michael Holoquist. Austin: U of Texas P, 1981.

Bhabha, Homi K. *The Location of Culture.* London: Routledge, 1994.

Bhabha, Homi K. *The Location of Culture.* London: Routledge, 1994.

Bizzell, Patricia. "Basic Writing and the Issue of Correctness, or, What to Do with 'Mixed' Forms of Academic Discourse." *Journal of Basic Writing* 19.1 (2000): 4–12.

—. "Hybrid Academic Discourses: What, Why, How." *Composition Studies* 27 (Fall 1999): 7–21.

—. "The Intellectual Work of 'Mixed' Forms of Academic Discourses." *ALT-DIS: Alternative Discourses and the Academy.* Eds. Christopher Schroeder, Helen Fox, and Patricia Bizzell. Portsmouth, NH: Heinemann, 2002. 1–10.

Borah, Eloisa Gomez. "The Filipino Landing in Morro Bay in 1587." *Filipino American National Historical Society Journal* 4 (1996): 15–18.

Comfort, Juanita. "A Rhetoric of 'Cultural Negotiation': Toward an Ethos of Empowerment for African-American Women Graduate Students." *Rhetoric, Cultural Studies, and Literacy: Selected Papers from the 1994 Conference of the RSA.* Ed. John Frederick Reynolds. Hillsdale, NJ: Lawrence Erlbaum Associates, 1995. 123–32.

Dobrin, Sidney. "A Problem with Writing (about) 'Alternative' Discourse." *ALT-DIS: Alternative Discourses and the Academy.* Eds. Christopher Schroeder, Helen Fox, and Patricia Bizzell. Portsmouth, NH: Heinemann, 2002. 45–56.

Felski, Rita. *Beyond Feminist Aesthetics: Feminist Literature and Social Change.* Cambridge, MA: Harvard UP, 1989.

Fraser, Nancy. "Rethinking the Public Sphere: A Contribution to the Critique of Actually Existing Democracy." *The Phantom Public Sphere.* Ed. Bruce Robbins. Minneapolis: U of Minnesota P, 1993. 1–32.

Hebb, Judith. "Mixed Forms of Academic Discourse: A Continuum of Language Possibility." *Journal of Basic Writing* 21.2 (2002): 21–36.

Logan, Shirley Wilson. "Identification and Resistance: Women's Civic Discourse Across the Color Line." Rhetorical Democracy: Discursive Practices of Civic Engagement. Eds. Gerard A. Hauser and Amy Grim. Mahwah, NJ: Erlbaum, 2004. 33–44.

McKinley, William (President). "Remarks to Methodist Delegation." Reprinted in *The Philippines Reader: A History of Colonialism, Neocolonialism, Dictatorship, and Resistance.* Eds. Daniel B. Schirmer and Stephen Rosskamm Shalom. Boston: South End Press, 1987. 22–23.

Morson, Gary Saul and Caryl Emerson. *Mikhail Bakhtin: Creation of a Prosaics.* Stanford, CA: Stanford UP, 1990.

Pezzullo, Phaedra C. "Resisting 'National Breast Cancer Awareness Month': The Rhetoric of Counterpublics and Their Cultural Performances." *Quarterly Journal of Speech* 89 (November 2003): 345–65.

Powell, Malea. "Rhetorics of Survivance: How American Indians *Use* Writing." *College Composition and Communication* 53.3 (February 2002): 396–434.

Revilla, Linda A. "Filipino American Identity: Transcending the Crisis." *Filipino Americans: Transformation and Identity.* Ed. Maria P.P. Root. Thousand Oaks, CA: Sage, 1997. 95–111.

Royster, Jacqueline Jones. "Academic Discourses or Small Boats on a Big Sea." *ALT-DIS: Alternative Discourses and the Academy.* Eds. Christopher Schroeder, Helen Fox, and Patricia Bizzell. Portsmouth, NH: Heinemann, 2002. 23–30.

Rusling, James (General). "Interview with President McKinley." *The Cristian Advocate* 22 January 1093, New York Ed.: 17. Rpt. in *The Philippine Reader: A History of Colonialism, Neocoloialism, Dictatorship, and Resistance.* Ed. Daniel B. Schirmer and Stephen Rosskamm Shalom. Boston: South End Press, 1987. 22–3.

Squires, Catherine R. "Rethinking the Black Public Sphere: An Alternative Vocabulary for Multiple Public Spheres." *Communication Theory* 12 (November 2002): 446–68.

Warner, Michael. "Publics and Counterpublics (abbreviated version)." *Quarterly Journal of Speech* 88 (November 2002): 413–25.

Wei, William. *The Asian American Movement: A Social History.* Philadelphia: Temple UP, 1993.

24

Public Portals, Catholic Walls: Teacher Training and the Liberal Arts at Two Western, Massachusetts Colleges for Women in the 1930s, The College of Our Lady of the Elms and The State Teachers College at Westfield

Beth Ann Rothermel
Westfield State College

In her essay "Faith, Knowledge, and Gender," scholar Jill Ker Conway reports that although Catholic women's colleges have received little attention from historians, 75 years ago they outnumbered other types of women's colleges and educated "a slightly larger cohort than Protestant or nondenominational institutions" (12). Ker Conway's essay along with others in Tracy Schier and Cynthia Russett's recent collection *Catholic Women's Colleges in America* begin to tell the "story of that relatively invisible yet significant set of institutions [...] the colleges sponsored by women's religious congregations" (6). These essays focus on such issues as the cultural and social phenomena that gave rise to such institutions, the diverse orders that founded them, and the innovative perspectives and practices that often characterized them. Schier and Russett note, however, that their collection is just a beginning and that more research is needed in a number of areas. Welcome are more histories of "individual colleges" to help "fill in blanks in our knowledge of how these institutions developed" and of the cultures that evolved at these schools (9). They also call for more comparative studies of these colleges with secular women's colleges, asking for example, how "the women who graduated from Catholic women's colleges differ (if they did) from those attending secular women's colleges" (10)?

This essay responds to this call by comparing the College of Our Lady of the Elms (in Chicopee, Massachusetts) to a neighboring public teachers college, The State Teachers College at Westfield, during the 1920s and 1930s. I examine the curricula offered by these institutions in relation to each school's mission. Of particular interest to me is each school's program of rhetorical study.

But why study the Elms alongside a public teachers college when, as Schier and Russett point out, Catholic women's colleges were more likely to model themselves on existing private women's colleges (10)? Although research shows that the Elms, founded in 1928 by the Sisters of Saint Joseph of Springfield, developed a curriculum of study more like that offered at another neighboring school, Smith College, the Elms grew out of an academy and normal school established in the late-nineteenth century (Aherne). As Elms College historian Thomas Moriarty reports, "a significant factor in Catholic school growth during the 1920s was development within religious communities, as well as within dioceses, of normal schools" (Unpublished 8). Furthermore, Westfield, which was a normal school until 1932, and the Elms served the same population of students, largely women of the lower-middle and middle classes, many of whom were first, second, and third generation Irish. As Mary Oates reports in a 1989 essay on Catholic lay women and the labor force, mid- to late-nineteenth-century Catholic women had "flocked to normal schools and colleges" (98). Religious orders had also sent sisters to these institutions as a way to prepare them to teach in the nation's many new parochial schools (Innes 9). One of the sisters who ran the normal school program at the Elms in the late 1910s was in fact a graduate of the nearby Worcester State Normal School (Moriarty, "History" 9), while a professor of education in the 1930s trained at the North Adams State Normal School (Personnel). As Kathleen A. Mahoney shows, the establishment of Catholic women's colleges was in part a response to the large number of Catholic women attending secular and Protestant institutions. Additionally, throughout the twentieth century, graduates from both institutions went on to varied careers in public schools in the area, a career field that graduates of institutions like Smith chose less and less often.

As I am engaged in ongoing research about Massachusetts Normal Schools/Teachers Colleges, studying these two institutions alongside one another has complicated my own understanding of the educational opportunities available to area women of the lower-middle and middle classes during the 1920s and 1930s. My research leads me to assert, for instance, that the opening of the Elms, first as normal school and then as college, provided women, many of whom would become teachers, with more rigorous training in the arts and sciences, particularly in rhetorical studies, than the twentieth-century public teachers college. In response to state pressure to adopt a course of study more professional than cultural in nature, the state teachers college had, in fact, revised its more progressive nineteenth-century program of study in a way that may have constrained women students' intellectual growth, particularly in the area of oral and written expression.

Following in the vein of Helen Lefkowitz Horowitz, who writes about architecture at noted women's colleges, let me begin by suggesting how descriptions of the academic spaces in school promotional materials reveal important differences in the two schools' missions. Emphasized by Westfield materials were the school's historical contributions to public education and its connections to the community—from its Romanesque portals "teachers of ability, character, and clear vision" consistently emerge (Massachusetts WPA 78). Catalogues from the 1930s celebrate founding father Horace Mann. The school building is "excellently situated, with good light and air," and "splendidly equipped for the purpose of educating teachers" (*Catalogue*, 1931–32). Also highlighted is the school's "assembly hall where the students meet daily," the school's proximity to various population centers, and its connections with a community training school that "furnishes students privileges of observation and practice." These descriptions reflect the school's "strictly professional" agenda: "to prepare in the best possible manner the pupils for the work of organizing and teaching the public schools of the Commonwealth." The 1931–32 curriculum then outlined, including a few general education courses, stresses over and over again how all course work is linked with the professional development of its student population. Not mentioned are the opportunities for more general academic study that Westfield's progressive nineteenth-century curriculum had offered to women of limited economic means.

A catalogue description of the Elms from the early 1930s is certainly more like that found in a Smith College catalogue. In focus is the spaciousness of the campus, "its forty acres of wood and lawn" for relaxation. The College Building, furthermore, is

> home of the liberal arts and the sciences [...] a majestic structure of pure collegiate Gothic [...] the Library, with its pleasant reading room, its shelves of 'learned lore,' both ancient and modern, and its storied stained glass windows, which at night, make the illuminated front of the tower a thing of beauty, casting a brilliant smile over the whole neighborhood. (*College*, c. 1931, 11)

Also noted are the Veritas Auditorium, where "fourteen hundred may enjoy lecture, oratorical entertainment, or drama" (12), and the College Chapel.

> Manifestly, the Campus buildings leave nothing to be desired that makes for the moral, mental, or physical development of the students who matriculate at The College of Our Lady of the Elms. [...] The welcoming arms of Our Lady, at the main entrance, symbolize an assurance to which the stately campus structures give confirmation. (14)

Not mentioned is the wall that enclosed the campus, a wall that came down some fifty years later as the school tried to improve its ties to the surrounding neighborhood. Such descriptions likely served a number of purposes. They assured anxious parents, and church officials, that the Elms, like other Catholic women's colleges, would provide a cloistered environment steeped in Catholic tradition—one that catalogues from the 1930s overtly state would protect women students from dangerous secular or Protestant influences. But descriptions also reveal the college's, and its founding order's, emphasis on the arts and sciences. The curriculum that follows includes intensive course work in philosophy, rhetoric, literature, some sciences, and religion, course work women at the state teachers colleges were encountering. Since the Elms saw itself as preparing women students both for "life" and a "living," courses in educational theory and psychology were also offered (*College*, c. 1931, 10).

I will provide a more detailed discussion of the curricula offered by these two neighboring schools, focusing in particular on the rhetorical program of study. Let me first give some relevant history. In 1928, the Elms College opened its doors to degree-seeking young women, mostly from surrounding communities, the result of the collaborative advocacy of Mother John Berchmans, Third Superior General of the Sisters of Saint Joseph, and the Reverend Thomas O'Leary, D.D., Third Bishop of Springfield, who would be the college's first president (Aherne 98-99). In preparing to open the college, Mother John Berchmans consulted with faculty from varied institutions, including the nearby Smith College and St. Catherine's in St. Paul, Minnesota. But the Sisters of Saint Joseph (SSJ) were not starting from scratch. They had a progressive history, one characterized by intensive work in the field of education and the exposure among its members to a variety of institutions. The SSJ had established and run parochial schools and other education programs throughout western Massachusetts since the 1880s. In 1899, they also established an academy where the Elms now resides, responding to a call for institutions where young women of modest means who did not have access to parochial schools could study (Moriarty, "History" 6). In 1904, the sisters began offering its normal school program in conjunction with the academy, a program which grew considerably through the teens and twenties (Moriarty, "History" 10).

The SSJ was a progressive order, with a "unique philosophy of education" when compared with other orders, as well as other educators (Aherne 83). Unlike other Catholic academies, which were often finishing schools, the Elms required both academy and normal school students to do work in the liberal arts and sciences. In order to take courses in music and the visual arts, which were staples at some Catholic academies, academy students paid extra (Moriarty, "History" 5). Normal school students pursued liberal arts course work during the first of two years, along with courses in educational psychology, music, physical education, and religion (Moriarty, "History" 6). Professional course work and practice teaching at area parochial schools occurred during the second year. The program of study the Elms offered resembled that called for by progressive Catholic reformer J. L. Spalding in his 1890 article, "Normal Schools for Catholics." Spalding had argued that the many women, most of whom were nuns, sent out to teach in parochial schools needed training in the "art and science" of teaching. The program of study he called for would include not just the "methods of education," but also "the history of education, the theories of education, physiology and psychology in their bearings upon education. [...] Philosophy and literature, and possibly the classical languages and physics" should also be taught. "[F]or the aim of a true Normal School is not merely to impart professional and technical knowledge and skill, but to give culture of mind, without which the teacher always works at a disadvantage" (96). Although the Elms was primarily preparing lay women to teach in public schools, such a philosophy seems to have prevailed.

Spalding, in fact, shares the views of many nineteenth-century progressive pedagogues establishing public normal schools like that of Westfield, views outlined in Mariolina Rizzi Salvatori's collection *Pedagogy: Disturbing History, 1819–1929*. The nineteenth-century Westfield, for instance, had a curriculum, with courses in philosophy, rhetoric, and various sciences, that provided students with the "mental culture" Spalding declared so important for teachers aiming to inspire their pupils to do "effective intellectual work." Of course, the school where that work occurred had a Protestant ethos, instead of a Catholic one. But early-twentieth-century state boards of education pressured public institutions like Westfield to develop programs purely professional in nature—programs that did not duplicate the liberal arts curricula of elite private colleges, or the more theoretically oriented education programs of state universities. Such directives were issued, interestingly, right around the time that the private Elms was establishing a program of study emphasizing broader intellectual training as well as professional course work.

To be sure, the Elms Normal School, and later College, did not serve as many young women as state normal schools like Westfield. Until the 1930s, no tuition was charged at Westfield. However, catalogues from both schools reveal that by the mid-1930s, students attending Westfield paid $75 a year, compared with the $150 required at Elms, likely making both within reach of the lower-middle and middle classes (Smith cost $500 a year for tuition). Whether or not some students were drawn to the Elms instead of Westfield because it offered a more progressive program of study is difficult to establish. What does seem most likely is that young women from Catholic (and often Irish) homes found in the Elms a culture more open to them than what they would have encountered at Westfield.

Plenty of research documents the extent to which anti-Catholicism thrived in places like western Massachusetts during the first half of the twentieth century, a period when large numbers of Catholics from Ireland, Poland, and Italy were settling in the area (Moriarty; McGreevey). Studies like those of Mary Oates show the efforts of second-generation Irish Catholic women to move from the industrial or domestic labor force into middle-class occupations such as teaching. While these women did attend places like Westfield, they encountered there not just a curriculum supported by Protestant and/or secular worldviews but also prejudice against their religious and ethnic origins. Graduates of area parochial schools who sought admission to Westfield in the 1910s had to jump over more hurdles than their public school counterparts, taking, for example, admissions tests (and typically receiving low scores) (Student Entrance Records 1910–15). Critic teacher reviews of these students' practice teaching, while not mentioning religion, criticize them for "incorrect language," "lack of forcefulness and enthusiasm," and as being not "attractive to children" (Student Records). Although evidence is primarily anecdotal, drawn from comments made by alumnae of that era both orally and in writing, some faculty expressed anti-Semitic views (Alumni Correspondence). It is likely that similar prejudice against Catholics found voice in a culture steeped in New England Protestantism. Certainly, an institution like the Elms would have been welcome for those young Catholic women seeking cultural and religious affirmation, at least those of the lower-middle and middle classes.

In the 1920s, the SSJ recognized in the Elms Normal School the foundations for a four-year college that would provide its students with a more complete liberal arts education. Many of the order's own members had been pursuing more advanced studies through colleges like Fordham University and Boston College, obtaining the degrees and the experience necessary to make the transition in 1928 (Aherne 122).[1] The Elms college still reflected the central mission of its founding order, graduating students who would become teachers and administrators in area public and private schools throughout the next 75 years. That central mission continued to show the order's own commitment to providing future teachers with rigorous intellectual training along with professional work that emphasized both theory and practice. Early catalogues make cautious claims about women's place, but they always emphasize the school's role in preparing women for work in the world as well as home. The school will aid women in "attain[ing] success in any chosen field of temporal effort […] religion, education, journalism, social work, and kindred fields which the complex exigencies of modern life have opened to women" (*College*, 1931, 10). For the SSJ, the appropriate foundations for such effort rested with a liberal arts program.

The program of rhetorical study required at the Elms in the late 1920s and 1930s reveals the extent of its focus on "formation" and not "information" (*College*, c. 1931, 9). Furthermore, a brief comparison of it with the program of rhetorical study required at Westfield suggests that the Elms may have provided more opportunities for women to develop intellectually powerful voices as well as minds. As noted earlier, although Westfield's nineteenth-century students studied rhetoric and oratory, along with philosophy and various natural sciences, as subjects in their own right, Westfield mission statements from the 1920s and 1930s emphasized the professional nature of all study. The Massachusetts Board of Education asserted, for example, that normal school English courses should concentrate more on fostering correct habits of speech and methods to teach them, and less on theories of discourse (Brodeur). While progressive era faculty did find some innovative ways to resist this pressure, a topic that space prevents me from developing at length, the curriculum they promote in the catalogues suggests this more limited focus.

The two semesters of oral and written expression that students took in the 1920s and 1930s aimed to develop students' ability to speak effectively before audiences, but it also stressed the "development and application of methods of the work of each grade," along with "technical grammar" and the "development of standards." The course in composition covered "the art of writing and speaking effectively," requiring students to work in varied real world genres, but these genres were ones they would use in their profession, "club papers, talks, reports, book reviews" (*Catalogue*, 1925). Students also completed courses in penmanship, library instruction, and children's literature (later, reading and storytelling were added). Courses in adult literature, and advanced writing and speaking, were largely unavailable even as the school began to offer a three-year program in the late 1920s and became a degree-granting teachers college in the early 1930s.

A look at an advertisement published in Catholic periodicals during the 1920s and 1930s, reveals richer intellectual goals, with a particular focus on rhetorical study. Students were to be immersed in the "seven Liberal Arts," which included "the Art of thinking clearly, the Art of reasoning logically, the Art of speaking convincingly, and the Art of writing gracefully" (Elms). The Elms required its students to engage in both curricular and extracurricular activities that involved thinking, reasoning, speaking, and writing. All curricular and extracurricular activities occurred in the "light of Catholic standards" (*College*, 1929, 10). How this light influenced the presentation of subject matter deserves more exploration, but my own study suggests that the Sisters of Saint Joseph encouraged the free play of ideas.[2]

Students enrolling at Elms in the 1930s completed a total of twenty hours of course work in literature and writing, about double what was required at Westfield.[3] Catalogues show that as at Westfield, students completed two courses in oral expression, but focused on "the psychology of the voice," "expressive gesture," and "dramatic reading and interpretation" (*College*, c. 1931, 32). All students were, in fact, required to give orations before the school community. These orations included not only "convincing delivery of masterpieces" but also "original orations" on work encountered in other areas of the curriculum (Oral). Yearly, the school held a dramatic reading contest, judged often by alumni as well as community members. The aim of work in expression was to provide students with "practice," but also to "lay foundations of future work in pedagogy, journalism, popular forms of prose composition, social welfare, etc., in all of which, effective public speaking is an essential prerequisite" (*College*, c. 1931, 44). The Elms' courses would have won the approval of Mabel Ford Yeomans of Grinnell College, who in a 1918 *English Journal* article "Women and Public Speaking," criticized the tendency of "oral English" courses, particularly for women, to divorce "manner from matter" (379).

Other required courses were Rhetoric and Composition, which included "[s]pecial study of modern English prose as well as argumentative prose" (*College*, c. 1931, 22), various literature courses (including courses on drama and contemporary Catholic literature), and by 1935, English methods courses for future teachers (*College*, c. 1935, 17). By the early 1940s, students not majoring in English (many electives were available at this point) were required to take an advanced writing course as well (*College*, c. 1941, 26). Among the faculty members who taught these courses was Helen Joseph Powers, a graduate of Smith College and Fordham University ("These Two").

Although early yearbooks or catalogues never render the teaching sisters visible, Sister Helen may have served as advisor to one of the main clubs created at Elms only a couple of years after the four-year college opened, the M.J.B. Debating Society, named after Mother John Berchmans, whose interest in debate and oratory is revealed in the journal she kept throughout her tenure. She frequently attended and sponsored oratorical contests and debates held at area parochial schools (Aherne 129). Among themselves and with neighboring coeducational and men's colleges, the society actively debated questions of social justice, including the growth of the National Rifle Association, labor union activities, and educational issues (Debating Club File). In the 1935 *Elmata* (the school yearbook), members of the society describe their activities:

> It is customary for most people, especially members of the masculine sex, to dismiss the attempts of members of our fair sex to debate as mere attempts and feeble ones at that. We call to witness our M.J.B. Debating Society to send any such hallucination scampering off to the four winds. We are proud of the work of this society. It gives us a tingle of pleasure to watch our class representatives hammer away at rebuttals, and, with fire in their eyes, equal any exhibitions we have attended at our brother colleges. The persuasiveness that constitutes forceful debating, the poise that marks a finished speaker, the logic that characterizes a well-planned argument are but a few of the points that the training in this club emphasizes. (77)

Perhaps it was the lack of public or institutional encouragement for women engaged in public speaking during the 1930s that had actually led Westfield's joint Drama and Debate Society to quit holding debates. But Elms students resisted such prohibitions. The wall that surrounded the Elms campus may have been to conservative Catholic forces a "moral and religious safeguard," but it also created a space where women students could explore and challenge the very myths behind that wall's erection.

Given its historical commitment to serious intellectual debate, I find it not surprising that today the Sisters of Saint Joseph of Springfield, along with Elms College graduates, are known for their public advocacy work, their efforts to use skillful discourse to educate the public on important national and international issues. Many of the students who attended the Elms in the 1940s were themselves members of the order. That is an issue worthy of future exploration. But what the above comparison suggests to me is that the Elms College, perhaps less beholden to state education officials and strongly committed to the value of a liberal arts education, was able to provide its students, many of whom would become teachers in western Massachusetts alongside graduates of Westfield, with richer opportunities for intellectual development. Given this observation, I think it worth remembering the anti-Catholic discourse generated by Reinhold Niebuhr and George Boas in the 1940s and 1950s. Niebuhr worried that the Catholic religion was a threat to people "doing their own thinking," while Boas saw the church as a "bitter opponent of the liberal tradition" (qtd. in McGreevey 167). Yet in western Massachusetts, it was a Catholic institution like the Elms, and not the neighboring public teachers college, that provided area women of the middle classes with greater access to the liberal tradition.

Local education officials did still play a role in the Elms' initial struggles to establish itself in the community. In 1967, Sister Mary Cornelius, a professor and administrator at the college since its founding, noted that "there was a time when, because of prejudice, it was very difficult for an Elms graduate to secure a position in the Springfield or Chicopee school systems. Now the college cannot fill the demand of school superintendents who almost wait in line for an Elms girl" ("These Two"). A review of the Alumnae Records shows the high number of graduates throughout the college's history who have pursued careers in area public schools as both teachers and administrators. Early graduates (1910s–1930s), facing the prejudice Sister Cornelius described, often began their careers as substitutes, or instead found places in evening adult education programs, nursery schools, and business schools.

Since the New England Association of Schools and Colleges did not accredit the Elms until the 1940s, Elms women wanting to teach in public schools enrolled in area teachers colleges like Westfield after completing their A.B degrees at Elms. That these women were in fact having to take education courses like those they may have already taken at Elms seems likely. By the early 1940s, however, Elms was granting B.S. degrees in education, making this practice less common.

During the early 1940s, Westfield also changed in significant ways, requiring its B.S. degree recipients to complete two years of courses "cultural" in nature before moving on to the professional curriculum. One catalogue (c. 1940) defends this change, arguing that "in order that a teacher may be an understanding guide to the youth of today it is necessary to have a broad fundamental knowledge in many fields [...] . The attempt is to broaden the background and interest, extend the experiences and assist students to observe, classify and reason." The English curriculum grew noticeably during the decade that followed, although more in the area of literary than rhetorical studies. While no documents exist claiming that Westfield altered its curriculum to be more like that of neighboring, and at that point competing, colleges like the Elms, research leads me to wonder whether the presence of such an institution as the Elms, with its strong desire to promote their students' intellectual as well as professional growth, helped create an atmosphere conducive to curricular revisions that would occur at institutions like Westfield. One might conclude that the Elms College, and the Sisters of Saint Joseph, while important for their contributions to the intellectual and professional growth of a number of area women, also helped inspire new confidence in the importance of study in the liberal arts for women and in connection with teacher preparation.

ACKNOWLEDGMENT

I would like to express my gratitude to the Alumnae Library at the College of Our Lady of the Elms, and to Sister Mary Gallagher, SSJ, their Archivist, without whose assistance I could not have written this essay.

NOTES

1. According to Aherne, Mother John Berchmans worked with the clergy at these and other institutions (Canisius, Villanova, and eventually the Catholic University of America) to facilitate undergraduate and graduate study. Much of this study was done in residence but through extension divisions. While completing their studies, the sisters were often housed in convents neighboring these colleges.
2. As noted, many of the sisters comprising the faculty at the Elms had received training at institutions founded and run by the Jesuits, who since the Renaissance had made work in rhetoric a central focus of men's education.
3. In its first few decades all courses at the Elms, with the exception of courses in philosophy and chemistry, were taught by the Sisters of Saint Joseph.

WORKS CITED

Aherne, Sister Consuelo Maria, SSJ. *Joyous Service: The History of the Sisters of Saint Joseph of Springfield.* Chicopee: Pond-Ekberg, 1983.

Alumnae Records. 1899–Present. The Elms College Archives. Alumnae Library. College of Our Lady of the Elms.

Alumni Correspondence Folder. Raymond G. Patterson Alumni Archive. Ely Library. Westfield State College.

Brodeur, Clarence. Letter to David Snedden, 1911. Clarence Brodeur Letter Books. Raymond G. Patterson Alumni Archive. Ely Library. Westfield State College.

Catalogue of the State Normal School at Westfield Massachusetts. 1844–1945. N. pag. Raymond G. Patterson Alumni Archive. Westfield State College Library.

College of Our Lady of the Elms. Catalogues. 1929–1945. The Elms College Archives. Alumnae Library. College of Our Lady of the Elms.

Elms College Advertisement. [c. 1930s]. The Elms College Archives. Alumnae Library. College of Our Lady of the Elms.

Debating Club File. The Elms College Archives. Alumnae Library. College of Our Lady of the Elms.

Elmata. Elms College Yearbooks. 1929–1945. The Elms College Archives. Alumnae Library. College of Our Lady of the Elms.

Horowitz, Helen Lefkowitz. *Alma Mater: Design and Experience in the Women's Colleges from Their Nineteenth-Century Beginnings to the 1930s.* Amherst: University of MA, 1993.

Innes, Donna. "Catholic Women's Colleges: Curriculum Development and Its Relationship to their Mission." Thesis, Catholic U, 1989. The Elms College Archives. Alumnae Library. College of Our Lady of the Elms.

Ker Conway, Jill. "Faith, Knowledge, and Gender." *Catholic Women's Colleges in America.* Ed. Tracy Schier and Cynthia Russett. Baltimore: Johns Hopkins UP, 2002. 11–16.

Mahoney, Kathleen A. "American Catholic Colleges for Women." *Catholic Women's Colleges in America.* Ed. Tracy Schier and Cynthia Russett. Baltimore: Johns Hopkins UP, 2002. 25–54.

Massachusetts WPA Writers' Project. *The State Teachers College at Westfield.* Boston: Jerome Press, 1941.

McGreevey, John T. *Catholicism and American Freedom: A History.* New York: Norton, 2003.

Moriarty, Thomas. "History of Our Lady of the Elms: Founding and Early Years." *Tribute to History: 100 Years of Education, Our Lady of the Elms, Chicopee, Massachusetts, for Life and for a Living. Annual Report, 1998–1999.* Annual Report, 1998–1999. The Elms College Archives. Alumnae Library. College of Our Lady of the Elms.

Moriarty, Thomas. Unpublished Address. The Elms College Archives. Alumnae Library. College of Our Lady of the Elms.

Oates, Mary J. "Catholic Laywomen in the Labor Force, 1850–1950." *American Catholic Women: A Historical Exploration.* Ed. Karen Kennelly, C.S.J. New York: Macmillan, 1989.

Oral Expressions File. *Springfield Union News*, Clipping, May 24, 1931. The Elms College Archives. Alumnae Library. College of Our Lady of the Elms.

Personnel Files, Sisters of Saint Joseph. Archives of the Sisters of Saint Jospeh of Springfield. Mont Marie. Holyoke, Massachusetts.

Salvatori, Mariolina Rizzi, ed. *Pedagogy: Disturbing History, 1819–1929.* Pittsburgh: U of Pittsburgh P, 1996.

Schier, Tracy, and Cynthia Russett, eds. *Catholic Women's Colleges in America.* Baltimore: Johns Hopkins UP, 2002.

Spalding, J. L. "Normal Schools for Catholics." *The Catholic World.* (April 1890): 88–97.

Student Entrance Records, 1890-1918. Raymond G. Patterson Alumni Archive. Ely Library. Westfield State College.

Student Records, 1904–1919. Raymond G. Patterson Alumni Archive. Ely Library Westfield State College.

"These Two Faculty Members Can 'Remember When.'" *The Catholic Observer.* September 1, 1967. The Elms College Archives. Alumnae Library. College of Our Lady of the Elms.

Yeomans, Mabel Ford. "Women and Public Speaking." *The English Journal.* 7.8 (August 1918): 377–82.

V

Publics

25

Rhetorical Landscapes
and Religious Identity

Gregory D. Clark
Brigham Young University

In 1941, F. O. Matthiessen published *American Renaissance*, a book that did much to explain the meaning of the national culture that emerged in the nineteenth century to Americans of the twentieth. While the primary objects of his attention are literary texts, Matthiessen treats them as lenses, looking through them to observe the formation of a national identity—an identity that is at once coherent and contradictory. For example, he describes the massive nineteenth-century project of pioneering expansion as a deliberate rush "from one rapid disequilibrium to the next," that was accompanied all along by a relentless "counter-effort" to create "islands of realization and fulfillment," of "communal security and permanence," that constitute the moments of "order and balance which [...] we can recognize as among the most valuable possessions of our continent." Some of those are moments are literary while others are material, notably, he suggests, "the New England green" and "Shaker communities" (172).

In keeping with the subtitle of his book, "Art and Expression in the Age of Emerson and Whitman," Matthiessen reads both the New England green and the Shaker community primarily as aesthetic expressions—expressions that are also assertions, essentially—of what those who inhabited them would have the world be. These are what I call rhetorical landscapes, by which I mean the environments and habitations that people create for themselves to both express and assert their identity. This concept is developed at length in my book, *Rhetorical Landscapes in America: Variations on a Theme from Kenneth Burke* (University of South Carolina Press, 2004). I use it in this chapter to examine American landscapes that express and assert identities that are specifically religious, as well as the rhetorical functions of such expressions and assertions in an insistently secular national culture. I will suggest that landscapes that are created by religious people express and assert a religious identity in ways that inflect the secular individualism that seems primarily to constitute the American character with the contradictory aspirations that follow from identification with a religious collectivity. American national identity is and always has been primarily secular and individualistic, but those values have always been tempered by, and even countered by, a persistently shared desire for citizenship in transcendent community. It is a contradiction that Americans seem to depend on to define who they are. I state that point now, directly, because what follows gets at it in a considerably more roundabout way.

RHETORICAL SCENES IN AMERICA

In a 1947 magazine article with the expansive title, "The American Way," Kenneth Burke observed that because "social status is not fixed or clearly defined" in the United States, its citizens must seek in their surroundings "objective evidence" of their individual and collective identity. That evidence takes the form of some shared environments and experiences that help to "place a person in his own eyes, as he surrounds himself with a scene which, he is assured, attests to his moral quality. For he can feel that he participates in the quality which the scene itself is thought to possess" (5). For Americans, their nation has always been a "scene" in Burke's dramatistic sense of that term—as a symbolic setting that both reflects and shapes the beliefs, the values, and thus the actions that identify the people who inhabit it.

Let me offer an initial example. In the first decade of the nineteenth century, a man who had been for some years one of the most prominent public opponents of the secular social order being put into place by ratification of the new U.S. Constitution stopped writing and speaking on religion and politics and, instead, started writing a travel book. Timothy Dwight, grandson of Jonathan Edwards, and long-time president of Yale (called "the Pope of New England" by his adversaries), envisioned a United States that would be built upon the foundation of the old Massachusetts Bay theocracy. But with Jefferson's election in 1800 and the ascendance of democratic ideologies, Dwight left pulpit and podium for his study where, over the next few years, he wrote a four-volume description of his own *Travels in New England and New York*. In that set of books, widely read throughout the nineteenth century after its publication in 1821, Dwight described that region as a rhetorical landscape that asserted, though not without contradictions, a distinctly religious identity.

The New England he described was a place where "the colonization of a wilderness by civilized men, where a regular government, mild manners, arts, learning, science, and Christianity have been interwoven from the beginning, is a state of things which the eastern continent and the records of past ages furnish neither an example nor a resemblance" (1: 177). As he describes the general scene in Massachusetts and Connecticut, "the people are very prosperous, the houses generally very good; the church, a new building, is handsome; and everything which meets the eye wears the appearance of industry and prosperity (1: 162–63). The source of that comfort and good order is, he explains, the fact that this place "exhibits openly and decisively the importance of religion to public happiness" (1: 185). In his description, "almost the whole country is covered with villages, and every village has its church and its suite of schools. Nearly every child, even those of beggars and blacks in considerable numbers, can read, write, and keep accounts." And all this follows from the fact that here "every child is carried to the church from the cradle nor leaves the church but for the grave" (1: 246). But that is the scene only until he crosses the state line into libertarian and secular Rhode Island. There the soil is "unusually lean, and the prospects are destitute of beauty." Dwight notes that throughout the state "the houses are almost all poor and ill repaired. Two or three small buildings resembling miserable barns were seen on the road, which we were informed were Baptist churches, and not more than perhaps half a dozen dwelling houses between the environs of Providence and Sterling of those which were visible to us could be termed decent" (2: 22). Indeed, Dwight knew immediately when he had crossed the unmarked state line back into Connecticut by "the sight of a village with a decent church and a schoolhouse at its center, and by the appearance of comfortable dwellings and better agriculture." While "the country was rough here also, [...] it wore the appearance of having been dressed. Everything looked as if the activity of man had been successfully, as well as diligently, employed to render life easy and desirable" (2: 22).

From its beginnings, the United States has been preoccupied with religion. And from those beginnings, it has also been persistently individualistic and libertarian. The consequence of that combination is that the United States has been, and continues to be, a fiercely secular culture that is permeated with a common belief that it and its citizens are favored by God—or some other source of cosmic order. Both individually and collectively, Americans seem to consider themselves at once favored by God and without need of a God because they believe themselves to be both self-made and self-governed. The scenes that Dwight describes encompass the contradictions that constitute that fractious identity. That identity seems constituted of majority and minority enclaves that express alternative, and even contradictory, values. Dwight's travel narrative reads as a sustained display of the scenes that assert the values that he finds self-evidently correct despite the contradictory evidence he encounters while crossing into Rhode Island. Despite that, it is his preference of the more pious part of New England as representative of that region that has lasted. Two centuries later, the sorts of landscapes he described encountering in Massachusetts and Connecticut remain the iconic images of that place. Such images of the ordered New England village where the white church dominates the peaceful green decorate the calendars that hang on the walls of apartments and row houses in the hectic cities of Boston and Springfield, Hartford and New Haven—walls decorated by people who would not be at all happy living on Dwight's terms.

In the rest of this chapter, I want to look at another religious landscape in America, one that is interesting to me because of the contrariety of the identity that it asserts in America—an identity that is composed of values that oppose almost everything that most people in the nation have stood for. Yet the scenes and artifacts that express this religious identity, one that confronts the prevailing values of the nation with their direct contradictions, have been objects of enduring popularity in this secular state. This is the landscape created in the nineteenth century by the United Society of Believers, known as the Shakers, in places ranging from Ohio to Massachusetts and Kentucky to Maine. This is a landscape that nonbelievers have worked carefully ever since to preserve. Indeed, what most Americans, then and now, have known about the Shakers *is* their landscapes, broadly understood—their farms, their architecture, their furniture and other products of their industry. These constitute landscapes that the Shakers created for the express purposes of asserting to themselves a set of religious doctrines that insistently separated them from the rest of the nation. Yet unbelieving Americans found then, and continue to find now, that Shaker landscapes express elements of an identity that they want to claim for themselves.

"A VISIT TO THE SHAKERS"

Throughout the nineteenth century, Shaker communities were separatist enclaves clearly set apart from the rest of America, and yet they were popular attractions for American and foreign tourists alike. Here is a typical encounter, this one from a British tourist.

> I stood upon high ground, which sloped gradually down to a valley of considerable extent, bounded by wooden hills; large masses of buildings [...] standing at some distance from each other, were surrounded by cultivated fields; there was nothing that could be called a village, (the name usually given to the Shaker's settlement,) but each large dwelling house in which a family of fifty persons is accommodated, had its barns, workshops, and other conveniences attached. The clear, rich valley was finely contrasted with the surrounding heights, while the extraordinary neatness of the roads and inclosures made the *detail* of the landscape more pleasing than is common on this side of the Atlantic. ("A Visit to the Shakers" 342–43).

After his visit to the Shakers the traveler then crossed the valley to fine accommodations in the neighboring New York town:

> After tea, I took leave of my kind hosts, and walked over to Lebanon Springs, a fashionable watering place, most frequented in summer by families from the Southern States. I put up at a very large tavern, where the company were sprawling upon the chairs and window-seats, smoking and drinking. [...] [T]o me, the noise of the place and the coarse style of conversation in which the men indulged, were so strongly contrasted with the serenity and decency of the scene I had just left, that I felt as if awakening from a dream, and could scarcely persuade myself that I was but a half hour's walk from the "Society of Union." (344–45).

This is, as I said, a typical encounter. Shaker life created idyllic places that were profoundly attractive to Americans throughout the nineteenth century—they considered them very nice places to visit, though they clearly didn't want to live there. But they visited, and when they visited they acquired elements of that landscape—Shaker wares—that they could then display in their homes. There was, and there remains, something about the Shaker landscape that speaks to secular Americans about who they are, or at least who they believe themselves to be.

So who were the Shakers? In his 1875 book, *The Communistic Societies of the United States*, Charles Nordhoff described them succinctly:

> They assert that the second appearing of Christ upon earth has been; and that they are the only true Church, "in which revelation, spiritualism, celibacy, oral confession, community, non-resistance, peace, the gift of healing, miracles, physical health, and separation from the world are the foundations of the new heavens" (quoting from "Autobiography of a Shaker," etc., by Elder Frederick W. Evans). (118)

For most Americans, then and now, this is a highly contrary set of beliefs—communitarianism, ready submission to ecclesiastical authority, nonrationalism, political passivity, and celibacy. In the context of the ambitious and opportunistic nineteenth-century nation, these seemed (and seem so now) to be profoundly un-American. But these beliefs describe who the Shakers were. In the words of Edward Deming Andrews, their mid-twentieth-century historian, for them "the [Christian] resurrection [...] was not a day of reckoning coming with catastrophic suddenness to all mankind. When any man confessed his sins, then he was personally saved and resurrected; when he entered into the life of the spirit, then for him the "world was at an end" (18). By that very attitude and act of separation, then, the Shakers identified themselves as *not* Americans.

So they created for themselves a world of their own in America, and secular Americans flocked to see it. Even now, restored Shaker villages attract people who want to visit an orderly, pastoral, somehow spiritual place. That's how I discovered them twenty years ago. My wife and I and our two small children were living in student housing in an upstate New York city while I was working on my degree at breakneck speed. One weekend we drove out into the country and discovered Hancock Shaker Village, a fully restored Shaker site in western Massachusetts. The buildings and surrounding farmlands, the lawns and paths and gardens, the rooms and even the food comforted and calmed us all. At Hancock, we found a place of order and peace, of serenity and beauty, and—though it was, of course, uninhabited—we recognized there a model for a better way of life where we could imagine ourselves happier. During our visits, we felt that we were more peaceful, that our lives were in greater order, and so we returned to Hancock frequently, just to *be* there. For us, the experience of being there wasn't particularly religious—at least we didn't think of it so. But it was comforting as it somehow transcended our daily life. Many others must have felt the same things—weekends could be crowded, and the facilities to accommodate us all were constantly being expanded.

The Shakers created their world for themselves, and they were deliberately rhetorical in doing so. Their landscape deliberately asserted to them their collective identity. They believed themselves to living in the Christian Millennium, and so located themselves apart in a heavenly order on earth. With that worldview, they did not distinguish between the spiritual and the physical. As one recent commentator put it, they "believed that the 'natural' world perceived by the five physical senses was an emblem or reflection of the real but intangible spiritual realm perceivable to the spiritual senses" (Sprigg 10). Manual work was thus sacred: "It was good for both the individual soul and the collective welfare," wrote their historian, Andrews, "mortifying lust, teaching humility, creating order and convenience, supplying a surplus for charity, supporting the structure of fraternity, protecting it against the world, and strengthening it for increasing service" (104). The products of their labors expressed those values. Consequently, their landscape was different from the rest of America, and Americans not only noticed that, they valued it. Here is William Hepworth Dixon writing in his 1867 book, *New America*:

> You see that the men who till these fields, who tend these gardens, who bind these sheaves, who train these vines, who plant these apple-trees, have been drawn into putting their love into the daily task; and you hear with no surprise that these toilers, ploughing and planting in their quaint

FIG. 25.1. Hancock Shaker village. From the collection of Hancock Shaker Village. Reprinted by permission.

FIG. 25.2.   Nineteenth-century view of Hancock. From the collection of Hancock Shaker Village. Reprinted by permission.

garb, consider their labor on the soil as a part of their ritual, looking upon the earth as a stained and degraded sphere, which they have been called to redeem from corruption and restore to God. (qtd. in Andrews 118)

Specifically, Andrews offers this lexicon for their landscape vocabulary that fuses the spiritual and material:

Architecture and craftsmanship alike reflected such principles as union (basic uniformity of design), the equality of the sexes (balance, proportion), utilitarianism (adaptation to needs, durability), honesty (mastery of techniques), humility and simplicity (absence of pretense or adornment), purity (a sense of pure form). (127)

So while Americans rejected Shaker doctrine, they embraced Shaker landscapes—and have continued to do so. They not only visited those landscapes, they imitated their material forms and acquired elements of them for themselves—Shaker furniture is the most prominent example. The Shakers were not always happy about that. They appreciated the ability to market their wares, but it was their doctrines that were important to them, not the artifacts that followed from those doctrines, and their visitors were rarely seriously interested in their doctrines. Indeed, as recently as 1989, one of the last Shakers, Sister Mildred Barker, reacted to the news that an original Shaker chair had sold at auction for $80,000 with the blunt statement, "I don't want to be remembered as a chair" (qtd. in Newman 321). But that is how Americans know the Shakers—by their chairs, their buildings, their landscapes, by the peaceful and orderly habitations they created for themselves that Americans never tired of visiting and imagining—for a moment—as their own. Not being able to afford an original

Shaker chair, I acquired at Hancock a print of a Shaker spirit drawing of the Tree of Life that hangs prominently in my living room. When I look at it, I identify with the simplicity, the order, and the peace it expresses.

Sister Mildred was a member of the last remaining Shaker community at Sabbathday Lake, Maine. She was also their representative to outsiders. By the time I visited there, six years ago, she was gone and only seven Shakers remained. Brother Arnold Hadd, who had taken over her responsibilities, expressed to me his perpetual disappointment when Shaker life and Shaker landscapes are inevitably described as "serene." Life as a Shaker is not serene, he said. It is hard physically and socially to live communally as brothers and sisters with people one has not chosen and might, in the world, not ever choose, to befriend. Serenity, he said, is not who the Shakers are.

But in secular America, serenity is what the Shakers have come to mean, and that is, I believe, what attracts Americans to the Shaker heritage. That is because in a society as secular, competitive, and hectic as this one, focus and order, clarity and community are hard to come by. Americans didn't then and will not now accept Shaker doctrines, but Shaker landscapes spoke then and speak now of a shared serenity that is within the reach of an American collective—serenity that comes from a common commitment to something greater than self that is, at least in aspiration, a part of who Americans consider themselves to be.

So to Sister Mildred I would suggest that it is actually a good thing to be remembered as a chair. That is because, to the rest of us, a Shaker chair is much more than a just a chair. It trails clouds of an identity that is entirely contrary to our individualistic and chaotic way of life that almost all of us want to claim as part of our own. Then and now, most Americans inhabit landscapes that speak loudly the very values that the Shakers worked hard to refute. And, then and now, most Americans love to visit those alternative landscapes that directly refute the ones they inhabit. Perhaps that is because such visits invite them to believe that they are not entirely the people their home landscapes identify. While most Americans never did and

FIG. 25.3.   A Shaker room. From the collection of Hancock Shaker Villaɡe. Reprinted by permission.

never will accept the particulars of Shaker doctrine, they have embraced and, indeed, cherished Shaker landscapes all along. In doing so, they seem to have continually recommitted themselves (at least vicariously) to a set of values—they might be called religious—that, though most of the time they do not inhabit as the Shakers inhabited them, remain a part of who they collectively understand themselves to be.

WORKS CITED

Andrews, Edward Deming. *The People Called Shakers: A Search for the Perfect Society.* New York: Dover, 1963.

Burke, Kenneth. "The American Way." *Touchstone* 1.2 (Dec. 1947): 3–9.

Dwight, Timothy. *Travels in New-England and New-York.* (1821). Ed. Barbara Miller Solomon. 4 vols. Cambridge, MA: Harvard UP, 1961.

Matthiessen, F. O. *American Renaissance: Art and Expression in the Age of Emerson and Whitman.* New York: Oxford UP, 1941.

Newman, Cathy. "The Shakers' Brief Eternity." *National Geographic* (Sept. 1989): 304–25.

Nordhoff, Charles. *The Communistic Societies of the United States.* New York: Schocken, 1875.

Sprigg, June. "Prologue." *Kindred Spirits: The Eloquence of Function in the American Shaker and Japanese Arts of Daily Life.* San Diego, CA: Minger International Museum of World Folk Art, 1995.

"A Visit to the Shakers," 341–47. *The Atheneum, or, Spirit of the English Magazines* 13, 1 Aug. 1823: 341–47.

26

The Doxicon: Image, Strategy, and the Undoing of Consent

Dana L. Cloud
University of Texas, Austin

This paper is about how images work rhetorically to reinforce dominant ways of seeing and, under some circumstances, to challenge them. I argue that certain iconic images resonate with and reinforce established ways of seeing. Such ways of seeing, in turn, direct interpretations of such images into established grooves of meaning. While counterpublics steeped in oppositional discourse may have the resources with which to resist or reframe such images in new terms, for a mass U.S. public, iconic images generally are doxastic, that is, capable of establishing, reinforcing, and deploying naturalized common sense about the world in the service of power.

This paper proceeds as follows. First, I will establish a theory of what I am calling the "doxicon" and argue that images working as doxicons may do so in either orthodox or heterodox ways. I will argue that orthodoxicons (orthodox icons), if you will, have enthymematic presumption in public discourse and that advocates of heterodoxy bear the burden of proof in the use of images. This means that counterhegemonic rhetors must generally provide some argumentative, propositional framing for images that can channel public response in unconventional directions. This chapter explores this problem in a series of examples: images of the toppling of the fall of Saddam Hussein's statue in April 2003, images of police in Miami during the 2003 Free Trade Area of the Americas (FTAA) protests, and images of torture of Iraqi prisoners at Abu Ghraib in 2004.

TOWARD THE DOXICON

First, an icon is a commonly remembered image that constitutes shared meaning for a public and reinforces shared identities. Thus, Hariman and Lucaites have argued that the photograph from the Vietnam War of a naked girl fleeing a napalm strike has constituted the American public as an aggregate of moral individuals responding as individuals to a historical atrocity (Hariman and Lucaites, "Public Identity," Ut). An icon is not only a commonly held, persistently memorable, culture-constituting image, but may also be defined as sets of commonly understood *types* of images. For example, while people may not recall any specific image of Afghan women during the U.S. war on terrorism, audiences recall the trope of the white man's burden, which is sedimented in U.S. popular memory. The series of images of Afghan women that saturated U.S. media after 9/11/2001 were iconic in the sense that they resonated with those set of commonly held, persistently memorable cultural and political scripts about Arab people, Islam, gender, and war (Cloud). Such scripts constitute the shared *doxa* of an imagined American national public.

Doxa is a concept originally worked through in Isocrates' *Antidosis*. In this work, Isocrates explained that *doxa* is a kind of social knowledge distinct from truth, or *episteme* (Isocrates; Poulakis). This sense of *doxa* defines the place of rhetoric in matters that are practical and contingent, guided by common sense rather than absolute, philosophical truth. However, *doxa* also may refer to the sets of unconsciously held but socially learned theories about the world that enable citizens to make sense of social relations (Poulakis 63). A critical-rational paradigm is insufficient to understand doxastic discourses; even so, rational, conscious reframing of images enables criticism of rhetors who mobilize *doxa* to undemocratic ends (Bordieu 168–69).

Critical scholar Pierre Bordieu has extended the concept of *doxa* in his work *Outline of a Theory of Practice*. There, he argues that controversy and heterodoxy are framed in terms of rhetorical principles limiting the range of contestation and naturalizing a bounded, partial set of beliefs. In other words, *doxa* is akin to but more specific than ideology; citizens and publics struggle over the parameters of naturalized common sense about particular topics, but with different degrees of agency in the process. When elite interests are successful in maintaining cultural hegemony, *doxa* defines the boundary of the real in ways that circumscribe questioning and dissent (Bordieu).

Doxicons are thus the link between image and *doxa*. In much the same way that ideographs sum up core social commitments in language, doxicons index and constitute core social commitments in the image (McGee). Images, especially images that operate within a rhetoric of realism (appearing to reflect reality, denying their rhetoricity; see Beer and Hariman) often are powerful shapers of an unreflexive doxiconic frame. Citizens are not always conscious of the doxiconic frames that organize their perceptions. The power of images can arise from their tendency toward condensation of complex matters into emotional frames; doxicons do not trigger the reflexivity characterized by responses to propositional argument. Bordieu notes, however, that the realm of *doxa* includes both ortho-doxy and hetero-doxy. Just as iconic images can be the subject of negotiation and appropriation for counterhegemonic purposes, so can the doxicon.

ORTHODOXICONS, ENTHYMEMES, AND THE BURDEN OF PROOF

Orthodoxicons work in the context of established enthymemes, or, to follow Aristotle, a set of premises that are taken for granted, shared in common, and thus needing no explicit articulation. Cara Finnegan has noted that photojournalistic images rest upon the enthymematic assumption that photographs reflect a transparent reality. Other enthymemes are also in play. For example, to see an iconic image of the Berlin Wall coming down today evokes meanings of capitalism as democracy. The image itself connotes freedom and victory over tyranny. Images whose meaning in the mass public depends upon such enthymemes tend to reinforce them. Thus, orthodoxicons have presumption in the popular imagination. They represent forms of enthymematic reasoning that may bypass logical reasoning in favor of resonance with common sense.

For this reason, rhetorical scholars and social movement actors alike must attend carefully to the conditions under which visual persuasion can be most effective in fostering social change. There is a significant and growing literature on the rhetorical strategies of images, particularly photojournalism, describing how images employ strategies of naturalization, reduction, condensation, and emotional appeal (Lucaites and Hariman, "Visual Rhetoric" 38; Sontag; Condit; Brummett; Jamieson). For the purposes of this essay, however, the central question in that literature is whether images argue. There has been a great deal of debate in our field on this question, with most scholars finding in the affirmative (see review in Biesecker). While the constitutive function of images, that is, their capacity to achieve collective, doxastic identification, is not argumentative in a dialogical sense, doxicons do represent already-established arguments; they are in themselves constitutive of a *prima facie* case.

Quite literally, given the "naturalistic enthymeme" of documentary photography, photographs seem "on the face of it" to prove their point (Finnegan; Sontag). Thus, rather than being non-arguments or anti-arguments, orthodox images simply have argumentative presumption. According to standard argumentation textbooks, presumption refers to the "momentum of decision makers"; presumption is the province of existing society standards (Rieke and Sillars 153), while opposition rhetors bear the burden of proof. So, the question is how to denaturalize common sense so that fundamental enthymemes become subjects open for debate. The examples below suggest that the degree to which a perspective is oppositional, the more explicit rather than enthymematic argumentation is required to win public adherence to novel interpretations of images and the points of view they represent.

Heterodoxicons may become the orthodoxicons of the future, but at the moment of their emergence into public visibility, they require explanation and framing for mass audiences. For example, an Austin photographer displays photographs of Iraqi and Afghan to represent the women as victims of war and occupation and to demonstrate their humanity to antiwar audiences (Pogue). Among antiwar counterpublics, this interpretation has presumption. However, if these images were to circulate more broadly, the photographer may want to include explanation: These women are opposed to war and do not welcome U.S. intervention; this woman's husband was killed by U.S. forces; on behalf of these women you must oppose the war, and so on. Otherwise, the images will likely be taken as evidence for the oppression of Afghan women by Islamic fundamentalists and as warrant for U.S. intervention (Cloud). The reverse is also true, namely, that orthodoxicons can under some circumstances erupt into heterodoxy.

HETERODOXY: CONDITIONS OF POSSIBILITY

The Berlin Wall and the Fall of Saddam

Images of the Berlin Wall have proliferated in U.S. culture since the fall of the wall in 1989. These images can be generic in so far as they commonly represent scenes of large numbers of youth and other activists actively hammering at the wall or standing on top of it in triumph over the tyranny of Stalinist communism.[1] In this case, the popular revolt against and economic and ideological collapse of Stalinism enacted the meaning of <freedom>,[2] at least from a liberal and/or procapitalist perspective. During the Iraq War (2003), pundits, politicians, and media attempted to establish the fall of the Saddam statue as a parallel occurrence and the photographs of that fall as meaningful icons of <freedom> and <democracy> for the U.S. public. The image of Marines and a few Iraqis pulling down the statue of Saddam Hussein on April 9, 2003 circulated widely in newsmagazines and other venues (Rebours).

On this occasion, *Time* magazine commented, "When a group of Iraqis took a sledge-hammer to the giant plinth beneath a Saddam statue opposite the international press head-quarters at the Palestine Hotel, journalists and TV anchors everywhere couldn't resist making the comparison with the tearing down of the Berlin Wall in 1989" (Karon). The Department of Defense publication *DOD LINK* revealed that major U.S. officials encouraged this iconic analogy, reporting Deputy Defense Secretary Paul Wolfowitz's remarks: "Seeing televised images of larger-than- life statues of Saddam Hussein tumbling over Iraq is like 'seeing the Berlin Wall come down all over again,' he said. 'Lovers of freedom everywhere can understand the joy of the Iraqi people and their hopes for the future'" (Rhem). Television reporters echoed the refrain that we were watching history being made on the scale of Communism's collapse.

The reporters did not mention that it was the Marines who initiated the demolition in a rather small crowd of Iraqi civilians; nor did they recognize the fundamental differences between the popular democratic resistance of Berliners and the efforts of an occupying army. Nonetheless, the iconicity of this image and all of the other similar images that circulated around the statue's fall depends upon its resonance with the collapse of Communism and the tearing down of the Berlin Wall in 1989. The attempt to make this image iconic failed. The large, international, antiwar protests of early 2003 provided an opening for criticism and questioning of this analogy.

This opening was given popular and national expression in an editorial cartoon that appeared in *Newsweek* on April 10, 2003:

FIG. 26.1.   By permission of Mike Luckovich and Creators Syndicate, Inc.

In this cartoon, humor makes sharp political criticism palatable to wider audiences. Providing a kind of perspective by incongruity makes the argument by analogy that the U.S. administration is a dictatorship like Saddam's (see Edwards and Winkler). This example drags the image of the statue's fall into a more explicitly propositional frame in which additional information and context may be elaborated and in which critical reading is further enabled by a lack of photographic realism. This example demonstrates how the circulation of critical movement discourses can generate challenges to orthodoxy even in mass popular culture. Further, the cartoon demonstrates how a critical perspective can take simultaneous visual and argumentative form.

WHO'S BARBARIC? IMAGES OF VIOLENCE AND VIOLATION

While propositional content may be necessary to the reframing of orthodox images most of the time, some images are so violating of prevailing doxa, and thus of an audience member's sense of self and commitments, that the images in themselves demand explanation and provoke the desire for more information and perhaps new critical thinking. As Hariman and Lucaites explain, the images of (a) a naked Vietnamese girl fleeing a napalm attack and (b) victims of the 1970 Kent State shooting are examples of such images (Hariman and Lucaites, "Public Identity"; "Dissent"). Such images may be provocative of a reworking of national identity and consciousness inside other, more stable frames (about individual responsibility, emotion, and gender, for example).

In Miami, Florida, in November 2003, students, labor union members, and other groups protested the talks taking place in that city to form the Free Trade Area of the Americas (an agreement among corporate and state representatives regarding Western-hemisphere trade). The protest against the undemocratic purposes and process of the meeting was met with severe police repression, and photographs of police taken during the demonstration circulated widely in popular and alternative media. One series of images shows a seated peaceful protester weaving something out of hemp attacked by a phalanx of police, who shoot her with a rubber bullet (Adame).

This image resonates strongly with both the "Accidental Napalm" and iconic images of protesters reacting to the attack by the National Guard at Kent State in 1970. As in the image of Kim Phuc fleeing a Napalm attack and the image of a young woman looking up in horror and grief from the site of a dead protester in the Kent State attack, the image of the FTAA victim deploys a gendered emotional appeal that could violate public views of protest and the role of the police in U.S. society. In my circle of friends, this sequence of images and the story they tell of a young, peaceful protester being shot in the head by the police provoked immediate strong outrage at the violation of human rights and the curtailment of the right to assemble and protest.

However, public response in Miami to coverage of the protest told a different story grounded in very different enthymemes. Although some progressives decried the police use of force, and there was later a board convened to investigate police conduct, most immediate coverage praised the police for keeping order and vilified protesters as "violent anarchists" (Nesmith). The implicit premises of enthymemes prevailing in Miami and the nation generally were: (1) We should fear protesters; protest is violence; and (2) Police did a great job keeping order; it is their job to keep order at all costs. In the daily papers and on television, news reports emphasized the meager "weapons" (a brick, e.g.) held by a few demonstrators and did not mention the three tanks, helicopter surveillance, and sniper patrol set up to defend the talks against an ostensibly free demonstration.

The question of audience is crucial. On commondreams.org or indymedia.org, the interpretation of these images as revealing outrageous police state behavior had presumption, but in a larger public arena, more explicitly argumentative discourse around the photos would be necessary to convey that meaning and perhaps shift public views of the police and protest. Thus, these images are heterodox only under certain circumstances and for particular audiences.

On the other hand, images that violate outright prevailing enthymemes may provoke a critical response in and of themselves. The widely circulated photographs of torture of Iraqi prisoners by U.S. troops at Abu Ghraib prison in Iraq in 2004 represent a stronger case in point where a prowar orthodoxy has been seriously challenged by images of violence.[3] Like images of lynchings (as they were received in the context of the civil rights movement), these photographs put the lie to a number of shared public assumptions in the United States: that the military is a force of liberation, that we are saving barbarians from themselves and that we exist in a clash of civilizations in combat with inferior, oppressive regimes. The Abu Ghraib torture participates in the logic of lynching in so far as the torturers dehumanized the victims in a racist frame and meant to make object lessons of those tortured. Similarly, both lynchers and the torturers in this case enjoyed the violent persecution of racialized Others.

However, I do not mean to equate the atrocity of the Abu Ghraib abuse with the horrors of lynching, only to point out how the imagery in both cases reveal racist barbarity and contradiction between the stated aims of our society and the actions of its leaders and institutions. Images of lynching emerged with new meanings out of and galvanized antiracist movements just as the Abu Ghraib photographs sparked outrage against the war around the world. These photographs enable a reversal of position on the part of audiences by challenging dominant enthymemes regarding the character of U.S. society and the value of U.S. intervention in Iraq.

Before the widespread publication of these photos, most U.S. citizens believed that the war was justified because our military supplanted a dictator who tortured his own people. Because torture is evil, he was evil, and "we" were good. The enthymemes of liberal democracy, especially the fundamental valuing of human rights, justified the war. Yet in the wake of the prison abuse scandal, this core value came to the foreground in a progressive way. As in previous social movements (for suffrage and against slavery, for example), basic ideographs of <equality> and <human rights> can serve as foundations for social change rather than as ideological covers for inequality and imperialism. Today, although we are arguably in a historical moment when human rights to liberty, personal security, and justice have been backgrounded in favor of national security and empire, these images inevitably bring the question of human rights to the foreground. For this reason, they enabled criticism and questioning of the motives and consequences of U.S. military intervention in Iraq.

As in the other examples, the effectiveness of this strategy depends on some contextual factors. One is, of course, audience. In the case of lynching, Southern white publics celebrated lynchings and the images of torturous death. White Southerners appeared in photographs of lynching carrying picnic baskets and wearing smiles of delight (Owen and Ehrenhaus). There was no enthymematic premise in circulation that subjecting a black person to such a death is wrong. In the case of these images of torture in Iraq, it is appears, similarly, that the soldiers who posed for and took the photographs took delight in the spectacle of abuse and dehumanization. Like the Nazis, too, they documented their actions extensively so as to enjoy the record in the future.[4] Amazingly, the perpetrators of the Abu Ghraib torture seemingly anticipated neither blame nor punishment for their actions.

It was only after the emergence of the civil rights movement that images such as photographs of Emmett Till's body circulated in new, democratizing frames among audiences increasingly critical of racial violence and segregation. There is no doubt, however, that images such as those of the torture at Abu Ghraib also galvanize movements. Since the photos were released, public support for the occupation dipped below fifty percent for the first time. There have been attempts to reframe the images in terms of a few bad apples and to scapegoat Rumsfeld and particular guards and commanders for these acts (Barry). However, those rationales are weak compared to the power and sheer volume of these images, which provide a *prima facie* case that the United States violated human rights. Thus, these images of torture turn orthodoxy, heterodox. For once, the administration's policy does not have presumption.

We must remember that, as Catharine MacKinnon explains in *Only Words*, that there is more than the image at stake here. Any photograph of enacted violence represents actual objects of that violence; no matter how the image is manipulated by journalists and others, there was still a real, suffering body before the camera. Publics inured to the daily bombardment of spectacular images of violence may forget that it is not just a matter of image combating an image, or critics making an argument to challenge images: It is a matter of us—in pedagogy and movements—using the openings provided by images and all of the available means of persuasion and material action to challenge the war and the barbarity it engenders.

CONCLUSION

Classical rhetoric and traditional argumentation theory can tell us a great deal about the work images do to sustain and challenge power. Grounded in *doxa*, mainstream photojournalism is difficult to contest by images alone. The concepts of the doxicon, enthymeme, and presumption can show, through particular cases, the conditions under which oppositional images may be persuasive. These conditions include the presence either of a movement and/or of documented horrific violation. It follows that progressives must do what they can to foster movements to expose atrocity and to make heterodoxy intelligible. In this chapter, I have argued that social movement actors should consider carefully audience and situation in the use of images. Further, progressives' successful use of images may depend upon the existence and circulation of counterdiscourses in movements. If we are to turn consent to contestation, we must answer the burden of proof with arguments—before the gruesome events and images of racist violence, torture, and war do the job for us.

NOTES

1.   See such images at <http://www.pohl-projekt.de/G_M_D/G_MD008b.jpg>.
2.   Concepts such as "freedom" are what Michael McGee called ideographs; they are indicated by framing the words in carats.
3.   I was denied permission by the *Washington Post* to reproduce the Abu Ghraib photos. I was told that the photos were not in the public domain and further, that they were not available for purchase or reproduction. However, these photos are compiled from various news sources at <http://www.antiwar.com/news/?articleid=2444>.

4. Again, I am not equating the Holocaust with the torture incidents. They are alike in kind but not in scale. However, the functions of images for perpetrators and public audiences are remarkably similar.

WORKS CITED

Adame, David. *Miami Police Open Fire on FTAA Protesters with Rubber Bullets.* 20 Nov. 2003 <http://commondreams.org/headlines03/1120-13.htm>.

Barry, John, Mark Hosenball, and Babak Dehghanpisheh. "Abu Ghraib and Beyond." *Newsweek* 24 May 2004 <http://www.msnbc.msn.com/id4934436/site/newsweek>.

Beer, Francis, and Robert Hariman, eds. *Post–Realism: The Rhetorical Turn in International Relations.* East Lansing: Michigan State UP, 1996.

Biesecker, Barbara. "Rhetorical Ventriloquism: Fantasy and/as American National Identity." *Argument in a Time of Change: Proceedings of the Tenth NCA/AFA Conference on Argumentation.* Ed. James Klumpp. Annandale, VA: NCA 1998. 168–72.

Birdsell, David S., and Leo Groarke, eds. "Toward a Theory of Visual Argument." Spec. issue of *Argumentation and Advocacy* 33 (1996): 1–10.

Bordieu, Pierre. *Outline of a Theory in Practice.* Trans. Richard Nice. Cambridge, UK: Cambridge UP, 1977. 168–69.

Brummett, Barry. *Rhetorical Dimensions of Popular Culture.* Tuscaloosa: U of Alabama P, 1991. 27.

Cloud, Dana L. "'To Veil the Threat of Terror': Afghan Women and the <Clash of Civilizations> in the Imagery of the U.S. War on Terrorism." *Quarterly Journal of Speech* 90 (2004): 285–306.

Condit, Celeste M. *Decoding Abortion Rhetoric.* Urbana: U of Illinois, 1990. 82.

Edwards, Janis L., and Carol K. Winkler. "Representative Form and the Visual Ideograph: The Iwo Jima Image in Editorial Cartoons." *Quarterly Journal of Speech* 83 (1997): 289–310.

Ehrenhaus, Peter, and A. Susan Owen. "Constructing Communities through Race Violence and Resistance: Rituals of Lynching and the Campaign for Anti-Lynching Legislation." Biennial Public Address Conference. Athens: U of Georgia, October 2002.

Figueras, Tere. "Big Police Presence, Few Clashes." *Miami Herald,* 21 Nov. 2003: 1A.

Finnegan, Cara A. "The Naturalistic Enthymeme and Visual Argument: Photographic Representation in the 'Skull Controversy.'" *Argumentation and Advocacy* 37 (2001): 133–49.

Fiske, John, and John Hartley. *Reading Television.* London: Methuen, 1978. 48–49.

Hariman, Robert, and John Lucaites. "Dissent and Emotional Management in a Liberal-Democratic Society: The Kent State Iconic Photograph." *Rhetoric Society Quarterly* 31 (2001): 5–32.

—. "Performing Civic Identity: The Iconic Photograph of the Flag Raising on Iwo Jima." *Quarterly Journal of Speech* 88 (2002): 363–92.

—. "Public Identity and Collective Memory in Iconic Photography: The Image of 'Accidental Napalm.'" *Critical Studies in Media Communication* 30 (2003): 35–66.

Isocrates. *Antidosis.* <http://classics.mit.edu/socrates/isoc.15.html>.

Jamieson, Kathleen Hall. *Dirty Politics: Deception, Distraction and Democracy.* New York, Oxford: Oxford UP, 1992. 16–42.

Karon, Tony. "Baghdad Falls." *Time* 9 April 2004 <http://www.time.com/time/world/article/0,8599,442046,00.html>.

Lake, Randall, and Barbara A. Pickering. "Argumentation, the Visual, and the Possibility of Refutation: An Exploration." *Argumentation* 12 (1998): 79–93.

Lucaites, John Louis, and Robert Hariman. "Visual Rhetoric, Photojournalism, and Democratic Public Culture." *Rhetoric Review* 20 (2001): 38.

MacKinnon, Catherine. *Only Words.* Cambridge, MA: Harvard, 1996.

McGee, Michael Calvin. "The Ideograph: The Link Between Rhetoric and Ideology." *Quarterly Journal of Speech* 66 (1980): 1–16.

Nesmith, Susannah. "Police Praise Selves on Absence of Chaos." *Miami Herald* 22 Nov. 2003: 1A.

Owen, A. Susan, and Peter Ehrenhaus. "Visual Rhetorics of White-on-Black Violence: Photographs." Presented at Western States Communication Association meeting. Albuquerque, NM. 15 Feb. 2004.

Perlmutter, David D. *Photojournalism and Foreign Policy.* Westport, CT: Praeger, 1998.

Pogue, Alan. Showing of Photographs of Iraqi and Afghan Women. Texas Center for Documentary Photography, 2003. <http://www.documentaryphotographs.com>

Poulakis, Takis. "Isocrates' Use of *Doxa.*" *Philosophy and Rhetoric* 34 (2001): 61–79.

Rebours, Laurent. *Saddam Falls.* AP <http://www.time.com/time/photoessays/iraq2003/saddamfalls>.

—. AP <http://www.time.com/time/world.article/0,8599,442046,00.html>.

Rhem, Kathleen T. "Seeing Saddam Statue Fall Like Seeing the Berlin Wall Come Down." *DefenseLINK* April 2003 <http://wwwdefenselink.mil/news/Apr2003/n0411 2003_200304115.html>.

Rieke, Richard D., and Malcom O. Sillars. *Argumentation and the Decision Making Process.* Glenview, IL: Scott Foresman, 1984. 153.

Sontag, Susan. *On Photography.* New York: Farrar, Strauss, and Giroux, 1973: 17.

Ut, Huynh Cong. *Naked Little Girl and Other Children Fleeing Napalm Strike.* 1963.

27

Representing Byron de la Beckwith in Film and Journalism: Popular Memories of Mississippi and the Murder of Medgar Evers

Kristen E. Hoerl
University of Texas at Austin

On June 12 1963, NAACP field secretary Medgar Evers was shot to death in front of his home in Jackson, Mississippi. Nine days later, police arrested avowed white supremacist Byron de la Beckwith for Evers's murder. Although prosecutors created a strong case against him, Beckwith was set free after two juries of white men could not reach a unanimous verdict (Nossiter unpaginated preface). The outcome of these trials fit within a broader pattern of state-sanctioned violence against activists and African Americans during the 1950s and 1960s. During these decades, state police frequently looked the other way when blacks and civil rights activists were beaten or killed. The state's legal system also failed blacks and activists; Beckwith's trials in 1964 were examples among many cases in which all white juries failed to convict whites of murdering blacks despite strong physical evidence against them.

Remarkably, the Jackson City Council asked the state to reopen the case against Beckwith in 1989. In 1994, thirty years after Evers's death, a jury comprising white and black jurists convicted Beckwith. Beckwith's conviction was unprecedented; never before had so much time lapsed between a homicide and the conviction of the person responsible for the crime. The trial against Beckwith is also remarkable for the media attention it garnered. Between 1989 and 2001, at least 376 articles in the nation's leading newspapers featured Beckwith. In 1996, the Hollywood film *Ghosts of Mississippi* recalled state district attorney Bobby DeLaughter's efforts to bring Beckwith to trial and have a jury find him guilty of Evers's death.

The media sources that attended to Beckwith's trial represented what Pierre Nora refers to as *lieux de memorie*, or sites of memory (1). As public memory scholarship attests, memories do not merely commemorate the past; they also ascribe meaning to these events for contemporary social and political life (see Ehrenhaus; Kammen; Lipsitz). Renewed interest in Beckwith suggests that memories of violence against civil rights activists and blacks have political roles in the present. Journalistic coverage and the film about Beckwith's conviction helped to constitute the unresolved case of Evers's death as a contemporary social injustice; media attention to Beckwith in the 1990s also brought the racism embedded in Mississippi's legal system during the 1960s into the national spotlight. By engaging memories of Evers's death as evidence for a contemporary trial, both Beckwith's conviction and commercial media attention to it demonstrate how popular memories are inextricable from the contemporary situations that evoke them.

Commercial media such as national newspapers and Hollywood entertainment films circulate broadly and are available to a wide range of audiences in the United States; thus, they constitute preeminent sites of memory about the past. Because the financial imperatives of commercial media frequently run counter to the interests of publics that observe them, I hesitate to describe these representations of the past as public memories, but I concede that these memories are popularized by mainstream media. In this chapter, I explain how the narrative within *Ghosts of Mississippi* constructed a particular memory about the history of racism in Mississippi's recent past. I also describe how this narrative resonates within the patterns of messages that appeared across coverage of Beckwith's trial in three prominent national newspapers: *The New York Times, The Washington Post,* and *USA Today.* By describing the commercially successful docudrama, *Ghosts of Mississippi,* and a range of national news media coverage surrounding Beckwith's trial, I argue that popular memory should be understood as intertextual rhetorical phenomena. Rather than explore newspaper articles and *Ghosts of Mississippi* as discrete rhetorical texts, I suggest that the relationship between these texts encouraged readers to draw particular meanings from Beckwith's trial. I also draw attention to the ways that commercial media function rhetorically by ascribing particular meanings to racially motivated violence from the past and to contemporary efforts to resolve them.

THE NARRATIVE OF A HERO: DE LAUGHTER'S TRIUMPH IN *GHOSTS OF MISSISSIPPI*

The narrative of *Ghosts of Mississippi* revolved around the efforts of Hinds County Assistant District Attorney, Bobby DeLaughter, to bring Beckwith to trial in the early 1990s. According to the film, DeLaughter initially resisted requests to bring Beckwith to trial because he believed little evidence remained to prove Beckwith was Evers's murderer. In addition to the lack of physical evidence tying Beckwith to the crime, DeLaughter's wife and parents objected to the state's interest in retrying the case. As the film accurately remembered, DeLaughter's father-in-law Russell Moore, who died before the case was revisited, was the judge who originally presided over the court proceedings in the 1964 trials that failed to convict Beckwith. Frequently, DeLaughter's family articulated racist beliefs, including the idea that integration had ruined their way of life. Despite these obstacles, De Laughter persisted in building a case against Beckwith. This film followed DeLaughter's efforts to attain evidence against Beckwith, gain the trust of Evers' widow, Myrlie, and convince a jury who finds Beckwith guilty in the film's final scene.

In contrast to the film's heroic image of DeLaughter, the film depicted Beckwith as a despicable character who spouted anti-Semitic, racist statements in almost every scene that included him. When jurists announced Beckwith's guilt, cheers resonated throughout the court house and among the crowd outside. Those who objected to Beckwith's conviction were not visible in the film's closing scene. Thus, this scene suggested that Beckwith and his racist sentiments had been eradicated from Mississippi. Indeed, as Myrlie Evers emerged from the courthouse with DeLaughter at her side, she announced to the crowd, "This is a new day for Mississippi." As this final scene suggested, Beckwith's conviction stood in metonymically for the value changes within Mississippi's social and political order.

Mississippi's civic identity was figuratively redeemed through DeLaughter's personal transformation as well. DeLaughter's conflicts with his family were central to the film's narrative about the history of racism in Mississippi. Because the racist ideology of DeLaughter's wife was fundamentally at odds with DeLaughter's ideals, his relationship with her dissolved. As the case against Beckwith progressed in the film, DeLaughter met and eventually married another woman, Peggy Lloyd, who applauded DeLaughter's efforts to bring Beckwith to trial. When DeLaughter began to doubt whether seeing the case to trial was worth the risk to his family's safety, Lloyd reminded him, "someday your children are going to be able to tell their children that it was their daddy that put away Byron de la Beckwith." Through Lloyd's conviction, DeLaughter was reassured that prosecuting Beckwith was "the right thing" to do.

The narrative of *Ghosts of Mississippi* represented what Janice Hocker Rushing and Thomas Frentz refer to as a social values myth in which the changes in the values of a society are symbolically represented through the struggles of characters featured in film (69-70). In the beginning of the film, DeLaughter was caught at a crossroads, forced to choose between his convictions in furthering the cause of social justice and his ties to his racist parents and wife. After he chose to pursue Beckwith's conviction, DeLaughter was able to build a new family. It is little coincidence that, within the film's narrative, DeLaughter's new family grew stronger as evidence against Beckwith mounted. Ostensibly, DeLaughter represented Mississippi's "new [white] man." Thus, the transformation of DeLaughter's personal life metaphorically represented a transformed Mississippi free from its racist, violent past.

MELODRAMA IN JOURNALISM:
LEAVING RACISM IN MISSISSIPPI TO THE PAST

The myth of social values transformation also emerged in journalistic coverage of Beckwith's trial. Collectively, *The New York Times, USA Today,* and *The Washington Post* covered the trial in ninety-five articles. These articles described the events leading up to Beckwith's arrest in 1990, the arguments made by attorneys defending and prosecuting Beckwith during his trial in 1994, and the Evers's celebration following Beckwith's conviction. As early as 1990, journalists acknowledged the significance of the case for public memory. According to one reporter from the *Washington Post*, Beckwith's "case has hung unresolved in the collective memory of a state where many attitudes about race have changed dramatically" (LaFraniere A1). Although newspapers set Beckwith's case in the context of Mississippi's violent and racist past, they featured Beckwith as central to that history. According to several reports, Evers's murder was one of the first killings of a well-known civil rights activist in Mississippi. (Dreifus 69; LaFraniere A1; Mayfield 38; Smothers A18). His was also one of the first deaths to galvanize the civil rights movement (Dreifus 69; Parker A1). Reporters frequently quoted DeLaughter, who told them, "This single, cowardly act of the person responsible for Medgar Evers's assassination has probably done more to hurt the state and the perception of Mississippi than any other single act I can think of" (LaFraniere, A1).

Coverage prior to Beckwith's conviction frequently characterized Beckwith and the 1964 trials against him in pejorative language or implicated him in the shooting. For example, a *New York Times* reporter described Beckwith as an "unregenerate hater" (Goodman C14), and a *USA Today* reporter stated that Beckwith's "grandfatherly [...] image falls apart as soon as he opens his mouth" (Howard 3A). Although negative portrayals of Beckwith were not isolated to coverage of the prosecutors' arguments against him during the trial, prosecutors' remarks provided some of the most colorful denunciations of Beckwith. According to one report, DeLaughter compared Beckwith to a snake when he told jurors, Beckwith's "venom has come back to poison him" (Booth, "Beckwith" A1). By characterizing Beckwith as a hate-filled man, as the obvious suspect in Evers's death, and in the image of a serpent, which is an archetypal symbol for evil, newspaper reports cast Beckwith as the villain centrally responsible for Mississippi's damaged reputation.

By describing Beckwith as a modern-day villain amid instances that highlighted institutional racism in the state's legal and justice system, newspaper coverage of the events that led to Beckwith's conviction positioned Beckwith as a metonymy for racist violence in Mississippi state history. Indeed, many reports acknowledged that the trial was not only about Beckwith; it was about "the Mississippi of the 1960s" (Mayfield, "Court" 3A; see also Booth, *Jackson* B1; Smothers, "30 Years" A12). According to several newspaper articles, Beckwith's conviction would not only undo a grave injustice from the past; it would rhetorically purify Mississippi's image. Individuals quoted in several newspaper articles stated that Mississippi "was growing up" (Smothers, "Supremacist" A18) and had begun a "cleansing process" (Nichols and Howlett A1). As Booth reported, "The guilty verdict was seen by many here as a sign that Mississippi [...] had moved far beyond the state-supported racism that almost tore the country apart in the turbulent 1960s" ("Beckwith" A1). George Smith told *Washington Post* reporters, "reopening the case shows that, even though you're black in Mississippi, our system works" (Mayfield, "Court" 38). Resonating with Myrlie Evers's final speech at the end of *Ghosts of Mississippi*, newspapers noted that, for many people, Beckwith's conviction demonstrated that racism in Mississippi had been left in the past.

RESACRILIZING MISSISSIPPI: HISTORY AS A FANTASY BRIBE

Ghosts of Mississippi and the news media framings of the trial suggested that Beckwith stood for something larger than himself; according to these texts, he was the embodiment of Mississippi's violent and racist past. Likewise, individuals such as DeLaughter and Evers were framed as heroes that embodied Mississippi's emerging identity. Popular memory surrounding Beckwith's conviction provided a melodrama whereby Mississippi was transformed by the state's efforts to convict Beckwith and embrace the goals of racial justice. Deming explains that heroes and villains who personify good and evil represent the urge toward achieving resacrilization in a modern age that has lost its faith in absolute value systems (6). By counterposing Beckwith and DeLaughter, *Ghosts of Mississippi* also portrayed a resacrilization of Mississippi's racist past. Because Beckwith represented the evils of Mississippi's racist past, the climax to narratives constructed in both the film and in journalistic coverage called for Beckwith's expulsion.

This framing of Beckwith's trial as a scapegoat for Mississippi's history of violence against African Americans and civil rights activists has implications for race relations and social injustice in the United States during the 1990s, when these memories were constructed. Although Beckwith was responsible for the death of Evers, he was not solely responsible for the injustices done to African Americans and civil rights workers during the 1960s. As the history of the civil rights movement attests, Evers's death was part of a larger pattern of violence against blacks and civil rights activists used to intimidate those who would challenge segregation and demoralize the movement.

The predominant framing of Beckwith as the cause for Mississippi's tarnished reputation also belies the poverty and de facto segregation of black and white neighborhoods in Jackson and elsewhere in the nation.[1] Popular memory's attention to Mississippi as the source of America's violence against African Americans also scapegoats one state for racial inequities and state-sponsored brutality against African Americans that have persisted throughout the United States. In 1995, African Americans were three times more likely to live in poverty than whites (Vobejda A1). During the early 1990s, as the case against Beckwith was growing, racial profiling was garnering news media attention as another incarnation of racism within America's justice system. News reports indicated that, although African Americans represented 12 percent of the population during the 1990s, they made up almost seventy-five percent of all routine traffic stops (Rogers, par. 2), comprised half of the nation's prisoners (Thomas A01), and were the most frequent victims of police shootings (Thomas A01).[2] Images of violence against African Americans were not relegated to memories of the 1960s either. The image of three white police officers beating Rodney King in 1991 bore resemblances to images of police officers beating activists and blacks in Southern states during the civil rights movement. Resonances between images of blacks abused by the justice system in the 1960s and the 1990s indicated that state authorities had not yet accorded equal status to blacks when Beckwith was convicted. Thus, memories of Mississippi drew attention to systematic racism in the United States that has persisted for decades.

In the context of ongoing racial inequities and contemporary instances of police brutality against African Americans, the popular memory of Beckwith's conviction offered media audiences what Jameson refers to as a "fantasy bribe." In contrast to images of King's beating, Beckwith was an easy social villain to capture the attention of the national imagination in the 1990s. At least in principle, Beckwith's anti-Semitic beliefs and his comments celebrating Evers's death were inimical to prevailing political sentiments of recent decades that celebrate the civil rights movement as a sign of progress for the United States. While popular memory of Evers's death and the struggles to prosecute Beckwith paralleled ongoing racial injustices in the United States' legal system, the narrative scapegoating of Beckwith in popular memory symbolically designated racism to memory. Consequently, this popular memory discouraged audiences from paying critical attention to contemporary instances of racially motivated violence.

The popular memory surrounding Beckwith's trial has implications beyond its significance for race relations at the end of the millennium. This study indicates that memories become popularized through the narrative patterns that run across documentary, or journalistic texts, and dramatic, or entertainment media. The omnipresence of the melodrama of the scapegoat and the social values transformation myth that ran across these texts indicates that narratives are not exclusive to fictional films or to individual texts, but constitute the broader frameworks in which commercial media encourage audiences to understand their place in history. The implications of popular memory of Beckwith for race relations in the 1990s warn us that, as narratives emerge through docudrama and in journalistic framings, they may become naturalized. In the absence of competing memories about the past, popular memories that emerge through news reports and film may acquire presence as an authentic representation of the past and obscure the selectivity of the narrative's frame. In order to challenge this narrative's ascendancy as the popular memory of institutionalized racism in recent U.S. history, activists and scholars must also seek to construct usable countermemories that hold present leaders and institutions accountable for contemporary social injustices. Such countermemories would more amenable to the cause of social justice that activists such as Medgar Evers struggled for.

NOTES

1. Booth presents coverage unique among articles covering Beckwith that explores the racial inequities that have persisted in Jackson into the 1990s ("Jackson" B1) .
2. In 1991, 33 of the 47 victims of Chicago police shootings were black. Likewise, 152 blacks in Indianapolis were shot by police, compared to 85 white victims (Thomas A01).

WORKS CITED

Booth, William. "Beckwith Convicted of Murdering Evers; White Supremacist Gets Life in '63 Shooting." *Washington Post* 6 Feb. 1994: A1.
—. "Jackson, Miss.: The City Time Remembers; Has it Really Changed Since the Murder of Medgar Evers?" *Washington Post* 11 Feb. 1994: B1.
Deming, Caren. "*Hill Street Blues* as Narrative." *Critical Studies in Mass Communication* 2 (1985): 1–22.
Dreifus, Claudia. "The Widow Gets Her Verdict." *New York Times* 27 Nov. 1994: 69.
Ehrenhaus, Peter. "Why We Fought: Holocaust Memory in Spielberg's *Saving Private Ryan*." *Critical Studies in Media Communication* 18 (2000): 3211–337.
Ghosts of Mississippi. Dir. Robert Reiner. Castle Rock Entertainment and Columbia Pictures, 1996.
Goodman, Walter. "TV Review: Medgar Evers and His Tragic End." *New York Times:* 11 July 1994: C14.
Howard, J. Lee. "Figure in Evers Case Battles 'Evil.'" *USA Today* 18 Dec. 1990: 3A.
Jameson, Frederick. "Reification and Utopia in Mass Culture." *Social Text* 1 1979: 130–48.
Kammen, Michael. *Mystic Chords of Memory: The Transformation of Tradition in American Culture*. New York: Knopf, 1991.
LaFraniere, Sharon. "Murder Charge Filed in Evers Case; Supremacist Faces Third Trial in 1963 Slaying of NAACP Official." *Washington Post* 19 Dec. 1990: A1.
Lipsitz, George. *Time Passages: Collective Memory and American Popular Culture*. Minneapolis: U of Minnesota P, 1990.
Mayfield, Mark. "Activists Gather to Mourn Evers, Civil Rights Hero." *USA Today* 11 June 1993: 38.
—. "Court OKs 3rd Trial in Evers' Death." *USA Today* 17 Dec. 1992: 3A.
Nichols, Bill, and Howlett, Debbie. "'Justice is Waking Up'; Miss. Tries Again to Close Evers Murder Case; Beckwith to Fight 'Tooth, Nail and Claw'." *USA Today* 19 Dec. 1992: A1.
Nora, Pierre. "Between Memory and History: Les Lieux de Memoire." *Representations* 26 (1989) : 1–6.
Nossiter, Adam. *Of Long Memory: Mississippi and the Murder of Medgar Evers*. Cambridge, MA: DeCapo Press, 2002.
Parker, Laura. "Reliving the Evers Death; Mississippi Haunted by '63 Murder of Black Activist." *Washington Post* 6 Feb. 1991: A1.

Rogers, Elizabeth. "Fear of Driving: Congress Considers Study of Racial Profiling in Police Traffic Stops." *ABA Journal* 86 (2000): 94.

Rushing, Janice Hocker, & Frentz, Thomas S. (1978). "The Rhetoric of 'Rocky': A Social Value Model of Criticism." *Western Journal of Communication* 41 (1978): 63–72.

Smothers, Ronald. "30 Years Later, 3d Trial Begins in Evers Killing." *New York Times* 28 Jan. 1994: A12.

—. "Supremacist Is Charged for 3d Time with Killing Medgar Evers in 1963." *New York Times* 19 Dec. 1994: A18.

Thomas, Pierre. "Police Brutality: An Issue Rekindled." *Washington Post* 6 Dec. 1995: A1.

Vobejda, Barbara. "U.S. Reports Decline in Number of Poor; Decrease Is First Since 1989." *Washington Post* 6 Oct. 1995: A1.

28

The Political Unconscious of Rhetoric: The Case of the Master-Planned Community

Thomas J. Kinney
University of Arizona

One of the commonplaces of the rhetorical tradition has been that democracy is dependent on rhetoric and vice versa. We see it in the great humanist myths of origins reproduced in Protagoras's Great Speech (Plato 320c–328d), Isocrates's Hymn to Logos (253-57), and Cicero's *De inventione* (I.i.2–I.ii.3) in which human beings, through the power of rhetoric, go from being uncivilized brutes to becoming civilized members of a self-governing society.[1] From the Roman republic and the Italian city-states to liberal democratic nation-states like the United States and now South Africa, the ability of rhetoric to democratize societies is an article of faith among scholars in rhetorical studies.[2] For example, in "The Origins of Rhetoric: Literacy and Democracy in Ancient Greece," Richard A. Katula argues,

> It has been said that rhetoric is the handmaiden of democracy. Whether in the courtroom, the legislature, or the public forum, free and intelligent speaking and writing are the lubricants that keep democracy running smoothly. Instruction in the arts of discourse affords each one of us the opportunity to participate in the public debate and thus to feel a part of the decisions that are made. (3)

With few exceptions, we in rhetorical studies have accepted the commonplace that rhetoric's fortunes rise under democratic states and fall under nondemocratic states.[3]

In this chapter, I argue, however, that rhetoric has a much stronger relationship with republicanism (also known as civic republicanism) than democracy. After describing the main tenets of democracy, republicanism, and liberalism, I build my argument on the following two premises: first, that democracy, republicanism, and liberalism are alike in one respect, namely their defense of private property; and second, that private property constrains the conditions of possibility for rhetoric. The conclusion, then, is that democracy, republicanism, and liberalism can be—and often have been—inimical to rhetoric. The belief that taxes are an individual burden rather than a civic duty, the erosion of public spending on social programs, the increasing commodification of all aspects of life, and the growing privatization of the public sphere have constrained not only the political freedoms enjoyed by citizens in the

United States and other liberal democracies but also the means of persuasion for these citizens to argue public issues. In order to specify how property and property rights affect the ability of citizens to engage in rhetoric, I offer an analysis of the master-planned community and the roles that rhetoric and public discourse have played in them. While there are many types of master-planned communities, some of which undoubtedly attempt to foster self-governance, most limit the conditions of possibility for rhetoric by creating a politics of exclusion and fear based on social inequalities; establishing centralized governance, surveillance, and restricted access; conflating ownership and sovereignty; and regulating "appropriate" public discourse.

Democracy, republicanism, and liberalism are not only different political theories but also different forms of government, which together have produced a variety of actual governments in practice. Both democracy and republicanism emerged in ancient Greece and Rome, though the former is more often associated with ancient Greece and the latter with ancient Rome.[4] Democracy is now widely accepted, mainly because it means different things to different people. In general, it is a political theory and a form of government that holds that "the people" should rule. Who the people are and what exactly they should rule, however, is the crucial question.[5] In the strongest sense, democracy is the direct participation of all people in self-governance; in the weakest sense, it is the universal suffrage of all citizens to choose political representatives. Unlike the positive freedom of democracy, republicanism holds that freedom is not the freedom to participate in self-governance but the freedom from domination. Republicanism argues that we human beings are, in Aristotle's famous phrase, political animals; that the rights of citizens (namely, life, liberty, and property) are protected not by God or nature but rather by the very institutions of the state; that we cultivate virtue by participating in self-governance; that some citizens are meant to be representatives and others are not; that these representatives should represent all factions; that the best government is a mixed one so that all citizens have an equal share of power; and that the goal of the state is to advance the common good.[6] Unlike democracy and republicanism, liberalism is less a form of government or a political theory than a philosophical tradition (hence why it is often combined with other terms, as in liberal democracy or liberal humanism). Liberalism holds that the role of the state is to protect the natural rights of individual citizens. Unlike the positive freedom of democracy (self-governance) or the negative freedom of republicanism (nondomination), liberalism holds that freedom is the freedom from interference.[7]

Even a cursory examination of the history of rhetoric, in particular classical and Renaissance rhetoric, reveals that rhetoric has a much stronger relationship with republicanism than democracy or liberalism. Historically, although it emerges out of the republics of Florence, Venice, Genoa, and other Italian city-states, republicanism has its roots in the works of the sophists; the civic humanists Isocrates, Cicero, and Quintilian; and the political philosophy of Aristotle in particular. Indeed, it is Cicero's mistranslation of Aristotle's *politeia* as *res publica* that gives rise to republicanism. Beginning with Cicero, republicanism becomes an alternative to tyranny and later monarchy. In the bourgeois revolutions, it becomes the foundation for modern nation-states. Indeed, in recent years, historians, political and legal theorists, and others have begun to reconsider the prominence that has been given to the liberal and democratic traditions (the former grounded in the political philosophy of Locke and Montesquieu, the latter grounded in the political philosophy of Rousseau) at the expense of the civic republican tradition (grounded in the political philosophy of Machiavelli, James Harrington, and others).[8] Republicanism can also be traced in the works of contemporary rhetoricians like Kenneth Burke, Richard McKeon, Wayne C. Booth, Ernesto Grassi, James

L. Kinneavy, Richard A. Lanham, George A. Kennedy, and Gerard A. Hauser. Not without notice have women been excluded from this list.[9]

Definitions aside, the political theories of democracy, republicanism, and liberalism do have one thing in common: the significance each theory gives to private property. Although the ways in which private property fits into them differs, it is given a prominence not found in other political theories like monarchy, socialism, or obviously communism. In a liberal democracy, the ownership of private property is conceived of as a guardian of every other right, and the primary role of the state is to protect the property and property rights of its private citizens. As Locke writes in *The Second Treatise of Government*, "The great and *chief end* therefore, of Mens uniting into Commonwealths, and putting themselves under government, *is the Preservation of their Property*" (350–51). Of course, for Locke, the term *property* means much more than what it does today (as in the phrase "life, liberty, and the pursuit of happiness," all of which for Locke were included in the term), but it does encompass the more materialist meanings we continue to ascribe to it. In a republic, the ownership of private property is conceived of as a means to facilitate an active and self-governing citizenry, as a means to enable citizens to cultivate their virtue and pursue the common good. Thus, in the *Politics*, Aristotle writes, "Property is a part of the household, and the art of acquiring property is a part of the art of managing the household; for no man can live well, or indeed at all, unless he is provided with necessaries" (I.iv). Without property, therefore, one was little more than a slave.

The relationship between rhetoric and property is a long and complex one, and a brief summary must suffice.[10] Rhetoric is said to have emerged in Syracuse (on the island of Sicily) during the second quarter of the fifth century BCE, when the tyrant Thrasybulus, who had confiscated all property, was overthrown in a popular uprising. When the exiles returned, they were forced to argue in court on their own behalf in order to reclaim their property, and since they had little or no experience in rhetoric, they sought the training of others who did. Thus was rhetoric born.[11] Throughout the history of rhetoric, such cases on property were commonplace both in the courtroom and the assembly, so much so that Isocrates remarks in the *Antidosis* that one of the charges against the sophists is that "when [their clients] gain this power [of rhetoric], they begin plotting to get the property of others" (198). Furthermore, many of the extant speeches of the ancient Greeks and Romans are legal cases dealing with property disputes. Yet, rhetoric's ties to property are much deeper than simple disputes over property, for how else but through rhetoric are property and property rights justified? Whether it is Aristotle, Aquinas, Locke, Bentham, Mill, or Nozick, any justification of them must engage in rhetoric.[12] And conversely, how else but through property and property rights do human beings gain the ability to practice rhetoric? Put another way, is not ownership of property and the access it affords the primary way one learns and/or uses rhetoric? As Roland Barthes observes in "The Old Rhetoric: An *aide-mémoire*," rhetoric is "that privileged technique (since one must pay in order to acquire it) which permits the ruling classes to gain *ownership of speech*" (13–14). Before we indict Barthes as a rhetorical *poseur*, who better to confirm Barthes's interpretation than Kenneth Burke? In *A Rhetoric of Motives*, in a section entitled "The Identifying Nature of Property," Burke writes, "In the realm of Rhetoric, such identification is frequently by property in the most materialistic sense of the term, economic property" (24–25). Property is, in other words, an essential part of the rhetor's ethos.[13]

Historically, both liberal democracy and republicanism have assumed that the best defense of political rights is achieved through a defense of property and property rights, the former because they are a means for individual liberty and the latter because they are a means for the common good. Both liberal democracy and republicanism argue that the ownership of property enables one to be a free and/or virtuous citizen. Yet, ownership of property is understood only in a private sense; in other words, they neglect public, common, or other forms of ownership, the neglect of which no doubt constrains the social practice of rhetoric. Furthermore, neither political theory deals sufficiently with the problem of the unequal distribution of property. In other words, in the practice of citizenship and hence rhetoric, all citizens are equal but some are more equal than others. More importantly, especially in terms of rhetoric, neither theory allows for a genuinely open public sphere in which citizens can argue public issues. While we may "live" in a democracy, we certainly don't work in one. And we don't shop in one either. Hence, the relationship between rhetoric and property is a contradictory one, and this contradictory relationship constrains the conditions of possibility for rhetoric, especially the type of rhetoric we mean when we talk about rhetoric and democracy.

While one of the commonplaces of liberal democracy and republicanism, then, is that property ensures political rights, one of the commonplaces of the rhetorical tradition is that equal access to the public sphere ensures political rights. In order to investigate this apparent contradiction, I will turn now to the case of the master-planned community. The incredible growth of master-planned communities (and most recently, gated communities) is part of a broader decline in the public sphere. This decline can be seen in the following trends: the proliferation of malls and Wal-Marts; the decline of the city center and/or main street, the rise of the suburb, and now the gentrification of the city center; the decline of and/or the corporatization of what Ray Oldenburg calls "the great good place"; the privatization of educational and social welfare programs like Social Security, Medicare, and Medicaid; the corporatization of the university; the monopolization of the media; and an increase in restricted access and surveillance. In short, late capitalism, felt both globally and locally. The master-planned community, however, is not a recent phenomenon. In fact, there have been master-planned communities throughout the history of many civilizations. In the West, one of the earliest master-planned communities was Miletus in Asia Minor, a prototype of the Enlightenment master-planned cities in the Americas, from Washington, DC, and Mexico City to Lima, Peru. Yet, there have been many other types of master-planned communities: company towns like Lowell, Massachusetts, and Pullman, Illinois; utopian communities like New Harmony, Indiana, and Salt Lake City, Utah; British Garden Cities like Radburn, New Jersey; New Deal-sponsored Greenbelt towns like Greenhills, Ohio, Greendale, Wisconsin, and Greenbelt, Maryland; New Towns like Park Forest, Illinois, and Reston, Virginia; and finally New Urbanist-inspired communities like Seaside, Florida (incidentally, where *The Truman Show* was filmed) and Celebration, Florida.[14]

Like the master-planned communities it eventually inspired, Thurii (an ancient Greek city based on Miletus) exemplifies their contradictions. Founded in southern Italy circa 444 BCE, Thurii had a rigidly orthogonal street layout and two separate but uniform residential zones. Between these two zones, there was an irregular zone of public buildings. In the rest of the city, there remained space to develop commerce and other public concerns. More importantly, every zone had a clear function, as well as a clearly functional relationship with the other zones and the surrounding areas. In addition to this master plan, which was devised by Hippodamus, Thurii also had a democratic constitution, which was crafted by Pericles, and an educational system based on the principles of rhetoric, which was established by Protagoras. Yet, these elements do not lead me to the argument, as it does for David Fleming, that Thurii was "an autonomous community of free and equal citizens who would govern themselves through their own practical, human capabilities" (6). On the contrary, I argue that the rationalist urban planning of Thurii became a means to, in the words of Harvey Yunis, "tame democracy." Not unlike the International Style of Albrecht Speer or Le Corbusier, it demonstrates a type of social engineering, an example of what the early Foucault calls the discourse of panopticism and the later Foucault calls biopower. In short, Thurii, like the Enlightenment master-planned communities that follow it, was a hegemonic means to control the populace: a place for everything and everything in its place, what Stephen Toulmin has critiqued as "cosmopolis," a view of society as rationally ordered as Newton's universe.[15] Of course, the proprietarian impulse in the master-planned community is akin to that same impulse in rhetoric (Fleming describes the Thurian project as the pursuit of *rightness*); in fact, both can easily be corrupted into a mastery of others based upon a politics of exclusion and fear.[16]

The case of Pullman, Illinois, offers a more striking example. Rather than a Thurian philosophical order, Pullman (both George Pullman, the capitalist, and Pullman, the city) sought to establish a capitalist economic order. Pullman was founded in 1880 on some four thousand acres just south of Chicago on Lake Calumet. Unlike Lowell, Massachusetts, which had been built a half-century earlier, Pullman included not only factories and dormitories but also private homes, row houses, and tenements for nearly eight thousand inhabitants; shops, offices, and markets; a hotel; schools, parks, playgrounds, a library, a theater, and even a church. Even more disturbing, there was no municipal government, and Pullman (George) refused to sell any of the land or properties to the residents, so as to maintain, in his words, "the harmony of the town's design" (qtd. in Walzer 296). Furthermore, home renovation was strictly controlled, churches were disallowed (the Presbyterian one sufficed), and there was only one bar, located in a hotel that most of Pullman's residents could not afford. Residents were also required to live in a certain way, with special attention to their appearance and behavior. Those who failed to meet Pullman's standards could be fined and/or have their leases terminated. Granted, the rents were lower than the surrounding areas, and the buildings were always kept in repair. Yet, as sociologist Michael Walzer explains, the residents were little more than serfs, a status at odds with democratic politics (297). Indeed, four years after the Pullman Strike of 1894, the Illinois Supreme Court broke up the town, arguing that it was "incompatible with the theory and spirit of our institutions" (Carwardine xxxiii). The problem with Pullman, not unlike the problem with many master-planned communities, is that sovereignty is conflated with ownership, citizenship with consumerism. And how can one practice rhetoric if all one is is a consumer?[17]

Unlike the philosophical order of Thurii and the economic order of Pullman, Celebration is an attempt to create an absolute social and cultural order, a sort of architectural *Gesamtkunstwerk* for the postmodern age. Celebration is owned and operated by the Walt Disney Company, and it was founded on November 18, 1995, which was, incidentally, Mickey Mouse's sixty-seventh birthday. It is located just south of Disney World on 27,000 acres. Incidentally, the land was bought from the state of Florida for $200/acre and quarter-acre lots now run as high as $80,000. Based loosely on the New Urbanism, Celebration has narrow, winding streets, which are both pedestrian- and bicycle-friendly; houses are placed on small lots with small yards and porches in the front and garages in the rear, all of which are meant to encourage visibility, interaction, and what is perceived to be small-town life. Yet, just as with Pullman, the dream of living with Disney has its pitfalls. There is no mayor or city council, no police or fire stations, no courthouse, and oddly enough no cemetery. Residents must sign a Declaration of Covenants, which is simply a homeowner's agreement disguised as a utopian declaration of independence. The agreement dictates rules by which residents must abide: for example, the size of political signs and the length of time they can be displayed, the number of yard sales permitted per year, and the areas where cars may be parked. The Celebration Board runs Celebration; it is composed of unelected officials, and they have the power both to fine and remove residents. More disturbingly, the Celebration School, though a public school in the Osceola County School District, is owned and partly operated by Disney. When some residents criticized the school, Disney responded that they were "just homesick for the towns they left" (qtd. in Giroux 77). The controversy led some in Celebration to move, but when they asked to be released from the homeowner's agreement they signed, Disney agreed "only on the condition of signing an agreement promising never to reveal their reasons for leaving Celebration" (Giroux 77). Obviously, in Celebration, the ability to engage in rhetoric or public discourse has been severely constrained, all in the name of safety, comfort, and protection from fear.[18]

The lesson to be learned from the master-planned community is not only that it constrains the conditions of possibility for rhetoric but also that, because of such constraints, we rhetoricians must pay close attention to the material conditions of rhetoric.[19] According to Edward James Blakely and Mary Gail Snyder, authors of *Fortress America: Gated Communities in the United States*, over eight million people in the United States now live behind gated communities, and nearly ten percent of all new homes are in such communities. Even more live in master-planned communities like the ones I analyzed above. If my argument holds, then the ability for people to engage in the practice of rhetoric is becoming more constrained than ever. It is my contention that while we can appeal to absolute democracy or the communitarian impulse in republicanism, only a materialist critique offers a genuine response. We must return to a genuinely Marxist critique, dare I say, "a ruthless criticism of everything existing" (Marx 12). Hardt and Negri's post-Marxist response in *Empire* is entirely inadequate:

> We do not intend here to weep over the destruction and expropriation that capitalism continually operates across the world, even though resisting its force (and in particular resisting the expropriation of the welfare state) is certainly an eminently ethical and important task. We want to ask, rather, what is the operative notion of the common today, in the midst of postmodernity, the information revolution, and the consequent transformations of the mode of production. It seems to us, in fact, that today we participate in a more radical and profound commonality than has ever been experienced in the history of capitalism. (301–02)

No doubt these are dangerous technophilic assumptions, especially in light of the Telecommunications Act of 1996.[20] In other words, we cannot put our faith in the proliferation of communication networks, the globalization of the workforce, and the production of new worker subjectivities to create absolute democracy. Theirs is *not* a ruthless criticism of everything existing, and neither is much of the work being done in rhetorical studies.

For too long, we in rhetorical studies have neglected the material conditions of rhetorical theory and practice. In response to this neglect, I argue for us to develop and strengthen our ties to Marxist and postcolonial theory. Historically, Marxism has been the main theoretical basis for analyzing the dialectical relationship between material conditions (the mode of production, i.e., the forces and social relations of production) and discourse (e.g., rhetoric). Postcolonial theory is also useful for analyzing the material conditions of rhetoric insofar as it offers a complementary theory for this dialectical relationship, based not on the relationship between capitalists and proletariat but rather colonizers and colonized. More specifically, I cite Fredric Jameson's theory of the political unconscious and Patricia Bizzell's use of it in "Marxist Ideas in Composition Studies" to critique the term *community* in the field of rhetoric and composition.[21] The political unconscious begins with the understanding that narrative—understood in Kenneth Burke's sense of symbolic action—is the form of our most basic experience of reality, and furthermore that narrative has an eminently collective function. Jameson appropriates and then historicizes the Freudian concept of the unconscious, arguing that it is not the lawless (and most importantly, individual) realm of repressed mental processes or states but rather the bourgeois (and hence collective) realm of repressed revolution. Hence, what is available for interpretation in most texts is the ideological structure that represses this revolution. The political unconscious is this ideological structure, which is expressed though the contradictions in the mode of production, and the means through which we access it is to historicize.

Just as narrative is a socially symbolic act, so too is rhetoric. Unfortunately, this political unconscious of rhetoric has been neglected in rhetorical studies. In this essay, I have developed one aspect of this political unconscious, namely the relationship between rhetoric and property, which undoubtedly has been neglected by scholars in rhetorical studies in favor of the relationship between rhetoric and democracy. To be sure, I do not mean to disparage such work on rhetoric and democracy; nevertheless, we must merge this "positive" critique of what goods rhetoric can do with an equally strong "negative" critique of what ills rhetoric has done or what goods rhetoric has been prevented from doing. It is not only unethical but also politically dangerous for us in rhetorical studies to study and teach rhetoric without reflecting on the material conditions of rhetoric. Throughout the rhetorical tradition, there are examples of rhetoric being used to bring about both freedom *and* oppression, both empathy *and* violence, both revolution *and* human suffering. Rhetorical studies must do more than simply theorize and analyze the means of persuasion; we must also theorize and analyze the means of production. Who controls the means of production often also controls the means of persuasion.

NOTES

1. See Kastely on these humanist myths of origins. His argument is that Cicero's myth reveals the ways in which he sees corruption not as an aberration but rather as "a philosophical problem that lies at the very heart of rhetorical practice" (236).
2. For examples of this commonplace in rhetorical studies, see Conley; Golden, Berquist, and Coleman; Hauser; Hauser and Grim; Herrick; Kennedy; Kennedy; Salazar; and Vickers.
3. One exception is Jeffrey Walker's *Rhetoric and Poetics in Antiquity*, which claims that "'rhetoric' (as broadly conceived in the sophistic/Isocratean tradition) does not depend on, rise, or fall with democratic institutions, as is often assumed; rather, 'rhetoric' (so conceived) may be democracy's condition of possibility" (x).
4. Although Athens and other ancient Greek *poleis* were democratic, many Greek philosophers, including Plato and Aristotle, were no friends of democracy. Indeed, their political philosophy is closer to republicanism, though such nomenclature is somewhat anachronistic and highly contested (cf. Nelson).
5. See Barrett, Charland, Hauser (*Vernacular Voices*), and McGee ("In Search") on rhetoric, public discourse, and the question of "the people."
6. See Pettit and Viroli for introductions to republicanism. See also Pocock and Skinner. For a critique of republicanism, in the context of rhetorical studies, see Fusfield.
7. See Viroli on the relationship between democracy, republicanism, and liberalism. "Republicanism," he argues, "is all too often seen as a province of democratic theory bordering on the large empire of liberalism. But it is historically more correct to regard both liberal and democratic po-

litical theory as provinces of republicanism, based in its classical form on the two principles of the rule of law and popular sovereignty" (7).

8. Cf. Alexander; Fallon; Kramnick; Rose.
9. For examples of republicanism in public discourse, see Bellah et al.; Eberly; Eberly; Putnam.
10. See Bethell and Pipes for introductions to property and property rights.
11. See Barthes, Cole, Enos, and Schiappa (1999) on this myth of origins of rhetoric.
12. See Rose on the rhetorical justification of property and property rights.
13. See also Pattison, who writes, "Like any other technology, rhetoric becomes a commodity. The knowledge of rhetoric has a cost to the student, unlike the knowledge of speech. If there were a price-tag on speech, half the world would be mute. There is a price-tag on the talent of rhetoric, and through history most men have not been able to afford it. The technologies of language follow rhetoric in this: they are all part of the economic nexus of civilization" (31).
14. See Blakeley and Snyder for an introduction to the master-planned community.
15. In addition to Toulmin's *Cosmopolis*, see also Angel Rama's *The Lettered City* for a critique of "the ordered city," the context of which is colonial Latin America.
16. See Ward-Perkins for more information on Thurii.
17. See Carwardine for more information on Pullman.
18. See Frantz and Collins, Giroux, and Ross for more information on Celebration.
19. See Cloud and McGee ("Materialist's Conception") for a defense of materialist critique in rhetorical studies. Though few in rhetorical studies draw on them, Rossi-Landi and Volosinov are foundational texts on the materialist approach to language.
20. See Logie for an interesting case study of the relationship between rhetoric and intellectual property.
21. See also Bizzell ("Frederic") where she develops her thoughts about the use of Fredric Jameson's work for rhetoric and composition.

WORKS CITED

Alexander, Gregory S. *Commodity and Propriety: Competing Visions of Property in American Legal Thought, 1776–1970*. Chicago: U of Chicago P, 1997.
Aristides. "To Plato: In Defense of Oratory." *The Complete Works*. Vol. 1. Trans. Charles A. Behr. Leiden: Brill, 1986. 78–150.
Aristotle. *Politics*. Vol. 2 of *The Complete Works of Aristotle*. 2 vols. Ed. Jonathan Barnes. Princeton: Princeton UP, 1984. 1986–2129.
Barrett, Harold. *Rhetoric of the People: Is There Any Better or Equal Hope in the World?* Amsterdam: Rodopi, 1974.
Barthes, Roland. "The Old Rhetoric: An *aide-mémoire*." *The Semiotic Challenge*. Trans. Richard Howard. Berkeley: U of California P, 1994. 11–93.
Bellah, Robert, et al., eds. *Habits of the Heart: Individualism and Commitment in American Life*. Cambridge: Harvard UP, 1985.
—. *The Good Society*. New York: Vintage, 1992.
Bethell, Tom. *The Noblest Triumph: Property and Prosperity through the Ages*. New York: St. Martin's, 1998.
Bizzell, Patricia. "Fredric Jameson and Composition Studies." *JAC* 16 (1996): 471–87.
—. "Marxist Ideas in Composition Studies." *Contending with Words: Composition and Rhetoric in the Postmodern Age*. Ed. Patricia Harkin and John Schilb. New York: MLA, 1991. 52–68.
Blakeley, Edward James, and Mary Gail Snyder. *Fortress America: Gated Communities in the United States*. Washington, DC: Brookings Institution, 1997.
Buder, Stanley. *Pullman: An Experiment in Industrial Order and Community Planning, 1880–1930*. New York: Oxford UP, 1967.
Burke, Kenneth. *A Rhetoric of Motives*. Berkeley: U of California P, 1969.
Carwardine, William M. *The Pullman Strike*. 4th ed. Chicago: Illinois Labor History Society, 1973.

Charland, Maurice. "Constitutive Rhetoric: The Case of the *Peuple Québécois.*" *Quarterly Journal of Speech* 73 (1987): 133–50.

Cicero. *De Inventione, De Optimo Genere Oratorum, Topica.* Trans. H. M. Hubbell. Cambridge: Harvard UP, 1949.

Cloud, Dana. "The Materiality of Discourse as Oxymoron: A Challenge to Critical Rhetoric." *Western Journal of Communication* 58 (1994): 141–63.

Cole, Thomas. *The Origins of Rhetoric in Ancient Greece.* Baltimore: Johns Hopkins UP, 1991.

Conley, Thomas M. *Rhetoric in the European Tradition.* New York: Longman, 1990.

Eberly, Don E. *America's Promise: Civil Society and the Renewal of American Culture.* Lanham: Rowman, 1998.

—, ed. *Building a Community of Citizens: Civil Society in the 21st Century.* Lanham, MD: Rowman and Littlefield, 1994.

Enos, Richard Leo. *Greek Rhetoric before Aristotle.* Prospect Heights, IL: Waveland, 1993.

Fallon, Richard H., Jr. "What Is Republicanism, and Is It Worth Revising?" *Harvard Law Review* 102 (1989): 1695–735.

Fleming, David. "The Streets of Thurii: Discourse, Democracy, and Design in the Classic Polis." *Rhetoric Society Quarterly* 32.3 (2002): 5–32.

Frantz, Douglas, and Catherine Collins. *Celebration, U.S.A.: Living in Disney's Brave New Town.* New York: Holt, 1999.

Fusfield, William D. "Refusing to Believe It: Considerations on Public Speaking Instruction in a Post-Machiavellian Moment." *Social Epistemology* 11 (1997): 253–314.

Giroux, Henry A. *The Mouse That Roared: Disney and the End of Innocence.* Lanham: Rowman, 1999.

Golden, James L., Goodwin F. Berquist, and William E. Coleman. *The Rhetoric of Western Thought.* 7th ed. Dubuque, IA: Kendall/Hunt, 2001.

Hardt, Michael, and Antonio Negri. *Empire.* Cambridge: Harvard UP, 2000.

Hauser, Gerard A. *Introduction to Rhetorical Theory.* 2nd ed. Prospect Heights, IL: Waveland, 2002.

—. *Vernacular Voices: The Rhetoric of Publics and Public Spheres.* Columbia: U of South Carolina P, 1999.

—, and Amy Grim, eds. *Rhetorical Democracy: Discursive Practices of Civic Engagement.* Mahwah, NJ: Lawrence Erlbaum Associates, 2004.

Herrick, James A. *The History and Theory of Rhetoric: An Introduction.* 2nd ed. Boston: Allyn and Bacon, 2001.

Isocrates. *Antidosis. Isocrates I.* Trans. David Mirhady and Yun Lee Too. Austin: U of Texas P, 2000. 205–64.

Kastely, James L. "The Recalcitrance of Aggression: An Aporetic Moment in Cicero's *De inventione.*" *Rhetorica* 20 (2002): 235–62.

Katula, Richard A. "The Origins of Rhetoric: Literacy and Democracy in Ancient Greece." *A Synoptic History of Classical Rhetoric.* Ed. James J. Murphy and Richard A. Katula. Mahwah, NJ: Hermagoras, 2003. 3–19.

Kennedy, George A. *Classical Rhetoric and Its Christian and Secular Tradition from Ancient to Modern Times.* 2nd ed. Chapel Hill: U of North Carolina P, 1999.

—. *A New History of Classical Rhetoric.* Princeton: Princeton UP, 1994.

Kinneavy, James L. "Restoring the Humanities: The Return of Rhetoric from Exile." The Rhetorical Tradition and Modern Writing. Ed. James J. Murphy. New York: MLA, 1982. 19–28.

Kramnick, Isaac. "Republicanism Revisionism Revisited." *American History Review* 87 (1982): 629–64.

Locke, John. *The Second Treatise of Government. Two Treatises of Government.* Ed. Peter Laslett. Cambridge: Cambridge UP, 1996. 285–447.

Logie, John. "Homestead Acts: Rhetoric and Property in the American West, and on the World Wide Web." *Rhetoric Society Quarterly* 32.3 (2002): 33–59.

Marx, Karl. "For a Ruthless Criticism of Everything Existing." *The Marx-Engels Reader.* 2nd ed. Ed. Robert C. Tucker. New York: Norton, 1978. 12–15.

McGee, Michael Calvin. "In Search of the 'People': A Rhetorical Alternative." *Quarterly Journal of Speech* 61 (1975): 235–49.

——. "A Materialist's Conception of Rhetoric." *Explorations in Rhetoric: Studies in Honor of Douglas Ehninger*. Ed. Raymie E. McKerrow. Glenview, IL: Scott, Foresman, 1982. 23–48.

Nelson, Eric. *The Greek Tradition in Republican Thought*. Cambridge: Cambridge UP, 2004.

Oldenburg, Ray. *The Great Good Place: Cafés, Coffee Shops, Community Centers, Beauty Parlors, General Stores, Bars, Hangouts and How They Get You through the Day*. New York: Marlowe, 1997.

Pattison, Robert. *On Literacy: The Politics of the Word from Homer to the Age of Rock*. New York: Oxford UP, 1982.

Pettit, Philip. *Republicanism: A Theory of Freedom and Government*. New York: Oxford UP, 1997.

Pipes, Richard. *Property and Freedom: The Story of How through the Centuries Private Ownership Has Promoted Liberty and the Rule of Law*. New York: Knopf, 1999.

Plato. *Protagoras. Collected Works of Plato*. Ed. Edith Grossman. Princeton: Princeton UP, 1963. 308–52.

Pocock, J. G. A. *The Machiavellian Moment: Florentine Political Thought and the Atlantic Tradition*. 2nd ed. Princeton: Princeton UP, 2003.

Putnam, Robert D. *Bowling Alone: The Collapse and Revival of American Community*. New York: Touchstone, 2001.

Rama, Angel. *The Lettered City*. Ed. and trans. John Charles Chasteen. Durham: Duke UP, 1996.

Rose, Carol M. *Property and Persuasion: Essays on the History, Theory, and Rhetoric of Ownership*. Boulder, CO: Westview, 1994.

Ross, Andrew. *The Celebration Chronicles: Life, Liberty, and the Pursuit of Property Value in Disney's New Town*. New York: Ballantine, 1999.

Rossi-Landi, Ferruccio. *Language as Work and Trade: A Semiotic Homology for Linguistics and Economics*. South Hadley, MA: Bergin and Garvey, 1983.

Salazar, Phillipe-Joseph. *An African Athens: Rhetoric and the Shaping of Democracy in South Africa*. Mahwah, NJ: Lawrence Erlbaum Associates, 2002.

Schiappa, Edward. *The Beginnings of Rhetorical Theory in Classical Greece*. New Haven: Yale UP, 1999.

Skinner, Quentin. *Liberty before Liberalism*. Cambridge: Cambridge UP, 1997.

Sloane, Thomas O., ed. *Encyclopedia of Rhetoric*. Oxford: Oxford UP, 2001.

Toulmin, Stephen. *Cosmopolis: The Hidden Agenda of Modernity*. New York: Free, 1990.

Vickers, Brian. *In Defense of Rhetoric*. New York: Oxford UP, 1988.

Viroli, Maurizio. *Republicanism*. Trans. Antony Shugaar. New York: Farrar, Strauss, and Giroux, 2002.

Volosinov, V. N. *Marxism and the Philosophy of Language*. Trans. Ladislav Matejka and I. R. Titunik. Cambridge: Harvard UP, 1996.

Walker, Jeffrey. *Rhetoric and Poetics in Antiquity*. New York: Oxford UP, 2000.

Walzer, Michael. *Spheres of Justice: A Defense of Pluralism and Justice*. New York: Basic, 1983.

Ward-Perkins, J. B. *Cities of Ancient Greece and Italy: Planning in Classical Antiquity*. New York: Braziller, 1974.

Yunis, Harvey. *Taming Democracy: Models of Political Rhetoric in Classical Athens*. Ithaca: Cornell UP, 1996.

29

Are the Weapons of Mass Destruction Here? Violence, Blowback, and the Rhetorical Agenda of WMDs

Kevin Douglas Kuswa
University of Richmond

We are always and suddenly in a time of crisis. New manifestations of violence and torture puncture the American womb, only to discover a growing fetus that resembles the same demons locked in deadly combat with the family itself. We take pride in these creations, these reproductions. Remember when we detected a rugged spirit of American-style independence and struggle for freedom in the Mujahadeen fighters in Afghanistan who were resisting the tyranny of communism in the 1980s? We nurtured that spirit, helped it to mature and grow into our own likeness. Heroes support heroes. There, in the hills of Nicaragua, Angola, Afghanistan, we could sense the pride and passion of democracy, the next wave of freedom born from the American spirit. For hundreds of years now, the ramifications of these imperial projects have been global in nature—the French and Germans in Africa, the Spanish Armada, the United States in the Philippines, struggles against colonialism in Haiti, Japan, India, and so on.

Something is currently intensifying these struggles; something that can be felt in the ongoing constitution of "us" versus "them." Local violence (Groznyy, Najaf, East Timor) is broadcast across the globe, while global violence (labor exploitation, escalating arms sales, environmental destruction) is obscured by a focus on local snapshots. The terrain of terror and violence, particularly in the wake of September 11th and the occupation of Afghanistan and Iraq, is shattering and intensifying the categories of global and local. Rhetorically, the terrain of terror and violence both links to and impacts this state of fluctuation—this state of political, ethical, spiritual, and overwhelmingly cultural crisis.

WEAPONS OF MASS DESTRUCTION

The theme of the Rhetorical Society of America's Eleventh Biennial Conference, "Rhetorical Agendas: Political, Ethical, Spiritual," calls into question existing theories of violence, terrorism, security, and rhetorical citizenship. Certain binary oppositions—comfortable and clean—do not match up with lived experience and global transformation. Our state of affairs, the state of the world, our state of influence, our governing state, our nation-state are all being organized (coded) by globalization and challenges or obstacles to globalization (Tsing). Distinctions between democracy and tyranny, security and warfare, guard and prisoner, promise and threat, hope and risk, or self and other generate false borders and dangerous oppositions. "The photographs *are* us" (Sontag). As Susan Sontag assesses the rhetorical aftermath of the Abu Ghraib photographs depicting the torture of Iraqi detainees, she contends, "The horror of what is shown in the photographs cannot be separated from the horror that the photographs were taken" (Sontag 26). The shifts we are now encountering are massive because they are partially of our own making. Whether an aberration or a continuation, 9/11 has magnified the stakes of our present condition.

The event encapsulated by the simple date, 9/11, has two components: the act itself and the act's effects. The event is both—the thing and its ripples (Derrida). One of the ripples is the reconceptualization of what constitutes a weapon of mass destruction and who has access to such weapons. Movies depicting "loose" nuclear weapons in the hands of few individuals may have foreshadowed the magnitude of the event (Baudrillard). Can we create what we see on the screen? The conventional understanding is that weapons of mass destruction (WMDs) are primarily in the hands of state actors and consist of complex nuclear, chemical, or biological elements—elements that require even more complicated methods of delivery. Conventional wisdom regarding WMDs began to change soon after the cold war, but a traditional notion of WMDs still guides many state policies, not to mention international regimes such as the Non-Proliferation Treaty, the Comprehensive Test Ban Treaty, and the Chemical Weapons Convention. Those institutions may not be able to ever plug the dam, for 9/11 may have ruptured an already cracking rhetoric of WMDs. Weapons of mass destruction are everywhere and they can be used in the United States. Delivery mechanisms have followed suit, particularly when the exchange only necessitates basic communication. In a *New York Times* article called "Bin Laden's Low-Tech Weapon," Nunberg reported that the cassette tape has become an easy way to create, smuggle, and exchange messages. In the same way that a small group of people armed with knives can commandeer a precise WMD, so too can a cassette recorder replicate the most sophisticated counterintelligence network. "High-tech countermeasures are of little use when the message comes in under the radar" (Nunberg).

Creativity allows these violent tendencies to circumvent resource constraints or new forms of surveillance. The human body itself, as seen in the West Bank and the rest of Palestine, can act as a WMD one suicide bomber at a time. The trope of the "weapon of mass destruction" has a unique relationship to the state's attempt to contain and deploy violence. Jonathan Schell, the Harold Willens Peace Fellow at the Nation Institute and Professor at Wesleyan University, states:

> No one had identified the civilian airliner as a weapon of mass destruction, but it occurred to the diabolical imagination of those who conceived Tuesday's attack that it could be one. The invention illumined the nature of terrorism in modern times. These terrorists carried no bombs—only knives, if initial reports are to be believed. In short, they turned the tremendous forces inherent in modern technical society—in this case, Boeing 767s brimming with jet fuel—against itself. (2)

Schell marks the broadening of the category of WMD, opening the door to the possibility of mass destruction throughout the domestic transportation infrastructure. At the right time and in the right place, car bombs, train bombs (Madrid), ship bombs (in Yemen), backpack bombs, and airplane bombs could all act as weapons of mass destruction. Schell goes on to associate the event of 9/11 with the concept of "blowback" and a state's suicidal tendencies. This is what Derrida refers to as an auto-immunitary response that induces a system to build in its own extinction. In Schell's words, "blowback" is "the use of a technical capacity against its creator—and, as such, represents the pronounced suicidal tendencies of modern society" (2). We will return to the very suggestive notion of blowback momentarily. In the meantime, it is important to follow the path of the rhetoric of WMD.

The "diabolical imagination" conjured up by Schell gestures to the WMD imaginary in multiple ways. It associates invention and creativity with the possibility of mass destruction—it is not simply the nuts and bolts precisely because it is only nuts and bolts, that is, the uncomfortable realization that "when there actually is a will, there is also a way." Of course, the anxiety behind the elimination of the possibility threshold and the capacity threshold for WMDs is a type of moral panic. If modernity has generated a virtually infinite source of WMDs, how can the war on terror ever win? This is an observation made many times since September 11th. What is interesting, though, is the surprise expressed by Schell that WMD privileges are no longer reserved to states and their personifications. Not only are those privileges being extended to stateless faces and faceless ideologies, but the capability to construct such weapons is more about micro-violence: box-cutters, security checks, seizing the cockpit, or otherwise exerting local violence to control mass transportation—knives and mass transportation assemble the WMD. This is the blurring of local and mass, of micro and macro, the line of flight that is also a line of suicidal fight, a regime of terrorism of mass destruction—the virtual and the actual—the accident that is inseparable from the machine. We do not imagine the Cuban missile crisis going awry and the button actually being pushed; rather, we imagine that the next wave of weapons will set in motion a blowback beyond comprehension—a mega-event beyond the day after tomorrow. Further complicating the macro and the micro, Ronald Greene (1998) uses Judith Butler (1997) to demonstrate that watching the bomb from afar is akin to becoming the bomb. Distances shrink as prime time forces an extension of mass violence into the living room through the television—mass violence leaking into the local. Is it unique to see the airliner as a weapon of mass destruction? Try the land mine, the automobile, the cigarette, the dollar bill, a gun, or a box-cutter. Or, even more disturbing, map the fertilizer we used to produce our food—our produce—on to the WMD responsible for the Murray Building in Oklahoma City; map the religious fervor of the Seventh-Day Adventists in Waco as the tinder ignited by a stockpile of rifles and the tactics of the FBI as a WMD; map the defoliants used in Vietnam as WMDs that transcend generations through genetic accumulation; map the global economy's creation of markets as a weapon of wage exploitation and mass poverty. Perhaps not mass destruction, but certainly "glocal" violence, can be seen in the planting of mail-bombs across the Midwest so that connecting the dots would form a giant smiley face on a map of the United States. Not Luke Skywalker, but a college student from Wisconsin–Stout, Luke Helder, drove across Big Sky Country in May of 2002 to deposit pipe bombs in specific mailboxes. These bombs would injure dozens of rural residents and postal workers, creating "dots of violence" that, connected together, gave the map of America a smiley face (Sonner; Taylor). Luke's twisted form of MTV-terror may represent the first weapon of mass construction.

"'BLOWBACK'"

From here, we confront the issue of mass violence. This is not to draw an empirical distinction between mass violence and "micro-" or "local" violence, only to mark a place in the imaginary and geopolitical landscape for the "mass" in WMD. The undercurrents of the weapon of mass destruction form a double double-articulation—the pincers of a lobster.

The pincer is split between mass and micro. The mass and the micro overlap in certain ways, but there is still a commonality between the violence of war, the rolling of tanks, the dropping of bombs, or even nature's violent array of hurricanes, tornadoes, earthquakes, and plagues of disease. This is mass violence in terms of scope, impact, magnitude, and complete destruction—violence as an effect of annihilation and mass disaster—both inflicted by humans and by nature. This violence stands in contrast to, yet inseparable from, micro- or local instances of violence—abuse, rape, torture, murder, oppression, perhaps the very edges of biopower.

That is why blowback has to take on contours outside of American exceptionalism, the recidivism of global incorporation, the flip-side, the way the covert and the public merge through warfare and violence. The state's attempt to maintain a monopoly over the production and imaginary of WMDs ensures the constant ratcheting up the firewall of the thing being blown back. We cannot pick and choose the types of blowback spawned by widespread militarism; and, when prediction is feasible, it is just as likely that mutations have transformed these reflections of military training and equipment—these moments of blowback—and made them undetectable to the very apparatus that played an instrumental role in their creation. The juxtapositions of blowback scenarios are almost too intertwined to trace. These include the capture of a commercial airliner full of the fuel that funded the Saudi elite who funded Bin Laden who learned from the CIA how to eventually attack the CIA, as well as the construction of an oil pipeline through Afghanistan into Turkey, a "safe" country that can ban the Kurdish language and continue to practice genocide—the manifestation of micro-violence as a WMD—simply because Turkey generally cooperates with the United States and belongs to NATO. Hypocrisy can be blown back just as easily as ammunition. Historical amnesia should not allow the United States to forget its imperial legacy and responsibility. Did the United States not deploy biological and chemical warfare in Korea and Vietnam? What else could magnify the trope of blowback more than the dioxins strewn across the Vietnamese countryside in the form of agent orange—an agent that entered the chromosomes of the Vietnamese and the Americans to extend the effects of this mass violence to future generations through countless birth defects and still-born births?

Blowback must confer agency on the architects of imperialism rather than being an excuse for inevitable collateral damage. It is instructive to offer Kolko's conception of blowback in opposition to Schell's. Gabriel Kolko, Professor of Political Science at York University in Toronto and author of *An Anatomy of War*, mentions Afghanistan as an example of blowback, but he does not stop there. Kolko's account gestures to a critical history that would move through the cold war and the use of proxies, the drug war and U.S. intervention in Central and South America, and the World Trade Center attacks as an effect of decades of Western imperialism. Kolko outlines a genealogical perspective on blowback:

> Afghanistan was scarcely the only place that the CIA produced "blowback," its expression to describe its foreign proxies who then turn on the United States and its interests—the unintended consequences of covert operations. President Ronald Reagan's "war on terrorism" meant arms for the contras in Nicaragua, who also peddled drugs to raise funds. On the other hand, Manual Noriega, CIA asset who was commander of the Panamanian Defense Forces and became that tiny but strategic nation's ruler, eventually required a brief American invasion in late 1989 to end his huge drug operation. (17)

All modern U.S. presidents have contributed to, and confronted, various forms of blowback. In Kolko's account, the history of U.S. imperialism can be traced back decades, including wars in Korea and Vietnam. Given this legacy, it is no surprise that Kolko would describe September 11th as "virtually inevitable" and see the event as a sign that "the United States itself is now on war's front line—and it will remain there permanently" (17).

But is blowback simply an ever-rotating cycle? The D.C. sniper exemplifies the cycle, the superpredator learning from a community of delinquents how to create fear. Such paternalism is the hallmark of American exceptionalism—a separate facility for those juveniles not committing crimes in states with the death penalty, joining other rogues such as Iran, Iraq, Syria, Libya, Saudi Arabia, and a few others. Now the state pays for an expert defense for John Lee Malvo, a 17-year-old who has confessed to pulling the trigger in some of the shootings—a machinic companion to the rifle in the trunk of a car operated by John Mohammed. They used the blue highways of William Least Heat Moon's experiential pilgrimage as the conduit for the brutal shooting of dozens of people, only to slip through road blocks multiple times. Caught primarily because of their decision to use the telephone, and demonstrating that blowback can work in both ways—recidivism also means learning how to get caught— John and John Lee remained callous and indifferent. Why? Because the state removed John Mohammed's children in a custody dispute resolved against him on September 4th, 2001? Bin Laden opposes U.S. troops in Saudi Arabia? So the retaliation for September 11 (perhaps itself blowback) results in American troops all over Afghanistan, Pakistan, and Iraq? But does blowback have to be unanticipated? Should the United States refrain from funneling American soldiers into the middle of the bull's eye? Ultimately, the best way to avoid blowback is to stop spitting in the wind.

STRUGGLE VERSUS CAPTURE AND THE MISSING WMD

The New Republic featured a cover article in October of 2003 called, "Blowback: The Kay Report Demolishes Bush's WMD Claims." In this article, Bob Drogin uses blowback to refer to the administration's own commission confirming the fabrication of evidence that Iraq was hiding WMDs (23). The turnabout of the Kay Report demonstrates what Drogin calls "friendly fire." Whereas the Kay Report was initially held up as conclusive proof that Iraq possessed WMDs, it eventually became the document that would invalidate the Bush administration's claims and Colin Powell's presentation to the United Nations. Although the manipulation of the Kay Report is interesting, blowback should not be seen as so many other examples of friendly fire. Blowback is more than an American GI using a grenade on his own troops. Blowback must assume its full stature as part of the state's regime of violence. Deleuze and Guattari distinguish between the ritualization of violence in a blow-by-blow order (struggle) and the state's act of policing or legislating violence. State violence, for Deleuze and Guattari, "consists in capturing while simultaneously constituting a right to capture" (448). The process of capture links into blowback because it is implied by the initial justification of military action. The legitimacy implied by the act of policing includes the unavoidable effects of blowback. But what is being conceded? Is the collateral damage more severe than the terror being challenged? As its own regime of violence, state militarism and its blowback "is an incorporated, structural violence distinct from every kind of direct violence" (Deleuze and Guattari 448).

Blowback is not simply the blow-by-blow of friendly fire when the fire includes weapons of mass destruction. In earlier work, Ronald Greene and I have worked through the material trope of Balkanization, mapping its conservative deployment to erase difference but also its possibility for inclusion in a public address rhetorical protocol that would emphasize settler narratives or colonial and imperial narratives. This new path helps to posit that violence is inevitable in the human condition, rhetoric is violent, and the only alternative is continued struggle. Within these recognitions, though, critical rhetoric can resist regimes of violence that attempt to legitimize their own authority. Deploying rhetoric as and through a different historical context—a critical genealogy—is a method that applies here in the intersection between terrorism and the war on terrorism, for blowback in an era of omnipresent weapons of mass destruction must be tempered by context.

The rhetoric of these large-scale weapons will return (and has returned) in violent and unpredictable ways. How can the United States continue the obsessive search for Iraq's WMD capability when that capability has already diffused itself across the globe? Weapons of mass destruction are here, requiring us to turn our attention to the motivations behind their use. Without intent—an intent produced by training and the infusion of an ideology that rests on violence—the trigger is never pulled. When the CIA and the U.S. military point to blowback, we should read "imperial violence." Instead of watching the United States convert its failed and fabricated search into an intervention for democracy and self-determination, we should instead continue to scrutinize the rhetoric of WMD in the context of its catastrophic blowback.

WORKS CITED

Baudrillard, Jean. "The Spirit of Terrorism." *The South Atlantic Quarterly* 1.2 (Spring 2002): 403–15.
Butler, Judith. *Excitable Speech*. New York: Routledge, 1997.
Deleuze, Gilles, and Guattari, Felix. *A Thousand Plateaus: Capitalism and Schizophrenia*. Trans. B. Massumi. Minneapolis: U. of Minnesota P, 1987.
Derrida, Jacques. "Autoimmunity: Real and Symbolic Suicides." *Philosophy in a Time of Terror: Interviews with Jurgen Habermas and Jacques Derrida*. Eds. Giovanna Borradori et. al. Chicago: U of Chicago P, 2003. 85–196.
Drogin, Bob. "Blowback." *The New Republic* 27 Oct. 2003: 23–27.
Greene, Ronald Walter. "Another Materialist Rhetoric," *Critical Studies in Mass Communication* 15 (1998): 21–41.
Greene, Ronald Walter, and Kuswa, Kevin Douglas. "Governing Balkanization: Liberalism and the Rhetorical Production of Citizenship in the United States." *Controversia* 1.2 (Fall 2002): 16–33.
Kolko, Gabriel. *Another Century of War?* New York: New Press, 2002.
Nunberg, Geoffrey. "Bin Laden's Low-Tech Weapon." *New York Times*, 18 Apr. 2004, W4.
Schell, Jonathan. "Terror's Aftermath." *Los Angeles Times*, 16 Sept. 2001, M4.
Sonner, Scott. "Bombing Suspect Wanted to Make 'Smiley Face.'" *Guelph Mercury (Ontario)*, 10 May 2003, A11.
Sontag, Susan. "The Photographs *Are* Us." *New York Times Magazine*, 23 May 2004, 24–29, 42.
Taylor, J. Bombs Add to Postal Service Costs. *Omaha World Herald (Nebraska)*, 11 May 2002, D2.
Tsing, Anna. "The Global Situation." *Cultural Anthropology*, 15.3 (2000): 327–60.

30

Emotion and Community Rhetorics: Victim Impact Statements as Cultural Pedagogy

Lisa Langstraat
Colorado State University

> If we think of emotions as essential elements of human intelligence, rather than just as supports or props for intelligence, this gives us especially strong reasons to promote the conditions of well-being in a political culture: for this view entails that without emotional development, a part of our reasoning capacity a political creatures will be missing.
>
> —Martha Nussbaum (*Upheavals of Thought* 3)

Nussbaum's insistence that emotions are integral to reasoning and political engagement reverberates within current scholarship in emotion cultures, scholarship that focuses on what might be called the *politics of affect*—how emotions influence and are influenced by the power relations that shape our daily lives. This scholarship[1] shares several, integral objectives: to resist the tropes of interiority that have, for so long, dominated Western discussions of affect; to historicize cultural perceptions about and corporeal expressions of emotions; and to gain new understanding of what philosopher Alison Jaggar calls "emotional hegemony"—the processes through which dominant groups struggle to regulate the epistemic potential of emotions, thereby determining which affective expressions are valued or devalued, in particular contexts.

Studies of the politics of affect, particularly in the humanities and social sciences, have proliferated at nothing less than an explosive pace in the last decade; as the study of emotions exceeded the realms of neurobiology and psychology, it has found firm ground in the realm of rhetoric. Consider, for example, anthropologists Lila Abu-Lughod and Catherine Lutz, who argue that innovative research on the sociocultural dynamics of affect must resist separating emotion and discourse, as if emotion pertains to individual, private consciousness, while discourse represents the public realm of culture. "Emotion talk," they claim, "must be interpreted as in and about social life, rather than as veridically referential to some internal state" (11). Abu-Lughod and Lutz maintain that exploring the social character of affect requires scrutinizing both "discourses on emotion"—including popular, specialized and scientific theories about affect—and "emotional discourses"—situated expressions of emotionality (13).

In this chapter, I explore the discourses on emotion and the emotional discourses associated with a particular community rhetoric: Victim Impact Statements (VIS).[2] VIS are narratives of the emotional, physical, and financial suffering that victims and their families experience as a result of the commission of a crime. Presented in either written form (a statement usually attached to a pre-sentence investigation report) or in a formal allocution to a judge or jury at a sentencing hearing, VIS can inform restitution judgments and, in a growing number of jurisdictions, they can influence sentencing decisions when they are presented at penalty hearings in criminal trials. While the use of VIS varies from district to district, one feature of VIS is consistent: they inspire heated debate among legal professionals and victim advocates. At the foundation of these debates are questions about emotions: first, whether VIS introduce improper emotionality in legal proceedings, thereby challenging the rationality of jurisprudence; second, whether VIS contribute to the objectification of victims, insofar as victims' emotional discourses are commandeered in the interests of the state; third, whether VIS sanction particular emotional expressions and efface other, less sanctioned emotions; and finally, whether VIS can, in fact, engender a new affective politics in juridical practices.

VIS epitomize a shift in contemporary emotion culture, a move toward overt affective expression in "official" institutionalized settings, explicit cultural pedagogies of emotion, and unequivocal attempts to wrangle with the politics of affect and the role of emotion in legal practices. In this chapter, I analyze several districts' guidelines for the creation of VIS, and I argue that while VIS pose significant challenges to the emotional hegemony of traditional legal discourse, the counterhegemonic potential of VIS is radically curtailed by an ongoing ahistoricity, naturalization, and privatization of emotions in both legal discourses on emotion and emotional discourses in legal settings. I thus explore VIS as a kind of case study, a representative of community rhetorics that are engaged in vexing new affective politics. As I explore these issues, I hope to not only contribute to our understanding of emotion in community rhetorics, but to also suggest methods for understanding the politics of affect when real human lives and healing are at stake.

EMOTION AND THE LAW:
THE CHALLENGE OF VICTIM IMPACT STATEMENTS

Most people have questions about the psychological effects of the crime. The following are some suggestions on how to approach this issue:

1. *Your life is most likely different today than it was prior to the offense. Some typical responses include changes in routines, changes in employment, or relocation. Relationships not only change, but sometimes end as a result of the crime.*

2. *Have you suffered any anxiety as a result of the crime? Sometimes people have nightmares, inability to sleep, headaches, eat too much or too little, develop fears that cause them to change routines. Are you now in counseling because of the offense?*

3. *How has this affected your family and loved ones? Is anything out of the ordinary happening with those relationships? (Virginia Beach Division of Victim Services, "Appropriate Information for Victim Impact Statements")*

VIS do not simply invite an explicit discourse on emotions. They require it. Consider the Virginia Beach Division of Victim Services VIS guideline, quoted above. Like most

VIS guidelines, it emphasizes the import of articulating the emotional repercussions of the crime, especially its lingering effects on the victim's psychological well-being. While guidelines do vary from district to district, all share a central feature: Each functions pedagogically, presenting heuristics that teach appropriate emotional topics and expression for legal proceedings.

Perhaps the most influential of these heuristics are those included in the National Center for Victims of Crimes (NCVC) report, "Victim Impact Statement Models—Improving Communications between the Justice System and Our Nation's Crime Victims." The report, intended to provide examples of and instructions for VIS procedures for all U.S. districts, suggests four topics for VIS, including emotional trauma, physical injuries, financial costs, and victims' commentary on appropriate sentencing for defendants. However, as one would expect from the most influential victim's rights organization, NCVC primarily emphasizes victims' affective needs and expression. Advice on page layout for VIS suggest that the victim be given "ample space to write as little or as much as he or she feels is necessary to convey emotional wounds, concerns, and fears to the sentencing and paroling authorities" (par. 10). Indeed, the organization of the VIS form should privilege the emotional well-being of the victim, such that statements of emotional impact should precede physical and financial impact: "Some victims find it insulting that the state or paroling authority would be primarily focus [sic] on the financial impact as opposed to the emotional impact of the crime." These guides even attend to rhetorical decisions about style and word choice, which "should demonstrate appropriate respect to victims by showing support and sympathy, and by avoiding impersonal or 'bureaucratic' language."

Perhaps most representative of the NCVC's concern for victim's emotional welfare are the NCVC's model "impact questions," heuristics designed to help victims express the emotional impact of the crime. The NCVC insists that such heuristics facilitate *individualized* emotional expression: "The state should not ask narrowly focused, specific questions regarding the impact of crime. It, rather, should ask victims to write about these issues by using open-ended questions that allow victims to identify what is important, not what the criminal justice system considers to be of importance to the victim." Most districts comply with these recommendations, and many reproduce the NCVC model heuristics verbatim, as is the case with Mississippi's VIS guidelines:

1.   How has the crime affected you and those close to you? Please feel free to discuss your feelings about what has happened and how it has affected your general well-being. Has this crime affected your relationship with any family member, friend, co-workers and other people? As a result of this crime, if you or others close to you have sought any type of victim services, such as counseling by either a licensed professional, member of the clergy, or a community-sponsored support group, you may wish to mention this.

2.   What physical injuries or symptoms have you or others close to you suffered as a result of this crime?

3.   Has this crime affected your ability to perform your work, make a living, run a household, go to school or enjoy any other activities you previously performed or enjoyed? If so, please explain how these activities have been affected by this crime. (Mississippi Department of Corrections)

These guiding questions, these prompts, reflect NCVC's central goal for VIS: "Such statements provide a means for the Court to refocus its attention, at least momentarily, on the human cost of the crime. They also provide a way for the victim to participate in the criminal justice process."

Indeed, consider Sanders et al's summary of the primary objectives for VIS:

1.   giving victims a "voice" for therapeutic purposes;
2.   enabling the interests and/or views of victims to be taken into account in decision making;
3.   ensuring that victims are treated with respect by criminal justice agencies;
4.   reducing the stress for victims of criminal proceedings;
5.   increasing victim satisfaction with the criminal justice system;
6.   increasing victim co-operation, as a result of any of the above being fulfilled. (448–49)

This list of objectives clearly demonstrates that improving victims' *affective* relationships with the legal system is paramount. Indeed, VIS function to affectively reeducate victims, to enhance their feelings that the legal system understands and respects the trauma of crime on an intimate, individual level. Proponents of VIS insist that members of the legal profession—particularly judges—are similarly affectively reeducated: to dehumanize victims, to dissociate crimes from their human consequences, is seemingly impossible when humans stand before a judge and recount their trauma. In this sense, victims' rights organizations have inspired a dramatic change in social definitions of the victim insofar as they insist that crimes are perpetrated not only against the state but also against individuals. This reconception of the victim—from the abstract concept of the state or governmental authority to the concrete presence of an individual who is a member of an embodied, local community—entails a concomitant reconception of the emotional dynamics of the law.

Certainly *emotional discourses* have always influenced judicial processes. Explicit *discourses on emotion*, however, have been rare, often reserved for judges who counsel laypeople on the dangers of emotionalism; for example, it is not unusual in capital punishment trials for judges to caution juries about the differences between mercy and sympathy (the former admissible, the latter not). In such cases, overt polemics on emotion (e.g., sympathy) usually function to reaffirm the rationality of legal/ethical concepts (e.g., mercy). As legal scholar Susan Bandes notes, the law has been devoted to the "myth of an emotionless, cognition-driven legal system" ("Introduction" 6). Indeed, Martha Minow observes that a central, long-standing purpose for public legal systems is to establish emotional control: The law is the designated body for channeling and reeducating emotions that would otherwise take destructive forms in society ("Institutions and Emotions" 271). Yet the *doxa* of legal discourse has historically pitted rationality against passion, insisting that emotionality is inherently dangerous, corrupting the comforting equilibrium of legal logic. Long-standing convictions about the import of judicial dispassion and the law's rational capacity have made conversations about emotionality in law difficult, and while emotions are an always-already feature of all legal proceedings, they have been conscripted to designated areas. Bandes remarks that the law has accepted "a finite list of law-related emotions—anger, compassion, mercy, vengeance, hatred—and each emotion has a proper role and a fixed definition" such that emotion doesn't encroach on the "true preserve of law: reason" ("Introduction" 2). VIS, however, are an explicit acknowledgment not only of the emotional impact of crimes, but that such emotionality should—and does—influence legal (i.e., sentencing and restitution) judgments.

GOOD VICTIMS AND RETRIBUTIVE JUSTICE:
THE LIMITS OF EMOTIONAL COUNTERHEGEMONY

Without question, the very existence of VIS, along with carefully constructed VIS guidelines and victim impact procedures, challenge the emotional hegemony of traditional legal discourse. However, as is the case with any discursive/procedural system engaged in a vexing and monumental change of affective politics, that counterhegemonic force is radically curtailed when discourses on emotion perpetuate tropes of interiority by casting certain affective expressions as natural, beyond the influence of culture, and when those discourses are appropriated in ways that reproduce the status quo. While legal scholars have voiced a number of serious and legitimate concerns about VIS,[3] I will focus the remainder of this chapter on two: the kinds of emotions deemed appropriate in VIS guidelines and the processes through which those "appropriate emotions" define and delimit "good victims." Despite Supreme Justice Scalia's claim that VIS "lay out the full reality of the human suffering caused by the defendant" (qtd. in Bandes, "Empathy" 405), we know, of course, that such a reality is mediated by language and the demands of the rhetorical situation.

As Minow explains, "Victim stories risk trivializing pain [because they] often adhere to an unspoken norm that prefers narratives of helplessness to stories of responsibility, and tales of victimization to narratives of human agency and capacity" ("Stories" 32). While Minow is discussing the narrative conventions informing stories by victims of hate crimes, her critique is certainly applicable to VIS. Indeed, one of the most strident condemnations of VIS is that they encourage "stock narratives" that curtail emotional complexity and privilege the expression of vengeance. Certainly, despite the NCVC's suggestion that guidelines be open-ended to allow victims to voice their own, rather than the states', concerns, many of the VIS guidelines I have included here could be accused of "leading" questions that seem to represent "typical" traumatic response: anxiety, nightmares, need for counseling, changes in relationships. I would argue, however, that while any heuristic for emotional expression risks normalizing appropriate affect, if we recognize that cultural conventions and emotional narratives influence our affective experiences, then we must also recognize that there is no "outside" of cultural constructs of emotional expression. Nightmares, anxiety—all are, indeed, "common" responses to criminal acts, and only if we adhere to some privatized notion of the unique individuality of emotional experience can we find fault with such "common" reactions.

Perhaps a more viable critique is that VIS guidelines risk appropriating victims' emotional expression for more traditional legal ends. Consider the following excerpt from the Virginia Beach Victim Witness Office's guidelines:

Inappropriate Information

You will notice the preceding information deals only with the impact of the crime on you. *This is the only information that is allowable by the Code of Virginia.* Here is another that needs to be handled with care:

ANGER

It is normal that you may feel angry about the crime and the offender who caused the changes you have talked about. It is OK to state that you feel very angry about what has happened, however, this is not the forum to vent that anger. Please do not use profanity or name-calling.

Many victims have strong feelings about the appropriate sentence. The only person to make this decision is the judge and while it is appropriate to ask for a lenient or severe sentence, remember that the judge is bound by the Code of Virginia and must follow the law.

The preceding is mentioned because unsuitable language or information can lessen the power of your statement.

In this rather extraordinary example of an explicit pedagogy of emotion, we can see the liminal space into which many victims are thrust. The difference between "stating" anger and "venting" anger is paramount, and it is a difference teeming with difference—especially in light of classed and raced expressions of affect. This excerpt also, however, reflects the difficulty of overtly classifying "appropriate" emotional expression, especially when that expression is imported into a venue which privileges rationalism.

Indeed, As Edna Erez and Kathy Laster argue, the ideal of objectivity still controls the assumptions and actions of many legal professionals. In their interviews with legal practitioners in South Australia (where victims' rights reforms parallel our own), Erez and Laster found that most *prided* themselves on handling VIS with objectivity: "Practically all interviewees emphasized the need to present victim input in a clinical manner, devoid of emotionality" (538–39). Many legal professionals also argued that social workers and victim advocates "lacked objectivity" and identified with victims' trauma in their reports and managerial efforts, leading many lawyers and judges to dismiss their recommendations (538; see also Davis and Smith).

Related to the problem of law professionals' training to resist and distrust emotional discourses is the issue of assumptions about who qualifies as a legitimate victim. As Jennifer Wood contends, "The irony of victim impact statements is that in the interest of giving victims a voice in the legal system in order to tell the stories of their suffering, many victims of crime may be silenced because their stories do not fit the dominant narrative of innocence that the Court's opinion imposes" (165). The "commonsense" conception of victims as vulnerable and innocent often reflects class-, race- and sex-based stereotypes (159). Middle-class, straight, white victims are normalized in many sample VIS, and victims who do not "fit" the category of innocence—victims of gay bashing or victims of domestic violence who have chosen not to leave their abusers—are not considered credible VIS narrators, and their suffering is rendered illegitimate. Such normalizing features operate subtly and overtly in many VIS heuristics. For example, the Minnesota Center for Crime Victim Services suggests that victims

Consider the following facts when writing or speaking to the court:

—[…] Your feelings about people who commit crime;

—Effect of sudden death to remaining family members—spouse, children, parents, siblings—loss of hopes, dreams, companionship, financial security; and

—The victim's accomplishments, awards, and activities—*photographs or family portraits may be helpful.* (emphasis in original)

While most of these prompts privilege the traditional nuclear family structure, the final recommendation here is particularly striking and clearly favors a particular kind of victim.

Moreover, VIS are often used to forward traditional features of retributive justice. Consider the 1997 trial of Timothy McVeigh in Denver. As *Nation* columnist Bruce Shapiro explains, the victim impact testimony at the trial received considerable media attention, attention focused on victims' opportunity for "closure." Yet those who took anti-capital punishment stances were not invited to testify at the trial; since the prosecution determines which VIS can be heard, and since the prosecution in this case was requesting the death penalty, those victims opposed to capital punishment were silenced. Shapiro contends that victims were relegated to the "narrow role as prosecutor's aides" and observes that "the interest of a victim and interest of the state are not necessarily the same" (par. 8).

Certainly, VIS procedures can objectify victims and their trauma in the service of a retributive form of justice structured to maintain the status quo. But, unlike many legal scholars and citizens, I am not willing to admit defeat. VIS' *are* valuable forms of affective (re)education, and they do hold much promise for revamping the affective politics of the law. Reaching that promise is as vexing and complicated as any other sweeping change of zeitgeist, but perhaps the most viable strategy for reaching VIS' counterhegemonic potential is precisely the kind of analysis I've conducted here. At base of this analysis is the import of understanding any discourse on emotion and emotional discourse within its historical, cultural context. Too often, as VIS are presented as opportunities for affective therapy, for "closure," they adhere to a form of a repressive hypothesis: as if, because legal discourse has eschewed overt emotionality in favor of an illusory rationality, just giving voice to feelings to an "authoritative" audience (judges, juries, lawyers, victim advocates) will, indeed, provide "closure" to victims and will lead to greater understanding and compassion on the part of legal professionals. Such an assumption—that merely expressing affect will evoke positive consequences—reflects the naivete of any privatized, acultural, ahistorical notion of emotions. And there is no room for naivete when human lives and the power of legal discourse are at stake.

NOTES

1. For a review of current scholarship on affect in the humanities and social sciences, see Scott McLemee's recent *Chronicle of Higher Education* article, "Getting Emotional."
2. In 1982, the Presidential Task Force of Victims of Crime recommended that crime victims be given an integral voice in criminal proceedings. By 1984, twelve states had passed victim impact laws, and by 1997, all fifty states had instituted provisions authorizing some form of victim participation in judicial processes (Davis and Smith 32). Official use of Victim Impact Statements and guidelines for those statements vary considerably from jurisdiction to jurisdiction; in some districts, VIS are used exclusively for discerning financial restitution. In other districts, VIS are presented at sentencing hearings and are often presented to judges as pleas for specific kinds or durations of sentences. See McCormick for a full history of victims' rights movements in the United States.
3. In 1987, in *Booth v. Maryland*, the Supreme Court ruled VIS unconstitutional in capital cases, arguing that VIS serve to "inflame the jury and divert it from the relevant evidence concerning the crime and its defendant" (482 U.S. 508). That decision was overturned in 1991 with *Payne v. Tennessee* (501 U.S. 808). These decision have led to considerable and heated discussion of VIS in light of death penalty issues (see Bandes, "Empathy"; Pillsbury; Sanders et al; Sigler; Wood).
4. For provocative and comprehensive discussions of the role of influences of race, class, sex, and gender on VIS reception, see Bandes, "Empathy" and Wood.

WORKS CITED

Bandes, Susan. "Empathy, Narrative and Victim Impact Statements." *University of Chicago Law Review*. 63.2 (1996): 361–12.

—, ed. "Introduction." *The Passions of Law*. New York: New York UP, 1999. 1–18.

Criminal Justice Intervention, State of Minnesota. "What a Victim Impact Statement Should Include." 24 May 2003 < http://www.letswrap.com/legal/impact.htm>.

Davis, Robert C., and Barbara Smith. "Victim Impact Statements and Victim Satisfaction: An Unfulfilled Promise?" *Journal of Criminal Justice* 22.1 (1994): 1–12.

Erez, Edna. and Kathy Laster. "Neutralizing Victim Reform: Legal Professionals' Perspectives on Victims and Impact Statements." *Crime and Delinquency* 45.4 (1999): 530–53.

Jaggar, Alison. "Love and Knowledge: Emotion in Feminist Epistemology. *Women and Reason*. Ed. Kathleen Okruhlik and Elizabeth D. Harvey. Ann Arbor: U of Michigan P, 1992. 115–42.

Lutz, Caherin A., and Lila Abu-Lughod, eds. "Introduction: Emotion, Discourse and the Politics of Everyday Life." *Language and the Politics of Emotion*. Cambridge UP, 1990. 1–23.

McCormack, Robert J. "United States Crime Victim Assistance: History, Organization and Evaluation." *Victims of Crime and the Victimization Process*. Eds. Marilyn McShane and Frank P. Williams III. New York: Garland, 1997. 197–209.

McLemee, Scott. "Getting Emotional." *Chronicle of Higher Education*. Feb 21, 2003. A14–A16..

McShane, Marilyn D., and Frank P. Williams III. "Radical Victimology: A Critique of the Concept of Victim in Traditional Victimology." *Victims of Crime and the Victimization Process*. Eds. Marilyn McShane and Frank P. Williams III. New York: Garland, 1997. 210–24.

Minnesota Center for Crime Victim Services. "Victim Impact Statement." 24 May 2003 <http://www.letswrap.com/legal/impact.htm>.

Minow, Martha. "Institutions and Emotions: Redressing Mass Violence." *The Passions of Law*. Ed. Susan Bandes. New York: New York UP, 1999. 265–83.

—. "Stories in Law." *Law's Stories: Narrative and Rhetoric in the Law*. Eds. Peter Brooks and Paul Gewirtz. New Haven: Yale UP, 1996. 24–36.

Mississippi Department of Corrections, Division of Victim Services. "Victim Impact Statement." 21 May 2003 <http://www.mdoc.state.ms.us/Victim%20Impact%20Statement.htm>.

National Center for Victims of Crime. "Victim Impact Statement Models—Improving Communications between the Justice System and Our Nation's Crime Victims." 24 May 2003 <http:///www.ncvc.org/resources/reports/impactstatements/models.html>.

Nussbaum, Martha. "Equity and Mercy." *Philosophy and Public Affairs*. 22 (1993): 83–125.

—. *Upheavals of Thought: The Intelligence of Emotions*. Cambridge: Cambridge UP, 2001.

Pillsbury, Samuel. "Emotional Justice: Moralizing the Passions of Criminal Punishment." *Cornell Law Review* 74 (1989): 65–710, 701.

Sanders, Andrew, et al. "Victim Impact Statements: Don't Work, Can't Work." *Criminal Law Review* (June 2001): 447–58.

Shapiro, Bruce. "Victim's Rights—and Wrongs." Salon Magazine 13 June 1997. 12 May 2004 <Salonmagazine.com/newsreal.html>.

Sigler, Mary. "The Story of Justice: Retribution, Mercy, and the Role of Emotions in the Capital Sentencing Process." *Law and Philosophy* 19 (2000): 339–67.

U.S. Department of Justice, Office for Victims of Crime. *Impact Statements: A Victim's Right to Speak, A Nation's Responsibility to Listen*. 24 May 2003 <http://www.ojp.usdoj.gov/ovc/help/impact/impact.htm>.

Virginia Beach, Virginia Victim Witness Office, . "Victim Impact Statement: Background and Helpful Hints for Preparation." 24 May 2003 <http://www.virginia-beachva.us/courts/oca/vw_impct.htm>.

Wood, Jennifer K. "Refined Raw: The Symbolic Violence of Victims' Rights Reforms." *College Literature* 26.1 (1999): 150–69.

31

Rhetorically Contained:
The Construction and Incorporation
of Difference in *Will & Grace*

Danielle M. Mitchell
Pennsylvania State University—Fayette

> The same hip public that revels in genderfuck also lauds Eminem, convinced by critics that there's something heroic about his harangues, something playful in the standing ovation he gets for shouting: "Hate fags? The answer's yes!" Here, the feelings liberals have taught themselves to deny are fully exercised. [And w]hatever guilt might attend that release is defused by the queer who attests to its harmlessness.
>
> —Richard Goldstein *(The Attack Queers* 4)

In a culture suffused with such blatantly homophobic discourse as the harangues of Eminem, NBC's Emmy-award-winning[1] prime-time show *Will & Grace* appears socially progressive. Until recently, for instance, it was the only first-run network situation comedy to feature a gay male as its lead character. It was also the only network show to depart from a heterocentric narrative that merely includes one gay character among many straight characters. Two of the show's four main characters are gay (Will, played by Eric McCormack, and Jack, played by Sean Hayes), and one of the female characters (Karen, played by Megan Mullally) is tenuously heterosexual at best. Moreover, the narrative includes gay bars, inside jokes, and blatant references to same-sex intimacy that abandon heterosexuality as the narrative default. With Max Mutchnick at the helm, then, the co-creator and executive producer who says that he feels a responsibility to the gay community to present realistic and positive images of cultural difference (Kaye), *Will & Grace* is a far cry from a hateful homophobic harangue. Rather, it is a business venture[2] and a public relations vehicle through which Mutchnick attempts to challenge a heteronormative television industry and alter unfavorable cultural understandings of sexual difference, thereby effecting social change.

Even given the significant distinctions between the ideological work of *Will & Grace* and the harangues referred to in the headnote, however, there is a potential point of commonality that I would like to explore in this paper—and that is how the TV program provides an opportu-

275

nity for viewers to exercise oppressive values of homophobia, racism, sexism, and classism. Dismissing the important work of *Will & Grace* is not my goal. But I do want to argue that the program be understood differently, as a contradictory site, rather than an exemplar of progressive politics. Reframing the show in this way is particularly important. In addition to the fact that its representations reach millions of viewers each Thursday night, even each day given its syndication, *Will & Grace* mirrors a larger process of sociopolitical negotiation central to current political debates. Namely, I believe the program relies on a "rhetoric of incorporation" that creates an image of socially progressive politics through its inclusion and apparent advocacy on behalf of the Other while actually functioning to contain transformative change.

To explore the program and establish a space for understanding its contradictory work, the remainder of this essay will be broken into three sections: the show's apolitical rhetorical stance and its use of homophobic humor; the construction of the gay male in relation to issues of class, patriarchy, and race; and the show's relationship to the paradigm of incorporation.

THE APOLITICAL STANCE OF COMEDY

Will & Grace's success rests on its rhetorical savvy. In a cultural climate where approximately "2% of the 540 lead or supporting" television characters are estimated to be gay (Shister, qtd. in Walters 103), where nonheterosexuality is deployed as a key issue in local, state, regional, and national politics, and where great pressure to increase lesbian, gay, bisexual, and transgender (LGBT) visibility in mainstream sites is applied by any number of advocacy groups, the program is able to appeal to the myriad values of a broad viewing audience. One way it does so is by creating an apolitical rhetorical stance.

Representatives of both *Will & Grace* and the NBC network have gone to great lengths to construct the gay-inclusive yet apolitical stance potentially offensive only to "extremists" (Natale 2).[3] Take the comments of network ad buyer Aaron Cohen, for example. Whereas "Ellen really wanted to make a statement" in her sit-com about the political and emotional legitimacy of same-sex relationships, he says, that's "far from what they do on 'Will and Grace'" (Freeman 35). McCormack underscores this point, asserting that *Will & Grace* is "not a political show" (Lipton 81). And as Debra Messing (who plays Grace) explains, "it's not a gay show," either (Natale 2). In fact, the program is not about gay issues at all, says NBC's programming chief, Warren Littlefield; it is about the relationship between a man and a woman (Natale 2). The title's work to heterosexualize the program is thus reiterated via publicity that simultaneously disavows any intent to produce a counter-hegemonic discourse of sexuality and constructs *Will & Grace* as an apolitical comedy about friends.

Perhaps this ideological positioning is a predictable maneuver given the show's rhetorical context. Any hope to successfully mainstream sexual difference into popular culture requires being accountable to multiple demographics as well as to pertinent genre conventions. Thus, in the case of *Will & Grace*, LGBT persons must feel adequately represented, straights must feel comfortable, and viewers must laugh. Rhetorical success in this scenario is based on what Sarah Schulman summarizes as a program's ability to "address [the] emotional need [of Others] to be accepted while selling a palatable image of homosexuality to heterosexual consumers that meets their need to have their dominance secured" (146). Developing an apolitical stance can be an effective strategy in this scenario. It creates LGBT visibility in prime-time television while also delimiting the sociopolitical agenda to the entertainment that results from such inclusion. But there is more at stake in the construction of an apolitical ethos than appeasing homophobic fears and securing an audience. In addition to stalling criticisms of *Will & Grace*'s inclusive content by separating the show from any political intent, the apolitical stance also de-emphasizes the show's ideologically conservative discourse. In other words, it's as if neither the inclusion of gay characters nor the homophobic humor should be taken too seriously because the show is an apolitical comedy—mere entertainment.

Yet the humor is no less political than is the show. And the show does include homophobic content, as the comedic structure of gay bashing is central to its rhetorical appeals. As Mullally asserts, for example, homophobia is a given: "the gay bashing is built into the show—[viewers] don't even have to do it. [...] The characters gay-bash each other" (O'Donnell 73, 75). It is not the homophobic humor itself that is the most troubling aspect of all of this, however. What's particularly disturbing is how humor that "manages to be rather offensive, claiming to offer realistic portrayals of gay men who [...] do little more than call each other 'homo' and 'queer' while mincing about," also happens to have "its deceptive charms (it feels smart)" (Wilonsky 2). I am certainly not in possession of the comedy de-coder ring that can definitively interpret the program's humor and once and for all ascertain its social effects. But while LGBT viewers may interpret the humor as camp, I fear that it works in broader audiences to secure the superiority of heterosexuality even as gayness is mainstreamed. As a number of my students recently reminded me, for instance, the extent to which they watch the program is dependent upon the extent to which gays are made fun of—the extent to which they (as viewers) are enabled to remain within homophobic discourse. To make matters worse, gay characters sanction this exercise of homophobia by normalizing verbal gay bashing as harmless, funny discourse.

STEREOTYPES AND THE CULTURAL IMAGINATION

Because a thorough explication of the program's characters is not possible here, I would like to focus specifically on how the program's construction of gayness tends to rely on stereotypes that efface sociohistorical realities of class, sex, and race.

Although close friends, Will and Jack are generally understood as foils for one another. Will is a well-employed, upwardly mobile, gender-appropriate-in-appearance man who many viewers could not tell was gay when the program first aired. Jack, however, is a frequently unemployed "screaming queen" who embodies stereotypes so well that Will says he is identifiably gay to both "dead men and dogs" (Holleran 65). While gender is certainly a significant issue here, so is the concept of gay affluence. At first glance, only Will appears to display the trappings of economic privilege. He is a successful attorney with a lucrative career; as such, he conforms to images of the conspicuously consuming gay man who has little to worry about other than where to spend his excess income. Yet both Will and Jack enjoy virtually the same lifestyle. That is to say that they eat in the same restaurants, go to the same bars, shop at the same stores, work out at the same gym, and live in the same building. Even though Jack may be shown on occasion taking money from his son or "dining and dashing" to avoid paying a bill, the ease with which he lives above his means renders him, too, suggestive of gay affluence—a prominent myth that much scholarship has debunked.[4] "Gay and bisexual men earn from 17 to 28 percent less than similarly qualified heterosexual men," according to economist M. V. Lee Badgett, for instance (45). And there are as many as three million "impoverished lesbians and gay men [living] in the United States" (Hennessy 140).

Will & Grace should not be expected to represent all of the social conditions and types of diversity associated with LGBT persons. But the perpetuation of economic myths seems counterproductive if the goal is to depict reality and to benefit an LGBT community living in a country where, among other things, federal legislation still allows employees to be fired based on their sexuality or gender performance.[5] Moreover, for all of the program's inclusive potential, by producing "a [narrative] world of well-dressed white gay men in which both lesbians and persons of color are introduced fleetingly and as the objects of derision" (Walters 103, 110), *Will & Grace* reproduces sexist and racist inequities that have plagued the LGBT community for years.

Lacking a recurring lesbian character, for instance, the show often relies on guest appearances by women such as Ellen DeGeneres, Rosie O'Donnell, and Sandra Bernhard to create images of lesbianism. Though Karen goes far to disrupt heterosexuality and to establish a bisexual stance, the one episode that specifically features lesbians has been soundly drubbed as so stereotypical and venomous that it is being re-edited for syndication. And no gay characters of color have been written into the show.[6] In fact, the one recurring character of color is Rosario, Karen's Salvadoran maid (played by Shelley Morrison).

Given her prominent position as *the* racial and working-class Other on the program, Rosario is a particularly important figure. There are times when the narrative makes her lack of power in the world quite clear, such as when Karen threatened her with deportation, had her arrested by airport security, and married her off to Jack. Karen is also just as likely to refer to Rosario as Maid as she is to call her by name. Even though these images are often softened by Karen's efforts to sexualize the relationship or to confide in Rosie as if she is a friend, the bottom line is that Rosario is a possession to be bought, sold, and wagered. Karen does, in fact, actually lose her in a game of pool.

But what I find interesting about the relationship is not its inequity, but how the narrative de-emphasizes the inequity through the deployment of humor. Rosario's sarcastic quips often work to establish a sense of intellectual superiority and independence, for example. Whether she is calling Karen a "drunken fool" or an "ass," she repeatedly uses witty, yet hostile, repartee to belittle and ridicule her employer. Asserting her agency via this verbal sparring, Rosario's humor suggests an ability to put Karen in her place and to equalize power relations. Yet this is an illusory power that does more to assuage viewer anxiety about class exploitation than to alter systemic relations of power. Understanding sarcasm as a means to virtual-ly equalize inequity, for instance, makes power itself a linguistic force, a matter of discourse. While this construction may pacify viewers by assuring them that she (and they) can successfully confront and undermine exploitation through the deployment of humor, this makes resistance a matter of personal perspective and individual action rather than a systemic critique of material conditions. Thus, such humor can deflect analyses of the systemic forces that construct Rosario as a commodity in the first place.

CONTAINING DIFFERENCE:
THE FUNCTION OF INCLUSION ON *WILL & GRACE*

To be clear, as a multifaceted cultural artifact, *Will & Grace* is neither wholly subversive of nor entirely complicit in hegemonic relations of power. Rather, like the larger culture in which it is produced, the program is a site of contradiction, a site of ideological contest where values, practices, and social norms are enacted, challenged, and negotiated. But the program's challenges to the prime-time heterosexual norm do not perforce produce anti-racist, anti-sexist, or anti-heterosexist counterknowledges that can be used to alter inequitable social conditions. In fact, the inclusion of sexual difference may enable the program to more effectively secure systemic social inequity because it appears progressive— because, as Robert Wilonsky suggested, it "feels smart," and it presents new kinds of characters on TV. But Raymond Williams's concept of incorporation provides a way to understand this phenomenon.

According to Williams, social change is a dynamic process of negotiation through which residual formations (such as heterosexism) and emergent knowledges (such as the fluidity of sexuality) collide, forcing changes to values and practices. As a process, however, incorporation mediates this collision, enabling change to take place while also delimiting what sort of change is possible. Thus, through incorporation, seemingly oppositional ideas can be absorbed and then re-deployed to reproduce hegemonic relations. As I suggested in previous sections, this framework is applicable to *Will & Grace*. It pushes the industry envelope, for instance, while also including gay subjects who are least likely to offend audiences. Its rhetoric of humor articulates gayness, but it does so through—not in opposition to—exploitative ideologies. By securing logics integral to systemic inequity, the program directs and manages social change such that oppression is actually reproduced through the inclusion of difference and the expansion of socially acceptable relationships. This is the upshot of the rhetoric of incorporation: it persuades us to consent to the perpetuation of oppressive ideologies and to the containment of transformative social change because they appear as something else. Consequently, programs like *Will & Grace* can appear to offer "recognition, acknowledgment, and thus a form of acceptance" through their inclusion of difference, while actually working to secure a "new phase of the dominant culture" (Williams 123, 125).

I would like to suggest that the rhetoric of incorporation provides an analytical concept for understanding other cultural sites of inclusion, as well. If we analyze same-sex marriage, for instance, we may come to understand it not as a simple assertion of equality, but, like *Will & Grace*, an ambivalent practice that could actually secure values central to the maintenance of systemic inequity. Same-sex marriage undoubtedly addresses critical social, personal, and familial needs. Hospital visitation and decision making, social security and inheritance rights, adoption privileges, and health care protections that accompany marriage are integral to the well-being of many couples and their children. These practical benefits of legalization ought not be dismissed. But linking such benefits specifically to marriage further entrenches the socioeconomic privileges afforded the nuclear family and further legitimizes the privatization of social services and rights. It is this ability to contain alternative methods of ordering social relations and understanding "intimacy," as well as same-sex marriage's promise to benefit most those persons in the upper middle class, that Judith Stacey says are responsible for the legalization movement getting as far as it has in this age of reactionary politics. Hegemonic ideology, she suggests, is thus being made to work through what appears as a progressive politics of inclusion and equality. In conclusion, it is only through a complex understanding of the contradictions that inhere in sites such as *Will & Grace* or same-sex marriage that it becomes possible to envision and produce a different social reality—a different paradigm of social order that may promote equity on a broader scale.

NOTES

1. Emmy Awards have been presented to the program and its actors over the last several years, and the show was honored by the Gay and Lesbian Alliance Against Defamation as the "best comedy for portrayals of gays" after its first season.
2. The business aspect of the program cannot be underestimated. Lifetime arranged a syndication deal in 2000, for instance, that guaranteed a fee of $600,000 per half hour of *Will & Grace* aired on the channel. Deals have been worked out with at least two other stations as well.
3. One prominent exception occurred on December 8, 2002, when a political advertisement included the main ensemble urging viewers to vote against California's Knight Initiative, a ballot item intended to curtail the rights of LGBT persons.
4. Scholars such as Alexandra Chasin and Fred Fejes trace the myth of gay affluence to the 1980s and 1990s, when several advertising firms associated gay identity with higher than average earnings in order to lure corporate clients with the promise of an economically powerful yet "un-

tapped minority market" (Lorch, qtd. in Chasin 32). See Altman, Badgett, Chauncey, Evans, Gluckman, Lukenbill, Peñaloza, and Vaid for more extensive analyses of the link between consumerism and the development of gay and lesbian identity, community, and market power.

5. The Employment Non-Discrimination Act (ENDA) remains in committee, years after its initial presentation before Congress. In the absence of federal protection from discrimination based on sexual orientation in public sector employment, LGBT persons must depend on antidiscrimination laws developed by individual states and localities.

6. At one point, Gregory Hines did a series of guest appearances as Will's employer and Grace's romantic interest. Jack assumed a black identity in "My Uncle the Car" when his parentage was under debate; his identity was based on allusions to black culture rather than an articulation of the realities of race politics, however. This should come as no surprise, of course, since Jack is the man who once made fun of his Asian date, joking about how "funny he talks."

WORKS CITED

Altman, Dennis. *The Homosexualization of America*. New York: St. Martin's, 1982.
Badgett, M. V. Lee. *Money, Myths, and Change: The Economic Lives of Lesbians and Gay Men*. Chicago: U of Chicago P, 2001.
Chasin, Alexandra. *Selling Out: The Gay and Lesbian Movement Goes to Market*. New York: Palgrave, 2000.
Chauncey, George. *Gay New York: Gender, Urban Culture, and the Making of the Gay Male World, 1890–1940*. New York: Basic, 1994.
Evans, David T. *Sexual Citizenship: The Material Construction of Sexualities*. New York: Routledge, 1993.
Fejes, Fred. "Advertising and the Political Economy of Lesbian/Gay Identity." *Sex and Money: Feminism and Political Economy in the Media*. New York: Routledge, 1995. 196–208.
Freeman, Michael. "For TV Characters, It's OK to be Gay." *Electronic Media* 18.38 Sept. 18, (2000): 3, 35. 14 Dec. 2001 <http://newfirstsearch.oclc.org>.
Gluckman, Amy, and Betsy Reed. *Homo Economics: Capitalism, Community, and Lesbian and Gay Life*. New York: Routledge, 1997.
Goldstein, Richard. *The Attack Queers: Liberal Society and the Gay Right*. New York: Verso, 2002.
Hennessy, Rosemary. *Profit and Pleasure: Sexual Identities in Late Capitalism*. New York: Routledge, 2000.
Holleran, Andrew. "The Alpha Queen." *The Gay and Lesbian Review* 7.1 (Summer 2000): 65–66.
Kaye, Lori. "Where Are the Funny Girls? This Season a Growing Number of Sitcoms Celebrated Gay Males—but TV Lesbians Were Confined to the Tears and Trials of Drama." *The Advocate* (Jan. 16, 2001): 85–89. 14 Dec. 2001 <www.advocate.com/html/stories/828_9/828_9tvlesbians.asp>.
Lipton, Michael. "Happily Married Eric McCormack Plays a Gay Lawyer." *Peoples Weekly* 26 Oct. (1998): 81.
Lukenbill, Grant. *Untold Millions: Positioning Your Business for the Gay and Lesbian Consumer Revolution*. New York: HarperCollins, 1995.
Natale, Richard. "Will Power." *The Advocate* (Sept. 15, 1998): 32–35. 17 Jan. 2002 <http://www.advocate.com/html/stories/799/799_98_fallpreview.asp>.
O'Donnell, Rosie. "Girl Talk." *Rosie* 129.5 (March 2002): 68–74.
Schulman, Sarah. *Stage Struck: Theater, AIDS and the Marketing of Gay America*. Durham: Duke UP, 1998.
Stacey, Judith. "Married to the Market: The Haves and Have Nots of Contemporary Conjugal Politics." School of Liberal Arts, and Women's and Gender Studies Program. Duquesne University, Pittsburgh. 5 Feb. 2004.
Walters, Suzanna. *All the Rage: The Story of Gay Visibility in America*. Chicago: U of Chicago P, 2001.
Will & Grace. Max Mutchnick and David Kohan, Producers. National Broadcasting Company.
Williams, Raymond. *Marxism and Literature*. New York: Oxford UP, 1977.
Wilonsky, Robert. "Blow Up the Box." *Phoenix New Times* 28 Dec. (2000). 16 Aug. 2001 <http://www.phoenixnewtimes.com/issues/2000-12-28/stuff.html>.

32

When Agonism Is Agony: Thomas Sloane, Controversia, and Political Discourse

Patricia Roberts-Miller
University of Texas at Austin

In *Donne, Milton, and the End of Humanist Rhetoric*, Thomas Sloane implicitly calls for a return to the pedagogical practice of controversia, or what is sometimes called pro-con argumentation. In *On the Contrary*, Sloane makes this call explicit. Sloane defines controversia as the play of both sides in the invention of one's argument. Not simply the presence of both sides, as in many argumentation readers, nor even the consideration of both in order to predict, and preempt, the opposition's argument, this is, he argues, a way of thinking. It is, he claims, a skeptical search for contingent solutions to issues of common concern.

On the whole, as is clear from how often I cite *On the Contrary* and *Donne, Milton, and the End of Humanist Rhetoric* in my own work, I agree with Sloane's argument that we should revive some form of pro-con argumentation. Whereas Sloane's major line of argument is that this is what humanist rhetoric really is and was, I would say that the same case can be made on the grounds that such thinking is absolutely necessary for democracy.

To make that argument, I would simply compare two debates: the 1787–88 controversy over the proposed constitution, typically called the Federalist-Antifederalist debate, and the recent decision and public wrangle (note that I do not call it a controversy) over the invasion of Iraq.

The three men generally called "the federalists," John Jay, Alexander Hamilton, and James Madison, were committed to getting the New York citizenry to support the constitution. They were not engaged in open-ended, consociational exploration of an issue; this was not the ideal speech situation. Whether their discourse can even be characterized as "good faith" argumentation is, for me, up for question, given their willingness to leave crucial terms undefined (e.g., *interest*), alternately invoke and dismiss the same premises (as in regard to human nature), and rely on arguments which can charitably be called casuistical (such as Madison's defense of the three-fifths compromise, or more relevantly, Hamilton's argument that a Bill of Rights was unnecessary). They wanted to persuade their readers to support the constitution, and it often appears that they would make any argument necessary to achieve that end. But, their controversial rhetorical training continually manifests itself—while not above taking serious swipes at the motives, intelligence, and even character of their opponents, in general, they do accurately represent the Antifederalists' arguments; specious as their responses sometimes are, the Federalists do respond to those arguments in the numerous prolepses scattered throughout; finally, and most important, Madison did eventually grant the justice of the strongest Antifederalist argument and acquiesce to a Bill of Rights.

Thus, the agonism of the public controversy did not cause one side or the other to win, nor did it lead to some kind of splitting the difference. The recurring topos of the need for a Bill of Rights, and the inability of the Federalists to dismiss that argument, meant that, while they did achieve their end (aided by some business-as-usual skullduggery), they had to concede on an issue of real principle.

It is quite possible that this concession was due not to highmindedness on the part of the Federalists but the demands of their audience; the very readers whom they were trying to persuade were themselves well-trained in pro-con argumentation. It may well be that the Federalists had to represent the Antifederalist arguments accurately, and had to respond to them as best they could, and even eventually had to concede on important points because their audience was reading both sides. The audience, therefore, would have recognized and been outraged by misrepresentation or evasion. It was easy for their readers to see the best arguments on both (really, various) sides because the newspapers of the day printed them, in full.

Compare this to the issue of the Iraq invasion. The Bush administration never granted that there was an informed, intelligent, patriotic opposition to their policies and never responded to the legitimate counterarguments. Precommitted to the invasion, Bush was willing to make any arguments that might work to support it. The Bush administration was equally committed to misrepresenting, if acknowledging at all, the opposition.

There were numerous arguments against the invasion: that Hussein was disarming, or did not have weapons of mass destruction, that he was not responsible for 9/11, that we would be mired in another Vietnam, that we should wait until we had the support of the United Nations, or that the United States could not manage the occupation of two countries. But Bush's 2003 State of the Union Address has *one* prolepsis: "Some have said we must not act until the threat is imminent." There may have been war opponents who made that argument; I don't claim to have read all of them, but I read a fair number, and I never saw that one.

Yet, the American people did not rise up in outrage; some did, certainly—the opponents of the war—but the general reading (and voting) public did not, and does not, demand of its rhetors that they represent fairly and respond legitimately to the opposition arguments. The general reading and voting public does not generally know what the opposition arguments are.

Certainly, the media are incapable of controversia, and, with the dropping of the Fairness Doctrine, governmental policy no longer supports it. People like Eric Altermann, Noam Chomsky, Edward Herman, and even George Orwell have argued that various qualities of the capitalist media preclude public discourse informed by diverse points of view; that may or may not be the first, final, or even any cause of the lack of controversia. There is, however, at least one other fairly obvious cause: the American public does not demand a controversial public debate because they have not been taught to. It seems to me that a fair amount of the blame for this situation must be laid squarely at the feet of the very people who teach the general voting public how to argue and what argument is.

We have met the enemy, in other words.

Thus far, it may seem, I have wholeheartedly endorsed Sloane's argument—my thesis seems to be that we should incorporate, if not debate, some form of disputation into all argument courses, as such a pedagogy will facilitate (if not cause) better political discourse. But there are several reasons to doubt that conclusion.

First, while Sloane is correct to note that the humanist understanding of language does resemble deconstruction (*On the Contrary* 65), attempting to teach that understanding through pro-con debate makes it a version of what is generally called "negative deconstruction." Negative deconstruction takes an opposition, usually one with privilege, and simply flips the privilege, leaving the opposition more or less intact. In a debate, unlike in humanist rhetoric, the sense of opposition not only remains, but is further strengthened at the end of the discourse—one side or the other may win, but the very method of argument accepts as a principle that questions can be answered in one of two ways. Sloane has dismissed this criticism as nit-picking, noting, in an aside, that the difference between two sides and many is trivial, but I will insist upon it.

That students' only experience with anything like pro-con thinking is likely to be in formal debate, or in the opinion pages of papers that have two columnists, or on television programs that claim to represent the political spectrum by having stooges from the Democrats and Republicans means that students are shifted away from the contingent, particular, and consequential thinking which serves democracy best. It means, further, that partisan arguments make sense: if there are two sides to an issue, and the Democrats represent one and the Republicans the other, then one can criticize the antiwar stance on the grounds that the Democrats' welfare policy is bad.

Second, one of the frequent consequences of debate training is to teach people to mistrust reason. Sloane discusses this objection as the age-old accusation of sophistry; John Locke calls it wrangling; James Crosswhite uses the Socratic term of logomachia. All of them seem similar to me, as they point to a sense that controversia takes straightforward issues and makes them unnecessarily complicated.

One might, as I would, argue that things only *seem* straightforward, and that the virtue of rhetoric is that its complicated and nuanced version of reality is more, well, realistic. But, still and all, the complication can be paralyzing. It can lead to a version of what used to be called liberal guilt, or might be thought of as political Antinomianism: if we get our theory straight, so that we are thinking about the issue in the correct way, then we have made political progress.

In addition, Sloane claims that humanist rhetoric presents argument as a way to contingent solutions, but it can simply be training in how to support any argument. Rather than a way to test precommitments, argument becomes a way to protect them.

Last summer, a high school friend happened to get in touch with me. We had known each other in Forensics—he was very successful in debate. The e-mail conversation drifted into politics, as it always had between him and me, but it was very strange. I had an odd feeling of arguing with someone who had no concern for what was true, or even likely, but who was willing to make any argument necessary to support his precommitments. That he argued badly was an odd disappointment to me, as I would think that someone as well-trained in debate as he had been would at least have been able to support his points more effectively. Genuinely disturbing, however, was that he was untroubled by the disconnect between basic levels of accuracy and his own political positions. He saw political stances as ultimately determined by something he called "irrational," yet his arguments relied heavily on using what passes for rationality in the service of attempts to intimidate (particularly fallacies of the false dilemma, argument by insult, straw man).

My latest project has been on antebellum rhetoric, especially regarding the issue of slavery, because, having been an advocate of the more classically oriented, debate-based training as a cure for much of what ails American political discourse, I have to face that this was a time with such a training and a fairly sickly public sphere. This whole puzzle is too complicated to present here, but I do want to say that the proslavery politicians, with their deep training in debate, behaved exactly like my friend. Their oratorical, if not rhetorical, skill was put completely in the service of trying to intimidate others into staying away from criticisms of slavery. There was the same strange intermixture of rational-like forms of argument, in the service of blazingly counterfactual and often internally contradictory stances.

Precommitted to slavery, they would not contemplate its long-term prospects, genuine consequences for the economics and politics of the southern states, or alternatives. Precommitted to slavery, they were committed to silencing public debate. They thereby operated against their own interests. A thorough discussion of slavery would have been in the best interests of the slave states.

Sloane discusses something similar to this, arguing that the issue is that debate and composition pedagogy have both dropped inventio (282–83). Inventio has two parts, which is not always made clear in the discussion of the five offices of rhetoric. One can invent one's argument, meaning one's stance on the issue, and one can invent one's argument, meaning the support for that stance. I'm saying that any pedagogy or political practice that restricts inventio to the second—that makes rhetoric training in how to support and protect one's precommitments—will not have the consequences Sloane advocates.

One response to my objection is that such a practice is not the good man speaking well, but the precommitted twit speaking well. But that raises the problem of whether Kenneth Burke's criticism of communism applies to humanist rhetoric. Were humans really as good as communism requires that we be, then communism itself would be unnecessary, as any political system would work. If humanist rhetoric requires that we be reflective and self-critical and open to argument, then isn't it presuming a model of human nature which would make any method of discourse work?

In fairness to Sloane, my objection is to an argument he does not quite make. He does not claim that training in pro-con thinking inevitably, invariably, or even necessarily *causes* rhetorical thinking—his language is carefully limited to verbs of association. So, let us grant that language: training in pro-con thinking is associated with a view of discourse, language, and humanity that would serve us well.

This is an unpopular argument in an era committed to "accountability," which amounts to testing education by students' performance on tests that cannot test thinking. As my students who are prospective high school teachers tell me when I advocate controversia, all of this is very fine, and they're persuaded of its merits, but teaching their students this method of thinking will not improve their performance on standardized tests. My students will, then, find themselves fired. And I'm not sure what to say to that.

One answer, and the one to which I keep returning, is entangled in the wrangling over the Iraq invasion. One of many counterarguments to which Bush never had to respond was that we could not manage an occupation of two countries. Rumsfeld sort of responded to that, by simply asserting that we would be welcomed as liberators by cheering crowds. There was no Plan B. Had the public insisted on better controversia, had the public known all sides of the argument, that piece of wishful thinking would have been treated as the pernicious silliness it turned out to be. Like the Federalists who had to formulate a Bill of Rights, the Bush administration would have had to formulate a Plan B. We would still be in Iraq—I am not claiming that a better public argument would have changed that outcome—but I think it plausible we would be in a better situation in Iraq because there would have been a plan for this outcome. Interestingly enough, the Bush administration would be in a better situation had they had less faith in their ability to construct reality, to lie with impunity, and to ignore undesirable outcomes. Like the southern slaveowners who worked to silence criticism, ultimately to their own disadvantage, so the Bush administration's resorting to invasion at all costs has hurt them.

WORKS CITED

Bush, George. "State of the Union." <http://whitehouse.gov/news/releases/2003/01/20030128-19.html>.

Crosswhite, James. "Conflict in Concert: Fighting Hannah Arendt's Good Fight." *JAC* 22 (Fall 2002): 948–59.

Sloane, Thomas O. *Donne, Milton, and the End of Humanist Rhetoric.* Berkeley: U of California P, 1985.

—. *On the Contrary: The Protocol of Traditional Rhetoric.* Washington, DC: Catholic U of America P, 1997.

33

Humanism and Cold War Rhetoric: The Ambiguous Rhetorical Legacy of Niels Bohr

Lisa Storm Villadsen
University of Copenhagen

> Looking back on those days, I find it difficult to convey with sufficient vividness the fervent hopes that the progress of science might initiate a new era of harmonious co-operation between nations, and the anxieties lest any opportunity to promote such a development be forfeited.
>
> —Niels Bohr ("Open Letter to the United Nations," par. 10)

In 1950, Niels Bohr was looking back at his first attempts in 1944 and 1945 to inspire political leaders to prevent a nuclear arms race following WWII. When looking around, he could note that his fears had come true: the world was in the midst of the cold war.[1] So he persisted in his attempt to motivate political leaders to work for increased openness in international political and cultural relations, and this time, he extended an appeal to the world community in the form of an open letter to the United Nations.

Niels Bohr's rhetorical legacy is about a tireless endeavor to turn the menaces of atomic technology to the good of mankind. It represents ambitious attempts to overcome barriers between the realms of scientific and political discourse and to bring these into dialogue in order to safeguard the world from total war. For this and other reasons, Bohr deserves the attention of scholars of rhetoric interested in questions of rhetorical agency, access to public debate, credibility across recognized fields of expertise (scientific/political), as well as the history of cold war rhetoric.

The Open Letter to the United Nations has traditionally been treated as a noble, albeit ineffectual, appeal to basic human interests in the face of the grotesque logic of the cold war. While recognizing the visionary quality of Bohr's thoughts, I wish, however, to also challenge the received understanding of this text. The overarching themes in my discussion are ambiguity and ambivalence. I shall argue that Bohr's Open Letter is a much more ambiguous document than hitherto perceived and that it reflects an attitude on Bohr's part which is more complex than the same tradition would have us believe. I see Bohr's letter less as an historical document transcending political quarrels in its appeal to reason and basic humanistic principles and more as a reflection of complex and conflicting interests—political as well as personal.

I shall forward this argument by first pointing to the seemingly unmotivated appearance of the Open Letter and the equivocal nature of its argumentation. Second, I will point to features in the text that offer alternative explanations of the purpose and content of the text, features that can account for the ambivalence characterizing it. In this context I shall discuss the audience of the letter, its authorship, the ideology informing the letter, and the question of personal and ethical motivations for it.

CRITICAL ANGLE OF THE DISCUSSION

My reading finds inspiration in the work of William Ray Arney as conveyed by Bryan Taylor in his article on the politics of biography of atomic spies (Taylor, 2002). Arney questions the ethical adequacy of "nuclear-narrative forms," especially in biographies of cold war personalities and argues that "we should resist traditional nuclear narratives that satisfy expectations for personality and closure, and instead endorse alternative forms characterized by ambivalence, evocation, inconclusiveness, and ambiguity" (qtd. in Taylor 45). I agree with Taylor who explains the motivation to heed Arney's call by pointing out that such "deliberately inelegant 'failures' potentially expose the contingencies underlying nuclear rationality so they might be exploited to develop more democratic systems of nuclear control"[2] (Taylor 45).

I find Arney's point about the need for more open-ended treatments of great figures of the atomic past equally well taken when it comes to rhetorical criticism because it forces us to think of Bohr's discourse in terms that de-center him as a speaking subject and opens up ways of understanding his texts that get beyond more traditional, instrumental conceptions of the isolated rhetor living up to ideals of a rational individual acting coherently and reasonably while dealing with a number of constraints. Hence, I will focus on issues that are likely to at least challenge Bohr's hitherto unquestioned status as somewhat of a misunderstood genius saint because I believe that such a rhetorical approach has the potential to add nuance to the historical accounts of Bohr and to contribute to the body of rhetorical scholarship on nuclear science and the cold war.

THE OPEN LETTER

Bohr's Open Letter to the United Nations might be regarded as the culmination of a very long and complicated endeavor on Bohr's part to influence the leading nations of the world in their long-term policy on nuclear energy research and arms development.[3] It is dated June 9, 1950.[4] The letter is about twelve pages long and falls roughly in seven sections. It consists of a narrative of Bohr's endeavor interspersed with quotations from his earlier texts, all held together with a few general comments and arguments for the importance of the idea being presented. The main point of the letter is an appeal to the nations of the United Nations to consider the adoption of a policy of openness, that is, an uninhibited access to sharing information and research, in particular on issues pertaining to nuclear weapons.

Taken literally as an appeal to the world community for action, the letter failed.[5] Regarded on its textual merits alone, this failure is not surprising. With its cumbersome prose, high level of abstraction, indirection in wording and extreme caution in expression generally, in addition to its several and lengthy quotations, it is not a compelling rhetorical utterance. While the letter repeatedly makes reference to urgent, serious, and concrete threats, the overall impression is almost the opposite, namely one of abstraction, distance, and vagueness. I now turn to the text proper in order to examine this elusiveness and aloofness.

THE ASSERTION OF A RHETORICAL SITUATION

The aim of the present account and considerations is to point to the unique opportunities for further understanding and co-operation between nations which have been created by the revolution of human resources brought forth by the advance of science, and *to stress that despite previous disappointments these opportunities remain* and that all hopes and all efforts must be centered on their realization. (Bohr, "Open Letter" par. 1 [emphasis added])

The Open Letter is marked by a conspicuous lack of a rhetorical situation in Bitzer's sense. This is interesting because there is plenty of evidence that Bohr recognized the need to contextualize his several appeals in the hope of making them more interesting to his audience.[6] In 1950, Bohr faced a great challenge in making his plea seem urgent and the moment right for dealing with the problem since the Soviets had demonstrated that they were in possession of nuclear weapons, and the cold war was an official fact. Bohr's fears of a divided world were thus already reality, and while he considered this the most powerful incentive to act in order to arrest further deterioration of East/West relations, international politics were operating under a different logic.

In the absence of an outside occasion, Bohr framed his letter as an answer to an (asserted) crisis, stating that the whole civilization is "presented [...] with a most serious challenge" and that "in the present critical situation," his "views and experiences may perhaps contribute to renewed discussion." Bohr wished to "point to the unique opportunities" created by "the revolution of human resources," to stress that "these opportunities still remain," and he emphasized this alleged occasion to act with a characteristic formulation, assuring that while the account of his previous (failed) attempts might seem discouraging, "it is in no way meant to imply that the situation does not still offer unique opportunities."[7]

With no particular historical occasion or event to motivate the Open Letter, Bohr had to explain its emergence at that time. He did so with the arguments that appeared most compelling to him, namely the frightening, absurd, and increasingly more dangerous division of the world into hostile blocks competing about the ability to destroy human civilization. However, in light of the international political climate at the time, this gesture was at best hopefully idealistic, at worst ill guided. It also rests uneasily with Bohr's use of quotations from earlier texts (a point I shall return to).

Aside from the fact that Bohr's accumulated message seems to have been vacillating between being premature and belated, at once attentive to specific historical events and suspended in time, and thus was characterized by a search for an ever-elusive rhetorical situation, my point is that this effort to "conjure up" a pretext to speak reflects ambiguously on the rhetorical agency of the text; at once a sign of rhetorical heroism—doing all things possible to gain a hearing for the message of peace and trust—and a sign of rhetorical solipsism—demonstrated by Bohr's inability to acknowledge the lack of interest and support his ideas were getting among policymakers. Moreover, the fact that the world was no longer/still not ready for Bohr's message raises the question of the purpose of the letter, and for that we must turn to the argumentation proper.

THE AMBIGUOUS CONTENT OF THE LETTER

It may be in the interest of international understanding to record some of the ideas which at that time were the object of serious deliberation. ("Open Letter," par. 2)

Even if it involves repetition of arguments already presented, it may serve to give a clearer impression of the ideas under discussion on these occasions to quote a memorandum, dated May 17th, 1948 [...] . ("Open Letter," Bohr, par.11)

Taken at face value as an address to the international political community, Bohr's text was ridden with ambiguity that contributes to its lack of compelling force. To find and investigate the presence of ambiguity and ambivalence in the text, a good starting point is with the significant amount of quotes mentioned earlier. Making up approximately one half of the letter, these quotes as a textual feature have serious consequences for the possible interpretations of the text.

As mentioned above, the Open Letter contains textual fragments dating from 1944, 1945, and 1948. From a rhetorical point of view, it is interesting that these fragments are used as part of the argumentation with no comment to the effect that the thoughts in them might need to be at least re-contextualized in light of the dramatic changes in world politics between 1944 and 1950. This is all the more noticeable given Bohr's keen attention to the opportunities of acting at the right moment and to the time pressure springing from this realization.[8] In combination, the uncontextualized use of older text fragments in a text that contains numerous traces of an intense awareness of issues of both time pressure and right timing adds to the ambiguous impression created by the text.

The large amount of quoting also renders the temporal direction of the letter's argumentation ambiguous: while arguing in the present about the future, the text is remarkably retrospective in its emphasis on opinions and analyses up to six years old. In a sense, Bohr's proposal thus presents itself as more *reactionary* than visionary, looking back and repeating old arguments rather than taking the current historical and political facts and conditions into account and presenting his idea in an argumentation springing from the status quo. While Bohr omits material from his earlier writings deemed irrelevant in the current situation, he nevertheless bases his argumentation on his earlier text fragments. In the absence of a more concrete discussion of the current potential hindrances for the realization of his plan, the argumentation in the open letter is hereby weakened. Unless the reader accepts the implicit claim that Bohr's first formulations of the problem were both comprehensive and timeless in their articulation of the political problems ensuing from a one-side knowledge of the atomic bomb, there is a risk that the letter would be read as either simply not addressing the problems facing the international community in 1950 or, perhaps worse, addressing the current problems in outdated language, thus opening for the question of whether Bohr was able to address the problems of the cold war adequately at all.

BOHR'S AUDIENCE FOR THE OPEN LETTER

I turn to the United Nations with these considerations in the hope that they may contribute to the search for a realistic approach to the grave and urgent problems confronting humanity. ("Open Letter," par. 15)

Participation in a development, largely initiated by international scientific collaboration and involving immense potentialities as regards human welfare, would also reinforce the intimate
bonds which were created in the years before the war between scientists of different nations.
("Open Letter," par. 7)

The addressee of the letter is both clearly identified and elusive. With the world public as
audience, it is not surprising that the letter only contains a very vague reflection of its audience as nations that are "supporters of international co-operation" and thus open to
Bohr's appeals concerning "the removal of obstacles for free mutual information and intercourse." Yet carefully read, the letter seems to appeal to a smaller audience with more
specific interests in common.

It has been pointed out from several sources that one reason Bohr had such difficulty in
persuading policymakers was that he was too settled in the scientific way of thinking and was
not able to understand the often conflicting and contingent elements that have a dominant influence on political decisions (see, e.g., Christmas-Møller 55). While there is reason to believe that individuals more politically astute than Bohr himself had a hand in composing the
open letter (a point I shall return to), I wish to show that Bohr's discussion seems to pose the
scientific community as a kind of prototype of international cooperation and brotherhood,
and that his argumentation in fact suggests that the real audience for the letter was the
(U.S.-based) scientific community.

This reading finds support in Danish historian Christmas-Møller's suggestion that Bohr's
letter was really intended for the (primarily U.S.) science community and the American media
rather than the politicians representing the nations of the world. Christmas-Møller bases his
thesis in part on Bohr's strategy for distributing the letter. At his own expense, Bohr had had
thousands of special editions of the letter printed, and via the Danish Ministry of Foreign Affairs and his son Aage's presence in the United States, these documents were distributed in the
scientific community in the United States (Christmas-Møller 195). I find Christmas-Møller's
thesis quite plausible and wish to point to some textual traits that might confirm it.

A striking aspect of the argumentation is the role Bohr sees for scientists in dealing with
the problems ensuing from the development of nuclear weapons. In spite of the high level of
abstraction, Bohr's basic plan is closely connected to his personal experiences as a scientist.
The international network of scientists sharing ideas and friendships that Bohr had been used
to be a part of in the years before WWII is presented as an ideal state, and Bohr envisions a
recreation of this community based on mutual respect and committed to expanding knowledge as the solution to the problems of the cold war.

It is thus characteristic of the letter that the argumentation takes its starting point in the
realm of science. Bohr's basic point is that while the current situation is the result of scientific discoveries, the proposed solution is also possible by means of technology springing
from scientific research. In arguing for an open world, Bohr thus takes his starting point in
the history of the atomic bomb stating that "the progress of science and technology has tied
the fate of all nations inseparably together."

Bohr's positioning of himself is noteworthy. Even though his part in the Manhattan Project was primarily advisory and that since 1945, he had "had no connection with any secret,
military or industrial project in the field of atomic energy," Bohr nevertheless positions himself as above all a scientist rhetor. In addition to mentioning his connection with the
Manhattan Project and thereby establishing some authority on the technical side of the issue,

Bohr even objectifies himself by referring to himself in the third person as "a scientist who had the opportunity to follow developments on close hand." I believe that this is very significant when we want to understand Bohr's argumentation.

It is clear that Bohr places great confidence in more science as a means of securing the world and establishing more trust between nations ("the fervent hopes that the progress of science might initiate a new era of harmonious co-operation between nations"). He does not question the value of scientific development ("as there hardly can be question for humanity of renouncing the prospects of improving the material conditions for civilization by atomic energy sources") but talks of "the promising industrial development," "such bright promises for common human striving," "the new situation brought about by the advance of science," and "the unique opportunities which, unknown to the public, have been created by the advancement of science."

The history of the development of the atomic bomb gives Bohr reason to imagine that at least the initial phase of the international control program could be facilitated by scientists in an international network, and the following comment is presented as a clincher to his whole argument. Here, Bohr comes very close to calling the atom bomb a blessing in disguise (at least for the scientific community) when he exclaims:

> Indeed, it need hardly be stressed how fortunate in every respect it would be if, at the same time as the world will know of the formidable destructive power which has come into human hands, it could be told that the great scientific and technical advance has been helpful in creating a solid foundation for a future peaceful co-operation between nations. (par. 9)

The passive construction might, of course, be interpreted as a sign of humility, but if we accept the idea that the letter really speaks to fellow scientists, it is rather an expression of considerable pride, implicitly investing science with formidable creative powers.

Science thus is presented as the answer to the problems of the world ("knowledge is the basis for civilization"). This argument seems a rather roundabout way of dealing with the concrete political issues dividing the world, and I find one comment in particular telling of Bohr's focus on the scientific community at the expense of a broader conception of society: "Participation in a development, largely initiated by international scientific collaboration and involving immense potentialities as regards human welfare, would also reinforce the intimate bonds which were created before the war between scientists of different nations." To anybody outside the scientific community, this argument would seem to put the cart before the horse, and I would argue that it is indicative of Bohr's rather exclusive understanding of the problems at hand that the international community should make it its purpose to improve contacts between scientists in different countries.

To sum up the question of the audience for the open letter, I have shown that there is textual evidence for the claim that Bohr was addressing a different audience than he claimed to be, namely the scientific community. On the level of argumentation, it explains some of the ambivalence with regard to the merit of nuclear weapons research, an ambivalence that must be buried in an overarching belief in the potential benefit of more scientific research. On the level of rhetorical agency, my reading of Bohr's privileging of the scientific community in his appeal leads to two, not necessarily exclusionary, ways of reading Bohr's positioning of himself as a scientist rhetor: positively phrased, Bohr not only takes responsibility for the terrible invention, but also takes the initiative to render it less dangerous by way of more scientific collaboration and control. Negatively phrased, Bohr seems unable to accept that nuclear weapons by 1950 primarily had become the responsibility of politicians and thus moved away from the control of the scientific community. However noble his idea of scientists being the right group to secure the nuclear weapons industry, this strategy would seem to risk being exclusive and not in accordance with the democratic principles of the United Nations.

AUTHORIAL VOICE(S) OF THE LETTER

In presenting here views which on an early stage impressed themselves on a scientist who had the opportunity to follow developments on [sic] close hand I am acting entirely on my own responsibility and without consultation with the government of any country. ("Open Letter," par. 1)

Throughout the letter, Bohr writes in the first person,[9] the account is framed by his personal involvement in the Manhattan Project, and his later efforts to influence the course of events, and he explicitly states that he is "acting entirely on [his] own responsibility [...]" (1).

While there can be no doubt that the letter is an integral part of Bohr's personal quest for improving the state of international politics and that he took the responsibility for it, there is reason to question the assertion that he did so "without consultation with the government of any country" (1). Christmas-Møller suggests the possibility that Bohr was in fact asked to present his ideas of an open world to an international public, possibly by David Lilienthal, chairman of the U.S. government's Atomic Energy Commission who was fighting a losing battle on the question of whether the United States should initiate the development of a hydrogen bomb (164). Whether this was the case or not, Christmas-Møller documents that the open letter was the result of many months' work where Bohr had sought the help of colleagues in the United States and, after returning to Denmark, had worked on the letter with a highly placed official in the Danish central administration, Hans Henrik Koch. Koch, who was savvy regarding the political system, believed that Bohr's ideas might form the basis of a Scandinavian foreign policy initiative on the subject of East/West relations. Their collaboration lasted several months, and the Danish government was likely informed about the preparation of the Open Letter.[10] The claim that Bohr's appeal had come without prior discussion with the government was strictly true but probably not a reflection of the actual political background for the letter.

The fact that Bohr's open letter had, if not coauthors, then at least a host of unofficial sponsors hoping to promote openness and stabilization of the nuclear arms problem takes nothing away from Bohr's legacy as a unique thinker and committed promoter of international cooperation, nor does it make his assertion of acting independently problematic— rather, they reflect basic conditions for introducing diplomatic initiatives. An understanding of this more complex background is relevant for a consideration of the political or ideological nature of Bohr's letter.

THE ETHICS AND POLITICS OF THE OPEN LETTER

The situation calls for the most unprejudiced attitude towards all questions of international relations. ("Open Letter," par. 14)

An open world where each nation can assert itself solely by the extent to which it can contribute to the common culture and is able to help others with experience and resources must be the goal to be put above everything else. Still, example in such respects can be effective only if isolation is abandoned and free discussion of cultural and social developments permitted across all boundaries.

Within any community it is only possible for the citizens to strive together for common welfare
on a basis of public knowledge of the general conditions in the country. Likewise, real co-operation between nations on problems of common concern presupposes free access to all information
of importance for their relations. ("Open Letter," par. 14)

Bohr's campaign for an open world has traditionally been read as an instance of great vision
and humanism. Although the Open Letter was the last major effort in this campaign, it is often made to represent the whole process, in part because it actually contains many of the
thoughts expressed earlier, and in part, no doubt, because of its public availability. In this
way, the rhetorical legacy of the letter has been somewhat decontextualized. The letter thus
is remembered as a grand statement to the nations of the world about the need for openness
and mutual trust. I wish to point to aspects of the open letter that challenge this received understanding of it as an almost transcendent expression of an ethical challenge to the madness of the nuclear arms race. In doing so, I will point out the ambiguous nature of the ethics
and politics of the text.

We remember Bohr as an eminent scientist who distinguished himself by showing critical distance to a project, which he in a sense could be said to be responsible for by virtue of
his groundbreaking research on the structure of atoms. Such a stance would normally command respect because it demonstrates not only critical thinking but also honesty and a set of
high ethical standards. However, there were limits to Bohr's criticism. Bohr did not condemn
the use of the atomic bomb over Japan or any subsequent detonation with its consequences of
destruction, fallout, and pollution. In fact, he explicitly did not comment on the use of nuclear weapons during WWII. Clearly then, Bohr had mixed feelings about nuclear weapons.
On the one hand, he was evidently willing to accept their use to defeat Japan and put an end to
WWII, and on the other, he considered the prospect of stockpiled nuclear weapons to be the
most awesome threat imaginable to the world.

As a poster boy for modern science and at the same time a political analyst worried about
the future safety of the world and stressing the "grave and urgent problems confronting humanity," Bohr experienced a difficult balancing act. Throughout the letter, Bohr emphasizes
the double nature of the results brought forth by science; again and again they are said to represent both a promise and a potential threat to humanity. Thus, the formal ambiguities discussed above (the nature of the situation and the use of quotations) are matched by
ambivalence at the semantic level in the wording of the letter. We find this ambivalence in
formulations such as, "At the same time as this development [of modern science and technol-
ogy] holds out such great promises for the improvement of human welfare it has, in placing
formidable means of destruction in the hands of man, presented our whole civilization with a
most serious challenge," and "the hopes and the dangers which the accomplishment of the
project might imply."

My point is that while Bohr was able to think beyond the immediate situation and the
most pressing needs in a truly visionary and humanistic spirit, his idealism was accompanied by more concrete, perhaps more cynical, utilitarian ethics, in effect based on the view
that the goal (winning WWII) had justified the means (bombing Hiroshima and Nagasaki).
Hence, in spite of his reputation as a great humanist, Bohr seems to have been subject to the
logic of war so well described by Bryan Hubbard in terms of Kenneth Burke's notions of
burlesque and entelechy. Hubbard explains that the fierceness of the war results in a burlesque rhetorical frame where "war is waged on an enemy who is not entirely human" and
thus "distorts ethics, creates caricatures of the enemy, and prevents exploration of more rational alternatives" (356). Moreover, the decision to use the atomic bomb was based on the

influence of entelechy, which Hubbard describes as driving "people toward the logical ends of their rhetoric and behavior," and he explains, "the development of the bomb always implied its use" (360). Hubbard's project is to explain the background for Truman's decision to use the atomic bomb, but it seems to be equally well taken with regard to Bohr's acceptance of its use.

Regardless of how we evaluate such wartime ethics, the question remains how Bohr positioned himself in the context of the cold war. The Open Letter expresses deep concern over the ongoing problems between East and West, but it does not condemn the development of atomic or hydrogen bombs or use hereof. Instead it places all its confidence in the deterrent effect of openness as well as in science's potential, but unspecified, positive contributions to civilization. In this light, the ethics of the Open Letter strike me as problematic: ambiguous at best but at worst misleading.

In this context, one might consider the Open Letter as a political document and thus as an expression of a certain ideology. This serves to suggest one more reason why the letter did not have the intended effect but also contributes to my overall argumentation about the letter, namely that Bohr's legacy as a great thinker capable of transcending nationalistic barriers for the greater sake of science and humanity needs to be nuanced.

The Open Letter operates in an ideological frame that is not committed to its own appeal to openness. As we have seen, the letter builds its argumentation partly on quotations from Bohr's 1948 memorandum to George Marshall. In his analysis of the career of Bohr's ideas from the war years to the 1960s, Christmas-Møller shows that this was not a politically neutral document, for although it would commit the United States according to its liberal ideological content, it was first and foremost a demand to the USSR to open up and thereby sacrifice one of its strongest points in negotiations with the United States. Christmas-Møller observes that Bohr in this respect was in line with one of the main goals of U.S. policy toward the Soviet Union and that many of his arguments show that he was aware of this (121–2). Christmas-Møller does not specify these arguments, but I wish to point to one in particular. In the excerpt from the memorandum to Marshall, Bohr emphasizes the value of appearances, what we might call the "signal effect" of his plan, saying:

> Nor should the difficulties in obtaining consent be an argument against taking the initiative since, irrespective of the immediate response, the very existence of an offer of the kind in question should deeply affect the situation in a most promising direction. In fact, *a demonstration would have been given to the world* of preparedness to live together with all others under conditions where mutual relationships and common destiny would be shaped only by honest conviction and good example. (par. 12, emphasis added)

Bohr continues,

> Such a stand would, more than anything else, appeal to people all over the world, fighting for fundamental human rights, and would greatly strengthen the moral position of all supporters of genuine international control. At the same time, *those reluctant to enter on the course proposed would have been brought into a position difficult to maintain* since such opposition would amount to a confession of lack of confidence in the strength of their own cause when laid open to the world. (par. 12, emphasis added)

I find in these excerpts signs of two things that compromise Bohr's alleged independence of any nation's government. First, the excerpts demonstrate a sense of alliance with the Western states, United Kingdom and United States in particular, that was perhaps natural at the time of WWII but less so in 1950. Bohr in effect councils especially the United States on how to win an international public relations campaign, and he therefore comes across as aligned with the West. More problematic is the second issue, namely, Bohr's apparent willingness to exert pressure on Soviet and the East block in order to place these governments in a bad light both internationally and in their own countries. This is only a weak version of the kind of pressure wielded in Eisenhower's 1953 "Atoms for Peace" speech so well documented by Martin Medhurst that I quote at length:

> On the diplomatic front, Eisenhower's speech was the opening salvo in an intensive persuasive campaign to put the Soviets at a public relations disadvantage by challenging them, in public, to join with the United States in the development of an International Atomic Energy Agency. The president hoped either to embarrass the Soviets and thus reduce their appeal to poor Third World countries or to start the Russians down the road of cooperation with the United States and thereby reduce the international tensions that could, he feared, lead to World War III. In either case, the United States' strategic position would be enhanced. (24–25)

Although Bohr is subtle and obviously in no position to threaten like Eisenhower was, his willingness to play the game of one-up-manship stands in conflict with the overall message of openness, respect, and collaboration with which we have traditionally associated the Open Letter.

In his discussion of the immediate reactions to Bohr's Open Letter, Christmas-Møller wryly comments that the Danish press immediately inscribed the Open Letter in a cold war pattern of discourse, something it was, according to Christmas-Møller, precisely meant to transcend and replace with trust (165). My reading shows that such possible intentions notwithstanding, the Open Letter was much more a product of the cold war than has been previously recognized.

BOHR AS AN AMBIGUOUS RHETOR

> I have been reluctant in taking part in the public debate on this question. In the present situation, however, I feel that an account of my views and experiences may perhaps contribute to renewed discussion about these matters so deeply influencing international relationship. ("Open Letter," par. 1)

> Until the end of the war I endeavored by every way open to a scientist to stress the importance of appreciating the full political implications of the project and to advocate that, before there could be any question of use of atomic weapons, international co-operation be initiated on the elimination of the new menaces to world security. ("Open Letter," par. 10)

My last comments concerning the elements of ambiguity and ambivalence in Bohr's Open Letter concerns Bohr himself as rhetor. In light of the rather unaccommodating political climate of the time, we can choose to regard Bohr's efforts in the Open Letter as an admirable initiative. Regardless of unfavorable odds, he demonstrated the possibility for an individual to take up rhetorical initiative in the interest of humankind. Unaffected by previous setbacks, Bohr persevered in his crusade for the cause of openness and trust between nations and did the only logical thing, namely bring the matter to the primary public forum of worldwide dimensions, the United Nations.

On the other hand, Bohr's Open Letter might be seen as a rather idiosyncratic document awkwardly pushed on the world public's agenda. Given the nature of international relations at the time, Bohr's insistence on bringing his ideas into a more public forum might be seen as a reflection of his inability, or lack of willingness, to admit that while honorable, his vision of an open world had not gained any practical support ever and likely wouldn't any time soon: Roosevelt wasn't really interested in it but was just being polite, Churchill was not polite and definitely wasn't in favor of Bohr's idea, and Marshall didn't put his political career at stake to promote it to Truman. In this light, the Open Letter as Bohr's personal project overshadows its stated aim as a humanitarian project.

This double nature of the function of the letter becomes more clear when we consider the text itself, for also in respect to Bohr himself, his quoting practice has ambiguous effects: on the one hand, he carefully and conscientiously details his earlier efforts in order to explain the background for the current address and bring the international public "up to speed" on his thinking on the matter (including his allowances for obstacles and hesitations regarding his plan). In doing this, he explicitly quotes from three of his earlier texts on the matter. In the following passages, he thus presents himself as a humble "servant of the world" merely putting his thinking at the disposal of the United Nations for the benefit of humankind: "I have felt that an account of my views and experiences may perhaps contribute to renewed discussion […]." "It may be in the interest of international understanding to record some of the ideas which at that time were the object of serious deliberation.[11] For this purpose, I may quote from a memorandum […]."

On the other hand, the practice of quoting himself at such length raises the question of Bohr's motivation for doing so as opposed to, for example, simply presenting his plan afresh with the necessary adjustments to the current situation. A statement like "Even if it involves repetition of arguments already presented, it may serve to give a clearer impression of the ideas under discussion […] to quote a memorandum […]" does not suggest any particular humility and appears to be a rather weak reason to reiterate. It suggests, rather, an interpretation of Bohr's practice of self-quoting as part of a self-vindicating effort. In this light, the quotations point to Bohr personally and his prophecy on the risk of an international arms race after WWII rather than to the problems at hand, and the letter becomes Bohr's political testament, a chronicle of his personal efforts made publicly accessible, Bohr in effect saying to the world: "I told you so!" In a sense, the letter becomes a declaration of hindsight, witnessing that Bohr's predictions of an international arms race had come true, and his expressions of humility to the contrary, Bohr comes across as still expecting as a matter of course to have the status and authority enough to gain the attention of the world community.

CONCLUSION

I have suggested a reading of Niels Bohr's Open Letter to the United Nations that privileges questions of ambiguity and ambivalence rather than aiming for a neatly summed up account of the motives and effects of the text. I have argued that Bohr's text is good material for such an analysis because it has a strong history of being interpreted as a testament to Bohr's noble personal effort to avoid the dangers of an atomic arms race and the problems of the cold war. Instead, I have identified some moments in the text that invite questioning by a rhetorical critic: the way the text mobilizes rhetorical agency in order to construct a rhetorical space and the way the text can be seen as a chronicle of previous texts rather than an argued response to its actual historical context. In addition, I have identified four aspects of the letter which alone and, to some extent, in combination add to its complexity and raise questions of its proper interpretation: the matter of the actual audience for the text, the question of actual authorship for the text, the ethical and political ambiguity informing the text, and finally the question of Bohr's personal motivation.

Bohr's creativity, courage, and persistence in working for a safer and better world were admirable, and the fact that this project was disconnected from his professional life as an atomic scientist makes it even more noticeable as an expression of individual beliefs and ideas. Nevertheless, I have shown that Bohr's text is more complex than first expected and suggested that it was driven by more mixed and personal motives than commonly believed.

NOTES

1. Niels Bohr (1885–1962) was a Danish physicist and the father of modern atomic physics. In 1922, he received the Nobel Prize for his work on the structure of atoms, and in the following decades he was a highly profiled scientist with a vast international network and enormous prestige. In virtue of his expertise in the field of nuclear physics, he was involved in the Manhattan Project, the American scientific program dedicated to developing an atomic bomb during WWII. Beside his considerable contribution to science, Niels Bohr was also a committed participant in public debate on political, social, and cultural issues.
2. The body of biographical works on Bohr would no doubt be rich material for the kind of work Arney proposes because of the remarkably homogenous nature of the received truth about Bohr's involvement in the Manhattan Project and his subsequent attempts to influence international politics on atomic research and arms control. However, I wish to translate Arney's critical project into the realm of rhetorical criticism.
3. The letter can be seen as the fourth major attempt Bohr made at promoting his ideas to international policymakers, and it is clear from the text that Bohr considered his various efforts over the preceding six years to be steps in a process that was now seeing its culmination. This continuity is very literally illustrated by the fact that the letter contains lengthy quotes from the previous three attempts, namely his memorandum of July 3, 1944, to President Roosevelt, the following memorandum of March 24, 1945, also to Roosevelt, and finally his memorandum to Secretary of Foreign Affairs George Marshall of May 17, 1948. These passages make up approximately one half of the letter, and this was the first time they were made publicly available.
4. A few days later, on June 12, 1950, Bohr held a press conference in his home in Copenhagen where he read the letter but declined to answer questions from the press. The press conference was scheduled for the afternoon (6 pm) to coincide with the presentation of the Letter to the General Secretary of the UN, Trygve Lie at 10 am in New York City. Immediately after the press conference Bohr forwarded a copy of the letter to the Danish prime minister, one to the American ambassador and at his own expense he had thousands of copies printed for distribution among diplomats, politicians, physicists, friends, and foreign newspapers.
5. In spite of the careful phrasing, rational arguments, and the humanistic nature of the appeal, the letter lacks compelling power. This was clear immediately after its publication. Outside Denmark and the other Nordic countries, the letter received little public attention. General Secretary Lie acknowledged the letter, but no initiative was taken to spread it around or stir debate on the views presented in it. Within a few weeks, the letter was overshadowed by other events: on June 24, the Korean War broke out, and later that year the United States detonated its first hydrogen bomb. The open letter was never the subject of discussion in the General Assembly and only reached it by way of a closing quotation in a speech by the Swedish representative in the plenary debate in October.
6. In the letter, there are in fact repeated references to the issue of time pressure and of the question of timing. In the 1944 memorandum, Bohr mentions "problems that call for most urgent attention," the need for an agreement "in due time," and he argues that the "potentialities of the project as a means of inspiring confidence just under these circumstances acquire most actual importance" and that "the momentary situation would in various respects seem to afford some quite

unique possibilities which might be forfeited by a postponement." He concludes in the 1944 memorandum, "The present situation would seem to offer a most favorable opportunity for an early initiative [...]."

    In the spring of 1945, the sense of urgency is even more pronounced when Bohr underscores the need to act "in due time," that mankind is "at a crucial moment of world affairs," and he claims that "the very novelty of the situation should offer a unique opportunity of appealing to an unprejudiced attitude" and finally warns that "all such opportunities may, however, be forfeited if an initiative is not taken while the matter can be raised in a spirit of friendly advice. In fact, a postponement [...] might [...] give the approach the appearance of an attempt at coercion." The quoted memorandum from 1948 still labors to establish a sense of urgency describing the "divergences in outlook" (between East and West) as "a most desperate feature of the present situation," the need for "a great issue" to "invoke the highest aspirations of mankind," and Bohr suggests "an offer, extended at a well-timed occasion, of immediate measures toward openness on a mutual basis."

7. The double negative seems very indicative of the actual basis for hope in the situation and is also a good example of Bohr's convoluted form of expression.

8. Thus, a crucial point in the first memorandum to Roosevelt was that America and England should share their secret of the atomic bomb with Russia *before* it was used in the war. The rhetorical situation then was, in other words, defined by the asymmetry in knowledge among the Allied nations. In Bohr's opinion, only an *early* initiative from America and England to share their secret would be fit to assure Russia that they had nothing to fear.

    The urgency of the 1944 memorandum was of course even more intensified in the spring of 1945 when WWII was coming to an end and the internal disagreements among the Allied nations were becoming ever more evident in connection with the Yalta conference and later the Potsdam conference. This was really the eleventh hour!

9. With the exception of the passage mentioned above where he refers to himself in the third person.

10. This prior knowledge allowed the Danish Prime Minister Hedtoft to issue a statement already a few hours after its publication stating that he gave the letter his full support. Christmas-Møller, 164.

11. This claim reflects Bohr's unfailing belief that especially Roosevelt had favored his ideas. Recent historical accounts, however, hold this to be false and point to evidence that Roosevelt on the one hand was committed to using the atomic bomb once it was developed, and on the other did nothing to bring Bohr's thoughts to the attention of his closest political advisers (see, e.g., Sherwin; Boyer).

WORKS CITED

Bitzer, Loyd. "The Rhetorical Situation." *Philosophy and Rhetoric*. (1968): 1–14.

Bohr, Niels. "Open Letter to the United Nations." Copenhagen: J. H. Schultz 12 Dec. 2004 <http://www.nbi.dk/NBA/files/gym/leth.htm>.

Boyer, Paul. *By the Bomb's Early Light. American Thought and Culture at the Dawn of the Atomic Age*. Chapel Hill: U of North Carolina P, 1994.

Christmas-Møller, Wilhelm. *Niels Bohr og atomvåbnet*. Gylling: Vindrose, 1985.

Hubbard, Bryan. "Reassessing Truman, the Bomb, and Revisionism: The Burlesque Frame and Entelechy in the Decision to Use Atomic Weapons Against Japan" *Western Journal of Communication* 62 (1998): 348–85.

Medhurst, Martin. "Rhetoric and Cold War: A Strategic Approach." *Cold War Rhetoric. Strategy, Metaphor, and Ideology*. Eds. Martin J. Medhurst, Robert L. Ivie, Philip Wander, and Robert L. Scott. New York: Greenwood, 1990: 19–27.

Sherwin, Martin J. *A World Destroyed. The Atomic Bomb and the Grand Alliance*. New York: Vintage Books, 1977.

Taylor, Bryan C. "Organizing the 'Unknown Subject': Los Alamos, Espionage, and the Politics of Biography." *Quarterly Journal of Speech* 88.1 (Feb. 2002): 33–49.

VI

Gender

34

The Persuasion of Esther: A Nun's Model of Silent, Seductive, Violent Rhetoric

Julie A. Bokser

DePaul University

In 1691, New Spain's famed nun and writer Sor Juana Inés de la Cruz offered the beautiful Biblical Queen Esther as a female exemplar because of her "gift of [...] persuasion" (*La respuesta* 77). Sor Juana was one of colonial Mexico's most prolific writers—a poet, composer of state ceremony, intellectual, and philosopher. In the larger project of which this chapter is a part, I illuminate the place of Sor Juana in the history and theory of rhetoric, using feminist rhetorical methodology to "extrapolate" Sor Juana's rhetorical theory from her seemingly nonrhetoric statements and activities (Ratcliffe 4). In that project, I argue that the text from which the allusion to Esther is drawn, Sor Juana's semi-autobiographical, exegetical, and proto-feminist manifesto, *La respuesta*, provides a theory of the rhetoric of silence. *La respuesta* is this nun's passionate defense of women's intellectual capacity and rights in response to a bishop who is trying to silence her scholarly activity and writing. Embroiled in a political battle with this bishop over issues of literacy, Sor Juana emerges as someone profoundly concerned with the acquisition, use, and effects of language in real-life contexts, especially contexts involving women and other nondominant speakers. She ultimately submitted to ecclesiastic authorities, but only after announcing her own impending silence and gesturing toward the rhetorical significance of this impending silence. Thus, following Krista Ratcliffe and Cheryl Glenn, this essay will use feminist historiography to contribute toward the ever-expanding "re-gendering" of rhetorical history (Glenn 2).

Sor Juana asserts that "one must name the silence, so that what it signifies may be understood" (*La respuesta* 41–43). She says she will speak "by way of the brief label placed on what I leave to silence" (43) and that "of those things that cannot be spoken, it must be said that they cannot be spoken, so that it may be known that silence is kept not for lack of things to say, but because the many things there are to say cannot be contained in mere words" (43). Then, after blatantly—yet humbly—interrupting the bishop to make these suggestive remarks in the form of extended apologia, she goes on to seemingly obey the bishop's injunctions by writing and publishing very little after this missive. She subsequently renounces humane studies, formally confesses her sins, and, four years later, dies at the age of 46. Hence, Sor Juana interrupts the bishop in order to explain her past reticence and to announce her impending silence so that she herself will be listened to—by those who know how to hear. A rhetoric of interruption merges with a rhetoric of silence. *La respuesta* is an act which reads as theory but which also constitutes her most critical and life-determining praxis. Sor Juana's rhetorical theory can be further illuminated by drawing out the implications of her allusion to Esther. These implications are two-pronged: first, through analogies between Sor Juana's position and Esther's we gain insight to Sor Juana's perspective on the complexities of her own rhetorical situation; and second, Esther's "gift" provides a model that can be interpreted as Sor Juana's more abstract consideration of rhetorical theory.

Sor Juana says that her "dull pen" initially stumbled over the problem of responding to the bishop's letter, which was so "immensely learned, prudent, devout, and loving" (*La respuesta* 39). Yet she manages to extricate herself from the trope of humility, which would entail submissive silence. She does this by extricating silence from submission when she announces the need to label it—to provide a "brief inscription." Immediately following this statement, she likens the bishop's permissiveness to that of the Biblical King Ahasuerus, and then lets this presumed permissiveness justify her reply. The enthymeme of this passage is that if the bishop is a "second Ahasuerus," then Sor Juana must be a second Esther, Queen to Ahasuerus. With characteristic subtlety, she identifies herself with Esther, the beautiful woman who saves the Jews from slaughter through wily politicking:

> Thus, sheltered by the assumption that I speak with the safe-conduct granted by your favors and with the warrant bestowed by your goodwill, and by the fact that, *like a second Ahasuerus*, you have allowed me to kiss the top of the golden scepter of your affection as a sign that you grant me kind license to speak and to plead my case in your venerable presence, I declare that I receive in my very soul your most holy admonition to apply my study to Holy Scripture; for although it arrives in the guise of counsel, it shall have for me the weight of law. (*La respuesta* 43–45, emphasis added)

This mention of the golden scepter references Esther's first recorded speech in the Bible, when she appears before the despotic Ahasuerus, risking her life if he does not extend the scepter. When license to speak is granted, she begins to carry out her subtle plot to get revenge on Haman, the king's powerful henchman and the persecutor of the Jews (Esth 5:4). Similarly, Sor Juana, *like a second Esther,* professes allegiance while in fact beginning her self-defense (in Sor Juana's words, pleading her case), which is also covert retaliation.

Later, Esther reappears, this time on Sor Juana's roster of significant women, a catalogue much like that of Christine de Pisan, whose works Sor Juana evidently did not know (Scott, "*'La gran turba'*" 222, note 1). Here, Sor Juana explicitly hails Esther for her "gift of [...] persuasion," a suggestive if brief allusion (*La respuesta* 77).[1] Susan Zaeske has argued that Esther "does not announce itself as rhetorical theory, but has operated as such" and was in fact employed as a rhetoric (194). Zaeske describes Esther as practicing an indirect, ingratiating rhetoric of submission (210). The book of Esther "teaches that direct, resistant rhetoric is ineffective, even dangerous, while clever, indirect, nonconfrontational methods will succeed in gaining the desired end—power" (202). When Esther receives the blessing of the golden scepter that allows her to speak, the transaction between king and queen is excessively submissive and public. Sor Juana also follows a path of rhetorical indirectness, submission, and public scrutiny.

Exactly what kind of persuasion does Esther practice? It is a rhetoric immersed in silence, where silence indicates deception. When she wins a place in the king's palace as one of his female companions, Esther keeps mum about her heritage. "And she would not tell him her people nor her country," we are told several times (Esth 2:10, see also 2:20).[2] Similar to Esther, Sor Juana was a lady-in-waiting in the viceregal court before she became a nun. She was also illegitimate, an aspect of her heritage she probably kept to herself or she wouldn't have enjoyed such prominence.[3] Esther's silence regarding her ethnic heritage is not broken until close to the end of the Hebrew narrative (implicitly in 7:4; explicitly in 8:1). When Haman precipitates a crisis by decreeing the massacre of all Jews, Esther reluctantly steps in, at the behest of Mordecai, her cousin and adopted father. Still, her speech proceeds slowly. "What is thy petition?," Ahasuerus continually asks (Esth 7:2; see also 5:3, 5:6, 9:12), and it is only at his third request that Esther finally reveals her objectives.

Esther's deferral exemplifies "strategic silence," which Barry Brummett describes in respect to political figures: "silence is strategic when someone has pressing reason to speak, but does not," instead enshrouding the silence with "mystery, uncertainty, passivity, and relinquishment" (289, 290). While the Biblical text is sparse in detail, it is easy to imagine Esther's encounters with Ahasuerus as employing mystery, passivity, relinquishment, and perhaps feigned uncertainty as a means of sexually induced pathos to obtain political gain. All Brummett's features of strategic silence are potentially enhanced by Esther's beauty—both natural and enhanced by "twelve month's treatment" undergone by all the king's harem (Esth 2:12 *Tanakh*, JPS translation). Using conventionally feminine wiles, Esther remains silent until the kairotic moment.

The first time she defers to make a "petition," Esther simply asks for Ahasuerus and Haman's presence at a feast she wishes to host. The next time, she again begs their attendance at another feast. Finally, at the end of the second feast, Esther responds to the king's request: "If I have found Favour in thy sight, O king, and if it please thee, give me my life for which I ask, and my people for which I request. For we are given up, I and my people, to be destroyed, to be slain, and to perish" (7:3-4). Lest he think she speaks too forwardly, she attests to her preference for silence. But these were extenuating circumstances: "And would God we were sold for bondmen and bondwomen: the evil might be borne with, and I would have mourned in silence: but now we have an enemy, whose cruelty redoundeth upon the king" (7:4). The floodgates of speech have opened and interruption is underway. Her petition for her people leads quickly to her revelation of Haman as the perpetrator, who is then hanged on the very gibbet Haman had intended for Mordecai.

Although Esther's language is still submissive when she meets with Ahasuerus and Haman at her feast, the men are now her guests and the banquet table becomes a bargaining table where it turns out Esther can exercise a surprising degree of gender equality and rhetorical power. So, by extolling Esther's gift of persuasion, Sor Juana offers clues for how a nondominant rhetoric can work around the traditional silence-submission contract. Interestingly, this reversal occurs in female, domestic space (Esther's banquet table). In *La respuesta*, Sor Juana pokes fun at Aristotle, wittily suggesting that his *curriculum vitae* might have been stronger had he suffered the female fate of having to study at home with only available instruments. She writes: "[W]hat can we women know, save philosophies of the kitchen? It was well put by Lupercio Leonardo that one can philosophize quite well while preparing supper. I often say, when I make these little observations, 'Had Aristotle cooked, he would have written a great deal more'" (75). I read this as a response to Plato's *Gorgias* and therefore as conscious entry into rhetorical theory. In the *Gorgias*, Plato castigates rheto-

ric as analogous to the lowly and base knack of cooking. On the contrary, Sor Juana implicitly replies, cooking is philosophical. Significantly, then, her rhetorical model Esther invites
Ahasuerus and Haman into her "kitchen," thereby enacting a rhetoric of the kitchen.

Listening for an audience's readiness and employing *kairos*, the timing of speech and silence, are key rhetorical principles we can extract from Sor Juana's work. By using Esther as
a rhetorical model, she underscores the operation of rhetorical silence, demonstrates the
need for savvy political pragmatism, and suggests an understanding of *kairos* that involves
waiting to speak until people are really ready to hear—regardless of their avowals of readiness. But these "lessons" obscure the full complexity of her theory. For Esther persuades
through dubious means: with her beauty, by deferring speech, and by withholding information about her ethnicity. By deferring her request to the king, Esther ensures his attention, inciting a desire to hear what she has to say through her very refusal. To put this in more
troubling terms, her "no" really does mean "yes." The line between seduction and persuasion
is blurred. Through Esther, Sor Juana acknowledges the reality of the politico-sexual nexus
in which persuasive-minded women become embroiled. Her use of the book of Esther indicates a pragmatic awareness that "selling out," that is, selling one's body (as some might say
Esther does) or one's soul (as some might say Sor Juana does), might become necessary in
certain circumstances. This offers a suggestive explanation for why Sor Juana ultimately
submitted to ecclesiastic authorities, who proved not as malleable as Ahasuerus.

Further, there are even more disturbing rhetorical implications in this tale than the impropriety of a nun endorsing deferred gratification to enhance seductive persuasion. For Esther
is not satisfied by the destruction of Haman or his ten sons. She continues to plead to reverse
Haman's decrees and allow the Jews to seek revenge on their enemies (Esth 8:5-11). A
bloody massacre ensues, in which Jews across the nation reverse expectations and slaughter
thousands of enemies, all authorized by Esther's decree. Esther then pleads for a second day
of violence in her own region. Finally, Mordecai records the events (9:20), and Esther and
Mordecai write another decree which sets in place the observation of the holiday of Purim
(9:29). From a reticent beauty in an alien court who hides belonging to an unpopular minority group, Esther transforms into a writing, speaking rhetor and national leader who wreaks
bloody havoc upon her enemies. While Sor Juana's own story is not respectively violent, to
examine her endorsement of Esther as a model of persuasion means considering a rhetorical
model that encompasses such violence. In other words, Sor Juana's understanding of rhetorical theory seems to acknowledge the slippery way in which violence encroaches upon
persuasive practice, and more to the point, acknowledges the way in which persuasion itself
can be quite violent.

Are the decrees Esther puts into effect different from the negotiated rhetorical exchange
with Ahasuerus? In other words, are there both "bad" and "good" models of rhetoric being
offered? Is the banquet negotiation an equilateral exchange, exemplifying democratic rhetoric, while the decrees represent autocratic rhetoric, univocal mandates of law from on high?
This interpretation is tempting, but the book of Esther seems to endorse the hierarchy and violence; it inaugurates the celebratory and joy-filled festival of Purim. Perhaps we can read
the story as a depiction of the violence that can ensue when rhetoric goes awry. And, like
many of those who have made use of the book of Esther as a rhetoric, Sor Juana may not be
intending the *entire* story to serve as model. Nonetheless, her use of Esther suggests a rhetori-

cal approach that raises significant ethical questions: it is a rhetoric for nondominant speakers grounded in deception, silence, pragmatism, conventional feminine wiles, a keen sense of *kairos*, and violence.

NOTES

1. Other Old Testament figures Sor Juana identifies include Deborah (whom Sor Juana praises for issuing laws and governing men), the Queen of Sheba (who goes unrebuked when she issues riddles to "the wisest of all wise men," Solomon), Abigail (who prophesies), Rahab (who has the gift of piety), and Hannah (the gift of perseverance) (77). A reference to Esther also appears in Sor Juana's play, *The Divine Narcissus*: Esther is a tiny stream which grows into a mighty river, which the character of Human Nature understands as a prefiguration of Mary. This allusion to Esther refers to a deuterocanonical portion of the book of Esther not found in the Hebrew text.

2. Unless noted otherwise, I am quoting from the Douay Rheims text of the Bible, which is based on the Latin Vulgate Sor Juana used. In the Vulgate, Jerome translated most of the book of Esther from the Hebrew text, and then, at the end of the Hebrew chronicle, added additional passages (known as deuterocanonical texts) found in the Greek Septuagint. The Hebrew text is far more cryptic and more strongly emphasizes Esther's silence, whereas the Greek version tries to explain Esther's motivations, frequently in her own words. It also brings in Mordecai and Esther's respect for Jewish law and God, while the Hebrew version makes no mention of divinity. Although the Greek additions belong within the narrative at various points, Jerome displaced them to the end of the text, where they make little narrative sense. He doubted their authenticity but bowed to the Septuagint's influence (*New Catholic Encyclopedia*, "Esther, Book of" 556). Thus, reading Jerome's translation, Sor Juana could still get a good sense of the mystique of silence in the Hebrew text.

3. Sor Juana's official Church biographer Diego Calleja cites Sor Juana's year of birth as 1651 when in fact her baptismal record indicates it was 1648. The latter lists only godparents, not birth parents, and says she was a "daughter of the Church," or illegitimate (Paz 65). In her convent's Book of Professions, she indicates that she was legitimate (Sabat de Rivers 39). Octavio Paz and Georgina Sabat de Rivers agree that while it was probably hard to admit illegitimacy on official documents, in practice it was often accepted. Sor Juana wrote an epigrammatic poem that seems to respond to disparaging accusations about parentage by asserting the influence of the mother in addition to the father on "honorable" parentage and by implying that the accuser's mother "solved" the problem for him by offering a number of fathers as possibilities (see "A Much-Needed Eyewash for Cleaning the Eyes of an Arrogant Myope," in Juana Inés de la Cruz, *Poems, Protest, and a Dream* 157). So, while she may not have always hidden the facts of her birth, it was clearly something she dealt with and attempted to finesse throughout her life.

WORKS CITED

Brummett, Barry. "Towards a Theory of Silence as a Political Strategy." *Quarterly Journal of Speech* 66 (1980): 289–303.

Glenn, Cheryl. *Rhetoric Retold: Regendering the Tradition from Antiquity through the Renaissance*. Carbondale: Southern Illinois UP, 1997.

Juana Inés de la Cruz. *The Answer—La respuesta: Including a selection of poems*. Eds. Electa Arenal and Amanda Powell. New York: Feminist, 1994.

—. *Poems, Protest, and a Dream*. Trans. Margaret Sayers Peden. New York: Penguin, 1997.

New Catholic Encyclopedia. New York: McGraw-Hill, 1967.

Paz, Octavio. *Sor Juana or, The Traps of Faith*. Trans. Margaret Sayers Peden. Cambridge: Harvard UP, 1988.

Ratcliffe, Krista. *Anglo-American Feminist Challenges to the Rhetorical Traditions*. Carbondale: Southern Illinois UP, 1996.

Sabat de Rivers, Georgina. *En busca de Sor Juana*. Mexico, DF: Universidad Nacional Autónoma de México, 1998.

Scott, Nina. "'La gran turba de las que merecieron nombres': Sor Juana's Foremothers in *La respuesta a Sor Filotea*." *Coded Encounters: Race, Gender, and Ethnicity in Colonial Latin America*. Ed. Javier Cevallos-Candau. Boston: U of Massachusetts P, 1994. 206–223.

Tanakh: The Holy Scriptures. The New JPS Translation According to the Traditional Hebrew Text. Philadelphia: Jewish Publication Society, 1985.

Zaeske, Susan. "Unveiling Esther as a Pragmatic Radical Rhetoric." *Philosophy and Rhetoric* 33.3 (2000): 193–220.

35

Classical Rhetoric and Nineteenth-Century American Clubwomen: Parallels of Feminist Rhetorics, Civic Reform, and Spiritual Agendas

Beth Burmester
Georgia State University

Nineteenth-century American clubwomen contribute to the history of what Anne Ruggles Gere has termed "the extracurriculum of composition," where "writing can make a difference in individual and community life" (78). In the accepted histories of English departments before the turn of the century, the extracurriculum, as Gere recognizes, is "solely a white male enterprise" (79), with literary societies and clubs at women's colleges and urban settings receiving no attention. "In addition," Gere argues, "each of these narratives positions the extracurriculum as a way-station on the route toward a fully professionalized academic department," with the express purpose of institutionalizing English studies, rather than the broader, civically oriented goals of bettering society. Gere's method in researching the study of clubs and writing groups is "to uncouple composition and schooling," so that for her, the extracurriculum "is constructed by desire, by the aspirations and imaginations of its participants. It posits writing as an action undertaken by motivated individuals who frequently see it as having social and economic consequences" (80).

I pick up Gere's call to look closer at histories outside classroom walls, to trace the legacy of women's involvement in public issues and rhetorics. To recover this heritage, we need to return to the affirmation and intellectual freedoms found in all-women associations that reach back to pre-Socratic Greece, where the contributions of women's rhetorical agendas construct a richer understanding of the role of conversation and relationships in knowledge building and collective public actions. The cultural dictum that enforced a strict separation of the sexes among the privileged citizen class in Athens also pertained to the middle and upper classes in the nineteenth century, where women's sphere was the home, and men's the public spaces of commerce, politics, and education. In both historical moments, the combination of social and political conditions provided the *kairos* and the exigence for women to connect civic welfare with feminine advancement. In the United States, a club culture that valued women's feminine identities led them to make major contributions in the name of civic duty and loyalty to other women, within—rather than counter to—the cult of domesticity and true womanhood.

Making strategic and rhetorical use of their feminine attributes gave women across history freedoms otherwise unavailable to them. Using feminist historiography, I examine the connections and parallels between women's lives and representations in classical Greece and those of the nineteenth-century clubwomen, recovering the images, practices, and lexicon that can serve as the groundwork for reimagining women's roles and their uses of gendered attributes. I also trace the roles of goddesses as part of the rhetorical heritage for women orators. Reclaiming these feminine and feminist rhetorical strategies and achievements can contribute to a richer understanding of the role of conversation and relationships in knowledge building and public rhetorics, and identify a legacy that did, and can continue to, influence women's agendas for spiritual, social, and political action.

The integration of religion, mass culture, and women's education in nineteenth-century life in the United States finds a correlation in ancient Mediterranean societies, where religious practices were entwined in women's lives through rituals associated with daily life, and seasonally with the well-being of the polis performed in festivals and rites. Most of these public ceremonies legally excluded men from observing or participating in any of the proceedings (see Dillon; Hamilton; this exclusion is highlighted in several of Euripides's dramas and in Cicero's forensic speeches and was a feature of both Greek and Roman religious practices). The women-only events created a basis for civic rhetorical performances for women and were vital to the functioning of the city, as well as offering women an opportunity to officiate and gather in public. The festivals were usually linked to fertility for both the land and the women, and celebrated reproduction and generation, as well as giving thanks for particular patron goddesses of the city for their past and future largesse. Women participating in these civic religious festivals in Athens as well as other city-states and colonies were referred to as "servants of Peitho," the Greek goddess of Persuasion (Kennedy 196; Kirby 213; Leach 426).

Their association with persuasion, embodied as a woman, shows that women were not entirely excluded from rhetoric (see Burmester; Connors; Glenn) and that in fact, they performed a kind of epideictic rhetoric, but only for audiences of women. As Matthew Dillon relates, on festival days, "women would proceed to the temples in groups to worship the gods without their menfolk [...] The male world of politics which excluded them [was] left behind as women made public statements of their piety" (4). Moreover, "It was not lawful for men to see the rites or to hear about them" (110). The secrecy of the all-women gatherings allowed women new roles, particularly for public speaking, though it may also have prevented women and their texts from entering the historical record, except for scattered archaeological evidence of engraved dedications in temple ruins and fragmented images in surviving artwork, as on friezes and pottery (Blundell 2; see also Dillon). Nineteenth-century American women also chose single-sex gatherings, where they delivered papers and speeches. The documents they produced as part of these clubs were often only distributed to members, and stored in women's houses—attics or basements, thus the small circulation and susceptibility to water, mold, fire, and other physical damage has prevented a print record from reaching larger audiences (see Sharer). While some clubs did keep meticulous archives that still exist, today they are deposited in special collections that continue to make the original and entire texts less accessible to a broad public audience. Thus the legacies of women's rhetorical acts hint at and suggest the vestiges of a once thriving culture outside but parallel to the public works by men (see Burmester, ch. 3).

Swearingen's research, coupled with recent studies using archaeology (Blundell; Dillon), demonstrate how the absence of women from historical mention does not equal their exclusion. As Swearingen observes, "Surviving traces of female wisdom figures and teachers, as well as figures of wisdom as feminine linger among the fragments of early Pythagorean and pre-Socratic philosophers," such as Hesiod, Empedocles, and Parmenides (129). Drawing on both textual evidence and the visual rhetorics on artifacts, "the historical reality of women teachers, priestesses, and wisdom figures of the seventh and sixth centuries B.C." along with "the literary representations of their speech invite attention to nuances of kinds of thought and language that were, and are, embodied in feminine qualities and characters" (Swearingen 129). The feminine attributes originated before Plato and Aristotle defined rhetoric.

As John T. Kirby asserts, before logos-ethos-pathos there was another "great triangle," one composed of peitho-bia-eros (213). Both Peitho and Bia were goddesses, with Bia being the personification of "force, physical strength, and (most especially) violence," and she serves as "an axis" between Peitho (persuasion) and Eros (sexual desire). Both Peitho and Eros are the children (daughter and son) of Aphrodite. Thus Greek culture prior to Plato and Aristotle represented love, persuasion, and physical passion as related, familial. Furthermore, as Kirby argues, "When *peitho*, *bia*, and *eros*, and their various combinations are traced through the Greek corpus, it becomes clear that they function as governing principles of both rhetoric and poetics, from Homer to Plato" (215), and that the masculine and feminine are joined.

The Coalition of Women Scholars in the History of Rhetoric and Composition chose *Peitho* as the name of their newsletter, and coeditors Susan Jarrett and Susan Romano introduce the new logo, a sketch of Peitho, in the Spring 2003 newsletter. Their description of why they chose her for the visual emblem of this women's organization uncovers her earlier position in Greek culture, as well as the potential gain from resuscitating her history:

> Peitho, Greek goddess of persuasion, merges her verbal power with the threat of seduction. In classical literatures, Peitho is connected with Aphrodite Pandemos and with Athena, goddess of the polis. Thus Peitho crosses from a feminized world of seduction into the public life of communities. We prize her for her ability to move across categories not easily violated in Western thought: religious and secular, male and female, seduction and reason, order and disorder, public in its several senses. (10)

Here, Peitho's connection with Athena opens up interpretations of the role of persuasion, and women, in public festivals aimed at civic harmony. While none of the nineteenth-century clubwomen discussed in scholarly studies mentions Peitho, many did wish to align themselves with goddesses and their attributes, and Athena was the popular choice. A variety of clubs across America invoked Athena, Minerva (her Roman incarnation), and Sophia, the Greek goddess of knowledge.

Athena is both goddess of wisdom and "goddess of domestic peace," since she "established courts of law (*Chiron Dictionary* 39). As "patron of the arts and sciences," she was worshipped by "poets and philosophers" (*Chiron* 39), so she embodied a link between rhetoric and poetics. Like Athena, Peitho was "associated with leadership and justice" (Leach 426), and both were "assigned by Zeus to 'bring young boys to manhood'" (Leach 426), primarily through mentoring. Athena is also the patron goddess of mentors. Mentoring in clas-

sical Greece indicated "education in relationships" (Young-Bruehl and Bethelard, sec. 1; see
Burmester, ch. 4). But equally significant, Athena joined the masculine and the feminine under her guise of war goddess, frequently depicted by her wearing of men's armor (helmet,
breastplate, and shield), on top of "a woman's robe" (Blundell 82). She was a virgin goddess
who, unlike the women who participated in her festivals, "was able to reject the roles of wife
and mother" (Blundell 83).

The goddess who embodied those roles, and who had strong connections to Peitho was
Aphrodite, particularly in her incarnations of Aphrodite Pandemos, and Aphrodite Hetaira
(Dillon 189). As Dillon points out, in Apollodorus's *On the Gods*, the goddess Aphrodite
Hetaira is cited as "The Companion," who "brought friends of both sexes together," and
"Hesychius mentions a shrine at Athens where male and female *hetairai*, friends, went,"
while "Athenaeus adds that Sappho called her friends *hetairai*" (qtd. in Dillon 189–90).
Pindar identifies *hetairai* as "the servants of Peitho" (Dillon 190), who were often affiliated
with Aphrodite Pandemos. So Aphrodite was not only the goddess of sexual love, but also
friendship among women, and harmony in marriage, generally achieved by the use of persuasion. Moreover, Aphrodite was a wife and mother: attributes that related her to citi-
zen-wives and gave them reason to celebrate her (alongside women from all walks of life)
with city festivals. She had the most to offer American clubwomen because they wished to
define feminism without rejecting motherhood or femininity, and because they wished to
cultivate friendships with other women; but Aphrodite's attributes and the definitions of
hetaira had, by then, shifted to mean loose morality and sexuality (Connors 68; Crockett 73;
Glenn *Rhetoric* 24-25; Glenn "sex" 182; Jarratt and Ong 12) .

Beginning in antiquity and up through the nineteenth century, strictures constraining
women's speech and their place in public life have continued virtually unabated. In order to
explain why women are not obvious in the practice of rhetoric, Patricia Bizzell notes, "This
apparent absence should not be surprising, considering the usual punishment for defying
prohibitions against women's use of rhetoric in public has been to be labeled unchaste. This
is an intriguingly gender-specific sanction" (31). Cheryl Glenn explains how women have
been "kept in their place" throughout history: "For the past 2500 years in Western Culture,
the ideal woman has been disciplined by cultural codes," and these are marked by closure: "a
closed mouth (silence), a closed body (chastity), and an enclosed life (domestic confinement)," when put together, eliminate women from participation in public life, as well as
judge their behavior on strictly gendered and sexual terms (Glenn "sex" 181).

Echoes of these codes can be detected in an incident recounted by Mary P. Ryan that occurred in 1862, where men with political power perceived "the women of New Orleans" to
have "abused the privileges of the public," hence "they were labeled prostitutes and
thereby rudely exiled to the most ignominious ranks of the citizenry" (4). LeeAnna Lawrence shows another perspective of these sanctions, arguing "A woman's style of discourse
had to conform to a specific etiquette which included the look in her eyes, the sound of her
voice, her way of carrying herself—all typed as 'womanly'. If she did not conform, she was
considered not just unwomanly, but immoral" (4). This could be an especial risk for African American women in the nineteenth century, as Floris Burnett Cash documents how
"the clubwomen had to prove that black women were virtuous [...] The most common
form of attack on the image of black women was to portray them as immoral," particularly
when they "refused to occupy the special place reserved for black women in the conven-

tional views of race progress" (8–9). In response to that criticism, Josephine Ruffin, editor of *Woman's Era* magazine "popularized the idea that a woman's place is where she is needed and where she fits in" (qtd. in Cash 9).

Fitting in while avoiding containment was a goal for many clubwomen, who were wives and mothers and committed church-goers (Blair 4). As historian Karen Blair emphasizes, "By invoking their supposed natural talents, women took the ideology of the home with them, ending their confinement and winning influence in the public realm" (4). Instead of defying the prevailing code, clubwomen tried to make it work for them. Jane Croly, founder of what many consider to be the first women's club, Sorosis, recognized the ways in which, as Blair states it, "Maternity seemed to be the greatest barrier to the admission of women to the public sphere" (18). Croly, who as a widow became "the first woman in the United States to teach newswriting" (Blair 16), lived in both public and private spheres, took the "maternal sensitivity, moral superiority, and domestic ability which she ascribed to women" and argued that these attributes "made them all the better equipped to influence the public sphere" (Blair 18). The "simple solution" to change the oppression women faced in and out of their homes, and to make a better society in general, was to "take control of their own lives and work together to demand the specific changes they desired" (Blair 19).

If women in their homes were the moral uplifters of society, then they were compelled to educate themselves to better carry out this edict. As Anne F. Scott makes clear, "Piety was linked to learning, and education to formation of moral character" (qtd. in Martin 34). While some women, younger and unmarried, were able to apply this line of argument to attend women's colleges, the older married women with children needed to find other outlets for their desire to read, write, and deliver speeches. The clubs became the ideal channel to satisfy their drive to learn and their drive to help others, while still maintaining their womanly identities. But the thousands of women joining clubs did so for another reason as well: "seeking in them the purpose, self-respect, and companionship they had previously found in their homes" (Martin 21).

I'd like to suggest viewing Sappho of Lesbos as something of a foremother of the clubwomen. Her *thiasos*, a word that translates literally to religious cult, not school, but can be interpreted in other contexts too, provides a space akin to Gere's extracurriculum. Sappho invited women to gather for conversation, celebration, and the resulting relationships became a kind of social and cultural education as well as a source of friendship. The women in her gatherings functioned in society and in this woman-centered space. Supporting a view that *thiasos* should not be read as "school," Holt Parker argues that the textual fragments of Sappho's poetry reveal her surrounded by "age-mates" or peers, not young pupils. David M. Robinson, a translator of Sappho, identified the hetairiai around her as "those ancient Y.W.C.A.'s for the cultivation of poetry and music" (245), intentionally connecting the idea of community and religious service or fellowship. Both Parker and Jarratt more recently have argued that Sappho should be regarded on the same level as the poet Alcaeus, "in a hetaira, an association of friends," (Parker 18), because she sang her songs not as cult rituals, but at public and private gatherings, like weddings and banquets, just like the male poets did" (Parker 178; see also Jarratt, "Sappho's Memory"). The elements of symposia, "cups, wine, wreaths, perfume," which usually denote all-male drinking parties, also appear throughout Sappho's fragments, perhaps alluding to "a women's society which was the mirror image of men's" (Parker 183, note 154). Parker concludes:

> Analagous to Alcaeus's circle. Sappho's society was a group of women tied by family, class, politics, and erotic love. Like any other association, it cooperated in ritual activities, cult practice and informal social events […]. This picture […] removes a distorting series of assumptions and reveals an exciting world, where women as well as men are concerned with love and politics. (183)

His conclusion firmly restores connections among peitho, pathos, and eros, in the teaching and practice of rhetoric. The association of friends also connects civic and political functions to private ones. Furthermore, looking at Sappho in this new role, other aspects about her come to view that have been obscured. While little is known of her life story, many scholars believe she did have a husband, and two poems mention a daughter, so while Sappho's identity remains woman-centered, her identity can expand to recognize her roles as wife and mother. Also, like the clubwomen after her, she saw herself and her work fitting into her society, and she made the most of the association with other women, since through the existing fragments we know how she cared for and loved the women she taught and celebrated life with.

Jane Cunningham Croly, the author of the 1200-page history of the club movement in the United States and a leading proponent of the women's club movement, expressed what many of her peers also experienced: "Sorosis has represented the closest companionship, the dearest friendships, the most serious aspirations of my womanhood" (qtd. in Martin 50–51; see also Blair, ch. 2). Her reflections also support Madeleine Grumet's insistence that "knowledge evolves in human relationships" (xix). The association of women espoused and practiced by both Sappho and Croly represent opportunities to realize Elisabeth Porter's proposal that feminist politics can "reiterate the Greek ideal of friendship" in its fullest sense for "women coming together to confirm a world held in common with […] other women" (65). What ultimately links the nineteenth-century clubwomen with classical rhetoric and Greek women is a new sense of the social importance and civic impact of associations of friends: women united for common goals.

The tradition of mythic women and their connection to persuasion and the polis was truncated when Aristotle systematically broke the union of rhetoric and poetics. When he distinguished persuasion as apart from rhetoric in his treatise, and when his definition became the accepted standard, the resulting tradition limited the encompassing woman-affiliated *peitho* while elevating the male-oriented *logos* (see Swearingen). Although the "connection between sex and rhetoric is commonplace in Greek and Latin literature," according to Kennedy (196; see also Calboli and Dominik 3), it took on distinctly gendered and negative connotations in later centuries. By the time Peitho appeared in Roman rhetoric, as "Suada," she is called "the marrow of Persuasion," but rather than evoking love, force, and power, Suada is "connected with *suavis*," meaning "sweet, pleasant" (Calboli and Dominik 3). Suada presages the personification of Folly and Eloquence during the Enlightenment, reducing the powerful Peitho to a collection of corrupting and wholly feminine attributes: superficial beauty in appearance, deception, and artifice (see Bizzell; Jarratt *Rereading*).

The associations of *peitho* with Athena's wisdom and her *metis,* or "cunning intelligence" (Blundell 82), fall away. It is time to bring them back. Jan Swearingen suggests, "The feminine aspects of persuading that have been denigrated as seduction can be similarly rescued through an examination of the close ties among emotion, love, adhesion, and persuasion in the Pre-socratic lexicon" (129). Into this lexicon, I put the term *hetaerae (hetairae)*. While its transformation through time and from Doric to Attic dialect leave us the common translation "courtesan," a reading that ensures the dismissal of women's roles as sexual instead of intellectual or relational, its earlier definitions of companion, friend, and pupil (Liddell and Scott 320) pave the way for exploring other legacies that may guide us back through history and forward again, expanding our views of women's contributions, by restoring representations and models of women's public collectivity and creativity.

WORKS CITED

Bizzell, Patricia. "Praising Folly: Constructing a Postmodern Rhetorical Authority as a Woman." *Feminine Principles and Women's Experience in American Composition and Rhetoric*. Ed. Louise W. Phelps and Janet Emig. Pittsburgh: U of Pittsburgh P, 1995. 27–42.

Blair, Karen J. *The Clubwoman as Feminist*. New York: Holmes and Meier, 1980.

Blundell, Sue. *Women in Classical Athens*. London: Bristol Classical, 1998.

Burmester, Elizabeth. "Beyond Masters and Mentors: Gender and Doctoral Education in Rhetoric and Composition." Diss. U of Illinois at Chicago, 2003.

Calboli, Gualtiero, and William J. Dominik. "Introduction: The Roman *Suada*." *Roman Eloquence: Rhetoric in Society and Literature*. Ed. William J. Dominik. New York: Routledge, 1997. 3–12.

Cash, Floris Burnette. *African American Women and Social Action: The Clubwomen and Volunteerism from Jim Crow to the New Deal, 1896–1936*. Westport: Greenwood, 2001.

Chiron Dictionary of Greek and Roman Mythology. Trans. Elizabeth Burr. Wilmette: Chiron, 1994.

Connors, Robert J. "The Exclusion of Women from Classical Rhetoric." *A Rhetoric of Doing: Essays on Written Discourse in Honor of James L. Kinneavy*. Ed. Stephen P. Witte, Neil Nakadate, and Roger D. Cherry. Carbondale: Southern Illinois UP, 1992. 165–78.

Crockett, Andy. "Gorgias's Encomium of Helen: Violent Rhetoric or Radical Feminism?" *Rhetoric Review* 13.1 (Fall 1994): 71–91.

Dillon, Matthew. *Girls and Women in Classical Greek Religion*. London: Routledge, 2002.

Gere, Anne Ruggles. "Kitchen Tables and Rented Rooms: The Extracurriculum of Composition." *College Composition and Communication* 45.1 (Feb. 1994): 75–92.

Glenn, Cheryl. *Rhetoric Retold: Regendering the Tradition from Antiquity through the Renaissance*. Carbondale: Southern Illinois UP, 1997.

—. "Sex, lies, and manuscript: Refiguring Aspasia in the History of Rhetoric." *College Composition and Communication* 45.2 (May 1994): 180–99.

Grumet, Madeleine R. *Bitter Milk: Women and Teaching*. Amherst: U of Massachusetts P, 1988.

Hamilton, Edith. *The Roman Way*. New York: Norton, 1932. Rpt. 1960.

Jarratt, Susan. *Rereading the Sophists*. Carbondale: Southern Illinois UP, 1991.

—. "Sappho's Memory." *Rhetoric Society Quarterly* 32.1 (Winter 2002): 11–43.

Jarratt, Susan, and Rory Ong. "Aspasia: Rhetoric, Gender, and Colonial Ideology." *Reclaiming Rhetorica: Women in the Rhetorical Tradition*. Ed. Andrea Lunsford. Pittsburgh: U of Pittsburgh P, 1995.

Jarratt, Susan C., and Susan Romano. "Peitho Revisited." *Peitho: Newsletter of the Coalition of Women Scholars in the History of Rhetoric and Composition* 7.2 (Spring 2003): 10.

Kennedy, George. *Comparative Rhetoric*. New York: Oxford UP, 1998.

Kirby, John T. "'The Great Triangle' in Early Greek Rhetoric and Poetics." *Rhetorica* III.3 (Summer 1990): 213–28.

Lawrence, LeeAnna Michelle. "The Teaching of Rhetoric and Composition in Nineteenth Century Women's Colleges." Diss. Duke University, 1990.

Leach, Marjorie. "Peitho." *Guide to the Gods*. Santa Barbara: ABC-Clio, 1992. 426.

Liddell & Scott's Greek-English Lexicon. 7th ed. Oxford, UK: Oxford UP, 1996.

Martin, Theodora Penny. The *Sound of Our Own Voices: Women's Study Clubs, 1860–1910*. Boston: Beacon, 1987.

Parker, Holt. "Sappho Schoolmistress." *Re-Reading Sappho: Reception and Transmission*. Ed. Ellen Greene. Berkeley: U of California P, 1996. 146–83.

Porter, Elisabeth. "Women and Friendships: Pedagogies of Care and Relationality." *Feminisms and Pedagogies of Everyday Life*. Ed. Carmen Luke. Albany: State U of New York P, 1996. 56–79.

Robinson, David M. *Sappho and Her Influence*. New York: Cooper Square, 1963.

Ryan, Mary P. *Women in Public: Between Banner and Ballots, 1825–1880*. Baltimore: Johns Hopkins UP, 1990.

Sharer, Wendy B. "Disintegrating Bodies of Knowledge: Historical Material and Revisionary Histories of Rhetoric." *Rhetorical Bodies*. Ed. Jack Selzer and Sharon Crowley. Madison: U of Wisconsin P, 1999. 120–42.

Swearingen, C. Jan. "Pistis, Expression, and Belief: Prolegomenon for a Feminist Rhetoric of Motives." *A Rhetoric of Doing: Essays on Written Discourse in Honor of James L. Kinneavy*. Ed. Stephen P. Witte, Neil Nakadate, and Roger D. Cherry. Carbondale: Southern Illinois UP, 1992. 123–43.

Young-Bruehl, Elisabeth, and Faith Bethelard. "Mentoring for Mentors: What is Mentoring?" 12 Dec. 2004 <http://www.mentoringformentors.com/>.

36

"Feeling" Sentimental: Politicizing Race and Gender in Harriet Jacobs' *Incidents in the Life of a Slave Girl*

Jami Carlacio
Cornell University

For the nineteenth-century female African-American autobiographer, writing was a performance of selfhood, an act of establishing her identity as "a woman and a sister"; it went beyond establishing a claim to woman- and sisterhood, however, and extended to the assertion of her right to be free from sexual exploitation. The themes of racism and sexual exploitation in fact dominated African-American women's autobiography during that century, whereby women expressed their virtue, their identity, and their self-worth, as well as negotiated the double bind of being Black and female (Carlacio). These women's narratives contained a political edge, particularly as they referred to the difficulties of satisfying the cultural expectations of true womanhood, for women's sexual exploitation under slavery and their unique struggles to provide a secure and safe haven for their (illegitimate) children made such a goal nearly impossible. In order for these women to communicate to their readers how they were challenged by these ideals, they needed to do more than chronicle their lives under slavery; thus, the slave narrative for women evolved into a political broadside against both the institution of slavery itself and the inhumane treatment Black women faced at the hands of their White masters and mistresses.

By mid-century, as a number of slave narratives, both spiritual and secular, made increasingly visible the issues women confronted while living in involuntary servitude, another genre—the sentimental novel—gained in popularity as White women legitimized their role in the maintenance of the virtuous home and in the security of the domestic haven. Many of these novels employed the seduction motif familiar to readers of the time, to elucidate the dangers of being female and therefore vulnerable to the potential abuses of lascivious males in a patriarchal society. Most, if not all, of these novels ended neatly, however, with the heroine transcending the trials and tribulations of her life through marriage or death. Harriet Jacobs took her cue from these immensely popular novels to tell her own story of seduction and freedom, but altogether revised the sentimental novel's fictionalized message and its tidy conclusion.[1] Unlike the stories that typified the sentimental genre, her story is not fictionalized, nor is it idealized. It ends, Jacobs explains, "not in the usual way, with marriage. I and my children are now free! [... A]nd though that, according to my ideas, is not saying a great deal, it is a vast improvement in *my* condition" (201). Blending the slave narrative genre with the immensely popular genre of sentimental fiction, Jacobs published *Incidents in the Life of a Slave Girl* in 1861, and in doing so, she performed at least two critical functions. First, she explicitly exemplified the brutality of slavery, particularly for women, through the strategy of empathetic identification; and second, she established a common ground that both African- and Anglo-American women could occupy. As a result of this identification, she could effectively urge her readers to take action, both materially and discursively, to eradicate that peculiar institution.

Using the pseudonym of Linda Brent, Jacobs details her life in slavery, her seduction, and her eventual escape. The thrust of the narrative illustrates how Linda must negotiate the reality of her sexual exploitation with the dominant cultural imperative that disapproved of women's sexual promiscuity even as it created the conditions that allowed it to occur. *Incidents* represents a critique of racism in the nineteenth century, where a system of moral values paradoxically elevated women to the highest position, even as it supported conditions that went strictly against them. Jacobs deftly discovered a way to articulate this dilemma in her story, whereby Linda rejects the sexual advances of her White master and demonstrates her agency in choosing her own (White) sexual partner. Although she must struggle with a new set of issues (bearing two illegitimate children and then providing for them once she is able to gain her freedom), Linda nevertheless reconciles her choices because she made them in the cause of freedom and self-preservation.

This reading of the novel is not new. A number of theorists, including Jean Fagan Yellin and Saidiya Hartman, have explored the political significance of Jacobs' work. Equally provocative is how Jacobs lends political force to her work by evoking an empathetic response from her audience. Specifically, Jacobs testifies about her life in slavery to establish an identification with readers across color and class lines in order to galvanize them into action. In the rest of the essay I will define empathy in its historical and its contextualized uses; then I will read Jacobs' text with an eye toward the author's ability to use empathy as a political tool to promote the abolitionist cause as the crisis of the Civil War peaked in 1861.

Feminist theorist Megan Boler has taken up the problem of empathy in the context of education, but her ideas are instructive for this project. She characterizes the increasing attention paid to the importance of "emotional literacy," and in particular its importance in the social and democratic order. Empathy (generally understood in its commonsense meaning as synonymous with sympathy) has become the *sine qua non* of social justice and curricula that foreground the importance of affective identification, locating their purpose in empathy's didactic qualities (cf. Cornell West in Boler 156). Boler further contends that "in the last 15 years of Western 'multiculturalism', empathy [has been] promoted as a bridge between differences, the affective reason for engaging in democratic dialog with the other" (156). But, Boler asks, does empathy—especially cross-culturally—invite risk? She argues that indeed empathy (as sympathy) does not "lea[d] to anything close to justice, to any shift in existing power relations" but rather lends itself to "passive empathy" and to "reading practices that do not radically challenge the reader's world view" (157). Understood in this context, Boler explains that empathetic relationships do entail risk, because, significantly, we tend to fear for *ourselves,* or we allow our emotional attachment to the text or to its writer to devolve into pity, which implies an unequal power relationship.

One of the most imminent risks I see associated with reader empathy is the inevitability of eliding the feelings (sentiments) of the other via proxy. In other words, the very act of substituting oneself for the other, in order to feel *for* the other, or, in an ideal world, *with* the other, enables a privileging of the one (reader) over the other (writer). One of the primary challenges facing us, then, as we read accounts of slavery such as Jacobs', is the risk we assume in trying to "empathize" with the writer, for indeed empathy is both slippery and difficult (Hartman 18). As Saidiya Hartman explains, "empathy is a projection of oneself into another in order to better understand the other or 'the projection of one's own personality into an object, with the attribution to the object of one's own emotions'" (Hartman 19; Peter Angeles qtd. in Hartman 19). At issue here is that the ease with which we identify with the enslaved body elides the reality of that body's suffering. We ultimately project our own feelings and thoughts onto the body of the other. Hartman rightly questions, "Can the white witness of the spectacle of suffering affirm the materiality of [B]lack sentience only by feeling for [ourselves]?" [...] Perhaps [B]lack sentience is inconceivable and unimaginable" (19).

While it may be impossible to inhabit the exact feelings or experience of another, Jacobs did invite identification. And to a great extent, her texts moved readers; as the sentimental novel gained in popularity as the nineteenth century progressed, writers like Jacobs were acutely aware of the "transformative capacities" of pain and suffering in that sentimental culture (Hartman 20). Indeed, as Jane Tompkins, Nina Baym, and Cathy Davidson have argued, writers of sentimental or domestic fiction appealed to their readers precisely because they wrote about issues that invited identification. Women shared common oppressions, and as a result of the immense popularity of domestic fiction, the distance between author/narrator and reader decreased; consequently, the "cultural work" (cf. Tompkins) that domestic fiction could accomplish became more acute. But while the conditions for identification were made more and more possible, they did not completely diminish the ostensibly unimaginable nature of suffering, particularly across racial and class boundaries. This insurmountability ultimately points to the "precarious nature of empathy," illuminating what Hartman identifies as the "thin line between witness and spectator": we as readers must substitute ourselves for the one suffering, thus foregrounding our own affective response (19). "It becomes clear," Hartman continues, "that empathy is double-edged, for in making the other's suffering one's own, this suffering is occluded by the other's obliteration" (19). In other words, "we feel ourselves into those we imagine as ourselves" (Jonathan Boyarin qtd. in Hartman 19–20).

Jacobs invites the risk of being obliterated by the very act of encouraging readers to *witness* and therefore participate in her life: her seduction, her betrayal by both White women and White men, her decision to be a fugitive (absent-present) mother,[2] and her eventual freedom from bondage. She risks, that is, becoming an "object-commodity" (Hartman) that would allow for the reader to consume and therefore annihilate her. Certainly, in granting her readers the power of witnessing, she risks losing any control she might otherwise retain; she could compromise her agency and subjectivity as the object of her readers' surveillance. And yet, while such a risk was great, it was an even greater one to forego the opportunity to imagine herself *as a self in control*: in control of her self through the very act of literacy which enabled her to write her life—to perform auto-bio-graphy—and, therefore, in control of establishing her identity via identification with her readers.

It would be correct to question how empathy-as-sympathy could ever be a tool of empowerment for someone like Jacobs, who ostensibly risks being subsumed by the reader's appropriation of her experience. But if we investigate empathy more radically, taking our cue from Boler, we may arrive at a nuanced definition of empathy that enables us to read

Jacobs' text and to appreciate how she skillfully invites readers into it in such a way that guards against the annihilation of her subjectivity. Writing about empathy in the context of teaching literature of the Holocaust, Boler argues for complicating the relationship between text and reader by requiring from the reader some responsibility and by encouraging an "empathetic response that motivates action: a 'historicized ethics' [...] that radically shifts our self-reflective understanding of power relations" (158). In order to effect such a shift, we must learn to "empathize across differences" through "testimonial reading." This kind of reading challenges the reader's relationship to the text vis-à-vis power. It allows for neither a kind of "passive empathy" that "imagines the other [...] too easily" nor an abdication of our responsibility for the conditions that produced or made possible the other's trauma in the first place (163).

"Testimonial reading," explains Boler, "emphasizes a collective educational responsibility" (164); "listening" to the text and its speaker, moreover, offers a way for us to interrogate not only our assumptions about that speaker or the event narrated but also our own (complicit) role in the situation, particularly from our "removed" position, our own cultural moment. Extending Boler's discussion from reading Holocaust literature to reading hybrid texts such as Jacobs', we can see the importance of listening empathetically, whether the readers were Jacobs' contemporaries or whether this includes those of us reading her in the twenty-first century. Testimonial reading requires us to pay attention to what is being said, to who is saying it, and generally to the rhetorical situation governing the problematic. Significantly, we are given the opportunity to bridge the distance between ourselves and the other by considering our analogous relationship to structures of power. Just as today we might recall our experience of gender-, race-, or class-based oppression, Jacobs specifically addresses her text to White, middle-class women in an effort to garner this kind of radical empathy—identification—by using the sentimental genre of fiction to produce a slave narrative that calls not for a passive and sympathetic readership but for an active constituency to voice their opposition and to act on it by "laboring to advance the cause of humanity!" (30).

Obviously, Jacobs must negotiate the tension between defining herself as a woman, a mother, and a sister at the risk of, paradoxically, effacing the very identities she seeks to create or appropriate. One the one hand, Jacobs effectively creates a (suffering) self in the very act of writing. On the other, Jacobs appropriates the monikers of woman, mother, and sister, thereby taking control of her self by choosing to identify with her readers on a level that they would understand and, indeed, identify with. Jacobs tries to preclude the possibility of "othering" herself by using the first-person narrative and by employing apostrophic address, both to prescribe and to proscribe the kind of empathy appropriate to her White, female, middle-class readers. Jacobs *risks* the co-optation of her pain, and indeed of her subjectivity, by encouraging her audience to identify with her. We might infer from her rhetorical strategies that she felt the risk to be worth it because her primary objective was to incite her readers to act, and they could not (or would not) act if they did not "feel" a certain kinship with her. Readers must, in order to identify with Jacobs, experience an affective relationship with her and her plight. Jacobs in fact prefaces her novel by assuring readers first that "this is no fiction" and that she

> earnestly desire[s] to arouse the women of the North to a realizing sense of the condition of two millions of women at the South, still in bondage, suffering what I suffered, and most of them far worse. I want to add my testimony to that of abler pens to convince the people of the Free States what Slavery really is. Only by experience can any one realize how deep, and dark, and foul is that pit of abominations. (1–2)

Clearly, Jacobs is offering her testimonial, based on her experience, to signify to readers that they can potentially identify with her suffering: they may come to a "realizing sense," or come to know and feel what she has known and felt. Early in the text, therefore, we see Jacobs taking control of their (our) affective response by instructing them (us) how to do so. Further, Jacobs demonstrates her knowledge of the previous abolitionist responses to it. She adds her voice to these "abler pens"—most likely this refers to Lydia Maria Child and the Grimké sisters—who have rather eloquently petitioned against the peculiar institution. Child and the Grimké sisters have testified, have listened empathetically. Just as their testimonials were models for Jacobs, so Jacobs' is a model for her contemporaries and for us.

Jacobs also demonstrates her authorial control by creating an alter ego, Linda Brent, who owns her sexuality. By refusing Dr. Flint's lascivious sexual advances, Linda lays claim to her virtue and her choice of suitors. Although she is forbidden to marry the "young colored carpenter" to whom she had become attached (37), she consents to the attentions of a "white unmarried gentleman," Mr. Sands, in order to "enrage" Dr. Flint and to "triumph over [her] tyrant even in that small way" (55). Before she offers an account of what she refers to as her "perilous passage," Jacobs attempts to pre-empt readers' judgment of her by inviting them to identify across the color line:

> I can testify, from my own experience and observation, that slavery is a curse to the whites as well as to the blacks. It makes the white fathers cruel and sensual; the sons violent and licentious; it contaminates the daughters, and makes the wives wretched. And as for the colored race, it needs an abler pen than mine to describe the extremity of their sufferings, the depth of their degradation. (52)

Here, Jacobs reaffirms her authority of experience by reminding readers that she is a bona fide witness to the horrors of slavery. Moreover, Linda [Jacobs] vindicates her decision to compromise her virtue by invoking what she believes are trumping sentiments common to all—the need for self-pride or self-esteem.

Jacobs goes on, providing a rationale for her sexual conduct:

> It seems less degrading to give one's self, than to submit to compulsion. There is something akin to freedom in having a lover who has no control over you, except that which he gains by kindness and attachment. A master may treat you as rudely as he pleases, and you dare not speak; moreover, the wrong done does not seem so great with an unmarried man, as with one who has a wife to be made unhappy. There may be sophistry in all this; but the condition of a slave confuses all principles of morality, and, in fact, renders the practice of them impossible. (55)

And in that same chapter, Jacobs employs both an ethical and a pathetic appeal to her audience:

> Pity me, and pardon me, O virtuous reader! You never knew what it is to be a slave; to be entirely unprotected by law or custom; to have the laws reduce you to the condition of a chattel, entirely subject to the will of another. [...] I know I did wrong. No one can feel it more sensibly than I do. The painful and humiliating memory will haunt me to my dying day. Still, in looking back, calmly, on the events of my life, I feel that the slave woman ought not to be judged by the same standard as others. (55–56)

In an adept rhetorical turn, Jacobs seeks the reader's pity, praises her virtue, and admits her "fall from grace"—all the while challenging the criteria on which Black women were to be judged, criteria to which White, middle-class women were not subject. Jacobs not only asserts her agency in choosing a lover and a potential father but also instructs her readers how to "read" the situation—in short, how to "feel" about it. Linda walks a fine line, to be sure, between choosing and refusing. She "chooses" Mr. Sands as she "refuses" Dr. Flint, and yet even her putative choice is only a choice between the lesser of two evils. In that context, Mr. Sands is not a "choice" at all; in fact, he represents a coerced choice, one that Linda [Jacobs] is able to defend. She does not willingly "give it up" to the "White man"; rather, she consents to her subjugation because her only other recourse is forcible rape. And that precludes any choice at all. In the end, we learn after all that Mr. Sands does not marry Linda, does not buy her and subsequently free her, and only marginally participates in the parenting of their children, Benny and Ellen. Jacobs reiterates, in her address to the reader, that sexual "freedom" is the province of the White and the free—it is therefore a class- and race-based political economy of exchange.

Jacobs turns the tables on her readers by describing her emotions and feelings about her impossible situation, presupposing what her readers might feel, and in effect instructing them how to feel *with* her—how to empathize. In her apostrophic address, to which I refer above, she tells readers that "it is not to awaken sympathy for myself that I am telling you truthfully what I suffered in slavery. I do it to kindle a flame of compassion in your hearts for my sisters who are still in bondage, suffering as I once suffered" (29). We might read Jacobs' use of the word compassion here as signifying empathy. She does not wish her readers to sympathize with or "feel badly" for her; rather, she invites them (and us) to identify affectively not only with her but also with her sisters, who remain in bondage. Her story does not, rightly speaking, refer only to a situation that has occurred in the past tense. Readers are ostensibly alerted to an ongoing injustice to which they ought to respond in the present. As Hartman explains, Jacobs effectively "pander[s] to [her readers'] sense of moral superiority only to topple the pedestal on which they stand and unmoo[r] them in the storm of events" (107).

Jacobs took a great risk in writing *Incidents in the Life of a Slave Girl*. By effectively blending the genres of the sentimental novel and the slave narrative, she produced an affective response in her readers that enabled them—and enables us today—to identify with her and her sisters as women subjected to one of history's worst evils. She explains to readers in her Preface that while her motives to produce "a sketch of my life" may have seemed "presumptuous," she nevertheless felt compelled to add her voice to the growing body of abolitionists who sought, mostly through moral suasion, to eradicate the bonds that held so many in involuntary servitude. As she wrote to her confidante Amy Post in October of 1853, "if it could help save another from my fate it would be selfish and unchristian in me to keep it back" (qtd. in Yellin xxix). As her friend William Nell wrote of the book's publication in a letter published in a January 1861 issue of *The Liberator*,

[*Incidents*] presents features more attractive than many of its predecessors purporting to be histories of slave life in America, because, in contrast with their mingling of fiction with fact, this record of uncomplicated experience in the life of a young woman, a doomed victim to [sic] America's peculiar institution ... surely need not the charms that any pen of fiction, however gifted and graceful, could lend. They shine by the luster of their own truthfulness—a rhetoric which always commends itself to the wise head and honest heart. (qtd. in Yellin xxiv)

Indeed, an honest and wise woman penned this work, and as her readers and her sisters, we must take our cue from Jacobs: we must use our "able pens" to testify to the multiple injustices women have suffered and continue to suffer, and we must actively seek to end them.

ACKNOWLEDGMENT

My thanks to Martin Kurth and Vicki Boynton for their careful review of this essay.

NOTES

1. A number of scholars point to the influence of the sentimental novel on Jacobs' work. See, for example, Jean Fagan Yellin; Thomas Doherty; Nina Baym; and Cathy Davidson.
2. By absent-present, I mean that Jacobs was both an "absent" mother because she could not actively mother her children and a "present" one because she lived in such close proximity to them in her grandmother's attic. The narrator in fact recalls, "Season after season, year after year, I peeped at my children's faces, and heard their sweet voices, with a heart yearning all the while to say, 'Your mother is here'" (148).

WORKS CITED

Baym, Nina. *Women's Fiction: A Guide to Novels by and about Women in America, 1820–1870.* Ithaca: Cornell UP, 1978.

Boler, Megan. *Feeling Power: Emotions and Education.* New York: Routledge, 1999.

Carlacio, Jami. "African American Women's Autobiography." *Encyclopedia of Women's Autobiography.* Ed. Jo Malin and Victoria Boynton. Westport, CT: Greenwood P. Forthcoming.

Davidson, Cathy. *Revolution and the Word: The Rise of the Novel in America.* New York: Oxford UP, 1986.

Doherty, Thomas. "Harriet Jacobs' Narrative Strategies: *Incidents in the Life of a Slave Girl.*" *Southern Literary Journal* 19.1 (Fall 1986): 79–91.

Hartman, Saidiya. *Scenes of Subjectivity: Terror, Slavery, and Self-Making in Nineteenth-Century America.* New York: Oxford UP, 1997.

Jacobs, Harriet. [Linda Brent]. *Incidents in the Life of a Slave Girl: Written by Herself.* Ed. Jean Fagan Yellin. Cambridge: Harvard UP, 1987.

Tompkins, Jane. *Sensational Designs: The Cultural Work of American Fiction, 1790–1860.* New York: Oxford UP, 1985.

Yellin, Jean Fagan. Introduction. *Incidents in the Life of a Slave Girl: Written by Herself.* Ed. Jean Fagan Yellin. Cambridge: Harvard UP, 1987. xiii–xxxiv.

37

Using the Needle as a Sword: Needlework as Epideictic Rhetoric in the Woman's Christian Temperance Union

Sue Carter
Bowling Green State University

Photographs of conventions, chapter meetings, and the like of the Woman's Christian Temperance Union (WCTU) in the late nineteenth and early twentieth centuries show recurring images of white ribbons tied to the bodices of women as a visual symbol of their support of temperance and stages decorated not only with flags and flowers, but also with a panoply of banners, shields, and quilts.[1] These images can be seen in Fig. 37.1, a photograph taken at the 1903 WCTU World Convention in Geneva.[2] These material artifacts typically were crafted by members of the Union and displayed over and over at local chapter meetings, in booths at state and county fairs, in parades, and at WCTU conventions at the state, national, and international levels. In their material forms, these handcrafted items publicly and simultaneously displayed women's support of the many social reforms advocated under Frances Willard's leadership, including suffrage, as well as women's accomplishment in the traditionally female art of fine needlework. This dual display was not simple stage dressing, for needlework was an important aspect of the rhetorical agenda of the WCTU under the leadership of Frances Willard in the last decades of the nineteenth century.

NEEDLEWORK IN THE RHETORICAL AND POLITICAL AGENDAS OF THE WOMAN'S CHRISTIAN TEMPERANCE UNION

This rhetorical strategy of juxtaposing the more radical calls for social reform with the more traditional notions of women's roles was widely used in temperance speeches in the late nineteenth century, as Carol Mattingly notes in *Well-Tempered Women* (52). One verbal example of this strategy is Frances Willard's strategic re-naming of woman's suffrage as "home protection." This slogan effectively yoked fundamentally different value systems

FIG. 37.1.   Photograph taken at the 1903 Woman's Christian Temperance Union World Convention in Geneva. Note that the stage is decorated with palm trees, ferns, flags, and banners. On the long banner running behind the row of seated women is the beginning of the WCTU motto, "For God and Home and Every Land." White ribbons can be discerned on the bodices of several of the women pictured. Photograph supplied by Archives of Ontario, F 885, image number 10006727. Women's Christian Temperance Collection. Archives of Ontario.

by arguing that because the public sphere already posed a threat to the home through male alcoholism, women needed the vote in order to protect their private sphere. Similarly, the making and displaying of handcrafted needlework can be viewed as rhetorical activities that yoked traditional, uncontroversial values to a wide-ranging social reform agenda that included not only temperance but also such issues as suffrage, child care for working women, prison reform, the eight-hour work day, federal aid to education, and the kindergarten movement. At the 1878 national WCTU convention in Baltimore, Willard consciously politicized one form of needlework, the quilt. When the commemorative Crusade Quilt was presented at this meeting, one speaker saw it as a symbol of the patience of women in matters of detail, a reiteration of conventional female values presumably needed in temperance work. Willard, in contrast, argued that the quilt should be placed as a symbol of protest alongside two powerful historical symbols of woman's oppression: the auction block on which women slaves had been sold and the death sentences of women burned as witches (Ferrero, Hedges, and Silber 87–88; Willard, *Woman and Temperance* 77–79). Willard's argument thus radicalized the traditional female arts of quiltmaking and needlework by reconceptualizing them as modes of women's social protest.

Willard's rhetorical agenda was a broad-based appeal to the traditional values of Christian morality, patriotism, and of women's "proper" sphere that was directed toward gaining support for the organization's political goals. The political agenda was pursued through an extensive network of rhetorical situations, including regular and numerous meetings at the local, state, national and international levels; temperance speaking tours; petition drives; and an extensive publishing industry. While temperance speeches, publications, petition drives and other forms of verbal rhetoric focused on accomplishing the political agenda of reform legislation, WCTU needlework can be viewed as forms of epideictic rhetoric that helped the organization create community among its membership and increase the intensity with which members identified themselves with that community. In their very fo ,a, such artifacts presented visual arguments that reinforced central values in shortened, epigrammatic or enthymatic form. These more general, less detailed visual arguments presented options for WCTU women to focus upon the ties that bound them, rather than the serious differences with which the organization's leadership and membership wrestled.[3]

What distinguished needlework as WCTU needlework was the use of symbols related to temperance and to the organization. Quilts, whether intended for home use, fund-raising, or as commemorative gifts, were often made in the official WCTU colors of blue and white. Some traditional quilt patterns came to be associated with temperance. The T or Double T pattern was readily associated with temperance, given its prominent visual image of the capital letter T. The pattern variously known as Solomon's Puzzle, Rocky Road to California, and Robbing Peter to Pay Paul gained the new name Drunkard's Path (Jenkins and Seward, 85), turning this wandering, intricate quilt pattern into a visual metaphor for the crooked path leading from the first sips of spirits to the moral downfall of alcoholism. This pattern was often made in the WCTU's official colors of blue and white, enforcing its symbolic association with temperance. The temperance slogan "Alcohol No Longer King" made on a tea towel illustrates that even everyday textiles were transformed into political banners (Ferrero et al. 82).

In discussing such forms of needlework as epideictic rhetoric, I draw on four aspects of theory and am particularly influenced by Cynthia Sheard's discussion in "The Public Value of Epideictic Rhetoric." First is the classical notion of epideictic rhetoric as ceremonial display of talent or artistry, which, with regard to WCTU needlework, involves the display of an appropriately feminine ethos. Second is the notion, drawn from Perelman and Olbrechts-Tyteca as well as others, of epideictic rhetoric as inculcating commonly held values and increasing the intensity of an audience's adherence to those values. The visual nature of and powerful symbols used in WCTU needlework clearly work to support the values explicated in more detail in temperance speeches and writings. The third, drawn primarily from Sheard and to a lesser extent from Takis Poulakos and Jeffrey Walker, is the notion of epideictic rhetoric as having a visionary quality. From this perspective, visual images in WCTU needlework can be seen as attempts to construct an idealized image of female reformers. And finally, drawn from Sheard, is the conception of epideictic rhetoric as "moving its audience toward a process of critical reflection" (787). On this point, I assess WCTU needlework on the basis of its potential to provide such a process for the women who contributed toward making it.

CONSTRUCTION AND DISPLAY OF A WOMANLY ETHOS

Considering WCTU needlework from the traditional perspective as display can involve recognizing the talent and artistry demonstrated in particular artifacts, and WCTU quilts and banners do support such an argument, although this is a line that I will not pursue at present. More relevant to the rhetorical agenda of Willard and the WCTU, instead, is the role of WCTU needlework in displaying an appropriate ethos, whether for individual speakers, for the stage on which they spoke, or for the WCTU as a whole. Mattingly discusses Willard's advice to female temperance speakers to present themselves in nonthreatening and womanly ways and dress accordingly: "Womanliness first—afterward what you will" (65–66), as well as the attention paid to Willard's own modest dress in public presentations (114–15). Likewise, Nan Johnson discusses the high prominence given to the performance of femininity for Willard and other temperance writers and speakers of her era (111–14).

In addition to advice about public speaking per se, Willard provided advice about how the stages and meeting halls should be decorated, a rhetorical strategy designed to bolster the feminine ethos of the speakers who would occupy the stage. Following Willard's instructions, WCTU members decorated stages with flowers, national flags, state shields, and banners they had designed and made, all powerful symbols of womanhood and patriotism (Willard, *Woman and Temperance* 632; Mattingly 67–68). Photographs of stages show the heavily decorated feel typical of Victorian interiors.[4] Meeting halls provided display space for WCTU needlework, such as embroidered and quilted samplers of the national motto (Mattingly 67–68) as well as banners, as in the photograph of a display from a WCTU national convention in the 1890s printed in Willard's autobiography (*Glimpses* 456ff.). Local chapters secured booths at expositions and at state and county fairs, where WCTU needlework was displayed (Ferrero et al. 86–87; Harker and Allen 63). As material artifact, then, WCTU needlework displayed a nonthreatening, conservative, and appropriately womanly ethos in various venues, from temperance stage to county fair booth to local Union meetings.

Willard herself provides an argument that suggests an additional way WCTU needlework functioned as a display of femininity. In her sketch "Our Many Sided Work," Willard praises the temperance women whom she dubs "'The silent sisters,' who do not help with voice or pen." Willard acknowledges that while the needs of temperance work are great, the talents of women are underestimated (*Woman and Temperance* 145–46). Using the war imagery common in temperance rhetoric, she continues: "Choice gifts indeed 'the silent sisters' bring into the common treasury. Largely from their wealth or industry we gather the sinews of war" (146). Needlework provided a material way for many women to contribute their industry to the temperance cause while simultaneously performing their femininity. As quilts and other forms of needlework were raffled, auctioned, or sold, a popular nineteenth-century fundraising activity (Cozart), the proceeds did help to line the WCTU war chest. While needlework is not mentioned in this passage, it is not hard to extend Willard's line of argument: The modest and gentle women who produced WCTU needlework waged war not with their words, but with their needles.

IDENTIFYING WITH COMMON VALUES

Producing WCTU needlework was a process—often a communal one—that allowed women to express their talents and artistry in a familiar medium associated with traditional gender roles, while simultaneously stitching ties to an organization that celebrated the traditional values of purity, Christianity, patriotism, and motherhood. Perelman and Olbrechts-Tyteca discuss the role of epideictic rhetoric in creating and maintaining a "sense of communion" centered on values that are taken as uncontested. A speaker's role is to promote "values that are shared in the community" and to "increase the intensity of adherence to values held in common by the audience and the speaker" (52). Epideictic rhetoric from this perspective is, in Sheard's words, "a rhetoric of identification and conformity" (766).

Promoting identification between the individual and the organization's values and identity is a central rhetorical function of WCTU needlework. "Chapter quilts" were made collaboratively by a local chapter, usually with each member responsible for making one square. At times, individuals signed their names, using colorfast ink popular among quilters in the late nineteenth century. Chapter quilts typically used the colors blue and white and the letters WCTU, signifying ties of the local group to the national organization. Once made, such quilts were used for display in a variety of settings, and at times when members of a particular chapter were unable to attend a prominent meeting, its chapter quilt might be sent and displayed. State Unions also made quilts, with individual squares representing local chapters. One such example is the 1887 Connecticut Shoo Fly quilt (Ferrero et al. 15). The initials WCTU are embroidered in blue on white squares, using the official colors of the organization. Four squares in the center honor the State officers by name and title. Local chapters are named individually in squares that make up the body and the border of the quilt. Crusade quilts also promoted identification between individual members or chapters with the organization. One made to honor the 1873 Women's Temperance Crusade in Ohio, led by Eliza Jane Trimble Thompson, was presented to her at the 1878 national WCTU convention. The quilt was made of squares of different colors for each state represented, and on the back of each square WCTU members inked their names—some three thousand altogether. It was the presentation and display of this quilt that prompted Frances Willard to comment upon the political symbolism of quilts (Ferrero et al. 85).

In addition to promoting identification, WCTU verbal rhetoric and needlework emphasized traditional, uncontested values central to the organization—purity, Christianity, patriotism, and womanliness. Purity is promoted in the ubiquitous white ribbon, while Christianity, patriotism, and motherhood are promoted in the WCTU motto "For God and Home and Native Land" or in international settings, "For God and Home and Every Land." Among WCTU needlework, these values are foregrounded most vividly in WCTU banners. Images and descriptions of banners are somewhat challenging to find, and photographs of decorated meeting halls often provide little detail about particular banners. Fortunately, images of twenty-one banners made by Canadian WCTU members between 1877 and 1932 are provided in *Gather beneath the Banner*, the catalog of an exhibit at the Textile Museum of Canada in Toronto in 1999. As a whole, the banners in this collection are a visual celebration of the identity of the organization and its central values. In fact, four banners in this collection include the WCTU motto, two with "Every Land" and two with "Native Land." The white ribbon, such a prominent symbol of the WCTU that temperance workers were sometimes referred to as "White Ribboners," is found in nine of the twenty-one banners in this collection. Figure 37.2, an Ontario banner with both symbols, is made of a deep blue velvet that contrasts starkly with the white painted letters of the motto and the painted image of the white ribbon.

The performance of femininity is demonstrated in the banners through their manner of construction and decoration. Made of lush velvets, silks, and satins, the banners have hand-painted lettering, satin-stitch and French knot embroidery, and elaborate fringes. Hand-painted images include floral borders, flowering tree branches, a dragonfly, yellow daisies, and grains such as hops and barley that represent alcoholic beverages. Figure 37.3,

FIG. 37.2. Ontario, Canada WCTU Banner, 1877. The values of purity, Christianity, patriotism, and womanliness are evoked through the WCTU motto and the painted images of the white ribbon and the Canadian maple leaves. *Gather beneath the Banner,* Plate 1, pp. 16, 51. Reprinted by permission of The Textile Museum of Canada, Toronto, Canada.

FIG. 37.3. Ontario Prize Banner, 1888. Made of beige satin with light and dark green velvet borders, the banner has painted lettering and thick coiled metal fringe along the lower edge and is hung from a green satin rope. Below the words "Prize Banner" is a hand-painted image of birds and tree branches. Some of the birds perch along the top of a column painted on the satin background, and several appear to be looking down, as though they are reading the WCTU motto below. *Gather beneath the Banner,* Plate 5, pp. 34, 53. Reprinted by permission of The Textile Museum of Canada, Toronto, Canada.

an Ontario Prize Banner from 1888, is made of beige satin and bordered with light and dark green velvet. Its top and bottom borders are overpainted. It includes a charming scene of little birds on tree branches, and some of the birds are looking down from their perch on top of a column, creating the impression that they are perhaps reading the WCTU motto below. These banners are an impressive performance of the feminine accomplishments of fine needlework and painting.

Christian values are evoked in these banners through words and through visual images, both usually painted on the cloth. Thirteen banners use Biblical slogans and Bible verses, some written out and others referred to by book, chapter, and verse. Four use slogans—"We Can Do All Things through Christ," "Workers with God," "In God We Trust," and "The World for Christ." Nine others use such inspiring and comforting Bible verses as these:

Fear not I am with you (Isaiah 43:5)

In the name of God we lift up our banner (Psalm 20:5)

Our God shall fight for us (Nehemiah 4:20)

Have faith in God (Mark 11:22)

Visual images are used as well: An 1894 banner features a painted image of a Bible opened to Psalm 23 ("The Lord is my shepherd; I shall not want"), and a 1909 banner shows a white dove of peace flying over a cross.

Patriotism is promoted likewise through patriotic symbols as well as through self-naming. The banners in this collection overwhelmingly name the communities they represent—such as Welland County, the Toronto district, Rosemount, Hamilton, Mount Forest. In fact, only one banner of the twenty-one does not name its provenance. In this Canadian collection, maple leaf symbols are painted on two banners, including the one in Fig. 37.2.

IDEALIZED VISIONS

Related to its function of promoting communally shared values, epideictic rhetoric can serve the function of assisting an audience in constructing images of reality, of one kind or another. As Sheard notes, "By bringing together images of both the real—what *is* or at least *appears to be*—and the fictive or imaginary—what *might be*—epideictic discourse allows speaker and audience to envision possible, new, or at least different worlds" (770). From this perspective, epideictic rhetoric can become "a vehicle through which communities can imagine and bring about change" (771). Images of this sort in epideictic rhetoric may well be more idealized than real (Poulakos 320; Sheard 770).

Idealized portraits of women are prevalent in temperance rhetoric. In discussing the genre of biographical sketches of female reformers written near the end of the nineteenth century, for example, Nan Johnson notes the prevalence of images of these women as "noble maids," "eloquent mothers," and "mother protectors." Johnson argues that these images underscore cultural beliefs at that time that "women speakers, and women in general, were eloquent not because they were skilled, but because they were moral and loving women who were naturally persuasive in their proper sphere" (114). Willard herself, in Johnson's analysis of her verbal rhetoric, "defines women's public involvement in politics as 'mothering' acts and persistently reinscribes an image of the nation as a home in crisis needing, more than anything else, the maternal intervention of women" (125). Certainly

FIG. 37.4.   Hamilton, Ontario "Workers With God" Banner, 1890. The striking painted image of the woman with a sword protecting a child illustrates the "noble maid" and "mother protector" images of WCTU women in temperance speeches and writings. The image represents a turn on the Biblical story of woman's fall after being tempted by Satan in the form of a snake. Here, the serpent in the nest of grains represents man's moral fall through alcoholism. *Gather beneath the Banner,* Plate 6, front cover and p. 54. Reprinted by permission of The Textile Museum of Canada, Toronto, Canada.

Willard's call for "the Home Protection ballot" and her repeated focus on reform through legislation highlight the sense of a nation in crisis, and her temperance rhetoric is rife with images of war and imminent peril.

The Canadian banner collection includes one particularly stirring banner that presents an epideictic vision of woman's power in the face of the peril of alcoholism. Figure 37.4, the Hamilton, Ontario "Workers with God" banner, is dominated by the painted image of a woman holding a sword raised as if to strike the forked-tongued, red-eyed, black snake emerging from a nest of grains. With her free hand she pushes back the small child at her side, in a gesture of protection. With her hair streaming in an imagined wind and her eyes blazing with the righteous necessity of the action she is about to complete, this woman presents a powerful visual image of Johnson's "noble maid" and "mother protector." In discussing epideictic in landscapes, Michael Halloran remarks on "a curious and typically late-nineteenth-century inversion" of the principle of display (240) wherein what is displayed is the audience's taste rather than the power of the orator. In perhaps a similar manner, this banner presents an inversion of the myth familiar to WCTU members of Adam's fall through Eve's being tempted by Satan in the form of a serpent. This banner presents instead a story about the redemption of man and the protection of child and the home from the evils of grain alcohol by the courageous actions of woman.

CONCLUSION:
EPIDEICTIC AS CONTINUED THOUGHT AND DISCUSSION

Sheard raises the consideration that idealized epideictic images present legitimate ethical concerns when depictions of the past or present are used to evoke changes in thought or action (784–85). Certainly the idealized image of the noble mother protector in the Hamilton banner can be seen as both an inspiring image as well as an unrealistic one. Its enthymatic argument conveniently distills the wide-ranging social reform agenda of the WCTU to a simple battle between Good and Evil. Likewise, the White mother pictured in this banner along with the pervasive white ribbons of the WCTU construct an idealized image of unity in an organization whose leadership engaged in strenuous debates about including suffrage in the political agenda and failed to deal adequately with their own racism (Mattingly, 73–76, 170–71; Johnson 176n). It seems certain that the symbolic forms and striking though abbreviated visual arguments used in WCTU needlework promoted the uncritical acceptance of cultural norms. Taken as a whole, WCTU needlework both supports the verbal rhetoric of the organization and mirrors its own shortcomings. Yet this very abbreviated form of argument enabled pious, conservative women to construct images of themselves as having a vital political voice that was consistent with their images of themselves as women.

Arguing for the public role of epideictic rhetoric, Sheard sketches a conception of it as inviting "continued thought and discussion as a prelude to decision and action" (788). Similarly, for Walker, epideictic "shapes the fundamental grounds, the 'deep' commitments and presuppositions that will underlie and ultimately determine decision and debate in particular pragmatic forums" (*Rhetoric* 9). There are anecdotal reports to suggest that at least some women engaged in an individual process of assessing their values as part of quilt-making projects, considering, for example, whether or not to sign a chapter quilt made in support of suffrage (Ferrero et al.). It also seems possible that in the process of constructing WCTU needlework—surely a type of "slow rhetoric," to borrow Lester Faigley's phrase (see ch. 1, this vol.)—individual women may well have examined and affirmed their own values, perhaps deciding they saw no contradiction between performing their roles as women and working for social reform. Sheard, Walker, and Perelman and Olbrechts-Tyteca note that epideictic rhetoric can function as a prelude to other types of discourse, particularly deliberative and judicial. Certainly as a component of the political and rhetorical agendas of the WCTU, this needlework played important roles, from constructing a feminine ethos for temperance speakers to constructing a political voice for those who stitched these stirring symbols of woman's power.

NOTES

1. I'd like to acknowledge Sharon Strand of Black Hills State University for first introducing me to WCTU needlework. I'd also like to acknowledge Inez Schaechterle of Buena Vista University for calling my attention to WCTU banners, particularly the collection I discuss here.

2. Photographs of WCTU leaders wearing white ribbons are readily found in both modern histories of temperance as well as ones from the late nineteenth and early twentieth centuries. *Gather beneath the Banner,* a catalog from the Textile Museum of Canada exhibition of WCTU banners, includes several photographs of decorated meeting halls. A few of these—along with images of several of the WCTU banners discussed later in this chapter—are available at the following web site: http://www.radio.cbc.ca/programs/Tapestry/temperance.html. Mattingly describes the WCTU's practice of decorating the public spaces where temperance meetings were held as a

"comprehensive rhetorical presentation" that not only provided a backdrop to the words of temperance speakers but also served rhetorical functions (67–68).
3. Mattingly's discussion of the racial tensions within the WCTU is especially enlightening in this regard (75–95). Bordin discusses strife within the WCTU's leadership (140–55).
4. *Gather beneath the Banner* provides several such photos (Harker and Allen 32, 35, 40, 49, 63); see also Willard, *Glimpses* 456ff., for a photograph of a display of banners at a WCTU national convention in the 1890s.

WORKS CITED

Bordin, Ruth. *Woman and Temperance: The Quest for Power and Liberty, 1873–1900*. Philadelphia: Temple UP, 1981.

Cozart, Dorothy. "The Role and Look of Fundraising Quilts, 1850–1930." *Pieced by Mother: Symposium Papers*. Ed. Jeannette Lasansky. Lewisburg: U of Pennsylvania P, 1988. 86–95.

Ferrero, Pat, Elaine Hedges, and Julie Silber. *Hearts and Hands: The Influence of Women and Quilts on American Society*. San Francisco: Quilt Digest, 1987.

Harker, Wendy, and Max Allen. *Gather beneath the Banner: Political and Religious Banners of the Woman's Christian Temperance Union, 1877–1932*. Exhibition Catalog. Toronto: The Textile Museum of Canada, 1999.

Halloran, S. Michael. "The Rhetoric of Picturesque Scenery: A Nineteenth-Century Epideictic." *Oratorical Culture in Nineteenth-Century America: Transformations in the Theory and Practice of Rhetoric*. Ed. Gregory Clark and S. Michael Halloran. Carbondale: Southern Illinois UP, 1993. 226–46.

Jenkins, Susan, and Linda Seward. *The American Quilt Story*. Emmaus: Rodale, 1991.

Johnson, Nan. *Gender and Rhetorical Space in American Life, 1866–1910*. Carbondale: Southern Illinois UP, 2002.

Mattingly, Carol. *Well-Tempered Women: Nineteenth-Century Temperance Rhetoric*. Carbondale: Southern Illinois UP, 1998.

Perelman, Chaim, and L. Olbrechts-Tyteca. *The New Rhetoric: A Treatise on Argumentation*. Trans. John Wilkinson and Purcell Weaver. Notre Dame: U of Notre Dame P, 1969.

Poulakos, Takis. "Isocrates's Use of Narrative in the Evagoras: Epideictic Rhetoric and Moral Action." *Quarterly Journal of Speech* 73 (1987): 317–28.

Sheard, Cynthia Miecznikowski. "The Public Value of Epideictic Rhetoric." *College English* 58 (1996): 765–94.

Walker, Jeffrey. "Aristotle's Lyric: Re-Imaging the Rhetoric of Epideictic Song." *College English* 51 (1989): 5–28.

—. *Rhetoric and Poetics in Antiquity*. Oxford: Oxford UP, 2000.

Willard, Frances E. *Glimpses of Fifty Years: The Autobiography of An American Woman*. 1889. New York: Source Book Press, 1970.

—. *Woman and Temperance*. 3rd ed. Hartford: Park, 1883.

38

Beyond Opposition: Reconceptualizing Social Movements Through the Spiritual and Imaginative Rhetorics of *This Bridge Called My Back* and *this bridge we call home*

Christa Jean Downer
Texas Woman's University

The multiple voices speaking their lives and experiences in both *This Bridge Called My Back: Writings by Radical Women of Color* and *this bridge we call home: radical visions for transformation* have taught me how to understand and respect differences among us and how to interrogate my own privileges as a light-skinned woman. Moreover, they have helped me to find ways in which I can work across differences in hopes of changing oppressive relationships existing within myself and in my world. Collectively, our rhetorics of transformation help to create Gloria Anzaldúa's concept of *El Mundo Zurdo*, the left-handed world where queer groups live together not in opposition but in interconnectedness and community to transform the world.[1] For Anzaldúa, the path to *El Mundo Zurdo* is a "two-way movement—a going deep into the self and an expanding out into the world, a simultaneous recreation of the self and a reconstruction of society" ("La Prieta" 232).

Believing that my efforts are indeed part of a "movement," I began to consider the rhetorics of transformation found in *Bridge* and *this bridge,* particularly those deriving from spiritual and imaginative activism, through a movement studies lens. In an attempt to categorize them as social movements, I turned to Charles J. Stewart's "Rhetoric of Social Movement." In his essay, published in the 1980 volume of *Central States Speech Journal,* a germinal collection of social movement criticism, Stewart defines social movements as "organized, uninstitutionalized, and expansive collectivities that mobilize for action to bring about or to resist programs for change primarily through rhetoric and that are countered by established orders" (301). Unquestionably, women-of-color feminists have formed multiple groups inside and outside of institutions.[2] For instance in academia, they have made great use of lesbian and feminist journals, small presses, and the multigenre anthology[3] to mobilize other justice-seeking individuals, including profeminist men and antiracist whites, in their efforts to transform oppressions within the academy and without. As expressed in both *Bridge* and *this bridge*, women-of-color feminists have always believed their theoretical and creative writings generate social movements. In fact, Anzaldúa believes that because writing is a way of activism "[w]riters have something in common with people doing grassroots organizing and acting in the community: it's all about rewriting culture" (Lunsford 277). When describing women-of-color feminism as a social movement, Anzaldúa claims, "Ours are individual and small group *movidas*, unpublicized *movimientos*—movements not of media stars or popular authors but of small groups or single *mujeres*, many of whom have not written books or spoken at national conferences" ("Haciendo Caras" xxvii).

I believe the theorists in *Bridge* and *this bridge*, these small groups and single *mujeres*, provide four important assumptions about the processes of building coalitions and creating social change through their *movidas* and *movimientos* that significantly contribute to our understanding of movement rhetoric. First, our identity labels and categories are effective strategies, but ultimately obstruct real social change; second, we need to base alliances in our commonalities and interconnectedness; third, we must change ourselves if we are to change the world; and, finally, we can create long-term, systemic social change through spiritual and imaginative strategies. This last principle—the use of spiritual and imaginative strategies—provides the energy that creates and sustains these *movidas* and *movimentos*. Enacting the spiritual and imaginative is a radical departure from traditional Western oppositional practices.[4] Keating, for instance, describes Anzaldúa's spiritual activism as a "metaphysics of interconnectedness [...] an alternate mode of perception, a holistic way of viewing ourselves and our world that breaks down self/other divisions and empowers individuals to work for psychic and material change on both personal and collective levels" ("Forging" 521). I believe this principle deserves greater attention from movement rhetoric studies for how its practices reconceptualize the ontology, cosmology, and epistemology of the "social movement/activist"; it is a different metaphysics—a metaphysics of relatedness and interconnectedness.

MOVING BEYOND LABELS AND CATEGORIES

Through their experiences with the civil rights movement, the women's movement, the gay rights movement, and nationalist movements, women-of-color feminists realize that labels and categories are important life strategies; they create visibility and break silences. However, women-of-color feminists understand, also, that the act of joining in uncomplicated solidarity around an identity category reifies oppressive relationships and, therefore, limits the efficacy of social movements that seek to change relationships of domination.[5] In the *Bridge* anthology, for example, theorists challenged the white women's movement for their uncomplicated solidarity around gender, a claim to sisterhood that refuses to take into account the different oppressions "women" suffer. As they sought to obtain visibility, break silences, and expose differences, women-of-color feminists began to conceptualize identity in increasingly complex ways,[6] engaging in self-reflective work and forming a "theory in the flesh," a feminism that would embody their experience and histories.

This self-reflective work complicated even their solidarity movements. Rosario Morales, for example, troubled the uncomplicated position of the oppressor. She writes,

I'm saying that the basis of our unity is that in the most important way we are in the same
boat   all subjected to the violent pernicious ideas we have learned to hate   that we must all
struggle against them and exchange ways and means hints and how tos that only some of us are
victims of sexism only some of us are victims of racism   of the directed arrows of oppression
but all of us are sexist   racist   all of us. (100)

Further, Anzaldúa represents our complex and interconnected identities in the persona
"Shiva," a mythological woman who rejects labeling herself in an either/or framework. She
understands herself as having "one foot on brown soil, one on white, one in straight society,
one in the gay world, the man's world, the women's, one limb in the literary world, another in
the working class, the socialist and the occult worlds" ("La Prieta" 228). Shiva represents a
self who lives in relation to others and not in opposition because, as Inés Hernández-Avila
writes twenty-one years later in *this bridge,* "We are related to all that lives" (532). The first
principle brought forth in the rhetorics of transformation, then, is to understand ourselves as
interconnected in complex ways rather than separated by our differences.

BASING ALLIANCES IN COMMONALITIES
AND INTERCONNECTEDNESS

Along with understanding our identities in relation, women-of-color feminism calls for
basing our alliances in our commonalities and interconnectedness. However, these theorists realize that to create communities of similar goals and interests is difficult work for
the very fact that even though our affinities may bring us together, our differences have
worked to keep us apart. In addition, they have realized that movement rhetoric must refuse to script a dominant narrative that all members should accept in the name of unity
and sameness; rather, they believe members must learn about each other's histories and
unite across these multiple stories.

Women-of-color feminism teaches us that to join in solidarity, then, we must first educate
ourselves about each other's stories and not rely on the "other" to teach us about their cultures. For example, in "—But I Know You, American Woman," Judit Moschkovich addresses how dominant groups often expect subordinates to instruct them about their lives.
She cites a white feminist who published an open letter in a national women's newspaper,
which asked Latin people to tell her what their struggles are. In her response, Moschkovich
suggests that the woman "read and listen" to the many sources available on Latin culture in
libraries and bookstores (84). She concludes:

> I would like us some day to get past the point of having to explain and defend our different cul-
> tures (as I am doing in this letter). For that to happen the process of learning about other cultures
> must be a sharing experience. An experience where American women learn on their own without
> wanting to be spoon-fed by Latinas, but don't become experts after one book, one conversation,
> or one stereotype. It is a delicate balance which can only be achieved with caring and respect for
> each other. (88)

The delicate balance of putting our identities in relation manifests in women-of-color
feminism movements when members align empathetically with different people and inte-
grate the diverse histories they learn into who they are and how they live (Violet 488).

TO CHANGE THE WORLD, WE MUST CHANGE OURSELVES

We can derive the next assumption in the rhetorics of transformation that informs social movements in Anzaldúa's words, "I believe that by changing ourselves we change the world" ("La Preieta" 232). This seems to be a very simple concept. If we seek to end oppression and to create socially just relationships, we must enact these relationships in our own lives. Yet, Anzaldúa writes in the same passage, "I am confused as to how to accomplish this" (232). Twenty-one years later, in *this bridge,* AnaLouise Keating writes that she too is confused about how to bring about these changes ("Forging" 522). She believes in Anzaldúa's vision of *El Mundo Zurdo* and the two-way movement of changing within and without but realizes the difficulty of achieving this visionary place:

> I can't offer pronouncements on how we can transform the world, or even how you can transform yourself. But I can tell you about my own efforts to engage in this two-way movement. I am a mother, a writer, a teacher. These relational identities give me specific locations where I can begin working for change—today [...] in my home, in the written word, in the classroom. (522)

Through their written words, Anzaldúa and Keating express the difficulty in achieving a spiritual transformation that is a deeply personal yet wholly social act. Yet this assumption is the binding principle in the rhetorics of transformation. It represents a way of being in the world that rejects living in opposition and, therefore, refuses reproducing relationships of domination and hierarchies of oppression.

Indeed, changing ourselves to change the world means *living with* contradiction and difference. It means *living in* relation and seeking more holistic ways of interacting with our environments. For example, Renée M. Martinez has transformed from a woman warrior to a peace activist. She writes,

> The process has meant trusting in the integrity of my principles and not relying on rigid categories of oppositional thinking. It has been about discovering the difference between having a critical analysis and simply being judgmental or condemning. I've learned not to focus exclusively on the gaps or conflicts, but on areas of intersection that will become pathways toward reconciliation. Slowly, I have become a Woman of Peace—Mujer de la Paz. (49)

For Martinez, her transformation begins within and moves outward into her environment. I imagine these social movements, *movidas* and *movimientos,* spreading outward from many points of center, connecting in increasingly intricate patterns and enfolding more and more of our global environment. Anzaldúa in "now let us shift [...]" explicates this process of transformation within and without in her seven stages of *conocimiento*. She points out, though, that far from a utopian vision, transformation has a "flaw": "it doesn't work with things that are insurmountable, or with all people at all times (we haven't evolved to that stage yet), and it doesn't always bring about immediate change" (571). However, she states, it does work with "las nepantleras, boundary-crossers, thresholders" (571). Therefore, by living in relation, as "nepantleras, boundary-crossers, thresholders," we create a new space where real, systemic change can occur.

SPIRITUAL AND IMAGINATIVE STRATEGIES
FOR SOCIAL CHANGE

As Anzaldúa points out, not all people desire to be *nepantleras*—boundary-crossers, thresholders. In the introduction piece to *this bridge,* Keating recalls, briefly, an experience at a recent National Women's Studies Association (NWSA) conference at which she conducted a roundtable about the original *Bridge* anthology. She shares that two contradictory trends came out of the roundtable and audience discussions; one was a continued reliance on identity politics: the need to self-name and claim a position from which to speak. The other trend represented a growing use of spiritual activism. These practitioners, Keating observes, enact "[a] spirituality for social change, spirituality that recognizes the many differences among us yet insists on our commonalities and uses these commonalities as catalysts for transformation" ("Charting" 18–19).

These trends represent only two of women-of-color feminism's many strategies for change. In fact, we may claim that they theorize and employ as many strategies and tactics as they initiate *movidas* and *movimientos.*[7] I am particularly interested, though, in the trend of spiritual activism for its reconceptualization of the oppositional framework in which most Western social movements are based. The spiritual activism that comes out of the theories found in *Bridge* and *this bridge* seeks to reconnect the mind/body/spirit split, an ontology that is the hallmark of Western rationality. Consequently, this spiritual activism manifests itself in various acts that refuse to privilege the scientific and rational over the intuitive and creative.

Many of the small groups and single *mujeres* speaking through the pages of these two anthologies choose to walk along the path of spiritual transformation to create real, systemic social change. However, they understand first, as Keating argues, that this spiritual activism unlike the solipsism of New Age spirituality "begins with the personal yet moves outward, acknowledging our radical interconnectedness" ("Charting" 18). These *nepantleras* make spiritual transformations through—as the subtitle of *this bridge* states—radical visions; an imaginative that moves beyond the dualistic, hierarchal ways of knowing embedded in Western culture. The imagination, Anzaldúa claims, is "a function of the soul, [with] the capacity to extend us beyond the confines of our skin, situation, and condition so we can choose our responses. It enables us to reimagine our lives, rewrite the self, and create guiding myths for our times" ("[Un]natural" 5). For spiritual activists, rational perceptions of reality—those filtered through predetermined screens—prevent them from perceiving beyond the many constraints, including cultural, social, economic, political, material, and physical, that bind us in relationships privileging one group over another: white/nonwhite, rich/poor, able/disabled, straight/gay. To imagine differently, the *nepantlera* moves beyond this way of thinking and creates new ways of understanding herself and her relationships with and in the world.

The *nepantlera's* strategies and tactics originate, Anzaldúa writes, in a new desired knowledge for the twenty-first century: "the inner exploration of the meaning and purpose of life" ("now let us" 540). She describes this way of knowing and existing in her seven stages of *conocimiento*; it is the process of "opening all of your senses, consciously inhabiting your body and decoding its symptoms" (542). Anzaldúa suggests that those walking along the path to *El Mundo Zurdo* enact this way of knowing and being "via creative acts—writing, art-making, dancing, healing, teaching, meditation, and spiritual activism—both mental and somatic (the body, too, is a form as well as site of creativity)" (Anzaldúa 42).

Imaging themselves and their perceptions of reality differently inspires the spiritual activists in *Bridge* and *this bridge*.[8] For many activists, this two-way path to *El Mundo Zurdo* requires taking responsibility for their perceptions of reality, enacting new ways of knowing and replacing the old ways that have proven unsuccessful in changing their lives, and extending this inner change out into the world. Irene Lara, in "Healing Sueños for Academia," exemplifies this spiritual activism. As an undergraduate student at Stanford University, she let her "shadow beast"—an internalized white man who is the personification of both Western modern thought and her mixed heritage—convince her that cultivating her reason and closing the door to her body's intuitive knowledge was her only path to success. After suffering several months of a severe headache that physicians attributed to stress, Lara decoded through her dreams of the "white man" that her physical pain was the manifestation of splitting her rational and feeling selves. With this knowledge, she began to heal her fragmented self. She writes, "I think and feel at once. Unlearning the western mind/body split and learning to listen to the wisdom of my whole self, my body/mind/spirit, is a perpetual process" (435). Lara sustains this process through prayer. But not in a traditional sense. Her prayers are questions for understanding and movements for change. She states, "I am learning how to use prayer to suture the ruptures that impede the collective hard work of personal, social, and cosmic transformation" (436).

Eight years later during her PhD qualifying exams, she writes a prayer to nourish her integrated self and to "[transform] the fragmenting processes of academia" (437):

May these words heal the de-spiritualization of the academy

May these words heal the de-politicization of the spiritual

May these words heal the de-eroticization of the body, mind, and spirit

May these words heal our separation from ourselves, each other, and the visible and invisible world

May these words "transfix us with love," so together we will soar

In Lak Ech

Through her prayer, Lara was able to bring her "whole powerful self to the committee table" (437). As a way of extending her spiritual activism outward, Lara says to the reader, "In the spirit of the Mayan philosophy 'In Lak Ech'—yo soy otro yo, I am your other I—I offer these words as a prayer for connection across difference and with the darkness, whiteness, and 'shadowbeasts' within" (437).

Similar to Lara, many of the authors in *Bridge* and *this bridge* offer that although oppositional politics have had some successes in combating oppression, they cannot be an end in themselves. These activists go beyond opposition by enacting the spiritual and imaginative in their lives. I believe that inherent in enacting the spiritual and imaginative is the promise that the *means* may well be the *ends*. However, even though these strategies may guide activists in their quest to connect across differences, Keating points out that they must not be "conflated with escapism" ("Forging" 529). She suggests that engaging in spiritual activism may even make us more vulnerable to the oppressions we face and fight against daily. Nevertheless, through this vulnerability, Keating asserts, we can also "forg[e] commonalities" (530).

CONCLUSION

In the introductions to both *Bridge* and *this bridge,* the editors gave their hopes for the future of their books. Cherríe L. Moraga and Gloria E. Anzaldúa wished the 1981 *Bridge* anthology would be a "catalyst, not a definitive statement on 'Third World Feminism in the US'" and a "revolutionary tool" in the hands of "people of all colors" (lv-lvi). In the 2002 *bridge* collection, coeditor AnaLouise Keating writes, "[m]ay this book be a threshold, a marker of change, a place of and invitation to transformation. May this book make a difference, jar us out of complacency, revitalize the dialogue, bring readers face-to-face with these thresholds, challenge you to choose, challenge *us* to cross over" ("Charting" 20, her emphasis).

To "revitalize the dialogue" and to bring the women-of-color feminism movement to people of all colors, my hope is that rhetorical scholars will take a serious interest in studying the movement's rhetoric. I have presented, here, only a brief outline of the movement, identifying but not analyzing the ways in which the rhetorics of transformation reconceptualize traditional social movements. Future studies could more closely investigate these differences; explore the various functions of the rhetorics of transformation; rhetorically analyze pivotal pieces in the movement's evolution; or investigate the efficacy of the movement in different institutions including the media, academia, and government.

NOTES

1. On May 18, 2004, before I began revising this chapter, I scanned the Women's Studies List Serv and caught the subject line "Moraga on Anzaldúa." When I opened the link, I was deeply saddened to learn that Gloria E. Anzaldúa had passed away on May 15. Those of us who read and learn from her contributions know that this world will sincerely miss her. I dedicate this chapter to her and her significant ideas about community, spirituality, peace, and love.
2. For an extensive discussion on the emergence of women-of-color collectives see Becky Thompson's "Multiracial Feminism: Recasting the Chronology of Second Wave Feminism." *Feminist Studies* 28.2 (2002): 337–60.
3. For an excellent discussion of the historical context from which the *Bridge* anthology emerges, see Cynthia G. Franklin's essay "Another 1981" in *Writing Women's Communities: The Politics and Poetics of Contemporary Multi-genre Anthologies.* Madison: U of Wisconsin P, 1997. 31–55.
4. For descriptions of the traditional characteristics and practices of Western social movements, see the collected essays in both *Central States Speech Journal* 31 (Winter 1980) and *Communication Studies* 42 (Spring 1991).
5. An essential characteristic of social movements in Western politics is an oppositional framework. The "We" in this binary opposition unite around an identity marker such as race, gender, class, or nationality, and oppose the "They." Within this context, we find what Leland Griffin calls the "aggressor and defendant rhetors" (*Central States Speech Journal* 31 [1980]: 225–32). What is more, the pervasiveness of movement rhetoric's oppositional ideology also leads to splits within the movement itself, as certain members begin to believe the main group is not addressing their concerns. Griffin theorized this as the natural result of the counter-movement (226-27). Consequently, the aggressor/defendant framework continues to reproduce itself.
6. The authors in today's women-of-color feminist works are not the first to theorize the complexity of identity. For instance, the great women-of-color rhetoricians of the nineteenth century spoke of their identities in terms of race and gender. For example, see Sojourner Truth's "Ar'n't I a Woman?" (*Ripples of Hope: Great American Civil Rights Speeches,* ed. Josh Gottheimer. New York: Basic Civitas Books, 2003. 43–44).

7. Chela Sandoval in "U.S. Third World Feminism: The Theory of Method of Oppositional Consciousness in the Post Modern World" argues that U.S. Third World feminists through differential consciousness move in and out of oppositional strategies, refusing to allow one collective ideology to represent the only truth or correct site of opposition. The differential mode of oppositional consciousness requires that subject-citizens "read" the situation of power and choose the appropriate ideological form to oppose specific oppressions. (*Gender* 10 [1991]: 1–24).

8. Diverse forms of spiritual activism weave through the works in *this bridge*. For instance, Helene Shulman Lorenz calls her activism "practice of self-in-community or self-in-participation with other people, the world, and what one could call the 'unknown sacred' flowing through us" (498). Luisah Teish's activism requires her to join her "kindred spirits" in a "sacred space," standing in a circle with other like-minded people, holding hands, informing their politics with their spirituality, and dancing for joy, kinship, and peace (510). Inés Hernández-Avila connects with "[l]as animas." The spirits of her loved ones and all creation teach her empathy, letting go, and connecting at multiple centers (536–38). Randy Conner and David Sparks embrace individually and collectively "earth-based spirituality" for their creativity, healing, and transformation (514–15).

WORKS CITED

Anzaldúa, Gloria. "Haciendo Caras, una Entrada." *Making Face, Making Soul: Haciendo Caras: Creative and Critical Perspectives by Women of Color.* San Francisco: Aunt Lute, 1990. xv–xxviii.

—. "La Prieta." *This Bridge Called My Back: Writings by Radical Women of Color.* Ed. Cherríe L. Moraga and Gloria E. Anzaldúa. Berkeley: Third Woman, 2002. 220–34.

—. now let us shift ... the path of conocimiento. ..." *this bridge we call home: radical visions for transformation.* Ed. Gloria E. Anzaldúa and AnaLouise Keating. New York: Routledge, 2002. 540–78.

—. "(Un)natural Bridges, (Un)safe Spaces." *this bridge we call home: radical visions for transformation.* Ed. Gloria E. Anzaldúa and AnaLouise Keating. New York: Routledge, 2002. 1–6.

Hernández-Ávila, Inés. "In the Presence of Spirit(s): A Meditation on the Politics of Solidarity and Transformation." *this bridge we call home: radical visions for transformation.* Ed. Gloria E. Anzaldúa and AnaLouise Keating. New York: Routledge, 2002. 530–40.

Keating, AnaLouise. "Charting Pathways, Marking Thresholds ... A Warning, An Introduction." *this bridge we call home: radical visions for transformation.* Ed. Gloria E. Anzaldúa and AnaLouise Keating. New York: Routledge, 2002. 6–21.

—. "Forging El Mundo Zurdo: Changing Ourselves, Changing the World." *this bridge we call home: radical visions for transformation.* Ed. Gloria E. Anzaldúa and AnaLouise Keating. New York: Routledge, 2002. 433–38.

Lunsford, Andrea. "Toward a Mestiza Rhetoric: Gloria Anzaldúa on Composition, Postcoloniality, and the Spiritual—An Interview with Andrea Lunsford" (1996). Rpt. *Interviews/Entrevistas: Gloria Anzaldúa.* Ed. AnaLouise Keating. New York: Routledge, 2000. 251–80.

Martinez, Renée M. "Del Puente al Arco Iris: Transformando de Guerrera a Mujer de la Paz—From Bridge to Rainbow: Transforming from Warrior to Woman of Peace." *this bridge we call home: radical visions for transformation.* Ed. Gloria E. Anzaldúa and AnaLouise Keating. New York: Routledge, 2002. 42–50.

Moraga, Cherríe L., and Gloria E. Anzaldúa. "Introduction, 1981." *This Bridge Called My Back: Writings by Radical Women of Color.* Ed. Cherríe L. Moraga and Gloria E. Anzaldúa. Berkeley: Third Woman, 2002. lii–lvi.

Morales, Rosario. "We're All in the Same Boat." *This Bridge Called My Back: Writings by Radical Women of Color*. Ed. Cherríe L. Moraga and Gloria E. Anzaldúa. Berkeley: Third Woman, 2002. 97–100.

Moschkovich, Judit. "—But I Know You, American Woman." Ed. Cherríe L. Moraga and Gloria E. Anzaldúa. Berkeley: Third Woman, 2002. 83–9.

Stewart, Charles J. "Rhetoric of Social Movements." *Central States Speech Journal* 31 (1980): 298–305.

Violet, Indigo. "Linkages: A Personal-Political Journal with Feminist-of-Color Politics." *this bridge we call home: radical visions for transformation*. Ed. Gloria E. Anzaldúa and AnaLouise Keating. New York: Routledge, 2002. 486–95.

39

The Perfected Mother: Listening, Ethos, and Identification in Cases of Munchausen by Proxy Syndrome

Julie Jung
Illinois State University

In both rhetoric and feminist studies, redefinitions of silence have galvanized research in listening. Rather than view listening as a passive act of reception, feminist theorists have interrogated the ways listeners both construct meaning and determine whose meanings will get heard. Feminist rhetoricians in particular have sought to understand the complex relationship among listening, ethos construction, and identity formation, especially in terms of how these processes might silence difference. Explaining her concept of rhetorical listening, Krista Ratcliffe, for example, advocates a listening that "proceed[s] from within a *responsibility* logic," a "performance" that "locate[s] identification in the discursive spaces of both *commonalities* and *differences*" (204, emphasis in original). By attending to both of these, Ratcliffe offers us a methodology for building alliances even as we recognize and contend with our differences. Her definition of rhetorical listening also reminds us of Kenneth Burke's edict: that "identification implies division" (45). To listen rhetorically, then, we must continually interrogate our processes of identification, examining how we both connect with and dis-connect from our discursive constructions of self and others.

In this presentation, I focus on the unique challenges of disconnection. Specifically, I seek to augment our understanding of the relationship among listening, ethos, and identification as I explore the limits of using dis-identification as a strategy for listening to difference. I argue that because a listener's construction of a speaker's ethos is inextricably tied to the listener's own sense of self, the process of dis-identification is complex. In situations where dis-identification undermines listeners' favorable views of themselves, the process can be even more difficult, tempting many listeners to *over*-identify—to emphasize commonalities and silence difference—in order to forego dis-identification altogether. In the majority of this paper, I examine how the failure to dis-identify can have potentially life-threatening consequences.

Specifically, I situate my analysis within a medical context and examine how doctors listen to—and why they believe—the often bizarre medical "facts" related to them by women suffering from Munchausen by Proxy Syndrome (MBPS), a form of child abuse where a caregiver—almost always the mother—fabricates or intentionally creates illness in her own child. After analyzing the rhetoric specific to cases of MBPS, I conclude by considering the implications of my argument within a classroom context, one where students are expected to dis-identify from the texts they read so that they might listen to difference more fully.

In their definitive study of MBPS, Herbert A. Schreier and Judith A. Libow describe the syndrome as follows: It is a disorder where caregivers

> systematically fabricate information about their children's health or intentionally make their children gravely ill. The children usually require extensive medical attention, often entailing serious and dangerous invasive medical procedures, intravenous medicines, or multiple X-rays. Well-versed in medical conditions, MBPS parents will seemingly stop at nothing to gain access to doctors and the inner circle of care in hospitals. Often they seek more general recognition of or public attention for their devoted caretaking of a sick child. […] We know, based on parents' own admissions as well as observations of some of these incidents taped by hidden cameras, that the mother's behavior is calculated, and performed calmly and carefully. These mothers are generally not psychotic and not in a dissociative state when they harm their children. (5–6)

According to the authors, children suffering at the hands of MBPS mothers present with a wide variety of medical symptoms, including

> abdominal pain, apnea, bleeding, diabetes, diarrhea, eczema, fevers, infections, lethargy, rashes, renal failure, seizures, shock, tachycardia, vomiting, and weight loss. […] Unfortunately, since these "illnesses" are nonexistent or induced by other substances or manipulations, they generally fail to respond to the physician's usual treatments, or show an unusual and unexpected course of recurrence or intensification. (15)

As such, doctors remain puzzled, investing enormous amounts of time attempting to solve a problem that doesn't make clinical sense. And, according to the authors, this is exactly what MBPS mothers want, as it enables them to exert control over doctors and obligates doctors to pay attention to them. As Schreier and Libow put it, MBPS mothers make their children sick in order to satisfy their "intense need to be in a relationship with doctors and/or hospitals" (13). While the authors' development of this theory is fascinating, it is not the focus of my study. Rather, I am interested in understanding how doctors identify with a particular mothering ethos in such a way as to make a correct diagnosis of MBPS difficult if not impossible.

In short, doctors believe these mothers (and therefore tirelessly pursue a nonsensical clinical case) because they are not ready to believe the alternative—that a mother who on the surface appears so caring and concerned could, in fact, be poisoning her own child (Schreier and Libow 40). Their *unwillingness* to believe the worst is, of course, tied to their *willingness* to embrace the prevailing cultural myth of The Good Mother, particularly in cases involving middle and upper class families. Although Schreier and Libow acknowledge that research on "social class distribution in cases of MBPS is sparse," they do report that "[c]ases have been reported in all social classes from the very wealthy to the very poor" (28). One study (Light and Sheridan, 1990) suggests that in those rare instances when doctors do suspect MBPS, they are most likely to distrust mothers who receive some form of welfare (28). In general, however, doctors remain extremely reluctant to view mothers, especially those whose social class most closely resembles their own, negatively and in terms that contradict a mother's "natural" function: to give and nurture life, not take it away.

These perceived "natural" life-affirming acts of mothering complement the goals of most Western doctors—to ameliorate pain, cure illness, and save lives. Consequently, doctors (particularly pediatricians) identify with mothers who perform the ethos of The Good Mother (Schreier and Libow 57). Explaining his principle of identification, Kenneth Burke writes:

> A is not identical with his colleague, B. But insofar as their interests are joined, A is *identified* with B. Or he may *identify* himself with B even when their interests are not joined, if he assumes that they are, or is persuaded to believe so. (20, emphasis in original)

In Burkean terms, then, because doctors believe they share with all mothers the goal of healing sick children, they identify with MBPS mothers as their allies in healing, failing to see how these mothers are, in fact, thwarting that very goal. These doctors' empathic identification validates their identities as authoritative healers as it reaffirms the myth of The Good Mother, both of which foil a correct MBPS diagnosis. As Schreier and Libow explain, "The physician is missing the fact that the very lack of clinical sense in the case, and not the symptoms he is attempting to track down, *is* the problem" (131, emphasis in original).[1] I argue that the inability to recognize this reality can be understood through the concept of over-identification.

For my purposes, I define over-identification as a process through which a listener focuses so much on the ways she and a speaker are alike that she fails to consider how they might be different. Many feminist scholars have theorized the ways in which an inability to recognize difference is a consequence of over-identification. In "The Reproduction of Othering," for example, Laura Brady problematizes early research in feminist composition that relies on the personal narratives of individual women to represent the experiences of all women. Despite feminist scholars' awareness of the problems associated with this kind of essentialist generalizing, Brady explains that the personal narrative continues to function as an appealing rhetorical strategy. Its appeal, she argues, "results from a reading strategy that emphasizes commonality to the exclusion of differences that might problematize the category of woman" (32). In analyses of their respective students' writing, Juanita Rodgers Comfort and Min-Zhan Lu reach a similar conclusion: that female students prefer to read in a way that allows them to identify along gender lines rather than risk disrupting that alliance by attending to differences in race, class, and/or sexual identity. As Lu explains, "their [her students'] interest in confronting sexism is accompanied by a general indifference to the interlocking of sexism with other forms of oppression" (240).

As these researchers make clear, over-identification occurs when a listener is intent on privileging an alliance with the speaker/writer, one in which the listener has a profound investment. What's on the line here is the listener's own identity, her own sense that she belongs to a group larger than herself. Challenging the terms of that alliance is difficult, not only because it demands that listeners recognize the differences that exist within groups, but also because it obligates listeners to interrogate *why they might resist doing so*. (For example, white female students in Comfort's and Lu's classes construct a seamless gender-only alliance because it does not require them to interrogate white privilege.)

The concept of over-identification in cases of MBPS helps explain why doctors fail to recognize mothers who poison their own children. As Schreier and Libow make clear, MBPS

TABLE 39.1
An Ethos-Identity Matrix in Cases of MBPS

Case	Doctor	Mother	Relationship
1. No MBPS present	Caring	Caring	Identification
2. MBPS remains undetected	Caring	Performance of Caring by Imposter Mother	Over-identification with mother's performance of The Good Mother Ethos
3. MBPS remains undetected	Caring	Not Caring	Unexplored Dis-identification
4. MBPS remains undetected	Not Caring	Caring	Unacceptable Dis-identification that leads to Over-identification with The Good Mother

Note. Shaded rows indicate options afforded by dis-identification. Notice that in Case 4, the doctor's own feared ethos fuels his desire to over-identify with The Good Mother. By over-identifying with the myth (Case 2), he is unable to see the reality (Case 3).

mothers are incredibly persuasive, using the myth of The Good Mother to their full advantage as they convince hospital staff, relatives and members of their communities, and sometimes even the rest of the nation, that they are wonderful mothers, women to be admired for their selflessness and tireless devotion. For doctors wooed by this performance, breaking their alliance with mothers as members of a group committed to healing sick children is thus an untenable task, obligating them as it does to question *their own* degree of selfless devotion, *their own* tireless pursuit of a medical cure. These doctors' professional identities are on the line, as their inability to solve the problem of the child's illness might be seen as evidence that they are not trying hard enough. So, what do they do? They *over*-identify with The Good Mother. They redouble their efforts to prove they belong. They order *more* tests, perform *more* invasive exploratory surgeries, immerse themselves even *more* fully in a tangled relationship with the child's mother—indeed, everything the mother *wants* them to do—in order to avoid being constructed in the manner they most fear: as incompetent, uncaring physicians.

The concept of over-identification also helps explain why directing doctors to simply listen better to their patients will not solve the problem of MBPS. In one particular case of abuse, for example, Schreier and Libow report that while doctors continued to believe the mother was caring and concerned despite mounting evidence to the contrary,

> it was the ward clerks who pointed out that they had always felt that something was wrong with this woman. In a case review and support conference later held with the nursing and ward staff, they said they had noticed that Ms. W. stayed around the hospital long after Anna [the child] was asleep for the night, despite the fact that she had another child at home. The ward clerks reported that she "loitered" by the nurse's station, seemed engrossed in the "medical gossip," and appeared unusually dependent, if inoffensive. It is not surprising that the health care workers with the highest level of suspicion about the mother were those who had prolonged informal contact

with her of a nonmedical nature. Their opportunity for observation of her social behavior stood in
sharp contrast to the medical focus of most nurse and physician interactions with Ms. W. (41)

For the ward clerks, there was no risk of over-identifying with Ms. W, a woman they perceived as needy and gossipy, as their professional ethos, unlike the doctors', was not on the
line. As such, they were better able to listen to her fully, to juxtapose her seemingly caring behaviors with those they registered as "wrong." Given that those furthest removed from the
medical specifics of a case are most able to see through an MBPS mother's performance,
Schreier and Libow advocate a collaborative approach to case management, one that allows
doctors, nurses, social workers, and other hospital staff to discuss together their concerns regarding cases that don't make clinical sense (213).

The challenges doctors encounter while trying to listen fully to MBPS mothers have implications in the context of the writing classroom, especially one where students are asked to
recognize and contend with—rather than silence or ignore—conflict and difference. First,
the problem of students' over-identifying with a particular argument or aspect of a character
may not be easily solved by directing them to "listen for difference." Indeed, as I hope my
analysis suggests, one of the causes of over-identification is the desire to *escape from* the
challenges posed by dis-identification. As such, asking students to contend with difference
may result in the very problem many of us are trying to avoid—the reductive homogeneity
afforded through over-identification. Furthermore, in situations where the terms of dis-identification are founded on cultural myths, the process of listening for difference is even more
complex. (For example, in cases of MBPS, doctors must question their assumptions not only
about what it means to be a mother, but also about what it means to be a doctor. Can a good
doctor admit confusion and uncertainty? Can s/he voice frustration and puzzlement and still
be regarded as competent? If not, why not?)

A few semesters ago, I experienced most vividly the problem of over-identification after assigning an essay by bell hooks in a first year writing course composed entirely of
white students. In their responses, most of my students reacted angrily to hooks's argument, contending that she unjustly stereotypes white people and is therefore guilty of reverse racism. In class discussions, I challenged my students to define "reverse racism" and
to contrast it with hook's definition of racism. My hope was that through such a process of
dis-identification, my students would understand how individual acts of stereotyping differ from systemic, institutionalized racism. What I did not realize at the time, however, was
that my students' feared ethoi as persons who are not hurt by labels and stereotypes led
them to over-identify with hooks as persons who are oppressed by racism. By over-identifying in this way, my students were able to avoid the hard work of contrasting the historical, material, and institutional contexts of their experiences with those of African
Americans. Their over-identification enabled them to avoid examining, for example, how
a prohibition against skateboarding through campus is quite different from being denied
access to that campus altogether. However, instead of starting from a position that acknowledged my students' frustration, their hurt over being stereotyped as reckless,
thoughtless teens, I hit them with the very thing they feared most: evidence that in the end
their pain didn't really matter all that much.

Listening for difference is a challenging process that requires students to recognize and
interrogate their own personal as well as cultural investments in and resistances to particular
ethos and identity formations. Given the complexity of such a task, I believe we set students
up for failure if we expect them to be able to dis-identify as they read on their own. Perhaps

instead we can practice with our students a more tolerant and necessarily collaborative approach to dis-identification, one where a student's initial inability to recognize difference is not interpreted as naiveté, ignorance, or a conscious decision to perpetuate oppression, but rather as *a first step toward* listening more fully.

NOTE

1. Throughout this paper I frequently use the masculine pronoun to refer to doctors because "approximately 75% of the physicians in MPBS cases [are] male. This is not decidedly different from the overall gender distribution in pediatric medicine" (Schreier and Libow 28). Additionally, I use the masculine pronoun in order to foreground unequal power relationships between men and women, as embodied by the figure of the paternalistic physician and the submissive female patient. According to Schreier and Libow, these gender dynamics play a significant role in MBPS cases (95). It's important to note, however, that the authors do not reference studies that track other kinds of differences among doctors, mothers, and abused children (e.g., ethnicity, sexual identity, age, etc.), most likely because this research has not yet been done.

WORKS CITED

Brady, Laura. "The Reproduction of Othering." Jarratt and Worsham 21–44.
Burke, Kenneth. *A Rhetoric of Motives*. Berkeley: U of California P, 1969.
Comfort, Juanita Rodgers. "Becoming a Writerly Self: College Writers Engaging Black Feminist Essays." *College Composition and Communication* 51 (2000): 540–59.
Jarratt, Susan C., and Lynn Worsham, eds. *Feminism and Composition Studies: In Other Words*. New York: MLA, 1998.
Lu, Min-Zhan. "Reading and Writing Differences: The Problematic of Experience." Jarratt and Worsham 239–51.
Ratcliffe, Krista. "Rhetorical Listening: A Trope for Interpretive Invention and a 'Code of Cross-Cultural Conduct.'" *College Composition and Communication* 51 (1999): 195–224.
Schreier, Herbert A., and Judith A. Libow. *Hurting for Love: Munchausen by Proxy Syndrome*. New York: Guilford, 1993.

40

Margaret Fell and the Problem
of Women's Ethos

Christine Mason Sutherland
University of Calgary

"For the Renaissance woman," writes Tita Baumlin, "ethos is problematic, since any use of public language risked the destruction of both her public and her private image" (230). It seems, then, that a strong ethos, recognized since the time of Aristotle to be a *sine qua non* of successful discourse, was impossible for women to achieve. They were caught in a vicious circle: the more they engaged in public discourse, the worse their public image was likely to become. However, in the seventeenth century a number of women effectively overcame this apparently crippling disadvantage to become successful writers. Each of these women found a different solution to the problem. Margaret Fell addressed the problem by identifying herself not with the current bourgeois culture but with the ancient tradition of women's spirituality.

An important element in this tradition had been prophecy, something that had from the earliest times been an embarrassment to institutional religion, both because it is uncontrollable by the authorities and because it so often calls into question the social practices of the time. Most of the Old Testament prophets challenged those in authority, particularly those who oppressed the weak. Few authorities, whether of church or state, then, have ever precisely welcomed prophets, yet they have often been afraid to ignore them; therefore, though suspicious of them, they have never entirely closed the door upon them, and from time to time have even listened to the prophetic voice.

From the earliest times, a few of these prophets have been women; in the seventeenth century there were many. At that time women were normally not allowed to preach. But prophecy was different: "For by claiming direct inspiration from God [...] a woman made it that much more difficult for her voice to be extinguished; there would always be those around her, credulous, or sympathetic, who believed that this extinction was suppressing the direct message from God" (Fraser 154). The subtle but important difference between a prophetess and an ordinary woman who voiced her opinions in public was that "the prophetess might challenge accepted notions concerning religion and society but she did not necessarily in her own person challenge accepted order" (250). The important words here are "in her own person."

If she claimed authority in her own right, she thereby challenged the accepted hierarchy upon which it was thought the stability of society depended. It was this that made the publicly speaking woman such a threat.

But prophecy, unlike the ordinary public speech, was a thing apart, an occasional phenomenon, and therefore less threatening. Because it was apparently random, it was hard for the secular authorities to legislate it; but—also because it was random— it was less likely to promote a coherent alternative ideology to disturb the *status quo*. The prophetic voice comes from another world, not this one. Yet the message carried by that voice is directly relevant to what is going on here and now: the prophets from ancient times have given messages that should alert the powers to current injustices, committed against the powerless. However, because they did not seek power for themselves but claimed to be speaking on behalf of God, they inspired a certain awe and were to some extent inviolate.

During the seventeenth century, and particularly during the civil wars and the interregnum, there had been many prophets—men of course, but also women. In fact, according to Phyllis Mack, in the seventeenth century there was an idea, particularly common among the sects, that women were especially receptive to the voice of God. It was the woman's place to be passive, to receive (23, 24). She was therefore more naturally inclined to allow the message from God to come into her soul without interference such as a man might be tempted to make. Women, then, had a particular credibility in this capacity that was denied them elsewhere. Phyllis Mack quotes the Puritan preacher, Daniel Rogers:

> [G]race makes that natural impotency of the woman, turne impotency for God [...] their nature (being fearfull) hath ever been prone to superstition [...] Men's spirits are hardier, doe not so easily feare Majesty, tremble at judgements, beleeve promises, shun sinne, love God, as women: so that when they are in the way, none are better. (qtd. in Mack 24, 41n23).

Not only were women thought thus to be more receptive: the very gift of prophecy itself was thought of as feminine. Many Protestant writers depicted prophecy as a feminine activity, whether the actual prophet was a man or a woman. Puritan ministers in Massachusetts went so far as to call themselves "the breasts of God" at which the congregation sucked the milk of the Word. "Such Ministers are your Mothers too," wrote Cotton Mather. "Have they not Travailed in Birth for you, that a CHRIST may be seen formed in you? Are not their Lips the Breasts thro' which the sincere Milk of the Word has pass'd into you, for your Nourishment?" (qtd. in Mack 24).

Margaret Fell, then, grounds herself initially in this liberating tradition of female prophecy. She then proceeds to build upon it to legitimize female utterance much more broadly interpreted. For although she places herself in the prophetic tradition, claiming its privileges, Margaret Fell most certainly does challenge the accepted hierarchy. Fell asserts a woman's legitimacy not only as a prophet, but also as a preacher, a teacher, and an advocate. In establishing women's ethos, she goes beyond merely proving from authority their right to prophesy. To quote Bonnelyn Young Kunze: "Her model of authoritative female public ministry was more enduring and effective than the model of the female prophetess, who was considered authoritative only while in a temporary and volatile state of religious enthusiasm" (233). To establish women's right to religious utterance beyond prophecy, she bypasses traditional interpretations of scriptural precept. Trusting in the "inner light" of Quaker belief, she reinterprets scripture in a way that legitimizes female authority.

The work in which Margaret Fell addresses the question of women's authority to speak—their ethos, in fact—is *Women's Speaking Justified, Proved, and Allowed by the Scriptures*. Arrested for holding illegal public meetings at her house, Swarthmoor Hall, she had been imprisoned because she refused to take an oath. Early in their history, the Society of Friends, later known as the Quakers, had decided to take literally Christ's command: "Swear not at all " (Matt. 5 :34). She was therefore imprisoned in Lancaster castle for four years, from 1664 to 1668, when she was released by the intervention of King Charles II himself. It was here, in the second year of her imprisonment, that she wrote *Women's Speaking Justified*. It was originally published in 1666, and reissued the next year with a further addition and a postscript.

She begins by tracing the status of women as represented in Scripture in the account of the creation of human kind in the book of Genesis. Now there are in Genesis two different accounts of the creation of woman, deriving from different Jewish traditions, the priestly and the prophetic. Here is part of the account as given in Genesis 1: "So God created man in his own image, in the image of God created he him; male and female created he them. [...] God said to them [...] have dominion over every living thing that moveth upon the earth." (Gen. 1: 26–29). The account given in Genesis 2 is quite different: it suggests a fundamental unity of man and woman, but it also is thought to imply the subordination of the woman, as the first account does not. In this account, Eve is created from Adam's rib expressly to be "an help meet for him" (Gen. 2: 18). Not surprisingly, it is the first account, not the second, that Margaret Fell uses as support for her argument. "Here God joins them together in his own image, and makes no such distinctions and differences as men do" (753a). Having deliberately ignored the other account of the creation of woman, Fell proceeds to deal with the matter of the Fall. Women's gullibility was often made the reason for their exclusion from public speaking and public office—like Eve, they were too easily deceived. Fell chooses to ignore this aspect of the story and rather to focus on what happens after the Fall, when God curses the serpent:

> I will put enmity between thee and the woman, between thy seed and her seed: it shall bruise thy head, and thou shalt bruise his heel (Gen. 3:15). [...] Let this word of the Lord , which was from the beginning, stop the mouths of all that oppose womens speaking in the power of the Lord: for he hath put enmity between the woman and the serpent; and if the seed of the woman speak not, the serpent speaks. (753b)

Ingeniously, if not quite convincingly, Fell attempts to identify those who question women's authority to speak with the devil himself!

More persuasively, Fell goes on to cite the very special regard that Jesus had for women. It was, she points out, the women who came to anoint the body of Jesus on the day after the Sabbath and the women to whom the message of the Resurrection was given. She next addresses certain vexatious passages in the New Testament that appear to undermine her position. Traditionally, the exclusion of women from preaching had been based upon certain verses in the Epistles, particularly those of St. Paul. Like many other Protestant reformers, Fell challenges not the authenticity of the texts themselves, but their interpretation. Borrowing her argument from George Fox, she suggests that the women who are exhorted to keep silence were "under the Law"; that is, they were as yet unconverted from their Jewish faith to Christianity, and therefore could not enjoy the liberty that was brought by faith in Jesus Christ (755a; Bacon, *Mothers* 12).

Fell next addresses the matter of New Testament prophecy. About ten days after the Ascension, the visible departure of Jesus Christ from the earth, the believers received the Holy Spirit (as he had promised they would). This was accompanied by the phenomenon of speaking in tongues: "And they were filled with the Holy Ghost, and began to speak with other tongues, as the Spirit gave them utterance [...]. Now when this was noised abroad, the multitude came together and were confounded, because that every man heard them speak in his own language" (Acts 2: 4, 6). There were present also, however, sceptics who simply thought the speakers were drunk. The Apostle Peter explains that what they are seeing is not drunkenness but something quite different: "These are not drunken as ye suppose, seeing it is but the third hour of the day. But this is that which was spoken by the prophet Joel: And it shall come to pass in the last days, saith God, that I will pour out of my Spirit upon all flesh: and your sons and your daughters shall prophesy" (Acts 2: 15–17). Daughters are included: the gift of prophecy is not limited to sons. Clearly, then, both the Old Testament (Joel) and the New (Acts) legitimize the prophetic utterances of women.

Furthermore, Margaret Fell argues that St. Paul himself had given instructions that women should pray or prophesy with their heads covered: "[I]f he had stopped women praying or prophesying, why doth he say: Every man praying or prophesying having his head covered, dishonoureth his head; but every woman that prayeth or prophesieth with her head uncovered dishonoureth her head? I Cor. 11: 4, 5." (755b). It seems, therefore, that there is scriptural authority for the prophetess, one that it is hard for the authorities to dispute. As for the instructions given in the Epistle to Timothy, that women should keep silence in church and ask their husbands to teach them at home, Fell believes this to apply only to married couples. Within marriage, the man is of course superior, and his wife must respect him. However, that subordination does not apply to all women in relation to all men. What about virgins and widows, she asks, those who have no husband to consult? Surely they are not forbidden to ask for enlightenment?

Fell concludes by citing famous women of the Old and New Testaments, from Sarah, whose advice God himself told Abraham to heed, to Elizabeth, mother of John the Baptist, and the aged Anna who prophesied over the infant Jesus (both mentioned in the Gospel of Luke), and the four prophesying daughters of the Evangelist, Philip, recorded in the Acts of the Apostles. One of the earliest of such women is Miriam, the sister of Moses and Aaron, who may have been the sister who watched over the baby hidden in the bulrushes. After the successful crossing of the Red (or, more properly, Reed) Sea, she led a chorus of women celebrating the victory of the Lord.

The Israelites, we must remember, were escaped slaves. They had no power in themselves to break their captivity; this is achieved by a series of miraculous plagues, sent by God to force the Egyptians to let them go. What is celebrated here is the intervention of God on behalf of the powerless and oppressed, something that prophets, whether male or female, typically reiterate throughout the ages. It is a theme that recurs throughout scripture and is particularly evident in the triumph songs of women. One of these is Hannah, mother of Samuel, who is born in answer to prayer: the triumph is over her husband's other wife, who has been blessed with children, and mocks poor barren Hannah. The birth of Samuel therefore validates Hannah as a woman and allows her to triumph over her enemy. Hannah also sounds a note that recurs again and again in scripture: the propensity of the Lord God to reverse the order of things, to act for the weak and put down the strong. Fell quotes part of the song of Hannah: "by [God] enterprises are established: the Bow and mighty Men are broken, and the weak hath girded to themselves strength" (759a). This note of triumphant reversal of the established order, the defeat of the oppressive powers, is clearly sounded in the song of Mary of Nazareth, known as the Magnificat: in fact, this whole song is a celebration of just such a reversal: "he (God) hath put down the mighty from their Seats and hath exalted them of low degree; he hath filled the hungry with good things and the rich he hath sent empty away" (758b). Fell points out (again borrowing the argument from George Fox) that this song of Mary is used daily by the Anglican church in the service of Evensong: "Are you not here beholding to the Woman for her Sermon, to use her words to put into your Common Prayer, and yet you forbid women speaking" (758b; Davies 221).

This empowerment of women, achieved by an alternative method of interpreting scripture that ignores mainline tradition, perhaps explains why so many of the early Quakers were the marginalized: women and the poor. Indeed, Stevie Davies believes that part of George Fox's appeal was precisely that he addressed those outside the power structures of society. "His secret lay in teaching the poor to value their own inner riches; women to esteem themselves; servants to free themselves inwardly—and all to bond to one another" (220). But this was no political revolution: it was a spiritual and religious one—one which used weakness itself as the ground of strength. It is not surprising, then, that the appeal to weakness is repeatedly used by religious women of the seventeenth century attempting to establish their ethos.

The appeal is quite different from the humility topos, frequently used by the men of the time, especially by inferiors to superiors, which attempts to establish ethos by appearing to deny it. It is usually insincere and often no more than a recognized ritual. The appeal to weakness is different because it is paradoxically a claim to strength. The triumph songs of women that Fell quotes are triumphs belonging not to themselves, but to God, who has a particular care for the weak, the helpless, those outside the power structures of their society. They identify with the oppressed Children of Israel and particularly with Jewish women; but they also claim this weakness as part of their strength, for God's strength is said to be available especially to the weak, and they believe themselves to be under his command and protection. "My strength is made perfect in weakness, " asserts St. Paul. "When I am weak, then am I strong" (II Cor. 12: 9, 10). When women such as Fell make this appeal, therefore, they may appear to be using the humility topos, but they are in fact taking the moral and religious high ground, as those especially favored by God. Margaret Fell uses the appeal at the beginning of *Women's Speaking Justified*. After referring to the creation of human beings, she continues:

> Here God joins them [man and woman] together in his image, and makes no such distinctions and differences as men do; for though they be weak, he is strong; and as he said to the Apostle [Paul] His grace is sufficient, and his strength is made perfect in weakness, 2 Cor. 12. 9 . And such hath the Lord chosen, even the weak things of the world, to confound the things which are mighty: and things which are despised, hath God chosen, to bring to nought things that are, I Cor. 1. And God has put no such distance between the male and female as men would make. (753a)

What Fell is attempting here is a reversal of accepted power structures: if the weak are, in God's eyes, the strong, then in fact good women are men and bad men are women. In her response to Judge Sawrey, who had accused her of pride and malice, she says, "thou art the woman that goes abroad and does not abide in thine own house" (Davies 232). With this reference to the Epistle to Titus 2:5, Fell reinterprets the scriptural injunction to women to apply instead to men. Stevie Davies presents their argument thus: "A woman is a weak person. The ministers are weak. Therefore the ministers are women." She goes on: "In a world whose norms are recognized as madness, such arguments turn the world upside down, i.e., the right way up" (233). This reversal of the established order was of course typical of the time, and particularly of the new religious sects, most of whom supported the revolutionary parliamentarians. At the head of his magisterial work on the period, *The World Turned Upside Down: Radical Ideas During the English Revolution,* Christopher Hill puts the following quotation from Henry Denne: "I may peradventure to many seem guilty of that crime which was laid against the Apostle, to turn the world upside down, and to set that in the bottom which others make the top of the building, and to set that upon the roof which others lay for a foundation" (qtd. in Hill 13).

In line with this reversal, Margaret Fell practices an alternative hermeneutic strategy, challenging not only accepted interpretations (as in her commentary on Genesis 3) but also the received meanings of words. As Barbara Ritter Dailey has said, "the transformation of the Quaker ethos is connected with the social meanings of language itself, and because language is the metaphor of experience that authorizes and legitimates our male and female identities, it simultaneously opens and closes possibilities for alternative behaviours" (68). By using the terms *man* and *woman* not literally but metaphorically, she changes the accepted meanings of the words and thereby legitimizes a new role for women. And by providing a deconstructive reading of scripture, interpreting it transgressively—transgressively, that is, in terms of the current bourgeois ideology—she opens up meanings that she believes are closer to the original liberating context of early Christianity. By doing so, she creates an ethos for women in general, and for herself in particular, by which she legitimates their practice not only of prophecy but also of instruction, preaching, and advocacy.

WORKS CITED

Baumlin, Tita. "'A Good (Wo)man Skilled in Speaking': Ethos, Self.-Fashioning and Gender in Renaissance England." *Ethos: New Essays in Rhetorical and Critical Theory.* Ed. James S. Baumlin and Tita French Baumlin. Dallas, Texas: Southern Methodist UP, 1994. 229–263.

Bacon, Margaret H. *Mothers of Feminism: The Story of Quaker Women in America.* 2nd ed.. Philadelphia: Friends General Conference, 1996.

Dailey, Barbara Ritter. "The Husbands of Margaret Fell: An Essay on Religious Metaphor and Social Change." *Seventeenth Century* 2 (1987): 55–71.

Davies, Stevie. *Unbridled Spirits: Women of the English Revolution: 1640–1660.* London: Women's, 1998.

Fell, Margaret. "Women's Speaking Justified, Proved, and Allowed by the Scriptures." *The Rhetorical Tradition: Readings from Classical Times to the Present.* 2nd ed. Ed. Patricia Bizzell and Bruce Herzberg. Boston: Bedford/St Martin's Press, 2001. 748–60.

Fraser, Antonia. *The Weaker Vessel.* New York: Knopf, 1984.

Hill, Christopher. *The World Turned Upside Down: Radical Ideas during the English Revolution.* Harmondsworth, UK: Penguin, 1975.

Kunze, Bonnelyn Young. *Margaret Fell and the Rise of Quakerism.* Stanford: Stanford UP, 1994.

Mack, Phyllis. "Women as Prophets during the English Civil War." *Feminist Studies* 8.1. (Spring 1982): 19–45.

Author Index

Note: Page numbers ending in *n* refer to endnotes.

Sorrentino, A., 79, *85*
Spalding, J. L., 216, *221*
Sparks, A., 18, *24*
Spellmeyer, K., 154, *156*
Sperber, D., 167, 168, *175*
Spolsky, E., 168, 169, *175*
Sprigg, J., 229, *232*
Squires, C. R., 211n5, *212*
Stacey, J., 279, *280*
Stern, F., 14, *24*
Stewart, C. J., 335, *343*
Stewart, M. W., 45, 46, *55*
Street, B. V., 106n12, *107*
Sullivan, D., 64, *67*
Swearingen, C. J., 311, 314, *316*

T

Tannen, D., 146, *150*
Tatsis, N., 146, *150*
Taylor, B. C., 288, *299*
Taylor, C., 12, *24*
Taylor, J., 263, *266*
Terrell, M. C., *55*
Thomas, P., 247, 248n2, *249*
Thoreau, H. D., 4, *9*
Tindale, C. W., 109, *113*
Tinkler, J. F., 88, *96*
Todorov, T., 23n2, *24*
Tompkins, J., 319, *323*
Toulmin, S., 255, 258n15, *260*
Traugott, E., 167, *175*
Trehub, S. E., 161, *163*
Trimbur, J., 98, *106*
Tsing, A., 262, *266*

U

Ulman, H. L., 109, *113*
Urquhart, B., 12, *24*
Ut, H. C., 233, *241*

V

Van der Poel, M., 26, 34, 38n4, *40*
Vanderjagt, A. J., 32, 38, *40*
Vatz, R., 104n6, *107*
Veith, G. E., 186, *191*
Verene, D. P., 78, *85*
Vickers, B., 159, 160, *163*, 257n2, *260*
Vico, G., 77, 78, 79, 80, 81, 82, 83, 84, *85*
Vielstimmig, M., 202, *203*

Violet, I., 337, *343*
Virgil, 26, 31, 38n5, *40*
Virilio, P., 6, *9*
Viroli, M., 257n6, 257n7, *260*
Vobejda, B., 247, *249*
Volosinov, V. N., 258n19, *260*
von Klemperer, K., 14, *24*

W

Walker, A., 45, 49, *55*
Walker, J., 257n3, *260*, 327, 333, *334*
Walker, R. J., 45, *55*
Wallat, C., 146, *150*
Walters, S., 276, 277, *280*
Walzer, A. E., 109, *113*
Walzer, M., 255, *260*
Ward-Perkins, J. B., 258n16, *260*
Warner, M., 208, *212*
Wei, W., 208, *212*
Weisser, C. R., 124, *129*
Wells-Barnett, I. B., 48, 51, *55*
Wesley, C. H., *55*
Wesley, J., 59, 60, 61, 62, 63, 64, 65, 66, *67*
West, C., 128, *129*
Whately, R., 137, 138, 139, 140, 141, 142, 143, 144, *144*
Whedbee, K., 88, *96*
White, D. G., *55*
Willard, F. E., 325, 326, 327, 328, 329, 331, 332, 334n4, *334*
Williams, F. P., III, *274*
Williams, R., 278, 279, *280*
Wilonsky, R., 277, 278, *280*
Wilson, D., 167, 168, *175*
Wilson, D., 185, 186, 187, 188, 190n3, *191*
Winkelmann, C. L., 201, 202, *203*
Winkler, C. K., 237, *240*
Woen, A. S., *241*
Wood, J. K., 272, 273n3, 273n4, *274*
Worsham, L., 152, *156*, 350

X

Xiao, X., 104n6, *106*

Y

Yellin, J. F., 318, 323n1, *323*

Subject Index

Note: Page numbers ending in *f* refer to figures. Page numbers ending in *t* refer to tables. Page numbers ending in *n* refer to endnotes.

A

Abolitionism, 45
Abu Ghraib prison, 22, 233, 238–239, 262
Academic capitalism, 179–184
Academic discourse, 200–201, 205–212
"Accidental Napalm," 237
Accountability, 284
Action
    and emotions, 154
    and ethos, 44–55
    motivators of, 154
    and rhetoric, 133, 135
Acumen, 77–85
Adbusters, 119
Aeneid, 26–28, 31
Afghan women, 234, 235
African Americans
    essays by, 44–55
    treatment of, 317–318
    violence against, 243–248
    voices of, 44–55
African National Congress (ANC), 19
"After Ten Years," 14
Agricola, Rudolph, 25–38
Al Qaeda, 13, 122, 125
Altermann, Eric, 282
Ambiguity, 289–298
American Renaissance, 225
"American Way, The," 226
Amplification, 30
Anatomy of War, An, 264
Ancient rhetorics, 189
Ancient Rhetorics for Contemporary Students, 186, 187

Andria, 31
Anger, 272–273
Antebellum rhetoric, 283–284
Antidosis, 234
Antinomianism, 283
Anxiety of Influence, 95
Anzaldúa, Gloria, 335–342
Apartheid, 18–21
Aphrodite, 312
Apolitical comedy, 276–277
Apparent, and real, 142–143
Areopagitica, 69–75
Argument
    beauty of, 81–82
    as comparison, 109–113
    defining, 80–81
    and style, 109–113, 194
Argumentation
    procon argumentation, 281, 283
    and science, 291, 294
    study of, 138, 194
    use of, 26–34, 38, 138
Aristotle
    on emotions, 29
    on ethics, 152–153
    on music, 158
    on passions, 138, 144
    on place, 117–119
    on politics, 152
    on rhetoric, 88, 314
    on virtues, 153
Arney, William Ray, 288
Asian American Studies, 208–209, 211
Astronomia Nova, 70
Athena, 311–312, 314

For Product Safety Concerns and Information please contact our EU
representative GPSR@taylorandfrancis.com
Taylor & Francis Verlag GmbH, Kaufingerstraße 24, 80331 München, Germany